PIERRE DE JEAN OLIVI
(1248-1298)

ÉTUDES DE PHILOSOPHIE MÉDIÉVALE

Collection fondée par Étienne Gilson

Dirigée par

Marta Cristiani
Jean Jolivet
Alain de Libera

ÉTUDES DE PHILOSOPHIE MÉDIÉVALE

LXXIX

PIERRE DE JEAN OLIVI
(1248-1298)

PENSÉE SCOLASTIQUE, DISSIDENCE SPIRITUELLE ET SOCIÉTÉ

Actes du colloque de Narbonne (mars 1998)

édités par

Alain BOUREAU et Sylvain PIRON

Ouvrage publié avec le concours du Centre National du Livre et de l'École des Hautes Études en Sciences Sociales

PARIS

LIBRAIRIE PHILOSOPHIQUE J. VRIN

6, Place de la Sorbonne, V^e^

1999

Imprimé en France
ISSN 0249-7921
ISBN 2-7116-1398-4

REMERCIEMENTS

Ce volume a bénéficié d'une généreuse aide à l'édition de la part de l'École des Hautes Etudes en Sciences Sociales et du Centre National des Lettres. Cécile Soudan a apporté à la révision éditoriale du texte et à la constitution de l'index et de la bibliographie un soin et une compétence remarquables.

Le colloque a pu se tenir grâce à de nombreuses aides de la part des institutions suivantes : Ministère de l'Éducation Nationale, de la Recherche et de la Technologie, Ministère des Affaires Etrangères, Ecole des Hautes Etudes en Sciences Sociales, Centre de Recherches Historiques (CNRS/EHESS), Commission Archéologique et Littéraire de Narbonne, Centre de Recherches Historiques sur les Sociétés Méditerranéennes (Université de Perpignan), Région Languedoc-Roussillon, Ville de Narbonne, Ville de Sérignan.

Nos amis Aline Rousselle et François Amigues ont apporté au comité d'organisation tout leur dévouement éclairé. L'accueil de Jacques Michaud, président de la Commission Archéologique et Littéraire de Narbonne a été chaleureux. Christiane Artz, Sophie Bily, Charles de Miramon et Stefano Mula ont efficacement organisé les déplacements et le séjour. Les membres du Comité (Giulia Barone, Nicole Bériou, David Burr, Jacques Le Goff, Alain de Libéra, Romain-Georges Mailleux, Agostino Paravicini-Bagliani, André Vauchez) nous ont fait bénéficier de leur appui.

A tous nous adressons nos chaleureux remerciements.

INTRODUCTION

INTRODUCTION

A l'occasion du septième centenaire de la mort de Pierre de Jean Olivi[1], décédé à Narbonne le 14 mars 1298, nous avons organisé, en cette ville, un colloque international qui a rassemblé la plupart des spécialistes de cet auteur. Parmi tant de célébrations et d'anniversaires possibles, pourquoi s'attacher à cette circonstance ? Parce qu'Olivi est probablement une des figures les plus importantes et les plus originales du XIIIe siècle, et qu'il reste encore largement méconnu. En outre, il présente l'étonnante singularité d'avoir été à la fois un profond penseur scolastique et l'inspirateur de dissidences spirituelles intenses aussi bien au sein de l'ordre franciscain que chez des laïcs parfois illettrés.

Né à Sérignan en 1248 ou 1249, entré à l'âge de douze ans chez les franciscains de Béziers, Olivi a étudié à l'Université de Paris dans les années 1267-1272, au moment de l'effervescence intellectuelle provoquée par la redécouverte de l'ensemble des œuvres d'Aristote et par la présence de Thomas d'Aquin et de Bonaventure. De retour en Languedoc, Olivi enseigna comme lecteur dans différents couvents : il exerça sans doute à Narbonne en 1278-1279, et à Montpellier en 1283. C'est là qu'il fut atteint par la censure d'une vingtaine de thèses erronées que l'ordre franciscain lui imputait. Cette condamnation visait d'abord à mettre au pas un esprit trop indépendant et elle ruina ses espoirs de carrière universitaire à Paris. Après avoir été suspendu d'enseignement pendant quatre ans (et peut-être assigné au couvent de Nîmes), il fut réhabilité en 1287, et nommé lecteur au couvent Santa Croce de Florence. Il revint à Montpellier en 1289, puis fut à nouveau nommé à Narbonne, où il enseigna jusqu'à sa mort le 14 mars 1298[2].

Malgré sa marginalité, largement due aux difficultés qu'il connut dans son ordre, cet homme qui n'a jamais enseigné que dans des *studia* franciscains, essentiellement à Narbonne et Montpellier, a néanmoins produit une œuvre

1. On trouvera dans ce volume diverses désignations de notre auteur : Pierre de Jean Olivi, Pierre Jean-Olivi, Peter Johannis Olivi, Peter of John Olivi, Peter John Olivi, Peter Olivi, Pierre de Jean Olieu, Pierre Déjean-Olieu. La seule forme attestée est latine : Petrus Johannis Olivi (le prénom suivi d'un génitif qui pouvait former nom de famille) ; la forme Pierre Déjean-Olieu est une reconstruction du nom languedocien probable. Mais l'incertitude demeure. Nous avons tenu à respecter le choix de chaque auteur, auquel il tient généralement. Pour le titre général, nous avons préféré parler de « Pierre de Jean Olivi », version française de l'appellation la plus courante et la plus aisément reconnaissable.

2. On se dispense d'une présentation moins sommaire d'Olivi en renvoyant à l'excellente synthèse de David Burr, *L'Histoire de Pierre Olivi, franciscain persécuté*. Traduction et préface de François-Xavier Putallaz, Fribourg/Paris, Editions Universitaires/Editions du Cerf, 1997.

systématique et immense selon le moule scolastique (une très longue suite de questions sur les Sentences de Pierre Lombard, qui constitue une véritable Somme, des commentaires analytiques de ces mêmes Sentences, des questions quodlibétiques, une vaste série de commentaires exégétiques). Mais la centralité de la pensée d'Olivi n'est pas que de forme : quant à sa substance, elle se situe au cœur du grand débat de la fin du XIIIe siècle entre aristotélo-thomistes et « néo-augustiniens ». Sous le point de vue philosophique, il s'agit de l'une des premières discussions méthodiques des thèses de Thomas d'Aquin, qui aboutit souvent à des solutions originales. Ainsi le traitement de l'ontologie du temps est saisissante de « modernité » (voir la contribution de Ruedi Imbach et de François-Xavier Puttallaz). Dans le domaine de l'exégèse, Olivi allie les sûres techniques du XIIIe siècle (voir Louis-J. Bataillon) et une hardiesse d'interprétation étonnante (voir Gilbert Dahan et Johannes Schlageter).

La seule filiation qu'il se reconnaisse est celle de saint Bonaventure; cette filiation ne doit pas masquer le fait que le défi opposé par Olivi à Thomas d'Aquin est d'une autre mesure: Olivi se campe plus décidément dans le champ scolastique et apparaît moins défensif que Bonaventure. Malgré l'interdit pesant sur la lecture de ses œuvres, la reformulation olivienne des questionnements traditionnels de l'école franciscaine (voir la contribution de Sylvain Piron) a pris une importante décisive dans les décennies suivantes. Pour l'historien de la pensée, Olivi apparaît depuis peu (depuis qu'on commence à découvrir ses textes) comme le maillon nécessaire entre Thomas d'Aquin et Duns Scot ou Guillaume d'Ockham. Il est probablement celui qui a le plus précisément construit cette révolution intellectuelle de la fin du XIIIe siècle, la critique de l'analogie de l'être au profit de l'affirmation de l'univocité de l'étant (voir l'article d'Alain Boureau). Au-delà du Moyen Age, certains de ses thèmes et de ses solutions se retrouvent dans la seconde scolastique des jésuites espagnols ou chez Descartes. Mais la restitution de connexions oubliées ne saurait masquer la très profonde originalité d'Olivi, qui, face aux dissensions et aux disputes, ne cessa de déplacer les questions et les réponses.

Si l'on a le goût du palmarès, on peut affirmer que dans le monde scolastique du XIIIe siècle (avant Duns Scot), les trois pensées les plus fortes furent celles de Thomas d'Aquin, d'Henri de Gand et d'Olivi. Or Thomas d'Aquin a bénéficié d'innombrables éditions, de milliers de publications; l'œuvre d'Henri de Gand, en cours d'édition scientifique, est souvent commentée, alors qu'en dehors d'un cercle limité, Olivi demeure peu connu et son œuvre est encore largement inédite.

Et pourtant, il y a plus encore, dans l'œuvre d'Olivi; le franciscain ne cessa de lancer des défis qui eurent bien des échos. On pourrait citer pêle-mêle son invention du mot « capital » dans le sens actuel du mot, dans un traité désormais célèbre qui tendait à justifier la légitimité de l'investissement économique et de sa rémunération (voir les contributions de Giacomo Todeschini et de Giovanni Ceccarelli), sa mise en place de la notion de « raison réelle », sa démonstration sur le fait que le Christ aurait reçu sa dernière blessure de son vivant, ou sa théorie physique de l'« impetus », qui remettait en cause un principe essentiel de la dynamique aristotélicienne.

C'est lui aussi qui, à la fin des années 1270, lança la fameuse controverse sur l'« usage pauvre » : est-ce que l'« usage pauvre » (c'est à dire la consommation très restreinte des biens de consommation) fait partie ou non de la règle de saint François. Olivi affirme que l'usage pauvre, dont le modèle se trouve dans l'Evangile, fait strictement partie de la Règle et doit faire l'objet du vœu franciscain (voir l'article de David Flood). Cette position suscita des réactions violentes dans l'ordre et provoqua les combats qui aboutirent à la formation du groupe des « spirituels » franciscains, dont certains membres se séparèrent graduellement de la branche « conventuelle » de l'ordre et formèrent, plus tard, l'Observance franciscaine. Le conflit portait moins sur l'enrichissement et l'installation de l'ordre que sur la nature même du vœu religieux. Les adversaires d'Olivi disaient que l'on ne peut émettre un vœu sur une matière indéterminée ; or l'usage pauvre dépend à l'évidence, de conditions externes (l'usage pauvre du vêtement n'est pas le même dans un pays froid ou un pays chaud, etc.). Alors que l'absence de propriété individuelle, le renoncement à la sexualité ou le respect de l'obéissance peuvent être pratiqués de façon certaine et absolue, l'usage pauvre et la vie évangélique ne se déterminent que relativement. Comment s'engager auprès de Dieu dans une relation dont les termes ne sont pas fixés ? Mais c'est précisément ce caractère essentiellement indéterminé du vœu qui en fait la valeur aux yeux d'Olivi : car l'homme y manifeste alors sa pleine liberté, maître-mot de la pensée d'Olivi, dans ses aspects métaphysiques (voir la contribution de Robert Pasnau) aussi bien qu'anthroplogiques (Vincenzo Mauro) et politiques (voir l'article de Luca Parisoli).

Un dernier aspect de son œuvre explique probablement le rôle d'inspirateur de groupes dissidents laïcs du Languedoc, les Béguins. Son grand commentaire exégétique, sur l'Apocalypse, achevé peu avant sa mort, poursuivait l'œuvre de Joachim de Flore (voir Warren Lewis) ; mais Olivi fut l'un des premiers commentateurs à envisager, après un premier combat contre l'Antéchrist, une période de paix et de compréhension spirituelle de 600 ans, moment d'une tranquille conversion des Juifs (voir Robert Lerner). Assuré de ce schéma d'ensemble et des persécutions et tentations qu'auraient à surmonter les franciscains, Olivi s'est retenu d'identifier avec précision la correspondance entre les événements contemporains et la série eschatologique, et il a maintenu comme principes l'obéissance au pape (voir sur ce point fort discuté la mise au point de Marco Bartoli) et l'unité de l'ordre franciscain (voir Roberto Lambertini), à la différence des franciscains spirituels qui voyaient l'influence de l'Antéchrist sur leurs adversaires.

Mais le commentaire, abrégé, traduit en langues vernaculaires assura à Olivi une réputation de sainteté prophétique parmi les Béguins, notamment dans le milieu narbonnais alors si dynamique (voir Gilbert Larguier). Les franciscains conventuels qui exhumèrent le corps d'Olivi à Narbonne et dispersèrent ses cendres n'agirent pas ainsi par simple rancune contre un adversaire pugnace. Ils entendaient mettre fin à un véritable culte sur la tombe de celui que des groupes de béguins provençaux et languedociens tenaient pour un saint (voir la contribution de Jean-Louis Biget). Des recherches récentes ont mieux fait connaître ce milieu et notamment cette disciple Na Prous Boneta qui comparut devant l'Inquisition (voir les articles de David Burr et de Louisa Burnham). A Marseille, on a la preuve documentaire de l'influence d'Olivi, notamment quant à sa doctrine sur la cinquième blessure du Christ, dans des milieux dévots de la ville. Il faudrait ajouter une influence plus diffuse mais néanmoins forte en Catalogne (où sa pensée rencontrait et croisait celles d'Arnaud de Villeneuve et de Raymond Lulle – voir Dominique de Courcelles) et en Italie, par le biais des franciscains entrés en rébellion contre l'Église ou par celui de son enseignement à Florence (voir l'étonnante connexion établie par Alberto Forni entre Olivi et Dante).

Notre colloque, dont le présent livre publie les actes, correspond à un moment particulier des études oliviennes, qui se caractérise par un foisonnement extrême. Après des siècles d'occultation et d'oubli, l'œuvre d'Olivi a été redécouverte par Franz Ehrle dans les années 1880; depuis, le travail d'édition et d'analyse a connu des phases alternées d'intensité et d'immobilité : dans les années 1920, B. Jansen publia les monumentales questions sur le seconde livre des Sentences de Pierre Lombard et M. Schmaus une fort longue question sur le premier livre. Dans les années 1950, Raoul Manselli fit connaître l'importance capitale du commentaire d'Olivi sur l'Apocalypse et des groupes dissidents d'obédience olivienne en Provence et Languedoc; Anneliese Maier, au même moment montrait les impulsions neuves que donnaient la pensée d'Olivi à la physique, en matière de mouvement et de temps. En 1959, Efrem Bettoni publia son importante somme sur la philosophie d'Olivi.

Mais depuis une trentaine d'années, le processus prend une ampleur et une vigueur nouvelles : citons l'œuvre considérable de David Burr depuis 1971, le travail de Brian Tierney (1972) sur l'infaillibilité pontificale, les analyses et éditions de Robert Lerner, Warren Lewis, Johannes Schlageter, Marco Bartoli, Paolo Vian, David Flood, Gedeon Gal et de plusieurs autres. A l'heure où ce volume sort des presses, de nouvelles éditions sont sous presse ou déjà préparées (le commentaire sur la Cantique par J. Schlageter, le commentaire sur les petits prophètes par G. Dahan, le commentaire sur les Romains par A. Boureau, le commentaire sur les Actes des Apôtres par D. Flood, la question XIV sur la perfection évangélique par M. Bartoli, plusieurs questions isolées et un nouveau texte du *Traité sur les contrats* par Sylvain Piron). D'autres suivront. Des thèses ont été soutenues (K. Murtagh, R. Pasnau, T. Madigan, L. Marazzi, S. Piron) [1].

Ces travaux ont souvent été produits isolément et un seul colloque avait réuni les oliviens, à Mönchengladbach en 1983. Mais l'année du septième centenaire a marqué un tournant : à la suite du colloque qui, sous la direction du Père Romain Mailleux a réuni les éditeurs de textes oliviens à Grottaferrata en décembre 1997, en coordination avec le colloque de Narbonne, a été constitué un

1. On trouvera en fin de volume une bibliographie 1988-1998 des éditions et des études oliviennes, qui complète les bibliographies de S. Gieben et de P. Vian.

comité scientifique en vue de l'homogénéisation des efforts éditoriaux[1]. Le présent volume a donc l'ambition de donner une vision globale de l'œuvre d'Olivi, en ce moment capital et passionnant, où elle commence à se dessiner plus fermement, tout en laissant des zones d'incertitudes et d'obscurité, gages de recherches futures sur une pensée forte et originale.

Alain Boureau et Sylvain Piron

1. Gilbert Dahan coordonne la partie des œuvres d'Olivi qui sera publiée dans le *Corpus Christianorum-Continuatio Mediievalis* des éditions Brepols.

OLIVI ON HUMAN FREEDOM

Robert Pasnau

THE TOP-DOWN APPROACH

The free will debate endures because there are two ways of approaching the issue: from the ground up and from the top down. Philosophers who take the ground-up approach provide comprehensive accounts of the various faculties involved in human action, and the causal relationships between those faculties. With their intricate theory established, these philosophers crown their efforts by explaining how all of this allows human beings to be free. Other philosophers take a top-down approach. They begin by declaring what human freedom requires, and proceed to construct theories that ensure these requirements are satisfied. Philosophers who work from the bottom-up take as fundamental certain causal assumptions, and certain principles of explanation. For them, any theory of human freedom must meet these fundamental constraints. Top-down philosophers take as fundamental the experience of freedom, and the reality of moral responsibility. For these philosophers, the details of action theory must be worked out in such a way as to honor the moral and experiential data. The free will debate will be settled when philosophers working from the ground-up manage to make contact, somewhere in the middle, with philosophers working from the top-down. So far, this has not happened.

One early instance of a philosopher committed to the top-down approach is Peter John Olivi (1247/8 – 1298), the colorful and controversial Franciscan who would eventually be condemned by his own order for overzealously advocating religious poverty. In his question commentary on Peter Lombard's *Sentences*, Olivi devotes several extended questions to the topic of free will, beginning with the question of whether human beings have free will (*liberum arbitrium*)[1].

1. I will be speaking of *free will* where scholastic authors generally speak of free decision (*liberum arbitrium*). Olivi himself does not put great weight on the distinction. The topic of *In II Sent.* q. 57 is « whether there is *liberum arbitrium* in a human being – that is, whether something should be postulated in a human being through which he can do things freely » (t. 2, p. 305). The answer, for Olivi, is simply that a free will (*libera voluntas*) must be postulated. For other scholastics, such as Aquinas, the distinction between *voluntas* and *arbitrium* is more important. For present purposes, nothing is lost by ignoring those subtleties.

Olivi's own argument for the affirmative conclusion begins by listing seven pairs of attitudes (*affectus*), each of which testifies to the existence of free will [1] :

1. Zeal and mercy
2. Friendship and hostility
3. Shame and glory
4. Gratitude and ingratitude
5. Subjugation and domination
6. Hope and distrust
7. Providence and negligence

Each of these attitudes, Olivi claims, is defensible only given the existence of free will. More specifically, they are « its distinctive products, or its distinctive acts and habits » [2]. As he runs through the list, explaining how each attitude entails free will, it becomes clear that many of these claims are familiar ones. Zeal, for instance, is an angry reaction to bad deeds, motivated « only against the bad that one judges to have been done voluntarily, and thus which could have been freely avoided » [3]. Without free will, this attitude is based on an assumption that is « thoroughly false and grounded on a thoroughly false object » [4]. As zeal goes, so do the related phonemona of accusations, excuses, blame, and guilt. Generally, « a human being could no more be accused of some vice than he could be accused of death, for he could avoid the one as little as the other » [5]. Providence and negligence, the last pair on the list, likewise become insupportable : « For it is foolish to be careful about things that will occur necessarily » [6]. It becomes pointless to be careful about deliberation, for instance, « because the deliberation itself will or will not happen necessarily, and even one's carefulness will or will not occur necessarily » [7].

These are familiar arguments. Other items on Olivi's list are more interesting, in particular the pairing of friendship and hostility. Olivi begins his discussion here on a rather elevated plane, declaring that « a human being can be drawn to another as a friend only by regarding and taking him as a being *per se*, standing on his own as an individual and a person » [8]. We might make this point differently by saying that one can be friends only with someone who is *autonomous*. The lack of free will would take away such autonomy, making us beings that do not wholly stand on our own, that do not act for our own sake, that are not under our own control, and that possess nothing good on our own. We « would seem to be possessed by another, as a servant is possessed by a master » [9]. All of this is inconsistent with genuine friendship and love, Olivi plausibly argues. One cannot

1. Q. 57, t. 2, p. 317.
2. *Ibid.*, p. 317.
3. *Ibid.*, p. 318.
4. *Ibid.*, p. 317.
5. *Ibid.*, p. 336.
6. *Ibid.*, p. 323.
7. *Ibid.*, p. 323.
8. *Ibid.*, p. 319.
9. *Ibid.*, p. 320.

be friends with things that lack reason, and likewise one cannot be friends with something incapable of returning the friendship. But friendship must be given freely, not forced or necessitated. Our feelings of friendship and love, then, presuppose the existence of free will. Human fellowship with God would likewise be impossible, since without freedom there can be no obedience, reverence, friendship, grace, or terror: « for God could no more be offended or dishonored by us than by beasts, no matter how much we blaspheme him by words or desires »[1].

For Olivi, these data stand as unshakeable evidence for the existence and nature of free will. He makes this clear from the beginning of his reply, when he introduces two premisses that « no one of sane mind ought to doubt »[2]. First, it is « impossible » for all of the attitudes of one's rational nature to be « thoroughly false and perverse and grounded on a thoroughly false and perverse object ». Since Olivi thinks that the attitudes that distinguish us as rational creatures are founded on free will, giving up on free will would be to abandon most of what makes us human. We would become, he later says, « intellectual beasts »[3]. Second, it is impossible for attitudes to be entirely illusory when human beings improve and perfect themselves by assuming those attitudes[4]. If the practices of zeal, deliberation, friendship, love, etc. were all founded on a false assumption, then surely these practices would not be so crucial to human well-being. Thus « no one of sane mind will believe that something could be the truth which so sharply puts an end to all good things and brings on so many bad things »[5]. In the face of these implications, we should reject whatever stands in the way of free will, whether that be the authority of Aristotle or some abstruse principle of metaphysics. « Even if there were no other argument establishing that [the denial of free will] is false, this alone ought to be sufficiently persuasive »[6]. Moreover, as he explicitly notes, we should be persuaded not just of our own free will, but of the free will of all human beings, since these arguments are based not on private experience, but on our relationships with others.

This top-down approach, beginning with the ethical and experiential data, leads Olivi to some provocative conclusions about the nature of will. He does not merely conclude that the will's choices are not necessitated; the further conclusion Olivi reaches is that the will, until it makes a choice, is entirely undetermined one way or another, and that it determines itself in the direction it chooses. This is something « every human being senses with complete certainty within himself »[7], a further datum of experience that adds to his top-down case. In arguing that the will determines itself, he means that it is a first mover, in need of no efficient cause other than itself. « Its free power is the cause of its motion,

1. *Ibid.*, p. 338.
2. *Ibid.*, p. 317.
3. *Ibid.*, p. 338.
4. *Ibid.*, p. 317.
5. *Ibid.*, p. 338.
6. *Ibid.*, p. 338.
7. *Ibid.*, p. 327.

when it is moved, and the cause of its rest, when it rests »[1]. If the will did not have this capacity for self movement, then the will would have to be determined by something else, hence it would not be making its own choices. But this violates the unshakeable assumptions from which Olivi begins, because it would then turn out that the will is not autonomous, not making its own choices, hence not a suitable object of one's zeal or friendship, among other things.

Olivi is well aware that the lack of autonomy does not entirely preclude a sort of pseudo-zeal or pseudo-friendship. One might be angry with someone, for instance, not out of the conviction that the bad action was that person's fault, but simply in an effort to change that person's ways. But this line of thought does violence to our conceptions of ourselves and our fellow human beings. We want people to do the right thing not because they have been effectively manipulated, but « solely and purely because of the love of justice »[2]. Further, when we urge people to do the right thing, « we do not intend simply to move someone toward what is good, but rather to make it that he voluntarily moves himself toward the good »[3]. These are large issues on which philosophers have been hard at work in the 700 years since Olivi's death. Despite these efforts, the ground on which the debate is waged has hardly shifted since that time. I now want to show how a closer look at Olivi and his contemporaries can help us get clear about precisely where that ground lies.

THE VOLUNTARIST SPIN

One scale along which the free will debate is often gauged runs from intellectualism to voluntarism. On this scale, Olivi clearly counts as a voluntarist. As we have seen, he explains freedom of choice in terms of the will's capacity to be a self mover. For Olivi, the scholastic power of *liberum arbitrium* (free decision) is entirely a power on the side of will, and this may seem dramatically different from how other scholastics understand *liberum arbitrium*. Thomas Aquinas, most notably, held that « the root of all freedom is found in reason »[4]; throughout his career, Aquinas accounted for the will's freedom of choice by appealing to the intellect's capacity to deliberate about the best possible action. As he writes in his *Compendium of Theology*, « that is free which is not bound to any one determinate good. But the appetite of an intellectual substance is not bound to any one determinate good *because it follows the apprehension of intellect* »[5]. Human freedom, in other words, comes from following intellect – not from the will's acting autonomously. Indeed, appetitive powers like the will are in general passive, not active : « an appetitive capacity is a passive capacity that is naturally

1. Ad 5, p. 341-342.
2. Ad 22, p. 368.
3. Ad 22, p. 369.
4. Thomas Aquinas, *Quaestiones de veritate* [=*QDV*] 24.2c.
5. I. 76.134.

suited to be moved by something apprehended »[1]. This means that the rational powers of intellect and will are related as prior to posterior, mover to moved, active to passive: « [T]he intellect is prior to the will, just as what produces movement is prior to the moveable, and the active to the passive. For the good that is an object of intellect moves the will »[2]. Aquinas even claims that the intellect is a higher, nobler capacity than the will[3].

Such « intellectualism » occasioned considerable criticism. The thesis that the will is passive was among the propositions condemned in Paris by Stephen Tempier in 1270. As for the claim that freedom stems from the intellectual side, Olivi himself condemned this as « insane » and « derogatory to our faith »[4]. Aquinas ran into still more trouble for claiming that the intellect is a higher capacity than the will. William de la Mare's widely circulated *Correctorium fratris Thomae* (« Correction of Brother Thomas », c. 1278) took specific issue with this thesis, holding that although it may not be « directly contrary to the faith or good conduct », still « it seems false and the forerunner of much that is false » (art. 34). Henry of Ghent too would describe the will as « the highest power in the whole governance of the soul, and thus higher than the intellect itself »[5].

The medieval debate is full of contention along these lines, and modern scholarship continues to measure scholastic theories of the will in terms of the degree to which a theory is or is not voluntarist[6]. But a close look at the theories themselves reveals that most of this talk of voluntarism and intellectualism is empty rhetoric. Aquinas's critics rallied to defend the will in the way that modern politicians rally to defend the flag, or family values. In actual fact neither Aquinas nor his more intelligent defenders ever denied that the will plays a leading role in the process of choice and action. If a voluntarist is someone who holds that the will is what controls human choices, then Aquinas is as much a voluntarist as anyone on the medieval scene.

Consider, for instance, the much-maligned claim that « intellect is superior to will »[7]. Even a cursory look at Aquinas's argument for that thesis reveals that it rests entirely on a comparison between the objects of intellect and the objects of will. Since the will concerns things insofar as they are good, whereas the intellect concerns the true essences of things, including the essence of goodness itself, the intellect has a certain conceptual priority. Whatever the significance of this line of

1. *Summa theologiae* [=*ST*] 1a 80.2c.
2. *ST* 1a 82.3 ad 2.
3. *ST* 82.3c.
4. Olivi, q. 57 ad 21, p. 365.
5. Henry of Ghent, *Quodlibet* I. 14.
6. On Aquinas see, *e.g.*, J. Hause, « Thomas Aquinas and the Voluntarists », *Medieval Philosophy and Theology* 6, 1997, p. 168 : « In my view, however, the debates among the voluntarist interpreters are all moot because Aquinas is not a voluntarist at all; he is a thoroughgoing intellectualist. » On Olivi, see F.X. Putallaz, « Pierre de Jean Olivi ou la liberté persécutée », in *Les philosophies morales et politiques au moyen âge*, t. 2, B. Bazán *et al.* ed., New York, 1995 : « On imagine volontiers que la doctrine olivienne de la liberté puisse être l'une des formes les plus radicales qu'ait pu prendre la tendance dite 'voluntariste' durant le XIIIe siècle » (p. 906). Putallaz discusses Olivi's views at greater length in *Insolente liberté. Controverses et condamnations au* XIIIe *siècle*, Fribourg- Paris, 1995.
7. *ST* 1a 82.3c.

thought, it certainly shows nothing about whether intellect or will plays the dominant role in human action. Here voluntarism is simply not the issue.

Voluntarism might more plausibly seem to be at stake in Aquinas's insistence that the will is passive, and that it must be moved by the intellect, which shows it the desirability of a certain course of action. For Aquinas, « it is necessary that every motion of the will be preceded by an apprehension »[1]. This would seem to be firmly at odds with Olivi's insistence that « the will does not need to be moved by anything else toward any act of willing »[2]. As its own first cause, the will seems to be independent, and in charge, in a way that is entirely alien to Aquinas's thinking.

Even here, however, there is little to choose from between Olivi and Aquinas, or between any of the scholastic disputants. Aquinas and Olivi agree that the intellect does not move the will as an *efficient* cause; instead, the intellect supplies information about the will's final cause, the object that has been judged to be good. « Something good that is grasped by intellect is the object of the will, and moves it as an end »[3]. Aquinas rejects the idea that the intellect determines the will's choice in the way « that which pushes moves that which is pushed »[4]. More revealingly, « the intellect rules the will not as if by inclining it toward what it tends toward, but by showing it where it ought to tend »[5].

This is not dramatically different from Olivi's view. He too acknowledges that « one cannot will, unless one first grasps with intellect that which one wills »[6]. Olivi of course agrees with Aquinas that neither the intellect nor its objects are efficient causes. In Olivi's technical causal vocabulary, such objects are required « only as the terminus of the attention (*aspectum*) of the agent's power »[7], a deliberately non-Aristotelian phrase, but one that in this context is not far from Aquinas's talk of final causes[8]. In less abstract terms, « The will (at least considered as free) receives nothing at all from the intellect and its act, nor is [the intellect] required for its act – except only for the representation of an object »[9]. Still, such representation is necessary. Olivi explicitly concedes, for instance, that the will's capacity for opposite actions requires that those opposites be shown to it by intellect[10]. So Olivi and Aquinas agree that the will needs the intellect, and they essentially agree on what the intellect is needed for.

Even if Olivi and Aquinas agree on these points, they may still seem to differ on the further question of how the will is moved. Olivi, as we have seen, believes

1. *ST* 1a 82.4 ad 3.
2. Olivi, q. 58 ad 12, p. 433.
3. Thomas Aquinas, *ST* 1a 82.4c.
4. Thomas Aquinas, *ST* 1a 82.4c.
5. Thomas Aquinas, *QDV* 22.11 ad 5.
6. Olivi, q. 59, p. 544.
7. Olivi, q. 58 ad 3, p. 419.
8. Olivi invokes this same causal account to explain perception : the senses, he argues, are active powers that have external sensible objects as the terminus of their attention. See R. Pasnau, *Theories of Cognition in the Later Middle Ages*, Cambridge, 1997, chs. 4-5. Olivi himself describes the terminus of attention as a kind of final cause (q. 72, t. 3, p. 36).
9. Olivi, q. 57 ad 12, p. 354.
10. Olivi, q. 58 ad 2.

that the will moves itself, and this may seem to be the crucial point of contention. But even here Aquinas can agree. In *ST* 1a2ae q. 9, he considers the things that can move the will, and he arrives at a list of four :

1. The will is moved by intellect (a. 1).
2. The will is moved by sensory appetites (a. 2).
3. The will is moved by itself (a. 3).
4. The will is moved by God (a. 6).

Of the four, only the last two exercise efficient causality; as he says elsewhere, « the will's movement comes directly from the will and from God »[1]. God's role in our voluntary actions must necessarily be rather remote : he creates us, but leaves us room to make our own choices. If God directly moved us to make a certain choice, the choice could hardly be voluntary[2]. What we are left with, then, is that the will itself is ordinarily the sole direct efficient cause of its own actions. Aquinas believes that the will is constantly moving itself: this occurs every time its choice to pursue a particular course is motivated by the desire to pursue a broader goal. I will to become healthier, for instance, and so I will myself to take a particular medicine[3]. « If someone wills an end with one act, and with another act wills the means toward an end, then willing the end will be for him the cause of willing the means toward the end »[4]. To stress the familiarity of the process, Aquinas compares it to the way the intellect moves through an argument from premises to conclusions[5]. Just as the will moves itself, so too does the intellect.

It may seem that these higher-order volitions will ultimately make little difference – not enough, at any rate, to warrant classifying Aquinas as a voluntarist. Although the maneuver focuses the attention on will for a moment, the ball may very quickly seem to be back in intellect's court. How are these higher-order volitions determined, after all, if not by intellect? I want the medicine because I want to be healthy, but surely I want to be healthy because reason favors this course. Higher-order volitions look like mere epicycles in a fundamentally intellectualist account.

To see how Aquinas is giving the will a real role in the process of choice, we need to focus not on sudden desires for a certain end, but on long-term dispositions that govern our day-to-day choices. The will does not simply endorse the passing judgments of reason, in a neutral fashion, but subjects those judgments to the higher-order aims that shape who we are. The will, in other words, contains habits or dispositions that influence the course of its operation[6]. Reason may tell us to cheat, but the will can insist on honesty; reason may counsel silence, but the will can urge us to speak. In such cases it is the will that is control,

1. Thomas Aquinas, *Quaestiones de malo* [=*QDM*] 3.3c.
2. Thomas Aquinas, *ST* 1a 2ae 9.6c.
3. Thomas Aquinas, *QDM* 6c.
4. Thomas Aquinas, *ST* 1a 19.5c.
5. *Ibid.*, 1a2ae 9.3c.
6. See *ST* 1a2ae 50.5.

in virtue of its fixed dispositions and desires. The will cannot entirely repudiate reason, but the will shapes reason just as much as reason shapes will.

No wonder Aquinas points to the will's capacity for self-movement as a requirement for *liberum arbitrium :* « The will is in control of its act, and has it to will and not to will. This would not be the case if it did not have the power to move itself to will » [1].

In the face of such remarks, it is hard to see the point of characterizing Aquinas as an intellectualist. In terms of ultimate causal responsibility, it looks like the will itself, as the efficient cause, plays the dominant role. (Recall from above how the role of the intellect lies in simply « showing [the will] where it ought to tend »). And in terms of psychological motivation, it looks as if Aquinas gives the will at least as large a role as he does the intellect. Our choices are of course influenced by rational deliberation, but they are just as much influenced by our long-term values and dispositions, which determine the sorts of options that reason will consider, the weight to which reason will give various factors, and the ultimate ends that we wish to pursue. All of this seems to have no greater claim to the label 'intellectualist' than does Olivi's account.

THE CAUSAL CRUX

Medieval proponents of the top-down approach distinguished themselves not by giving the will a larger role in human action, nor by describing the will as a self mover. Their distinctive claim, instead, was that the will functions as an unmoved mover, a first cause that is entirely sufficient as an explanation of free choices. Olivi may not have been the first to treat the will as an absolutely first cause or unmoved mover, but his account is sufficiently clear and detailed to warrant attention. He argues that the will has such autonomy that it can move itself and other things no matter what the countervailing inclinations :

> It is necessary that free will have the character of a first mover and be such that it could impel and move and restrain itself and other powers and active virtues subject to it, and this not only when there is nothing impelling it toward the contrary, but even when there *is* something inclining it toward the contrary [2].

The will's power is such that it can, on its own and without any prior cause, choose to do one thing or the opposite. In such cases the causal story simply ends with the will, and there is nothing more that *needs* to be said, as well as nothing more that *can* be said :

> In order to produce one effect there is no need to provide a fuller cause than one that is completely sufficient, and this is so certain that one who would want to provide something more will not find what more there is that he *could* provide. Therefore when one cause is posited to have complete sufficiency with respect to

1. *ST* 1a2ae 9.3sc ; *Cf. ST* 1a 105.4 ad 3.
2. Olivi, q. 58, p. 411.

> opposites – *e.g.*, with respect to action and rest – then if one asks why it ceases or what the reason for its ceasing is, it is entirely sufficient to reply by saying that it was completely and sufficiently able to cease [...]. Therefore, although there was no greater reason for acting than for ceasing, and conversely, it was nevertheless sufficient for each of those, taken disjunctively [1].

The will is not entirely self-sufficient. God must create it, for starters, and the intellect must show it the various options among which it chooses. But when supplied with these various choices, the will itself is « completely sufficient » as a cause of one choice or another. The will could go in one direction or another, without there being any further cause explaining that choice.

It has become commonplace, in modern libertarian accounts, to hold that the will has the capacity, at a given moment, to do one thing or the opposite. Olivi takes this view himself, as is clear, but (surprisingly enough) he does not think that this capacity is either necessary or sufficient for free will. The capacity for opposites is a « secondary » characteristic of freedom, not itself sufficient for freedom « unless it obtains because of the thing's operating by itself, not driven by another » [2]. Primarily, then, freedom is characterized by something's being its own first cause : « The will is said to have freedom, first and *per se*, because that which it does it does by itself. It is not driven and moved by another, but rather it drives itself toward what it does » [3]. The will can be free, then, even when it is not capable of doing opposites. Even though the will necessarily wills happiness, for instance, it does so freely. God's love of himself is likewise both necessary and free [4].

Olivi takes care to distinguish this position from the mere claim that the will moves itself. For Aquinas and others, the will is a self mover in the sense that one volition can give rise to another. Olivi of course does not deny that this can happen. But he insists that the will is capable of self movement of an altogether different sort : that the will is capable of spontaneously moving itself, without any prior act of will, simply as a consequence of the will's power. In taking this position, he has to confront Anselm's distinguished opposition. In *De casu diaboli* chapter 12, Anselm seems to maintain (as Olivi himself puts it) that « the will [...] cannot go from not willing to willing, unless there is something that moves it from not willing to willing » [5]. Ordinarily, Anselm thinks that the will moves itself, willing itself to will. But he imagines an angel that was created so as to be, at this moment, « ready to will but not yet willing anything » [6]. This angel

1. *Id.*, q. 57 ad 5, p. 342.
2. *Ibid.*, ad 17, p. 358-359.
3. *Ibid.*, p. 358 ; *Cf.* q. 116, t. 3, p. 341.
4. *Ibid.*, p. 359.
5. Q. 57 obj. 12, p. 399.
6. « *[...] iam sit aptus ad habendum voluntatem sed nondum velit aliquid* » (*De casu diaboli* ch. 12). Literally, Anselm says that this angel is « ready to have a will », but what this in fact means is that the angel is ready to be actively willing something – ready to have a volition. (This represents an older usage of the word *voluntas*.) If Anselm meant that the angel entirely lacked the capacity of will, the case would not bear on Olivi's thesis. The point, instead, is that even though the angel has a will, it nevertheless has nothing within it that could generate a first volition.

could not move itself to that first act of willing, because « whatever moves itself to willing, first wills itself so to move ». Since the angel, *ex hypothesi*, does not will anything, it cannot move itself to will, and so it needs something else to move it.

Olivi wants to deny these inferences. If Anselm is right, then the will « cannot move itself except through some will given to it in advance » [1]. This goes directly against Olivi's view that the will is a « completely sufficient » first cause [2], and so he immediately (and tactfully) explains how it seems to « some » that Anselm went wrong. Anselm's mistake was his assumption that the only way a thing can move itself to will is through some prior act of willing. This sometimes happens, as when our desire for an end motivates a desire for the means to that end [3]. But some acts of will are produced by the will itself, without any prior volition. Contrary to Anselm's assertion that the will, if not willing, cannot move itself to will [4], Olivi holds that the will can move itself by an impulse, and that this impulse just is the volition itself [5]. In other words, there is no need for any prior cause, other than the faculty of will itself. No prior internal volition is needed, and no external cause is needed.

Anselm causes still more trouble when he claims that « the will moves itself through its affections » [6]. Olivi sees a threat to his own view here, if this is read as meaning that the will moves itself solely by means of prior dispositions [7]. This is how, above, we saw Aquinas describe the will's capacity for self movement. The will moves itself in that it has certain dispositions to pursue certain ends. We are responsible for our actions insofar as we are responsible for those dispositions.

Olivi finds such accounts inadequate : « Not all of what is done through such dispositions (*habitus*) is done freely, but only when it is brought to action by the will, freely » [8]. Although he acknowledges a role for dispositions in making one's choices easier and more reliable, he holds that at other times the will embarks on a new course, and in such cases « the will moves itself through its own free power » [9] rather than through any prior disposition. His example is loving one's enemy for the first time : « Nothing else preceding need to be supplied through which I am moved to this, especially since it is through this motion that I would generate within myself a dispositional love of him, and not *vice versa* » [10].

Even in cases where the disposition is already in place, Olivi thinks free will requires a capacity for self movement that is independent of that disposition. For

1. Olivi, ad 12, p. 434.

2. Olivi actually denies that this goes « directly against us », since Anselm at least agrees that the will moves itself to an act of willing (q. 57 ad 12, t. 2, p. 434). But he is clearly struggling to put the best face on things.

3. Olivi, ad 12, p. 435.

4. « *Si dixero quia moveatur non volens, consequens erit ut non a se sed ab alio moveatur [...]* » (*De casu diaboli*, ch. 12).

5. « *Idcirco, quando voluntas exit in actum volendi, qui simul est impulsus voluntatis et eius motio, dicimus quod movet eam ad volendum* » (q. 57 ad 12, t. 2, p. 434).

6. *De concordia praescientia et praedestinationis et gratia dei cum libero arbitrio* III. 11.

7. See q. 57 obj. 28, p. 315.

8. Q. 59 ad 15, p. 564.

9. Q. 57 ad 28, p. 376.

10. *Ibid.*

one thing, the will must have the capacity to act against its dispositions: « otherwise the virtuous could not fall from virtue toward vice, nor conversely »[1]. Moreover, the will is rarely if ever so unified in its desires as to be subject to just a single disposition. Appealing to the case of Augustine's *Confessions*, Olivi holds that we often experience ourselves to have « two wills » in conflict[2]. In such cases, we cannot explain choices simply in terms of the will's being moved by some higher-level disposition. This « does great harm to freedom of the will »; the will would be « entirely compelled to act, in the way brute animals are »[3]. Again Olivi is working from the top-down, using experiential data to reach conclusions about the causal story that must be told.

A final remarkable feature of Olivi's view is that he wants to apply this experiential data across the board: so that it applies not just to the will, but also to the soul's cognitive faculties. Olivi digresses at length, in the middle of his discussion of free will, to argue against the traditional Aristotelian conception of the senses and intellect as passive. « That which in my judgment above all else moved many to believe that our will is entirely passive was and remains this: that they firmly held that all other capacities are passive »[4].

Like his opponents, Olivi agrees that it would be odd to make the will a special case, a uniquely active power surrounded by entirely passive faculties. But rather than rejecting self motion as metaphysically incoherent, Olivi preserves the data of experience by insisting that self motion should be embraced across the board. On Olivi's full account, there turns out to be nothing suspiciously *sui generis* about the will's capacity for self movement. The will is entirely active, but so are the soul's other capacities[5].

1. Q. 58, p. 411.
2. See *Confessions* VIII.v. 10, VIII.x. 24.
3. Q. 57 ad 29, p. 385.
4. Q. 58 ad 14, p. 461.
5. I discussed Olivi's views on the active nature of cognition in *Theories*, *op. cit.*, ch. 4. But there I failed to understand Olivi's motivation for linking his treatment of will and the cognitive capacities, referring to this linkage as « curious » (p. 157).

OLIVI ET LE TEMPS

Ruedi Imbach et François-Xavier Putallaz

INTRODUCTION

Depuis les travaux d'Anneliese Maier[1] il y a près d'un demi-siècle, la conception du temps chez Pierre de Jean Olivi n'a guère retenu l'attention des historiens de la philosophie, à l'exception peut-être d'un chapitre que lui a consacré Udo Jeck en 1994[2].

Notre intention est de reconsidérer certains aspects de cette analyse en l'abordant ici par le biais d'un manuscrit inédit : le *Codex Vatican Borghese 322* (f° 195va-198rb)[3], dont le contenu peut être rapproché du *Quodlibet I, 3* d'Olivi. Si ces deux textes vont principalement retenir notre attention, il existe néanmoins d'autres passages dont il faut commencer par rappeler brièvement l'existence.

II Sent. q. 9

La q. 9 des *Quaestiones in Secundum librum Sententiarum* est consacrée au problème de l'*aevum*[4] : il s'agit de déterminer la durée propre aux réalités spirituelles qui, tels les anges, ne sont pas éternelles[5]. Alors que Thomas d'Aquin voyait dans l'*aevum* une mesure des réalités ne supposant en elles-mêmes aucune succession[6], Pierre Olivi se rattache à l'interprétation de Bonaventure pour qui

1. A. Maier, « Die Subjektivierung der Zeit in der scholastischen Philosophie », *Philosophia naturalis* 1, 1951, p. 361-398 ; A. Maier, *Metaphysische Hintergründe der spätscholastischen Naturphilosophie*, Roma, 1955, p. 47-137.

2. U.R. Jeck, *Aristoteles contra Augustinum. Zur Frage nach dem Verhältnis von Zeit und Seele bei den antiken Aristoteleskommentatoren, im arabischen Aristotelismus und im 13. Jahrhundert*, Amsterdam-Philadelphia, 1994.

3. Nous remercions Sylvain Piron pour nous avoir fourni d'utiles indications à propos de ce manuscrit.

4. *Cf.* P. Porro, *Forme e modelli di durata nel pensiero medievale. L'« aevum », il tempo discreto, la categoria « quando »*, Leuven, 1996.

5. Cette question a fait l'objet d'une assez curieuse étude de O. Bettini, « La temporalità delle cose e l'esigenza di un principio assoluto nella dottrina di Olivi », *Antonianum* 28, 1953, p. 148-187. D. Burr y a consacré quelques lignes dans *Pierre Olivi, franciscain persécuté*, Fribourg-Paris, 1997, p. 78-80.

6. Par exemple, à la question « *utrum duratio angeli habeat prius et posterius* », Thomas d'Aquin répond notamment : « *Sic ergo si attribuatur mensura [durationis] angelo quantum ad substanciam tantum, illa non habet prius et posterius : sic enim mensuratur eorum esse euo* ». *Quodl.* X, q. 2,

l'*aevum* suppose une succession selon un *prius* et un *posterius*, quand bien même il n'implique aucun changement.

Pourquoi cette interprétation ? Si Olivi introduit une succession dans l'*aevum*, c'est pour souligner la réalité créaturale des substances spirituelles et sauver au mieux l'absolue transcendance de Dieu. A ses yeux les *sequaces Aristotelis*, ayant suivi le philosophe païen qui ne posait pas de succession dans les intelligences, l'ont abandonné lorsque Aristote faisait de ces dernières des dieux, et ils ont dès lors adopté une position bancale et contradictoire [1].

II Sent. q. 10

La question qui suit, la q. 10 des *Quaestiones in Secundum librum Sententiarum*, demande combien il existe de forme de temporalités ? Y en a-t-il une, deux ou plusieurs ? L'analyse permet à Olivi de rejeter deux opinions, dont l'une est longuement combattue. La critique de cette opinion s'achève sur une remarque lapidaire : « *Ista autem via longe est ab aula, quia a nullo magno communiter hodie, quod sciam, tenetur* » [2]. La moisson est mince, car on ne trouve là aucune explicitation positive de la conception olivienne du temps.

Quodl. I, 2

La deuxième question du *Quodlibet I* est quant à elle consacrée au problème de la relation du temps à l'instant qui passe : « *Quaeritur utrum tempus sit idem quod nunc fluens* ». Pour y répondre, Olivi présente trois opinions.

La première opinion tient que l'instant reste toujours identique à lui-même dans son essence (*secundum essentiam*), mais qu'il varie selon qu'il est sujet de modes d'exister différents (*secundum varia esse que accipit*). C'est ainsi que d'aucuns ont soutenu que toute l'essence du temps réside dans cet instant en mouvement : il s'agit de ceux qui identifient le temps au *nunc fluens* dont parle la question.

On signalera une constante dans la critique de cette position, puisqu'on la trouve dans le *Quodlibet I, 2* aussi bien que dans le *Borgh. 322 : « [...] et inde est*

art. un. ; Thomas d'Aquin, *Quaestiones de quolibet*, Léonine t. 25, 1, Rome-Paris, 1996, p. 129, l. 88-91. *Cf.* aussi Thomas d'Aquin, *Summa theologiae* I, 10, 5.

1. « *Via autem philosophorum paganorum, quantum credo, decepit istos ; illi enim coacti fuerunt ponere in intelligentiis durationem simplicem, quia posuerunt eas exire a Deo necessario et aeternaliter. [...] Posuerunt etiam in eis operationes intrinsecas invariabiles et aeternas, immo etiam eis consubstantiales, sicut apparet inspicienti subtiliter dicta eorum et maxime sequacium* Aristotelis ; *nec mirum, quia posuerunt eas tanquam deos, licet inferiores Deo summo. Istis autem positis quae directissime evacuant totam catholicam fidem necessarium fuit tenere durationem earum esse simul simplicem et actu infinitam ; isti autem in parte dicta eorum accipientes, pro quanto videlicet visa sunt eis non repugnare fidei, visi sunt non attendisse quod contradictio implicabatur in accipiendo partem dicti cum abiectione partis alterius quae fidei aperte contrariabatur* ». P.I. Olivi, II *Sent.*, q. 9, I, 175 (= Petrus Iohannis Olivi, *Quaestiones in Secundum librum Sententiarum*, ed. B. Jansen, 3e vol., Quaracchi, 1922-1926).

2. II *Sent.*, q. 10, I, 193.

quod dicunt aliqui, quod instans fluens est tota substancia temporis [...] »[1]. Le *aliqui* renvoie très vraisemblablement à Henri de Gand, lequel affirmait notamment que « *ipsum enim nunc est tota substantia temporis, in quo consistit totum esse temporis [...]* »[2]. Nous y reviendrons.

La deuxième opinion affirme seulement que le *fluens* ajoute quelque chose d'essentiel à l'instant.

Mais c'est à la troisième opinion que se rallie Olivi : il n'est pas possible qu'un instant puisse demeurer d'un bout à l'autre du temps. En réalité il n'existe aucun instant séparé en acte, exactement comme une ligne ne comporte aucun point en acte. Cette idée du *Quodl. I, 2* se retrouve identiquement dans le *Quodl. I, 3*[3], et se lit une nouvelle fois dans le *Borgh. 322* :

> *Unde vere, quod in toto tempore non est dare instans nisi illud in quo incipit et in quo desinit motus; illud enim est indivisibile, eo quod est continuum rei, et ideo vere habet racionem instantis. Sed quia in qualibet parte posset motus cessare et ita posset ibi tempus variari, ideo in qualibet parte est instans in potencia [...]*[4].

Bref, pour Olivi, le temps ne peut être identifié à l'instant[5].

Mais alors, qu'est-ce que le temps ? Cette question fait l'objet du *Quodl. I, 3* et du *Borgh. 322*, qui nous intéressent, mais elle y est posée sous une autre forme. En effet, les penseurs du XIIIe siècle acceptaient d'ordinaire la définition du temps léguée par Aristote : le temps, c'est la mesure du mouvement selon l'avant et l'après[6], et le problème portait moins sur la définition du temps que sur son mode d'exister. Aussi nos deux textes posent-il l'un et l'autre la question dans les termes suivants : « *Utrum tempus sit aliquid [reale] extra animam* ».

Mais d'où vient cette question et quel en est l'intérêt ? Pour le comprendre, il faut opérer un petit détour historique.

1. *Borgh. 322*, f° 196va. La comparaison entre les deux textes montre en effet un parallélisme intéressant : « *[...] et inde est quod dicunt aliqui, quod instans fluens est tota substancia temporis, quod tamen aliquo modo possit esse verum, ut dictum est, tamen valde improprie dicitur quod instans sit tota substancia temporis [...]* ». *Borgh. 322*, f° 196va. « *Dicendum quod quibusdam visum est idem nunc secundum essentiam in toto tempore semper esse, licet differat secundum varia esse que accipit in suo fluxu; et horum quidam dixerunt quod tota essentia temporis est illud nunc* ». *Quodl.* I, 2; Venetiis, 1509, f° 2rb.

2. Henri de Gand, *Quodl.* III, 11 (Jeck 475, 7-8). Henri de Gand affirme plus loin que « *revera necesse est ponere instans sive praesens esse in natura rei extra animam* ». Henri de Gand, *Quodl.* III, 11. Dans l'étude mentionnée ci-dessus, U.R. Jeck a établi une édition critique de ce texte; c'est elle que nous citons ici.

3. « *Falsum est igitur illud quod vulgariter dicitur, scilicet quod de tempore non habemus nisi nunc, loquendo de nunc indivisibili, licet sit verum sumendo nunc pro tempore presenti et divisibili, quia post debet dici quod in toto tempore non est actu aliquod nunc indivisibile nisi in sui initio et fine* ». *Quodl.* I, 3, f° 2vb.

4. *Borgh. 322*, f° 196va.

5. Si le temps s'identifiait à cet instant fluent, le *fluxus*, l'écoulement justement ne signifierait jamais une corruption de quoi que ce soit, et rien par conséquent ne cesserait jamais d'être : « *Preterea, secundum hoc [scil. si tempus esset idem quod nunc fluens], in toto tempore nihil realiter corrumpitur aut desinit esse, ac per consequens non est ibi aliquis fluxus dicens realem corruptionem aut desinitionem et preteritionem* ». *Quodl.* I, 2, f° 2rb.

6. Aristote, *Physique* IV, 11, 219a34-b1, et 220a24-25.

ORIGINE HISTORIQUE DE LA QUESTION

Une première constatation s'impose : dans sa célèbre condamnation du 7 mars 1277, Étienne Tempier a condamné un article qui vise une problématique proche de celle de nos deux questions. L'article 200 est en effet formulé comme suit[1] : « *Quod aevum et tempus nihil sunt in re, sed solum in apprehensione* ».

Plusieurs questions se posent à propos de cette thèse. D'abord on peut se demander qui était visé par cet article, et ensuite s'il existe un lien quelconque entre cet article condamné et les deux questions dont nous parlons. Pour ce qui est de cette seconde interrogation, nous ne l'aborderons pas ici. Quant à la première question posée, on peut rappeler qu'Udo R. Jeck et Roland Hissette ont renvoyé l'un et l'autre à Siger de Brabant et plus précisément à la *q. 8* de son commentaire du *De causis*, qu'ils considèrent comme l'une des sources possibles de l'article ; en effet, le terme « *apprehensio* » se rencontre à la fois dans le texte de Siger et dans l'article incriminé. R. Hissette en conclut que « cette insistance sur l'*apprehensio* a sans doute éveillé l'inquiétude d'un censeur »[2]. Mais si l'on examine d'un peu plus près la q. 8 de Siger, force est de constater qu'il s'agit d'une sorte de compilation-plagiat de la *Somme de théologie* I, 10, 1 de Thomas d'Aquin, ce qui nous autorise à conclure que l'article condamné concerne Thomas tout autant que Siger.

Mais les choses sont bien plus complexes encore, car en condamnant l'idée que le temps n'est pas une réalité hors de l'âme, les censeurs de 1277 pouvaient viser trois conceptions d'origine et de couleur fort différentes malgré leur parenté.

1. Il y avait d'abord Aristote. Après avoir livré la définition classique du temps entendu comme nombre du mouvement selon l'avant et l'après, le IVe livre de la *Physique* formule une aporie. Dans la *Translatio vetus*, ce texte célèbre débute comme suit : « *Utrum autem cum non sit anima, erit tunc tempus aut non. Dubitabit enim aliquis* »[3]. Aristote soulève ainsi le problème du rapport entre l'âme et le temps, problème suscité par sa propre définition du temps : le temps existerait-il si l'âme n'existait pas ?

2. Cette difficulté, Averroès l'a affrontée dans son grand *Commentaire de la Physique*, à la suite d'ailleurs de tous les commentateurs grecs de la *Physique*. Averroès dit ici très clairement que, sans l'âme, il n'y aurait pas de temps à strictement parler. Mais il introduit un nouvel aspect en se servant de la distinction entre acte et puissance : le temps en acte n'existe que par l'activité de l'âme, mais le temps existe imparfaitement et en puissance hors de l'âme[4].

1. Nous suivons la numérotation de Mandonnet, reprise par R. Hissette, *Enquête sur les 219 articles condamnés à Paris le 7 mars 1277*, Louvain-Paris, 1977.

2. R. Hissette, *op. cit.*, p. 154 ; *cf.* aussi U.R. Jeck, *op. cit.*, p. 329-338.

3. Aristoteles, *Physica* IV, 14, 223a21-22 ; *Aristoteles Latinus*, VII, 1, fasc. Secundus, éd. F. Bossier et J. Brams, Leiden-New York, 1990, p. 188, l. 10-12 ; *cf.* aussi le texte proposé par U.R. Jeck, *op. cit.*, p. 187.

4. « *[...] et quaeritur de tempore, utrum inveniatur extra animam, sicut est in anima [...] Et est impossibile, aliquid aliud numerare praeter animam et de anima intellectus. Manifestum est, quod si*

Thomas d'Aquin lui-même adoptera cette solution élégante, au moins dans son *Commentaire des Sentences*[1].

3. Il y avait une troisième solution. C'était la célèbre doctrine d'Augustin, telle qu'il l'avait formulée dans le XIe livre des *Confessions*. La position d'Augustin, affirmant le non-être du temps, repose à la fois sur l'inexistence des parties du temps (passé et futur) et sur l'inexistence de l'instant. Or cette théorie explicite du non-être du temps amène Augustin à postuler que le temps n'existe que dans l'âme; aussi affirme-t-il que le temps est une *distentio animi*.

Dans l'état actuel de nos recherches, nous ne pouvons déterminer avec certitude si les censeurs parisiens visaient plutôt la variante aristotélico-averroïste de la négation de la réalité du temps en dehors de l'âme ou au contraire la variante augustinienne.

Pour ce qui est du problème de la réalité du temps avant la condamnation de 1277, on peut noter que la position d'Averroès aussi bien que celle d'Augustin ont été largement débattues[2]. De plus, Robert Grosseteste[3] et Albert le Grand[4] ont l'un et l'autre sévèrement critiqué l'approche augustinienne du problème, alors que nous ne trouvons aucune discussion sur ce point chez Thomas d'Aquin. Précisons enfin que le dominicain allemand rejette également la doctrine d'Averroès, alors que nous en trouvons des traces incontestables chez Thomas et chez Gilles de Rome[5].

anima non fuerit, non erit numerus. Et cum numerus non fuerit, non erit tempus. [...] Idest, et motus erit, et si anima non erit. Et secundum quod prius et posterius sunt in eo numerata in potentia, est tempus in potentia. Et secundum quod sunt numerata in actu, est tempus in actu. Tempus igitur in actu non erit, nisi anima sit. [...] Et tempus nihil aliud est quam prius et posterius in motu, sed secundum quod sunt numerata. Et ideo indiget in hoc, quod sit in actu anima, scilicet secundum quod est prius et posterius numerata. [...] Secundum igitur hunc modum dicitur tempus habere esse extra animam simile perfecto, et si non sit perfectum» Averroes, *In Aristotelis Phys.* IV, t. comment. 131, nous suivons l'édition établie de ce passage par U.R. Jeck, *op. cit.*, p. 125-127; *cf.* aussi l'édition de Venise (Junctina), vol. IV, 1562, f° 202ra-va.

1. « *Ex quo patet quod illud quod est de tempore quasi materiale fundatur in motu, scilicet prius et posterius; quod autem est formale, completur in operatione animae numerantis; propter quod dicit Philosophus,* IV Phys., text. 131, *quod si non esset anima, non esset tempus* » Thomas d'Aquin, *In Sent.* I, d. XIX, q. 2, a. 1, sol. Il est à noter que Thomas remplace la terminologie de l'acte et de la puissance par celle de forme-matière; quant au fond, il reste toutefois fidèle à la doctrine du philosophe arabe.

2. *Cf.* à ce propos l'ample analyse de U.R. Jeck, *op. cit.*, p. 200-328.

3. Grosseteste discute ces problèmes dans son *Commentaire de la Physique* IV (Roberti Grosseteste Episcopi Lincolniensis, *Commentarius in VIII libros Physicorum*, éd. R.C. Dales, Boulder, Colorado, 1963); voir l'analyse détaillée de U.R. Jeck, *op. cit.*, p. 206-211.

4. La question *De tempore*, dans le *De IV coaequavis* (datée d'avant 1246) comporte une critique ouverte de la position augustinienne comme l'a montré de manière convaincante U.R. Jeck, *op. cit.*, p. 219-232.

5. Jeck affirme que le *Commentaire des Sentences* de Gilles de Rome (*In* I *Sent.*, d. XIX, p. 1, q. 2, a. 1, Venise, 1521, f° 106ra) défend une position ouvertement « averroïste » sur la question du temps. Elle sera approfondie dans le *Commentaire de la Physique;* à ce propos, *cf.* U.R. Jeck, *op. cit.*, p. 296-302 et 314-322.

LA RÉPONSE DE PIERRE OLIVI

Quodl. I, 3

A la question si discutée de la réalité extramentale du temps, le *Quodl. I, 3* d'Olivi répond avec tranchant: « L'existence du temps peut s'entendre de deux manières ». D'une part, on peut prendre le temps dans sa totalité, lorsque ses différentes parties sont données simultanément; dans ce sens, le temps n'existe pas hors de l'âme, et Augustin a ici raison. D'autre part, on peut prendre le temps dans le sens où ses parties existent l'une à la suite de l'autre; dans ce sens, le temps existe dans les choses hors de l'âme[1].

La réponse donnée par Olivi est donc rapide et incisive. Néanmoins la distinction entre ces deux façons de concevoir le temps n'est pas explicitée dans le *Quodl. I, 3;* on se sentirait pourtant en droit d'en attendre un commentaire. Or cette explication existe, mais il faut la lire dans le *Borgh. 322*[2].

1. « *Dicendum quod de existentia temporis possumus loqui dupliciter : primo scilicet eam simul totam accipiendo, ac si tota instar permanentium esset simul, et sic non est nisi in consideratione nostra. Et hoc modo verum est quod Augustinus dicit. Secundo modo secundum quod una eius pars vere fit et existit post alteram, et secundum quod una inde preterit, et alia vere advenit. Et sic vere est in rebus extra apprehensionem anime* » *Quodl.* I, 3, f° 2va.

2. Voici le plan détaillé de la question consacrée à ce problème dans le *Borgh. 322* (*Utrum tempus sit aliquid reale extra animam*, f° 195va-198rb) qui, sept ou huit fois plus long que le *Quodl. I, 3*, est forcément beaucoup plus complexe et détaillé :

1.Prima opinio : tempus nihil est extra animam
1.1. Primum argumentum : ex quiditate temporis
1.2. Secundum argumentum : ex existentia parcium temporis
1.3. Contra primam opinionem
1.3. 1. Primum argumentum : comparando tempus ad motum
1.3. 2. Secundum argumentum : comparando tempus ad animam
2. Secunda opinio : tempus est res extra animam
2.1. Quatuor consideraciones
2.1. 1. Quomodo se habet tempus ad instans
2.1. 2. Quomodo se habet tempus ad motum et quietem
2.1. 2.1 Quatuor genera toti
.
2.1. 2.2 Motus comparatur ad mobile et ad magnitudinem
.
2.1. 2.3 Duplex divisibilitas
.
2.1. 2.4 Divisio rei temporalis
.
2.1. 2.5 Quomodo tempus causetur a motu
.
2.1. 2.6 Tempus et quies
.
2.1. 3. Quomodo se habet tempus ad animam
2.1. 3.1 Totalitas completa in anima
.
2.1. 3.2 Totalitas non completa in rebus extra
.
2.1. 4. Quid est tempus
2.2. Responsio

Borgh. 322

Le *Borgh. 322* reprend donc la même idée. Il y a en effet, répète l'auteur, deux manières de considérer l'existence de la temporalité dans son ensemble [1] : ou bien on la prend comme une totalité *complète*, et le temps dépend alors de l'âme ; ou bien on la prend comme une totalité *incomplète*, et le temps existe alors hors de l'âme. Commençons par cette seconde approche.

Le temps hors de l'âme

Si nous considérons les choses dans leur devenir, c'est-à-dire dans leur *succession*, la totalité du temps n'est jamais donnée de telle manière que ses parties (passé, futur) existent simultanément ; la totalité du temps se présente seulement comme une continuité où une première partie d'un mouvement est suivie continuellement et réellement par une autre partie, et ainsi de suite, comme c'est le cas pour le mouvement lui-même : « *Certum enim est, quod post primam partem motus continue et realiter sequitur altera, et post illam iterum altera, et sic continue quousque motus fuerit terminatus* » [2]. La réalité du temps ainsi entendue est une sorte d'écoulement (*fluxus*) qui se présente comme une *continuité* réelle, où les parties se relaient les unes les autres sans discontinuité (*sine interpolacione*). Bref, tout l'être et toute l'essence [3] du temps sont un flux continu et un devenir existant *dans les choses* : « *Tempus enim unum quodammodo [?] est et quicquid realiter tempus est totum extra animam, eo quod totum esse eius est continuatum fieri* » [4].

Le temps dans l'âme

Mais nous pouvons considérer la totalité du temps d'une autre manière et l'entendre comme un tout constitué de plusieurs parties existant ensemble, comme une totalité formée de passé et de futur. Évidemment, une telle totalité n'existe pas dans les choses ; elle n'existe que dans l'âme :

> *Uno enim modo potest sumi totalitas completa, ut intelligatur successivum esse unum totum ex*[5] *pluribus partibus simul existentibus, ut tempus ex preterito et futuro ; et sic nunquam est ipsa dare in rerum natura, eo quod vere non essent successiva, sed habent isto modo hoc, quod sunt in re extra animam et suam totalitatem ab anima*[6].

Comment cela se fait-il ? Lorsque le passé était réellement présent, il a pu être appréhendé par l'âme ; aussi lorsqu'il est devenu réellement passé, il n'a pas pour

1. *Cf.* Thomas d'Aquin, In *Phys. IV*, lect. 23, n. 629 : « *Sic igitur et tempus non habet esse extra animam, nisi secundum suum indivisibile : ipsa autem totalitas temporis accipitur per ordinationem animae numerantis prius et posterius in motu* ».

2. *Cod. Borgh. 322*, f° 198ra.

3. « *[...] sic vere ita est in re, sic est tota essencia temporis et totum esse eius* » *Cod. Borgh. 322*, f° 198ra.

4. *Cod. Borgh. 322*, f° 198ra.

5. ex] quod *Cod. Borgh.*

6. *Cod. Borgh. 322*, f° 198ra.

autant passé aux yeux de l'âme qui l'avait appréhendé : l'appréhension des choses demeure dans l'âme après leur destruction. C'est ainsi que l'âme peut rapporter ce qui a été saisi auparavant à ce qui l'a été après (*conferendo postea prius ad posterius*).

C'est cette totalité-là, et elle seulement, qui dépend de l'âme : « *Et isto modo loquendo totalitas temporis totaliter dependet ab anima, non tamen eius essencia, quia*[1] *realem essenciam parcium invenit anima in re, non tamen eorum totalitatem, que simul non sunt* »[2].

Pour illustrer la différence qui existe entre ces deux manières d'envisager le temps, Olivi propose un exemple, celui d'un groupe de trois personnes. Prenons trois hommes. Ceux-ci existent bien dans la réalité ; aucun d'eux cependant n'est à lui seul trois personnes ; le nombre trois n'est en rien un accident de chacun d'eux. Il n'empêche qu'ils sont vraiment trois : les trois unités en question existent dans la réalité, mais leur *totalité* n'existe que par l'âme qui les réfère l'un à l'autre et dit que ces unités sont au nombre de trois[3].

Il en va de même pour le temps : le temps est quelque chose de réel qui existe dans les choses comme un devenir continu (*continuatum fieri*). Mais si on y distingue des parties discontinues, c'est-à-dire un *prius* réellement distinct d'un *posterius*, le temps, qui est la mesure de ce changement selon un avant et un après, est alors analogue au nombre de tout à l'heure et n'existe que dans l'appréhension de l'âme.

En conclusion :

> *Totalitas tamen eius [scil. temporis] dependet ab anima conferente prius ad posterius : totalitas dico simultatis parcium. Sed hec totalitas non est de natura successivi, sed de natura apprehensionis [...]. Totalitas autem successiva, inquantum successiva est, non dependet ab anima, eo quod illi sufficit realis successio parcium*[4].

1. quia] quod *Cod. Borgh.*

2. *Cod. Borgh. 322*, f° 197vb-198ra. Dans la réalité (*in re*), les parties de cette totalité ne peuvent être données en même temps que dans le cas des réalités permanentes : « *In permanentibus enim sumitur totalitas ex aggregacione multarum parcium simul existencium [...], et ideo eorum totalitas nullo modo dependet ab anima ; unde habent completam racionem totalitatis et absolutam ab altera, scilicet prima a secunda.* » *Cod. Borgh. 322*, f° 197vb. Pour ce qui est soumis au devenir, une telle totalité n'est jamais donnée *in re*, et elle n'existe que *in anima*. Telle est la signification de la très courte allusion aux réalités permanentes qui se lit dans le *Quodl. I, 3* : « *Primo scilicet eam simul totam accipiendo, ac si tota instar permanentium esset simul, et sic non est nisi in consideratione nostra.* »

3. « *Exemplum autem huius manifestum est : numerus enim quidam accidens est constans ex multis mutacionibus ; si igitur velis sumere numerum realiter, non [?] inconveniens de eo in re ; nisi indivisibile videt unitatem utpote summum esset tres homines uterque unus est et tamen nullus est tres ; et tamen verum est quod illi sunt tres cum nullus eorum sit nisi unus ; tota igitur essencia vere in re est quod tres unitates in illis tribus sunt, et tamen eius totalitas non est nisi ab anima, inquantum enim anima conferret unum cum altero et invenit quelibet esse unum in se distinctum, et ita invenit tres unitates et ita dixit illas esse tria ; sumitur hoc quod dico ternarius non ut unum accidens* ». *Cod. Borgh. 322*, f° 198ra.

4. *Cod. Borgh. 322*, f° 198ra. On pourra également se rapporter à la réponse générale donnée par le *Cod. Borgh. 322* à la question du début : « *Ad questionem igitur patet responsio, quod tempus est realiter extra animam totum, licet hoc quod est essencialiter et quoad suam totalitatem completam, que est ex unione omnium parcium insimul, que competit solum permanentibus, habet esse ab anima,*

Olivi et Henri de Gand

Si l'on veut comprendre cette position d'Olivi dans son contexte doctrinal, c'est-à-dire dans la discussion sur la nature du temps après la condamnation de 1277, il convient de rappeler qu'Henri de Gand a lui aussi consacré une question au problème qui nous préoccupe; c'était à Pâques 1278 : « *Utrum tempus possit esse sine anima* ». Henri conclut son très long exposé de la position augustinienne en disant ceci : « *Et sic secundum Augustinum non nisi eo, quod est in anima, metimur id, quod est extra, et non nisi secundum esse, quod habet in anima* » [1].

Quant à la solution différenciée et fort nuancée qu'Henri donne à la question posée, elle peut être interprétée comme une reformulation de la conception reçue d'Averroès, celle que Thomas avait lui aussi adoptée : « *Tempus ergo secundum suum esse quasi materiale et in radice instantis habet esse in rebus extra, sed secundum suum esse formale et completum secundum partes prioris et posterioris habet esse in anima* » [2]. Henri fonde cette conception sur une triple analyse du mouvement en exposant d'abord la continuité du temps; dans un second moment il montre que l'âme distingue des seuils dans cette continuité en y introduisant ainsi la discrétion; finalement Henri considère un troisième moment et parle de discrétion dans la continuité; il désigne de la sorte la synthèse des deux aspects précédents [3].

Pour ce qui est de la position d'Augustin, Henri la critique en reprochant à l'évêque d'Hippone d'avoir conçu l'instant de manière trop isolée, le privant de réalité et s'interdisant ainsi de le comprendre comme l'articulation du passé et du futur :

> *Sed illa eius consideratio multum insufficienter respexit naturam temporis in praeterito et futuro includendo ipsa inter instantia praeterita et futura et non copulando ad instans praesens, sicut in sua consideratione copulavit ea Aristoteles et valde bene* [4].

Selon Henri, Aristote a su mieux comprendre le *nunc* qui est le lien entre le passé et l'avenir. Toute la critique d'Augustin repose donc sur la thèse que l'instant existe hors de l'âme. C'est pourquoi Henri peut affirmer que « *ipsum enim nunc est tota substantia temporis* » [5].

Il est incontestable que la question quodlibétale d'Henri de Gand et les deux textes que nous suivons (le *Quodl. I, 3* d'Olivi et le *Borgh. 322*) s'insèrent dans cette même discussion : partout on cite les mêmes autorités à propos d'une même question, une critique comparable est adressée à la conception augustinienne et averroïste niant l'être extramental du temps. Nous pouvons même dire que la

que tamen totalitas non est secundum naturam successivi, sed secundum naturam apprehensionis, quia [?] nichil apprehendit, nisi quod est, non nec totum sic [?], nec eo modo, quo apprehendit ». *Cod. Borgh. 322*, f° 198rb.

1. Henri de Gand, *Quodl.* III, 11 (Jeck 468, 20-22).
2. Henri de Gand, *Quodl.* III, 11 (Jeck 476, 4-7).
3. *Cf.* U.R. Jeck, *op. cit.*, p. 376-396.
4. Henri de Gand, *Quodl.* III, 11 (Jeck 475, 3-7).
5. Henri de Gand, *Quodl.* III, 11 (Jeck 475, 7).

réponse est substantiellement la même ici et là, car Henri aussi bien que le *Cod. Borgh.* et le *Quodl.* plaident pour une solution mixte qui tente de combiner l'objectivité et la subjectivité du temps.

Il convient toutefois de noter quelques différences importantes : l'auteur de la question du *Borgh. 322* n'accepte pas la distinction entre «*materialiter*» et «*formaliter*», distinction qui guide la solution henricienne ; il rejette pareillement l'idée selon laquelle l'instant serait le point d'ancrage réel du temps. Il insiste en revanche avec force sur la réalité de la succession, et donc sur la spécificité de l'être successif. On peut même dire que l'auteur du *Borgh.* esquisse une ontologie de la temporalité des créatures. Décidément, sa prise de position est plus réaliste que celle d'Henri.

La critique d'Augustin

Chez Henri de Gand aussi bien que dans les deux textes que nous examinons, la critique de la position subjectiviste du temps joue un rôle important. Si cette critique vise à la fois Averroès et Augustin, c'est seulement l'opposition à Augustin qui nous retiendra ici.

Notons d'abord que la discussion avec Augustin dans le *Quodlibet* est beaucoup plus succincte, car dans le *Cod. Borgh.*, l'auteur ne se contente pas de résumer la thèse adverse, il présente également des arguments avancés en sa faveur. Puis il expose deux groupes d'arguments à l'encontre de cette opinion. Mais il y a d'autres différences significatives entre nos deux textes. Dans le *Quodl.*, Augustin est nommé, alors que le *Borgh.* ne mentionne pas le nom de l'adversaire visé. En revanche, il tient à faire remarquer : «*Hec autem opinio est plene contra Aristotelem*».

Pour ce qui est de la présentation de la thèse augustinienne, les deux textes insistent sur l'idée que les parties du temps n'existent pas[1], et relèvent l'importance de la thèse augustinienne selon laquelle c'est l'activité de l'âme qui mesure le temps[2]. On signalera enfin que les termes «*memoria*» et «*expectatio*», si

1. «*Circa secundum arguo sic : penes naturam totalitatis et particularitatis omne compositum [ex non] entibus est non ens. Sed tempus est compositum ex preterito, quod non est, quia est tempus presens, et sic esset in presenti, et ex futuro, quod nondum est, quia sic esset presens et non futurum ; ergo tempus non est extra animam, cum eius partes non sunt extra animam.*» *Cod. Borgh. 322*, f° 195va.

2. «*Item Augustinus libro XI* Confessionum, *querens multis sermonibus, quid est tempus. Cum quicquid de eo est preteritum vel futurum, nihil sit ; presens autem nullum spacium habeat. Et finaliter determinat : non ergo ipsa, que iam non sunt, sed aliquid in memoria mea metior, quod infixum manet in animo meo, in quo, inquam, tempora metior affectione, quam res pretereuntes in ipso faciunt, que quidem manet, cum ille pretereunt, ipsam affectionem metior presentem non ea, que pretereunt ipsam metior, cum tempora metior. Et iterum post. Quis igitur negat et preteritum non esse ? Sed tamen iam est in animo expectatio futurorum, et memoria preteritorum. Et quis negat presens tempus carere spacio, quia in puncto preterijt ? Sed tamen perdurat attentio, per quam pergat ad esse, quod aderit*». P.I. Olivi, *Quodl* I, 3, f° 2va. «Quidam *enim voluerunt aliquando dicere, quod tempus nichil est extra animam, sed est tantummodo quedam distinccio non alicuius rei existentis extra animam, sed distinccio quedam affeccionis animi, distinccio, dico, derelicta in anima ex rebus transeuntibus sive affeccio animi, per quam affeccionem anima habet intuitum rerum presencium et memoriam rerum preteritarum et expectacionem futurarum ; distinccio igitur, qua animus extenditur ad memorandum*

centraux chez Augustin, se rencontrent dans le *ms. Borgh.*, et le terme « *attentio* », dans le *Quodl.*

C'est bien sûr la critique proprement dite de la position augustinienne qui importe le plus. Quels en sont les arguments majeurs ? Dans le *Quodl. I, 3*, Olivi reproche à Augustin de ne pas bien comprendre l'*esse successivum* qui est engagé dans un continuel devenir. Il critique en même temps Augustin pour avoir isolé l'instant en l'interprétant comme un maintenant indivisible (*tale instans non sumitur nisi in sola imaginatione*). Dans le *Borgh.*, cette discussion sur l'instant a passé dans l'argumentation autour de la deuxième opinion.

L'argumentation anti-augustinienne du *Borgh.* comporte quant à elle deux moments essentiels. D'abord l'auteur fait remarquer qu'aucun homme sensé ne peut nier la réalité du mouvement à laquelle la réalité du temps est directement liée[1]. Cet argument se rencontre également dans le *Quodl.* : « *Qui enim negat motum esse in rebus extra animam negat sensum, quia indubitabiliter sentimus et videmus multas res moveri et multos motus fieri* »[2].

Le second groupe d'arguments que le *Cod. Borgh.* avance contre la thèse augustinienne met en perspective une subjectivation radicale de la perception du temps : « *Si enim tempus haberet solum esse secundum percepcionem ipsius anime, ergo quod michi esset tempus, tibi non esset tempus* »[3]. Cet argument ne se retrouve pas tel quel dans le *Quodl.* où Olivi dit seulement que notre appréhension perdrait toute fiabilité si Augustin avait raison.

Un constatation s'impose donc d'elle-même : il y a dans les deux textes et de manière semblable une double stratégie : d'une part on insiste sur l'absurdité qui consiste à nier l'existence du mouvement et d'autre part on esquisse les conséquences, également absurdes, qui résulteraient si l'on soutenait que le temps n'existe que dans l'appréhension du sujet.

Il faut noter cependant que l'un et l'autre textes insistent sur la vérité partielle de la position combattue. Dans le *Quodl.* Olivi affirme que la doctrine d'Augustin est vraie si l'on considère le temps comme une totalité simultanée. Dans l'autre texte, il est dit ceci : « *Sed forte vellent hii dicere, quod totalitas temporis esset ab*

preterita et raciocinandum presencia et expectandum futura ; talis, dico, extencio et distinccio, quam anima habet ex rebus transeuntibus, quas aspicit vel intuetur vel memoratur vel expectat, dicitur tempus. Hec autem distinccio et est ab anima, que se extendit ad res, et in anima, que extenditur ad intelligendum ipsas res. Extensio enim est in re extensa ut in subiecto et ideo tempus est in anima solum ut in subiecto et est ab anima se ad res intuendas virtualiter. » *Cod. Borgh. 322*, f° 195va.

1. « *Item : certum est, ut ad oculos videmus multos motus fieri continue et successive, ergo realiter ante partem, que videtur esse facta, alia prius et realiter fieret, alia posterius ; et hoc totum videmus ad sensum fieri. Si ergo in motu realiter una pars precessit et alia est futura, est non solum quoad animam, sed realiter, ut videmus. Ergo in motu realiter est prius et posterius. Sed tempus nichil aliud est quam prius et posterius in motu ; ergo tempus est realiter extra animam sicut motus, quia si tempus non [est], nec motus* ». *Cod. Borgh. 322*, f° 195vb.

2. *Quodl.* I, 3, f° 2va.

3. « *Circa secundum sic arguo comparando tempus ad animam, penes apprehensionem anime. Si enim tempus haberet solum esse secundum percepcionem ipsius anime, ergo quod michi esset tempus, tibi non esset tempus, nisi ut faceres per eamdem apprehensionem ipsa nunc que tempus terminant, et ita te dormire per unam noctem, cum non percipias, non est verum te domisse per unam noctem, quod falsum est.* » *Cod. Borgh. 322*, f° 195vb.

ipsa anima [...]; hoc enim verum est, ut patebit in sequenti opinione, licet hoc non sonent eorum opiniones» [1].

CONCLUSION

En conclusion, nous voudrions relever trois points qui concernent respectivement la question doctrinale, l'authenticité du *Borgh. 322* et la datation de l'œuvre.

1. Nous avons examiné un certain nombre de documents sur la question du temps. Mais quel en est l'enjeu philosophique? Quelle est cette ligne doctrinale qui assure la continuité entre ces différentes approches? Les textes d'Olivi ainsi que le *Borgh. 322* s'accordent sur un point fondamental: tous combattent l'attitude consistant à annihiler le temps dans la réalité (c'est l'attitude augustinienne notamment); et s'ils la critiquent, c'est pour garantir une ontologie des êtres créés qui, par ce qu'ils sont, sont des êtres successifs. Tous les textes insistent sur cette réalité extramentale de la succession qui est le signe de la condition créaturale de tout ce qui existe, aussi bien les choses temporelles que les réalités spirituelles et éviternelles. Comme on l'a dit, on voit s'esquisser ici une ontologie de la temporalité des créatures.

En outre, il n'est pas impossible que cette insistance très marquée sur la réalité extramentale du temps chez Olivi soit une exigence formulée par sa théologie de l'histoire [2] : comment serait-il possible d'évoquer la marche de l'histoire selon ses différents âges, si le temps n'était pas une réalité indépendante de l'appréhension humaine?

2. Pour ce qui est de la question de l'authenticité du *Cod. Borgh. 322*, dont Anneliese Maier se disait presque certaine [3], il nous est difficile d'avancer une preuve quelconque.

Certes les indices sont nombreux, car il y a convergence doctrinale sur plusieurs points centraux concernant la conception du temps: tous nos textes présentent la thèse augustinienne et averroïsante afin de la critiquer; la réponse générale à la question de la réalité du temps se retrouve partout, et il existe d'autres parallélismes mineurs. Néanmoins les approches des différents textes sont variées, et il n'est pas possible par exemple de tirer un parallélisme absolu entre le *Quodl. I, 3* et le *Borgh. 322*.

1. *Cod. Borgh. 322*, f° 196ra.

2. *Cf.* D. Burr, *Pierre Olivi*, *op. cit.*, p. 41-63.

3. «*Die Stelle findet sich in der schon erwähnten Quaestio des Borgh. 322, die sehr wahrscheinlich Petrus Johannes Olivi angehört. Der Codex enthält eine Sammlung von etwa 60 Quaestionen, die fast alle von ihm sind, so dass schon der äussere Zusammenhang für seine Autorschaft spricht. Überdies zeigt unsere Quaestio – sie beginnt: Circa istam quaestionem qua quaeritur utrum tempus sit aliquid reale extra animam fuerunt duae opiniones – nicht nur in der doktrinalen Haltung, sondern auch in der ganzen Art der Präsentation unverkennbar die Eigenart Olivis*». A. Maier, *Metaphysische Hintergründe*, *op. cit.*, p. 51 n. 6.

Il existe d'ailleurs un problème : c'est la référence presque exclusive à l'autorité d'Aristote dans le *Borgh. 322*, comme lorsque l'auteur achève sa présentation de la première opinion (celle d'Augustin-Averroès) en se plaignant que « *hec autem opinio est plene contra Aristotelem*[1] ».

Que signifie cette présence massive d'Aristote dans le *Borgh. 322* qui permet à l'auteur de rejeter la position adverse, celle d'Augustin rappelons-le, et de la rejeter justement parce qu'elle est anti-aristotélicienne ? Ce fait serait d'autant plus troublant s'il s'agissait d'Olivi, puisque l'auteur du *Borgh. 322* achève le développement de sa thèse sur le rapport entre le temps et le mouvement en affirmant sans ambages : « *Et hec omnia dico sequendo doctrinam Aristotelis* »[2].

3. A supposer néanmoins que le *Borgh. 322* soit d'Olivi, il faut remarquer que le *Quodl. 1, 3* aussi bien que le *Borgh. 322* semblent présupposer une connaissance directe du *Quodl. III, 11* d'Henri de Gand : en disant que « *inde est quod dicunt aliqui, quod instans fluens est tota substancia temporis* »[3], l'auteur du *Borgh. 322* semble faire allusion à la thèse d'Henri de Gand qui affirmait que « *ipsum enim nunc est tota substantia temporis*[4] ». Or le *Quodl.* d'Henri date de 1278 ou 1279, ce qui soulève un problème de datation : cette question du *Borgh. 322* serait évidemment postérieure à la condamnation de 1277 et, si Olivi en est l'auteur, on ne pourrait donc pas la situer durant ses premières années d'études.

Nous serions donc tentés de dire que cette question du *Borgh. 322* est bel et bien un texte d'Olivi ; mais le dossier des œuvres oliviennes et celui du problème du temps au XIIIe siècle sont dans un tel état qu'on ne peut rien affirmer d'autre qu'une forte probabilité, et surtout inviter les chercheurs à poursuivre l'examen du *Codex Borgh. 322*.

1. *Cod. Borgh. 322*, f° 196ra.
2. *Cod. Borgh. 322*, f° 197vb.
3. *Cod. Borgh. 322*, f° 198va.
4. Henri de Gand, *Quodl.* III, 11 (Jeck 475, 7-8).

LE CONCEPT DE RELATION CHEZ PIERRE DE JEAN OLIVI

Alain Boureau

L'ontologie de Pierre de Jean Olivi présente d'emblée un caractère résolument « moderne » : on y trouve un nombre limité de substances et des réseaux complexes et multiples de relations entre ces substances. Contre l'exubérance ontologique scolastique, se construit un univers sobre de l'essence rare et de la complexité structurale. Le concept de relation y occupe donc une place centrale. Il suffit de penser aux vertigineuses pages de la question *Quid ponat ius ?*[1] *(Summa IV)*, où sont mis en regard la propriété, le pouvoir princier, le langage et le sacrement, entités auxquelles Olivi refuse le statut d'essences ajoutées au réel, et dont l'existence dans le monde relève de la relation entre des substances préexistantes. Plus généralement, Olivi multiplie les questions *Quid addit?* (« qu'ajoute au monde telle ou telle chose ? ») pour y répondre négativement (*nihil,* « rien », c'est-à-dire aucune essence séparée, mais un nouveau déploiement du réel, une nouvelle relation). Pourtant, on ne trouve guère, chez Olivi, de travail philosophique précis et technique de la notion de relation, alors même que la pensée scolastique du XIIIe siècle y a consacré d'immenses efforts[2] : aucune question de la *Summa* n'y est consacrée pleinement; seule une brève question quodlibétique en traite[3]. Comment expliquer cette dyssymétrie entre l'usage et la théorie ? La notion de relation est-elle une notion floue ou bien un instrument souple ? S'agit-il d'un désintérêt pour un concept jugé trop philosophique ou du sentiment d'une évidence immédiate, qui n'a pas à être mesurée à l'aune de raisonnements spécifiques ? Il est difficile de répondre à cette question, car, dans l'œuvre d'Olivi, on ne sait que rarement comment ordonner les priorités de l'enquête entre philosophie, théologie et exégèse. Je voudrais

1. « *Questio quid ponat ius vel dominium* ou encore *De signis voluntariis, (Summa IV)* », éditée par F. Delorme, *Antonianum* 20, 1945, p. 316-330.

2. Voir le commode et brillant petit livre de Mark G. Henninger, S.J., *Relations. Medieval Theories, 1250-1325*, Oxford, Clarendon Press, 1989. On peut regretter toutefois que soient trop exclusivement prises en compte les dimensions philosophiques de la question, au détriment des considérations théologiques, qui ont joué un rôle essentiel dans le traitement de la relation, comme j'espère le montrer. Les chapitres du père Henninger prennent en compte les plus brillants penseurs de l'ontologie philosophique du Moyen Age central, de Thomas d'Aquin à Guillaume d'Ockham sans s'arrêter sur des doctrines moins élaborées, mais peut-être plus décisives.

3. « *Queritur an relatio addat aliquid realiter differens ab illo in quo immediate fundatur* », *Quodlibeta* II, 2, Venise, 1509, f° 20V a et b.

suggérer ici que la notion de relation a une telle importance dans la théologie trinitaire et la christologie d'Olivi que l'auteur renonce volontairement à la cantonner à son emplacement usuel, dans la discussion philosophique sur les catégories d'Aristote.

UNE CRITIQUE DE L'ONTOLOGIE DE LA RELATION

Dans la pensée scolastique, la relation apparaît principalement comme une des dix catégories d'Aristote. La liste des catégories de l'être n'avait sans doute pas, chez Aristote, de consistance absolue[1], et les médiévaux ont certainement durci cette liste des catégories ou prédicaments en en faisant une sorte de carte d'identité de l'être, dont les rubriques avaient une réalité intangible. Dans le système « classique » des catégories, une première distinction doit être opérée entre la première catégorie, celle de substance et les neuf autres qui ont statut d'accidents par rapport à la première, distincts par une *ratio* propre. La relation partage avec ces huit autres catégories son inhérence dans la substance. Sa *ratio* spécifique est constituée par son « orientation vers » (*ad quid)*, son « *respectus* ». La relation constitue une sorte d'accident au second degré, puisqu'elle s'accroche à un « fondement » (« *fundamentum* ») qui est lui-même un accident de la substance : dans la relation exprimée par la phrase : « Pierre est plus grand que Paul », l'accident relationnel (supériorité de taille) inhère dans la substance de Pierre en se fondant immédiatement dans son accident « taille », tandis que l'accident relationnel symétrique (infériorité de taille) inhère dans la substance « Paul » en se fondant immédiatement dans son accident « taille »[2]. Une telle relation est dite « réelle », parce que les termes corrélés, ainsi que les fondements de la relation, constituent des réalités extra-mentales du monde[3]. Ce réalisme de la relation impose de décrire, en chaque cas de corrélation entre A et B, deux relations complémentaires, R qui inhère en A par son fondement et s'oriente vers B et R' qui fait de même dans l'autre sens en inhèrant en B.

La première raison du désintérêt théorique d'Olivi pour la relation tient sans doute au scepticisme qu'il manifeste vis-à-vis de la notion de catégorie[4] en général, même si c'est surtout sur la catégorie de quantité qu'on connaît le mieux ses positions originales, qui lui valurent de sérieux ennuis lors de la persécution

1. Voir O. Hamelin, *Le Système d'Aristote*, Paris, Vrin, 2e éd., 1931, p. 97-110.

2. Je suis bien conscient que cet exposé d'une théorie commune de la catégorie de relation est forcément sommaire et faux, puisque chaque auteur l'a modulée différemment.

3. Nous verrons plus loin que toutes les relations ne sont pas réelles : certaines ne sont que de « raison ». Il faut noter aussi que les catégories ont joué un rôle essentiel dans les diverses querelles sur les universaux ; cet aspect ne nous retiendra que fort indirectement.

4. Voir Efrem Bettoni O.F.M., *Le dottrine filosofiche di Pier di Giovanni Olivi*, Milano, Vita e pensiero, 1959, p. 201-215.

de 1283[1]. On le sait, il fut, en tous domaines, un adversaire de l'aristotélisme chrétien[2]. En l'occurrence, la catégorie lui paraît être une notion vide et arbitraire. Ce scrutateur des signes chiffrés de la Providence se moque du fétichisme du chiffre dix chez les commentateurs d'Aristot: « car certains sectateurs d'Aristote, croyant qu'Aristote a voulu que les dix prédicaments soient dix genres des choses essentiellement distinctes entre elles ont accepté en guise de premier principe qu'il en allait bien ainsi »[3]. Pour Olivi, la catégorie n'est qu'un instrument de description dépourvu de toute nécessité ontologique :

> Etablir la série successive des éléments [catégoriels] ne revient pas à prouver (*probare*) le nombre des prédicaments, mais seulement à en donner le récit (*narrare*) ; car si quelqu'un souhaitait ajouter ou retrancher quelques éléments au chiffre parfait des prédicaments, il pourrait, par le moyen d'une narration semblable, établir un plus grand ou plus faible nombre de prédicaments[4].

Sur ce point comme sur d'autres, Olivi reproche aux aristotéliciens moins la fausseté de la doctrine que le renversement d'ordre dans la dignité des concepts : un simple instrument descriptif ne doit pas prétendre à une dignité de principe premier de la métaphysique. Dès lors, Olivi ne suit pas la première attaque critique produite par la scolastique contre la notion de catégories, celle d'Henri de Gand[5], qui proposait de voir dans les catégories des modes d'être (« *modi essendi* »).

A ce stade, Olivi semble critiquer un excès de réalisme chez Henri de Gand :

> La diversité des modes de prédication [qui produisent les prédicaments ou catégories] n'entraîne pas nécessairement la diversité des modes d'être, puisque le mode de prédication suit le mode d'intellection plutôt que le mode d'être ; c'est pourquoi nous attribuons aux choses certains traits selon le mode de notre intellection, qui ne correspondent nullement au mode d'être qui est dans la chose[6].

Parmi les catégories, la relation illustre clairement cette réduction « mentaliste » opérée par Olivi. Sa petite question quodlibétique (« Est-ce que la relation ajoute quelque chose de réellement différent de ce sur quoi elle se fonde ? »[7]) montre bien cette orientation : le premier argument en faveur de la réponse

1. Voir David Burr, *L'Histoire de Pierre Olivi, franciscain persécuté.* Traduction et préface de François-Xavier Putallaz, Fribourg-Paris, Editions Universitaires de Fribourg-Cerf, 1997 (original de 1976), p. 156-179.

2. Voir David Burr, « Petrus Ioannis Olivi and the Philosophers », *Franciscan Studies* 31, 1971, p. 41-71.

3. *Summa* II, q. 28, éd. B. Jansen (*Quaestiones in secundum Librum Sententiarum,* Quaracchi, Collège Saint Bonaventure, 1922-1926), t. I, p. 483.

4. *Ibid.*, p. 486.

5. Voir J. Paulus, *Henri de Gand. Essai sur les tendances de sa métaphysique,* Paris, Vrin, 1938. Il faut sans doute être plus prudent en parlant d'une première attaque scolastique. Mais j'entends par là une attaque sur le terrain même de la métaphysique, et non sur la question de l'applicabilité des catégories en théologie et spécialement en théologie trinitaire. Nous le verrons, dès le XIIe siècle, certains souhaitaient séparer nettement les domaines.

6. *Summa* II, p. 485.

7. Voir note 3 plus haut.

négative de l'auteur repose sur le fait que la relation, comme processus, intervient dans beaucoup de genres ontologiques, distingués de la catégorie de relation par les aristotéliciens et pourtant construits par le principe de relation : action et passion (cinquième et sixième catégories d'Aristote) n'existent qu'en relation[1]. Mais il en va de même de la matière et de la forme (dont l'union est essentielle à la substance, première des catégories), de la partie substantielle et de son tout, de l'accident et de son sujet propre, de la représentation et du représenté, de l'habitus d'amour ou de science et de son objet (et plus généralement de tout habitus en rapport avec un acte spécifique). Il en va encore de même, dit Olivi, de la notion d'union ou de continuité, de situation ou de détermination des dimensions et des corps (il s'agit implicitement des septième et neuvième catégories), de l'ordonnancement de l'antérieur et du postérieur (définition, on le sait, du temps selon Aristote, rapportée ici à la huitième catégorie, le *quando*). Autrement dit, la relation, partout présente, neutralise toute prétention à l'autonomie ontologique des catégories.

Comment qualifier cet état de choses qui ne s'ajoute pas à l'existant, mais le réorganise comme mode d'intellection ? Un passage des *Principia* d'Olivi énumère sept « divisions de l'être » (*divisiones entis*) où la relation intervient tout en étant partie du processus qui constitue les autres, si l'on suit la démonstration de la question quodlibétique ; à propos des sept sceaux de l'Apocalypse, Olivi note :

> Ces sept signes peuvent, sur un plan général, être compris selon les sept divisions de l'être, auxquelles les autres peuvent être ramenées, à savoir : l'un et les multiples, l'acte et la puissance ; l'absolu et le déterminé ; l'universel et le particulier ; ce qui est par soi-même et ce qui est par accident ; l'absolu et le relatif ; ce qui est selon le réel et ce qui est selon notre saisie[2].

Un autre chapitre des *Principia* donne une autre liste de sept « formes très générales et très hautes de division »[3] : or cette liste correspond à la précédente, à quelques variations près : le couple « conformité en rapport avec la contrariété et la difformité » est ajouté, alors que le couple « universel/particulier » disparaît. La relation demeure à la même place, sous une dénomination différente (« la relation

1. Là encore, je simplifie, mais en suivant Olivi. Les théories scolastiques « classiques » connaissaient bien la question de cette interférence entre les diverses catégories et notamment à propos de l'action de de la passion ; elles y apportaient leurs propres réponses.

2. *Principia quinque in sacram scripturam*, édités par David Flood, O.F.M. et Gedeon Gàl, O.F.M., dans *Peter of John Olivi on the Bible*, Franciscan Institute Publications, St. Bonaventure, 1997, p. 133.

3. *Ibid.*, p. 51. Le texte fait problème : les éditeurs déchiffrent ainsi : « *secundum generalissimas et altissimas [formas]* dicentis (*dividens* dans le manuscrit du Vatican). On peut penser à une mauvaise lecture de copiste pour *divisionis*. J'ai vérifié le texte sur le manuscrit latin 15 588 de la Bibliothèque Nationale de Paris : la lecture est indéniable ; mais ce manuscrit que j'utilise pour mon édition du commentaire sur l'épître aux Romains par Olivi comporte de nombreuses erreurs évidentes de copistes, malgré les corrections souvent justes de Pierre de Limoges. A moins que le *dicentis* ne doive se comprendre comme « celui qui énonce » : en effet les êtres conceptuels et non réels sont souvent nommés « *secundum dici* » (en tant qu'ils sont objets d'un discours). Mais ce vocabulaire ne se trouve pas, à ma connaissance, chez Olivi.

ou comparabilité relative, en rapport avec l'absoluté ou avec l'acception absolue »).

Ainsi, Olivi se compose sa propre liste de « catégories », avec une nuance considérable : tant qu'à faire de les nombrer, autant se référer à un chiffre réellement sacré, le « sept » apocalyptique ; ensuite, ce nombre est indexé sur les « *signacula* » de l'Apocalypse, ce qui les réduit ou les exhausse au niveau de signes. Le terme de « division » mentionné dans la première liste évoque d'ailleurs une imposition de signification, plus qu'une répartition ontologique essentielle. Les variations dans les objets et les dénominations des deux listes confirment ce caractère instrumental des sept divisions de l'être.

Est-ce à dire que nous avons affaire à la première « internalisation » nominaliste des catégories et de la relation en particulier, annonciatrice de Guillaume d'Ockham et de Henry de Harclay ? Ce n'est pas exclu et on trouverait là un des nombreux points sur lesquels Olivi prépare la voie à Ockham. En fait, les choses sont plus compliquées, parce que, dans sa critique d'Henri de Gand, au livre second de la *Summa*, Olivi mentionne à plusieurs reprises que les catégories et la relation en particulier ne produisent pas une quiddité nouvelle dans l'être, mais en livrent une *ratio realis* (une raison réelle) :

> Le fait que chaque prédicament ait un mode d'être réellement divers des autres n'est pas davantage prouvé que le fait qu'il ait des essences diverses ; car, étant donné que certains d'entre eux ne diffèrent que selon *les seules raisons réelles*, il est sûr qu'ils ne pourraient avoir de mode d'être différent en réalité [1].

Après avoir renvoyé dos à dos les tenants de la position classique (les catégories créent des essences) et Henri de Gand (les catégories désignent un « mode d'être »), Olivi introduit son célèbre concept de *ratio realis*. La *ratio realis* est du côté d'une appréhension de l'être, car c'est d'abord une *ratio* et non une *res ;* mais, pourtant, elle n'est nullement un pur mode d'intellection (de type nominaliste ou conceptualiste, pour dire vite), car elle saisit du réel objectif. La *ratio realis* se situe non du côté de l'esprit qui saisit l'être, mais du côté de l'être lui-même qui se donne à saisir sous un certain angle, certes limité, mais sans se déformer, sans s'enclore dans une représentation, sans se modaliser. La *ratio realis*, c'est cette présence de la chose en cette situation. Cette notion pourrait apparaître à l'historien comme une simple forme de transition entre deux ontologies, l'une réaliste, l'autre nominaliste, si elle ne jouait un rôle essentiel dans la théologie d'Olivi.

LA RELATION COMME ARGUMENT THEOLOGIQUE

La relation constitue un instrument décisif dans trois domaines de la théologie d'Olivi, qui concernent la Trinité, la création et le Christ. Mon ordre de présen-

1. *Summa II*, q. 28, t. I, p. 486.

tation est assez arbitraire, car il est bien difficile d'établir une hiérarchie en ces trois domaines.

Une des rares questions conservées de la première partie de la *Summa* traite fort longuement de la relation à propos de la possibilité pour l'essence divine d'engendrer ou d'être engendrée. C'est sur cette question qu'Olivi rencontra ses premières censures, dès 1283[1]. Innocent III, au concile de Latran IV (1215) avait répondu à certaines critiques adressées par Joachim de Flore à Pierre Lombard, qui, selon l'abbé calabrais, aurait créé une quaternarité en distinguant trop nettement le Dieu Trine du Dieu Un, et en attribuant trop de choses à l'essence divine commune aux trois personnes. En retour, Joachim fut parfois accusé de « trithéisme ». Innocent III prit résolument parti en faveur de Pierre Lombard, en distinguant d'une part l'essence divine unique, et d'autre part Dieu qui, en tant que Père, engendre ou, en tant que Fils, est engendré. L'essence n'engendre ni n'est engendrée. Cette position ne souleva guère de problèmes au XIIIe siècle, non pas tant par respect pour l'autorité du Concile que parce que cette solution simple était assez souple pour s'accorder avec diverses théologies trinitaires sans revenir aux positions sulfureuses de Pierre Abélard, de Gilbert de la Porrée et de Joachim de Flore. Seul Guillaume d'Auvergne sembla vouloir réduire la portée de l'essence divine en proposant, pour la Trinité, l'image des trois sommets d'un triangle[2]. Mais le caractère constamment métaphorique de la pensée de Guillaume d'Auvergne empêche de savoir s'il s'agit là d'une proposition véritablement construite. Olivi fut donc sans doute le premier penseur scolastique à vouloir proclamer que l'essence divine engendrait. Il fut suivi, sur ce terrain, par l'auteur anonyme du *Liber contra Lombardum*, qui, quelques années plus tard, prit radicalement parti contre la position d'Innocent III[3]. L'opinion d'Olivi est plus nuancée, puisqu'il propose de concilier Pierre Lombard et Joachim de Flore en montrant que la notion d'essence divine renvoie à deux significations, car elle exprime tantôt la *ratio entis* tantôt la *ratio existentis* de Dieu; dans le premier sens, l'essence n'engendre pas. Dans le second sens elle engendre ou est engendrée.

Dans la question sur la production dans l'essence divine, l'*opponens* entend d'abord montrer que la production (ou plus particulièrement l'engendrement) entraîne forcément une *composition* de l'essence divine : en effet, ce en quoi les personnes divines diffèrent est ou bien une essence (ou quiddité) ou bien rien. S'il s'agit d'une essence, alors on aura bien une composition, proposition inacceptable, puisque l'essence divine est absolument simple. Si l'on cherche à dire que ce en quoi elles diffèrent n'est rien d'absolu, mais quelque aspect ou orientation (*respectus*), alors cette distinction, cette *personalitas* ne serait rien d'autre qu'une

1. Voir David Burr, *L'Histoire de Pierre Olivi, op. cit.*, p. 139-148.

2. Voir Guillaume d'Auvergne, *De trinitate*, édité par B. Swiltaski, Pontifical Institute of Medieval Studies, Toronto, 1976, p. 142.

3. *Liber contra Lombardum (Scuola di Gioacchino da Fiore)*, édité par C. Ottaviano, Reale Accademia d'Italia, Studi e Documenti, 3, Rome, 1934. Un article important de Fiana Robb a rétabli la chronologie de ce texte et l'a ôté du milieu de Joachim : « A Late Thirteenth-Century Attack on the Fourth Lateran Council : the *Liber contra Lombardum* and Contemporary Debates on the Trinity », *R.T.A.M.*, 1995, p. 110-144.

relation (de fait, le *respectus* désigne, on l'a vu, la *ratio* propre de la catégorie de relation). On aboutit à une contradiction, car les relations distinctes se fondent sur des termes distincts, qu'on doit pouvoir saisir avant les relations. La distinction des orientations sera donc causée par la distinction des personnes qu'elle serait supposé causer[1]. La réponse d'Olivi consiste, d'une part, à proposer la distinction entre les deux types d'essence, différenciés selon des *rationes reales*, d'autre part à affirmer la parfaite adéquation de sa critique de la notion de relation à la résolution des difficultés soulevées. On retrouve ici tous les éléments de la critique philosophique de la relation aristotélicienne déjà rencontrés dans la partie II de la *Summa* et dans la question quodlibétique (arbitraire des catégories, qui n'ajoutent aucune essence à leur fondement). La relation est pourtant soigneusement préservée en étant considérablement étendue, tout à fait hors de son cadre initial : elle devient le mode de saisie de toute *ratio realis*. En effet, si Olivi maintient un sens restreint de la relation pour désigner précisément la *production* (paternité, filiation, spiration) des personnes, conformément à la tradition théologique, et s'il dit clairement que ce type de relation n'est pas constitutif de la *personalitas* (pas plus, dit-il, que la blancheur de Socrate ne constitue sa socratéité), c'est sous le mode de la relation étendue que nous percevons tous les attributs de la divinité, puisque la distinction entre les personnes, la création (comme action et passion) ne se manifestent que par cette orientation de l'objet vers ce qui peut le saisir comme *ratio realis*. Ainsi, l'action et la passion « en plus de leur essence ou de leur être, n'ajoutent que cette condition « par quelque chose d'autre » (*ab alio*) ou « en quelque chose d'autre » (*in alio*). C'est pourquoi c'est en cela seul qu'elles semblent se différencier des autres relations qui sont dit proprement être dans le prédicament (la catégorie) de relation et non d'action et de passion, parce qu'elles ne sont pas saisies comme postérieures à leur sujet ni comme quasiment causées par eux, mais plutôt comme antérieures et comme causales, bien qu 'en vérité elles ne puissent les précéder »[2]. Dans le paragraphe suivant, Olivi enchaîne immédiatement sur sa critique favorite du fétichisme des catégories aristotéliciennes : « en cette matière, nous ne rencontrons de difficulté que du fait des opinions des hommes ». Cette généralisation de la relation, sous le nom de « condition », par le biais des prépositions grammaticales, désignant des orientations de la substance, n'est pas sans rappeler quelques tentatives antérieures de détournement de la notion de relation.

En effet, depuis le XIIe siècle (et probablement bien avant[3]), l'application de la notion de relation à la théologie trinitaire avait posé problème. Les *Theologiae* de Pierre Abélard avaient traité avec hardiesse de la question; le modèle trinitaire d'Abélard, qui juxtaposait la division pouvoir/sagesse/bonté à la distinction entre paternité/filiation/procession, empruntait le vocabulaire de la relation sans trop

1. *Summa I*, question éditée par A. Schmaus, « Der Liber Propugnatorius des Thomas Anglicus », *B.G.P.T.M.A.* 19, 1930, p. 144*.
2. *Ibid.*, p. 194.
3. Voir John Marenbon, *From the Circle of Alcuin to the School of Auxerre. Logic, Theology and Philosophy in the Early Middle Ages*, Cambridge University Press, Cambridge, 1981.

de peine[1], d'autant que l'auteur accordait une large place aux intuitions préchrétiennes de la trinité et relativisait la possibilité d'un langage adéquat à l'évocation de Dieu. Mais cette théologie trinitaire, qui accordait tant à la séparation des personnes fut âprement critiquée. Thierry de Chartres et Clarembaud d'Arras rejetèrent la possibilité d'une adéquation du langage des catégories d'Aristote à l'Etre qui est au-delà de l'idée de substance[2]. Robert de Melun et surtout Pierre Lombard, afin de sauver l'éminence de l'essence divine, modérèrent les analyses des propriétés substantielles des personnes divines et tentèrent de retrouver, chez Augustin, les emplois grammaticaux (Donat, Priscien), et non ontologiques de l'idée de relation[3]. Mais l'originalité forte d'Olivi consiste à étendre ce déplacement à tous les emplois des catégories et de la relation, sans se limiter aux relations divines.

On comprend aisément comment le traitement de la création bénéficie de cette redéfinition de la relation. En effet, dans la tradition thomiste, la création, comme processus, relève de la catégorie de la relation. La pensée scolastique, en se référant au cinquième livre de la *Métaphysique* d'Aristote[4], ce petit glossaire de termes philosophiques, distinguait trois types de relations. Le premier type comprend les relatifs de nature numérique, étendue par Aristote à des cas connexes (identité spécifique, similarité qualitative et égalité quantitative). Le deuxième type inclut les relations causales, fondées sur les accidents d'action et de passion. Enfin la troisième classe n'est esquissée que sommairement « comme le rapport du mesurable au mesuré, du connaissable à la connaissance et du perceptible à la perception ». Pour saint Thomas[5], ce troisième type de relation prit une grande importance, car il y vit une classe de relations non-mutuelles : la relation R qui va du connaissant au connu est réelle, tandis que la relation R', du connu au connaissant, n'existant que dans l'esprit du connaissant, est une « relation de raison », non « réelle ». Ce caractère asymétrique de la relation « épistémique » en faisait un cadre propice pour y loger les relations entre Dieu et la créature. On put admettre sans difficulté que si la créature entretenait une relation réelle avec Dieu, à l'inverse Dieu n'avait de relation que de raison avec la créature. La pure puissance créative de Dieu ne saurait inhérer dans un fondement spécifique de la substance divine. C'est à partir de cette troisième classe des relations, étendue par la scolastique, qu'Olivi trouva les moyens de redéfinir le principe relationnel. Non seulement, il y trouva la question des relations avec Dieu, mais aussi les reliquats, recueillis par saint Thomas, de la formulation purement situationnelle, et non catégorielle, de la relation, évoquée plus haut à propos des emprunts faits par Pierre Lombard à saint Augustin et aux gram-

1. Pierre Abélard, *Theologia christiana,* 3.174, 4.50, 4.154-56, éd. P. Buytaert, *Corpus Christianorum, Continuatio Medievalis* 12, Brepols, Turnhout, 1969, p. 260, 287, 342-343.

2. Voir Enzo Maccagnolo, *Rerum universitatis : saggio sulla filosofia du Tedorico di Chartres,* Le Monnier, Florence, 1976.

3. Voir Marcia Colish, *Peter Lombard,* Brill, Leyde, 1994, t. I, p. 91-154.

4. Aristote, *Métaphysique,* V, cap. 15 (1020 b25-1021 b11). J'utilise le texte, traduction et commentaire de Marie-Paule Duminil et Annick Jaulin : Aristote, *Métaphysiques. Livre Delta,* Presses Universitaires du Mirail, Toulouse, 1991, p. 81-85.

5. Voir A. Krempel, *La Doctrine de la relation chez saint Thomas,* Paris, Vrin, 1952.

mairiens. Thomas, en effet, énumère trois figures de la relation non réelle : un des deux termes au moins peut n'être pas réel (cas des relations entre concepts); les termes corrélés ne sont pas distincts (cas de l'identité à soi-même) ou encore, le fondement réel de la relation n'existe pas : Thomas cite le cas de l'animal qui se trouve être à droite de cette colonne[1]. L'effort d'Olivi consista à faire de cette partie de la relation situationnelle ou de la partie non-réelle de la relation de création le modèle de toute la relation de création, et, finalement de toute relation.

Comme le remarquait le Père Bettoni, les deux membres de la relation de création, chez Olivi, deviennent « de raison »[2]. Mais il faut ajouter que ce retournement ne put se faire que grâce à cet instrument remarquable qu'était la raison réelle. Ce recentrage de la relation de création sur sa partie divine importait afin de manifester clairement que la création comme processus n'ajoutait rien à l'essence de ce qu'elle crée et dont elle n'est qu'une raison réelle. Il donnait aussi l'occasion de rejeter la thèse de l'exemplarité de la création dans les idées divines[3] : la sixième objection à l'opinion de l'*opponens* sur l'ajout d'essence au fondement de la relation, dans la question quodlibétique sur la relation, le note clairement :

> Sixièmement, ils [en fait Olivi] prouvent leur opinion à partir des orientations générales de toute essence créée par rapport à Dieu, parce qu'ainsi [si on acceptait la thèse adverse], chaque chose, selon sa propre raison et sa propre essence, serait la similitude de quelque idée divine. Or chacune est immédiatement créée par Dieu, du moins quant à celles qui viennent par la seule création. En effet, la création n'est pas une action ou une passion réellement intermédiaire entre Dieu et l'essence créée[4].

Sur cette « dé-réalisation » de la relation, Olivi pouvait appuyer une thèse à laquelle il tenait particulièrement, au point de lui consacrer toute une question du livre second de sa *Summa* : l'identité entre création et conservation, ou création continue du monde par Dieu. Cette thèse originale ne pouvait en effet admettre un ajout permanent d'essence aux substances originellement créées.

La localisation du principe de relation dans le modèle de la relation épistémique se trouve confirmée et illustrée dans le troisième mode d'ancrage théologique de la notion de relation, c'est à dire dans la christologie d'Olivi, telle qu'elle apparaît au livre III de la *Summa*[5]. La question qui porte sur la possibilité de l'union personnelle entre la nature humaine et Dieu, induit une objection de l'*opponens* quant au fondement de la relation d'union : toute relation doit se fonder sur quelque chose d'absolu. Si l'on prend la nature humaine comme un tel

1. Saint Thomas d'Aquin, *Summa Theologica*, I, q. 13, art. 7.

2. E. Bettoni, *op. cit.*, p. 213 n. 194. Le père Bettoni parle de relation « logique » là où je préfère employer le terme de relation « de raison », qui situe mieux le point précis où s'insère la nouveauté d'Olivi.

3. Sur ce point, voir la contribution de Sylvain Piron à ce volume.

4. *Quodlibet, op. cit.* (voir note 3 plus haut).

5. Partiellement éditée par A. Emmen et E. Stadter, *Questiones de incarnatione et redemptione. Questiones de virtutibus*, Collège Saint Bonaventure, Grottaferrata, 1981 (désormais citée comme *Summa III*, suivi du numéro de la question et de la pagination de l'édition Emmen et Sadter).

fondement dans la relation d'union, alors elle ne peut s'extraire de cet investissement divin, ce qui est absurde[1]. La réponse d'Olivi nous est désormais familière : l'« absolu » se dit ou bien de ce qui n'est, en son essence, relié à rien d'autre, (acception impossible, en ce cas de l'union avec Dieu) ou bien de ce qui « en plus de ses raisons d'orientations (*rationes respectivas*) contient en soi quelque raison absolue (*aliquam rationem absolutam*) ». On reconnaît là le principe des « raisons réelles ». Mais immédiatement, Olivi y conjoint immédiatement le modèle de l'acte de savoir (*actus sciendi*) : « l'acte de savoir est essentiellement relié à un objet et à un sujet, en tant que sujet, et à son principe effectif ; et pourtant, à côté de ces orientations (*respectus*), il exprime une certaine essence qui porte de telles orientations »[2]. De façon elliptique, Olivi ajoute : « et l'on trouve la même évidence dans le mouvement local » : comme si la relation ne constituait au fond qu'un équivalent ontologique du mouvement auquel sont soumises les substances créées (fulgurant parallèle avec le thème de la création continuée).

La relation généralisée comme instrument du salut

Pourtant la relation joue un rôle capital et précis dans l'histoire du salut. La question II de la *Summa III*, qui porte sur la rédemption de l'homme par les mérites du Christ en donne les raisons. Dieu et ses créatures sont à tel point incommensurables que seul un processus relationnel instauré par Dieu nous fait accéder à sa grâce :

> Nous pouvons méditer sur la façon dont, quant au satut de grâce et de gloire, aussi bien ici-bas que là-haut, les hommes, par le mérite du Christ, sont tous reliés aussi bien à Dieu qu'au Christ-homme et aussi à eux-mêmes. Car si nous considérons d'abord le statut de gloire, Dieu ne regarde personne comme digne de gloire, si ce n'est sous la relation continue du mérite du Christ participé par le bienheureux lui-même ; et par conséquent, ce regard essentiel de Dieu et cet amour béatifiant de tous ne se portent sur aucun humain, si ce n'est grâce au regard actuel (*aspectu*) et à l'orientation tendue (*respectu*) vers le Christ en tant qu'il est en relation avec nous[3].

De façon précise, l'institution relationnelle résout l'incommensurabilité entre Dieu et la créature ; le second mode de relation :

> [...] implique une relation infinie, c'est à dire à l'infini ; car [...] l'offense faite à Dieu [par le péché] n'a pas d'essence infinie, ni n'est fondée en une essence infinie, mais elle est infinie dans la mesure où elle offense un bien infini et où elle est digne d'une peine infinie.

1. *Summa III*, q. 1, p. 8.
2. *Ibid.*, p. 43.
3. *Summa III*, q. 2, p. 115.

Or, une fois établie cette relation de dette infinie, le mérite du Christ a été communiqué aux hommes sous un triple mode (*ratio*) : mode causal, mode intentionnel et mode juridictionnel. Ces trois modes peuvent se décrire comme des relations (on se souvient que la deuxième classe des relations est précisément de type causal), mais c'est la « mise en rapport juridictionnelle » (*ratio jurisdictionalis*) qui spécifie précisément la relation comme lien entre l'homme et Dieu. La juridiction doit se comprendre ici comme processus actif, comme une « ouverture de droits » : la communication des mérites du Christ s'effectue « sous le mode juridictionnel, parce que si l'homme peut donner sa personne ou ses biens sans qu'une mutation réelle se produise en lui ou en ses biens, en sorte qu'un autre homme ait un droit véritable sur lui et sur ses biens, à plus forte raison le Dieu-homme peut, selon sa volonté propre, nous donner sa personne et ses mérites, en sorte que le Christ aussi bien sa grâce et sa charité puissent être dits nôtres, plus pleinement et véritablement que le château donné par un roi à un chevalier peut être dit appartenir au chevalier lui-même, ou plutôt que la puissance du roi, donnée par lui à son bailli ou son préfet, peut être revendiquée par le préfet comme véritablement sienne »[1]. Ce texte présente l'intérêt de montrer l'unité profonde de la pensée d'Olivi : comme dans la question *Quid ponat ius ?*, le transfert de droits, grâcieux ou onéreux, unilatéral ou contractuel, constitue la relation fondatrice de l'histoire humaine, dans la société comme dans les rapports avec la divinité. Le renoncement au monde (se donner soi et ses biens), opéré dans le vœu de pauvreté absolue, aussi bien que le contrat marchand, construisent le mouvement du monde, vers le salut ou l'enrichissement. Les finalités divergent, mais l'aspect créateur de la relation est le même. Au paragraphe qui suit, Olivi mentionne que, par prédestination, les mérites du Christ ont été communiqués avant d'avoir été accomplis, mystère qu'il illustre par un parallèle avec les pratiques marchandes, qui pourrait contribuer à expliquer la fameuse énigme du *Traité sur les contrats :*

> Dans la donation d'un droit, quelque chose de futur peut être donné, comme, par exemple, je peux donner à quelqu'un, par contrat notarial (*instrumento*) une maison, que je vais construire et je peux même m'obliger à la construire; de même, je peux céder un gain, que je dois réaliser à l'avenir[2].

La généralité du modèle de la relation est encore précisée dans la question suivante de la *Summa III*, qui porte, à propos du baptême des enfants, sur l'identité entre le fait d'avoir droit au mérite du Christ et la possession de la grâce[3]. Pour Olivi, il s'agit essentiellement de réfuter l'idée de grâce comme *habitus* (comme état acquis et permanent) au profit de la notion d'*habitudo*, c'est à dire « prise en charge » (passive ou active), dérivant d'un don grâcieux, dans

1. *Ibid.*, p. 111.

2. *Ibid.*, (dans l'édition de A. Emmen, le *possunt* de la ligne 27, p. 111 doit être corrigé en *possum*). Sur le *Traité des contrats*, voir la thèse et l'édition de Sylvain Piron, en préparation. Une première édition critique complète a été donnée par G. Todeschini, *De emptionibus et venitionibus, de usuris et restitutionibus*, Rome, 1980. Voir la contribution de G. Todeschini au présent volume.

3. Question « *An habere ius ad meritum Christi sit idem ac habere gratiam ?* », éditée en annexe à la question II de la *Summa III*, p. 143-185.

l'instantanéité sans cesse renouvelée de la relation. Le transfert juridictionnel, comme toute relation selon Olivi, n'ajoute aucune essence nouvelle, et pourtant, dans le cas du baptême, il engendre à nouveau; il fait renaître. Ce paradoxe (déjà observé à propos de la création) est illustré par une belle série d'exemples :

> Si donc quelqu'un condamné à mort par un roi est soudain réinstallé dans la faveur du roi au point que ce dernier lui donne droit de succession au royaume, on pourra dire que le roi l'a créé de nouveau et qu'il l'a fait à partir de rien, bien qu'en la circonstance, il n'ait rien reçu qu'un être relatif et juridictionnel, à plus forte raison quelqu'un pourra être dit né à nouveau et regénéré par l'être relatif et juridictionnel qu'il reçoit par le mérite du Christ.

Le deuxième exemple concerne la « relation de bénédiction épiscopale », qui fait d'une maison un temple, par le seul fait juridique que tout acte d'irrespect désormais effectué en ce lieu crée le nouveau délit de sacrilège. L'adoption pratiquée en droit civil fournit un troisième exemple.

La source de cette préminence de la relation réside dans le fait qu'elle s'origine soit dans la volonté humaine soit dans le vouloir divin : « bien que les relations semblent avoir un faible degré d'entité (*modicum entitatis*), néanmoins elles sont au plus au point *pesées* par Dieu et par l'intellect et l'affect humains » [1] : le verbe *pensare* employé ici est d'une grande richesse, car il désigne à la fois la pensée, la pesée et l'échange. Il implique donc le jugement de prédestination :

> Comme il faut peser cette prise en charge de la prédestination du vouloir divin, selon laquelle il se porte de façon individuelle vers les prédestinés [...]. Et elle est bien fausse, cette opinion de ceux qui estiment que des relations de ce type ont peu d'entité. Car ce n'est pas du fait qu'elles n'ajoutent pas une essence diverse aux choses auxquelles elles le rapportent immédiatement qu'elles doivent être estimées avoir un faible degré d'entité, mais bien au contraire, sauf pour celui qui estime davantage la diversité et l'accidentalité que l'identité et la consubstantialité [2].

On comprend donc pourquoi la relation, chez Olivi, constitue un concept fondamental sans faire l'objet d'une enquête technique approfondie. Elle transcende très largement son emploi ontologique ou logique initial. Mais l'absence de distinction réelle entre la relation et son fondement suspend toutes les interrogations scolastiques sur les rapports entre substances, accidents et fondements.

La conception de la relation chez Olivi dérive donc étroitement de son orientation spirituelle et théologique [3]. On a noté sa grande originalité. Est-ce à dire qu'elle est totalement singulière et isolée au XIIIe siècle ? Sans doute pas, car on peut repérer au moins un antécédent et quelques reprises postérieures. On n'en

1. *Ibid.*, p. 156.
2. *Ibid.*, p. 157.
3. Ceci serait confirmé par une étude précise de l'usage de la notion de relation dans l'exégèse d'Olivi, qu'on peut, à bien des égards, qualifier de « relationnelle » (notion qu'il faudrait distinguer de son « joachimisme » interprétatif). Sur l'originalité de l'exégèse d'Olivi, je renvoie à l'étude de Gilbert Dahan publiée dans le présent volume.

donnera ici que quelques linéaments, faute de place et faute d'une recherche plus avancée.

Le premier *quolibet* de John Peckham, tenu en 1270, débute par une question curieuse, mais hélas fort brève sur la relation. Plus précisément, le docteur franciscain est interrogé sur le point suivant : « est-ce que, dans ce qui est dit sur Dieu en temporalité, la relation d'intellection est un accident de la créature ? »[1]. Certes, le propos est limité et la réponse donnée n'a rien pour surprendre : cette relation, qui ne saurait être un accident de la divinité, constitue bien un accident de la créature. Nous avons là une nouvelle occurrence du schéma asymétrique de la relation entre Dieu et la créature ; nous sommes apparemment bien loin d'Olivi. Cependant, les attendus sont moins banals, pour trois raisons.

En premier lieu, le schéma de la relation épistémique est inversé ; chez Thomas d'Aquin, la relation qui va du connaissant au connu, de la mesure au mesuré est réelle, tandis que la relation inverse est « de raison ». Appliqué aux rapports entre Dieu et les créatures, le schéma se retourne : la relation de Dieu à la créature est « de raison » et la relation inverse est réelle. Or Peckham homogénéise l'ensemble des relations sur le modèle de la relation divine : la relation se produit du côté de la mesure ou de l'intellection *secundum dici,* selon le mode « de raison », non réel. Ceci annonce le renversement olivien noté par le père Bettoni.

La deuxième curiosité tient au caractère très particulier de l'accident de relation dans la créature. Peckham doit en effet réfuter un argument de l'*opponens* qui affirme qu'on ne peut comprendre une chose sans son accident. Or on ne comprend pas la créature sans son *respectus*, sa relation d'intellect en direction de la divinité. Donc ce *respectus* n'est pas un accident de la créature. La réponse du maître consiste à dire qu'on peut fort bien comprendre une chose par son essence sans connaître son être ; or l'être n'est qu'un acte de l'essence. Mais, au passage Peckham réfute, en sens contraire, un propos d'Avicenne, qui affirme que la relation est tout simplement un accident de la chose. Le franciscain oppose alors les accidents absolus de la créature que Dieu peut supprimer par miracle et l'accident relatif que Dieu ne peut supprimer sans évacuer son fondement, la substance. Cette limite à la puissance de Dieu n'est pas en soi surprenante, car elle relève du principe de non-contradiction logique que la plupart des théologiens du temps place au-delà du pouvoir absolu de Dieu[2] : « car il n'y a pas de similitude de

1. « *Utrum in dictis de deo ex tempore respectus intellectus sit accidens creaturae ?* », *Quodlibet* I, édité par F. Delorme, O.F.M. et G.J. Etzkorn, *Fr. Ioannis Pecham, ofm, Quodlibeta quatuor*, College Saint-Bonaventure (Bibliotheca Franciscana Scholastica Medii Aevi, tome XXV), Grottaferrata, 1989, p. 3-5.

2. Voir E. Randi, *Il sovrano e l'orologioaio : due immagini di Dio nel dibattito sulla « potestas absoluta » fra XIII e XIV secolo*, Nuova Italia, Florence, 1987. L. Moonan, *Divine Power. The Medieval Power Distinction up to its Adoption by Albert, Bonaventure and Aquinas*, Clarendon Press, Oxford, 1994. William J. Courtenay, *Capacity and Volition. A History of the Distinction of Absolute and Ordained Power*, Pierluigi Lubrina Editore, Bergame, 1990. Voir aussi la commode anthologie de textes rassemblée sous la direction de Olivier Boulnois, *La Puissance et son ombre. De Pierre Lombard à Luther*. Textes traduits et présentés par O. Boulnois, J-F. Genest, E. Karger, A. de Libera, C. Michon, M. Ozilou, J-L. Solère, Aubier, Paris, 1994.

blancheur ou il ne peut y en avoir s'il n'y a pas de blancheur». Mais Peckham ajoute : «en sens contraire, la substance ne peut être sans quelque relation de convenance ou de différence par rapport aux autres créatures, ou du moins sans relation d'ordre par rapport au Créateur».

On peut se demander si Olivi n'a pas connu ce texte et ne lui apporte pas dans une réponse dans son *Quolibet*[1] : le septième argument du maître, malheureusement assez obscur et bref, s'énonce ainsi :

> Ils prouvent leur opinion du côté de la puissance divine : parce que si la relation dit une essence différente des autres [essences accidentelles], alors, semble-t-il, Dieu, par miracle, peut faire sa substance et son essence sans telle autre et principalement parce que sa substance sera par nature antérieure à cette autre. Mais cette raison entraîne des complications que je n'ai cure d'expliquer pour le moment.

Malgré la très mauvaise qualité de cette reportation, on peut deviner que l'argument se place sur le même terrain que celui de Peckham. Malgré les dénégations de ce dernier, l'autonomie ontologique de l'accident relation peut conduire Dieu à le créer seul, sans la substance dont il est l'accident. Il faut donc se débarrasser de ce statut catégoriel. La désinvolture de la phrase finale tiendrait à la fois au respect pour Peckham, franciscain de sensibilité proche d'Olivi, malgré de grandes différences doctrinales, mais aussi et surtout au fait que le débat débouchait sur la question de la puissance absolue de Dieu, épineuse et dangereusement agitée dans les querelles entre mendiants et séculiers[2].

Au deuxième argument de l'*opponens*, sur l'incongruité d'une médiation entre la substance et le créateur, Peckham rétorque que la substance lui est relié «causalement», et «formellement» par la relation qui s'y attache : «elle [la substance] n'est pas une relation et n'est pas capable d'immédiateté; et cette relation ne crée pas de distance entre la créature et Dieu mais dit une *habitudo* de la créature par rapport à Dieu». On reconnaît là le terme qu'employait Olivi pour désigner la relation de grâce entre la créature et la divinité; il ne s'agit pas là d'une simple homonymie : chez Peckham, le désir de singulariser et de privilégier la relation épistémique par rapport à Dieu le conduit à vider presque complètement la notion d'accident, en la rapprochant de l'immédiateté de la substance. En somme, il ne manque à Peckham que le concept de *ratio realis* pour élaborer une description analogue à celle d'Olivi.

Notons enfin un dernier trait : le corps de la réponse de Peckham débute par une longue citation du *De trinitate* de saint Augustin[3] qui use d'une métaphore pour montrer que la substance immuable de Dieu peut être dite reliée à la créature sans rien perdre de son incommutabilité. L'image est celle du sou (*nummus*) qui devient prix (*pretium*) ou cesse de l'être sans aucune mutation de sa substance. Cette métaphore pourrait nous introduire au monde vertigineux de l'échange

1. *Quodlibet, op. cit.* (voir note 3, p. 41).

2. Voir A. Boureau, «Le vœu monastique et l'émergence de la notion de puissance absolue du pape (vers 1270)», *Cahiers du Centre de Recherches Historiques* 21, 1998, p. 23-34.

3. Augustin, *De Trinitate*, V, cap. 16, n. 17, *Patrologie latine* 42, col. 922-923.

généralisé et immédiat chez Olivi. Elle nous rappelle aussi que les théories contractuelles du sacrement dont Olivi fut l'un des plus remarquables théoriciens s'inscrit dans un certain augustinisme franciscain qui passe par Bonaventure, Guillaume de Méliton et bien d'autres [1].

Je serai encore plus rapide sur la possible postérité de l'analyse olivienne de la relation. Richard de Mediavilla, le censeur franciscain d'Olivi, tout en maintenant la relation dans le domaine catégoriel, se détourna de la question de l'inhérence de la la relation (aspect accidentel) au profit de l'orientation vers (*ad quid*) [2]. Cette position le rapproche à la fois de John Peckham et d'Olivi. La distinction de Jean Duns Scot entre relations catégorielles et relations transcendentales, même si elle est esquissée chez Thomas d'Aquin, me paraît avoir bénéficié de l'apport d'Olivi [3]. Guillaume d'Ockham a pu trouver chez Olivi la suspension d'un aspect central de la définition scolastique de la relation: la relation réelle entre deux choses suppose que ces deux choses soient distinctes et extra-mentales [4]. Même si la pensée d'Olivi demeure fort singulière dans sa connexion étroite entre les domaines de la philosophie, de la théologie et de la spiritualité, le franciscain avait sérieusement ébranlé l'édifice scolastique et ouvert de nouvelles voies.

1. Voir les travaux de William Courtenay et d'Irène Rosier. J'en donne une petite synthèse dans A. Boureau, « Naaman, son mal et son secret. Un patient biblique examiné par l'Église (XIIe-XVIe siècle) », *L'Evolution psychiatrique* 58, 3, 1993, p. 515-522.

2. Voir M. Henninger, *Relations, op. cit.*, p. 59-67.

3. Voir J.P. Beckmann, *Die Relationen der Identität und Gleichheit nach J. Duns Scotus*, Bonn, 1967.

4. Voir G. Martin, « Ist Ockhams Relationstheorie Nominalismus? », *Franziskanische Studien* 32, 1950, p. 31-49.

LA QUESTIONE DELLA *RATIO LIGATA* E PIETRO DI GIOVANNI OLIVI

Vincenzo Mauro

INTRODUZIONE

Una notte il filosofo cinese Chuang-tzu, contemporaneo di Aristotele, sognò di essere una farfalla che volava felice. Improvvisamente si svegliò e scoprì di essere di nuovo Chuang-tzu. Da allora andava dicendo di non sapere più chi in realtà egli fosse, se un uomo che aveva sognato di essere una farfalla, o una farfalla che stava continuando a sognare di essere un uomo [1].

Circa 15 secoli più tardi il vescovo parigino Guglielmo d'Alvernia definiva la follia come uno stato mentale in cui le immagini della realtà, percepite in maniera alterata, allontanano il soggetto da se stesso, condizionando fortemente il suo modo di essere. Guglielmo raccontava in particolare d'aver visto un alienato di mente che, convinto d'essere un uccello, si comportava come tale [2].

Lo strano effetto confusionale tra realtà e fantasia che sembra caratterizzare lo stato dell'*amens* e quello del *dormiens* è considerato essere dalla Scolastica uno dei principali aspetti di quella situazione psico-fisiologica denominata *ratio ligata*, *ligatio rationis* o *ligatio intellectus*. Queste formule stanno ad indicare appunto quegli stati mentali nei quali l'uso della ragione si troverebbe parzialmente o totalmente impedito. Per questa loro peculiarità *dormientes* e *amentes* (o *furiosi*) [3], ma anche *infantes* ed *ebrii*, costituirono, fin dall'antichità, oggetto d'interesse da parte di discipline come il diritto, la medicina, la teologia e la filosofia.

I primi accenni di rilevanza filosofica si ritrovano già in Aristotele [4], ma una vera e propria problematizzazione si avrà soltanto con Agostino [5]. La teologia e il

1. *Cfr. The Complete Works of Chuang Tzu*, B. Watson tr., New York-London, 1968, p. 49. Il paradosso relativistico serviva ad esemplificare la non necessaria distinzione tra uomo e farfalla nell'eterno processo di traformazione delle cose che è il Tao.

2. *Cfr.* Guillelmus Alvernus, *De universo*, p. III, 2, c. 13, in *Opera omnia*, Parisiis, 1674 (rist. an. Frankfurt a. M., 1963), t. 1, p. 1041a.

3. Il termine *dormiens* indica chiaramente « colui che dorme », ma spesso sottintende anche « colui che sogna ». Il termine *furiosus*, che non rimanda ad una precisa malattia mentale isolata dalla medicina antica e medievale, indica semplicemente il pazzo scatenato, al quale si affianca un altro tipo generico di follia, quella che colpisce l'*amens* o il *demens*.

4. *Cfr.* Aristoteles, *De anima*, III, 3, 429a2-8.

5. *Cfr.* Augustinus, *De Genesi ad litteram*, XII, *P.L.* 34, 453-486 e *infra*, n. 79.

diritto canonico si occupano della *ratio ligata* in riferimento all'amministrazione dei sacramenti e più precipuamente in relazione alla dottrina del peccato.

Poiché la *ratio ligata* si oppone concettualmente a quella libertà che dovrebbe caratterizzare l'agire morale, nel Duecento molti dei contributi a tale tema sono rintracciabili nei Commenti alla XXV *Distinctio* del II *librum sententiarum*, in cui il *Magister* sviluppava il significato di libero arbitrio [1].

Accanto ai testi tratti dai Commenti alle Sentenze compaiono però anche svariate questioni disputate e quodlibetali, redatte tra gli altri da autori come Gerardo d'Abbeville, Tommaso d'Aquino, Matteo d'Acquasparta, Enrico di Gand, Riccardo di Mediavilla e Pietro di Giovanni Olivi, tanto per citare i più noti. Se l'elenco di questi nomi è indicativo del fatto che attorno al problema della *ratio ligata* il XIII secolo aveva sviluppato un certo dibattito, si tratta ora di vedere quali fossero i termini di tale dibattito.

Nel caso della follia i problemi possibili da risolvere si riducono, secondo i medievali, ai seguenti quesiti : può il folle ricevere i sacramenti ? E' in grado di esercitare l'uso del libero arbitrio, ovvero è moralmente e penalmente responsabile degli atti che compie ? E, infine, qual è la causa del suo impedimento ?

La *ligatio* generata dal sonno rimanda a problemi pressoché analoghi. La conoscenza degli stati intellettuali del dormiente è ritenuta importante per poter determinare in primo luogo se il libero arbitrio sia perfettamente operante oppure no, e se in secondo luogo i sogni possano davvero mettere in comunicazione con entità spirituali superiori. La questione del libero arbitrio nel sonno ha una duplice implicazione : da un lato quella della responsabilità morale e giuridica di fronte alle azioni compiute da chi dorme (polluzioni notturne e sonnambulismo), dall'altro quella del merito durante il sonno (l'esempio ricorrente si riferisce al sogno di Salomone) [2].

L'*excursus* che qui intendo proporre si limiterà ad offrire qualche cenno solo su alcuni di questi problemi, per poi lasciare spazio all'analisi del contributo di Olivi.

1. All'inizio degli anni '50 Bonaventura si chiede *Utrum liberum arbitrium propter ineptitudinem corporis ligari possit quoad usum* (Bonaventura, *In II librum Sententiarum*, d. 25, p. II, a. un., q. 6, PP. Collegii S. Bonaventurae ed., Quaracchi, 1885, t. 2, p. 620-624). Qualche anno più tardi Pietro di Tarantasia rispondeva al quesito *An liberum arbitrium possit impediri per corporis impedimentum* (Petrus de Tarantasia, *In II librum Sententiarum Commentaria*, d. 25, q. 4, a. 2, Tolosae, 1649, p. 221a-b), cui faceva eco Guglielmo de la Mare con la *quaestio* dal titolo *Utrum liberum arbitrium possit impediri per impedimentum corporis* (Guillelmus de la Mare, *Scriptum in II librum Sententiarum*, d. 25, q. 9, H. Kraml ed., München, 1995, p. 342-345). Riccardo di Mediavilla si concentrerà invece sull'impedimento che interessa lo stato fisiologico del sonno : Richardus de Mediavilla, *In II librum Sententiarum*, d. 25, a. 5, q. 2 (*Utrum per naturam possumus in somnis habere usum liberi arbitrii*), Brixiae, 1591 (rist. an. Frankfurt a. M., 1963), t. 2, p. 333a-335a.

2. *Cfr. III Rg* 3, 4-14.

INTELLIGERE EST CONIUNCTI

Uno dei principali postulati della psicologia razionale scolastica afferma che le operazioni intellettuali non sono svolte da alcuna parte organica del nostro corpo. Gli autori impegnati nelle indagini sulla *ratio ligata* devono pertanto spiegare in primo luogo come mai un disturbo o una indisposizione del corpo possa ostacolare l'attività mentale.

Bonaventura è dell'avviso che l'impedimento delle attività razionali, e segnatamente del libero arbitrio, si possa spiegare nel modo seguente. L'anima e il corpo insieme concorrono a costituire un terzo elemento : il composto, cui si riferiscono tutte le operazioni, *intelligere* incluso. Se quindi il corpo ha qualche impedimento, questo si ripercuote sul composto. L'anima, in tale prospettiva, non dipenderebbe dal corpo soltanto per il sentire, ma anche per l'*intelligere*, nel senso che fino a quando essa si trova nel corpo le sue operazioni intellettuali non possono aversi senza una determinata disposizione da parte del corpo stesso [1].

Una risposta del tutto simile si ritrova in Matteo d'Acquasparta [2], e dello stesso tenore è anche la posizione di Guglielmo de la Mare, il quale sottolinea che gli atti razionali richiedono particolari condizioni fisiologiche del corpo, affinché possano svolgersi nel migliore dei modi [3]. La struttura gerarchica della natura umana è tale che tutto quanto segue deve servire a quanto precede ; ciò ha però l'inconveniente che se quanto deve essere di ausilio presenta dei problemi, questi si ripercuotono necessariamente su ciò che si sarebbe dovuto avvalere di quell'ausilio [4].

PERCHÉ IL CORPO CONDIZIONA LE ATTIVITÀ INTELLETTUALI

Spiegato l'assunto aristotelico secondo cui l'intelletto opera *sine corpore, sed per corpus*, i medievali devono precisare come mai l'attività intellettuale venga ostacolata solo in occasione di particolari indisposizioni corporali.

Gerardo d'Abbeville [5] individua tre fattori che determinano l'impedimento dell'*intelligere* nel sonno. Il primo fattore è dovuto al potere limitato dell'anima. Quando essa si trova impegnata in una certa operazione, si distrae da tutte le altre. Nel sonno infatti essa si concentra sulla parte vegetativa, abbandonando le operazioni della parte intellettiva [6]. Il secondo fattore è dovuto ad un mutamento di complessione che influenza direttamente l'attività superiore dell'anima : la natura dei sogni dipenderebbe appunto dal tipo di mutamento organico in atto in

1. *Cfr.* Bonaventura, *op. cit.*, p. 623a.
2. *Cfr.* Matthaeus ab Aquasparta, *Quaestiones disputatae de cognitione*, q. 10, PP. Collegii S. Bonaventurae ed., Quaracchi, 1957, p. 399.
3. *Cfr.* Guillelmus de la Mare, *op. cit.*, p. 343.
4. *Cfr. ivi.*, p. 344.
5. *Cfr.* Gerardus de Abbatisvilla, *De cogitationibus*, q. 18, A. Pattin ed., Louvain, 1993, p. 315-330.
6. *Cfr. ivi*, p. 320.

quel momento[1]. Il terzo fattore, connesso al secondo, consiste infine nella dissoluzione temporanea di quel rapporto che tiene insieme tutte le facoltà cognitive. In particolare si interrompe il collegamento tra intelletto e immaginazione. Un analogo fenomeno si verificherebbe anche nei dementi, a causa dell'occlusione di alcuni canali che trasmettono le informazioni dei sensi al cervello[2].

Secondo Riccardo di Mediavilla l'uso della ragione è impedito nel sonno, perché, a causa dei vapori e del ritrarsi degli spiriti verso l'interno, si produce un certo ingrossamento e una certa compressione negli organi dei sensi interni[3]. Ciò provocherebbe un'alterazione delle condizioni richieste da questi organi per l'estrinsecazione dell'atto secondo dell'anima intellettiva : il raziocinare[4]. Nella fattispecie il movimento alterato degli spiriti prodotto dai vapori creerebbe un certo disordine tra i fantasmi, cosicché la facoltà cogitativa sarebbe indotta ad operare a sua volta in modo disordinato. Da qui l'impossibilità per l'intelletto di svolgere perfettamente le proprie operazioni[5].

SPECIES PRO REBUS

La ricorrente analogia tra follia e sogno si fonda, come accennato, sul fatto che in entrambi i casi il soggetto non è in grado di capire se le immagini che gli appaiono appartengano alla realtà oppure no[6]. Furiosi e dormienti, ricorda Matteo d'Acquasparta, confondono parimenti « *similitudines et species pro rebus* »[7]. La sola differenza tra i due stati 'confusionali' consiste essenzialmente

1. *Cfr. ivi*, p. 321-322.

2. *Cfr. ivi*, p. 322-323.

3. Per i concetti di *spiritus* e di senso interno nella filosofia medievale si vedano rispettivamente J. Hamesse, « *Spiritus* chez les auteurs philosophiques des XIIe et XIIIe siècles », in *Spiritus. Atti del IV Colloquio Internazionale del Lessico Intellettuale Europeo, Roma 7-9 gennaio 1983*, M. Fattori, M. Bianchi ed., Roma, 1984, p. 157-190 e R.E. Harvey, *The Inward Wits : Psychological Theory in the Middle Ages and the Renaissance*, London, 1975.

4. *Cfr.* Richardus de Mediavilla, *op. cit.*, p. 334a. Il motivo per cui secondo Riccardo di Mediavilla l'intelletto necessita dell'ausilio dei sensi interni si deve al fatto che l'intellettiva è per essenza forma della materia sensibile. Ciò spiegherebbe perché un impedimento in atto nel corpo generi un impedimento nelle operazioni della forma che dovrebbe perfezionare la materia di quel corpo ; *cfr. ivi*, p. 334b.

5. *Cfr. ivi*, p. 334a.

6. *Cfr.* ad es. Guillelmi Altissiodorensi, *Summa aurea*, tr. 16, c. 4, J. Ribaillier ed., Paris-Roma, 1982, t. 2, p. 565 ; Guillelmus Alvernus, *De vitiis et peccatis*, c. 6, in *Opera, cit.*, t. 1, p. 272b e *Id.*, *De anima*, VI, 32, in *Opera, cit.*, t. 2, p. 192a ; Alexander Halensis, *Quaestiones disputatae « antequam esset frater »*, q. 67, m. 1, PP Collegii S. Bonaventurae ed., Quaracchi, 1960, t. 3, p. 1349. Chi sogna, come chi vaneggia, secondo Tommaso d'Aquino confonde il piano della realtà con quello della fantasia e così facendo non distingue più le cose dalle loro immagini (*cfr. Summa theologiae*, I, q. 54, a. 5, P. Caramello ed., Torino, 1952, t. 1, p. 270b).

7. Matthaeus ab Aquasparta, *op. cit.*, p. 397.

nella durata, ammetterà Riccardo di Mediavilla: *ad tempus* nel sonno, *semper [...] in simpliciter furiosis*[1].

Il motivo per cui secondo Pietro di Tarantasia i fantasmi sono percepiti « *ut res, non ut signa* » risiede nel legamento del senso comune, che non trasmette più i dati sensibili alla fantasia sotto forma di *rerum similitudines*[2].

Con il ricorso alle teorie mediche, Guglielmo de la Mare pensa che nella follia tale confusione sia determinata da un malfunzionamento dell'immaginazione[3]. Nel sonno invece tale confusione sarebbe causata dal blocco della facoltà cogitativa, divenuta per questo incapace di giudicare se sta considerando delle immagini o dei corpi[4].

D'accordo con Pietro di Tarantasia, o meglio, con Aristotele[5], anche Enrico di Gand sostiene che sia il blocco del senso comune a rendere la facoltà immaginativa incapace di percepire nel sonno le immagini come tali[6]. Siccome nel sonno le specie sensibili non vengono trasmesse alle facoltà interne, le specie preesistenti rifluiscono dalla memoria fino al senso comune, dove l'immaginativa le scorge e le giudica essere cose concrete[7]. Dal momento quindi che la specie si dà *sub ratione rei*, diviene impossibile l'astrazione dell'universale[8].

A tale proposito valeva la lezione aristotelica ripresa da Tommaso e dai tomisti: *nihil potest homo intelligere sine phantasmate*. Pertanto quando la specie fantastica non può essere astratta dalla specie sensibile, anche le operazioni intellettuali si trovano impedite[9].

Possibilità di peccare nel sonno

Il fenomeno della *ratio ligata* dovuto allo stato fisiologico del sonno costituiva un problema di non poco conto per il clero del Duecento. L'impegno verso il

1. *Cfr.* Richardus de Mediavilla, *Quodlibeta*, I, a. 5, q. 2, ed. cit., t. 4, p. 24a. I teologi medievali, come i giureconsulti romani, attuano una distinzione tra colui che soffre fin dalla nascita di disturbi mentali e chi invece ha di tanto in tanto momenti di lucidità (*dilucida intervalla*). La distinzione assume particolare importanza nel decidere se un furioso può o meno accedere ai sacramenti, o se sono da ritenere peccaminosi certi suoi comportamenti.

2. *Cfr.* Petrus de Tarantasia, *Quodlibet* I, q. 16, in P. Glorieux, « Le Quodlibet de Pierre de Tarentaise », *R.T.A.M.* 9, 1937, p. 257.

3. Secondo i medici la frenesi rappresenterebbe un'infiammazione nella parte anteriore del cervello, in cui veniva riconosciuta la sede dell'immaginazione; *cfr.* Gualteri Agilonis *Summa medicinalis*, c. 7, P. Diepgen ed., Leipzig, 1911, p. 100-104.

4. *Cfr.* Guillelmus de la Mare, *op. cit.*, p. 343. Guglielmo ricorda che una spiegazione della *ligatio rationis* durante il sonno era stata offerta anche da Agostino nel XII libro del *De genesi ad litteram*, ma non la riporta, perché ammette di non averla capita bene: « *est satis difficile intelligere dictum suum* » (*ivi*, p. 344).

5. *Cfr.* Aristoteles, *De somno et vigilia*, cap. 2, 455b 7-13.

6. *Cfr.* Henricus de Gandavo, *Quodlibet VI*, q. 9, G.A. Wilson ed., Leuven, 1987, p. 84.

7. *Cfr. ivi*, p. 84-85.

8. *Cfr. ivi*, p. 85-86.

9. *Cfr.* Thomas Aquinas, *In librum De memoria et reminiscentia commentarium*, l. 2, R.M. Spiazzi ed., Torino, 1949, p. 92 n. 314.

celibato e la condanna dell'onanismo accresceva evidentemente la frequenza dei sogni erotici e delle polluzioni notturne [1]. Per questo uno dei dubbi che sembrano assillare di più i pensatori del XIII secolo, quando affrontano la questione della *ratio ligata*, concerne la possibilità di peccare dormendo. Il principio agostiniano secondo cui il peccato nasce soltanto da un atto della volontà [2], richiedeva la dimostrazione che nel sonno non si danno atti di libero arbitrio [3].

La questione del sonnambulismo

Oltre a problemi di carattere morale, in certi casi l'attività onirica poteva sollevare anche questioni di carattere giuridico, come si evince da una questione quodlibetale di Giovanni Peckham, nella quale ci si chiede *Se sia tenuto alla riparazione dei danni colui che nel sonno ferisce qualcuno* [4].

Secondo Peckham solo chi ignora di soffrire di questo disturbo non è tenuto a tale riparazione. Chi invece sospetta o è a conoscenza delle proprie peregrinazioni notturne è da ritenersi responsabile degli atti che compie, perché avrebbe dovuto prevenirli [5]. Peckham pensa che il fenomeno del sonnambulismo si verifichi in persone dall'intelletto debole e dalla forte immaginazione, capace di stimolare i sensi esterni nel sonno [6].

La logica dei sogni

Un argomento ricorrente nei testi che trattano della *ratio ligata* è quello che mette in dubbio l'impedimento del libero arbitrio nel sonno per il fatto che

1. Fin dai primordi del Cristianesimo il sogno venne visto come terreno incontrollabile su cui si realizzavano, sotto forma d'immagini, desideri lussuriosi repressi nello stato di veglia. Alla questione è dedicata un'intera *distinctio* del *Decretum Gratiani*, *Cfr.* Friedberg, I, cc. 9-11.

2. *Cfr.* Augustinus, *De vera religione*, c. 14, 27, K.D. Daur ed., Turnholt, 1962, p. 204.

3. Nel trattato *De cogitatione* Gerardo d'Abbeville si chiedeva *utrum dormiens possit cogitare et per consequens dormiendo peccare* (q. 18), *ed. cit.*, p. 315-330. Nella Pasqua del 1264 Pietro di Tarantasia aveva tenuto una discussione quodlibetale dal titolo *Utrum dormiens possit in sompnis peccare* (*Cfr. Quodlibet* I, q. 16, *ed. cit.*, p. 256-258). Nella sostanza emergeva che « *quia ligatur usus rationis, ligatur potestas peccandi* » (*ivi*, p. 257). Analogamente si era espresso anche Tommaso d'Aquino (*Cfr. Summa theologiae*, IIa, IIae, q. 154, a. 5, *ed. cit.*, p. 669a-b).

4. *Cfr.* Joannis de Pecham, *Quodlibet romanum*, q. 6, F.M. Delorme ed., Roma, 1938, p. 87-88. In merito alla responsabilità degli atti compiuti dal sonnambulo una lunga tradizione giuridica e poi canonistica (che culminerà nel canone *si furiosus* di Clemente V) assimilava la sua incapacità mentale a quella dei bambini e dei folli. Per l'analisi di alcuni problemi connessi al fenomeno del sonnambulismo nel XIII secolo, *Cfr.* A. Boureau, « La redécouverte de l'autonomie du corps : l'émergence du somnambule (XIIe-XIVe s.) », *Micrologus* 1, 1993, p. 27-42.

5. *Cfr. ivi*, p. 88.

6. Lo stato dei sonnambuli ricorda quello delle persone sveglie, ma distratte al punto da non percepire quanto accade loro intorno ; *Cfr. ibid.*

l'esperienza mostra ad ognuno di noi che talvolta nel sogno è possibile svolgere ragionamenti e costruire sillogismi [1].

Tommaso sostiene che ciò accade in particolari momenti del sonno e cioè quando i sensi interni non sono del tutto oppressi dai vapori. In questi casi l'immaginazione e in parte anche il senso comune non si trovano impediti. L'uomo è in grado allora di ragionare e di giudicare quanto gli appare in sogno, ma solo in modo parziale e fallace. Per questo chi sogna di comporre dei sillogismi, una volta sveglio si accorge che questi, per un verso o per l'altro, sono errati [2].

Pietro di Tarantasia crede invece che sillogizzare in sogno significhi svolgere un'operazione simile a quella del ragno quando tesse la ragnatela: sembra che compia un'opera d'arte mentre invece si tratta di un atto meccanico e ripetitivo. Analogamente quindi queste attività pseudorazionali che si manifestano nel sogno sarebbero dovute alla consuetudine, non ad un atto ponderato. Se si sillogizza nel sonno è perché da svegli si è soliti ordinare termini e proposizioni [3].

Secondo Matteo d'Acquasparta sarebbe il caso all'origine di ragionamenti logici e versi poetici nel sonno; mai ad ogni modo un atto deliberato della ragione. E proprio perché sono frutto del caso – argomenta Matteo – questi ragionamenti e questi versi ci sembrano banali e imperfetti una volta svanito il sogno [4].

Enrico di Gand ritiene che il sillogizzare e il comporre versi durante il sonno siano l'effetto di una qualche *impressio*, prodotta dall'abitudine a svolgere da svegli quelle stesse attività sotto il controllo della ragione. La facoltà immaginativa compie atti apparentemente razionali perché segue appunto i dettami di questa impressione, come se fosse la ragione stessa [5].

Riccardo di Mediavilla parla invece di una certa abitudine da parte della facoltà cogitativa a muoversi in modo ordinato in rapporto all'intelletto. Egli riconosce tuttavia che talvolta tale *ordinatio* possa anche essere un effetto del caso [6].

RATIO LIGATA E RIVELAZIONI CELESTI

Nonostante che la *ratio ligata* sia all'origine di tutti questi problemi, i pensatori del XIII secolo non sono tuttavia convinti che tale stato mentale rappresenti un handicap *tout court* per il soggetto. Il legame dei sensi interni e l'astrazione dalla realtà sensibile, che impediscono al soggetto un uso naturale della ragione,

1. Agostino riconosceva che nel sogno fosse possibile immaginare conversazioni e dispute fondate su *verae rationes*, per quanto fossero false, ovvero irreali, le circostanze; *Cfr. De immortalitate animae*, c. 14, W. Hörmann ed., Wien, 1986, p. 124.

2. *Cfr.* Thomas Aquinas, *Summa theologiae*, I, q. 84, a. 8, *ed. cit.*, p. 415a.

3. *Cfr.* Petrus de Tarantasia, *Quodlibet* I, q. 16, *ed. cit.*, p. 257-258. Una spiegazione simile ricorre anche in Guillelmus de la Mare, *op. cit.*, p. 345.

4. *Cfr.* Matthaeus ab Aquasparta, *op. cit.*, p. 401-402.

5. *Cfr.* Henricus de Gandavo, *op. cit.*, p. 86.

6. *Cfr.* Richardus de Mediavilla, *Quodlibeta* I, a. 5, q. 2, *ed. cit.*, p. 25a-b.

vengono infatti a costituire le condizioni psico-fisiche ideali per un contatto con le entità celesti. Autori come Gerardo d'Abbeville[1], Guglielmo de la Mare[2], Enrico di Gand[3], e Riccardo di Mediavilla[4] si sforzano di dimostrare che il sogno può rappresentare il luogo d'incontro tra Dio e creatura umana, tra presente e futuro, tra naturale e sovrannaturale.

Non si tratta però di una peculiarità propria del sogno. Anche la follia, come riconoscono Guglielmo d'Alvernia[5], Tommaso d'Aquino[6] e Giovanni Peckham[7], può facilitare la preveggenza e il contatto con le sostanze angeliche[8]. Il dormiente divide quindi con il furioso non soltanto lo stato di confusione mentale, ma anche il privilegio di una vicinanza alle verità celesti.

IL CONTRIBUTO DI OLIVI

Quelli passati in rassegna nei precedenti paragrafi costituiscono, nella sostanza, i principali problemi connessi al fenomeno della *ratio ligata*. A questo punto si tratta di vedere quale sia stato il contributo di Pietro di Giovanni Olivi. Egli si occupa di questo tema in tre diversi scritti, il primo dei quali, in ordine di tempo, è rappresentato dalla 59ª questione *In II Sententiarum*. Qui Olivi si chiede *Se i bambini, i dormienti e i furiosi siano in grado di esercitare l'uso del libero arbitrio*. Studiata finora solamente come luogo in cui ricorre la formulazione della sfortunata teoria psicologica, la *quaestio* 59, lunga ben 50 pagine nell'edizione Jansen, per la sua articolazione e la sua complessità costituisce un ulteriore esempio – caso mai ce ne fosse ancora bisogno – di quel vigore intellettuale e di quell'autonomia di pensiero che caratterizza l'opera del maestro provenzale. Un'autonomia di pensiero che anche in questo testo si trincera prudentemente dietro l'uso di pronomi indefiniti (*alii*, *aliqui*), ai quali viene attribuita questa o quella data tesi.

In merito alla questione della *ratio ligata*, Olivi si mostra in pieno accordo con altri pensatori, se si tratta di riconoscere che durante il sonno e le crisi di follia il soggetto non è in grado di compiere azioni *cum pleno dominio*[9]. L'accordo viene

1. *Cfr.* Gerardus de Abbatisvilla, *Quaestiones quodlibetales*, XIV, q. 11, *ed. cit.*, p. 106-109 e *Id.*, *De cogitatione*, q. 18, *ed. cit.*, p. 324.

2. *Cfr.* Guillelmus de la Mare, *op. cit.*, p. 345.

3. *Cfr.* Henricus de Gandavo, *op. cit.*, p. 86.

4. *Cfr.* Richardus de Mediavilla, *Quodlibeta* III, q. 11, ed. cit., t. 4, p. 101a-104a.

5. *Cfr.* Guillelmus Alvernus, *De universo*, p. III, c. 20, *ed. cit.*, p. 1053a.

6. *Cfr.* Thomas Aquinas, *Summa theologiae*, I, q. 86, a. 4, *ed. cit.*, p. 427b.

7. *Cfr.* Joannis de Pecham, *Quodlibet romanum*, q. 7, *ed. cit.*, p. 89-90.

8. Secondo Ruggero Marston le anime alienate dei frenetici vedono quello che altri non possono vedere soprattutto quando sono prossime alla morte (*Cfr.* Rogerus Marston, *Quaestiones disputatae de emanatione aeterna, de statu naturae lapsae et de anima*, q. 7, PP. Collegii S. Bonaventurae ed., Quaracchi, 1932, p. 372).

9. *In II Sent.*, q. 59, t. 2, p. 530.

meno però quando si tratta di spiegare invece « *modum et causam huius impedimenti* »[1].

Olivi confuta diverse soluzioni, prima di proporre la propria. Secondo alcuni l'impedimento del libero arbitrio procederebbe da un'eccessiva *conversio* dell'anima verso il proprio corpo, nello sforzo di governarlo e di reggerlo[2]. Ma se così fosse, si obietta, l'impedimento del libero arbitrio si avrebbe anche in occasione di forti dolori fisici. Un'altra posizione sostiene che tale impedimento sia dovuto ad un errore prodotto dalla fantasia « *in accipiendo speciem suam pro re* »[3]. Questa ipotesi, dice Olivi, sembra fondarsi però su di un falso concetto di errore, il quale è un atto compiuto dall'intelletto che giudica, non dalla fantasia. Olivi rifiuta quindi quello che anche molti autori francescani avevano sottoscritto. Secondo lui l'apprendere la specie come la cosa non può costituire la causa del *ligamentum liberi arbitrii*, perché altrimenti si dovrebbe ammettere che anche nella veglia può darsi tale problema. Talvolta infatti capita davvero di fare questa confusione. Olivi fa l'esempio di chi preso dai propri pensieri emette dei suoni come se stesse vivendo effettivamente quelle situazioni che si sta immaginando[4].

La causa dell'impedimento del libero arbitrio è da ricercare invece, secondo Olivi, nel tipo di unione che lega la parte intellettiva dell'anima al corpo umano. La psicologia oliviana insegna, com'è noto, che non è la parte intellettiva a costituire la forma sostanziale del corpo umano, bensì la parte sensitiva, o piuttosto l'anima razionale attraverso la parte sensitiva. L'intellettiva e la sensitiva si trovano unite come due nature formali in una stessa materia e danno luogo pertanto ad un rapporto di consustanzialità tale da spiegare teoricamente l'unione metafisica del composto umano.

La digressione psicologica, che occorre qui tralasciare, serve ad Olivi per proporre la soluzione del quesito fondata su due punti : in primo luogo l'anima ha bisogno del corpo per avere una perfetta sussistenza e un perfetto modo di essere ; in secondo luogo ogni operazione dell'anima razionale dipende in qualche modo dal corpo e dalla sua buona disposizione[5]. Come si vede siamo vicini alla soluzione fornita da Bonaventura. Ma in Olivi ciò costituisce uno dei passaggi intermedi rispetto alla soluzione vera e propria, che emerge dopo aver analizzato il processo da cui scaturiscono gli atti dell'intelletto e della volontà. In termini oliviani, perché l'attività razionale abbia luogo è sì necessaria l'operatività della potenza, ma si richiede anche un *aspectus* debito, ovvero il rivolgersi intenzionale da parte della facoltà verso l'oggetto[6]. L'*aspetto*, secondo Olivi, è cioè

1. *Ibid.*
2. *Cfr. ivi*, p. 531.
3. *Ibid.*
4. *Cfr. ivi*, p. 536.
5. *Cfr. ivi*, p. 542.
6. « *[...] aspectum [...] voco conversionem virtualem seu intentionalem potentiae ad objectum* » : *ivi*, p. 543. La dottrina oliviana dell'« aspectus » è stata studiata da O. Bettini, « Fondamenti antropologici dell'attivismo spirituale in Pietro di Giovanni Olivi », *S.F.* 54, 1957, p. 12-39 ; ma sono da vedere anche E. Bettoni, « I fattori della conoscenza umana secondo l'Olivi », *Rivista di filosofia neoscolastica* 47, 1955, p. 21-22 e A. Krömer, *Potenzenhierarchie und Dynamismus des Geistes. Ein*

una particolare modificazione dell'anima che permette ad una data potenza di convergere la propria attenzione su di un oggetto specifico[1]. L'atto del vedere è determinato dalle condizioni di salute dell'occhio e dal suo convergere verso l'oggetto sensibile. Si potrebbe dire che nel caso della vista l'*aspectus* sia la messa a fuoco operata dall'occhio.

La discussione sulla natura e la funzione dell'*aspectus* si protrae per diverse pagine. Nella sostanza Olivi dichiara che il libero arbitrio, nella follia come nello stato di sonno, si trova impedito per via di un'alterazione dell'aspetto[2], provocata da una trasmutazione del corpo, la quale si comunica dalla parte sensitiva alla parte superiore dell'anima[3].

Olivi specifica che l'*aspectus* può risultare inadeguato, riguardo agli atti di libero arbitrio, o per una eccessiva ritrazione, o per una eccessiva conversione. La *retractio* si verifica nel sonno, quando le facoltà animali si ritirano verso l'interno, con la conseguente sospensione dell'attività sensoriale. Durante il sonno infatti quand'anche gli occhi fossero aperti e davanti a noi vi fosse un oggetto alla debita distanza, noi non saremmo in grado di vederlo. La *conversio* si verifica invece nei frenetici, poiché la facoltà immaginativa o quella cogitativa si trovano inclinate, ovvero rivolte, *immoderate* verso le loro *species*[4]. In queste due situazioni il dominio del libero arbitrio viene meno. Per una « eccessiva ritrazione » infatti l'*aspectus* si altera, cosicché la potenza o non si rivolge affatto all'oggetto o vi si rivolge in modo debole[5]. A causa di una « conversione inadeguata » invece la potenza si accosta all'oggetto in modo errato, cosicché l'*aspectus* non si troverà a quella distanza e altezza debita che di norma esige la potenza rispetto al suo oggetto[6].

Beitrag zur Erkenntnismetaphysik des Petrus Johannis Olivi (1248/49-1298), Freiburg i. Br., 1974, p. 137-150.

1. La dottrina dell'*aspectus*, secondo cui l'anima protende verso le cose e ciò facendo permette alle potenze di incontrarsi con la realtà, si trova strettamente connessa ad un'altra tesi altrettanto singolare di Olivi, quella della « causa terminativa ». Con entrambe Olivi sperava di poter definire i rapporti tra mondo fisico e spirituale senza dover ricorrere alla dottrina aristotelica dell'intelletto agente. Le soluzioni di carattere gnoseologico formulate da Olivi, lungi dal seguire l'*opinio communis* delle scuole, rappresentano uno degli aspetti più interessanti e più studiati della sua riflessione filosofica ; oltre ai contributi già citati mi limito a ricordare B. Jansen, *Die Erkenntnislehre Olivis. Auf Grund der Quellen dargestellt und gewürdigt*, Berlin, 1921 ; S. Belmond, « Le mécanisme de la connaissance d'après Pierre Olieu, dit Olivi », *F.F.* 12, 1929, p. 291-323, 463-487 ; E. Bettoni, « Pier di Giovanni Olivi critico dell'intelletto agente », *S.F.* 52, 1955, p. 19-41 ; W. Hoeres, « Der Begriff der Intentionalität bei Olivi », *Scholastik* 36, 1961, p. 23-48 e C. Bérubé, « Olivi, critique de Bonaventure et d'Henri de Gand », in *Studies honoring Ignatius Charles Brady Friar Minor*, R.S. Almagno, C.L. Harkins ed., St. Bonaventure (N.Y.), 1976, p. 57-121.

2. Più precisamente, l'impedimento conseguirebbe da un'alterazione dell'aspetto universale (*Cfr. In II Sent*, q. 59, t. 2, p. 543). Secondo Olivi infatti gli « aspetti » possono essere universali o particolari. Quello universale consiste in una « *[generalis conversio] ad omnia obiecta quae sibi praesentia dici possunt* », l'aspetto particolare è invece « *[determinata conversio] ad certum obiectum* » : *ivi*, p. 544.

3. *Cfr. ivi*, p. 547.

4. *Cfr. ivi*, p. 550.

5. *Cfr. ibid.*

6. *Cfr. ibid.*

Ritrazione e conversione, per quanto interessino la parte sensitiva dell'anima, si ripercuotono immancabilmente sulle potenze superiori, proprio perché la sensitiva si trova intimamente unita all'intellettiva. Ne segue dunque che l'ordine superiore è sconvolto da un disordine che si verifica ad un livello inferiore [1].

Olivi ha con questo chiarito che il *ligamentum* nel sonno e nella follia ha gli stessi effetti, ma cause differenti : nei dormienti risulta da una ritrazione che produce un affievolimento delle capacità sensoriali ; nei folli sorge invece da una inadeguata conversione naturale delle potenze verso la realtà esterna.

Adesso resta da capire per quale ragione la specie venga confusa con l'oggetto. La risposta di Olivi è che in questi casi l'atto della facoltà immaginativa è scambiato per l'atto dei sensi particolari. In quei momenti il soggetto non conosce la cosa esterna in atto, né conosce lo stato dei sensi particolari. Poiché non è in grado di riferire in modo sufficiente le percezioni alle potenze relative, la specie fantastica viene considerata dall'immaginazione con un *aspectus* simile a quello che il senso comune adopera nei confronti dei sensi particolari quando questi sono in funzione [2].

Nella veglia tale confusione accade soprattutto quando si rivolge troppa attenzione alla specie. La differenza è che nella veglia il soggetto può capire immediatamente che si sta ingannando, nel sonno invece no [3].

Qualche tempo dopo la stesura della *quaestio* 59, Olivi ritorna a trattare del problema della *ratio ligata* in due questioni quodlibetali. Questa volta però l'attenzione è rivolta soltanto allo stato mentale del sonno. Nella prima questione Olivi si chiede se nel sogno possano essere svolte operazioni razionali [4]. Nella seconda questione viene affrontato invece il problema del sonnambulismo [5]. Come si vede si tratta anche in questo caso di temi già discussi da autori precedenti. Ma anche qui Olivi non si limita affatto a riproporre le soluzioni di altri.

In merito alla prima questione viene confutata la tesi, sostenuta qualche anno prima da Enrico di Gand, secondo cui gli atti apparentemente razionali del sogno sarebbero in realtà prodotti dalla fantasia, che conserverebbe della veglia una certa *impressio ratiocinationis*. Il motivo per cui Olivi rigetta questa tesi è che l'*impressio*, per sua natura, si riferisce soltanto ai termini universali derivati dalla realtà sensibile, quando invece è noto che nel sogno compaiono anche termini universali puramente intellettuali (come il concetto di grandezza, di castità, di amore, di fede, ecc.) che trascendono la realtà sensibile e che non possono quindi

1. La ritrazione che interessa la parte sensitiva può avere due cause : lo sviluppo incompleto dei suoi organi e l'abbandono, da parte degli spiriti animali, delle facoltà sensitive. Le normali condizioni di funzionamento di una facoltà esigono infatti un organo sano e completo e una debita disposizione degli spiriti. Il primo genere di *retractio* si verifica nell'infanzia, il secondo durante il sonno, quando il venir meno degli spiriti animali rende inoperative le facoltà (*Cfr. ivi*, p. 550). La *conversio improportionalis* può anch'essa originarsi in due modi : o a causa di un'alterazione naturale del corpo o per l'azione di un demone (*Cfr. ivi*, p. 551). In entrambi i casi questa conversione si ha per mezzo di un irregolare movimento degli spiriti, che impedisce alle facoltà sensitive di operare correttamente.

2. *Cfr. ivi*, p. 554.

3. *Cfr. ibid.*

4. *Cfr. Quodl.* I, q. 6, f° 3va.

5. *Cfr. Quodl.* I, q. 7, f° 3va-4ra.

essere rappresentati dalla fantasia, in quanto non costituiscono l'oggetto di alcuna facoltà sensoriale[1].

Olivi prosegue la sua critica confutando anche la tesi di quanti sostengono che durante il sonno non vi possano essere atti di ragione a causa del fatto che le *species*, allora, non si presenterebbero come immagini di cose assenti, ma come oggetti concreti e presenti. La specie cioè non si offrirebbe alla ragione come si conviene per continuare il processo di astrazione, ovvero *sub modo abstractibili et intelligibili*, ma si presenterebbe *sub modo brutali seu corporali*. E tale *modus* sarebbe secondo costoro ben distante dall'astrazione intellettuale che opera l'intelletto agente[2]. Olivi, autore tra i più critici nei confronti della dottrina dell'intelletto agente, ritiene questa spiegazione *ridiculosa et nulla*. Egli non è affatto convinto che l'immagine del sogno non possa costituire l'oggetto da cui la ragione muove per attuare il processo di astrazione, anche perché in quanto specie, quella del sogno non dovrebbe differire per grado di astrazione da quella della veglia[3]. Se poi nel sogno le immagini vengono percepite come *res* – prosegue Olivi – ciò non dipende dall'immaginazione, ma da un difetto della *ratio conferentis*, che in quei momenti non è in grado di giudicare se la rappresentazione sia reale o fittizia[4].

Ad ogni modo la dimostrazione che durante i sogni la ragione non sia inattiva Olivi la individua nel fatto che spesso il *dormiens* svolge ragionamenti completamente estranei a quelli effettuati durante la veglia. Questi ragionamenti, che non possono certo essere dovuti a delle impressioni che sopravvivono nella fantasia, talvolta poi sono così fini e inventivi che mai forse saremmo stati in grado di produrli da svegli[5].

Come si vede, su questo punto Olivi ha respinto tutte le soluzioni precedentemente elaborate. Comporre versi o costruire sillogismi in sogno non sarebbero atti dettati dal caso, dall'abitudine o derivati da qualche *impressio*, bensì il frutto di una certa attività mentale vera e propria.

Riguardo alla questione del sonnambulismo, ricordata poco sopra, Olivi nota una stretta analogia tra i *semidormientes* e i ciechi. Che alcuni ciechi possano muoversi e agire meglio di quanto sappiano fare molti vedenti non desterebbe infatti meno meraviglia del fatto che alcune persone durante il sonno possano vedere, ascoltare, parlare, camminare e andare a cavallo assai meglio di quanto farebbero se fossero svegli[6].

Olivi ricorda che qualcuno ha ritenuto di individuare la causa del sonnambulismo in un funzionamento parziale del senso comune, che consentirebbe ad alcuni sensi particolari di svolgere le loro funzioni.

1. *Cfr. Quodl.* I, q. 7, f° 3vb.
2. *Cfr. ivi*, f° 3va-vb.
3. *Cfr. ivi*, f° 3vb.
4. *Cfr. ibid.* Per *ratio conferentis* si deve intendere la facoltà cogitativa.
5. *Cfr. ibid.*
6. *Cfr. ivi*, f° 3va. L'importanza di questo testo è già stata ricordata da A. Boureau, « Pierre de Jean Olivi et le semi-dormeur. Une élaboration médiévale de l'activité inconsciente », *Nouvelle revue de psychanalyse* 48, 1993, p. 231-238.

Olivi obietta dicendo che i sensi particolari non possono mai essere in atto senza che prima non lo sia anche il senso comune. L'esperienza ci dimostra inoltre che quando i nostri sensi interni sono rivolti completamente ad altro, le percezioni dei sensi esterni non vengono minimamente avvertite, e di esse non resta traccia nella nostra memoria [1]. Il senso comune deve quindi necessariamente presiedere agli atti dei sensi particolari.

Ma come si spiega allora il fenomeno del sonnambulismo? Com'è possibile che alcuni *semidormientes* siano così infallibili in quello che fanno? Secondo Olivi ciò dipende dalla *certitudo* della facoltà estimativa, che facendo compiere le azioni in modo meccanico, come avviene negli animali, rende i sonnambuli sicuri e impavidi [2]. Sembra di capire quindi che quella sicurezza con la quale i sonnambuli possono svolgere certe azioni tipiche della veglia, ma meglio di quanto farebbero se fossero svegli, sia dovuta nella sostanza alla mancanza della componente emotiva.

Se la spiegazione del sonnambulismo che qui Olivi propone appare essere approssimativa, bisogna dire che i risultati raggiunti dalla scienza medica del tempo non erano poi molto più esaurienti.

Vincenzo de Beauvais individuava la causa del sonnambulismo in un sogno particolarmente vivido o in un riscaldamento accidentale del corpo, che avrebbe liberato in parte i sensi precedentemente immobilizzati dal freddo-umido proveniente dal cervello [3].

Rogerio Frugardi, un medico della Scuola salernitana e Guglielmo de Congenis, un medico attivo a Montpellier all'inizio del XIII secolo, ritenevano che il sonnambulismo fosse la conseguenza di una lesione cranica e che un intervento chirurgico avrebbe rimosso tale disturbo [4].

Un altro medico, Bernardo de Gordon, allievo di Arnaldo da Villanova, individuava invece la causa di tale fenomeno in una complessione cerebrale caldo-umida che, accrescendo il vigore dell'immaginazione e paralizzando quasi gli organi di senso, agirebbe sui nervi motorei.

Data l'eventuale pericolosità di questo fenomeno Bernardo consigliava vari rimedi. Raccomandava ad es. di far annusare dell'aceto al soggetto durante le sue crisi, ma soprattutto riteneva efficace qualche frustata, quando il sonnambulo fosse stato in procinto di alzarsi dal letto. La sferza, come l'aceto, avrebbe avuto la funzione terapeutica di distrarre il soggetto preso da una sì forte immaginazione [5].

1. *Quodl.* I, q. 7, f° 4ra.
2. *Cfr. ibid.*
3. *Cfr.* Vincentius Bellovacensis, *Speculum naturale,* l. 26, c. 27, Duaci, 1624, (rist. an. Graz, 1964), t. 1, c. 1858.
4. *Cfr.* Rogerius de Frugardo, *Chirurgia*, XXII, e Guilelmus de Congenis, *Chirurgia*, XIII, K. Sudhoff ed., in *Beiträge zur Geschichte der Chirurgie im Mittelalter* 2, 1918, p. 167-168, 320-321.
5. *Cfr.* Bernardus Gordonius, *Lilium medicinae*, c. 18, Parisiis, 1542, f° 106r.

CONCLUSIONE

Quali conclusioni si possono trarre da questo breve *excursus*? In primo luogo emerge chiaramente che la questione della *ratio ligata* assume, nel corso del XIII secolo, una fisionomia dalle molteplici sfaccettature. Inoltre, se le preoccupazioni che inducono gli autori ad affrontare tale questione sono spesso preoccupazioni di carattere teologico e morale, si deve riconoscere che le soluzioni che vengono poi elaborate acquistano una valenza prettamente filosofica e scientifica, formandosi alla luce di modelli gnoseologici. Si può anzi dire che la questione della *ratio ligata* costituisca in un certo senso un banco di prova della teoria della conoscenza di un autore, come dimostra proprio l'analisi approfondita proposta da Olivi. Da un punto di vista storico si deve però rilevare anche un altro dato : le indagini relative alla *ratio ligata* rimasero spesso confinate a interessi di carattere pratico e applicativo, più che teoretico e speculativo. Soprattutto non venne messo ben a fuoco quel problema già intravisto da Agostino nelle *Confessioni*, quando riconosceva la sua impotenza di fronte al vigore di certi sogni :

> [...] in quella mia memoria di cui ho tanto parlato sopravvive la visione di quelle concupiscenze : la consuetudine ve le ha stampate e mi si affacciano, prive, sì, di forza durante la veglia, nel sonno invece sufficienti non solo fino al piacere, ma anche al consenso e al compimento dell'atto. E quella vana immagine ha tanta forza nel mio spirito e nella mia carne che, mentre dormo, quelle false apparenze ottengono ciò che quelle vere non possono ottenere da me sveglio. Forse che allora non sono più io, o Signore? Vi è dunque tanta differenza tra me e me in quel momento in cui passo dalla veglia al sonno o da questo ritorno alla veglia? Dove si trova la ragione in quei momenti che pure resiste vigile a tali suggestioni e non si lascia impressionare nemmeno dalla realtà? Si chiude insieme con gli occhi? Si assopisce insieme con i sensi del corpo?[1].

« *Ubi est tunc ratio ?* », si domandava dunque Agostino. Qui la *ratio* veniva a coincidere con la coscienza, intesa come consapevolezza di essere e di operare, senza la quale l'uomo perde la propria essenza, la propria identità, divenendo altro da sé : *tunc ego non sum*, specificava il vescovo d'Ippona. Ed è appunto questo l'aspetto più drammatico della *ratio ligata* che a mio avviso non venne colto in tutta la sua portata dai pensatori medievali, neppure dagli agostiniani più convinti come Olivi[2].

Falsch Gebild und Wort verändern Sinn und Ort (Goethe, *Faust*)

1. *Cfr.* Agostino, *Confessioni*, X, c. 30, C. Vitali tr., Milano, 1988, p. 287-288.

2. Olivi citava il brano di Agostino a dimostrazione del fatto che durante il sogno possono verificarsi atti somiglianti allo scegliere e al consentire, pur non essendo espressione del libero arbitrio ; *cfr. In II Sent.*, q. 59, t. 2, p. 521.

LA LIBERTÉ DIVINE ET LA DESTRUCTION DES IDÉES CHEZ OLIVI

Sylvain Piron

Comme l'écrit Camille Bérubé, la critique des théories de l'illumination que mène Olivi contre Henri de Gand et l'ensemble des penseurs franciscains de son temps constitue un « tournant d'histoire »[1]. La thèse, presque universellement partagée par les frères mineurs dans les années 1260-70, s'est trouvée totalement abandonnée à la fin du siècle. Pierre de Trabibus lui-même, le principal disciple d'Olivi en théologie spéculative, reconnaît n'avoir accepté cette critique qu'à contrecœur, après avoir compris le danger que représentait le thème d'une vision dans les raisons éternelles[2]. De fait, avant de rédiger l'*Ordinatio* de son commentaire des *Sentences*, dans des questions disputées contemporaines de sa *Lectura* donnée à Santa Croce en 1294-95, il l'avait très clairement rejetée[3]. On se souviendra sans doute que c'est sur ce terrain qu'Étienne Gilson avait choisi de

1. Camille Bérubé, « Olivi, critique de Bonaventure et d'Henri de Gand », dans *Studies honoring Ignatius Charles Brady Friar Minor*, R.S. Almagno, C.L. Harkins éd., St. Bonaventure (N.Y.), Franciscan Institute Publications, 1976, p. 57-121, repris dans *Id.*, *De l'homme à Dieu selon Duns Scot, Henri de Gand et Olivi*, Rome, Istituto storico dei Cappucini, 1983, p. 19-79.

2. « *Sed licet credam Augustinum in praefata sententia piam et rectam intentionem habuisse, fateor tamen me non intelligere quomodo ista positio habeat veritatem, licet quandoque tenuerim et adhuc, si veram eam caperem tenere sim paratus. Sequitur enim ex positione ipsa [...] quod divina lux quae non est aliud quam divina essencia, naturaliter ob omni intelligente modo aliquo videatur. Et hoc Augustinus sensit quod invalida et exilis videatur [...] Hoc autem manifeste est contra alios sanctos et contra Dionysium [...]* », éd. dans A. Di Noto, *La Théologie naturelle de Pierre de Trabibus, O.F.M*, Padoue, 1963, p. 107.

3. « *[...] dixerunt aliqui quod praeter generalem Dei influentiam vel providentiam non requiretur aliud ad intelligendum, sed anima suo naturali lumine potest intelligere veritates. Sed quia bene advertunt dicta Augustini, dicunt [...] Sed haec sententia utrum sit vera vel non nescio, sed tamen scio quod bene stare non potest cum verbis Augustini alibi dictis [...]*, quaestio *utrum lux aeterna sit nobis ratio cognoscendi* », éd. dans Efrem Longpré, « Nuovi documenti per la storia dell'Agostinismo Francescano », *Studi Francescani* 9, 1923, p. 333. Je reprends les désignations d'*Ordinatio* et de *Lectura* (sur les livres II et III, contenue dans le cod. Florence, Bibl. Naz. Conv. Sopp. D. 6. 359) de H.A. Huning, « Die Stellung des Petrus de Trabibus zur Philosophie nach dem zweiten Prolog zum ersten Buch seines Sentenzenkommentars. Ms 54, Bibl. Communale, Assisi », *Franziskanische Studien* 46, 1964, p. 193-286 ; 47, 1965, p. 1-43. Une question du deuxième *Quodlibet* présent dans le même manuscrit donne comme date présente l'année 1296, mais des renvois internes montrent que les lectures des livres II et III ont été données la même année que le premier *Quodlibet* et donc, probablement, en 1294-95.

présenter l'essentiel de la nouveauté thomiste[1]. Pourtant, dans sa critique, Olivi ne prend guère appui sur le maître dominicain. Il pense même, à juste titre, être plus radical encore que Thomas d'Aquin. C'est ce que confirme une importante question inédite sur la volonté divine, jamais encore étudiée, qui mène sur un problème connexe une critique directe de Thomas, et atteint aussi bien l'ensemble des maîtres franciscains de l'époque. Cet article a pour objet de donner une simple présentation de ce texte, la sixième question conservée de la première partie de sa *Summa*[2].

Le thème d'une connaissance certaine dans les « raisons éternelles », quelles que soient les variantes sous lesquelles il se présente, suppose qu'un fondement de ces raisons puisse être atteint sans que l'essence divine soit vue. Ce fondement, ce sont les « idées divines » à travers lesquelles Dieu connaît éternellement sa création. Or l'un des axes du texte qui sera présenté ici consiste proprement à vider ces idées de tout contenu[3]. A ce titre, il faut le lire dans le prolongement de textes qui avaient cherché à disjoindre les problèmes de la connaissance humaine et de la connaissance de Dieu. Ces trois questions (I, 2-4), rédigées vers 1277[4], peuvent être comprises comme une réaction presque instantanée, menée dans un couvent du Midi, à la publication parisienne des premiers articles de la *Summa* d'Henri de Gand, principale cible de la question I, 2. La preuve de l'existence de Dieu *a priori* par la voie des « propositions universelles intelligibles »[5] a semblé particulièrement dangereuse à Olivi. En faisant correspondre les notions premières d'Avicenne aux « raisons éternelles » de saint Augustin, elle suggère que les notions qui s'impriment en premier dans l'esprit apportent une certaine connaissance de Dieu. Elle s'expose à une critique radicale : comment la vision dans les raisons éternelles ne serait-elle pas une vision naturelle de l'essence divine ? C'est en fonction de cette conséquence inacceptable qu'Olivi cherche à détruire toute possibilité de tirer des textes de saint Augustin l'identification de ces « raisons éternelles » à « quelque chose qui serait Dieu »[6].

1. Étienne Gilson, « Pourquoi saint Thomas a critiqué saint Augustin », *Archives d'histoire doctrinale et littéraire du Moyen Age* 1, 1926, p. 1-127.

2. Josef Koch, « Der Sentenzkommentar des Petrus Johannis Olivi », *Recherches de théologie ancienne et médiévale* 2, 1930, p. 290-310, repris dans *Id.*, *Kleine Schriften*, Rome, Storia e Letteratura, 1973, t. 2, p. 168-189. Je montre que ce texte était suivi d'autres questions, non retrouvées, sur la volonté divine, dans « Les œuvres perdues d'Olivi : essai de reconstitution », à paraître dans *Archivum Franciscanum Historicum* 91/2, 1999.

3. C'est à une destruction du même ordre que se livre, bien plus tard, Ockham, *cf.* Armand Maurer, « The Role of Divine Ideas in the Theology of William of Ockham », dans *Studies Honoring Ignatius Charles Brady*, *op. cit.*, p. 357-377.

4. Je présente dans ma thèse une chronologie générale des écrits d'Olivi : *Parcours d'un intellectuel franciscain. D'une théologie vers une pensée sociale : l'œuvre de Pierre de Jean Olivi (ca. 1248-1298) et son traité* De contractibus, Paris, EHESS, 1999, première partie, ch. 3 et 4.

5. *Cf.* Pasquale Porro, *Enrico di Gand. La via delle proposizioni universali*, Bari, Levante, 1990, p. 99-105 ; Camille Bérubé, « Olivi, critique de Bonaventure », *op. cit.*, p. 84-94 ; Jean Paulus, « Henri de Gand et l'argument ontologique », *A.H.D.L.M.A.* 10, 1935, p. 265-323.

6. Voir l'intitulé de la q. I, 2 : « *[...] an aliquid directe et immediate seu positive a nobis apprehensum sit Deus. Quod non est aliud quaerere quam an Deus videatur a nobis* », *II Sent.* t. 3, p. 455.

Cette critique est loin de se réduire aux seuls problèmes de la connaissance. Elle atteint aussi bien l'ontologie réaliste sur laquelle repose la démarche d'Henri de Gand. Pour celui-ci, si les propositions universelles demeurent vraies en l'absence de tout individu dans lequel elles se vérifient, c'est qu'elles atteignent l'être d'essence (*esse essentiae*) du sujet sur lequel elles portent, qui n'est autre que l'idée formelle de ce sujet en Dieu, connu par l'intellect divin comme possible avant d'être créé[1]. Olivi résout le problème de manière non-réaliste. Les propositions nécessaires n'ont qu'une nécessité conditionnelle : elles ne sont vraies que pour autant qu'elles sont formées par un sujet pensant[2]. Leur nécessité signifie seulement qu'elles ne peuvent être formées par l'intellect sans être vraies[3]. Que soit posée l'existence d'un sujet (*homo*), ou qu'il soit saisi par l'intellect comme simple quiddité, sa raison ne peut être formée sans qu'un prédicat (*animal*) lui soit associé[4]. Mais le concept universel qui se forme de la sorte ne correspond en rien à l'idée que Dieu en a de toute éternité. Ce que Dieu connaît de sa création n'est pas ce que nous en connaissons[5].

La critique de l'illumination proprement dite est menée dans la question suivante (I, 3) de manière plus diplomatique. Au lieu d'une attaque frontale, Olivi réclame une série de précautions qui ont pour effet de vider de tout contenu la connaissance « dans les raisons éternelles ». Avant de réclamer ces précautions, et après avoir sommairement présenté les variantes des théories de l'illumination, Olivi rappelle que selon « d'autres grands » – c'est-à-dire Thomas d'Aquin – Augustin était sur ce point platonicien[6]. Certes, Olivi refuse d'adopter pour autant une théorie aristotélicienne de la connaissance. Sa discussion est remise à plus tard, pour des textes qui présenteront une théorie de la connaissance comme activité, dans laquelle les objets ne sont requis qu'à titre de cause « terminative », en rupture totale avec toutes les traditions médiévales[7]. Le bref appel à Thomas permet du moins de disqualifier un platonisme d'Augustin, selon un jugement

1. Henricus a Gandavo, *Quodlibet I*, R. Macken éd., Leuven-Leiden, Leuven U.P.-Brill, 1979, q. 9, p. 49 : « *[...] habens tamen formalem ideam in Deo, per quam in Deo est ens quoddam antequam fiat ens in propria natura* ».

2. *II Sent.* q. I, 3, ad 6, t. 3, p. 484 et ad 24, p. 495 ; q. II, 13, ad 12, t. 1, p. 255.

3. *II Sent.* q. I, 2, ad 2, p. 481 ; q. 12, ad 1, t. 1, p. 228 ; q. 13, t. 1, p. 255.

4. *II Sent.* q. I, 2, ad 6, p. 484.

5. « *Rationes autem earum ideales, quamvis maneant rebus destructis, non tamen sunt illae rationes quae a nobis certitudinaliter apprehenduntur, quando cogitamus de perfectionibus et conditionibus rerum, etiam universaliter [...] Illam tamen veritatem qua sic ab aeterno erant verae nos non videmus* », *id.*, q. I, 2, ad 6, p. 483-484.

6. « *Alii autem, etiam magni, voluerunt et volunt quod Augustinus in hac parte fuerit Platonicus [...]* », *II Sent.* q. I, 3, t. 3, p. 503, paraphrasant Thomas d'Aquin, *Summa Theologiae*, Ia, q. 84, art. 5. C. Bérubé, « Olivi, critique de Bonaventure », *art. cit.*, n'identifie pas cette allusion.

7. D'abord dans la q. II, 58 (vers 1278) puis dans les qq. II, 72-75 (vers 1282). Effrem Bettoni, *Le dottrine filosofiche di Pier di Giovanni Olivi. Saggio*, Milano, Vita e pensiero, 1959, p. 471 et Camille Bérubé, *La connaissance de l'individuel au Moyen Age*, Montréal-Paris, Presses de l'Université de Montréal-PUF, 1964, p. 100 voient à juste titre dans ces textes l'aspect le plus « révolutionnaire » d'Olivi.

qu'Olivi reprend plus clairement à son compte ailleurs [1]. Il est d'autre part certain qu'il pense, avec Thomas, que la seule lumière naturelle offre une connaissance suffisante, capable de fournir ses propres règles de certification [2]. Et pour cette raison, elle n'atteint pas tous ses savoirs avec le même degré de certitude [3]. Toutefois, et c'est le point sur lequel on voudrait attirer l'attention, Olivi pense être plus radical encore que Thomas sur ce terrain.

En effet, s'il refuse de suivre Thomas, ce n'est pas seulement en raison de ses réticences philosophiques et méthodologiques à l'égard d'Aristote, ni par une fidélité d'apparence envers ses maîtres, ou parce que Thomas ne connaît pas l'esprit d'Augustin [4]. C'est également que celui-ci n'échappe pas non plus aux difficultés des théories de l'illumination, surtout s'il veut qu'Augustin ait voulu dire « que les espèces de l'intellect proviennent des idées comme de leurs premiers objets » [5]. C'est effectivement ainsi que Thomas comprend Augustin, et qu'il le rejette en montrant que les espèces intelligibles doivent être actuées par l'intellect agent à partir d'espèces sensibles. Mais il ne s'agit là que d'un détour par le sensible. Les formes intelligibles ainsi dégagées émanent toujours des idées divines [6]. La critique menée par Olivi sur ce thème dans ses questions d'angélologie le dénonce plus fortement encore [7]. Comme il le note enfin, la nature participée de la lumière noétique permet également à Thomas de prétendre pouvoir s'accorder à saint Augustin [8]. C'est précisément ce que celui-ci à cru faire [9] et la critique qu'en fait ici Olivi suggère que ce n'était pas par illusion. Les théories de l'illumination sont rejetées parce qu'elles ne rendent comptent, ni de l'absolue transcendance divine, ni de l'activité propre de l'intellect humain. Du point de vue d'Olivi, la variante thomiste ne vaut guère mieux. Pour lui, aucune causalité extrinsèque naturelle n'est admissible : l'action d'intelliger commence

1. « *Beatus Augustinus tamquam in parte sequens dogma Platonicum credidit omnem intellectum illustrari a luce aeterna et immediate contueri aliquas aeternas regulas eius ac deinde cetera in regulis illis [...]* », *II Sent.* q. 38, ad 2, t. 1, p. 679.

2. « *[...] dicendum quod pro quanto essentialis lux intellectus est recta et ad rectum et Dei recta imago, pro tanto habet vim rectae regulae* », *II Sent.* q. 74, p. 131.

3. Le texte le plus intéressant à cet égard apparaît dans *II Sent.* q. 55, p. 289 ; voir aussi *Lectura super Isaiam*, dans David Flood, Gedeon Gál éd., *Peter of John Olivi on the Bible*, St Bonaventure (N.Y.), Franciscan Institute Publications, 1997, p. 198.

4. « *[...] non sapit mentem Augustini* », *II Sent.* q. I, 3, t. 3, p. 505.

5. « *istorum expositio satis parum videtur distare a modo illo erroneo superius improbato, maxime si ipsi intenderent Augustinum voluisse quod species intellectus essent ab ideis sicut a primis obiectis* », *II Sent.* q. I, 3, t. 3, p. 505.

6. Voir *De substantiis separatis*, c. 16, dans *Opera Omnia*, Romae, Ad Sanctae Sabina, 1969, t. 40, p. 69, et *Summa Theologiae*, Ia, q. 84, art. 4, ad 1 ; q. 105, art. 3.

7. *II Sent.* q. 35-36, t. 1, p. 626-653 et *Lectura super librum De angelica hierarchia*, B.A.V., Urbinat. lat., 480, f° 147vb-149ra.

8. « *Dicunt enim quod lumen intellectus agentis de quo, ut dicunt, scriptum est, signatum est per lumen vultus tui super nos, est similitudo primae veritatis. Et ideo quae videntur in isto lumine dicuntur ab Augustino in lumine primae veritatis [...]* », *II Sent.* q. I, 3, t. 3, p. 505.

9. *Quaestio disputata de spiritualibus creaturis*, art. 10, ad 8 (*Opera Omnia*, Parme, Fiaccadori, t. 8, 1856). Le témoignage d'Olivi donnerait donc raison sur ce point à Édouard-H. Weber, *La personne humaine au treizième siècle*, Paris, Vrin, 1991, p. 326, contre Gilson, *art. cit.*, p. 119-120.

par nous, et ne dépend que de nous[1]. Sur ce point, la ligne de fracture ne dépend pas de la prééminence relative de la volonté sur l'intellect, mais de l'attribution complète des actes de ces deux puissances au sujet humain[2].

Olivi tire de ces premières critiques une affirmation centrale. Pour l'énoncer de la façon la plus générale, la création n'est pas intelligible par dérivation de l'intelligibilité qu'elle a pour son créateur. C'est également ce que montre une longue question inédite sur le vouloir et le savoir divin. La question I, 6, « si Dieu avait pu ne pas vouloir ce qu'il a voulu et veut, et ne pas savoir ce qu'il sait »[3], fait partie d'une série de questions rédigées peu après les condamnations parisiennes de mars 1277, auxquelles elles ne font pas ouvertement référence, qui visent autant certains articles condamnés qu'un ensemble de positions thomistes[4]. En l'occurrence, la question I, 6 fournit une réponse aux thèses du *syllabus* portant sur la nécessité des actions divines[5]. Il faut dire, tant selon la foi que selon la raison, que Dieu aurait pu vouloir ou savoir autre chose que ce qu'il sait et veut, sans quoi son acte ne serait pas libre[6]. Il faut le dire, mais il faut surtout le démontrer.

L'un des traits les plus intéressants de ce texte est d'aborder simultanément les thèmes de la volonté et du savoir divin. La position même du problème en révèle les présupposés. Si vouloir et savoir peuvent être conçus séparément, ils doivent l'être ensemble, aussi bien dans leur distinction que dans leur entrelacement. Deux doutes, soulevés dans le cours de la discussion, s'inquiètent de savoir s'il découle, de la thèse proposée, que l'intellect suit la volonté ou l'inverse. Il est remarquable qu'Olivi signale que sa position puisse donner lieu à l'une ou l'autre interprétation. Mais pour autant, ces doutes portent à faux. La

1. « *Sed actio intelligendi dependet a nobis, et nos primo incipimus insistere ad intelligendum quam ratio aeterna nobis cooperetur, et ratio et causa huiusmodi actionis incipit a nobis et non ab ipso ratione aeterna* », *II Sent.* q. I, 3, t. 3, p. 510. Cette critique vaut aussi bien contre la coopération des espèces intelligibles émanées des idées divines, et atteint Thomas à ce titre, *cf. Summa Theologiae*, Ia, q. 105 a. 3.

2. De ce point de vue, Olivi est du même côté de cette fracture que Thierry de Freiberg, *cf.* Ruedi Imbach, « Prétendue primauté de l'être sur le connaître. Perspectives cavalières sur Thomas d'Aquin et l'école dominicaine allemande », *Lectionum varietates. Hommage à Paul Vignaux (1904-1987)*, J. Jolivet, Z. Kaluza, A. de Libera éd., Paris, Vrin, 1991, p. 121-132.

3. « *Utrum Deus potuerit nolle que voluit et vult et velle que noluit nec vult et idem, queritur de scientia eius, utrum scilicet, utrum potuerit nescire seu non prescire ea que scivit et scit debere fieri et esse et econverso* », B.A.V., Borgh. 322, f° 169rb-179vb et Borgh. lat. 358, f° 154ra-165ra. La question sera citée à partir de ce deuxième témoin, éventuellement corrigé à l'aide du premier. Le troisième témoin connu, Montefano, cod. 19, f° 135v-138r, n'a pu être consulté.

4. Ces questions, *II Sent.* q. 4-6, 16, 33-36, 50-51, 57-58, connaissent déjà le *Correctorium fratris Thomae* de Guillaume de la Mare, mais sont antérieures aux premières *Quaestiones de perfectione evangelica*, elles-mêmes antérieures à l'été 1279.

5. En particulier l'art. 20, « *Quod Deum necesse est facere quidquid immediate fit ab ipso* », dans Roland Hissette, *Enquête sur les 219 articles condamnés à Paris le 7 mars 1277*, Louvain-Paris, Publications Universitaires-Vander-Oyez, 1977. p. 51.

6. « *[...] dicendum quod necesse est, tam secundum fidem catholicam quam secundum rationem rectam, ponere quod Deus potuerit nolle facere eas res quas facere voluit et vult, et potuit velle multa que noluit et idem dico de divino scire [...] Nam si Deus nullo modo potuit in rebus condendis aut non condendis aliquid aliter velle quam voluit, nichil omnino libere et imperiose dominationis super ipsas res habuit aut habet* », *I Sent.* q. 6, f° 154va.

réponse note qu'il ne peut y avoir en Dieu aucun rapport de consécution ou de prééminence. Le vouloir exprime l'être de Dieu tout autant que son savoir. Une pleine intelligibilité de l'acte divin réclame qu'il soit saisi selon ces deux « raisons réelles », mais celles-ci ne correspondent pas à deux aspects, ni réellement, ni formellement distincts. Bien plus, elles se recoupent nécessairement, et sont mutuellement inclues l'une dans l'autre, puisque l'activité divine implique tout autant le vouloir que le savoir[1]. Un autre trait notable tient à l'emploi insistant de formes verbales infinitives : il s'agit du *velle* et du *scire* divin, pas de la *voluntas* ou *scientia divina*. Ce choix signale l'impossibilité de penser le vouloir et le savoir comme deux puissances ou facultés divines. Olivi les distingue à l'aide de sa fameuse notion des « raisons réelles », qui ne correspondent ni à des modes d'être, ni à des modes d'intelliger, mais à des modes d'intelligibilité des choses mêmes[2]. Il en offre, dans les dernières pages de cette question, l'une des formulations les plus claires :

> Chacune dit le même tout, mais aucune ne le dit totalement. Quand nous disons qu'une raison n'est pas l'autre, et qu'elles ne sont pas identiques mais diverses, c'est ce défaut de totalité ou cette absence de signification totale, qui est supplée par l'autre raison, que nous entendons signifier[3].

La réponse principale contient une série de remarques sur la source des erreurs commises sur le sujet. Elles consistent à formuler des propositions universelles au Créateur et à la créature au moyen de similitudes fondées sur des traits qui sont en vérité dissemblables[4]. L'argument « ceci est dans la créature,

1. « *[...] dicendum quod nichil quod in Deo sic sequitur secundum rem aliquid quod sit in Deo, vel in aliquo alio, unde nec intelligere sequitur ibi velle nec econverso, cum secundum rem sint id ipsum, in ratione, tamen unius includitur aliquando ratio alterius et non econverso* », *id.*, f° 163rb ; « *dicendum quod non debet poni quod divinum intelligere eodem modo et eisdem causis representet obiectum divinum velle quibus illi ponebant hic de ydeis respectu divine intelligere ; non enim hoc fit ad hoc quod Dei voluntas possit prodire in actu volendi, cum Dei velle a nulla potentia producatur, sed sit absolute ipsum esse Dei et secundum rem idem quod intelligere. Sed solum debet per hoc intelligi quod divinum velle exigit in ratione sui obiecti quod includatur in ea ratio cogniti. Unde divinum velle ex se et immediate fertur in ipsum rem sicut et divinum intelligere, quamvis non feratur in rem nisi ut cognitam a divino intellectu* », *id.*, f° 163va.

2. La définition des « raisons réelles » comme modes d'intelligibilité partielle n'exprimant aucune différence réelle apparaît dans *II Sent.* t. 1, q. 7, ad 5, p. 144 : « *Si tamen daretur una ratio includens in se totam plenitudinem essentiae et omnes modos intelligibilitatis eius, talis ratio non posset plurificari ; nihilominus tamen haberet intra se plures rationes partiales, quia continet in se omnes rationes rei* » ; *id.*, t. 3, q. I, 2, ad 29, p. 497-498 : « *Quamvis enim in una simplici essentia duae rationes comprehenduntur, illa essentia potest intelligi secundum unam illarum rationum, non intelligendo eam secundum alteram, quamvis secundum totam intelligibilitatem suam non intelliatur, nisi intelligatur secundum omnes rationes suas quas habet* ».

3. « *Quando enim dicimus quod rationes in quantum tales non sunt eedem rationes, non intendimus simpliciter significare per hoc quin sint simpliciter eadem res et quin sint realiter omnino idem, sed intendimus significare per hoc quod nulla earum in quantum talis dicit divinam essentiam secundum totalitatem sue perfectionis seu secundum totam suam significatam. Unde omnes dicunt idem totum sed nulla earum dicit idem totaliter. Defectum ergo totalitatis seu totalis significationis qui per alias rationes suppletur intendimus significare per hoc quod dicimus quod una ratio est non est alia et quod non sunt eedem sed diverse* », *id.*, f° 179va.

4. « *Ad evidenciam huius veritatis et omnium argumentorum est primo notandum quod maior pars argumentorum que contra hoc fiunt, aut fieri possunt, sumitur a propositionibus que in sua plena*

donc c'est en Dieu» est vicié. Il confond ce qui relève d'une imagination des propriétés divines à partir de l'expérience humaine, et d'une pure intelligence de Dieu dans sa différence spécifique[1]. Une brève typologie de ce qui est commun et de ce qui est propre à Dieu permet de mettre en relief trois différences essentielles : l'acte divin ne procède d'aucune puissance. Alors que la liberté humaine relève d'une puissance active, Dieu est libre dans son acte même. Enfin, il ne peut y avoir en lui aucun rapport de dépendance ou de domination sur des actes internes[2].

Toutefois, Dieu n'est pas seulement caractérisé comme «acte pur». Il l'est surtout comme «acte le plus absolu», qui n'est de lui-même ordonné à rien, ni soumis à aucune cause formelle interne[3]. C'est sur ce point qu'apparaît la principale critique portée ici contre Thomas d'Aquin, pour qui le vouloir divin est déterminé par sa bonté[4]. Olivi y oppose son refus de poser une cause interne au vouloir divin. S'il faut dire avec Augustin que Dieu veut *propter bonitatem suam*, il ne faut pas comprendre qu'il veut à cause de sa bonté, mais à travers sa bonté[5]. Dieu n'est pas déterminé à s'aimer lui-même, mais s'aime dans un surexcès de bonté[6]. L'allusion faite dans ces pages aux questions contemporaines sur la

universalitate sunt false et a convenciis que a simili in eo quod est dissimile inferunt suum simile, seu potius suum dissimile», *id.*, f° 155rb.

1. «*Secundo est notandum quod id quod super omnia turbat intellectum quorumdam in pura intelligencia huius veritatis, et etiam consimilium, est defectus distinguendi inter actum et obiectum ymaginationis et intellectus, et inter proprium et commune*», *ibid.*

2. «*Proprium vero sibi soli habet tria ad presens, quorum primum est quod in eo non est aliqua exitus, seu aliqua productio. Non enim est actus progrediens a potentia vel a quocumque alio [...] Secundum est quod sicut in nobis potentia nostre voluntatis est potens immediate super actus oppositos et ipsis mediantibus super obiecta opposita, sic actus divini velle est immediate potens super obiecta opposita et super effectus extrinsecos oppositos [...] Tertium est quod in Deo non est libertas seu dominium super actus intrinsecos oppositos nec super aliquid intrinsecum, sicut est in nobis, quia hoc non posset esse ibi sine diversitate essentiarum et etiam graduum. Esset enim ibi subiectio et dominatio [...]*», *id.*, f° 155rb. Une série de distinctions symétriques est présenté dans le *Tractatus de Verbo*, Robert Pasnau éd., *Franciscan Studies* 53, 1993, p. 121-153.

3. «*[...] cum Deus et totus eius actus sit de se absolutissimus nec ad aliquam rem sit de sua natura protensus aut applicatus aut etiam ordinatus [...]*», *id.*, f° 154vb.

4. «*Ex eisdem autem potest improbari illud aliud dictum eorum quod in eodem predicto argumento est tactum, quod scilicet Deus nichil vult nisi volendo suam bonitatem*», q. I, 6, f° 158vb. *Cf.* Thomas d'Aquin, *Summa Theologiae*, Ia, q. 19 art. 3; *Summa contra Gentiles*, I, 80, 87 et II, 23; *Quaestiones disputatae de Veritate*, Romae, ad Sanctae Sabinae, 1973, t. 3, q. 23, art. 4, p. 662-663.

5. «*Divinum enim velle immediate fertur super omnia sua obiecta, nec preter se habet aliquam aliam rationem que sit sibi causa formalis vel finalis vel quecumque alia ad hoc quod velit istam vel illam rem. Unde et quando dicitur quod 'omnia vult propter suam gloriam', non est sensus quod sua bonitas vel gloria sit ratio motiva aut causa finalis illius velle quo Deus vult illam rem fieri, quia impossibile est dare in Deo aliquod velle quod habeat aliquam causam moventem vel finalem. Unde sensus est quod Deus vult res taliter fieri quod ipse res ad suam gloriam tamquam in suum finem ultimum ordinentur. Est enim sensus quod bonitas ipsius divini velle seu eius benignissima libertas est tota causa quare res fiunt. Unde quando dicimus 'Deus vult hoc propter suam bonitatem', idem est quod dicitur vult hoc ex suam bonitatem; et iterum huius sensus est quod divinum velle sola sua bonitate habet hoc vel illud pro obiecto, non ex aliqua utilitate vel necessitate*», *id.*, f 158vb.

6. «*Si autem contra hoc instetur quod divina voluntas est determinata ad Deum diligendum et divinam essentia est determinata ad productionem personarum, patet quod instantia hec frivola est, quia hoc non est per aliquam determinacionem seu determinatam applicationem divine nature et voluntatis, sed solum per excessivam sufficentiam bonitatis et actualitatis que est in ei, quia divina*

volonté (II, 57-58) est particulièrement éclairante[1]. C'est bien la thèse de la volonté cause d'elle-même qui est à l'arrière-plan de l'ensemble de cette affirmation de la liberté divine[2]. Pour cette raison, tout au long de la question n'apparaît pas la distinction entre puissance absolue et puissance ordonnée, dont Olivi fait usage dans d'autres textes[3]. L'ensemble de la question se situe exclusivement dans le domaine d'une volonté illimitée, qui ne considère pas la convenance ou la justice de ses choix.

La principale distinction sépare l'acte divin pris dans un sens absolu, et pris en tant qu'il vise tel ou tel objet[4]. De lui-même et absolument, Dieu n'a pas le moindre vouloir ou non-vouloir[5]. En revanche, tout aussi absolument, le savoir divin s'étend à tout objet connaissable, à tel point qu'il ne peut pas ne pas les connaître[6]. Mais il s'agit d'un savoir qui considère uniquement les quiddités des choses intelligibles, et l'existence qui peut leur être donnée[7]. De la sorte, et sans contradiction, il peut viser *sub disiunctione* des objets opposés[8]. Sous cette

voluntas non posset non diligere summum bonum, nisi deficiendo a ratione summe bonitatis, unde hec posse non esset posse, sed potius deficere a vero posse, et idem est de productione personarum », *id.*, f° 154vb-155ra.

1. *II Sent.* q. 57-58, t. 2, p. 305-517.

2. Sur la volonté selon Olivi, *cf.* Feliciano Simoncioli, *Il problema della libertà humana in Pietro di Giovanni Olivi e Pietro di Trabibus*, Milan, 1956; Effrem Bettoni, « *La libertà come fondamento dei valori umani nel pensiero di Pier di Giovanni Olivi* », dans *Atti del XII congresso internazionale di filosofia*, Florence, 1960, p. 41-47; François-Xavier Putallaz, *Insolente liberté. Controverses et condamnations au* XIIIe *siècle*, Fribourg-Paris, Presses Universitaires-Le Cerf, 1995, p. 127-162; Olivier Boulnois, « *Vouloir, vœu et noblesse de la volonté selon Olieu* », *Cahiers du Centre de Recherches Historiques* 16, 1996, p. 57-64.

3. Par ex. : « *Loquendo de potentia Dei absoluta, prout scilicet rescipit ens absolute absque respectu ad convenientiam vel disconvenientiam ordinis decentis et indecentis [...]* », *III Sent.* q. 1 (*Quaestiones de incarnatione et redemptione. Quaestiones de virtutibus*, A. Emmen, E. Stadter éd., Grottaferrata, Coll. S. Bonaventura, 1981), p. 42. L'étude des différents passages dans lesquels Olivi y a recours offre une image plus complexe que celle que résume William J. Courtenay, *Capacity and Volition. A History of the Distinction of Absolute and Ordained Power*, Bergame, Lubrina, 1990, p. 98.

4. « *[...] dicendum quod per velle et nolle possumus significare actum divini velle secundum suam essentiam absolutam [...] Aut possumus per hoc significare ipsum actum in ordine ad obiecta opposita seu prout est huius vel illius obiecti* », *I Sent.* q. 6, ad 2, f° 155vb.

5. « *Deus ex se et absolute non habuit nolle alicuius, ita parum sicut velle non habui* », *id.*, ad 5, f° 156rb, « *bene potest dici quod Dei velle quantum est de se seu ex vi absoluta sue nature non erat huiusmodi, nec est, sed solum ex libertate sua* », *id.*, ad 7, f° 156va.

6. « *Cum enim scientia, quantum est de se, se extendat ad omne scibile, dicere quod divina scientia non possit extendere se ad omne scibile est idem quod dicere quod in eo non est omnis ratio et perfectio scientie* », *id.*, f° 154vb.

7. « *Unde de se et absolute omnis terminos et quiditates cogitabiles divinus intellectus de sui nature et necessarie intellexerit et intelligit. Hoc est dicere quod divinum intelligere de se et necessario fuit intelligere talium obiectorum. Semper enim scivit, et non potuit non scire, quid est res quecumque scibilis seu possibilis et quid est ipsum existere quod eis dare potuit [...] Sed hoc non est scire eam ut actualem, unde non ex se et necessario alteram illarum scivit ut veram et actualem* », *id.*, f° 159ra.

8. « *Oportet igitur quod divinus actus habeat in se equivalenciam, seu potius prevalenciam actuum oppositorum. Sed hoc est impossibile nisi sub distinctione possit esse oppositorum obiectorum, aut nisi sub disiunctione possit esse et non esse eiusdem obiecti absque alia sui variatione* », *id.*, f° 155rb; « *Potest enim divinus intellectus obiecta contradictoria aliquo modo simul*

disjonction, Dieu connaît simultanément A et non-A, non en tant qu'existants actuellement, mais en tant qu'intelligibles, et également susceptibles d'être produits : à ce titre, il connaît comme vraies l'une et l'autre partie de la contradiction [1]. C'est par la liberté de son vouloir que Dieu choisit l'une ou l'autre partie de la contradiction, sans être aucunement déterminé par l'intellect [2]. Ce choix n'implique aucune négation, il affirme la partie positive ou la partie négative de la contradiction : Dieu veut A ou non-A [3]. Pour autant, ce vouloir n'est pas contingent mais libre ; seuls les objets de son vouloir sont contingents [4]. Ces négations, qui n'affectent que les objets possibles qui n'ont pas été voulus, ne nient ou diminuent rien de Dieu [5].

Cette indifférence première, décrite comme « prévalence » sur des objets opposés, est la condition même de la liberté du vouloir. On en trouve une image très déformée dans le libre arbitre humain, qui possède une même prévalence, non dans ses actes (qui sont toujours successifs), mais dans sa puissance [6]. En dépit de cette dissemblance, c'est bien la même affirmation d'une souveraineté de la volonté qui amène Olivi à adopter une conception synchronique de la contingence [7]. Les circonstances dans lesquelles il l'a fait méritent d'être signalées. Le thème apparaît pour la première fois dans la question sur le libre-arbitre (II, 57), à l'occasion de la réfutation d'un argument provenant

apprehendere et aliquo modo hoc potuit disiunctive, et consimiliter potest dici de divino velle », *id.*, f° 156ra.

1. « *[...] unde et de iis quae fecit potuit scire oppositum, potuit enim scire sub disiunctione utramque partem contradictionis esse veram [...]* », *II Sent.* q. 3, p. 58, dans un passage qui résume la q. I, 6.

2. « *[...] illud quod Deus quantum est de se et absolute non volebat, per libertatem suam voluit* », q. I, 6, f° 156rb.

3. « *Licet etiam odire vel nolle videantur in se implicare negationem vel quadam contrarietatem secundum rem, tamen semper dicunt velle affirmativum. Non enim aliud dicunt quam velle prout fertur super partem contradictionis negativam, unde non est aliud nolle hoc fieri quam velle hoc non fieri* », *id.*, ad 14, f° 157rb.

4. « *Si autem queratur an saltem ex hac ratione debeat concedi quod divini velle fuerit huius vel illius obiecti potentialiter vel contingenter, dicendum quod magis proprie debet dici quod fuerit libere huius vel illius. Contingentia enim, proprie accepta, includit aliqua defectibilitatem circa eius cuius est, unde illi qui posuerunt eam in divino velle, credo quod non aliud voluerunt significare nisi libertatem divini velle qua libere et non ex aliqua necessitate vel naturali determinacione est huius vel illius obiecti* », *id.*, f° 156vb.

5. « *[...] per negationem qua in Deo negamus aliquod scire vel velle, dicendo hoc quod scit et vult nescire vel nolle, non intendimus negare essentiam divini actus nec aliquid sibi essentiale, sed solum per hoc intendimus negare respectu eius, hec vel illa obiecta, aut ipsum a talibus obiectis. Sensus enim est : potuit enim hoc nescire et nolle, idest divinum scire et velle in se ipso semper manens absque aliqua sui desitione et variacione potuerunt non esse actus istorum obiectorum quorum nunc sunt actus. Per huius igitur negationes nichil in Deo reale adimitur, nec per contrarias affirmationes aliquid reale sibi additur* », *id.*, f° 156rb.

6. « *Quod autem dicitur quod non possunt esse in Deo successive bene concedo, nichilominus tamen pro toto illo nunc eternitatis pro quo unum fuit, potuit sub disiunctione esse et reliquum, sicut et in exemplo dissimili dicimus quod voluntas nostra respectu eiusdem nunc potuit disiunctive in opposita* », *I Sent.* q. 6, f° 171ra.

7. La dépendance de Duns Scot à l'égard d'Olivi sur ce point a été relevée par Stephen D. Dumont, « The Origin of Scotus's Theory of Synchronic Contingency », *The Modern Schoolman* 72, 1995, p. 149-167.

d'Averroès, portant sur l'impossibilité de deux actes contraires simultanés. L'affirmation d'une « prévalence » de la puissance sur ces actes opposés permet de sauvegarder la liberté d'une action qui aurait pu, au moment même où elle choisit l'un des opposés, accomplir l'autre [1].

Mais cette liberté humaine n'offre qu'un miroir très déformé de la liberté divine. Le pouvoir (*posse*) qui est dit de Dieu ne correspond pas à une puissance (*potentia*), au sens propre du terme, à une capacité dont procéderaient les actes. Il s'agit au contraire du pouvoir (*potestas*) de produire comme effets les objets de son vouloir. Ce pouvoir exprime seulement le fait que le vouloir est immédiatement efficace, et nécessairement redoublé par la production de l'objet voulu [2]. Ce qui est d'abord l'objet du vouloir divin est ensuite son effet. De la sorte, la distinction entre volonté et puissance est interne au vouloir divin [3]. Comme Olivi le signale ailleurs, à proprement parler, on ne peut penser Dieu que sous les raisons de la volonté et de l'intellect, et toutes les autres raisons ne lui sont attribuées que dans un sens très métaphorique [4].

L'absolue liberté divine permet d'affirmer sans difficulté que Dieu aurait pu ne pas vouloir ce qu'il veut. La réponse est plus complexe pour ce qui est de son savoir. Comme on l'a vu, Dieu connaît nécessairement tout connaissable, de

1. « *Ad tertium dicendum quod bene concedo quod nihil potest simul in opposita, nisi habeat potestatem non solum aequivalentem, sed etiam praevalentem duabus virtutibus contrariis [...] sed tamen non propter hoc debet dicere quod habeat in se contrarias rationes [...] Si autem dicatur quod Averroes ponit primam, super VIII Physicorum et alibi [...] quaero quomodo probant eam, sciens quod eam supponut, non probant. Ad quartum dicendum quod licet Averroes maiorem huius ponat et ex dictis Aristotelis eam trahat, ipsa tamen est falsa nec ab aliquo eorum probata [...] Non enim oportet quod illud quod potest in opposita sub disiunctione, hoc est, quod in eadem hora habet potentiam pro quocunque illorum, ita tamen quod, si unum agit, tunc ab altero cesset, non, inquam, oportet quod simul agat utrumque vel simul cesset ab utroque; sed potius sequitur quod sic agat alterum quod potuerit pro eodem nunc agere aliud cessando a primo et e contrario. In hoc autem nulla contradictio implicatur, sed potius vera libertas potentiae astruitur* », *II Sent.* q. 57, ad 3 et 4, p. 340-341. Cette question, de très peu antérieure à la question I, 6, se situe également dans le contexte des condamnations de 1277. Plus précisément qu'Averroès, cette critique pourrait viser l'un des *Averroistae*, mentionné peu après : « *Hoc est igitur quod latuit Averroistas* », *id.*, p. 343.

2. « *[...] quando dicimus Deum posse vel potuisse quod vult et non vult, per hoc verbum 'posse' non intendemus significare potentiam aliquam respectu divini velle, proprie sumendo potentiam. Sed solum per hoc intendimus significare quod divinum velle est potentissimum et imperiosissimum ad hoc ut dicit huius vel illius obiecti [...] Non enim dicimus quod quia Deus facit rem esse, vult eam esse, sed potius quia vult eam esse, facit eam esse, et ita non sequitur quod divinum velle sit effectus vel actus divine potestatis, sed potius quod sit ipsa potestas* », *I Sent.* q. 6, f° 156vb-157ra. Voir aussi : « *Non enim est actus progrediens a potentia vel a quocumque alio. Sed potius ipse actus in quantum est per se ipsum ens, et super effectus creatos per se ipsum potens, habet non solum rationem actus, sed etiam potentie* », *id.*, f° 155va.

3. « *[...] efficacia divini velle semper redundat super suum obiectum volitum [...] Unde quando in Deo distinguimus scientiam, voluntatem et potentiam, per potentiam non significamus aliquam rationem potentie que sit a voluntate diversa, eo modo quo in nobis sunt potentie motive et exsecutive eius quod imperat nostram voluntas, sed solum per hoc significamus ipsam voluntatem prout est efficax super suos effectus* », *id.*, f° 157va-vb.

4. « *[...] sed intellectus et voluntas videntur in his conditionibus excedere omnes formas creatas, in tantum quod nullam rationem formalem possumus in Deo ponere nisi valde metaphorice nisi quae spectant ad rationem intellectus et voluntatis. Unde et secundum isti duo dicimur facti ad imaginem Deo* », *II Sent.* q. 54, t. 2, p. 250.

même qu'il connaît nécessairement tout ce qu'il produit [1]. C'est précisément dans l'écart entre le possible et le voulu que se tient la possibilité d'un non-savoir divin. Dieu ne connaît pas comme existant ce qui n'a pas été voulu comme tel. Le savoir qu'il a des choses existantes lui vient de la vérification de l'efficace du vouloir divin qui se porte sur tel ou tel objet [2], mais il ne connaît pas comme tel ce qui n'a pas été voulu, et c'est à ce seul titre que son savoir est libre [3]. Il y a donc un double rapport du savoir au vouloir : le savoir détient une relative précédence dans l'appréhension des quiddités possibles, mais il suit le vouloir quant à l'appréhension des existants effectivement voulus. Pour autant, ce n'est qu'une attribution de notre mode d'intelliger, qui ne correspond à aucune consécution réelle en Dieu [4].

C'est dans ce cadre, afin de préciser de quelle façon l'exemplaire divin se rapporte uniformément à ses objets, qu'Olivi introduit une question annexe sur le statut des idées en Dieu. La critique porte en premier lieu sur une opinion que l'on peut reconnaître comme celle de Thomas d'Aquin, ramenée à son expression la plus concise : l'exemplaire signifie l'essence divine en tant qu'elle est participable et imitable par les diverses créatures. Chaque idée représente une « raison d'imitabilité » par laquelle les créatures participent de l'essence divine [5]. Après avoir présenté l'opinion de Bonaventure, puis deux autres (dont nous réserverons, comme il le fait lui-même, la discussion pour plus tard), Olivi avance une cinquième opinion que l'on peut reconnaître comme la sienne. Elle présente l'acte divin, intelligence actuelle des choses possibles et devant être créées, comme l'exemplaire en tant qu'il est l'intelliger actuel de chaque chose [6]. La

1. « *[...] sicut immensitas divine essentie sic in se existit quod nichil potest fieri quin sit ei presens, sic immensitas divini intelligere tante claritatis est quod nihil potest habere entitatem aut veritatem quin sit ei presens* », *I Sent.* q. 6, f° 157vb.

2. « *Aliter igitur potest esse divinum velle diversorum obiectorum, et aliter divinum scire. Divinum enim velle habet hec ex sua libertate, divinum vero scire ex obiecti verificatione quam accipit a divino velle quando sua eterna efficacia in certo tempore determinatur ad esse creatum* », *id.*, f° 157vb.

3. « *Divini igitur scire potuit non esse huius obiecti per hoc quod ipsum obiectum potuit non esse, si Deus oppositum voluisset. Potuit autem esse multorum aliorum, per hoc quod Deus potuit multa alia velle facere que noluit* », *ibid.*

4. « *Licet enim intellectus divinus secundum modum intelligendi nostrum precedit actu divini velle quoad quiditates obiectorum absque actualitates essendi acceptas, sequitur tamen ipsum quantum ad apprehensionem actualis existentie rerum* », *id.*, f° 158ra.

5. « *Quidam enim volunt quod exemplar significet divinam esssentiam prout est diversimode participabilis et imitabilis a diversis creaturis, una vero ratio ymitabilitatis, unam dicit ydeam et specialiter respectu illorum que Deus fieri disposuit seu voluit* », *id.*, f° 158ra, *cf.* Thomas d'Aquin, *Summa theologiae*, Ia, q. 15, a. 2 : « *Unaquaeque autem creatura habet propriam speciem, secundum quod aliquo modo participat divinae essentiae similitudinem. Sic igitur inquantum Deus cognoscit suam essentiam ut sic imitabilem a tali creatura, cognoscit eam ut propriam rationem et ideam huius creaturae* », et *Summa contra Gentiles*, I, 54. *Cf.* L.B. Geiger, « Les idées divines dans l'œuvre de St Thomas », dans A. Maurer, E. Gilson *et al.* éds, *St Thomas Aquinas 1274-1974. Commemorative Studies,* Toronto, Pontifical Institute of Mediaeval Studies, t. 1, p. 175-209, François-Xavier Putallaz, *Le sens de la réflexion chez Thomas d'Aquin*, Paris, Vrin, 1991, p. 218-220.

6. « *Quidam vero alii volunt quod actus divinus qui est intelligere in quantum est actualis intelligencia seu actuale intelligere omnium rerum Deo possibilium et etiam fiendorum, est exemplar rerum in quantum vero est actuale intelligere huius vel illius rei, ita proprie sicut si totus esset determinatus ad ipsum, est illius ratio rei, vel ydea* », *I Sent.* q. 6, f° 158ra.

réponse générale, donnée un peu plus loin, laisse entrevoir un léger flottement, une hésitation entre les deux niveaux du savoir divin (absolu, *sub disiunctione*, ou actuel, par vérification des objets voulus). Dans un sens large, l'exemplaire peut être pris comme représentation des seules quiddités possibles, mais plus proprement dit, il est le discernement et la vérification de l'existence actuelle des choses voulues, pour le moment du temps dans lequel elles seront créées [1]. En ce sens, les idées ne sont pas autre chose que la connaissance actuelle et unique que Dieu a de tout ce qui sera créé dans le cours du temps. Le commentaire sur les premiers versets de Jean, lieu d'accueil majeur du néoplatonisme dans les évangiles, permet de confirmer qu'il s'agit là d'une destruction de toute réalité intermédiaire entre le Créateur et la création. *La vie était en lui*, mais seulement au sens où le connu et le voulu sont dans un sujet connaissant et voulant. Ceci ne pose réellement aucun mode d'être, sinon la seule similitude exemplaire, la connaissance, la volonté et la puissance active de ce sujet connaissant et de l'exemplé [2]. Comme on le verra, Olivi conserve le vocabulaire bonaventurien de l'exemplarité et de l'expression, mais le sens en est profondément transformé. L'expression est immédiate, elle n'indique que la relation qui lie le vouloir éternel à ses objets voulus qui apparaissent dans le cours de l'histoire [3].

La critique de Thomas est menée du point de vue de l'absolue simplicité et liberté de l'acte divin. Présenter les idées comme les principes formels par lesquels l'intellect divin, s'inspectant lui-même, se reconnaîtrait comme imitable, revient à introduire une étape superflue. Si Dieu avait besoin de telles raisons pour accéder à la connaissance de ses objets, une dépendance interne apparaîtrait au sein de l'acte divin [4]. L'intellect humain a certes besoin d'espèces mémoriales pour saisir les choses absentes. En revanche, l'intellect divin, éternellement présent à toute chose, n'a nul besoin de telles raisons, mais peut se

1. « *Divinum intelligere potest dici quorumdam ratio representativa seu actualis representatio quorumdam, vero magis proprie debet dici ratio diiudicativa et affirmativa seu negativa seu potius actualis diiudicatio seu affirmacio eorum, sicut enim in nobis simplex apprehensio quiditatum seu terminorum est per quandam seu cum quadam representatione earum* », *id.*, f° 158vb.

2. « *Nota quod potius dixit* erat vita in ipso *quam erat in ipso, ne credatur quod esset in ipso secundum propriam essentiam, sed quam existit in suo esse creato. Non enim erat ibi nisi sicud exemplatum seu representatum vel cognitum est in representante et cognoscente, et sicud volitum et excogitum est in volente et excogitente. Hic autem modus essendi nihil realiter ponit, nisi solam exemplarem similitudinem et cognitionem et voluntatem et activam potentiam ipsius cognoscentis et exemplatis, quia nec divinum scire et velle non solum sunt actus vite sicud in nobis, ymo etiam sunt totum esse et vivere Dei, et tota essentia et vita ipsius [...] Hoc autem potius dixit de rebus factis in quibus etiam omnia fienda tamquam iam apud Deum quasi facta includit, potius quam de possibilibus fieri, quia facta et fienda pro tanto plus ceteris in Deo existunt et vivunt pro quanto eorum actuale existere est preceteris volitum et previsum a Deo, ita quod tota actualis causalitas eorum eternaliter fuit in Deo, eque perfecte sicud est in ipso in ipsa hora qua fuerit ab ipso* », *Lectura super Iohannem*, 1, 4, Florence, Bibl. Laur., Plut X dext. 8, fol. 6vb.

3. A ce titre, la critique des idées est strictement corrélative de l'extraordinaire extension qu'Olivi donne aux relations. Sur ce point, voir la contribution de Alain Boureau à ce volume.

4. « *[...] erit dare in Deo aliquid dependens ab altero et naturaliter posterius illo et aliquod essentiale productum ab altero. Huiusmodi enim rationes se habebunt sic ad actum divini intelligere quod sine ipsis et sine aspectu earum non poterit esse* », *id.*, f° 158rb.

porter immédiatement sur ses objets. La critique de méthode est d'avoir indûment comparé l'intellect divin à l'intellect humain sans tenir compte de leur dissemblance sur ce point[1].

Par ailleurs, ce savoir procédant par une inspection interne ne parvient pas à exprimer suffisamment la connaissance effective d'objets distincts. Un rapport (*respectus*) ne peut être connu avant son terme, puisque c'est lui qui constitue ce dernier comme terme d'un rapport. De la sorte, la découverte d'un rapport d'imitabilité ne suffit pas à faire connaître la chose imitable, puisqu'il la supposerait en fait déjà connue[2]. Il conviendrait alors de donner deux idées de chaque chose, l'une selon laquelle la chose est imitable, et l'autre selon laquelle elle est connue[3]. De plus, il paraît impossible de donner un fondement à ces rapports d'imitabilité dans l'essence divine[4]. La connaissance par inspection interne apparaît bien comme insuffisante et superflue. Enfin, cette position ne permet pas d'exprimer la connaissance distincte que Dieu possède d'individus d'une même espèce, dans la mesure où ceux-ci participeraient de l'essence divine selon la même raison d'imitabilité[5]. De la même façon, une connaissance qui passerait d'abord par des rapports d'imitabilité, éternels par principe, ne permettrait pas d'exprimer de quelle façon Dieu connaît les choses pour le moment dans lequel elles seront créées, ou distingue entre les choses qui seront crées et celles qui ne le seront pas[6]. Dieu connaît immédiatement les choses qu'il crée; en les

1. « *Unde isti qui modum illum posuerunt videntur divinum intellectum comparasse nostro* », *ibid.* De fait, Thomas d'Aquin, *Summa Theologiae*, Ia, q. 15, art. 2 : « *Sicut aedificator speciem domus concipere non potest nisi apud ipsum esset* », et q. 44, art. 3.

2. « *Preterea, prius oportet intelligere extremum alicuius respectus quam ipsum respectum, aut saltem simul, nec ipsum extremum intelligo per ipsum respectum, ergo per aliud oportebit intelligere creaturam quam per respectum ymitabilitatis secundum quam divina essentia diversitate refertur ad creaturas, seu potius creature ad ipsam; oportebit ergo prius intelligere ipsa extrema seu terminos huius respectus* », *I Sent.* q. 6, f° 158rb-va. Voir aussi, *II Sent.* q. 57, t. 2, p. 346 « *Certum enim est quod relatio non potest naturaliter praecedere sua extrema* », et q. 37, t. 1, p. 658.

3. « *[...] secundum hoc oportebit dare in Deo uniuscuiusque rei duas ydeas, ita quod duobus modis erit Deus exemplar omnium, uno modo secundum quod sua essencia est diversimode imitabilis, alio vero modo secundum hoc quod in Deo est actuale intelligere omnium seu actualis intelligentia omnium rerum* », *I Sent.* q. 6, f° 158rb.

4. « *Preterea, quomodo et per quid divina essentia representat huiusmodi imitabilitates diversas, maxime cum ipsa non sit participabilis ab aliquo univoce, nec in ydemptitate numerali ? Videre enim divinam essentiam, ut ita dicam totam intentionem eius in quantum talem, non est videre aliquam aliam essentiam et maxime non sibi univocam, nec huius imitabilitas ponit aliquid in divina essentia, etiam secundum rationem realem, nisi solum ipsam Dei essentiam* », *id.*, f° 158va.

5. « *Preterea individua unius speciei in nullo sibi dissimilia, quomodo per hunc modum intelligetur a Deo, cum eodem modo Dei essentiam imitentur [...] Diversus autem gradus participandi istas aut diversus gradus participandi rationes generales entis non sufficiat ad apprehendum diversitatem omnium specierum creabilium aut creatarum, non videtur quomodo per hanc viam Deus possit plene omnia intelligere* », *id.*, f° 158rb.

6. « *Non enim video quomodo exemplari universaliter se habente in representando omnia possit Deus idem scire et nescire. Non video etiam quomodo divina essentia per hunc modum possit representare esse rerum pro tempore pro quo vult Deus eas fieri magis quam per alio, aut quando Deus vult eas fieri potius quam quando non vult [...] Non video quomodo videat esse rerum fiendarum potius quam non fiendarum et econverso* », *id.*, f° 158va. Voir aussi *Quodlibet* II, 2, cité par Alain Boureau, « Le concept de relation chez Pierre de Jean Olivi », *supra*.

créant, il les exprime parfaitement et distinctement, sans qu'il y ait lieu de poser la moindre réalité intermédiaire [1].

En dépit de leur visée apparente, ces critiques sont loin de n'atteindre que la position thomiste. En réalité, Thomas affirme une connaissance divine des singuliers – au nom de sa connaissance de la matière par laquelle les singuliers sont individués – aussi bien qu'une connaissance des futurs contingents pour le temps dans lequel ils seront en acte. Mais il est vrai que sur ces deux points, sa démonstration se passe totalement du concept d'idées, et s'oppose précisément à une connaissance divine à travers des causes universelles [2]. C'est justement sur ce terrain que Guillaume de la Mare a fait porter l'une des critiques de son *Correctorium*. Il reproche à Thomas d'affirmer que Dieu connaît les futurs contigents, non pas à travers leurs causes idéales, mais au nom de la coexistence de l'éternité divine à chaque partie du temps [3]. De la sorte Dieu est éternellement et immédiatement présent à chacune des choses créées, pour le seul temps dans lesquelles elles seront ou sont en acte.

Olivi connaît cette objection. Mais, loin de l'employer contre Thomas, il la reprend comme objection à sa propre thèse, et consacre de longues pages à la réfuter, en n'hésitant pas à la présenter comme « hérétique » [4]. Cette objection repose avant tout sur une incompréhension de l'immensité de l'éternité divine, en semblant l'imaginer comme un instant antérieur au temps [5]. Il faut au contraire comprendre que l'éternité englobe toutes les parties du temps (y compris ses parties possibles et non advenues), en coexistant à chacune par une raison différente – chacune de ces raisons étant elle-même fondée dans le savoir divin antérieurement à l'advenue de cet instant dans le cours du temps [6]. Il est vrai,

1. « *Nemo enim sane poterit negare quin divinum intelligere in quantum actualiter intelligit res, perfecte exprimens eas, cum ipsum in quantum tale, sit actu actualissima obiectorum expressio et representatio et distinctio seu discretio* », *I Sent.* q. 6, f° 158rb.

2. Thomas d'Aquin, *Summa Theologiae*, Ia, q. 14, art. 11 et art. 13.

3. Guillelmus de Mara, *Correctorium fratris Thomae*, dans Palémon Glorieux, *Les premières polémiques thomistes. Le Correctorium Corruptorii Quare*, Kain, Le Saulchoir, 1927, art. 3, p. 18-20.

4. « *[...] quidam ex illis rationibus moti fuerant ad dicendum quod Deus non videt res futuras propter aliquam presenciam sui aspectus ad illas, sed solum propter rationes ydeales representantes futura. Unde et volunt quod Dei eternitas non attingit presencialiter omnia tempora et temporalia in ipsis suis naturiis quamdiu non sunt in se ipsis, nisi solum pro tanto quia rationes causales et ydeales omnium temporum et temporalium sunt Deo presentes ab eterno. Hoc autem meo iudicio est simpliciter hereticum et contra omnem opinionem omnium magistrorum, sicut in scriptis eorum solempnibus patet et est expresse contra dicta sanctorum* », *I Sent.* q. 6, f° 159rb.

5. « *Ostendit hoc quidem primo Dei eternitas que non est sic ymaginanda quasi non sit nisi unum nunc actualiter non excedens ambitum unius nunc temporalis [...] Hec enim ymaginatio manifeste ponit Deus eternitatis actualem et presencialem ambitum non esse immensum* », *id.*, f° 160ra.

6. « *Oportebit ut credo responderi ad questione premissa quod sicut tempus preteritum, presens et futurum non habent nec habitura sunt simul esse, sed sunt ad se invicem distancia, quod sic secundum alium ordinem, seu secundum aliam rationem unum sit presens Deo et aliud secundum alia, unumquodque scilicet in suo ordine; unum scilicet in ordine prioris et aliud in ordine posterioris. Aliqua igitur rationem ambitus divini nunc attingit unum et aliud aliam, sed veritas istarum rationum erat in divino nunc antequam ipsa essent, ita quod quamvis in eis non sit ordo prioris et posterioris, tamen secundum unam erat Deus attingibilis a preterito, secundum aliam a futuro. Sed iste rationes non dicunt aliud quam coexistentia Dei cum diversis temporibus, ergo huiusmodi coexistentia secundum quam Deus coexistit omnibus temporibus, attigendo unumquodque*

reconnaît Olivi, qu'une telle coexistence du passé et du futur excède toute expérience humaine, mais la difficulté même à la comprendre prouve davantage la vérité de la chose que sa fausseté[1]. Cette longue explication est complétée par d'autres arguments qui refusent une connaissance divine par des raisons causales. L'efficace immédiate du vouloir divin prouve qu'il ne peut être absent des effets qu'il produit[2]. L'indétermination des futurs contingents avant qu'ils ne se réalisent signale qu'ils ne sont pas déterminés par une cause éloignée[3]. L'intelligence divine, enfin, n'affirme pas l'être des choses créées nominalement (ce qui pourrait être un être d'essence distinct de l'existence actuelle), mais un être effectif qu'elle connaît de toute éternité[4].

Avant d'engager la critique de la position thomiste, puis de réfuter l'objection de Guillaume de la Mare, Olivi avait cherché à sauver la position de Bonaventure. De celui-ci, il ne propose qu'une paraphrase des questions *De scientia Christi*, présentant la lumière divine comme expression de toutes choses[5]. Bien comprise, cette formulation peut s'accorder à la position d'Olivi, à condition d'entendre la

in suo ordine, erat prius tota simul in Deo », *id.*, f° 160ra-rb. Ces passages méritent d'être rapprochés de l'analyse de la réalité du temps présentée dans une question inédite étudiée par Ruedi Imbach et François-Xavier Putallaz, *supra*. La question I, 6 y fait expressément référence : « *Pro quanto autem dictum Augustinum de existentia temporis preteriti et futuri possit verificari, ex questionibus de tempore satis potest haberi, ubi dictum est quod esse simpliciter, quale est esse permanens et presentiale secundum omnes suas partes non habent nisi in anima ; esse vero in fieri seu sumptum pro fieri habent veraciter in rerum natura* », *id.*, f° 177vb.

1. « *[...] omnia experimenta que nos experimur sunt contraria huius rei. In nullo enim potest nobis occurrere quod prior duratio sit eadem cum futura, ita quod simul et semel attingat preterita et futura. Et certe huiusmodi difficultas et singularitates magis attestantur veritati rei quam falsitati aut dubietati quia nunquam Deus meus occureret in meo intellectu ut verus et summus Deus, nisi aliquo modo occurreret mihi ut summe et inaccessibilis et ut summe singularis* », *id.*, f° 162ra.

2. « *Ostendit hoc etiam secundo Dei activa efficacia seu potestas. Nulla enim causa est sufficienter efficax ad producendum effectum nisi pro quanto est presens. Nunquam enim absens in quantum tale est efficax, sed Deus fuit efficax ab eterno ad producendum omnia tempora et temporalia, ergo sua efficacia fuit eis presens* », *id.*, f° 160vb.

3. « *Ostendit etiam tertio hoc futurorum contingentium variabilitas. Contingentia enim pro toto tempore pro quo precedunt eorum actualem esse, nullam habent determinacionem ad esse nec in se nec in aliqua causa, etiam in voluntate Dei. Alias non evenirent contingenter et per alias cause eorum essent determinate ad eorum productionem* », *id.*, f° 161ra.

4. « *Ostendit etiam quarto divine intelligencie veritas. Quicquid enim Deus videt in re et de re quando est actu, videt ab eterno. Ergo eius esse, non solum nominaliter sed verbaliter acceptum, et realem affirmationem ipsius esse de re quam presencialem ita re esse videt quando res est, vidit ab eterno* », f° 161rb.

5. « *Alii vero volunt quod lux divini intellectus pro eo quod est exemplar genus, est potens exprimere non solum unum genus rerum, sed omnia ; ipsa igitur, ut est lux omnia exprimens, est exemplar omnium ; expressiones vero eius determinate sunt rationes rerum determinate, quas respectu fiendorum quidam ydeas vocant. Dicuntque quod quia divina lux est sua expressio, ideo ipse expressiones sic determinate exprimunt unamquaque rem, quod tamen non sunt plura lumina sed solum una lux [...]* », q. I, 6, *ibid. Cf.* Bonaventura, *De Scientia Christi*, q. 2 in *Opera Omnia*, t. 5, p. 9 : « *[...] quia enim ipse intellectus divinus est summa lux et veritas plena et actus purus, sicut divina virtus in causando res sufficiens est se ipsa omnia producere, sic divina lux et veritas omnia exprimere [...] et quia expressio est quaedam assimilatio, ideo divinus intellectus, sua summa veritate exprimens, habet aeternaliter omnium rerum similitudines exemplares, quae non sunt aliud ab ipso, sed sunt quod est essentialiter* », et q. 3, p. 13 « *Potens est autem divina veritas, quamvis sit una, omnia exprimere per modum similitudinis exemplaris, quia ipsa est omnino extra genus* ».

« lumière divine » comme actualité et clarté de l'intelliger divin, et « ses expressions » comme ce même intelliger en tant qu'expression actuelle de ses objets. L'erreur serait de concevoir ces termes comme désignant une puissance intellective et son acte[1]. A s'en tenir à cette seule citation, on pourrait penser à une relative fidélité. Mais en réalité, Olivi ne retient des questions *De scientia Christi* que la seule solution au problème de la pluralité des idées (q. 3) : l'expression est unique en tant qu'elle est la vérité divine; elle exprime une pluralité en tant qu'elle se rapporte aux choses[2]. Dans le même temps, l'essentiel des réponses aux questions précédentes est rejeté. Bonaventure y affirme en effet que Dieu ne connaît pas les choses par leur essence, mais par leurs similitudes qu'il a en lui sous la forme de leurs raisons éternelles[3]. Pour Bonaventure comme pour Thomas, toute connaissance requiert que l'agent possède une similitude des objets à connaître, afin que l'intellect puisse s'assimiler à l'objet intelligible[4]. Dans le cas présent, puisque ces objets ne sauraient préexister à leur connaissance, ni en être la cause, Dieu doit posséder en lui-même les formes des êtres qu'il crée. C'est en se connaissant lui-même qu'il se reconnaît comme imitable ou capable d'exprimer toute chose. En dépit de la différence de vocabulaire, la structure des deux argumentations est identique, et c'est celle-ci qu'Olivi récuse globalement.

La q. I, 6 suggère en effet que ce type d'inspection n'est pas un préalable nécessaire à la connaissance des êtres possibles, mais qu'au contraire Dieu les connaît immédiatement. On ne peut pas prendre pour une concession le thème de la vérification par l'intellect des objets voulus, par considération de la puissance qui les crée[5]. Ce trait ne dit pas que Dieu doit se connaître avant de créer, mais qu'il connaît les objets de son vouloir avant que ceux-ci n'existent en acte dans le temps. Le savoir divin n'a pas besoin de se convertir sur lui-même pour les

1. « *[...] et forte est idem cum secundo modo bene intellecto* », f° 158ra; « *Secundus autem modus potest sane intelligi si 'lux divina' sumatur pro actualitate et claritate divini intelligere, et si nomine 'expressionum suarum' non aliud intelligatur quam ipsum Dei intelligere, ut est actualis expressio unucuisque obiecti secundum suam propriam rationem, et hoc modo non differt ab ultimo modo* », f° 158vb.

2. « *[...] expressio secundum id quod est nihil aliud est quam ipsa veritas, sed secundum ad quod est, tenet se ex parte rerum quae exprimuntur. Unde expressio unius rei et alterius rei in divina vel a divina veritate, secundum id quod est, non est aliud et aliud, sed secundum id ad quod est, plurificari dicitur* », *De scientia Christi*, q. 3, p. 14.

3. « *[...] divinus aspectus in cognoscendo non desilit extra se, sed aspiciendo se ut veritatem [...] per rationes aeternas, quae sunt idem quod ipse, cognoscit quaecumque cognoscit [...]* », *id.*, q. 1, p. 5; « *Deus cognoscit res per rationes aeternas [...] Hae autem sempiternae rationes non sunt rerum essentiae verae et quidditates, cum non sint aliud a creatore; creatura autem et Creatore necessario habent essentias differentes et ideo necesse est quod sint formae exemplares, ac per hoc ipsarum rerum similitudines representativae, et ideo cognoscendi rationes sunt, quia cognitio hoc ipso quod cognitio, assimilationem dicit et expressionem inter cognoscentem et cognoscibile. Et ideo ponendum est, secundum quod sancti dicunt et rationes ostendunt, Deus cognoscere res per earum similitudines* », *id.*, q. 2, p. 8.

4. *Cf. id.*, p. 7, arguments 3 et 4 en faveur de la connaissance par les similitudes.

5. « *[...] potius deberet dici quod Deus videt res diversas per hoc quod videt totam suam potentiam per quam potest facere diversa quam per hoc quod videt suam essentiam et diversimode participabilem, et tamen ipsi hoc non concedunt, quod Deus sufficienter res videt per hunc modum* », q. I, 6, f° 358va.

connaître. Il les connaît d'emblée, comme distincts de lui-même, par leur essence et non par leurs similitudes. Il faut donc bien conclure que le débat engagé avec Thomas atteint directement les thèses de Bonaventure. En rejetant la solution de la question 2 *De scientia Christi*, c'est l'ensemble de la question 4 qui est ruiné, dans laquelle la coopération des raisons éternelles (les idées comme similitudes des choses) est présentée comme nécessaire à la certitude de la connaissance humaine.

Après avoir présenté les opinions de Thomas et Bonaventure, Olivi signale également deux autres opinions, dont la discussion est reléguée à la fin de la question. La première, qu'Olivi dit avoir vue soutenue, postule une pluralité réelle des idées en Dieu[1]. Il en a entendue une autre qui prétendait éviter cette erreur, en niant toute réalité des idées en Dieu[2]. Or cette dernière position correspond exactement à celle tenue par Arnaud Gaillard[3], telle qu'Olivi la prend à partie dans l'*Impugnatio*, en faisant explicitement référence à cette question[4]. De son côté, Arnaud avait également dénoncé Olivi sur ce terrain, non pas en critiquant sa propre position, mais en lui attribuant l'opinion que lui-même cherchait à combattre, à savoir la thèse de la pluralité réelle des idées en Dieu. La réponse d'Olivi dans la *Lettre à R.* est lapidaire : « j'ai expressément soutenu et écrit le contraire, en montrant que cet énoncé était hérétique et profane »[5]. C'est effectivement les termes qu'il emploie à ce propos dans la question I, 6[6]. La dénonciation d'Arnaud est donc purement réactive, et sans se fonder sur un texte rédigé, attaque Olivi en fonction de ce qu'il a perçu du débat qui les opposait : si Olivi n'accepte pas sa thèse, c'est qu'il tombe dans l'erreur que lui-même parvient à éviter. La réponse fournie par la *Lettre à R.*, est probablement identique à la confession donnée devant son ministre provincial Arnaud de Roquefeuil, qui fut sans doute transmise au général de l'ordre, Bonagratia de San Giovanni in Persiceto.

1. « *Vidi tamen quemdam dicentem, et ut credo non multum catholice, quod huius rationes seu expressiones habeant in Deo aliquam veram pluritatem* », *id*, f° 173ra. Il s'agit d'une position que Bonaventure critiquait déjà, *In I Sent.*, dist. 35, q. 2, p. 605, qui correspond approximativement à celle de Richard Rufus. *Cf.* Rega Wood, « Distinct Ideas and Perfect Solicitude : Alexander of Hales, Richard Rufus and Odo Rigaldus », *Franciscan Studies* 53, 1993, p. 7-46.

2. « *Quemdam vero audivi qui hanc caripdim volens stulte effugere, negant omnem realitatem rationum in Deo* », *id.*, f° 173ra.

3. Pour l'identification de ce personnage, généralement désigné comme frater Ar., voir mon introduction à Petrus Ioannis Olivi, « Epistola ad fratrem R. », *A.F.H.* 91/1, 1998, p. 37-38.

4. *Cf.* « *Dixit etiam, prout per eosdem intellexi, quod rationes attributorum divinorum aut idearum non sunt in Deo aliquo modo realiter, arguens quod si veritas eorum esset in Deo realiter, necessario sequeretur quod essent ibi realiter et essentialiter distincte. Vult igitur quod sint solum intellectibus creatis et in obiectis seu connotatis, et quod loco omnium illarum sit solum in Deo unica ratio sue essentie et sue veritatis* », *Impugnatio*, art. 24, f° 49rb. On voit que le verbe « *audivi* » doit se comprendre comme relation faite par des auditeurs d'Arnaud. Une trace d'un débat direct entre les deux frères, un ou deux ans plus tôt, transparaît dans le remaniement de la question II, 11 (*II Sent.* t. 1, p. 181-187).

5. « *Contrarium huius expresse asservi et scripsi, dictum hoc ostendens esse hereticum et prophanum* », *Epistola ad fratrem R.*, art. 17.

6. « *[...] modus ille qui ponit aliquam realem differentiam in ydeis [...] est omnino impossibile et ut credo hereticum* », *I Sent.* q. 6, f° 164ra-vb.

En examinant, tant le texte de cette question, les dénonciations d'Arnaud Gaillard que la réponse d'Olivi, la commission des maîtres et bacheliers franciscains réuni au couvent parisien en mai 1283 n'a pas pu prendre au sérieux l'accusation de son adversaire. En revanche, la critique de Thomas atteignait un grand nombre de maîtres franciscains[1]; elle fut reprise dans la *Lettre des sept sceaux*. Dans le même temps, l'affirmation d'une co-présence de Dieu à chaque partie du temps fut également retenue contre Olivi[2]. Comme le nota l'un des censeurs en marge d'un codex utilisé à cette occasion: « ici, il parle sottement contre frère Guillaume de la Mare et l'opinion commune »[3].

Toutefois, Olivi n'était sans doute pas le seul franciscain à proférer de telles sottises en ces années. À deux reprises, lors de ses sessions quodlibétiques, en 1285-87, Richard de Mediavilla eut à s'expliquer sur des thèses typiquement oliviennes qu'il avait contribué à censurer, au sujet de la quantité et du caractère sacramentel[4]. Une troisième question, « Les choses futures sont-elles réellement présentes à l'éternité ? »[5], cherchait sans doute autant à l'interroger sur la censure d'Olivi sur ce point, que sur la valeur de cet argument du *Correctoire*. Cette fois, sans prétendre condamner absolument cette position (et prenant ainsi ses distances face à la sentence prononcée contre Olivi), Richard fait son possible pour montrer comment doit être comprise l'autorité de Guillaume de la Mare[6], tout en reconnaissant que le thème d'une co-présence de l'éternité à chaque partie du temps, tel que le défendent Olivi et Thomas d'Aquin, peut être recevable. Il est possible qu'Olivi ait alors eu des émules au sein de couvent parisien. Il est également possible que sa censure ait provoqué des remous dans le monde intellectuel parisien. Comme on a cherché à le suggérer, ses textes, rédigés dans un lointain couvent du Midi, étaient en prise sur les débats intellectuels les plus pressants de la fin des années 1270. A l'opposé des critiques purement réactives de Guillaume de la Mare, ils proposaient une nouvelle voie qui cherchait à discuter, textes en mains, les difficultés posées par les *Averroistae* et Thomas

1. Par exemple, Guillelmus de Mara, *Scriptum in primum librum sententiarum*, H. Kraml éd., Munich, Verlag der Bayerischen Akademie der Wissenschaften, 1989, d. 35, q. 2, p. 409, repris par Johannes Pecham, *In primum Sententiarum*, d. 35, q. 2, Florence, Bibl. Naz. Conv. Sopp. G. 4. 854, f° 99ra.

2. « *Item, dicere quod ydea dicit essentiam divinam imitabilem a creatura, non est contrarium fidei nec etiam rationi, sed est potius communis opinio; et licet idem sint re intelligere divinum et ydea, differunt tamen secundum rationem. Item dicere quod res que non sunt sint presentes Deo in sui propria natura et essentia, et aliter quam per ydeam vel per suam causam, est falsum; et dicere quod sit hereticum, est erroneum* », Geroldus Fussenegger, « *Littera septem sigillorum contra doctrinam Petri Ioannis Olivi edita* », *A.F.H.* 47, 1954, p. 51.

3. « *[...] hic loquitur stulte contra fratrem G. de Mara et communem opinionem* », B.A.V., Borgh. 322, f° 159rb.

4. « *Utrum quantitas dicat rem aliquam ultra substantiam, cuius est quantitas, loquendo de re absoluta* », *Quodlibeta*, Brixiae, 1591, repr. Frankfurt, Minerva, 1963, Quod. II, art. 2, q. 2; « *Utrum character dicat aliquid absolutum in anima* », *id.*, III, 15, p. 108-109, qui reprennent et discutent les positions d'Olivi, sans faire toutefois référence à la censure.

5. *Id.*, q. III, 1, p. 84-86.

6. « *[...] et sic debet intelligi verborum quorundam magnorum qui negant futura esse realiter praesentia aeternitatis* », *ibid.*

d'Aquin, en accueillant parfois certains acquis de ce dernier, tout en tentant de sauver ce qui pouvait l'être du vocabulaire de Bonaventure.

La révision drastique du statut des idées en Dieu qu'il propose procède d'une affirmation de la liberté divine. Elle permet de mieux faire ressortir l'abîme qui sépare le Créateur des créatures. Dieu ne crée pas les choses selon des similitudes qu'il aurait en lui, mais les crée immédiatement hors de lui. Si les humains sont dôtés d'une lumière intellectuelle, par laquelle ils sont fait à l'image de Dieu, c'est elle seule qui leur permet de connaître la création. Aucune entité intermédiaire, aucune influence noétique naturelle ne leur sert de point d'appui. Ce monde composé de choses singulières doit être connu et reconnu comme tel. Les concepts universaux, les propositions scientifiques ne rejoignent en rien la connaissance que Dieu a de l'univers créé. Olivi conserve malgré tout le concept d'idées divines. Leur unique utilité est liée à la caractérisation des divers degrés de la vision béatifique. La vision des bienheureux est d'autant plus intense que sont nombreuses les idées divines qu'ils aperçoivent[1]. Mais en cette vie, Dieu se tient dans une totale invisibilité. Seul le miroir des créatures offre un chemin pour reconnaître qu'elles dépendent d'autre chose que d'elles-mêmes.

1. « *Preterea, si in Deo non sunt realiter ydee et rationes in quantum sunt proprie huius vel illius, tunc omnes videntes Deum non videbunt eum nisi secundum unam rationem, ita quod visiones eorum non poterunt differe, nisi solum secundum magis et minus, non autem penes hoc quod unus videat unam ydeam quam alius non videt, immo omnes necessario videbunt illam ydeam quam alicuius videbit, ac per consequens et illam rem creatam quam alius videt in Deo quamquam unde possit intensius eam videre quam alius* », *id.*, f° 164va. Voir aussi *Lectura super De angelica hierarchia*, cap. 5, B.A.V. Urbinat. 480, f° 144va : « *Constat enim quod senior beatus videt aut videre potest plures rationes ydeales rerum in verbo quam alius. Quis etiam dicit quod anima Christi non attingat in Deo plures rationes divinas seu non videat Deum sub pluribus rationibus quam ceteris ? [...] Ex hoc autem sequitur quod visio Dei que est in superioribus, plures rationes divinas in se comprehendat, ita quod sit plurium rationum Dei actualiter expressiva seu actualis expressio quam faciat illa visio que est in inferioribus* ».

L'EXÉGÈSE DES LIVRES PROPHÉTIQUES CHEZ PIERRE DE JEAN OLIEU

Gilbert Dahan

Dans mes recherches sur l'exégèse de la Bible au XIIIe siècle, j'ai souvent rencontré Pierre de Jean Olieu, trouvant toujours beaucoup de choses intéressantes dans ses commentaires, notamment dans celui de la Genèse, qui fait de cet auteur l'un des exégètes majeurs de son temps. Or, en lisant les études récentes sur Olieu, il m'a semblé que le travail quotidien de l'exégète a été quelque peu délaissé au profit des points de sa doctrine qui ont suscité des polémiques. Aussi voudrais-je vous proposer une approche quelque peu différente de celle à laquelle sont habitués les « olivistes » mais qui, malgré son caractère technique et son formalisme, me paraît féconde; elle permettra de mieux situer notre auteur dans l'exégèse de son temps et, par là-même, de jauger la spécificité de son apport; pour la raison que l'on verra, je m'en tiendrai ici aux livres prophétiques de l'Ancien Testament – excluant donc notamment la *Lectura super Apocalypsim*, qui pose des problèmes variés et me paraît ainsi moins représentative de son exégèse [1].

OLIEU DANS L'HISTOIRE DE L'EXÉGÈSE CHRÉTIENNE

Pierre de Jean Olieu rédige ses commentaires bibliques dans le dernier quart du XIIIe siècle. C'est le moment où domine l'« exégèse universitaire »; prenant des options radicalement différentes de celles de la *lectio* monastique, elle fait aboutir les nouveautés de l'exégèse des écoles, notamment de celle des écoles parisiennes de la fin du XIIe siècle et du début du XIIIe [2]. Mise au point dans

1. Pour la liste des œuvres exégétiques d'Olieu, voir F. Stegmüller, *Repertorium Biblicum Medii Aevi*, IV, Madrid, 1954, p. 341-353, ainsi que la « Liste des œuvres de Petrus Ioannis Olivi » établie par S. Piron, 1997.

2. Pour une caractérisation de ces « genres », je me permets de renvoyer à mon étude « Genres, forms and various methods in Christian exegesis of the Middle Ages », dans *Hebrew Bible / Old Testament : The History of its Interpretation*, t. I/2, *The Middle Ages*, éd. M. Saebo, Göttingen (sous presse), et au chapitre II de mon ouvrage *L'Exégèse chrétienne de la Bible en Occident médiéval*, Paris, 1999. On aura, bien sûr, toujours recours aux grands ouvrages de C. Spicq, *Esquisse d'une histoire de l'exégèse latine au moyen âge*, Paris, 1944, de B. Smalley, *The Study of the Bible in the*

l'enseignement de l'Université, elle est rapidement adoptée dans les *studia* des ordres mendiants. Je la caractériserai par les points suivants, qui seront expliqués et illustrés par les commentaires de Pierre de Jean Olieu : l'exégèse universitaire se distingue par des caractéristiques de degrés, de formes, de techniques ou de méthodes exégétiques, d'herméneutique, avec particulièrement le problème des *modi*, qui mène à une analyse du langage plus large que celle que procurait l'exégèse des écoles, laquelle s'en tenait à une approche plus strictement grammaticale et rhétorique. Toujours dans les questions d'herméneutique, le problème du passage au sens spirituel, déjà présent dans l'exégèse des écoles, qui s'efforçait de lui trouver une solution avec l'étude de la *translatio*, fait l'objet d'une constante réflexion au sein de l'exégèse universitaire; elle cherche à le résoudre notamment par une étude du champ de la métaphore.

Voilà donc à peu près définies les différentes directions de notre recherche – mais nous réglerons rapidement les deux premiers points, qui concernent les caractéristiques les plus extérieures de l'exégèse universitaire. La simple lecture des commentaires de Pierre de Jean Olieu montre amplement qu'ils appartiennent totalement à ce type d'exégèse. Comme chez d'autres auteurs (Thomas d'Aquin, par exemple), on y retrouve les deux degrés de l'enseignement scripturaire : en laissant de côté l'enseignement sur les *Sentences*, je rappellerai que l'enseignement biblique se fait en deux phases [1] :

– un enseignement *cursorie*, assuré par un bachelier biblique, qui consiste en une explication rapide des livres bibliques;

– un enseignement *magistraliter*, assuré par un maître, qui consiste en l'étude approfondie d'un ou deux livres bibliques pendant l'année universitaire.

Alfonso Maierù et d'autres ont montré que cette structure bi-partite déterminée à l'Université se retrouve également dans les *studia* des Mendiants (du moins, les *studia generalia*, qui délivrent ce que nous appellerions un enseignement supérieur) [2]. Bien que Pierre de Jean n'ait pas reçu le grade de maître en théologie, nous trouvons chez lui des commentaires qui illustrent les deux niveaux, lecture *cursorie* (par exemple, le commentaire des Petits Prophètes), lecture *magistraliter* (par exemple, celui d'Isaïe). Il n'y a pas lieu de s'en étonner : si, pour des raisons qui nous échappent, il n'a pu ou voulu obtenir la maîtrise, ses compétences étaient reconnues dans son ordre et la réglementation des *studia* ne

Middle Ages, 3e éd., Oxford, 1983, et de H. de Lubac, *Exégèse médiévale. Les quatre sens de l'Écriture*, Paris, 1959-1964.

1. Voir H. Denifle, « Quel livre servait de base à l'enseignement des maîtres en théologie dans l'université de Paris ? », *Revue thomiste* 2, 1894, p. 149-161 ; P. Mandonnet, « Chronologie des écrits scripturaires de saint Thomas d'Aquin. 3° Enseignement de la Bible 'selon l'usage de Paris' », *Revue thomiste* 34, 1929, p. 489-519 ; P. Glorieux, « L'enseignement au moyen âge. Techniques et méthodes en usage à la Faculté de Théologie de Paris au XIIIe s. », *A.H.D.L.M.A.* 35, 1968, p. 65-186 (voir p. 109-111 et 119-120).

2. A. Maierù, « Tecniche di Insegnamento », dans *Le Scuole degli Ordini Mendicanti (sec. XIII-XIV)*, Todi, 1978 (Convegni del Centro di Studi sulla Spiritualità medievale, 17), p. 305-352 (surtout p. 324-332). Voir aussi dans le même recueil les études de J. Verger, « *Studia* et universités », p. 173-203 ; G. Barone, « La legislazione sugli *studia* dei predicatori e dei minori », p. 205-247 ; S. Severino Polica, « Libro, lettura, 'lezione' negli studia degli ordini mendicanti (sec. XIII) », p. 373-413.

reprenait pas toutes les dispositions de l'enseignement universitaire. On ne doit pas s'étonner davantage que la chronologie ne soit pas significative et que l'on trouve des lectures *cursorie* postérieures à des commentaires magistraux : dans les *studia* (et plus encore dans les *studia* éloignés de Paris), les professeurs répondent à des besoins précis et réels.

Une autre caractéristique apparaît clairement à la première lecture des commentaires de Pierre de Jean Olieu : ceux-ci utilisent les formes propres de l'exégèse universitaire, tant dans leur composition externe que dans leur structure interne. Le commentaire universitaire *magistraliter* est précédé d'un prologue généralement assez ample, bâti sur un thème scripturaire, qui peut être étranger au livre commenté et qui, divisé selon les techniques des *artes praedicandi*, amène l'exposé des quatre causes aristotéliciennes, par lesquelles se trouvent définis successivement l'auteur du livre, son sujet, sa forme et son objectif. Comme divers autres commentateurs, Pierre de Jean Olieu adopte ce schéma avec souplesse, ainsi que le montrent les prologues d'Isaïe[1] et d'Ezéchiel[2]. La structure des prologues des commentaires *cursorie* est moins significative : aussi bien dans les Lamentations que dans les Petits Prophètes, Olieu livre un certain nombre de règles d'interprétation, sur lesquelles on reviendra. Les prologues sont ainsi l'occasion de réflexions herméneutiques. Celles-ci apparaissent également, même si elles y ont souvent une place assez réduite, dans une autre forme propre de l'exégèse universitaire (et qui s'apparente au prologue du commentaire magistral) : les *principia*, autrement dit les exposés introductifs au cours faits théoriquement par les bacheliers bibliques mais en réalité par l'ensemble des chargés de cours de Bible. Inspirés peut-être des *principia* de la faculté des Arts, ils obéissent à des règles strictes et doivent contenir un éloge et une division de l'Écriture[3]. Les *principia* de Pierre de Jean Olieu, qui viennent d'être publiés par David Flood et Gedeon Gál[4], témoignent d'une plus grande maturité que la plupart des autres *principia* qui nous sont conservés (y compris ceux d'Albert le Grand et de Thomas d'Aquin). Tout en restant fidèle aux exigences de la *recommandatio* et de la *divisio Scripturae*, Olieu développe des considérations moins formelles, où la réflexion herméneutique trouve sa place.

Après le prologue, le commentaire universitaire se découpe en un certain nombre de *lectiones*, qui correspondent ou non aux chapitres du livre et qui ont généralement une structure fixe :

1. Dont le thème est Eccli. 48, 27 : *Spiritu magno vidit ultima et consolatus est lugentes in Sion usque in sempiternum* (il s'agit, bien sûr, d'un verset de l'éloge du prophète fait par le Siracide).

2. Dont le thème est Ez. 28, 12-13 : *Tu signaculum similitudinis plenus sapientia et perfectus decore, in deliciis paradisi Dei fuisti.*

3. Peu de travaux ont été consacrés à ces *principia*. Je n'ai pu encore lire la thèse de N. Spatz, *Principia : A Study and Edition of Inception Speeches delivered before the Faculty of Theology at the University of Paris, ca. 1180-1286*, Ithaca, 1992. Voir *L'Exégèse chrétienne de la Bible*, p. 403-407. Pour les rapports avec les *principia* de la Faculté des Arts, voir G. Dahan, « Une introduction à l'étude de la philosophie : *Ut ait Tullius* », dans *L'Enseignement de la philosophie au* XIIIe *siècle. Autour du « Guide de l'étudiant »*, éd. C. et J. Lafleur, Turnhout, 1997, p. 3-58 (voir p. 5-7).

4. *Peter of John Olivi and the Bible. Principia quinque in sacram Scripturam. Postilla in Isaiam et in I Ad Corinthios*, éd. D. Flood et G. Gál, St. Bonaventure, 1997.

– *divisio* du texte ; j'ai montré ailleurs l'intérêt herméneutique de la *divisio*, qui ne correspond nullement au « plan du texte » mais éclaire l'intention de l'exégète et propose immédiatement les lignes majeures de sa lecture du livre étudié [1] ; on distingue des divisions générales, concernant la totalité du livre, et des divisions spécifiques à un chapitre, une partie de chapitre, voire un verset ; Olieu utilise avec beaucoup de finesse cette technique ;

– commentaire explicatif verset par verset ou mot à mot ;

– *quaestiones* ou *dubia*, permettant d'exposer les problèmes théologiques ou philosophiques suscités par la *lectio* commentée.

La *quaestio* appartient principalement au commentaire *magistraliter* ; les leçons *cursorie* lui donnent une place plus restreinte [2]. La lecture des commentaires d'Isaïe et d'Ezéchiel permet de distinguer ces structures globales.

Dans l'ensemble des commentaires, on retrouve ce que j'ai appelé les « microstructures » fondamentales de l'exégèse médiévale (elles sont communes à l'exégèse des écoles et à l'exégèse universitaire) ; je me contenterai de les énoncer, les parties suivantes de mon exposé fournissant des exemples pour chacune d'elles :

– la glose explicative : brève, elle vise à dissiper les obscurités du texte lu ; chez Pierre de Jean Olieu, elle joue un rôle majeur, le commentateur ne laissant passer aucune difficulté, grammaticale, sémantique, historique, contextuelle ou autre ;

– la *quaestio*, comme microstructure (et non comme forme complexe constituant une partie de la *lectio*) : à l'inverse de la glose, qui explique linéairement le texte, la *quaestio* souligne les aspérités dues à des contradictions, divergences, problèmes de chronologie ou exégèses opposées ; caractéristique de l'exégèse des écoles parisiennes de la fin du XIIe siècle, cette microstructure poursuit sa carrière dans la partie centrale de la *lectio* universitaire, tant *cursorie* que *magistraliter*, y compris chez Pierre de Jean Olieu, où elle se trouve souvent signalée (comme dans l'exégèse scolaire) par une abréviation *q°* en marge ;

– les *distinctiones :* avec l'essor des recueils de *distinctiones*, l'exégèse universitaire utilise très volontiers la technique de la *distinctio*, développant en marge du commentaire les différentes significations données à un vocable biblique (il s'agit d'une forme plus systématique de ce que dom Leclercq appelait l'« exégèse par concordance » [3]) ; chez Olieu cependant, cette structure reste assez rare, même si la disposition particulière du commentaire d'Ezéchiel dans le manuscrit de Padoue donne l'impression d'une certaine fréquence.

1. G. Dahan, « Nommer les êtres : exégèse et théories du langage dans les commentaires médiévaux de Genèse 2, 19-20 », dans *Sprachtheorien in Spätantike und Mittelalter*, éd. S. Ebbesen, Tübingen, 1995 (*Geschichte der Sprachtheorien* 3), p. 55-74 (voir p. 55-56) ; *L'Exégèse chrétienne de la Bible*, p. 269-273. Voir également M.M. Rossi, « La *divisio textus* nei commenti scritturistici di S. Tommaso d'Aquino : un procedimento solo esegetico ? », *Angelicum* 71, 1994, p. 537-548.

2. Elles n'en sont pourtant pas absentes, comme le montrent les commentaires d'Osée, Jonas (dans lequel Olieu renvoie à plusieurs reprises à l'une de ses « questions textuelles »), Habacuc, Aggée et Zacharie.

3. J. Leclercq, *Initiation aux auteurs monastiques du moyen âge. L'amour des lettres et le désir de Dieu*, 2e éd. 1963, Paris, p. 76-77.

Voilà donc Pierre de Jean Olieu bien situé dans l'histoire de l'exégèse médiévale : il apparaît comme un auteur qui se plie aux règles et aux usages de l'exégèse de son temps [1], comme un commentateur universitaire, qui suit les lois d'un genre précis. Cela ne diminue en rien ses mérites, non plus que ceux des autres exégètes de la seconde moitié du XIIIe siècle, qui coulent leurs réflexions dans ce moule commun. Ces aspects extérieurs étant décrits, nous allons pénétrer davantage dans l'œuvre exégétique du Languedocien, en étudiant précisément ses techniques et en développant quelques réflexions à propos de son herméneutique. J'ai choisi les commentaires des livres prophétiques, qui posent avec acuité les problèmes qui se trouvent au cœur de l'exégèse des maîtres du XIIIe siècle : se donnant d'emblée à déchiffrer, ils suscitent par eux-mêmes la réflexion et obligent à s'interroger sur le problème du niveau de sens. La place de la prophétie dans la pensée d'Olieu [2] vient conforter ce choix, qui prendra en compte les commentaires d'Isaïe [3], des Lamentations [4], d'Ezéchiel [5] et des XII Prophètes [6].

LES TECHNIQUES D'EXÉGÈSE

L'une des caractéristiques les plus fortes de l'exégèse universitaire est l'utilisation de techniques précises, qui tendent à faire de l'exégèse de la Bible une science – voire une science exacte. Les maîtres universitaires ont, là encore, mené à son terme une évolution qui se dessinait dès l'exégèse des écoles ; mais la constitution d'outils et l'aspect systématique du traitement leur sont propres. Ces techniques concernent aussi bien l'approche littérale du texte que l'approche spirituelle. Commençons par la première.

Les techniques littérales

L'approche littérale a la place la plus grande dans l'exégèse universitaire ; au début de notre siècle, plusieurs discussions ont tourné autour de ce problème, particulièrement à propos de l'exégèse de Thomas d'Aquin [7]. En fait, la dimen-

1. R. Manselli, *La « Lectura super Apocalipsim » di Pietro di Giovanni Olivi. Ricerche sull'escatologismo medioevale*, Rome, 1955, p. 146, en faisait déjà la remarque (« *come egli è inquadrato perfettamente nei suoi tempi [...]* »).

2. Voir, en dernier lieu, D. Burr, « Olivi on Prophecy », *Cristianesimo nella Storia* 17, 1996, p. 369-391.

3. Dans l'édition récente de D. Flood et G. Gál, *op. cit.* (p. 93), p. 162-347.

4. Ed. M. Bartoli, *La Caduta di Gerusalemme. Il commento al Libro delle Lamentazioni di Pietro di Giovanni Olivi*, Rome, 1991.

5. J'utilise le ms. Padoue, Bibl. Univ. 1540, f° 123ra-177va.

6. Edition collective sous presse dans la *Continuatio mediaeualis* du *Corpus Christianorum ;* je citerai ici le ms. de base, Paris, BnF lat. 507.

7. A. Blanche, « Le sens littéral des Écritures d'après saint Thomas d'Aquin [...] », *Revue thomiste* 14, 1906, p. 192-212 ; P. Synave, « La doctrine de saint Thomas d'Aquin sur le sens littéral des Écritures », *Revue biblique* 35, 1926, p. 40-65.

sion spirituelle demeure le but essentiel de l'exégèse chrétienne mais la difficulté de fonder le « saut herméneutique » incite les commentateurs du XIIIe siècle à élargir le plus possible le champ de l'exégèse littérale; cela est vrai pour Olieu, avec les nuances et restrictions que l'on va voir. En tous cas, si, dans les commentaires d'Olieu, l'on se réfère à des données quantitatives, fondées sur l'identification faite par l'auteur lui-même (passages désignés expressément *mistice* ou *allegorice*), la place accordée à l'exégèse spirituelle est réduite, voire presque nulle dans certains commentaires des Petits Prophètes. Le soin apporté à l'exégèse littérale n'en paraît que plus grand, comme le montre l'utilisation des techniques auxquelles je faisais allusion.

L'attention portée à la qualité du texte

L'un des acquis les plus remarquables de l'exégèse universitaire est l'assimilation, devenue presque banale, des techniques de critique textuelle. L'adoption par l'université de Paris, au début du XIIIe siècle, d'un texte biblique contesté avait suscité une littérature de correctoires, fondés sur une riche documentation et utilisant une méthodologie rigoureuse [1]. Non seulement les exégètes recourent à ces correctoires dans leurs commentaires mais, surtout, une attitude de sensibilité critique à l'égard du texte biblique devient assez courante dans la seconde moitié du siècle. Les franciscains disposent notamment du travail remarquable de Guillaume de Mara, excellent hébraïsant et helléniste, dont le correctoire est d'une richesse admirable. Pierre de Jean Olieu l'utilise souvent: il s'agit de celui qu'il appelle, ici et là dans son commentaire des Lamentations, le *corrector solemnis*, mais il ne le suit pas aveuglément et semble parfois utiliser d'autres correctoires (dominicains?) [2]. On trouve chez lui les trois démarches caractéristiques de cette « attitude critique », que j'ai étudiée plus précisément ailleurs, en mettant à contribution du reste aussi des textes d'Olieu [3]. Je me contenterai ici d'un exemple pour chaque catégorie.

La première démarche rapproche entre eux plusieurs *codices latini;* c'est précisément le constat de divergences entre les textes qui avait fondé l'analyse critique, devenue pratique courante à l'époque de Pierre de Jean Olieu. Ainsi, dans cet exemple, sur *Osée* 9, 7 où le texte hésite entre *scitote* et *scito te :*

> O Israel, scito te stultum. *Scito etiam illum quem tu estimabas virum spiritualem [...]. Potest legi : et scito te esse prophetam insanum [...]. Quidam legunt le* scito te *in plurali, ut sit una dictio et Israel sit accusativi casus, et sic dicuntur habere antiqui et ebrei [...].*

1. Voir G. Dahan, « La critique textuelle dans les correctoires de la Bible du XIIIe s. », dans *Langages et philosophie. Hommage à Jean Jolivet*, éd. A. de Libera, A. Elamrani-Jamal et A. Galonnier, Paris, 1997, p. 365-392.

2. Sur ces correctoires, demeure fondamental le travail ancien de H. Denifle, « Die Handschriften der Bibel-Correctorien des 13. Jahrhunderts », *Archiv für Literatur- und Kirchengesch. des Mittelalters* 4, 1888, p. 264-311 et 471-601.

3. *L'Exégèse chrétienne de la Bible*, chapitre IV.

La remarque vient de Guillaume de Mara : « *scitote Israel stultum.* Heb[rei] et anti[qui] habent *scitote* in plurali » [1]. Le texte parisien avait la leçon au singulier, *scito te*, de même que Hugues de Saint-Cher (dans sa Postille); l'édition des moines de Saint-Jérôme[2] (que j'appellerai désormais *Editio maior*) adopte le pluriel, conforme en effet à l'hébreu *yed'u*.

Une autre démarche consiste en la confrontation entre la traduction de saint Jérôme et le texte originel de l'Écriture; avant même la littérature des correctoires, elle était fréquemment utilisée par André de Saint-Victor et Olieu s'inspire parfois de lui pour ses rapprochements avec l'hébreu dans le commentaire d'Isaïe, dette qu'il reconnaît clairement (*secundum Andream, Hebrei habent [...]*). Mais cette démarche comparative ne se limite pas à de tels emprunts; dans ses autres commentaires, la source n'est manifestement pas André. Mon exemple sera pris au commentaire des Lamentations (Lam. 2, 1); au-delà de la critique textuelle, il se fonde sur une connaissance de la syntaxe hébraïque :

> Proiecit inclitam Israel *[...]* de celo *[...]* terram *[...]. Hebrei et nostri antiqui non habent hic* in; *est autem aliquando mos in hebreo ponere sic accusativum sine prepositione, quamvis subintelligatur, iuxta quod nos dicimus* Vado Romam[3].

Olieu doit encore cela à Guillaume de Mara : « *Heb[rei] et anti[qui]* de celo terram; *iuxta heb[reum] potest sonare quasi in terram, sicut Abdie primo* quis detrahet me in terram ». L'hébreu a en effet le nom de la terre, *erets*, seul, sans préposition *hishlikh mi-shamayim erets*, de même qu'en Abd. 3, *mi yordeni arets*, traduit pourtant *quis detrahet me in terram*.

Troisième démarche, la confrontation de ce que nous appelons la vulgate avec les traductions antérieures (dites « vieilles latines »), désignées génériquement dans les textes du XIIIe siècle par *Septuaginta*. Un exemple remarquable – parce que cette comparaison textuelle débouche sur une interprétation spirituelle – est fourni par le commentaire de Jonas (3, 4); là où Jérôme traduisait *adhuc quadraginta dies et Nineve subvertur*, Pierre Olieu note : « *Septuaginta habent adhuc tres dies, quorum littera mistice verificatur* ».

En effet, le grec des LXX (passé dans les vieilles latines) a bien : ἔτι τρεῖς ἡμέραι. La note n'est pas fournie par Guillaume de Mara mais il s'agit d'une notation fréquente qui remonte à Jérôme et que l'on trouve, par exemple, dans la *Postille* de Hugues de Saint-Cher.

J'espère que ces exemples rapides auront suffit à montrer le sérieux de l'approche de Pierre de Jean Olieu. Les points suivants confirmeront qu'il s'agit bien d'un exégète professionnel, en possession des techniques et des outils à la disposition des biblistes de son temps.

1. Pour Guillaume de Mara, j'utilise le ms. Vatican, lat. 3466 (pour les Petits Prophètes, f° 106v-111v).

2. *Biblia sacra iuxta latinam vulgatam versionem [...]*, vol. XIII-XVII (Prophètes), Rome, 1969-1987. On utilise couramment l'*editio minor* de R. Weber *et alii*, *Biblia sacra iuxta vulgatam versionem*, Stuttgart, 2e éd. 1975.

3. Ed. Bartoli, p. 39 (texte corrigé).

L'analyse grammaticale et linguistique

Les exemples précédents nous montraient déjà l'attention d'Olieu aux questions de grammaire et de langue. Il s'agit toujours d'expliquer le texte, d'en dissiper toutes les ambiguïtés. Si, dès l'exégèse monastique, l'attention philologique est toujours en éveil chez les exégètes, mes lectures des commentaires du XIIIe siècle m'y font constater souvent une plus grande technicité et des développements qui vont au fond des problèmes. Chez Pierre de Jean Olieu de tels passages sont assez fréquents. Je relève, par exemple, au début d'Osée (1, 2), *Principium loquendi Domino in Osee*, son analyse de la préposition *in*, qui peut signifier *ad Osee*, ou bien *intra cor Osee* ou bien *per Osee ad populum*[1]. De même, encore dans le commentaire d'Osée (3, 4), l'explicitation du sens de la conjonction *quia :*

> [Et ego expectabo te. Quia dies multos sedebunt filii Israel sine rege]. *Et secundum hoc id quod subditur potest dupliciter legi. Primo scilicet ut le* quia *sit coniunctio expletiva solum serviens de ornatu ac si absque ipsa absolute subdatur pena captivitatis :* Dies multos *etc. Secundo, ut le* quia *sit coniunctio causalis et velut reddens causam precepti dati, ut sit sensus : ideo inter cetera tibi precipio ut me diu expectes et cum deo falso non forniceris, quia in captivitate diu stabis [sine] rectore et cultu dei desolata*[2].

Olieu est sensible aux hébraïsmes que la traduction de saint Jérôme a conservés ; il en est ainsi notamment de ce qu'il appelle le nominatif absolu *more hebreorum* et que les philologues appellent parfois *nominativus pendens;* par exemple en Nahum 1, 3, *Dominus in tempestate et turbine vie eius*, que Pierre de Jean commente : « *le* Dominus *stat hic absolute et non servit nisi de antecedente ad hoc pronomen relativum* eius »[3].

La recherche sémantique occupe également une place dans les préoccupations de Pierre de Jean Olieu. Non seulement les termes hébraïques passés dans la langue de Jérôme (et souvent déjà expliqués par lui, comme *Baali* et *Baalim* en Osée 2, 16) mais également les termes latins rares suscitent une glose plus ou moins longue ; je retiendrai ce qu'il dit de *bruchus*, en Nahum 3, 15[4] : « *Et sic devorabit cuncta eius sicut bruccus multus devorat totam herbam et eius radices. Est autem bruccus fetus locuste* [« une larve de criquet »] *que plus rodit et vastat omnia quam locusta* ». Cette attention aux problèmes de sens se manifeste aussi par l'utilisation ponctuelle de l'*Elementarium* de Papias, nommé ici ou là (dans les Lamentations et dans Zacharie, notamment)[5].

1. Ms. BnF lat. 507, f° 1va.
2. Ms. cité, f° 2va.
3. Ms. cité, f° 17ra. Sur cet hébraïsme, voir W.E. Plater et H.J. White, *A Grammar of Vulgate. An Introduction to the Study of the Latinity of the Vulgate Bible*, Oxford, 1926, p. 19, § 19.
4. Lemaistre de Sacy traduit ce terme par « insectes » puis par « hannetons ». L'hébreu a *yeleq*, traduit par « criquets » dans la Bible de Jérusalem, par « hannetons » dans la Bible du Rabbinat.
5. *Cf.* sur Lam. 2, 11, éd. Bartoli, p. 42 : « *Secundum enim Papiam, oppidum dicitur ab oppositione murorum vel a dando opem contra hostem et subdit quod magnitudine et menibus differt a vico et castello* » ; sur Zach. 13, 7, ms. BnF lat. 507, f° 32vb : « O framea, *id est secundum Papiam spata vel lancea seu hasta longa, et secundum eum dicitur framea quasi ferrea. Vel dicitur a fremo, -is, quia fremendo vibratur* ».

L'analyse rhétorique

Une autre technique connue dès l'exégèse monastique (où elle avait reçu son premier manuel, le *De tropis et schematibus* de Bède le Vénérable) est l'analyse rhétorique : il s'agit d'identifier les différentes figures de style et, surtout, de pensée du texte biblique pour ne pas égarer le commentaire sur de fausses voies. Comme dans le cas de l'analyse grammaticale, l'exégèse universitaire adopte cette technique mais elle lui fait subir une mutation importante en l'orientant vers la définition des *modi*, c'est-à-dire vers une analyse plus complexe du style et des intentions de l'auteur. On y reviendra ; je m'en tiens pour le moment à l'identification simple des figures, en laissant aussi de côté le problème de la métaphore, qui me paraît fondamental. Deux figures reviennent d'une manière particulièrement fréquente dans les commentaires de Pierre de Jean Olieu, l'ironie et la synecdoque ; l'une et l'autre ont évidemment une importance spécifique pour les questions de sens. Ainsi, le début de la prophétie contre Ninive en Nahum 2, 1 est interprété *yronice et irrisorie*[1]. Les identifications de synecdoques sont généralement accompagnées d'une définition de cette figure ; par exemple, Olieu voit une synecdoque en Osée 9, 7, à propos du prophète fou, et note que Dieu ne désignant qu'une partie vise en fait la totalité d'Israël[2]. On rencontre également ici ou là le nom d'autres figures, et notamment l'hyperbole[3].

Le contexte historique et archéologique

Bien que l'*Historia scholastica* de Pierre le Mangeur ne soit plus dans l'exégèse universitaire le manuel de base qu'elle était au début du XIIIe siècle, elle a laissé une empreinte profonde ; les maîtres de la seconde moitié du siècle en effet accordent la même importance que le Mangeur à l'étude historique et archéologique du texte biblique. Ce souci est prépondérant chez Pierre de Jean Olieu ; j'allais dire « d'une manière étonnante » mais nous verrons que cette attention portée à l'explication de la narration biblique est un caractère fondamental de son exégèse. De la sorte, ses commentaires ont une allure très « moderne » et pourraient constituer une bonne introduction historique à l'étude des Prophètes. Ainsi les règles énoncées dans le prologue au commentaire des Petits Prophètes ont-elles pour objet principal la chronologie absolue et relative de ces textes. Les commentaires mêmes sont avant tout une élucidation historique et archéologique du récit : identification des personnages nommés et des lieux, situation dans l'histoire biblique, etc. Voici quelques exemples. A la fin d'Abdias, Olieu identifie les toponymes, notamment Sarepta, située au sud de Sidon et mise en relation avec I Rois 17 (épisode de la veuve de Sarepta)[4]. Au début d'Aggée, Olieu distingue le Darius qui y est nommé du personnage

1. Ms. BnF lat. 507, f° 17va : « *Contemplare, yronice et irrisorie dicit ad Ninive quod diligenter contempletur viam per quam sui hostes ad eam veniunt [...]* ».

2. Ms. cité, f° 4rb : « *Vel ut per synodochem, quod est partis, id est pseudoprophetarum, attribuatur toti Israeli* ».

3. En voici un exemple, sur Joël 2, 10 : « A facie eius moti sunt celi, sol et luna optenebrati sunt. *Hoc dicit tum yperbolice et exaggerative, tum quia [...]* ».

4. Ms. cité, f° 11ra : « *Sarepta enim erat locus sub urbe Sydonis, in qua erat vidua que pavit Helyam, III° Regum xvii* ».

apparaissant aux chapitres 9 et 13 de Daniel[1]. En Sophonie 1, 5, c'est un détail archéologique qui suscite l'intérêt: il y est question de « ceux qui adorent au-dessus des toits l'armée du ciel »; Olieu fait observer qu'en Palestine les toits étaient plats et donc les étoiles, mieux visibles, y étaient adorées[2].

Pierre de Jean Olieu renvoie beaucoup à Jérôme et utilise l'*Historia scholastica* (peut-être par l'intermédiaire de Hugues de Saint-Cher). Comme l'ensemble de ces sources et comme la plupart des auteurs du XIIIe siècle, il cite à l'occasion des interprétations juives. Je ne développerai pas ici ce point; dans mes études sur l'utilisation de l'exégèse juive, j'ai plusieurs fois cité des passages d'Olieu[3]; il ne me semble pas qu'il cite de première main, et comme ses contemporains, il ne distingue pas interprétations littérales et interprétations midrashiques (ou plutôt il les distingue intuitivement en parlant dans le premier cas plutôt de *traditiones*, dans le second plutôt de *fabulae*); je reviendrai cependant dans la dernière partie de cet exposé sur son attitude à l'égard de l'exégèse juive.

L'analyse philosophique et théologique

Je mettrai enfin au nombre des techniques d'exégèse littérale l'approche philosophique ou théologique du texte commenté. L'exégèse universitaire, plus encore que l'exégèse des écoles, tend à expliciter les données idéologiques suggérées par le texte scripturaire. Bien sûr, c'est dans la leçon *magistraliter* que l'exploitation est la plus complète, avec l'utilisation de la forme de la question dite scolastique. Le commentaire d'Isaïe de Pierre de Jean Olieu en fournit plusieurs exemples; la *lectio* sur le titre du livre s'accompagne de deux questions liées entre elles; la première, sur le caractère certain de la vision prophétique, met en jeu le problème des futurs contingents; la seconde, sur le mode de la vision prophétique, permet à l'auteur d'exposer les différentes thèses sur la perception intellectuelle, y compris sur la vision angélique[4]. Les commentaires *cursorie* n'ignorent pas ce type de réflexions, même si elles y ont nécessairement une place plus restreinte. Un exemple remarquable est fourni par le commentaire de Zacharie 1, 9, *et dixit ad me angelus qui loquebatur in me*, où précisément l'emploi de l'expression *loquebatur in me* soulève le problème du rôle des anges dans l'inspiration prophétique; en fait, le verset de Zacharie est presque toujours cité dans les discussions sur ce sujet[5]; Olieu rappelle notamment que l'*illatio*

1. Ms. cité, f° 23rb : « In anno secundo Darii, *non illius qui cum Ciro corregnavit Babilonemque cepit, qui Danielis 9° dicitur filius Assueri et Danielis 13° vocatur Astiages, sed alterius Darii, dicti filii Ydaspis* ».

2. Ms. cité, f° 21va : « Super tecta, *que in Palestina erant plana, et forte ibi magis adorabant stellas, quia inde liberius eas videre poterant* ».

3. Voir « L'utilisation de l'exégèse juive dans la lecture des livres prophétiques au XIIIe s. », dans *Neue Richtungen in der hoch- und spätmittelalterlichen Bibelexegese*, éd. R.E. Lerner, München, 1996, p. 121-138; « La connaissance de l'exégèse juive par les chrétiens, du XIIe au XIVe s. », dans *Rashi et la culture juive en France du Nord au moyen âge*, éd. G. Dahan, G. Nahon et E. Nicolas, Louvain-Paris, 1997, p. 343-359.

4. Ed. D. Flood-G. Gál, p. 192-200.

5. *Cf.* par exemple la question 481 du ms. Douai 434 (Hugues de Saint-Cher) publiée par J.P. Torrell, *Théorie de la prophétie et philosophie de la connaissance aux environs de 1230. La contribution de Hugues de Saint-Cher*, Louvain, 1977, p. 7-8 et 16-17.

mentis ne s'applique pas aux anges; il propose deux solutions à ce problème: 1) que le *in* doit être compris comme *ad* (« ut le *in* sumatur pro *ad* »); 2) comme le montre l'exemple de Luc 8, avec les démons, même s'il n'y a pas *illatio mentis,* il peut y avoir une certaine présence angélique, de sorte que la parole de l'ange soit saisie *ab extra* ou *ab intra;* et Olieu dit avoir vu « une sainte personne » qui pouvait distinguer chacun de ces deux modes [1].

Si, sur ce point encore, Pierre de Jean utilise les mêmes procédures que ses contemporains, il s'en distingue cependant par la rareté du recours aux *auctoritates* philosophiques: ainsi, dans le commentaire d'Isaïe, Aristote n'est-il nommé qu'une fois [2] et il me semble ne l'avoir jamais rencontré sur les XII Prophètes ni sur les Lamentations. Du reste, Olieu ne nomme vraiment que ses sources immédiates: Jérôme, la *Glossa*, André de Saint-Victor pour Isaïe, Pascase Radbert pour les Lamentations, Grégoire le Grand pour Ezéchiel, tout en se référant parfois à des *quidam* non identifiés.

Les techniques spirituelles

A la suite de Hugues de Saint-Victor, l'exégèse des écoles avait cherché à fonder l'interprétation spirituelle sur des règles aussi objectives que celles de l'interprétation littérale; il s'agissait en fait de codifier un certain nombre de procédures utilisées depuis longtemps, en tâchant de réduire la part de l'arbitraire ou de l'intuition [3]. L'exégèse universitaire fait siennes ces exigences mais elle ne recourt qu'avec prudence à ces techniques. Dans le cas de Pierre de Jean Olieu, la réticence à les utiliser est particulièrement nette. Mon exposé sur ce point sera donc forcément beaucoup plus court qu'à propos des techniques littérales (je rappelle que je n'envisage pas ici les *thèmes* de l'exégèse olivienne mais seulement ses *méthodes*).

Exégèse des verba

Une première catégorie concerne l'exégèse des mots; l'étymologie et l'*interpretatio* des noms étaient dans la pratique exégétique du XIIe siècle un

1. Ms. BnF lat. 507, f° 25rb: « *Tercio queritur quomodo dicit quod angelus loquebatur in me, cum nullus angelus possit illabi menti* ». Qui est la « sainte personne » dont il parle à la fin de la *questio: « Unde et quandam sanctam personam aliquando vidi, que has differentias et quasdam alias in se discernebat seu potius sentiebat* »? D. Burr, « Olivi, Apocalyptic Expectation, and Visionary Experience », *Traditio* 41, 1985, p. 273-288, cite un passage de la *Lectura super Mattheum* (« *A viro valde spirituali audivi revelatum esse quod [...]* ») et un autre de la *Lectura super Apocalypsim* (« *Audivi etiam a viro spirituali valde fide digno et fratri Leoni confessori et socio beato Francisci valde familiari [...]* ») faisant certainement allusion au même personnage.

2. Ed. D. Flood-G. Gál, p. 204: « Filios enutrivi [Is. 1, 2]. *Et in hoc tria beneficia innuit quae filii a patre habent, quorum nullum recompensare potest, secundum Aristotelem in Ethicis* »; *cf. Eth. Nic.* VIII, 16, 1163b20-28. Bien sûr, il ne s'agit pas d'ignorance; Olieu, comme beaucoup de ses contemporains théologiens, connaît parfaitement ses *auctoritates;* les philosophes sont cités surtout dans le commentaire des Sentences. Sur son attitude à l'égard de la philosophie, voir son petit traité *De perlegendis philosophorum libris*, éd. F. Delorme, *Antonianum* 13, 1941, p. 37-44, et l'étude de D. Burr, « Petrus Ioannis Olivi and the Philosophers », *F.S.* 31, 1971, p. 41-71.

3. Voir *L'Exégèse chrétienne de la Bible*, chapitre VI.

procédé courant permettant le passage au sens spirituel, allégorique ou tropologique [1] ; bien que les *artes praedicandi* du XIIIe siècle leur consacrent encore des réflexions intéressantes, leur rôle est le plus souvent bien moindre dans l'exégèse universitaire, y compris chez Pierre de Jean Olieu. De plus, chez celui-ci on relève un certain nombre d'*interpretationes nominum hebraicorum* utilisées non pas sur le plan spirituel mais à l'appui de la lettre, ce qui est assez remarquable. Par exemple, sur Amos 1, 15, traduit par Jérôme *Et ibi Melchom in captiuitatem*, Olieu explique que *Melchom* désigne une idole des Ammonites ou bien leur roi, puisque *Melchom* a pour *interpretatio* « *rex eorum* » [2] (comme le comprend la Bible de Jérusalem, qui traduit « et leur roi s'en ira en exil »). Même le nom de Ninive, dont l'*interpretatio* « *speciosa* » donne généralement lieu à des commentaires tropologiques, reçoit, sur Nahum 3, 4, une note plutôt littérale [3]. Quant aux étymologies, elles sont rares et, sauf inattention de ma part, ne jouent pas leur rôle habituel d'enclenchement de l'exégèse spirituelle [4].

Exégèse des nombres

L'arithmologie était aussi un procédé de base pour l'exégèse spirituelle, les nombres faisant partie de ces catégories signifiantes énumérées par Hugues de St-Victor et d'autres après lui. Olieu n'en fait qu'un usage modéré et on constate encore que ses réflexions sur les nombres s'inscrivent plutôt dans une démarche d'exégèse littérale. Ainsi, dans le long commentaire d'Osée 3, 2, « Je l'achetai [il s'agit de la femme adultère que Dieu demande à Osée de prendre pour épouse] pour quinze sicles d'argent, et un muid et demi d'orge », après l'identification des mesures, le nombre obtenu de 45 puis de 50 est mis en rapport avec le temps qui sépare la sortie d'Egypte du don de la Loi [5]. Nous sommes loin, je crois des considérations arithmologiques sur la valeur « symbolique » des nombres, qui fondent des interprétations allégoriques. Cependant, la suite du même passage nous ramène à une arithmologie plus courante, avec des considérations sur le 15, produit de 10 + 5 (la totalité de la loi : dix commandements et cinq livres de Moïse) ou de 5 x 3 (les trois classes de commandements donnés dans les cinq livres) ou de 7 + 8 (lettre et esprit) [6].

1. G. Dahan, « Lexiques hébreu-latin ? Les recueils d'interprétations des noms hébraïques », dans *Les Manuscrits des lexiques et glossaires, de l'Antiquité à la fin du moyen âge*, éd. J. Hamesse, Louvain-la-Neuve, 1996, p. 481-526.

2. Ms. BnF lat. 507, f° 6rb : « *Melchon vero est ydolum eorum vel stat pro rege eorum, quia Melchon interpretatur 'rex eorum'* ». L'*interpretatio 'rex eorum'* est donnée par la liste *Aaz apprehendens* (ms. BnF lat. 36, f° 347rb : « *Melchom rex eorum vel principans eis* »).

3. Ms. BnF lat. 507, f° 17vb : « *Propter multitudinem fornicationum meretricis speciose et grate [...]. Vocat autem eam speciosam tum alludens ad nomen eius, quia Ninive interpretatur 'speciosa', tum quia fuit nimis pulcris et amena* ».

4. *Cf.* cependant cet exemple, sur Am. 6, 7, *et auferetur factio lasciventium :* « [...] Vel factio, id est 'ficta actio' seu prodicio eorum aufferetur », ms. cité, f° 9rb.

5. Ms. cité, f° 2rb.

6. *Ibid.*, 2va : « *[...] ut per quindecim argenteos eis datos intelligatur eminens noticia decalogi, id est tocius legis in quinque libris Moysi scripte, ut sic decem et quinqe sint quasi quindecim. Vel ut pro quindecim sumamus ter quinque : in prefatis quinque libris est eis data lex et noticia moralium et cerimonialium et iudicialium, quasi lex trina seu tria genera mandatorum. Vel constituendo*

Exégèse des res

On devine ainsi que l'une des procédures les plus courantes de l'interprétation spirituelle n'aura qu'un rôle réduit chez Olieu : je veux parler des réalités signifiantes, dont le décryptage peut fonder le sens spirituel. Les quelques recours à la typologie sont rapides : ainsi Olieu nous dit-il en peu de mots et sans y revenir, qu'Osée est une figure du Christ, qui épousa l'Église à partir de la fornication des nations[1]. Autre chose l'intéresse dans les réalités : pourrait-on parler de « suggestion symbolique » ? Au lieu d'une rupture ontologique entre la réalité et sa signification, je vois une continuité, qui serait de l'ordre de la métonymie – mais il faudrait approfondir cela. Le passage d'Osée cité plus haut et relatif à l'achat de la femme adultère donne un exemple qui me paraît éclairant : il est question d'orge et non de blé ; l'orge, aliment destiné au bétail, nous oriente vers la matière, le blé, aliment du partage humain, vers l'esprit[2]. Il me semble ainsi que l'on a une connaissance réelle et une utilisation ponctuelle des procédures de l'exégèse spirituelle – mais radicalement transformées par Olieu, dans un sens, qui, on le verra, s'accorde parfaitement avec ses options herméneutiques.

Autres techniques

Les autres techniques de l'exégèse spirituelle, plus subtiles et faisant peut-être moins appel à de simples automatismes (ou en tous cas aux mécanismes de l'allégorie), jouent un rôle plus important chez Pierre de Jean Olieu. Je veux parler notamment des différentes techniques de concordance, la concordance verbale et la concordance thématique. Dans mon livre sur l'exégèse médiévale, où je tente de décrire ces procédures, des exemples pris dans le commentaire des Lamentations d'Olieu illustrent chacune de ces catégories. Je les redonne ici tels quels, mais la réflexion que je proposerai sur l'herméneutique d'Olieu permettra de mieux en comprendre la fonction. Comme exemple de concordance verbale, je citai le commentaire de Lamentations 3, 56, « Tu entends mon cri, ne sois pas sourd à ma prière, à mon appel » ; par l'intermédiaire du terme *clamor*, Olieu met ce verset en relation avec Hébreux 5, 7, où le Christ écoute cet appel, exauce cette prière[3] : effet d'écho, de résonance – puisque l'Ecriture est une, ses affirmations s'éclairent les unes les autres. Comme exemple de concordance thématique, je citai le commentaire allégorique du chapitre I des Lamentations, dans lequel Olieu définit un *modus concordantie*, qui lui permet une construction polyphonique dans laquelle la captivité de Babylone, celle provoquée par les Romains

quindecim ex septem et octo intelligitur per septem littera vel noticia status legis seu debiti regiminis huius vite, per octo vero prophetica et mistica noticia status gracie aut eterne resurrectionis et glorie ».

1. Ms. cité, f° 1rb : « *Geritque [Osee] figuram Christi, qui ex fornicatione gentium sibi ecclesiam assumpsit* ». Il s'agit d'un emprunt à la *Glossa ordinaria*.

2. Ms. cité, f° 2va : « *Quia vero prefata beneficia et documenta fuerunt terrenis admixta et, ut plurimum, corporalia vel sensualia, idcirco non dicuntur fuisse tritici sed ordei, tanquam iumentis et hominibus animalibus data* ».

3. Ed. M. Bartoli, p. 72.

et celle que feront subir à l'Église les dix cornes de la Bête ou l'Antéchrist se lisent sur la même partitition[1].

Mais que l'on considère comme provisoire cette analyse; il me semble que l'herméneutique de Pierre de Jean Olieu se situe au-delà de l'application de techniques, fussent-elles parfaitement maîtrisées, et qu'elle transcende totalement le clivage lettre/esprit. On a l'impression que l'application des automatismes de l'exégèse spirituelle ne l'intéresse pas – et c'est pourquoi l'allégorie a une place réduite dans son système herméneutique, au bénéfice de la métaphore, véritablement au centre de son exégèse. Olieu connaît parfaitement les procédures habituelles de l'exégèse spirituelle : mais, pour lui, il s'agit d'une démarche que le premier lecteur venu peut assumer; sur Osée 2, 15, après un commentaire littéral extrêmement développé, il conclut négligemment : « *Pro tempore tamen Christi et eterne patrie adapta hec, prout decet* »[2]; l'interprétation allégorique est une *adaptation* (le mot est fréquent chez lui) que l'on qualifierait volontiers d'automatique. Le passage au plan spirituel se fait pourtant ici et là – mais il ne s'agit plus d'allégorie: il s'agit, je crois, de mise en concordance de plans différents de réalité, pour laquelle les mécanismes de la métaphore ou de la métonymie seraient davantage de mise. J'emprunterai un exemple au même commentaire du chapitre 2 d'Osée, où l'enchaînement des causes naturelles devient pour Olieu une métaphore (il dit *mistice*) de l'« ordre hiérarchique selon lequel les dons de Dieu descendent d'abord de Dieu vers les êtres excellents qui les recherchent et les méritent, puis par leur intermédiaire vers les moyens et enfin vers ceux qui sont au bas de la hiérarchie »[3]. Nous sommes loin de la démarche allégorique à laquelle nous avait habitués l'exégèse spirituelle classique. Il paraît donc utile et prometteur de s'interroger sur la réflexion herméneutique de notre auteur.

UNE HERMÉNEUTIQUE

Ma tentative de définir l'herméneutique de Pierre de Jean Olieu se fera en deux temps. Tout d'abord, j'examinerai ses propres affirmations, en mettant en relief quelques points majeurs de sa théorie de l'exégèse. Celle-ci nous mènera dans un second temps à l'intérieur de son système, au cœur duquel nous trouverons l'analyse de la métaphore, axe essentiel de son herméneutique, voire plus généralement de sa pensée.

1. *Ibid.*, p. 31-32. Voir *L'Exégèse chrétienne*, p. 351-353.

2. Ms. cité, f° 2ra.

3. *Ibid.* : « *Per hoc mistice innuat ierarchicum ordinem secundum quem Dei dona primo descendunt a Deo in suppremos illa digne querentes et promerentes, et per suppremos in medios et per medios in postremos* ».

Les lieux

Pierre de Jean Olieu expose ses idées concernant l'exégèse aussi bien dans des textes théoriques que dans les commentaires mêmes; malgré leur dispersion et leur brièveté, les remarques éparpillées dans les commentaires sont tout aussi révélatrices que les grandes réflexions des textes théoriques. Comme textes théoriques, j'entends les *principia* et les prologues. Ainsi que dans le reste de cet exposé, je m'en tiendrai ici à ce qui concerne l'exégèse des livres prophétiques (qui me paraît de toutes les façons être le plus significatif dans l'ensemble de la réflexion de Pierre de Jean). Parmi les *principia* que viennent d'éditer David Flood et Gedeon Gál, deux ont une importance particulière dans la perspective présente[1]. Il s'agit des textes qu'ils ont intitulés *De doctrina Scripturae* et *De Christo medio Scripturae*. Le thème est dans les deux cas tiré d'Ezéchiel, livre dont les stimulations herméneutiques ont été souvent reçues par les exégètes chrétiens. Pour les quatre commentaires considérés ici, les prologues sont de deux sortes: d'une part, ceux des Lamentations et des Petits Prophètes (commentaires *cursorie*) donnent chacun une série de règles concernant particulièrement l'exégèse des livres considérés, surtout sur le plan littéral. Les huit règles des *Prophetae minores* concernent particulièrement des questions de chronologie[2]. Les sept règles des Lamentations constituent davantage un *accessus* au livre[3]. D'autre part, les prologues d'Isaïe et d'Ezéchiel utilisent la même structure complexe que les *principia*, avec un thème scripturaire, et fournissent une riche moisson d'éléments herméneutiques[4]. Je n'analyserai pas les textes mais présenterai ces éléments d'une manière synthétique.

La notion de medium

Les deux *principia* procurent une notion-clé dans l'exégèse d'Olieu. Tous deux exploitent en effet le terme de *medium*, fourni par les versets d'Ezéchiel: *Cum essem in medio captivorum iuxta flumen Chobar, aperti sunt caeli et vidi visiones Dei* (Ez. 1, 1); *Ingredere in medio rotarum que sunt subtus cherubim [...]* (Ez. 10, 2). Cette notion de *medium* implique ce qui me paraît être le présupposé majeur de l'exégèse chrétienne : le fait qu'un message transcendant (puisque venant de Dieu) soit véhiculé dans un langage humain. Le théologien s'interroge sur la possibilité d'une telle situation, qu'il appartient à l'exégète de gérer: comment l'infini peut-il être circonscrit dans les limites des mots de l'homme? La solution donnée au début du XIIIe siècle se fondait sur un

1. *De doctrina Scripturae*, éd. citée, p. 78-123; *De Christo medio Scripturae*, *ibid.*, p. 127-142.
2. Ms. BnF lat. 507, f° 1ra-b.
3. Ed. M. Bartoli, p. 1-9. On observera que la présentation est la même dans les deux prologues: Lam.: « *Circa expositionem Lamentationum Ieremie prophete VII sunt prenotanda* »; XII Proph.: « *Ad succinctam et summariam elucidationem libri duodecim prophetarum [...] in summa octo ad presens nota* ».
4. Isaïe, éd. D. Flood-G. Gál, p. 162-174; Ezéchiel, ms. Padoue, Bibl. Univ. 1540, f° 123ra-125rb.

approfondissement de la *translatio*[1]; au cours du XIIIe siècle, les écrits pseudo-dionysiens permettaient aux auteurs occidentaux d'assumer le caractère poétique du langage scripturaire – c'est-à-dire de recevoir d'emblée la parole biblique comme texte à interpréter[2]. Le pseudo-Denys soulignait le caractère ineffable de la Révélation mais aussi la nécessité qu'elle parle à l'homme : d'où le thème de la *manuduction* et celui des images dissemblables, qui déclenchent le processus exégétique et « conduisent par la main » l'exégète vers une réflexion qui ne s'arrêtera pas aux mots. Les deux *principia* de Pierre de Jean Olieu citent le pseudo-Denys et utilisent ces thèmes; dans son commentaire de la Genèse, Olieu proposait une forme différente au thème de la manuduction – non pas l'enfant pris par la main mais le bébé à qui sa mère s'adresse en « balbutiant » pour être plus à sa portée[3].

Mais en fait, chez Olieu, ces thèmes servent à exposer le problème, non à lui donner une solution (comme c'est le cas chez Thomas d'Aquin, par exemple). La solution est justement cette notion de *medium*, expliquée dans les deux *principia*. L'ambiguïté apparente de l'identité du *medium* – le Christ, l'Écriture – exprime bien la complexité et la richesse de la solution. Le *medium*, c'est le moyen terme, l'intermédiaire, le médiateur entre le message transcendant et l'immanence du vécu ou du pensé humain. Car, ainsi que l'affirme Olieu dans son prologue à Ezéchiel, l'intention des textes prophétiques est bien « de nous décrire Dieu et son royaume », « de nous enseigner l'essence de Dieu, sa prescience, ses jugements et ses bienfaits »[4]. A l'autre bout, il y a l'homme, dans son agir et sa connaissance : comment passer de l'infini au limité, de l'effort humain à l'essence de Dieu? Au-delà du thème théologique familier (mais qui conservera toujours son air de scandale dans une réflexion sur la Révélation) de la médiation du Christ Jésus, s'affirme une herméneutique, qui ne s'affadit pas, me semble-t-il, dans l'affirmation de l'accomplissement des Écritures en le Christ, mais qui pose audacieusement le Christ comme maître d'Écriture ou comme règle des Écritures – ou, mieux encore, comme Écriture même[5].

Livre scellé, livre ouvert

La notion de *medium* va donc jouer un rôle considérable dans l'herméneutique olivienne, non seulement sur le plan des options mais aussi sur celui de

1. Voir par exemple I. Rosier, « *Res significata* et *modus significandi* : les implications d'une distinction médiévale », dans *Sprachtheorien in Spätantike und Mittelalter* (cité n. 9), p. 135-168.

2. *L'Exégèse chrétienne*, p. 422-424.

3. Ms. Paris, BnF lat. 15559, f° 25v : « *Scriptura sepe utitur tali modo loquendi. Loquitur enim de Deo humano more, quasi mater balbutians cum infantulis suis* ».

4. Ms. Padoue, Bibl. 1540, f° 125rb : « *Est enim eorum intencio describere nobis Deum et eius regnum magnifice, recte et pie ordinatum. Et in hiis docent nos Dei essenciam, prescienciam, iudicia et beneficia* ».

5. Un autre franciscain avant Olieu, Antoine de Padoue, fondait aussi son herméneutique sur le thème du Christ maître d'Ecriture; *cf.* G. Dahan, « Saint Antoine et l'exégèse de son temps », dans *Congresso internacional Pensamento e Testemunho. 8° Centenario do Nascimento de Santo Antonio. Actas*, éd. M.C. Pacheco, Braga, 1996, p. 147-177.

la pratique exégétique. Elle va notamment nous expliquer comment l'Écriture est à la fois livre scellé et livre ouvert : objet à interpréter et clé d'interprétation. L'image, prise à Ezéchiel et à l'Apocalypse [1], revient fréquemment chez Olieu. Que l'Écriture soit un livre scellé, il le redit sans cesse, particulièrement dans le *principium De doctrina Scripturae*, qui analyse la *septuplex clausura* du texte sacré [2]. Le constat même de ce septuple scellement engage l'herméneute dans son effort d'interprétation, puisque ce sont des caractéristiques opposées qui génèrent l'opacité du texte biblique : par exemple, sa matérialité (le caractère matériel, physique, humain du récit) et, en même temps, son inaccessibilité, ou, mieux, sa proximité et son étrangeté [3]. Je m'attarderai un peu sur ce point, trouvant, dans ce constat de Pierre de Jean Olieu, l'une des expressions les plus admirables de la spécificité de l'exégèse biblique : la proximité est un facteur d'opacité, parce que le risque est grand de tomber dans les séductions d'un texte facile, réduisant tout à la dimension de l'homme, risquant de faire oublier la dimension transcendante du message. Car c'est aussi un texte autre, qui nous dit des choses radicalement différentes de ce que nous enseigne notre expérience humaine ; que cette altérité soit facteur d'opacité est sans doute plus facilement perceptible. Mais c'est l'opposition elle-même proximité / étrangeté qui va permettre l'ouverture, être la première clé qui brisera les sceaux, écartera les voiles, nous fera entrer à l'intérieur du texte. Une affirmation centrale du même *principium* le dit nettement :

> C'est aussitôt par le *medium* de ce qui est suprêmement abstrait que s'éclaire toute matérialité. Quiconque en effet verra ce *medium* absolument immatériel à partir du point culminant de son immatérialité, aussitôt luira [pour lui] d'une manière surabondante dans la matérialité pleine des saintes Écritures la clarté des réalités divines, immatérielle et au-delà de l'intellect [4].

Nous ne sommes pas loin du pseudo-Denys – mais s'entend aussi l'écho d'un siècle de réflexion sur la nature particulière du texte sacré.

Les principes exégétiques seront alors de deux sortes. D'une part, des principes pratiques, comme ceux qu'expose le commentaire de Zacharie :

> Parce qu'il fallait que dans l'Ancien Testament ce qui concernait le Christ fût dit en partie clairement, en partie d'une manière voilée (*adumbrate*), Dieu ordonna que cela fût écrit en des termes très précis mais qui fussent triplement voilés. Premièrement par la dispersion de ces données à travers des textes divers, de sorte qu'elles fussent comme des paillettes d'or brillantes dispersées et cachées

1. *Cf.* Ez. 2, 9 et Apoc. 5, 1-9.

2. Ed. D. Flood-G. Gál, p. 87-97.

3. *Cf. ibid.*, p. 87 : « *Erat enim ibi septuplex clausura, quam aperiri oportebat ad hoc quod divina claritas ibi plenarie refulgeat. Erat enim clausa sub miranda materialitate, sub miranda mutabilitate et extraneitate, et sub miranda propinquitate et carnali amicabilitate, sub vana exultatione et iucunditate, sub apparenti discordantiarum et contravietatum falsitate, et sub miranda impossibilitate, et sub inexplicabili inapprehensibilitate et inexperientia et invisibilitate* ».

4. Ed. citée, p. 89 : « *Statim in medio summae abstractionis aperitur omnis materialitas. Quicumque enim intuetur medium illud quod est immaterialissimum secundum altitudinem immaterialitatis suae, statim in tota materialitate Scripturarum sanctarum relucet abundantissime immaterialis et superintellectualis claritas divinorum* ».

dans le sable. Deuxièmement, par la mise en rapport de ces données avec des sujets divers de l'écorce littérale de l'Ancien Testament. Troisièmement, du fait que ces termes précis peuvent, la plupart du temps, être compris selon un sens plus commun[1].

Démarche triple à laquelle est invité l'exégète : attention au texte, exégèse par concordance, analyse sémantique ou, dirait-on, socio-linguistique (la troisième règle nous rappelant un principe du droit canon appliqué à la théologie dans le *Sic et non* d'Abélard[2]). De telles directives pratiques apparaissent ici ou là dans les commentaires[3].

D'autre part, Olieu propose une série de principes théoriques d'exégèse, qui permettent d'ouvrir le livre en résolvant les oppositions sur lesquelles le *De doctrina Scripturae* fondait l'opacité de l'Écriture et par lesquelles le prologue *Super Ezechielem* posait la tension du texte prophétique[4]. Je résumerai très rapidement ces principes, en les répartissant en deux catégories :

– l'analyse historique, qui permet de constater la progression de l'homme, dans le cadre défini des sept âges ; il ne s'agit pas d'une transposition allégorique de faits d'un âge à l'autre, mais d'une réflexion sur le sens de l'histoire, dans laquelle le texte biblique, *medium* par excellence, est à la fois objet et sujet – en ce qu'il renvoie à l'étude objective d'un passé mais se trouve aussi sujet de l'évolution historique, selon le principe défini dans une page célèbre de Grégoire (qu'Olieu reprend dans son commentaire d'Ezéchiel), qui veut que « l'Écriture avance avec son lecteur »[5] ;

1. Sur Zach. 12, 10, ms. BnF lat. 507, f° 32rb : « *Nota quod, quia in Veteri Testamento oportuit propria Christi dici partim clare, partim adumbrate, idcirco ordinavit Deus quod sic verbis propriissimis sepissime scriberentur, quod tamen tripliciter adumbrarentur. Primo scilicet ex dispersione eorum per varia loca, ut essent sicut grana auri prefulgida inter cumulos arene dispersa et abscondita. Secundo ex coniunctione eorum ad varias materias corticis litteralis Veteris Testamenti. Tercio ex eo quod verba propria possunt plerumque sumi sub significatione communiori [...]* ».

2. *Cf.* Abélard, *Sic et non*, prologue, éd. B.B. Boyer et R. McKeon, Chicago-Londres, 1976-1977, p. 95-96 (*P.L.* 178, 1343-1344).

3. Par exemple, à la fin de Joël, cette *nota* remarquable, ms. BnF lat. 507, f° 6vb : « *Nota etiam quod verba prophetarum coaptanda sunt omnibus captivitatibus et reductionibus populi Dei ad tempus prophete usque ad ultimam, que fiet in fine mundi, et est ubique diligenter attendendum cui illorum magis concorditer et magis proprie coaptantur ; nam aliquando plus uni et aliquando plus alteri [...]. Ei autem qui in huiusmodi coaptationibus est subtiliter exercitatus occurrunt ita cito plures sensus, sicut et unus, et longe sub armonia maiori quam quando solus unus occurrit. Nam ex omnibus insimul sumptis et adinvicem comparatis resonat admirabilis ordo Scripture* ».

4. Voici un passage caractéristique du prologue d'Ezéchiel, ms. Padoue, BU 1540, f° 125rb : « *Est enim eorum [prophetarum] intencio describere nobis Deum [...]. Et hoc faciunt per quatuor genera misteriorum [...]. Quedam enim sunt magnifica, stupenda et adunata [?] ; quedam autem sunt archana et profunda ; quedam sunt autem seva et terribilia ; quedam vero benigna, placida et demulcentia [...]* ».

5. Grégoire le Grand, *Homélies sur Ezéchiel* I, VIII, éd. et trad. fr. Ch. Morel, Paris, 1986, p. 245 : « *Diuina eloquia cum legente crescunt, nam tanto illa quisque altius intellegit, quanto in eis altius intendit. Vnde nec eleuantur rotae, si non eleuantur animalia, quia nisi legentium mentes ad alta profecerint, diuina dicta, uelut in imis, non intellecta iacent* ». Sur ce principe herméneutique, voir P.C. Bori, *L'Interprétation infinie. L'herméneutique chrétienne ancienne et ses transformations*, trad. fr. F. Vial, Paris, 1991, p. 37-49.

– l'analyse ontologique ; la rapide classification des sciences fournie au début du *De doctrina scripture* montre que l'Écriture couvre, sur le plan de la connaissance, l'ensemble des niveaux de la réalité, de la métaphysique à la politique, la théologie assurant l'unité[1]. Qu'est-ce à dire ? On va plus loin que dans les classifications fournies traditionnellement aux XIIe et XIIIe siècles dans les prologues des livres salomoniens où, d'une manière un peu artificielle, chaque livre est considéré comme illustrant l'une des trois parties de la division stoïcienne de la science[2]. Il s'agit pour Olieu de montrer que l'Écriture couvre l'ensemble du réel connaissable (et inconnaissable) et que l'exégète, passant d'un plan de connaissance à un autre (par exemple, de la physique à la métaphysique) peut ainsi desceller le livre – au moyen des clés mêmes que lui fournit le livre.

Herméneutique stupéfiante, qui témoigne de la maturité d'une réflexion et d'un engagement entier dans le travail d'exégèse. Si bien des aspects de l'œuvre de Pierre de Jean Olieu sont attachants, je me demande si celui-ci n'est pas le plus surprenant et le plus novateur. Mais prenons garde : Olieu ne bâtit pas son exégèse à partir de rien et, surtout, il ne la fonde pas sur une déconstruction du travail des générations antérieures. Bien au contraire : sa réflexion s'appuie sur l'immense et passionnant travail de ses prédécesseurs, y compris dominicains, travail sur lequel on a souvent disserté sans percevoir les éléments *dramatiques* qu'il faisait naître, particulièrement dans une recherche pathétique du « saut herméneutique » ou dans la tension née de l'opposition (implicite mais réelle) entre exégèse confessante et méthodes scientifiques, au risque de mener à un constat d'échec dans la définition d'une exégèse *et* spécifiquement chrétienne *et* fondée comme science. Ce qui me paraît propre à Olieu est d'avoir pris en compte l'ensemble des données et d'avoir proposé des solutions, quelque audacieuses qu'elles paraissent. Voilà pour l'herméneutique. Mais nous ne sommes pas au bout de nos surprises, puisque l'examen du travail même de l'exégète va nous entraîner encore plus loin.

LE DÉCHIFFREMENT DES MÉTAPHORES

Plus encore que les autres, les livres prophétiques se prêtent à l'herméneutique de Pierre de Jean Olieu : inscrits dans l'histoire, ils se donnent immédiatement à interpréter[3]. Les recherches du milieu du XIIIe siècle avaient fait assumer leur langage poétique : l'effort de l'exégète ira vers le déchiffrement des méta-

1. Ed. D. Flood-G. Gál, p. 79 (à la ligne 10 lire *methafisicum* au lieu de *mechanicum : « Est enim medium methafisicum, et hoc est medium essentiae, quod est abstractissimum »*).

2. *Cf.* S. Leanza, « La classificazione dei libri salomonici e i suoi riflessi sulla questione dei rapporti tra Bibbia e scienze profane, da Origene agli scrittori medioevali », *Augustinianum* 14, 1974, p. 651-666 ; G. Dahan, « Origène et Jean Cassien dans un *Liber de philosophia Salomonis* », *A.H.D.L.M.A.* 52, 1985, p. 135-162 (notamment p. 139-144).

3. Voir nos « Réflexions sur l'exégèse des livres prophétiques à la fin du moyen âge », dans *Pensée, image et communication en Europe médiévale. Les Apôtres et les Prophètes au Credo*, éd. P. Lacroix et A. Renon, Besançon, 1993, p. 193-198.

phores. La métaphore se trouve ainsi au centre du travail herméneutique d'Olieu. Il la désigne de différents noms, dont le caractère commun est d'indiquer la nécessité du passage à un sens second : *tipus*, *metaphora*, *tropus*. Mais, dépassant la figure de rhétorique, qui implique un « sens figuré » au-delà du « sens propre », la métaphore n'est-elle pas aussi porteuse d'une vérité au-delà de l'histoire, ne va-t-elle pas provoquer le basculement vers le sens spirituel, comme chez saint Thomas, ainsi que j'ai tenté de le montrer[1] ? Autrement dit, l'effort herméneutique va-t-il se satisfaire du déchiffrement d'une figure de style ou doit-il aller plus loin ?

Quelle est la portée du texte prophétique, où va sa vérité ? Est-elle contenue dans la bi-polarité que lui assigne l'exégèse juive, d'une histoire immédiate ou micro-histoire et d'une réalisation eschatologique[2] ? La ligne traditionnelle de l'exégèse chrétienne ramenait au Christ la vérité prophétique : développant les suggestions du récit des pélerins d'Emmaüs, les exégètes lisent les prophéties dans la vie du Christ – et de l'Église ; autrement dit, récusant le passé de la micro-histoire, aboli, épuisé dans son accomplissement, ayant perdu sa consistance, aussi bien que le futur idéel ou potentiel de l'eschatologie, ils prennent pour axe de lecture l'avènement historique du Christ, dans sa complexité et sa présence continue, puisque cette lecture dit aussi une communauté ou une Église constamment contemporaine. Pierre de Jean Olieu ne se satisfait pas de ce schéma, fait éclater le cadre de la lecture traditionnelle. D'abord, en assumant pleinement la vérité historique du texte prophétique – sa situation dans une micro-histoire : les règles énoncées en tête des Douze Prophètes, le soin qu'il prend à établir un synchronisme, l'examen minutieux concernant l'identification d'un personnage ou d'un lieu montrent le sérieux et l'importance qu'il accorde à ce niveau de vérité du texte biblique. En outre, l'accomplissement eschatologique est aussi pris en compte par lui, non pas à la manière du « prophétisme » illuminé qu'on a voulu voir dans sa *Lectura in Apocalypsim*, mais à la manière de l'exégèse juive, en tant que réalisation littérale des prophéties. Mais si, de la sorte, deux des dimensions que l'exégèse traditionnelle avait eu tendance à négliger retrouvent chez Olieu toute leur force, son exégèse des Prophètes recouvre aussi la dimension christique, à laquelle s'ajoute une application particulière à saint François et à l'Église de son temps ; encore une fois, il convient de relever le caractère spécifique de cette démarche et, surtout, de se garder de l'assimiler par exemple à l'« allégorie historique » d'un autre franciscain, Alexandre le Minorite[3], ou d'y voir l'application ecclésiale habituelle de l'exégèse allégorique

1. « Saint Thomas d'Aquin et la métaphore. Rhétorique et herméneutique », *Medioevo* 18, 1992, p. 85-117. Cette tentative ne me satisfait pas entièrement aujourd'hui ; justement parce que, comme saint Thomas, j'avais voulu y trouver le moyen d'accéder au sens spirituel. A la lumière de l'exégèse de Pierre de Jean Olieu, je me demande si la métaphore ne permet un épanouissement *du* sens (dépassant, je crois, l'opposition sens littéral / sens spirituel) plus que le passage à *un* sens dit spirituel. Mais l'étude se terminait par une interrogation, qui demeure...

2. Voir « L'utilisation de l'exégèse juive » (cité n. 36), p. 130-131.

3. *Alexander Minorita. Expositio in Apocalypsim*, éd. A. Wachtel, Weimar, 1955 (n. éd. Munich, 1983) ; voir S. Schmolinsky, *Der Apocalypsenkommentar des Alexander Minorita [...]*, Hanovre,

traditionnelle. Ainsi, on a l'impression d'un déchiffrement à quatre niveaux (essentiellement différents des quatre sens classiques, dont je n'ai pas parlé et qui n'ont chez Olieu aucune pertinence opératoire), par addition ou couches successives : micro-histoire, le Christ, saint François, eschatologie. Même si une approche superficielle peut nous tenter de le faire, il n'est en effet pas question de réduire ce schéma à celui des quatre sens canoniques – déjà parce que le passage d'une « couche » à une autre se fait par un mécanisme métaphorique et non par une application allégorique.

On observera que le schéma ainsi défini englobe les axes constitutifs de l'exégèse juive; celle-ci ne se trouve pas disqualifiée chez Olieu (alors qu'elle l'est durement chez Albert le Grand [1], par exemple, non par antipathie particulière pour le judaïsme mais par cohérence herméneutique). Le peuple juif (Israël ancien et juifs contemporains) joue un rôle dans le déchiffrement de l'histoire chez Pierre de Jean Olieu [2] – son exégèse reste valide même si elle est incomplète (et contestable dans son détail, comme Olieu ne se prive pas de le dire [3]).

Lettre / esprit ?

Dans cette partie de l'exposé, j'ai évité d'utiliser l'opposition lecture littérale / lecture spirituelle, fondatrice de l'exégèse chrétienne. Si j'ai écarté péremptoirement le principe des quatre sens (ils n'apparaissent pas dans les *principia* et là où l'on s'attendrait à un couplet à leur sujet, à propos d'un aspect quadruple de la réalité par exemple, Olieu ne cède jamais à une suggestion dans cette direction), je ne saurais nier que l'opposition lettre / esprit apparaît assez souvent chez lui, les deux termes les plus spécifiques de son vocabulaire étant *umbratiliter* et *mistice*. Cependant, comme je l'ai fait observer plus haut, la part des développements identifiés comme spirituels est réduite; dans les Lamentations, ils ont quelque raideur; le commentaire des XII Prophètes se termine sur cet aveu :

> J'omets l'application de tout ce qui a été dit au triple avènement du Christ, parce qu'elle peut s'éclairer à partir de ce qui a été rapporté ici et ailleurs. Mon intention n'a pas été d'exposer longuement les XII Prophètes mais seulement de jeter les bases de la lettre et de proposer une introduction à l'intelligence spirituelle [4].

Je me demande si cette désinvolture (qui s'explique sans doute principalement par le genre de la *lectio cursoria*) ne recouvre pas autre chose, de plus

1991 ; la même, « Merkmale der Exegese bei Alexander Minorita », dans *Neue Richtungen* (cité n. 36), p. 139-148.

1. Exemples dans les deux études citées n. 36.

2. Voir ici même la contribution de Robert E. Lerner.

3. Par exemple, sur Zach. 2, 9, ms. BnF lat. 507, f° 26rb : « *Iudei tamen stultizant hoc tempore Messie, quod adhuc falso exspectant esse implendum* ».

4. Ms. cité, f° 36vb : « *Applicationem autem omnium predictorum ad trinum Christi adventum omitto, quia ex hic et alibi traditis satis inclarescere potest. Non enim fuit mee intentionis.xii. prophetas hic diserte exponere sed solum aliqua fundamenta littere iactare et aliqualem introitum specialis [*lire *spiritualis ?] intelligentie apperire* ».

grave, voire de bouleversant en exégèse chrétienne : il n'y aurait pas de cloison entre lettre et esprit, tout est lettre ou tout est esprit. Plusieurs indices me laisseraient croire cela ; je ne pense pas qu'il s'agisse d'une option consciente de l'herméneutique de Pierre de Jean Olieu, mais cette tendance apparaît ici et là au fil de son travail d'exégète. Par exemple, en Aggée 2, 10, le prophète parle du Temple reconstruit, dont la gloire dépassera celle du premier; cela ne peut s'entendre à la lettre, nous dit Olieu; cette prophétie ne se vérifie qu'au sens mystique; argument contraire : Jésus s'étant rendu *corporaliter* dans ce Temple et y ayant prêché, n'y a-t-il pas ainsi réalisation littérale de la prophétie ? N'y a-t-il pas ainsi un mouvement d'aller/retour entre lettre et esprit ? Bien sûr, ici Olieu ne fait qu'appliquer le principe courant dans la seconde moitié du XIIIe siècle selon lequel l'accomplissement des prophéties en le Christ est de l'ordre de la lettre. Ce même principe explique le caractère littéral de la polémique sur Isaïe 7, 14, à laquelle Olieu accorde un intérêt particulier et où il manifeste une connaissance précise de l'argumentation juive – la cible étant cependant l'exégèse d'André de Saint-Victor[1]. Le débat sur la réalisation des prophéties messianiques se situe sur le plan de la lettre et non de l'exégèse spirituelle. Mais Olieu incite le lecteur à briser la coquille de la noix littérale, à dépasser l'annonce ombreuse pour atteindre la lumière d'une vérité d'un autre ordre.

L'emploi de *mistice* me semble alors impliquer la démarche herméneutique même de Pierre de Jean Olieu – le fait que l'on passe de la micro-histoire des textes prophétiques à autre chose, cet autre chose étant, comme l'indiquait le passage cité plus haut, le triple avènement du Christ.

Mistice

Je ne reviendrai pas sur le principe qui fonde ce point : la lecture quadruple, telle que je l'ai définie, s'appuyant sur une interprétation exigeante et précise de la micro-histoire pour développer une vision ample de l'histoire humaine, rythmée par les trois avènements du Christ. Cet aspect propre de la pensée olivienne est bien connu[2] et je me contenterai de citer quelques textes qui illustrent l'application au second avènement, en saint François d'Assise et en l'observance de la règle. On remarquera qu'il n'y a pas application systématique, mais seulement ici ou là quelques indications dans ce sens.

Dans le commentaire d'Isaïe, un seul passage exploite ce type d'exégèse ; à la fin du commentaire d'Isaïe 8, 1-10, Olieu affirme que tout le passage sur la naissance virginale peut être appliqué *mystice* au troisième et au quatrième temps :

1. Ed. D. Flood-G. Gál, p. 235-256.

2. Voir notamment R. Manselli, *La « Lectura super Apocalipsim »*, p. 192-219; D. Burr, *L'histoire de Pierre Olivi, Franciscain persécuté*, trad. fr. F.X. Putallaz, Fribourg-Paris, 1997, p. 41-63.

« En effet, au troisième temps, au stade de saint François (*in statu Francisci*), la vie du Christ a été conçue en sainte Marie des Anges »[1].

La prophétie de Sophonie sur l'humble Reste d'Israël (Soph. 3, 11-13) reçoit une application similaire :

> Bien que cette prophétie ait été accomplie lors du premier avènement du Christ en les apôtres, elle doit bien plutôt se réaliser lors du second avènement, parce qu'Israël sera tout entier sauvé par l'esprit de pauvreté, d'humilité et de simplicité porteur du Christ, suscité en François[2].

Enfin, le *planctus* évoqué en Zacharie 12, 11, qui reçoit généralement une interprétation en relation avec la Passion, est aussi compris eschatologiquement par Olieu, quand tout Israël sera sauvé; mais à ce salut contribue spécialement « François, marqué d'une manière étonnante des stigmates du Christ »[3]. Mon étudiante Dominique Turbé, qui a préparé l'édition du commentaire de Zacharie, a analysé judicieusement ce passage, en le situant dans la pensée olivienne et en étudiant également avec précision les supputations chronologiques qui l'accompagnent[4].

CONCLUSION

Les commentaires des livres prophétiques nous révèlent donc un exégète à la fois singulier et s'inscrivant totalement dans son temps. Il maîtrise parfaitement les formes et les techniques de l'exégèse universitaire mais il se situe aussi dans la lignée propre de l'exégèse franciscaine[5]. Celle-ci prend son essor avec Antoine de Padoue, se développe avec Bonaventure et s'épanouit avec Pierre de Jean Olieu. Exégèse franciscaine, non seulement par une thématique spécifique (qu'il conviendrait de développer) et par le rôle conféré à la personnalité de saint François d'Assise, mais aussi par quelques caractères notables, comme l'assimilation des techniques contemporaines à une démarche spirituelle propre (je crois l'avoir montré à propos d'Antoine de Padoue) et, surtout, une attention très vive à

1. Ed. D. Flood-G. Gál, p. 260 : « *Tota ista pars de Christi virginali conceptu et ortu posset mystice aptari ad tertium tempus et deinde ad quartum. Nam tertio tempore, in statu Francisci, concepta est vita Christi in sancta Maria de Angelis* ».

2. Ms. BnF lat. 507, f° 23ra : « *Licet autem hec in primo Christi adventu sint in apostolis impleta, potissime tamen sunt in secundo implenda, quia omnis Israel salvus fiet per spiritum christifere paupertatis et humilitatis ac simplicitatis in Francisco suscitatum et in tempore antichristi tam mistici quam aperti plenius suscitandum* ».

3. Ms. cité, f° 32rb : « *Et ideo tunc perfectissime renovabitur passio et lamentatio mortis Christi, propter quod et missus est nobis et toti orbi et specialiter omni Israel salvando Franciscus, Christi stigmatibus modo mirifico consignatus* ».

4. D. Turbé, *La « Lectura super Zachariam » de Pierre Jean Olivi*, mémoire de D.E.A., Paris, École pratique des hautes études (section des sciences religieuses), 1996, p. 56-63.

5. Voir I. Brady, « Sacred Scripture in the Early Franciscan School », dans *La Sacra Scrittura e i Francescani*, Rome-Jérusalem, 1973, p. 65-82 ; G.L. Potestà, « I Frati Minori e lo Studio della Bibbia. Da Francisco d'Assisi a Nicolo di Lyre », dans *La Bibbia nel Medio Evo*, éd. G. Cremascoli et C. Leonardi, Bologne, 1996, p. 269-290.

la lettre du texte, qu'il s'agisse de sa qualité matérielle ou du sens (et ainsi l'on n'est pas surpris de trouver au XIVe siècle un prolongement de cette exégèse avec la *Postilla litteralis* d'un autre exégète franciscain majeur, Nicolas de Lyre).

Je parlais d'un épanouissement de l'exégèse du XIIIe siècle dans l'œuvre de Pierre de Jean Olieu : je ne crois pas exagérer. Il me semble voir en son herméneutique l'aboutissement de la réflexion bouillonnante de son temps. Aux problèmes posés, au problème fondamental du « saut herméneutique », il propose une solution audacieuse, l'abandon presque radical de la démarche allégorique comme fondatrice du sens spirituel au profit d'une démarche métaphorique (ou métonymique), dont les modalités précises restent à étudier; solution que déterminait déjà Thomas d'Aquin comme théoricien mais qu'il appliquait moins radicalement comme exégète au travail. Cependant, la solution olivienne pouvait-elle avoir une postérité ? Sans compter les problèmes qui ont entouré la mémoire du Languedocien, le travail extrêmement dense et l'implication existentielle qu'elle exigeait du commentateur rendaient difficile la diffusion d'une telle herméneutique. Peut-être aujourd'hui seulement sommes-nous mieux armés pour comprendre et admirer sa richesse et sa force.

OLIVI UTILISATEUR DE LA *CATENA AUREA* DE THOMAS D'AQUIN

Louis-J. Bataillon

La position de Pierre Jean-Olivi (ou Olieu) sur la théologie de l'essence divine avait été critiquée dans le rapport de la commission des « *septem magistri* » franciscains réunis par le ministre général Bonagrazia en 1283. Le frère mineur théologien s'est défendu dans un mémoire justificatif de 1285[1], dans lequel il disait qu'avant les arguments rationnels, il citerait en faveur de sa thèse les *auctoritates sanctorum*, c'est à dire non seulement l'opinion d'Augustin, Hilaire et Anselme, mais aussi celle de nombre de Pères Grecs parmi lesquels il nomme Théophylacte[2].

Il est probable que, malgré sa forte culture patristique, le maître languedocien pensait qu'il s'agissait de quelque vénérable Père des premiers siècles et ne savait pas qu'il s'agissait en fait d'un évêque byzantin du XIe siècle, qui se consolait d'un semi-exil chez les Bulgares en commentant la Bible d'après les Pères, spécialement d'après Chrysostome, tout en critiquant volontiers les Latins avec une modération souvent quelque peu méprisante.

Ce qui est important ici est que les commentaires de Théophylacte sur les trois derniers Evangiles[3] n'ont été connus dans l'Occident médiéval que par les traductions faites à la demande de Thomas d'Aquin. Celui-ci l'a utilisée pour composer sa *Glosa continua* (plus connue comme *Catena aurea*) sur Marc, Luc et Jean; il s'est aussi servi pour commenter Marc de la compilation de Victor d'Antioche, qu'il prenait pour Chrysostome, et pour gloser Luc et Jean, des chaînes grecques de Nicétas. La citation du théologien grec, qui sert d'argument à Olivi[4] correspond littéralement à un morceau d'un passage qui figure dans la *Glosa in Iohannem*[5].

1. D. Laberge, « Fr. Petri Ioannis Olivi, O.F.M. tria scripta sui ipsius apologetica annorum 1283 et 1285 », *A.F.H.* 28, 1935, p. 126-155, 374-407; 29, 1938, p. 98-141, 365-395; l'article a été publié à part en un seul volume avec une pagination continue nouvelle mais en conservant entre crochets l'ancienne pagination.

2. D. Laberge, *op. cit.*, p. 80 [100].

3. Robert Grosseteste a connu le commentaire de Théophylacte sur l'Epitre aux Galates (J. McEvoy, *Gli inizi di Oxford. Grossatesta e i primi teologi*, Milan, 1996, p. 87-88).

4. D. Laberge, *op. cit.*, p. 106 [126] l. 36 – 107 [127] l. 4.

5. *Catena in Io,* XV, 26 (ed. A. Guarienti, Thomas d'Aquin, *Catena aurea in quatuor Evangelia*, II, Turin-Rome, 1953, p. 535a. Tout en renvoyant désormais à cette édition, je donnerai les textes

Quand il commente l'Evangile de Jean, Olivi ne reprend pas cette citation, mais cela ne veut pas dire qu'il n'ait pas consulté à cette occasion la *Chaîne* de Thomas. Bien au contraire, les emprunts à cet ouvrage ne sont pas rares dans le commentaire du théologien franciscain. Pour établir qu'Olivi a eu recours à la *Catena* et non au texte original, trois cas sont possibles. Le premier est quand, comme dans le cas de Théophylacte, le texte cité ne pouvait être connu autrement que par la *Glosa continua*. Le cas ne vaut pas seulement pour Théophylacte, mais pour plusieurs autres auteurs tirés par Thomas des chaînes grecques traduites pour son usage et qui semblent ne pas avoir circulé en dehors de la *Catena :* pour Marc, le maître dominicain a eu à sa disposition la compilation de Victor d'Antioche, qu'il identifiait à Chrysostome; pour Luc et Jean, les chaînes de Nicétas dans lesquelles on trouve des passages d'ouvrages inaccessibles par ailleurs à l'époque, comme le commentaire de Cyrille d'Alexandrie sur Luc, ou ceux de Titus de Bostra ou d'Isidore de Péluse. Le second type de preuve est quand une série de citations se retrouve exactement dans le même ordre dans les deux ouvrages. Le troisième cas, qui donne un degré de certitude meilleur que le précédent, est lorsque Thomas a abrégé ou modifié sa source, ce qui lui arrivait assez souvent comme lui-même l'explique dans sa lettre-préface à la chaîne sur Matthieu :

> *In assumendis autem Sanctorum testimoniis, plerumque oportuit aliqua rescindi de medio ad prolixitatem uitandum, nec non ad manifestatiorem sensum, uel secundum congruentiam expositionis littere ordinem commutari; interdum etiam sensum, uerba dimisi.*

C'est souvent le cas pour les *Homélies* authentiques de Chrysostome, «*propter hoc quod est translatio uitiosa*». Un examen rapide du commentaire d'Olivi sur Jean montre un bon nombre de citations empruntées à Théophylacte d'après la *Catena*[1]. Voici un cas entre autres[2] :

(Io. 4, 33)

Olivi, *In Iohannem*
Firenze, Laur. S. Croce Plut. X d. 8, f° 33va

Adhuc theophilatus dicit quod Dominus cibos ab aliis oblatos suscipere solebat non quia alieno ministerio indigeret qui dat escam omni carni sed ut deferentes meritum consequerentur, simulque formam tradens non erubescere paupertatem neque graue putare ab aliis nutriti; proprium enim et necessarium est doctoribus alios habere procuratores ciborum ut ipsi de nullo curantes uerbi ministracionem procurent sollicite. Hec theophilatus.

Catena in Iohannem
Linz 449, f° 48ra. Ed. p. 389b

Theoph.[3] *In hoc autem quod dicunt discipuli Numquid aliquis attulit ei manducare? considerandum est quod cibos ab aliis oblatos Dominus suscipere solebat, non quod alieno ministerio indigeret qui dat escam omni carni, sed ut deferentes meritum consequerentur, simulque formam tradens non erubescere paupertatem neque graue putare ab aliis nutriri; proprium enim et necessarium est doctoribus alios habere procuratores ciborum ut ipsi de nullo curantes uerbi ministrationem procurent sollicite.*

d'après les manuscrits *Linz, Studienbibliothek.* 446 (Matthieu), 448 (Luc), 449 (Jean). Ces manuscrits sont parmi les meilleurs témoins du texte universitaire parisien.

1. J'ai relevé dix-sept cas évidents, mais il y en a certainement plus.

2. J'utilise pour le commentaire d'Olivi sur Jean le manuscrit *Firenze, Laur. S. Croce,* Plut. X, d. 8.

3. PG 123, 1247 CB.

Plusieurs fois Théophylacte est associé à des auteurs qui le suivent ou le précèdent dans la *Catena*. Ainsi, sur Jean 10, 22-23, Olivi cite, aussitôt après l'exégèse de Théophylacte, celles de Grégoire le Grand et d'Alcuin. Si on se reporte à la *Catena* on voit que les trois passages se suivent dans le même ordre avec l'insertion de Chrysostome entre Grégoire et Alcuin, mais ce passage du docteur grec est très proche de Théophylacte – et pour cause car, nous l'avons vu, l'évêque byzantin s'inspirait avant tout du saint patriarche –; ainsi s'explique aisément qu'Olivi l'ait laissé de côté.

(Io. 10,22-23)

Olivi, *In Iohannem* Firenze, Laur. S. Croce Plut. X d. 8, f° 62ra	Catena Linz 449, 108rb. Ed. p. 477a
Et hyems erat. *Secundum Theophilatum tempus hyemis euangelista exprimit ad ostendendum quod proximum erat passionis. Nam in uere sequenti passus est Dominus et ideo Iherosolimis conuersabatur.*	Theoph.[1] *Tempus autem hiemis Euangelista exprimit ad ostendendum quod proximum esset tempus passionis : nam in uere sequenti passus est Dominus et ideo Hierosolymis conuersabatur.*
Secundum uero Gregorium idcirco uere tempus hyemis curauit exprimere ut inesse Iudeorum malitie frigus indicaret. Ante porticum Salomonis.	Gregorius, Moralium. *Vel idcirco hiemis curauit tempus exprimere ut inesse Iudeorum cordibus malicie frigus indicaret.*
Secundum Alchuinum porticus Salomonis dicitur porticus illa in qua Salomon ad orandum stare consueuerat.	Crisostomus [...] *Alcuinus Porticus Salomonis dicitur ubi rex ille ad orandum stare consueuerat*

Si le passage de Grégoire est cité littéralement dans les deux textes, avec seulement *Iudeorum* dans la *Catena* au lieu d'*audientium* dans Grégoire, en revanche le passage d'Alcuin[2] a été sérieusement abrégé dans la *Catena* : « *[...] porticum in quo rex quanto moralis et terrenus, quamuis potentissimus et sapientissimus ad orandum stare solebat* ». Il y a donc eu emprunt pour les trois citations.

De même, dans le commentaire de Jean 18, 10, Théophylacte est cité aussitôt après Chrysostome dans le même ordre que dans la *Catena*. Certains groupement d'autres auteurs semblent eux aussi avoir leur origine dans la *Glosa continua*, ainsi, sur Jean 6, 27, des passages d'Hilaire, Alcuin et Chrysostome sont cités dans le même ordre et dans les mêmes termes chez Thomas et Olivi.

La même chose se constate dans le commentaire un peu postérieur sur Luc dans lequel j'ai compté au moins vingt-huit citations tirées de la *Glosa*. Ici les auteurs cités sont plus nombreux, car Thomas a beaucoup plus utilisé la chaîne grecque pour Luc que pour Jean; si Théophylacte reste le plus souvent invoqué, avec 14 passages, Cyrille d'Alexandrie est cité 6 fois et on rencontre aussi Basile, Grégoire de Nazianze, Titus de Bostra, Eusèbe de Césarée et des auteurs appelés « *Grecus* » par Thomas et « *Grecus glosator* » par Olivi[3].

1. PG 124, 73 C.
2. *Comm. In S. Ioannis Euang.*, l. V, c. 6 (PL 100, 891 D).
3. Il s'agit de différents auteurs dont une bonne part a été identifiée au XVIIe siècle par Jean Nicolai (S. Thomae Aquinatis, *Opera omnia*, t. XVII, *Expositio continua super quatuor Euangelia [...] Catena aurea*, Paris, 1660), mais ces précisions n'ont été retenues par les éditions postérieures que

Voici un cas dans lequel Théophylacte est associé à un autre théologien grec, anonyme dans la *Catena*[1] :

(Lc 1 56)

Firenze, Laur. Plut. X. d. 4, f° 120ra.	Linz 448, f° 12ra – Ed., p. 22b
Theophilatus uero dicit quod quando Helisabeth paritura erat uirgo recessit propter multitudinem que ad partum congregari debebat. Inconueniens enim erat in talibus uirginem esse presentem. Item Grecus glosator dicit : mos enim est uirginibus sedere (sic pro cedere) quotiens pregnans parit.	Theoph.[2] *[...] propter multitudinem que ad partum congregari debebat;. inconueniens autem erat in talibus uirginem ibi esse presentem.* Grecus. *Mos est enim uirginibus cedere quociens pregnans parit.*

Dans ses citations, Olivi donne toujours son vrai nom à Théophylacte[3], quitte à l'abréger Theo^tus^, alors que d'autres emprunteurs de la *Catena*, tel Jacques de Voragine[4], l'appellent ordinairement *Theophilus*. En effet, dans la plupart des manuscrits de la *Catena*, notamment dans ceux qui dépendent de l'exemplar universitaire parisien, le nom est abrégé Theo^us^ ou Theoph^us^. Pour la *Catena sur Luc*, je n'ai repéré jusqu'ici que deux témoins, tous deux d'origine napolitaine[5], à avoir écrit en entier le nom de l'exégète byzantin; pour celle sur Jean, je ne connais que trois cas[6]. Cela semble indiquer qu'Olivi a eu entre les mains un manuscrit de très bonne qualité.

Pour les autres évangiles, Olivi n'a commenté de Marc que le prologue attribué à Jérôme et celui-ci n'a pas trouvé place dans la *Catena* et donc il n'y a pas à chercher de relation dans ce cas. Pour le commentaire de Matthieu, la situation est plus difficile en ce sens que ce premier livre de la *Glosa continua* n'utilise comme sources que des auteurs latins ou des Pères grecs aisément accessibles au XIIIe siècle en traditions latines comme Origène et Chrysostome. Mais une étude de Kevin Madigan permet de constater l'usage assez abondant de la *Catena* par Olivi dans le chapitre 16 de Matthieu[7]. Des séries de citations patristiques se recoupent de très près. Ainsi le premier verset du chapitre selon la division médiévale qui est selon l'usage moderne le dernier du chapitre 15 et qui

jusqu'à celle de Parme (1871, t. 11-12). Les éditions postérieures de Vivès (Paris, 1876, t. 16-17) et de Marietti, ont laissé tomber ces précieuses indications. Pour la chaîne grecque de Nicétas sur Luc, l'ouvrage le meilleur est celui de X. Th. Kritônis, Συναγωγη Πατερων εισ το κατα Λουκαν Ευαγγελιον, Thessalonique, 1973.

1. Il s'agit en fait de Syméon Métaphraste ; PG. 115, 534 D ; *cf.* Krikônis, *op. cit.*, p. 103.

2. PG 123, 713 AB.

3. Cela est vrai surtout des manuscrits de Florence; le manuscrit *Vatican, Ottob. lat.* 3302 écrit généralement « theophilus » ou « theophi. », une fois seulement (f° 186r) « theophilatum ».

4. *Cf.* L.J. Bataillon, « Iacopo de Varazze e Tommaso d'Aquino », *Sapienza* 32, 1979, p. 22-29 ; réimprimé dans *Id. La prédication au* XIIIe *siècle en France et Italie*, Aldershot, 1993, n. XVIII.

5. *Napoli*, Naz. VII AA 3 et 17. *Cf.* H.V. Shooner, *Codices manuscripti operum Thomae de Aquino*, t. III, Montréal-Paris, 1985, p. 4 n. 109 et p. 5 n. 111.

6. *Firenze, Laur. S. Croce* Plut. 28 f° 8 : *cf.* H.F. Dondaine, H.V. Shooner, *Codices, cit.*, I, Rome, 1967, p. 312 n. 863 ; *ibid.*, *Fiesol.* 96, p. 329 n. 906 ; *Linz, Studienbibl.* 449 ; *Cf.* H.V. Shooner, *Codices, op. cit.*, II, Rome, 1973, p. 217 n. 1480. Ce dernier manuscrit comporte de nombreuses indications de *pecie*.

7. K. Madigan, « Peter Olivi's *Lectura super Mathaeum* in Medieval Exegesis and Context », Doctoral dissertation, University of Chicago, 1992, p. 248-252.

parle de Jésus montant en barque après la seconde multiplication des pains, Olivi donne une série d'*auctoritates* qui se retrouve un peu plus abondante mais dans le même ordre dans la *Catena*.

(Mt. 15, 39)

Olivi	Catena in Mattheum
Firenze, Laur. S. Croce, Plut. X dext. 4. f°68rb	Linz 446, f° 145vb ; ed. Guarienti, p. 247
Dicit ergo : Dimissa turba. *Crisostomus, Sicut post miraculum quinque panum Dominus turbas dimisit, ita et nunc, nec recedit pedes, sed nauigio, ne turba eum sequatur.* *Et uenit in fines Macadan.*	Crisos. : *Sicut post miraculum quinque panum Dominus turbas dimisit, ita et nunc ; nec autem pedes recedit sed nauigio, ne turba eum sequatur [...]*
Mc. 8° *dicitur : Venit in partes Dalmanuta. Sed dicit Augustinus quod idem locus per utrumque nomen significatur. Vnde dicit quod plerique libri habent Macedii.*	Augustinus[1]. *Marcus autem dicit quod in Dalmanuta, nec est dubitandum eundem locum esse sub utroque nomine, nam plerique codices non habent, etiam secundum Marcum, nisi Mageda.*
Est autem Maceda secundum Rabanum regio circa Gerasam.	Rabanus[2]. *Est autem Mageda regio circa Gerasam et interpretatur poma [...]*

Voici maintenant le texte de Chrysostome, tel que Thomas pouvait le lire dans la traduction de Burgundio, seule alors accessible pour cette partie des *Homélies*[3] :

> *Et tunc enim et nunc turbas dimittens recessit in nauigium, sed et Iohannes hoc ait [...] Discessit post huius miraculi operationem, et neque pede abiit ut non sequerentur sed in nauigium.*

La citation d'Augustin n'est pas littérale dans la *Catena*, et bien que celle de Raban Maur le soit, il est clair qu'ici Olivi s'est servi de la *Catena* sans recourir directement aux *Homélies*.

Un cas particulièrement intéressant se présente, à propos de Mt. 10, 9-10 sur l'envoi en mission des Apôtres. Olivi fait ici usage des questions sur la pauvreté évangélique et critique longuement Thomas d'Aquin qui, dans sa *Somme de Théologie*[4], avait enseigné, *secundum aliorum sanctorum expositionem*, que les interdictions faites aux prédicateurs d'emporter besace ou vêtements en double n'étaient que provisoires et destinées à la première formation des Apôtres et avaient été abrogées après la Cène en Luc 22, 35. Dans sa longue critique, Olivi a cru identifier ces *alii sancti* grâce à la *Catena* sur Luc[5]. Il écrit donc[6] :

1. Augustinus, *De consensu euangelistarum*, II, 51, *C.S.E.L* 43, p. 215, ligne 5 : « *Hic sane ordinem etiam Marcus [...] hoc idem subicit quod Mattheus nisi quod Dalmanutha, quod in quibusdam codicibus legitur, nam dixit Mattheus, sed Mageddon. Non autem dubitandum est eundem locum esse sub utroque nomine, nam plerique codices non habent, etiam secundum Marcum, nisi Magedan* ».

2. Hrabanus Maurus, l. 5, ch. 15 *Comm. in Matth.*, *P.L.* 107, 986 C.

3. *Vaticano, BAV, Vat. lat.* 343, f 173rb.

4. Iª IIᵉ, q. 108, a. 2, ad 3.

5. Ed. Guarienti, II, p. 290b. L'extrait est tiré de la seconde homélie de Chrysostome *In illud : Salute Priscillam et Aquilam*, 2, *P.G.* 51, 199, *cf.* Krikônis, *op. cit.*, p. 480.

6. *Firenze, Laur. S. Croce*, Plut. X, d. 4, f 50ra.

Puto quod ipse <Thomas> hoc sumpsit ex uerbis Crisostomi que ipse recitat super illud Luce 22 : Quando misi uos sine sacco, etc. Dicit enim Crisostomus quod si docens natare supponit in principio manus suas ad sustinendum illum quem docet, postea uero manus abstrahens ut sibi opituletur, quinimmo et paulatim ipsum permergi permittit, ita Christus fecit discipulis. In exordiis quidem parans eis uberrime affluentiam omnium, unde dicit quod nichil defuit eis, et ubi oportebat proprias uires obstendere subtraxit eis aliquantulum gratiam iubens eis ex se non nulla peragere.

La citation de la *Catena* continue encore assez longuement et est presque littérale, ensuite de quoi Olivi donne brièvement sa propre interprétation de Chrysostome et passe à l'extrait suivant de la *Glosa*, tiré de Bède et également cité *ad litteram* et commenté. Il semble qu'Olivi a bien identifié, au moins en partie, les *alii sancti* de la *Somme* à la différence des différents éditeurs de celle-ci.

Il ne faudrait pas d'ailleurs croire qu'Olivi n'utilisait que la *Catena*. Dans le commentaire de Jean il lui arrive de se référer à Hugues de Saint-Cher[1]. Dans le commentaire de Matthieu, il cite parfois directement, tantôt l'*Opus Imperfectum* inauthentique[2], tantôt les homélies authentiques, données avec indication de leur numéro[3]. Une recherche plus attentive montrerait probablement la même chose pour d'autres Pères.

La *Catena* n'est pas la seule œuvre exégétique de saint Thomas utilisée par Olivi : il s'est aussi largement servi, dans son commentaire de Job, de celui du maître dominicain, quitte à le critiquer au passage[4]. On sait que c'était là une attitude normale chez les auteurs médiévaux.

Pour revenir à la *Catena,* il semble que l'usage qu'en fait Olivi soit dicté avant tout par un désir d'enrichir sa connaissance des écrits patristiques et d'y trouver des exégèses autres que celles qu'il trouvait dans les *auctoritates* latines classiques. La recherche des sources patristiques d'Olivi dans ses différentes œuvres ne sera probablement pas très aisée, mais elle sera aussi très probablement extrêmement intéressante. De toute façon nous avons vu dans cette comparaison un double témoignage, d'une part sur la rapide diffusion de la *Catena*, de l'autre sur l'emploi intelligent que pouvaient en faire des théologiens qui n'avaient pourtant aucune sympathie pour beaucoup de positions de saint Thomas.

1. Petrus Iohannis, *Super Iohannem* 4, 5 : *Firenze, Laur. S : Croce* Plut X, d. 8, f. 30rb. ; *Catena in Io.* ed. Guarienti, II, p. 382.

2. Petrus Iohannis *Super Mt.* II, 2, f° 11rb. – Ps.- Chrysostomus, *Opus imperfectum in Mt. P.G.*, 56, 657-658.

3. Petrus Iohannis, *Super Mt :* II, 2, f° 11rb. ; Ioh. Chrys. *Hom. In Mt.* 6, *P.G.* 57.

4. Saint Thomas d'Aquin, *Opera omnia*, t. 26, Rome, 1965, p. 17*, 36*-37*.

VON GÖTTLICHER IN MENSCHLICHER LIEBE ÜBERLEGUNGEN ZUM CANTICUM-KOMMENTAR DES FR. PETRUS JOHANNIS OLIVI O. MIN.

Johannes Schlageter O.F.M.

OLIVIS HOHELIEDKOMMENTAR IN DER GESCHICHTLICHEN ENTWICKLUNG SEINES DENKENS

Die neueren Arbeiten über Geschichte und Denken des provençalischen Franziskaners Petrus Johannis Olivi führen bereits zur Frage, wo die Dynamik seines Lebens geistlich-religiös verwurzelt ist[1]. Er ist ja nicht nur Parteigänger und theologischer Gewährsmann einer bestimen Richtung in Orden und Kirche, der von der Endzeitprophetie Joachims von Fiore beein flußten franziskanischen Reformbewegung[2]. Olivi ist ein geistlicher Denker im eigentlichen Sinn, der ganz von Einsichten und Optionen einer biblischen Spiritualität ausgeht, wie vor allem David Flood in seinen Arbeiten deutlich gemacht hat[3].

Schon von Anfang an hat für den jungen franziskanischen Lehrer das Studium besonders der Heiligen Schrift den entscheidenden Beweggrund in der « *Glut der Liebe* ». Es « *muß bewegen die Glut der Liebe. Denn die Erkenntnis des Göttlichen bringt der Liebe vielfältige Nahrung ihrer Glut. Denn sie unterstützt*

1. Vgl. etwa J. Schlageter Ed., *Das Heil der Armen und das Verderben der Reichen. Petrus Johannis Olivi – Die Frage nach der höchsten Armut*, Werl, 1989, 17f Anm 2, 25f Anm 33; Petrus Ioannis Olivi, *De usu paupere. The* Quaestio *and the* Tractatus, D. Burr ed., Firenze – Perth/Australia, 1992, XXXI-XXXIV; D. Burr, *Olivi's Peaceable Kingdom. A Reading of the Apokalypse Commentary*, Philadelphia, 1993 [= University of Pennsylvania MA Series(besonders « Preface » (IX-XII). Abkürzungen nach S. Schwertner, *Internationales Abkürzungsverzeichnis für Theologie und Grenzgebiete*, Berlin-New York, 1976.

2. Diese Seite Olivis ist besonders eindringlich dargestellt bei D. Burr, *The persecution of Peter Olivi*, Philadelphia, 1976. Vgl. für die Literatur S. Gieben, *Bibliographia Oliviana (1885-1967)*, *CFr* 38, 1968, p. 106-170 und Pietro di Giovanni Olivi, *Scritti scelti*, ed. P. Vian, Roma, 1989 [= Fonti christiane per il terzo millenio 3], p. 47-61.

3. Vgl. dazu schon J. Schlageter « Petrus Johannis Olivi », in : H. von der Bey, J.B. Freyer, (Hg.), *Die Franziskanische Bewegung. Bd.: Geschichte und Spiritualität*, Mainz, 1996, p. 113-117. Besonders aber siehe D. Flood, « Peter John Olivi. A Search for a Theology and Anthropology of the Synoptik Gospels », in : K.B. Osborne Ed., *The History of Franciscan Theology*, St. Bonaventure / N.Y., 1994, p. 127-184. *Grundlegend* für Olivis geistliche Option sind seine « *Principia quinque in Sacram Scripturam* », die neu ediert sind : Peter of John Olivi on the Bible : *Principia quinque in Sacram Scripturam, Postilla in Isaiam et in I ad Corinthios,* Appendix : *Quaestio de Oboedientia et Sermones duo de S. Francisco*, ed. by D. Flood and G. Gál, St. Bonaventure / NY, 1997 (*Olivi on the Bible*).

sie mit Gründen: mit den Gegenstand betreffenden, ohne die die Liebe nicht bestehen kann; mit anleitenden, ohne die die Liebe nicht richtig vorgehen kann; mit anregenden, ohne die die Liebe nicht leicht aufwallen und erglühen kann; mit vertiefenden, indem sie ihr ihres Geliebten unermeßliche und unzählige, übersteigende, entzückende und hinaufführende Gründe darbietet. Wie sie einmal sagt: 'Schön an Gestalt vor den Menschenkindern' (vgl. Ps 45, 3 Vg.). *Und im Hohenlied: 'Mein Geliebter ist hell glänzend und rötlich schimmernd'* (Hld. 5, 10) *usw. 'Seine Kehle ist sehr süß, und er ganz ersehnenswert'* (Hld 5, 16). *Zu Recht sagt daher der Apostel im 1. Brief an Timotheus: 'Die Erfüllung des Gebotes ist die Liebe'* (vgl. 1 Tim 1, 5 Vg). *Und Christus sagt bei Matthäus im 22. Kapitel, daß an den beiden Geboten der Liebe das ganze Gesetz hängt und die Propheten»* (Mt 22, 40)[1]. Daß Olivi hier auf den «*Geliebten*» des Hohenliedes hinweist, macht deutlich, daß dieses Bild ihm schon für seinen geistlichen und theologischen Weg der Liebe als wesentliche Zielorientierung vor Augen steht. So sieht er in ähnlichem Zusammenhang gerade in den kanonisch (hebräisch) tradierten Büchern «*Salomos*» die maßgebende Wegstrecke mit der Heiligen Schrift vorgedeutet[2]:

> Den Anfängern im Aufstieg zu Gott begegnet die Schrift als allgestaltig, und ihnen steht es zu, die vielen Sprichwörter Salomos zu lesen und seine vielgestaltigen Gleichnisse. Denen aber, die voranschreiten bis zum Ende der Stufenleiter, wann auch die Leiter selbst zurückzulassen ist, begegnet sie als nichtgestaltig, und ihnen steht es zu, Kohelet zu lesen, der von der Nichtachtung der Welt handelt. Denen aber, die eintreten in Gottes Brautgemach, begegnet sie ganz als eingestaltig, und das im Hohenlied [...] Sie (die Schrift) aber ist schöner gestaltet als die Sonne. Über alle Ordnung der Sterne findet man sie im Vergleich des Lichtes ursprünglicher. Wie sie nämlich im Blick auf ihren Ursprung heller Glanz des ewigen Lichtes ist und im Blick auf ihre Materie Spiegel von Gottes Majestät, so ist sie gemäß ihrer Form Bild seiner Güte.

1. Siehe *Principium I. in Sacram Scripturam* [De studio] § 6: «*Tertio debet movere caritatis ardor. Notitia enim divinorum administrat caritati multiplex fomentum ardoris. Subministrat enim sibi rationes: obiectivas, sine quibus caritas non potest subsistere; directivas, sine quibus caritas non debet recte incedere; incitativas, sine quibus caritas non potest faciliter ebullire et inardescere; inabyssativas, tradendo videlicet sibi sui dilecti rationes immensas et innumeras, transcendentes, exstaticas et anagogicas; ut quando ait* (Ps 44, 3): Speciosus forma prae filios hominum. *Et Canticum* (Ct 5,10): Dilectus meus candidus et rubicundus usw. Guttur illius suavissimum, et totus desiderabilis (Ct 5, 16). *Propter quod merito Apostolus I ad Timotheum 1, 5 dicit:* Finis praecepti est caritas. *Et Christus, Matthaei* (Mt 22, 40), *dicit quod in in duobus mandatis caritatis universa lex pendet et prophetae*». Nach: *Olivi on the Bible*, a.a. O. 21.

2. Vgl. *Principium II. In Sacram Scripturam* [De Causis] § 46-47: «*Inchoantibus igitur divinas ascensiones occurrit scriptura ut omniformis, et istis competit legere multa proverbia Salomonis et multiformes parabolas eius. Progredientibus vero usque ad finem scalae, quando et ipsa scala est reliquenda, occurrit ut nulliformis, et istis competit legere Ecclesiasten, qui est de contemptu mundi. Intrantibus vero Dei thalamum occurrit tota uniformis, et in Canticis (?) Canticorum [...] Haec igitur est speciosior sole. Super omnem stellarum dispositionem luci comparata invenitur prior. Nam sicut per respectum ad suam originem est candor lucis aeternae, et per respectum ad materiam est speculum Dei maiestatis, sic secundum suam formam est imago bonitatis illius*» (*Olivi on the Bible*, a.a. O. 62). Nach dem bei Olivi üblichen Sprachgebrauch muß es hier wohl heißen «*in Cantico Canticorum*».

Der Primat der Liebe, wie ihn Olivi in der Heiligen Schrift entdeckt, bestimmt seine Auseinandersetzung mit dem zeitgenössischen Denken wie auch seine Auffassung evangelischer Armut und seine geschichtstheologische Parteinahme[1].

Bereits als der franziskanische Lehrer über die «Sentenzen des Petrus Lombardus» zu lehren beginnt, geht es Olivi in seiner grundlegenden Auseinandersetzung mit dem philosophischen Menschenbild damaliger Aristoteles-Rezeption um die Verteidigung der menschlichen Freiheit, wobei er die ungeheuere Bedeutung der Liebe betont[2]:

> Im Streben und im Lieben nämlich hat das Sinnen eine solche Höhe und Weite, daß keine größere Macht zu lieben oder zu streben erdacht werden kann. Selbst Gott und universal allen Sinngrund irgendeines Guten kann das Sinnen auf unaussprechliche Weise erstreben. Und es kann nicht irgendeine Weise zu lieben uns begegnen, die der Wille nicht auf irgendeine Weise haben kann. Im Vergleich zur Liebe ist kein höherer und erfreulicherer Akt zu finden. Und im Vergleich zur Liebe, wodurch Gott geliebt wird, das einfachste, unbedingteste, erhabenste Gut, ist kein einfacherer, unbedingterer, erhabenerer Akt zu finden, ja vielmehr kann ihm keiner darin verglichen werden.

Allerdings gibt es für Olivi im Menschen die liebende Freiheit und die freigewählte Liebe in unterschiedlicher individueller und sozialer Verwirklichung; denn von Gott her läßt sich eine heilsgeschichtliche Steigerung ihrer Dynamik und Wirklichkeit erhoffen, ja erfahren[3]. Und dafür ist Olivi gerade als franziskanischer Lehrer engagiert.

1. Vgl. besonders die Arbeiten von E. Stadter, «Das Glaubensproblem in seiner Bedeutung für die Ethik bei P.J. Olivi. Ein Beitrag zur Geschichte der Ethik und Religionsphilosophie im Mittelalter», *F.S.* 42, 1960, p. 225-296; «Das Problem der Theologie bei P.J. Olivi. Auf Grund gedruckter und ungedruckter Quellen», *F.S.* 43, 1961, p. 113-170; «Offenbarung und Heilsgeschichte nach P.J. Olivi», *F.S.* 44, 1962, p. 1-13, 129-191; «Die spiritualistische Geschichtstheologie als Voraussetzung für das Verständnis von fides und auctoritas bei P.J. Olivi», *F.S.* 48, 1966, p. 243-253; *Psychologie und Metaphysik der menschlichen Freiheit. Die ideengeschichtliche Entwicklung zwischen Bonaventura und Duns Scotus*, München-Paderborn-Wien, 1971.

2. *Summa quaestionum* (In Sent. II.) q. 57 R: «*In appetendo enim et in amando tantam habet mens altitudinem et latitudinem quod non potest excogitari maior potestas amandi seu appetendi; nam et Deum et universaliter omnem rationem cuiuscumque boni potest mens ineffabiliter appetere, nec potest nobis occurrere aliquis modus amandi quem voluntas non possit aliquo modo habere. Si igitur amore non potest aliquis actus altior neque iucundior, nec amore quo Deus amatur qui est bonum simplicissimum et absolutissimum et abstractissimum potest invenire aliquis actus simplicior, absolutior et abstractior, immo nec aliquis sibi potest aequari in istis*» (P.I. Olivi: *Quaestiones in Librum II. Sententiarum*, ed. B. Jansen, Bd. 2, Quaracchi, 1924, 330f).

3. Vgl. J. Schlageter, «Die Auseinandersetzung zwischen griechischem und biblischem Menschenbild im franziskanischen Freiheitsverständnis des Petrus Johannis Olivi», *Wissenschaft und Weisheit* 60, 1997, p. 65-86.

Den «erhabensten Grad des Gottesliebe» sieht deshalb Olivi in der «höchsten Armut»[1], in einem voll verwirklichten evangelischen Armwerden[2]:

> Wer um der Liebe Gottes willen die Höhe und Schwierigkeit solcher Armut annimmt, erweist seine Liebe zu Gott unvergleichlich umfassender, als wer zu ihr nicht hinaufsteigt, außer wenn er in etwas anderem ihr Gleichwertigem das übersteigt. Daher schließt diese Armut, um Gottes willen angenommen, den erhabensten Grad der Gottesliebe in sich ein wie eine Wirkung ihre Ursache, und sie übt ihn ein [...] Deswegen heißt es im Hohenlied letztes Kapitel: 'wenn ein Mensch das ganze Vermögen seines Hauses für die Liebe gäbe, achtete er es für nichts' (Hld 8, 7). Dabei will es, daß die Gottesliebe, wenn sie glühend ist – und von ihr spricht es vorher –, alles Vermögen der Welt für nichts achtet. Und weil sie durch diese Nichtachtung das Sinnen trennt vom Weltlichen, wie der Tod die Seele vom Leib, deswegen sagt es vorher: 'stark wie der Tod ist die Liebe' (Hld 8, 6). Und weil sie durch diese Nichtachtung alles Begehren verzehrt wie ein starkes Feuer Fäden oder Hölzer, daher heißt es vorher: 'hart wie die Unterwelt ist die Eifersucht', die dasselbe ist wie ungestüme Liebe Gottes, und 'ihre Fackeln sind wie Fackeln voll Feuer und Flammen' (ebd.).

Den «*erhabensten Grad der Gottesliebe*», wie er sich in der von Franziskus erneuerten Armut Jesu Christi manifestiert, sieht Olivi also schon nahegelegt durch die Schriften des Ersten Testamentes, ganz besonders durch die Liebeslyrik des Hohenliedes. Denn gerade es führt in seinem geistlichen Verständnis in die höchste Liebeseinigung mit Gott in Jesus Christus.

1. Von der «*Erhabenheit der* höchsten Armut», spricht Franziskus im 6. Kapitel der «Bullierten Regel», und für ihn besteht sie in Erneuerung des armen Lebensweges Jesu im Leitbild der «Herrin Armut» für seiner und seiner Brüder Jesusnachfolge. Vgl. RegB VI in: *Opuscula S. P. Francisci Assisiensis*, ed. C. Esser, Grottaferrata 1978, 232; *Die Schriften des hl. Franziskus v. Assisi*, hg. v. L. Hardick, E. Grau, 6. Aufl., Werl 1980, 165f.

2. *Quaestio de Perfectione Evangelica* (QPE) *VIII.* (R. I. 11.5): «*Ergo qui propter Dei amorem altitudinem et difficultatem tantae paupertatis assumit, amplius incomparabiliter Deum diligere comprobatur quam illie qui ad eam non assurgit, nisi forte in aliquo alio huic aequivalenti excedat. Paupertas igitur haec pro Deo assumpta altissimum gradum divini amoris videtur in se includere sicut effectum suam causam et altissimum gradum divini amoris exercitare [...] Propter quod Canticum ultimo capitulo dicitur quod* 'si dederit homo omnem substantiam domus suae pro dilectione, quasi nihil despiciet eam' (Ct 8, 7). *In quo vult quod Dei dilectio, si sit fervens – quia de hac loquitur sicut ex praecedentibus patet – despicit totam mundi substantiam quasi nihil. Et quia per hunc despectum separat mentem a mundanis sicut mors animam a corpore, ideo praemiserat quod* 'fortis est ut mors dilectio' (Ct 8, 6). *Et quia consumit omnem cupiditatem per hunc despectum sicut ignis fortis fila vel ligna, ideo etiam praemiserat quod* 'dura sicut infernus aemulatio' *– quae est idem quod vehemens Dei amor – et quod* 'lampades eius sunt lampades ignis atque flammarum'» (ib.). Siehe J. Schlageter, ed.: Das Heil der Armen, a.a. O. 110. Vgl. auch Olivis Auslegung zu Hld 8, 6-7 in: Petrus Johannis Olivi, *Expositio in Canticum Canticorum*, § 338-341. Hier wie dann in der kritischen Edition selbst werden die Paragraphen nach der Edition von B. Bonelli, *S. Bonaventurae Operum omnium Supplementum*, Tom. I, Trentino, 1772, p. 50-281, angegeben. So bleibt ein Vergleich mit dieser Edition möglich. Vgl. schon J. Schlageter: Die Bedeutung des Hoheliedkommentars des Franziskanertheologen P.J. Olivi (+1298). Argumente für eine neue Edition, in: *Wissenschaft und Weisheit* 58, 1995, p. 137-151.

DIE ZENTRALE BEDEUTUNG VON OLIVIS HOHELIED-AUSLEGUNG

Olivi distanziert sich nun grundsätzlich von einer Deutung des Hohenliedes auf *bloß* «*fleischliche Liebe*» und verwirft sie im Einklang mit kirchlicher Tradition als «*ketzerisch*»[1]. Damit scheint er die von alters her überlieferten Vorwürfe gegen Theodor von Mopsuestia (+ 428) aufzugreifen[2], die er dann noch zuspitzt. Denn in der biblisch überlieferten Hochzeit zwischen König Salomo und einer Pharaonentochter (1 Kö 3, 1), auf die hin Theodor das Hohelied gedeutet hatte, geht es nach Olivi um keine *natürliche* menschliche Liebes-Beziehung, sondern um eine verwerfliche, «*verderbte Liebe*», die selbstsüchtigen («*fleischlichen*») Interessen und wollüstigem Sich-Ausleben dient. Doch Olivi will nicht jedweden Bezug des Textes auf den erotisch-sexuellen Bereich einer menschlichen Liebes-Beziehung abstreiten[3]:

> Solltest du nun einwenden, daß es in diesem Buch vieles gibt, was nach fleischlicher Liebe schmeckt, das aber könnte man anscheinend nicht übertragen auf eine geistliche Liebe hin, weil sie einander sehr gegensätzlich sind und in vieler Hinsicht unähnlich und ungleichförmig. Dann gilt es zu wissen: Es ist sinnvoll, daß uns die Heilige Schrift genau belehrt, alles Sinnenhafte führe uns zu Gott zurück, jedoch in ehrenhaften und keuschen Weisen. Gott hat es ja erschaffen zu seiner Vergegenwärtigung und zu unserer Führung. Daher enthält das alles seiner Natur und Bestimmung nach gewiß nichts Unehrbares, es sei denn infolge unseres Gebrechens. Demgemäß werden wir also in diesem Buch wie an vielen anderen Stellen durch sinnenhafte Liebe hingeführt zu geistlicher, ganz und gar göttlicher Liebe sowie durch sinnenhafte Form und Schönheit zu geistigem Glanz. Und es ist nicht verwunderlich, weil auch aus göttlicher Einsetzung die fleischliche Ehe und deren fleischliche Vereinigung Sakrament Christi und der Kirche sind.

Insofern also das «*Fleischliche*» nichts anderes meint als die leibliche, sinnenhaft wahrnehmbare Dimension einer menschlichen Liebes-Beziehung gerade auch in ihrem erotisch-sexuellen Vollzug, ist es durchaus *natürlich* und von Gott geschaffen. Mag es auch zu verderben sein durch menschliche Gebrechlichkeit, so bleibt es doch aufgrund seiner geschöpflichen und sogar gottgesetzten Bestimmung Sakrament und Symbol, transparent für seine

1. Vgl. *Exp. in Ct.* Prologus §. 14.
2. Siehe dazu etwa H. Haag, K. Elliger, « *Und wenn er mich doch küßte [...]* » Das Hohe Lied der Liebe, Solothurn-Düsseldorf [2]1993, 100.
3. Ebd. § 19 : « *Si vero obiicias quod in libro isto multa sunt quae carnalem amorem sapiunt, talia autem non videntur posse transumi ad spiritualem amorem, cum sint sibi valde contrarii multumque dissimiles et difformes : sciendum quod decuit per scripturam sacram nos edoceri, omnia sensibilia nos in Deum reducere sub modis tamen honestis et castis. Si enim Deus ea condidit, et hoc ad sui repraesentationem et nostram manuductionem : constat quod secundum suam naturam et secundum rectam institutionem eorum nihil continent inhonestum nisi solum ex nostro vitio. Secundum hoc ergo tam in libro isto quam in plerisque aliis locis per sensibiles amores ducimur ad sprituales divinissimosque amores et per sensibiles formas et pulchritudines ad intellectuales decores. Nec mirum, quia etiam ex divino instituto coniugium carnale et eius carnalis copula sunt sacramentum Christi* ».

geistig-geistliche, ja eigentlich göttliche Tiefendimension, die Liebes-Beziehung zwischen Gott und dem Menschen[1]:

> [...] der Zitherspieler bringt so aus den Sehnen eines toten Tieres sowie aus einem zerbrechlichen und ausgehöhlten Holzstück harmonischen Klang und süße Melodie hervor. Was wundert es also, wenn es der Heilige Geist versteht, durch den Mund seiner Heiligen in einer Art geistlicher Übertragung von der ehelichen Vereinigung her uns das Lied der göttlichen Liebe zu dichten? Daher ist es beachtlich und bemerkenswert, daß du in diesem Buch kein Wort findest, in dem die Abscheulichkeit eines schamlosen Tuns anklingt. Wundersam ehrenhaft werden ja die Beispiele aus den sinnenhaften Formen und Wonnen genommen, die man in einer königlichen Vermählung zu finden pflegt.

Ein solches Verständnis ist für Olivi keine ins Hohelied hineingetragene *künstliche* Allegorese[2], sondern ist der geistliche, eigentliche Sinn jener Liebe zwischen Bräutigam und Braut, die oberflächlich gesehen nichts anders ist als menschliche Liebe[3]. Daß gerade hier menschliche Liebe sich in Metaphern, in Bildern und kühnen Vergleichen ausdrückt, die den Bereich des bloß und einfach Menschlichen weit zu übersteigen scheinen, kommt der tieferen, geistlichen Deutung Olivis entgegen.

Mit der Distanz gegenüber einer zu allegorischen Deutung erhält sich Olivi die Offenheit für möglichst alle Sprachformen menschlicher Liebe im Hohenlied. Denn alle Sprache menschlicher Liebe, jedenfalls sofern sie nicht sittlich fragwürdig oder gar unannehmbar erscheint, kann transparent werden für das eigentliche Geschehen göttlicher Liebe. So sehr Olivis Auslegung von seiner mystischen Einsicht und geschichtstheologischen Konzeption bestimmt ist, kann er doch flexibel mit dem Text selbst arbeiten. Daher verkraftet er es z. B. auch, daß die von ihm konzipierte Fruchtbarkeit göttlicher Liebe bei den Liebenden des Hohenliedes nicht so deutlich zum Vorschein kommt: Aus jetziger Sicht stehen eben individuelle wie universale Vollendung noch aus[4].

Diese Offenheit für das Text-Geschehen selbst wird erst recht deutlich, wenn man Olivis Auslegung etwa mit der vorhergehenden des Johannes Peckham in Beziehung setzt[5]. Bei Peckham wird der Text durchweg christologisch gedeutet, was die Bilder der Liebe zwischen Bräutigam und Braut weithin zu einer

1. Ebd. § 20: « *Sic etiam citharaedus ex nervis animalis mortui et ligno fragili et concavo trahit cantum harmonicum et melodiam suavem. Quid igitur mirum, si de copula coniugali Spiritus Sanctus per ora sanctorum suorum sciverit nobis per quasdam spirituales transumptiones depromere Canticum divini amoris? Unde notanter est animadvertendum quod in toto libro isto non invenies unum verbum quod sonet foeditatem actus impudici, sed sub mira honestate trahuntur exempla a sensibilibus formis et deliciis quae in regali connubio inveniri solent* ».

2. Das meint Olivi wohl, wenn er zum Schluß in seinem « *Epilogus* » das tiefere « moralische Mysterium », « frei von Allegorischem », vorführen will (ebd. § 361). Das ist ein anderes Verständnis von Schriftauslegung, als es in den späteren Zusätzen wie etwa in der Edition B. Bonellis auftaucht.

3. Das ist eben der « *tropus* », die bildhafte Redeweise, in der nur von menschlicher Liebe die Rede zu sein scheint, die aber Olivi auf ihren tieferen, eigentlichen geistlich-göttlichen Sinn zu deuten versucht.

4. Das erklärt wohl auch Olivis Zurückhaltung im Schlußsatz des « *Epilogus* », sich diesen letzten Aufstieg der Liebe selbst zuzuschreiben (siehe *Exp. in Ct.* Epil. § 370).

5. Vgl. dazu Johannes Peckham: *In Canticum Canticorum* (Siena, Bibl. Com. U. V. 2, f°1v-64v).

vorgefaßten und bestimmten Deutung bringt. Bei Olivi ist zwar die Beziehung auf die Geschichte Christi und seiner Kirche in der Geschichte göttlicher Liebe stets gegeben, weil sie schon in ihrem Ursprung darauf hinausläuft. Aber im Hohelied erscheint die Menschwerdung Christi *ausdrücklich* nur an «*passenden*»[1] Punkten des Textes. Gerade die noch unerfüllte *Sehnsucht* der Liebe, die in diesen Texten so deutlich zur Sprache kommt, soll in Erinnerung und Feier neu gegenwärtig werden. So erst wird die ersehnte Erfüllung selbst neu zu Tage und zum Tragen kommen. Für Olivi ist das die Basis genug für eine mystische Deutung seines Geschicks und geschichtstheologische Deutung seiner Zeit.

Davon spricht Olivi in seiner Hohenliedauslegung eher verhalten. Doch weil er hier die Liebe auf ihrem Weg in einem schmerzhaften Ablösungsprozeß sieht, kann das zuerst auf die Trennung der Urkirche von der Synagoge angewandt werden, aber ähnlich auf die Aus-Einander-Setzung, in die er selbst verwickelt wird[2]:

> Wenn die « Hüter » (5, 7a) oder Wächter der « Stadt » hier als die verwerflichen Vorgesetzten und Lehrer genommen werden, dann bedeutet, daß die Braut von ihnen geschlagen und verletzt wird, die starke Verwerfung ihrer beschaulichen und forschenden Glut, die die fleischlichen und verwerflichen Vorgesetzten verabscheuen. Doch deswegen wird das Sinnen, das glüht vor Sehnsucht nach dem Bräutigam, mit einem stärkeren Pfeil der Liebe verwundet. Denn ein Hindernis, das man einem großen und ungestümen Fluß in den Weg stellt, läßt dessen Überschwemmung und treibende Wirkung anwachsen. So bricht das Hindernis, wenn es nicht vorher entfernt worden ist, und dann wird er viel ungestümer als zuvor übersprudeln und herabstürmen. So ist es auch im vorliegenden Fall. Mit dem « Entreißen » des « Mantels » (7d) ist das Entfernen der Hülle jener Zeit zu verstehen. Denn infolge der Verfolgung, die der Kirche von Schriftgelehrten und Priestern der Juden angetan wurde, wurde die fellartige Hülle der Gebräuche und des tötenden Buchstabens kraftvoller von ihr zurückgelassen. Und so sieh ähnliches in jeder ähnlichen Zeit. Sie nehmen ihr auch weg den « Mantel » der Scham, wodurch sie nicht so ungescheut wagte, öffentlich allem nachzugehen, was höher ihrem Stand entspricht. Daher wird sie

1. Das ist wohl gemeint, wenn es in der vermutlich besseren Version des «*Incipit*» heißt: «*In speculo brevi et* apto» (*Exp. in Ct.* Prol., § 1).

2. Vgl. besonders *Exp. In Ct.* Cap. V, § 228-229: «*Si enim* 'custodes' (7a) *seu vigiles 'civitatis' pro malis praelatis et doctoribus hic sumantur, tunc sponsae ab eis percussio et vulneratio significat fortem exprobrationem sui contemplativi et inquisitivi ardoris quem praelati carnales et reprobi abominantur. Et tamen ex hoc mens sponsi desiderio ardens fortiori amoris iaculo vulneratur; quia sicut obstaculum flumini grandi et impetuoso appositum eius inundantiam et impulsivam efficaciam excrescere facit ita quod irrumpit obstaculum, nisi sit prius amotum, ac deinde longe impetuosius quam prius insilit et decurrit, sic et est in proposito [...] Per ablationem vero* 'pallii' (7c) *intelligitur amotio velaminis illius temporis. Sicut enim ex persecutione illata ecclesiae a scribis et sacerdotibus Iudaeorum pelliceum velamen caeremonialium et litterae occidentis est fortius ab ea relictum, sic et in omnibus consimilibus consimilia intuere. Tollunt etiam sibi* 'pallium' *erubescentiae quo non sic inerubescibiliter audebat publice prosequi omnia altius competentia statui suo. Unde ex persecutionibus inerubescibilior redditur ad quaerendum, et hoc in tantum quod etiam a communi vulgo imperfectorum non erubescit quaerere sponsum et sui amoris languorem quasi quamdam sui miseriam eorum subsidio relevandam eis absque erubescentia propalare*».

> aus den Verfolgungen ungescheuter zurückkehren zur Suche, und das so sehr, daß sie sie auch vor dem allgemeinen Volk der Unvollkommenen nicht schämt, den Bräutigam zu suchen und die Schwäche ihrer Liebe gleichsam als ihre Not, die durch deren Hilfe zu beheben ist, ohne Schamröte bekannt zu machen.

Hier kommt Olivis eigenes Geschick in Erinnerung, wie er es besonders deutlich in seinem «*Brief an R.*»[1] geistlich verarbeitet. Die persönliche Bedrängnis, die ihm im Orden widerfährt, feuert Olivis Eifer für den geistlichen Höchststand der gemeinsamen Lebensform eher an. Denn die Bedrängnis, die er erleben muß, und die Demütigung, die ihm zugemutet wird, wird für ihn geradezu zum Wahrheits-Zeichen, daß er Jesus Christus besonders nahe kommt[2]:

> O heller Vernunft-Grund, fruchtbar an himmlischen Mysterien und voll überweltlicher Weisheit, die die Fürsten dieser Welt nicht erkennen (vgl. 1 Kor 2, 5). Wenn sie erkännten, liebten sie über alles die Demut Christi. Meine geliebtesten Brüder! Wo keine Furcht ist, da zittert nicht vor Furcht, sondern freut euch eher mit mir, der ich bis zu den Zeichen der Wahrheit durchtrage. Darum beginne ich, von den Menschen verworfen zu werden, damit ich erst gänzlich lerne, ja sogar gezwungen werde, mit den Demütigen zusammen zu spüren, wo der Sitz der Wahrheit ist und wo die Wurzel der Weisheit offenbart wird.

Es ist die «*Verwerfung*» durch die Vorgesetzten und Lehrer, auf die und deren Unkenntnis der «*überweltlichen Weisheit*» Olivi mit dem Hinweis im Präsenz auf die «*Unkenntnis der Fürsten dieser Welt*» anspielt[3]. Aber erst durch diese Verwerfung gelangt er mit den Demütigen auf dem Weg Jesu Christi zum «*Sitz der Wahrheit*» und zur «*Wurzel der Weisheit*», wo Gottes demütige Liebe sich im äußerstem Einsatz und Durchtragen menschlicher Liebe offenbart.

Das ist es, was Olivi anhand seiner Erfahrung in des alle Hindernisse überwindenden Liebesdynamik des Hohenliedes erkennen kann. Es ist also

1. Siehe Petrus Johannis Olivi: *Quodlibeta. Impugnatio. Defensiones*, Venedig, 1509 (Druckerei: Lazaro de' Soardi), 51va-53rb; dazu auf anderer handschriftlicher Basis Gratien de Paris, «Une lettre inédite de P. de Jean Olivi», *Etudes Franciscaines* 29, 1913, p. 412-422. Vgl. zum Ganzen D. Burr, *The persecution of P. Olivi*, a.a. O. p. 35-40. Wer der Adressat des Briefes war, ist immer noch nicht klar, wenn auch der Hinweis des einen Manuskripts (Paris, Bibl. Nationale, Nouv. acqu. 774, f°94r) auf *Raimundus Gaufredi* (Generalminister 1289/95) nicht ohne Wert scheint. Jedenfalls richtet sich der Brief offensichtlich an Gesinnungsfreunde, die Olivi in einigen sie beunruhigenden Punkten über seine Rechtgläubigkeit aufklären möchte. Vgl. auch Gratien de Paris, *Histoire de la Fondation et l'Evolution de l'Ordre des Frères mineurs au XIIIe siècle*, Roma, 1982, 364f.

2. Olivi, *Quodlibeta [...] Defensiones*, ebd. 51va, «*O luculenta ratio caelestibus mysteriis fecunda et supermundana sapientia plena, quam principes huius mundi ignorant* (cf. 1 Cor 2, 8). *Si enim cognoscerent, super omnia humilitatem Christi amarent. Fratres mei dilectissimi! Ubi non est timor, nolite trepidare timore, sed mihi potius congaudete, qui usque ad signa veritatis perfero, quod ab hominibus reprobari incipio, ut omnino addiscam, immo et cogar cum humilibus consentire, ubi est sedes veritatis et ubi solum radix sapientiae revelatur*». Siehe Gratien de Paris, «Une lettre inédite», a.a. O. 416.

3. Daß auch die Höheren an Autorität gelegentlich einmal dem Urteil eines Untergebenen oder Jüngeren weichen müssen, erweist Olivi hier mit Argumenten, die die sonst anerkannte Hierarchie in Frage stellen (siehe ebd. 52vb; Gratien de Paris, «Une lettre inédite», a.a. O. 420). Vgl. dazu D. Burr, *The persecution of P. Olivi*, a.a. O. 39.

gerade die Verfolgungs situation, die Olivi, wie die Braut des Hohenliedes, den Gang an die Öffentlichkeit nicht mehr scheuen läßt und diesen Durchbruch inmitten von Bedrängnis als Weg göttlicher in menschlicher Liebe versteht und mitteilt.

Das ist zentral ein *spirituell-mystischer* Weg, aber durchaus mit *geschichtstheologischer* Basis und Konsequenz. Zu den Anklagen gegen Olivi gehörte ja schon, daß er « *wie ein Wahrsager Träumen und fantastischen Visionen folgt und es unternimmt, verwegen über zukünftige Ereignisse Voraussagen zu machen* »[1]. Ohne nun auf Olivis Verteidigung seiner geschichtstheologischen Konzepte im « *Brief an R.* » näher einzugehen, hier interessiert das *eine* Zukunftsdatum, das er seinen Freunden gegenüber ausdrücklich bekräftigt[2] :

> [...] dennoch ein gewisses allgemeines Zukunftsereignis halte ich mit Sicherheit fest, daß nämlich der Franziskus-Orden, nachdem er zuerst geschüttelt, gesiebt oder gesäubert wurde, auf dem ganzen Erdkreis die Gottesverehrung aufs höchste wiederherstellen wird oder vielmehr Gott durch ihn, sodaß er nach Überwindung der wilden Tiere die Gesamtheit oder die gesamten Reste der Juden und Völker in Christi Kirche hinein und zu Christi Sitz hin führen wird.

Das ist eine Überzeugung, die durch Olivis Werk hindurch geht[3]. Diese Überzeugung wirkt sich selbst in der Dynamik göttlicher in menschlicher Liebe aus, wie sie Olivi im Hohenlied zu erkennen glaubt. Aber Olivi formuliert seine geschichtstheologische Zukunftserwartung in seiner Auslegung des Hohenliedes sehr viel vorsichtiger und grundsätzlicher, als er das *Bild* auslegt, nach dem die Braut zweimal ihren « *Geliebten* » « *ins Haus ihrer Mutter* » einlädt[4] :

1. Olivi, *Quodlibeta [...] Defensiones*, a.a. O. 52vb-53ra : « *[...] a quibusdam mihi impingitur, quod instar augurii somnia sequor et quasdam fantasticas visiones et de futuris eventibus praedicendis temerarie me intermitto [...]* ». Siehe Gratien de Paris, « Une lettre inédite », a.a. O. 421. Vgl. dazu D. Burr, *The persecution of P. Olivi*, a.a. O. 39.

2. Olivi, *Quodlibeta [...] Defensiones*, a.a. O. 53ra-rb : « *Tamen quoddam universale futurum certitudinaliter teneo, scilicet quod ordo Francisci flagellis et tentationibus innumeris primitus excussus, cribratus aut expurgatus in universo orbe divinum cultum altissime reparabit seu potius Deus per eum, ita ut bestiis efferis expugnatis universitatem seu universa reliquias Iudaeorum et gentium in Christi ecclesiam introducat et ad Christi sedem adducat* ». Siehe Gratien de Paris, « Une lettre inédite », a.a. O. 421.

3. Vgl. etwa J. Schlageter, ed., *Das Heil der Armen*, a.a. O. 45ff, 158ff. Siehe auch : La caduta di Gerusalemme, *Il commento al Libro delle Lamentazioni* di Pietro di Giovanni Olivi, a cura di M. Bartoli, Roma, 1991 [=Nuovi Studi Storici 12] 32; *Olivi on the Bible: [...] Postilla in Isaiam [...]*, a.a. O. 166f, 278, 285.

4. Vgl. Hld 3, 4c und 8, 2ab. Dazu *Exp. in Ct.* Cap. VIII. § 324-325 : « *Signanter ponitur hoc hic et ibi, quod omnis spiritualis sponsa vel ecclesia circa suae spiritualis immutationis et transformationis solemne primordium singulariter afficitur ad consimilem transformationem ecclesiae vel religionis aut etiam parentalis cognationis de qua est naturaliter vel spiritualiter nata. Et idem est circa finem, quia tunc tamquam de hoc mundo cito abitura singularius anxiatur, si antequam abeat, non videat illos secum in Christo [...]. Hoc autem expressius et generalius locum habet in ecclesia Christi respectu synagogae matris suae quae – postquam per primum trinum ascensum fuit spiritus Christi lumine et dulcedine plenius confirmata – singulariter institit et optavit Christum introducere in domum et in cubiculum synagogae, ita ut Paulus ad Romanos nono dicat :* 'Optabam ego anathema esse pro fratribus meis' (Rm 9, 3), etc. *Et licet tunc ecclesia in toto non obtinuerit, obtinuit tamen in aliqua sui parte. Circa finem autem debet idem desiderium in ea fortius renovari et spes convertendi matrem suam non qualitercumque, sed ad Christi transformativam et ecstaticam unionem dabitur ei.*

> Bezeichnend steht das hier wie dort, da jede geistliche Braut oder Kirche im bedeutungsvollen Anfangsstadium ihrer geistlichen Umwandlung und Umgestaltung sich besonders um eine ähnliche Umgestaltung kümmert für die Kirche oder religiöse Gemeinschaft oder elterliche Verwandschaft, aus denen sie natürlich oder geistlich geboren wurde. Und dasselbe ereignet sich gegen Ende. Denn da sie rasch aus dieser Welt scheiden mag, geriete sie ganz besonders in Angst, sähe sie nicht, bevor sie scheidet, daß jene mit ihr in Christus sind [...] Das aber findet noch ausdrücklicher und allgemeiner seinen Raum in der Kirche Christi im Blick auf die Synagoge, ihre Mutter. Denn nachdem sie durch den ersten dreifachen Aufstieg mit Licht und Lieblichkeit des Geistes Christi voller bestärkt wurde, drängte sie besonders danach, Christus in das Haus und Ruhegemach der Synagoge einzuführen. So konnte Paulus im Römerbrief 9. Kapitel sagen : 'Ich wünschte, selbst verflucht zu sein um meiner Brüder willen' (Röm 9, 3) usw. Und mag die Kirche das damals nicht insgesamt erhalten haben, erhielt sie es doch zu einem Teil. Gegen Ende aber muß dieselbe Sehnsucht in ihr noch stärker erneuert werden, und es wird ihr die Hoffnung gegeben, ihre Mutter zu bekehren – nicht auf beliebige Weise, sondern zur umgestaltenden und ekstatischen Vereinigung mit Christus. Und was sie dann wünscht, wird sie in Fülle erhalten, wie der Apostel bezeugt : 'dann wird ganz Israel gerettet werden' (Röm, 26).

Der Wunsch, den Geliebten ins Haus der Mutter zu führen, bedeutet für Olivi nicht bloß eine Bestärkung und umfassendere Erfüllung menschlicher Liebe. Er sieht darin die geschichtliche Dynamik göttlicher Liebe selbst. Denn der Wunsch, jene Gemeinschaft oder Verwandschaft, aus der man hervorgangen ist, an der verwandelnden und umgestaltenden Kraft der Liebe teilhaben zu lassen, ergibt sich ja aus der Kraft der geistlichen Umgestaltung und Verwandlung selbst. So erscheint sie auf einem ersten geistlichen Höhepunkt bei Paulus, aber wird – wie dort schon vorausgesehen – am Ende neu aktuell. Und diese Erwartung einer « *umgestaltenden und ekstatischen Vereinigung mit Christus* », die möglichst umfassend auch Israel einbezieht, will Olivi nicht einfach auf unabsehbare Zeit vertagen. Durchaus im Sinne der urchristlichen Apokalyptik legt er sie drängend möglichst nahe und setzt sich schon gegenwärtig dafür ein[1]. Diese apokalyptische *Naherwartung* wird hier zum Glück nicht als franziskanisches Programm der Judenmission formuliert, wie es im « *Brief an R.* » und wohl auch in anderen Olivi-Texten aufgefaßt werden könnte. Sie erscheint grundsätzlicher als Ausdruck liebender Hoffnung für möglichst alle. Denn so taucht sie in der Erfahrung eigener geistlicher Verwandlung und

Et tunc quod optat, ita obtinebit ad plenum; ut teste Apostolo 'tunc omnis Israel salvus fiat' (Rm 11, 26). Siehe auch *Exp. in Ct.* Cap. III, § 143.

1. Es mag diese Nähe Israels zur urchristlichen und damit jüdischen Apokalyptik sein, die Olivi die apokalyptische Vision des Paulus der Rettung von ganz Israel so positiv aufnehmen läßt. Jedenfalls besteht hier eine Nähe Olivis zur apokalyptisch-messianischen Hoffnung des Judentums, die heute wieder aktuell werden könnte. Vgl. dazu unten Anm 29f, sowie J. Schlageter: Das Verhältnis von Philosophie und Theologie am Beispiel der « Frankfurter Schule », besonders bei Jürgen Habermas, in: S. Bonk, A. Lazzari (Hg.), *Ideen zu einer Integralen Anthropologie*, FSch K. Mácha, München, 1991, p. 385-400, besonders die Ausführungen über Walter Benjamin, 399f.

Umgestaltung allein aus Gottes Liebe und Erbarmen schon bei Paulus auf, und so wird sie bei Olivi im Anschluß an Joachim von Fiore [1], im Sinne des Franziskus von Assisi [2] neu Gegenwart.

Daß diese Hoffnung leider wieder verloren gehen konnte, zeigt sich im *Kontrastbeispiel* eines Textes von Johannes Duns Scotus, der die Zwangsbekehrung der Juden befürwortet [3]:

> [...] ich möchte glauben, es geschähe in religiöser Weise, wenn man die Eltern selbst mit Drohungen und Terror zwänge, die Taufe anzunehmen und sie nach ihrer Annahme zu bewahren. Denn mag es sein, daß sie in der Gesinnung nicht wahrhaft gläubig würden, wäre es dennoch für sie ein geringeres Böses, nicht ungestraft ihr unerlaubtes Gesetz ausüben zu können, als es frei ausüben zu können. Ebenso wären ihre Kinder, wenn man sie gut erzöge, in der dritten und vierten Generation wahrhaft gläubig. Und magst du sagen: nach der Prophetie Jesajas, die Paulus im Römerbrief 9. Kapitel zitiert: 'Am Ende wird der Rest Israels sich bekehren' (vgl. Jes 10, 21f; dazu Röm 9, 27) [4], dürften die Juden nicht insgesamt gezwungen werden, die Taufe anzunehmen und ihr Gesetz zu verlassen, antworte ich: ich zweifle nicht an der Wahrheit der Prophetie Christi, die Christus im Johannesevangelium 5. Kapitel anführt: 'Ich bin im Namen meines Vaters gekommen, und doch lehnt ihr mich ab. Wenn aber ein anderer in

1. Vgl. dazu J. Schlageter, «Olivis Sicht der Endzeit und Joachim von Fiore; Apokalyptisches Denken bei P.J. Olivi», *Wissenschaft und Weisheit* 50, 1987, p. 150-163, 13-27.

2. Vgl. dazu J. Schlageter, «Evangelisation im Verständnis der frühen franziskanischen Bewegung»; H. von der Bey, «Franziskanische Evangelisierung in den indianischen Kulturen Altamerikas» *Thuringia Franciscana NF* 51, 1996, p. 311-337, 447-487.

3. Johannes Duns Scotus, *Opus Oxoniense* IV d 4 q 9: «*Crederem religiose fieri si ipsi parentes cogerentur minis et terroribus ad suscipiendum Baptismum, et ad conservandum postea susceptum, quia esto quod ipsi non essent vere fideles in animo, tamen minus male esset eis, non posse impune legem suam illicitam servare, quam posse libere servare. Item filii eorum, si bene educerentur in tertia et quarta progenie, essent vere fideles. Et si dicas quod secundum prophetiam Isaiae quam recitat Paulus Rom. 9.* Reliquiae Israel convertentur in fide; *et ideo Judaeos non oportet cogere totaliter ad Baptismum suscipiendum et reliquendum legem suam. Respondeo, non dubito, quin vera sit prophetia Christi, quam recitat Christus Joan. 5.* Ego veni in nomine Patris mei, et non accepistis me; si alius venerit in nomine suo, illum suscipietis; *ergo ex verbo Christi erunt pervertendi, quia adhaerebunt illi pessimo Antichristo, de quo est sermo Christi praedictus. Et si dicas, quod visa destructio Antichristi, illi qui sibi adhaeserant, convertentur, dico pro tam paucis, et sic tarde convertendis, non oporteret totos Judaeos in tot partibus mundi, tantis temporibus sustinere in lege sua persistere, quia finalis fructus de eis Ecclesiae est, et erit modicus. Unde sufficeret aliquos paucos in aliqua insula sequestratos permitti legem suam servare, de quibus tandem illa prophetia Isaiae impleretur*» (Ed. Vivès XVI, 489). Ausgehend von der Frage nach der Erlaubtheit einer «Zwangstaufe» nichtchristlicher Kinder geht es besonders um den Einsatz von Zwang und Terror zur «*Judenkonversion*». Vgl. zum geschichtlichen Kontext (z. B. Vertreibung der Juden aus England 1290), J. Cohn, *The Pursuit of the Millenium. Europe's Inner Demons*, New York, 1970; J. Cohen, *The Friars and the Jews. The Evolution of Medieval Anti-Judaism*, London, 1970; H. von der Bey, «Dunkles Erinnern – Juden und Franziskaner», in H. von der Bey, J.B. Freyer (Hg.), *Die Franziskanische Bewegung*, Bd. 1, a.a.O. 148-157.

4. Die andere Aufassung, auf die hier Duns Scotus sich bezieht, könnte von Olivi stammen. Allerdings käme dann eher Olivis Auslegung des Jesaja-Buches in Frage, wo Olivi mit den entsprechenden Schriftstellen argumentiert. Vgl. dazu *Olivi on the Bible: [...] Postilla in Isaiam [...]*, a.a.O. 278, 285 (In Isaiam 10, 21f).

seinem eigenen Namen kommt, werdet ihr ihn aufnehmen' (Joh 5, 43)[1]. Zumindest nach dem Wort Christi werden sie sich verschlimmern, weil sie sich jenem schlimmsten Antichrist anschließen, von dem bei Christus die Rede ist. Und magst Du sagen: nachdem sie die Vernichtung des Antichrist sahen, werden jene, die ihm angehangen, sich bekehren, sage ich: wegen so weniger, die sich erst so spät bekehren, muß man nicht so viele Juden in so vielen Teilen der Welt so lange Zeit aushalten, daß sie in ihrem Gesetz beharren. Denn die schließliche Frucht von ihnen für die Kirche ist und wird nur gering. Daher genügte es, wenn man einige wenige auf irgendeiner abgesonderten Insel ihr Gesetz bewahren ließe, bei denen schließlich sich die Prophetie Jesajas erfüllen würde.

Ein solcher Text erwächst leider aus einer Zeit verstärkter Intoleranz gegenüber Andersgläubigen und besonders gegenüber den Juden. Denn es triumphiert ein Systemdenken, das den « Anderen » nicht mehr aushält, die Liebe und ihre gewaltlos-dienende Hoffnung nicht mehr durchträgt[2], sondern eher auf die Effizienz von Gewalt und Unterdrückung setzt. Dagegen findet sich in der Linie, die über Joachim von Fiore, über Franziskus noch bis zu Olivi geht, die möglichst umfassende Heils-Hoffnung auf eine verwandelnde und umgestaltende göttliche Liebe, die in menschlich-geistlicher Liebe zum kraftvollen Durchtragen und Einsatz kommt.

Schluß

Olivis Hoheliedauslegung läßt eine große spirituelle und theologische Kraft erkennen, die in einer biblisch inspirierten, tiefen mystischen und geschichtlichen Erfahrung wurzelt, sich aus der Erinnerung an die Prophetie Joachims von Fiore und an den franziskanischen Neuaufbruch nährt, aber durch Olivis persönliches Geschick der Bedrängnis und Demütigung ihren hier besonders reifen Ausdruck findet. Olivi konnte die Dynamik göttlicher Liebe in menschlicher Liebe, wie er sie im Hohenlied zu entdecken glaubt, zwar nicht einfach dem Buchstaben des Schrifttextes entnehmen. Das ergab sich für ihn aus dem traditionell vorgegebenen Programm einer geistlichen Schrifterschließung, das ihm aber existentiell *neu* bedeutsam wurde. Daher wollte Olivi keine bloße Allgorese betreiben, sondern im Buchstaben und in der menschlichen Redeweise einer Liebes-Dichtung den tieferen, typischen, geistlichen Sinn aufdecken, der Gottes Liebe und ihre Dynamik meint. M.E. kann man im Sinne Olivis immer noch fragen, wie in menschlicher Liebe zutiefst, umfassend und alles übersteigend göttliche Liebe zum Ausdruck kommt. Gerade um «*fleischliche*» Perversionen von Liebe im Streben nach Herrschaft und Aneignung zu überwinden, sowie um liebende Zuneigung, Zuwendung, Hingabe in der

1. Vgl. zu dieser Deutung ebenfalls *Olivi on the Bible: [...] Postilla in Isaiam.* Introductio, a.a. O. 166f.

2. Vgl. dazu J. Schlageter, «Gewaltverzicht und Friedensmitteilung in franziskanischer Spiritualität», *Thuringia Franciscana N.F.* 50, 1995, p. 521-554.

Einigung mit dem « Anderen » zu fördern, ist diese Sicht biblisch in der Geschichte Gottes mit den Menschen neu zu entdecken. Das gilt m. E. gerade für einen Text, der dem *Augenschein* nach « *nur* » von menschlicher Liebe spricht wie das Hohelied, aber gerade so der Dynamik göttlicher Liebe ganz nahe ist. Bei solcher Neuentdeckung biblischer Intentionen kann m. E. Olivis Auslegung des Hohenliedes bis heute anregend sein [1].

1. Das ist die Absicht meiner neuen kritischen Edition von Olivis Hoheliedauslegung mit Einführung und deutscher Übersetzung, die zur Zeit für den Druck vorbereitet wird (Grottaferrata 1999). Daß es sich jedenfalls erneut lohnen könnte, einem solch *spirituellen*, nicht bloß historischen und nicht bloß allegorischen Verständnis der Hl. Schrift nachzugehen, dazu siehe I. De la Potterie, « Le sens spirituel de L'Ecriture », *Gregorianum* 78, 4, 1997, p. 627-645 und die dort gegebenen Hinweise auf H. de Lubac, *Catholicisme. Les aspects sociaux du dogme chrétien*, Paris, 1938, p. 119 : « Les réalités *historiques* ont donc une profondeur, elles sont à comprendre *spirituellement :* υστορικα πνευματικως : et en revanche les réalités *spirituelles* apparaissent en devenir, elles sont à comprendre *historiquement :* πνευματικα ιστοριως ». Vgl. hier auch Angelus Silesius, *Der cherubinische Wandersmann*, II. Buch, 137 (eingeleitet und erläutert v. W.E. Peuckert, *Leipzip o. J.* [= Sammlung Dieterich 64, 1938] 57 : « *Schrift ohne Geist*. Die Schrift ist Schrift, sonst nichts. Mein Trost ist Wesenheit./ Und daß Gott in mir spricht das Wort der Ewigkeit ».

PETER JOHN OLIVI, AUTHOR OF THE *LECTURA SUPER APOCALIPSIM* : WAS HE HERETICAL ?

Warren Lewis

HOW NOT TO READ THE LECTURA SUPER APOCALIPSIM

In the early 1930s, on the eve of a frightful nightmare, L. Jarraux, of France, made a speech about our beloved Olivi before Bonaventura Marrani, of Italy, Minister General of the Order of Friars Minor, at the Palazzo Barberini *Institut de Culture franciscaine*. That speech, by a Frenchman to an Italian, is a splendid example both of how historical studies can be used to cement international relationships during difficult times, and of how « reader response theory », whether in biblical or literary or historical studies, is a violation of the text and a reduction of historical consciousness to the psychologism of a Rorschach test that tells us more about the speaker than it does about the topic [1].

The elegant Jarraux granted Olivi plenary indulgence for any supposed entanglements with the Franciscan Spirituals. Before an imaginary court of inquisition, he pardoned him with exclamation of the charges of heresy : « *Mais que l'on ne dise pas qu'il avait une âme d'hérétique!* » He pronounced Olivi to be a good Catholic boy, speaking of his « *[...] complète et fervente soumission au magistère vivant du Souverain Pontife, gardien des âmes et guide de leur foi [...]* » Jarraux proclaimed the desecration of Olivi's tomb to have been « [une] *détestable, odieuse profanation [...] absolutement injustifiée [...]* » Avoiding the issue of whether Olivi's *Lectura super Apocalipsim* contained doctrinal errors, Jarraux emphasized that the Apocalypse commentary was not condemned until after Olivi's death. (But of course it was not! Olivi died perhaps no more than three or four months after he completed his *magnum opus vitae eschatologicum*). In fine French taste, Jarraux concluded his personal reconstruction of Olivi's reputation : « *On reconnaît sans peine le Languedocien mâtiné de Provençal : un peu d'ail [...] un peu de lavande [...] un bon vin généreux !* » [2].

Two generations later, we have come a long way towards a better understanding of Olivi's *Lectura super Apocalipsim* (hereinafter : *L.S.A.*). My

1. See Warren Lewis, « Patron Saints of Reader-Response Criticism », Indiana University, Bloomington : *Simploké* 1/1, Winter, 1993, p. 93-100.

2. L. Jarraux, « Pierre Jean Olivi, sa vie, sa doctrine », *Études Franciscaines* 45, 1933, p. 129-153, 277-298, 513-529.

edition of the text[1], though imperfect, has been helpful in this advance, for « everyone » has a pirated copy of it – and, yes, you are welcome ! Based on a critical reading of all the manuscripts that were extant in the 1970s, the *L.S.A.* is now (in the long-lamented phrase of Raoul Manselli, of blessed memory) « *in corso di stampa* ». An English translation will be published at the Scarecrow Press in 1999, and the Latin will appear as a « working text » online at David Burr's Olivi webpage[2]. Placing the *L.S.A.* electronically before us will make remaining errors painfully obvious, but it will also make them easily corrigible. Could Friar Olivi himself but have imagined that we would be able to make his *L.S.A.* universally accessible, it would have seemed a further proof that the Third Age of the Holy Spirit was just around the corner. Now, at the end of the 700-year-long Third Age – just as Olivi prophesied – we live no longer in the world of either the Catholic scriptorium or of the Protestant press but of the Pentecostal internet. The Scarecrow Press's publication in English will, for being in print and permanent, be a more Protestant event.

WHAT IS THE QUESTION ?

Olivi was persecuted in his own time for supposed heretical doctrines ; he was suspected of being himself a heretic ; he was tried and condemned posthumously for having been a heresiarch of Spiritual Franciscans, Beghards, and Beguines. Would we, now, agree with those judgments ? From a different perspective, however, the question : « Was Olivi heretical ? » may now be a profoundly uninteresting question.

In our time, comfortable as we have become with notions of « progress », « development », « innovation », and truth (according to scientific method) as something ever being discovered, rather than something to be preserved, will we not praise Olivi, rather than anathematizing him, for having been a pivotal figure in the intellectual evolution of the 13th century, the most significant interpreter in the Joachite tradition, and forerunner of a whole host within the Third Force of Christendom – not Catholic, not Protestant, but those radicals who, more than others, have put the reading of the Apocalypse and Christian eschatological expectation back on the tracks of history and hope.

David Burr, whose published work on Olivi makes him the reigning scholar on Olivi's eschatological vision, rightly warns against the « dangerous assumption » that somehow early-14th-century foes and friends alike may have

1. Warren Lewis, *Peter John Olivi, O.F.M. (1248-1298) : Prophet of the Year 2000 – Ecclesiology and Eschatology in the* Lectura super Apocalipsim *(1297)*, Eberhard-Karls-Universität, Tübingen, 1972, vol 1, historical-critical introduction ; vols 2 & 3, critical edition of the text. I began the work upon leaving Harvard Divinity School at the suggestion of my friend and mentor, Heiko Augustinus Oberman ; edited the Prologue at the *Pontifical Institute of Medieval Studies* in Toronto ; and continued the edition of the whole *L.S.A.* and wrote the introduction under Oberman as Doktorvater at Tübingen.

2. http ://dburr.hist. vt.edu/OliviPage/Olivi_Page.html.

misread the *L.S.A.* When thinking about the negative report of 1318, and the 1326 condemnation of the *L.S.A.*, Burr tentatively suggests that « we may find it hard to decide what the fuss was about »[1]. When, on the other hand, one does focus the question in terms of heresy, and especially in terms of Olivi's times, back when folk took their heresies seriously, then one can understand without difficulty what the « fuss was about ». No matter whether one be a willing Euro-Christian Catholic of the early-14th century with an affinity for the pope and Rome, or a tolerant, historical-critical exegete of scripture and liberal historian, it takes more, I suggest, than olive oil, a little lavender, and a good red wine for us to swallow Olivi on the Apocalypse, heretic or not.

HERESIARCH ? HERETIC ? OR MERELY HERETICAL ?

« When in doubt », as St. Bonaventure, another famous 13th-century Franciscan, is said to have said, « make a distinction ». To answer the question whether Olivi were heretical, we need make the distinction that one can be « heretical » (what one thinks) without being an « heretic » (what one teaches) and without being an « heresiarch » (what one does). One can be heretical in thought and hope, faith and feeling, but unless one urges one's heretical notions on others, then one is not a heretic. By teaching others one's heretical notions, and thereby undermining their faith, one takes the half-step from being internally heretical to being outwardly a heretic, a teacher of heresy. The next half-step is to become a heresiarch, one who urges and leads others down the path of heresy in a way that undermines social and ecclesiastical structures (a potentially lethal thing to have done in Olivi's time, a dangerous thing in any century).

Which one, then, was Olivi ? Heresiarch ? Heretic ? Merely heretical ? All of the above ? And if his *L.S.A.* did smack of heresy, is that bad ? Ought we to « fuss » at him or praise him for having been innovative and beneficial both in Church history and in the history of humane exchange ?

In early-14th-century Christian Europe, a heresy was any teaching in disagreement with Catholic faith as expressed in tradition and scripture and creed, and held in stubborn defiance of the Church, whose principal see was Rome and which was considered to be indefectible in matters of faith. (It was not yet possible to make facile reference to the infallibility of the Bishop of Rome, for that dogmatic expression was as yet a « work in progress » during the Avignon papacy of John XXII himself, the « heretical » pope who condemned Olivi). Did Olivi, author of the *L.S.A.*, think or teach or do anything contrary to the Roman version of the Euro-Christian tradition, scripture, or creed and in defiance of the Church ?

1. David Burr, *Petrus Iohannis Olivi : Selections from the Apocalypse Commentary* (http : //www.majbill.vt.edu/history/burr/Olivi_Apoc.html) : « *When we examine Olivi's writings today, we may find it hard to decide what the fuss was about* ».

NEITHER HERESIARCH NOR HERETIC

Taking the last part first, we can say that Olivi never intentionally defied either the Church or the Order of Friars Minor. Time and again – before Jerome of Ascoli in 1278; in 1279 with Olivi's indirect assistance in the production of *Exiit qui seminat;* in his response to the attack of « Friar Ar. » in 1280; in his acquiescence to (not agreement with) the demands of the *Rotulus* and the *Littera septem sigillorum* of 1282/1283; in the Parisian aftermath of Milan, 1285-1287; in 1292 at the Chapter General before Raymund Gaufredi; and as late as 1295, in Olivi's canonical argumentation on the case of Pope Coelestine V and in Olivi's mollifying advice to Conrad of Offida and the other hot-headed Italian Spirituals – that is to say, throughout his entire life – Peter John Olivi remained in heart and mind, deed and example a true brother of Francis and a true son of the Church. This means that he was neither a heresiarch (he did not rebelliously lead others into heresy) nor a willful heretic (he did not stubbornly believe anything contrary to the teachings of the Catholic Church). Here and there in the *L.S.A.*, Olivi wrote that he neither « knew » nor « asserted » his exotic notions. Was this the disingenuous spirit of a clever heretical teacher sweetly and smoothly seducing his readers? If so, then I am going too easy on Olivi, but I think he meant what he said.

Nevertheless, Olivi was condemned roughly a quarter-century after his death for having been a leader of the heretical Franciscan Spirituals. The verb « to make a person to become a Beguine » (*imbeguiniri*) was coined in reference to Olivi's intellectual leadership of people who, everyone agrees, were heretics. Notwithstanding that influence, no thinker or believer ought to be condemned for the use, misuse, or abuse of his or her teaching after he or she has died. If we were responsible for the heretical use of our ideas, then Jesus would be the biggest heretic of all (which, of course, he may be).

LITTERA MAGISTRORUM: HOW THE EIGHT MASTERS OF AVIGNON READ THE *L.S.A.*

Taking the first part last, were Olivi's thinking and teaching unintentionally heretical? Did Olivi teach anything contrary to tradition and scripture and creed? It is here that we espy our heretical thinker.

The work of the eight examiners who produced the *Littera magistrorum* of 1318 points us, moreover, in the right direction to focus upon the implicit heresies in the *L.S.A.*, even though these masters of Avignon did not always get it right. Jeff Gardner has provided us with a succinct summary of the ten matters, plus one, considered by those eight learned doctors to be either « heretical » (49 of the 60 numbered articles so labeled) or otherwise variously damnable. I myself cannot distinguish the many fine points that they saw: What is the difference between something that is merely « rash » and something else that is

« audacious » ? One must, nevertheless, appreciate the extent of their vocabulary of doctrinal detestableness. One gathers the impression that they disapproved :

> [...] rash, imprudent, irrational fiction, presumptuous assertion, supported neither by reason nor authority, a position already condemned, ridiculous, insane, audacious, fabricated, false, impudent, frivolous, proving nothing, noxious, absurd, senseless, foolish, of erroneous methodology, malevolent, not supported by probable reasoning, not stated in any authentic scripture, schismatic, blasphemous, exaggerating, and therefore to be rejected [1].

In the following list, I juxtapose the ten matters, plus one, from the *Littera magistrorum* (hereinafter : *Litt. mag.* ; the item numbers are internal references) together with page references to my edition of the *L.S.A.* alongside chapter-and-verse locations in the Apocalypse. This brief guide indicates that Olivi's text bears out the accuracy – more or less – of the reading by those eight masters in the majority of points they made against him.

1. Olivi declared the Roman Church [through her opposition to Francis and the Rule] to be the Great Harlot Babylon, or the Beast, and he suggested that, therefore, the Church should be condemned and that she would be rejected, overturned, and replaced by the coming new Spiritual Church, as the church of Christ had replaced the rejected synagogue of the Jews.

Litt. mag.	*L.S.A. page*	Apoc
III	32-3	P[2]
IV	54-5	P
(X)[3]	99	P
XII	187-8	2:5
XX	310	5:1
XXII	393	6:12
(XXIII)	394	6:12
(XXIV)	397-8	6:12
(XXV)	401-2	6:12
XXVI	402-7	6:12
XXVII	410-1	6:12, 14
XXX	424-8	7:3
XXXIII	492	8:3
(XXXVII)	538	9:14
XLVI	754-7	14:7-8
(XLVIII)	801-2	16:10
(XLIX)	805	16:12
(LIII)	818-9	16:18, 19
LIV	826	17:1

1. Jeff B. Gardner, « The Condemnation of Peter John Olivi's *Lectura super Apocalypsim* as contained in *Littera Magistrorum :* A Translation and Review », Lawrence : University of Kansas, 1993, premised on the edition by Stephen Baluze, in *Miscellanea*, vol. II, p. 258-270.

2. Some references are to Olivi's lengthy prologue, not to a specific verse in the Apocalypse.

3. Gardner does not assign each of the 60 articles of the *Litt. mag.* to one of his ten numbered areas ; for the sake of completeness, I have added those which he omitted, placing them in parentheses.

Litt. mag.	*L.S.A. page*	Apoc
(LV)	860-1	18:3
(LVI)	862-4, 866	18:4, 5
LVII	882	19:1

Olivi's frequent, consistent, historically pointed, and locally topical references to aspects of the *carnalis ecclesia Latinorum,* as opposed to the *ecclesia spiritualis, viri evangelici, nova sponsa,* and other images, are unfavorable to the Church of Rome. He contrasted Franciscan preaching and living of the pure and restored gospel of evangelical perfection with the luxury, simony, avarice, and moral turpitude of the clerical and monastic establishments of the Church. He traced historically the *genetic* perpetuation of evil from ancient, imperial Rome through contemporary, papal Rome. He counterposed two women – one bad woman : meretricious Rome, the Great Whore, *versus* one good woman : the Woman Clothed with the Sun, *i.e.*, the early Church, Mary, and the *nova sponsa*. He associated the Church of Rome with John's Apocalyptic menagerie of beasts, evil spirits, demons, dragons, snakes, scorpions, frogs, and many-headed critters. The croaking frogs included Averroistic philosophers jumping out of the mouth of the Mystical Antichrist; to Olivi that meant Thomas Aquinas, among others [1].

At the heart of Olivi's eschatological ecclesiology, he was pointing to a big change already taking place in the Church, and he said that it had been prophesied in the Apocalypse of John. In text after text, sometimes literally and obviously, sometimes obliquely and by intimation, Olivi made abundantly clear that he was talking specifically about the Church of Rome, the Church whose principal see was Rome and whose head was the successor to Peter. In Olivi's diatribes against the tribes of Apocalyptic enemies, he occasionally named individual personal names, but not always. For example, Olivi stopped short of writing this accusation : « Boniface VIII is the Antichrist! » although Olivi did call Pope Coelestine by name and then pointed obliquely to « his successor », adding that things were « now getting worse and worse » [2].

1. *L.S.A.*, p. 623-881.

2. At *Apoc.* 12 : 6, *L.S.A.*, p. 656-57 : *Ex tunc autem omnis persecutio sui [sc. Francis] evangelici status spectat ad persecutiones antichristi et secundum hoc insequenti XLII generatione cepit Parisius persecutio quorundam magistrorum condemnantium evangelicam mendicitatem [...].*

Prout autem inchoantur a Christi baptismo, id est post XXX annos a primo initio, sic in XLI generatione cepit ordo evangelicus per totam latinam ecclesiam esse in doctrina famosus ; et in XLII cepit persecutio seu error dicentium statum religionis esse inferiorem statu seculari clericorum curam animarum habentium, et iterum error dicentium quod habere aliqua in communi est de evangelica perfectione Christi et apostolorum ac per consequens quod nichil tale in communi habere non est de evangelica perfectione. Insurrexerunt etiam alii non modici contra evangelicam paupertatem errores, contra quos est declaratio seu decretalis domini Nicholai III in eadem generatione edita. In eadem etiam Parisius prodierunt errores philosophici seu potius paganici, qui a doctoribus estimantur magna seminaria secte magni antichrist, sicut et precedentes sunt seminaria et etiam plante errorum mistici antichristi. Prout vero inchoantur a Christi morte vel ascensione, sic in initio XLI apparuit circiter per tres menses stella comata valde grandis et stupenda. Tuncque Manfredus, Frederici filius, usurpatorie regnum Sicilie contra ecclesiam tenens, est per Carolum devictus et occisus et paulo post Colradus filius Colradi filii Frederici. Et in XLII generatione Petrus

2. Olivi asserted that the true Church is embodied in the practice of evangelical poverty by the Franciscan Order, and that the Rule of Francis contains the restored Gospel of Christ (along with other schismatic ideas about Francis and interpretations of the Rule).

Litt. mag.	*L.S.A. page*	Apoc
VII	88	P
XXII	393	6:12
(XXIII)	394	6:12
XVII	241	3:10
(XXV)	401-2	6:12
(XXVIII)	416-8	7:2
(XXIX)	423	7:3
(XXXI)	432	7:4
XXXV	525-6	9:11
(XL)	564-5	10:1-3
LXI	576-8	10:11
L	805-6	16:12
LVII	882	19:1

Olivi identified Francis with specific images in the Apocalypse, *e.g.*, the angel of the sixth seal in Apoc 7 : 2 (following Bonaventure). Olivi defined points of *concordia* between Christ, his Apostles, and the early church and Francis, his Friars, and the 144,000 sealed servants. Olivi contrasted the Johannine nature of the Franciscan Order and the emerging *ecclesia spiritualis* with the Petrine nature of the Church of Rome in moral decline [1].

Olivi's career-long quarrel with the Conventual forces of the O.F.M. and with the popes and cardinals who sided with them, has been discussed in the literature on Olivi more than any other one subject. The fine points of his position on the *usus pauper* take us beyond my concern in this presentation. The eight masters of Avignon accurately had their collective finger on a neuralgic spot that had been the point of contention for years, whatever one's judgment may be on who was right.

3. Olivi suggested that the sixth and seventh stages of the Church were more important and holy than the first five stages had been.

Litt. mag.	*L.S.A. page*	*Apocalypse*
I	10-2	P
(II)	45	P
VI	76	P
IX	95-6	P

rex Aragonum invasit Sicilie regnum et ex tunc secuta sunt multa discidia inter reges et regna, que quibusdam non indoctis videntur esse preparatoria magni mali. In fine autem huius XLII generationis contigit novitas electionis Celestini pape et successoris eius et quorundam aliorum nunc ingravescentium [...]

1. *L.S.A.*, p. 169-170, 247, 393, 416-420, 557-568.

Litt. mag.	*L.S.A. page*	*Apocalypse*
XII	159, 187-8	2:5
XVII	241	3:10
XXXVI	536	9:14
LX	968-70	21:21

Olivi had a certain preference for the sixth and seventh stages of the church, believing that he was living in the penultimate moment of the sixth stage, and that the seventh stage would be a time of earthly bliss. For the critics in Avignon to have said, however, that the latter times were « more holy » than the age of the apostles or the age of the martyrs and doctors, was to have put the matter wrongly.

Like many other biblical Christians, Olivi had first-century Christianity up on a pedestal in his mind. As a restorationist, Olivi believed that St. Francis had restored the Church in terms both of doctrine (true following of evangelical poverty) and life (living the poor and humble life of Christ and Francis); this, according to Olivi, was the pure and pristine, revealed and re-revealed, New Testament pattern. Like other restorationists and fundamentalists who imagine a « golden age » in the past, Olivi was nostalgic for a time when Christ and the Apostles had followed the presumptive rule of poverty purely and simply. Like other apocalypticists who imagine a « golden age » in the future, Olivi was progressively eschatological in his belief that Christ had come again spiritually in Francis and that, now, the *nova sponsa* was emerging and the Third World Age of the Holy Spirit was about to begin. Putting the two mindsets together (nostalgia and eschatology), we can say that Olivi was afflicted with *eschatalgia*, a malady of trying to get to the future by way of the past[1,2].

4. Olivi falsely predicted future events with heretical implications.

Litt. Mag.	*L.S.A. page*	*Apoc*
VIII	91-2	P
XXVIII	416-8	7:2
(XXXIX)	563	10:1-3
XLIV	735-7	13:18
XLV	737-8	13:18
LI	806-7	16:13
LVIII	922-3	20:3
LIX	956	21:12

Olivi was predicting the downfall of the Church of Rome as the masters of Avignon knew and loved it: That prophecy and all its details had to be considered heretical by them. Among the « future events » that Olivi « predicted » (in fact, he speculated – « *quod nec assero nec scio nec censeo asserendum* ») was the

1. I acknowledge Therese Stewart, formerly the Dean of *Unification Theological Seminary*, as the neologist of « eschatalgia » in her attempt to explain certain aspects of the Rev. Sun Myung Moon's theology.

2. *L.S.A.*, p. 10-13, 28-30, 144, 159-164, 225-239, 244-247, 558-568.

possible resurrection of Francis, based on what Conrad of Offida had told him that Brother Leo had said[1].

5. Olivi foresaw that the primacy of the Roman Catholic Church was to be transferred to a true *ecclesia spiritualis* (the *nova sponsa*) of the sixth and seventh stages.

Litt. mag.	*LSA page*	Apoc
XII	187-8	2:5
XVIII	245-6	3:11
XIX	246	3:11
(XLIII)	632-3	12:3
XLVII	770-2	14:15
L	805-6	16:12

Olivi adduced a number of biblical metaphors to convey the transfer of primacy from « Babylon » to the *nova sponsa, e.g.* transfer of kingship from Saul to David[2]; transfer of the priesthood from the lineage of Eleazar to that of Ithamar[3]. Perhaps his favorite was the transfer of primacy from a church in the image of Peter to a church in the image of John. The latter is characterized (in contrast to the prevailing church of Olivi's time) by the peace and effortless knowledge of God (*spiritualis intelligentia*); influence of the special charismas and *claritas* of the Holy Spirit; Franciscan rule of the church through missionary work, contemplation, evangelical and egalitarian humility, and spiritually experiential worship[4].

6. Olivi said that the wisdom and truth of the church of Christ, at last to be revealed in the sixth and seventh stages of the Church, had not been so fully revealed in the previous five stages[5].

Litt. mag.	*L.S.A. page*	Apoc
V	57	P
VII	88	P
XXII	393	6:12
(XLVIII)	801-2	16:10

The masters of Avignon misunderstood Olivi at this point. *Eschatalgist* Olivi believed that the wisdom and truth of Christ's poverty and gospel had been fully revealed during his First Advent « in the flesh », but that it had been re-revealed through his coming « in spirit » in his Second Advent through Francis, and that it would now be revealed sevenfold in the Third Age of the Spirit with the blazing light of the sun of seven days, and this would lead up to Christ's Third and final

1. *L.S.A.*, p. 417-418.
2. *L.S.A.*, 397.
3. *L.S.A.*, p. 50-51.
4. *L.S.A.*, p. 108-113, 227-231, 265-270, 557-558, 580 s, 770, 891-895, 975-981, 993-994.
5. I would prefer, I think, to conflate n° 6 with n° 3 : The logic of the argument and the effect are identical under both heads, but I follow Gardner's numeration here.

Coming « to judgment », perhaps 700 years later (the Year 2000). The revelation of poverty and the gospel in Francis was not a latter-day revelation of something new, but a new revelation of something old[1].

7. Olivi rejected the first two world ages in favor of the Third Age – that is to say, he saw God rejecting the Old-Testament Age of the Father and the New-Testament Age of the Son in favor of the coming Age of the Holy Spirit.

Litt. mag.	*LSA page*	Apoc
VII	88	P
XIII	229	3:7
XIV	233	3:7

Olivi did not « reject » the Ages of the Father and the Son; he saw them, rather, as divine, revealed, essential phases in the staged and progressive creation by God of history. Olivi did believe that God changes things, and from his Euro-Christian perspective on Judaism, the following analogy was apt: Israel, Moses' Law, and the synagogue of the Jews had once been God's revealed will during the First World Age of the Father, but that had given way historically – « was rejected by God » – to Christianity, the Gospel, and the church of Christ in the Second World Age of the Son. So, now, with a further changing of the times, as the first had yielded to the second, so the second was yielding to the third. The church of the Age of the Son « was being rejected by God », that is, the Church of Rome, grown unfaithful to her original calling, was now to be replaced by the restored gospel of poverty, the Rule and Order of Francis, and the *nova sponsa* in the Third World Age of the Holy Spirit. Olivi was throughly Joachite in his use of the three world ages[2]. In the *L.S.A.*, Olivi betrayed no evidence of ethnic anti-Semitism; his use throughout of Rom 11 : 25-26 as a literal prophecy of the endtime, however, indicates his prophetic expectation that the Jews would be converted as part of Franciscan missionary work.

8. Olivi said that the existing Church of his own time, rather than being a pathway to salvation, was leading people into sin, and that the pope was, in fact, a pseudo-pope who guided the faithful into spiritual error.

Litt. mag.	*L.S.A. page*	Apoc
(XLII)	600-1	11:7
XLIV	735-7	13:18
XLV	737-8	13:18
(LII)	809	16:13

Mostly resisting the urge to name names and go into detail, Olivi painted with broad and vigorous strokes a picture of the moral failures, philosophical errors, and ecclesiastical misadventures of his century. Wherever Babylon is damned,

1. *L.S.A.*, p. 58-61, 100-102, 394-407, 739-750, 917-919.
2. *L.S.A.*, p. 46-48, 52-55, 917-919.

the *nova sponsa* is praised, and the perfections of Christ are explained. One ought not to think, however, that Olivi's prophetic agenda was that merely of moral reformation of the Church (like the 11th century Gregorian / Hildebrandine reformation is said to have been); it was eschatologically too late for that. Olivi had gone beyond being a prophetic moralist reformer to being an eschatological apocalyptic restorationist: God's apocalyptic clock was ticking, and Olivi foresaw a doctrinal change *de fide et moribus* from top to bottom, a change as drastic as the change from the Jewish synagogue to the Christian Church had been.

9. Olivi saw that the privileges that the Church of Rome had extended to the Franciscan Order were in fact destroying the Order.

Litt. mag.	*L.S.A. page*	Apoc
XXX	424-8	7:3

The litmus test of the doctrinal / moral « fall of Babylon » is the Church of Rome's failure to uphold Franciscan poverty as Olivi understood it and, indeed, had indirectly contributed to the Church's formulation of it[1].

10. Olivi taught that the Apostles had owned no material possessions and that they, therefore, practiced absolute poverty.

Litt. mag.	*L.S.A. page*	Apoc
XXXIV	522-23	after 9:11

The old quarrel over the nature of true Franciscan poverty surfaces in the *L.S.A.*, though not in detail. To Olivi's mind, that issue was settled. The masters of Avignon, then, had only to remind their principal reader (Pope John XXII) that Friar Olivi's notions of poverty, while they might have been papally approved a century before, were now outmoded orthodoxy – and that is one definition of heresy[2].

11. Outside of Gardner's formal numbered list of ten areas, he suggests an eleventh category: « Olivi's denial of papal power », a theme « so prevalent that it appears in fourteen of the sixty articles ».

Litt. mag.	*L.S.A. page*	Apoc
IV	54-5	P
V	57	P
VI	76	P
VII	88	P
XI	159	2:1
XIII	229	3:7
XIV	233	3:7
XV	235	3:7
XVI	238	3:8

1. *L.S.A.*, p. 398s, 538s, 579-584, 805.
2. *L.S.A.*, p. 10-13, 28-30, 144, 560.

Litt. mag.	*L.S.A. page*	Apoc
XVII	241	3 : 10
XVIII	245-6	3 : 11
XXI	389-90	6 : 11
XXXVIII	560, 562-3	10 : 1-3
(XLII)	600-1	11 : 7
LX	968-70	21 : 21

Olivi, who had made suggestions for the writing of *Exiit qui seminat* (1279), believed that in its promulgation Pope Nicholas III had put the Roman seal of approval on Franciscan poverty; therefore, any subsequent pope who might deny that reaffirmation of the gospel of poverty, would thereby become a heretical pope (*papa haereticus*) or false pope (*pseudopapa*). Olivi did not (*contra* Tierney[1]) believe in papal infallibility « in the future tense », such that popes could not commit errors *de fide et moribus*, become heretics, and fall from their papal dignity and Christian faith. Because the theologians of John XXII at the papal court in Avignon during 1318 were at work on this new dogmatic formulation, however, they quite consistently took umbrage at Olivi's suggestions that a pope could become false, heretical, and an antichrist.

Out of the rich Apocalyptic mixture of whores, beasts, false prophets, pseudopopes, and antichrists, Olivi distilled that there would be two antichrists, an « invisible and mystical » one and an « open and great » one. He closely associated approval of the Arab philosophy of the Averroists with the emergence of these historical figures of evil. At Apoc 9 : 14, thinking of the « great apostasy » prophesied in II Thessalonians, Olivi coupled the power of the pope with heresy and Averroistic philosophy and labeled the result with the apocalyptic image of the Euphrates River[2,3].

Heretical in Eschatology and Ecclesiology

As I read it, the text of Olivi is clear that he taught in opposition to the understanding of the nature of the church as it had been developed – and was being developed – by the Roman tradition of ecclesiastical triumphalism in Olivi's time. This trajectory runs from at least the 8th-century papacy through Innocent III to Boniface VIII and – past Olivi – to John XXII and after that to the 19th-century dogmatic definition of papal infallibility at Vatican I.

The Roman triumphalists in Avignon who read Olivi's Apocalypse commentary did not foresee what Olivi foresaw: they believed that the

1. Brian Tierney, *Origins of Papal Infallibility, 1150-1350: A Study in the Concepts of Infallibility, Sovereignty and Tradition in the Middle Ages*, Leiden : Brill, 1972.

2. *Potestas enim pape et multitudo plebium sibi obediens et favor ipsius est quasi magnus fluvius Euphrates impediens transitum et insultum emulorum evangelici status in ipsum. Designatur etiam per Euphraten multitudo sapientium virorum et sapientie theologice et humane resistentis erroribus hereticorum et Sarracenorum et consimilium [...]. L.S.A.* 538.

3. See Olivi's attack on the papacy in many places: *L.S.A.*, p. 159-160, 184-89, 357-382, 407, 513-518, 538, 600-602, 720-738, 757, 806-809.

hierarchical, clerical, canonical, authoritarian, Christocentric, Petrine Church of Rome was to be eternal. Olivi, to the contrary, believed that the Church of Rome as he had known it was about to give way to a charismatic, evangelical, pentecostal, humble, Pneumatocentric, Johannine Spiritual Church. The masters of Avignon were aggravated that Olivi was so willing to speculate about such things: Francis, prophesied in the Apocalypse as the angel who preaches the Everlasting Gospel of Poverty, had already appeared once to fulfill that prophecy, and he might well appear a second time in a glorious resurrection like Christ's to confirm it. Olivi, said the masters, was not only wrong but also rash in his interpretation of Francis and his Rule. The doctors of Avignon, like traditionalists of other stripes, thought that things would remain the same. Our Olivi thought that things would have to change, if they were to remain the same. By the standards of his time, therefore, Olivi was heretical in his ecclesiology and his eschatology.

HERETICAL IN HERMENEUTICS?

If Olivi were heretical in his reconstruction of the Roman Christian ecclesiastical tradition, was he also heretical in his interpretation of scripture, specifically of the Apocalypse of John? To do justice to this complicated question would require more space and time than we have today.

Even the eight masters of Avignon dealt with Olivi not so much in terms of hermeneutics as in the language of systematic theology, but occasionally faulting him for teachings that were not « according to the scriptures of the apostles »[1]; teachings « supported neither by reason nor authority »[2], not by biblical « evidence »[3], and not by « authentic scripture »[4]; for being less adept at interpretation than was Richard of Mediavilla[5]; and, once, for « a foolish, rash, and erroneous methodology that proves nothing » when – as happens many times in the *L.S.A.* – Olivi's propensity for tortuous application of Joachim's principle of *concordia* got out of hand[6]. The attack of the eight men of Avignon is far more adequately verbalized as a blast at Olivi's processive, progressive vision of history than it is as a quarrel with his biblical hermeneutics.

The eight masters wisely declined to commit themselves to detailed interpretations of specific passages in the Apocalypse. Like their non-Joachite contemporaries, their hermeneutical starting point would have been the Augustinian norm of seeing the City of God moving through history, that Heaven-bound community whose love of God is greater than their self-love or their love of this world; and it includes the faithful both of Israel and of the

1. II.
2. VIII.
3. XXII.
4. XXXVIII.
5. XXXII, Apoc 7 : 17, *L.S.A.*, p. 455-456; LV.
6. XXXVI.

Christian church. The Augustinian view was, to be sure, of God's eschatological train, but without any published schedule of stops and starts, derails or intersections [1]. Like the majority [?] of biblicists, credalists, confessionalists, and fundamentalists in all centuries and of all denominations who think that the first century was the Golden Age of the church, the Avignon Eight looked backwards rather than forwards. Hermeneutics not yet being a specific locus of theological debate, Olivi's critics excoriated him theologically for his Sabellian modalism of history [2] – the idea that the Age of the Old Testament might somehow belong more to the Father; the Age of the New Testament, more to the Son, and the Third World Age, more to the Holy Spirit, rather than seeing all of history as belonging equally to the one whole holy trinity of divine persons.

Both the infrequency and inadequacy of the hermeneutical critique reminds us that both Olivi and his detractors were reading their Bibles before the invention of the scientific, ideally objective, historical-critical method of biblical exegesis. Both contenders in this fray were equally susceptible to the kind of gratuitous self-help in the interpretation of scripture that allows the reader to interpolate his or her own concerns into the text.

It is not that medieval interpreters did not aspire to understand scripture according to the *sensus litteralis* (which Olivi called the *sensus principalis*) at the historical level. Rather, the medievals lacked a well articulated historical-critical method. Doing their work in the time before the Humanists had issued their cry, « *Ad fontes!* » and before the men of the Enlightenment had taught Europe the benefits of objectivist reductionism, the medieval exegetes were ill-equipped to search out historical meanings (*exegesis*). With this lack of hermeneutical equipment, they – like naive readers of the Bible today – sprang too easily to so-called « spiritual » (*i.e.*, subjectivist) meanings, and this was their plenary indulgence for reading anything into the text (*eisegesis*) that they jolly well pleased. That is no different from the blank check filled in at will by today's reader-response theorists in their subjective overdrafts on the Bank of Textual Meaning. These « Post-Modern » theorists congratulate themselves on the novelty of their hermeneutics, but the habit was as old as the moralizing apologists who read Homer's epics and excused the gods of their immoralities by way of allegory. This was the liberal method and defensive mode imported by Philo the Jew of Alexandria to excuse the literary and moral crudities of the Hebrew scriptures, once again by reading the text through allegory-tinted spectacles. The *sensus quattuor scripturis* was an ancient tradition, and Olivi had been totally immersed in it.

Olivi, the first great interpreter of the Apocalypse in the Joachite tradition after Joachim of Fiore himself, thought that, like Canticles (where everything seems to be about sex, but cannot possibly be !) [3], the *Book of Revelation* has no proper *sensus litteralis*, for that would involve one in a *sensus zoologicus* about

1. See Article LV of the *Littera magistrorum*.

2. XIII ; see Gardner's n° 3 and n° 6.

3. Olivi established this hermeneutical approach in his commentary on *Canticles* (*Song of Songs*) ; see *Praefatio*, p. 1-25, B. Bonelli, *Operum S. Bonaventurae Supplementum*, Trent, 1772-1774 : I 1-66.

literal horses, frogs, beasts, dragons, and the rest of St. John's Apocalyptic zoo. Instead, reasoned Olivi, the *sensus principalis* of the Apocalypse starts already one rung higher up the ladder of signification than the usual literal-historical level: According to Peter John Olivi, Church History – past, present, and future – is the literal meaning of the Apocalypse. (Ordinarily, the prophetic sense of scripture is understood to be one of the three spiritual levels, presumably the anagogical)[1].

With this as his starting point, Olivi then went on to make the same mistake that every other post-Olivi Joachite has made, whether chiliast, millennialist, premillennialist, left-wing Radical Reformer, Cromwellian, Shaker, Millerite, Adventist, Jehovah's Witness, Moonie, Rapturist of the Evangelical Right, or suicide victim no longer willing to wait at Heaven's Gate. Olivi and his ilk find their own times and pet issues prophesied in the *Book of Revelation;* they locate themselves as standing in the ante-penultimate moment; they congratulate themselves either on some special revelation or some improved vantage point in history; consequently, they over-interpret the details of John's Apocalypse in the service of their own historical-theological agendas. Joachite interpreters of the Apocalypse are, therefore, classic examples of reader-response theorists who see themselves reflected in the ink blots on the page of defenseless scripture. They twist the texts until the silent letter is forced to cry out in subjectivist testimony to the interpreter him- or herself (« What it *means* to me »), instead of the other way around, namely, the interpreter crying out in historical-critical witness to the text (« What it *meant* when it was written »)[2].

Following Joachim, Olivi's *contribution* – if we can call it that without choking – is his equation of Franciscan history with the future tale as foretold by the Seer of Patmos. This gratuitous reading of oneself into the text is the mistake that every subjectivist exegete of Revelation has made ever since. Whether trumped-up notions of « the tribulation » or out and out interpolations of the « rapture », since Joachim and Olivi, have all been wrong, historically speaking, in their hasty expectation that « the Lord is coming soon ». When it comes to the interpretation of « 666 », for example, whether it was some Protestant damning some pope, some 19th-century preacher fuming about Mary Baker Eddy, some German Confessing Christian agonizing over *der Führer*, or some Republican targeting the blue eagle symbol of Franklin D. Roosevelt's New Deal, from Joachim and Olivi to the latest radio preacher, they have all been wrong.

If we change the term of our judgment to ask whether Olivi were *mistaken* (rather than *heretical*), then the question becomes easier to answer. The Apocalypse of John is no more about the Franciscan Order than it is about Christian Science or the New Deal or *der Führer*. There is no more evidence in 1998 than there was in 1298 that Heaven favors absolute poverty like that of Francis or that God has rejected Roman Catholicism. History has not borne out

1. See *L.S.A.*, p. 5.

2. I acknowledge Krister Stendahl, Professor of New Testament at *Harvard Divinity School* when I studied there, 1962-1965, for the distinction between « What it means » and « What it meant ».

Olivi's interpretation of the *Book of Revelation* as a future-history text on decisive Franciscan events. If you are a historical-critical exegete, the *Book of Revelation* is about none of the above; if you are a reader-response *eisegete*, it may be about all of the above. The next logical question, then, would be this: Does « to be mistaken » equal « to be heretical? » If so, then we are all heretical, for we are all mistaken, and even the most objectivist of critical historians sometimes reads and responds subjectively. Reading scripture is about the most dangerous thing a believer can do!

The juxtaposition of world history and church history with the images of the Apocalypse in Olivi's hermeneutics proves only one thing: the state of the mind of the interpreter. Most of us present at the International Olivi Colloquium in Narbonne in 1998 will still be alive to see whether Olivi's prediction of the Year 2000 comes to pass as a likely date for Jesus' Second (Third, according to Olivi) Advent « in judgment ». One desperately refreshing aspect of this date-setting style of reading the *Book of Revelation* is that it is easily falsified, which is more than one can say about most theology. When the appointed doomsday arrives and the calendar date is passed, the important question then becomes whether the apocalypse-struck « Joachites » will have the decency to acknowledge their error, or whether – to keep their operation going – they will spiritualize the historical miscalculation into some Heavenly non-event. Olivi had the decency to die before his predictions had a chance not to come true.

Heretical in confessing the creed

Olivi's greatest heresy, I suggest, was another heresy of the creed, a matter which the authors of the *Litt. mag.* seem but barely to have glimpsed, and which they did not adequately spell out. The Apostles Creed teaches that Christians believe not only in « one Church » (as opposed to « two women », bad old Babylon and the good *nova sponsa*) but also in « one Lord, Jesus Christ ». Accordingly, the person expected in the Second Coming is the same person who has already come, namely, Jesus, « who was crucified under Pontius Pilate », and not someone else, not even someone else who may look very like Jesus in life, teaching, and suffering. Olivi, by contrast, heretically taught in the *L.S.A.* that St. Francis was the Second Coming of Christ « in spirit ».

A partial glimpse of this heresy flickered in the minds of the eight masters of Avignon in Article #2, and by implication in all the articles where Olivi's hostile readers were incensed at his doctrine of the *nova sponsa*. Where there is a new bride, there is also a new groom, and for Olivi, that new groom was Francis of Assisi. The *L.S.A.* proof-texts cited above at *Litt. mag.* Articles #2 & 4 speak directly to this issue.

Olivi marshaled scripture to prove that at the transition between the Age of the Son and the Age of the Holy Spirit, there would be a second, intermediate coming of Christ; hence, there would be three advents: the First Advent of Christ « in the flesh », the Second Advent of Christ « in spirit », and the Third Advent of Christ

« to judgment ». To make clear what, he said, is not clear in scripture, Olivi suggested that history is like a mountain range with three peaks : At a distance, one cannot distinguish the peaks and the valleys in between from one another, but now that Olivi enjoyed the improved historical vantage point of standing where he could see both the Second Advent in Francis (past) and the Third Advent of Jesus (future), he could see what others had missed [1].

With an intermediate Second Advent « in spirit » as his hermeneutical starting point, Olivi found prophecies in the Apocalypse of St. Francis as the Second Coming of Christ, much in the way that believers in the *N.T.* found Jesus all over the *O.T.* anywhere they looked. For example, at Apoc 3 : 3, the « thief at the door », usually interpreted as a prophecy of Christ's coming at an unexpected hour, becomes a prophecy of the « occult » coming of Christ in Francis [2]. At Apoc 7 : 2, like Bonaventure before him, Olivi interpreted « another angel, having the sign of the living God » as Francis. Going beyond Bonaventure's, Olivi coupled Christ and Francis such that Francis becomes the spiritual Second Coming. Invoking Joachim's principle of *concordia,* and with an oblique reference to Olivi's own hermeneutical principle set forth in the discussion of Three-Peak Mountain, Olivi paralleled in detail the life and work of Francis with the life and work of Christ [3]. Olivi carried the parallel of Francis's being Christ's angelic other in life and teaching and death so far as to suggest that Francis might also become just like Christ by rising again from the dead. To support this amazing suggestion, Olivi cited the *viva vox* of Franciscan oral tradition by way of Conrad of Offida back to Brother Leo; it is at this point, however, that Olivi also softened his novel suggestion by saying that he neither knew for sure nor was he asserting anything [4].

Olivi worked out this revised version of the Second Coming at a variety of other spots throughout the *L.S.A.* [5], and in so doing, Olivi reinvented the *théologie*

1. *Et hinc est quod in hiis visionibus presentatur trinus Christi adventus : Primus scilicet in carnem passibilem, mundum redimens et ecclesiam fundans ; secundus in spirituam evangelice vite, reformans et perficiens ecclesiam primitus iam fundatam ; tertius ad iudicium, glorificans electos cunctaque consummans [...]* (*L.S.A.*, p. 57 ; see the whole of the eighth hermeneutical note in the Prologue, *L.S.A.*, p. 55-62).

2. *Nota quod correspondenter prefigurat hic occultum Christi adventum et iudicium in fine quinti status et in initio sexti fiendum, prout infra in apertione* sexti *signaculi explicatur* (*L.S.A.*, p. 225).

3. *L.S.A.*, p. 560-568.

4. *Audivi etiam a viro spirituali valde fide digno et fratri Leoni confessori et socio beato Francisci valde familiari quoddam huic scripture consonum, quod nec assero nec scio nec censeo asserendum, scilicent quod tam per verba fratris Leonis quam per propriam revelationem sibi factam, perceperat Franciscus in illa pressura temptationis bablilonice, in qua eius status et regula quasi instar Christi crucifigetur, resurget gloriosus, ut sicut in vita et in crucis stigmatibus est Christo singulariter assimilatus, sic et in resurrectione Christo assimiletur, necessaria tunc suis discipulis confirmandis et informandis, sicut Christi resurrectio fuit necessaria apostolis confirmandis et super fundatione et gubernatione future ecclesie informandis* (*L.S.A.*, p. 417-418).

5. See Olivi's delightful meditation on the difference between « dinner » and « supper » (a distinction that Mediterraneans make more easily than do Northerners) as a way to explain the Second and Third Comings (*L.S.A.*, p. 890) ; Francis who, like Christ, upholds the Church (*L.S.A.*, p. 169-170) ; Francis who, as the « strong angel » of Apoc 10 : 1, has divine power to withhold the winds and constrain demons (*L.S.A.*, p. 535-536, 557-558) ; Francis who, like Christ, combines in

archaïque[1] of « angel Christology ». A Catholic thinker could afford to lavish this exotic Christology of the ancient church on Francis because now, after more than a millennium of Christological development, the elements of angel Christology could be applied to a « mere man » (such as Francis) without threat of compromising better-known Christological *loci communes*, such as the hypostatic union and consubstantiality of the Father and the Son. A pattern familiar to phenomenologists of religion seems also to have been at work here : Just as the *deus otiosus* of Israel had been repersonalized in Jesus, who then himself was deified, so Jesus, the *deus otiosus* of Christianity, was repersonalized by Olivi in Francis, and this might well have led to a similar deification of Francis, had the Spiritual Franciscan tradition been more successful. Olivi's hitherto unparalleled Christology of Francis did surely influence Giotto and the other artists of Franciscanism, who loved nothing better than to paint the seraphic, stigmatic, cruciform Francis in iconic parallel with the crucified Christ.

The following analogy may help to make the degree of Olivi's heresy clear : Our beloved Olivi was a 13th-century Moonie. Members of the Unification Church, founded by the Korean messiah, Sun Myung Moon, believe that their leader is the Lord of the Second Advent, the Third Adam, husband of the Second Eve, and the spiritual Second Coming of Christ; and that the Unification Church is « Third Israel »[2]. Shakers, by the way, who proclaimed their foundress, Mother Ann Lee, to be « the Second Appearing of Christ according to the female line », made a similar mistake. A number of other zealous followers of messianic figures have done likewise. Moonies and Shakers alike responded to the need to repersonalize the *deus otiosus* of Christianity. Olivi, similarly, pronounced Francis to have been the Second Coming of Christ in some spiritually historical, doctrinally eschatological sense that muddies the creedal confession about the Second Coming as much as the Christology of Moon or the Christology of Mother Ann muddied theological waters for Shakers and Moonies. The thickness of the mud in Olivi's case can be measured in terms of how far astray those went who followed Olivi's idolatrous thoughts about Francis, for they learned to think

himself all the offices of the Church (*L.S.A.*, p. 560) ; Francis who, like Christ, is the cloud-rider and the lion, the doer of perfect deeds, one who descends from Heaven wrapped in clouds, one preaches at home and abroad, and the one who, like Christ, has the full power of the Gospel (*plena potestate* – a fuller plenitude of power, in Olivi's mind, than the papal successors of Peter had). With this *plenitudo potestatis*, Francis becomes the mediator who delivers and teaches the *spiritualis intelligentia* that will characterize the holy minds of the Third Age – that is, Francis, like Christ, sends the Holy Spirit (*L.S.A.*, p. 560-568).

1. See Jean Daniélou, *Théologie du judéo-christianisme* (Tournai : Desclee, 1958; English editions, 1964, 1977), *passim*.

2. I am personally acquainted with the Rev. Moon and with many leaders of his Unification Church. When I showed them the relevant passages in Olivi's *Lectura*, they became instantly curious about, and appreciative of, Olivi's mind and method which seemed to them to resemble Rev. Moon's approach to interpreting the Second Advent. See Warren Lewis, « Is the Rev. Sun Myung Moon a Heretic ? Locating Unification Theology on the Map of Church History », in *A Time for Consideration*, M. Darroll Bryant and Herbert Richardson, eds., Toronto & New York, Edwin Mellen Press, 1978, p. 275-289.

idolatrously not only about both Francis and Olivi but also about themselves. I am remembering Sister Prous Boneta.

Granted, Olivi – unlike Rev. Moon – still believed in a future, cataclysmic Advent of Christ « in judgment », the eschatological event mentioned in the creed. Indeed, Olivi calculated that if the Age of the Holy Spirit were to begin, as he thought it well might do, in the Year 1300, and last 700 hundred years (an appropriate number of perfection for the Holy Spirit, especially in the Apocalypse where one reads of the « seven spirits of God » [1]), then Christ might come to judgment in or around the Year 2000[2]. This is why I titled my introduction to the *Lectura super Apocalipsim* as I did : « Peter John Olivi, O.F.M., Prophet of the Year 2000 ».

Nevertheless, when one considers that Olivi's reading of the Apocalypse of John allowed him to insert a « second » and « spiritual » coming of Christ in between the first coming « in flesh » and the third and final coming « to judgment », and that the implication of this novelty was that the popes would become heretics and antichrists, and that the Church of Rome would fall, and that the ecclesiastical norm would change from the synagogue of Christ to the *nova sponsa* of Francis, then one must conclude that our Franciscan was changing the unchangeable : Olivi was amending the creed, sticking a Second Coming in between the First and Last; and that is what made him heretical in his own time and place, and also in ours.

THE HISTORICAL GOOD USES OF HERESY

With this evidence before us, one need register but little difficulty in understanding « what the fuss was about ». Just because our Olivi was heretical, however, does not lessen the fondness that we have for him. In fact, we appreciate him even more when we realize that his heresies helped him « think outside the box » of his century. Olivi & Co. were the first Joachite version of the countless fissiparous sectarian separatists, charismatic groups, spiritual conventicles, and schismatic reformers – beginning with the Beguines – who, in the centuries following Olivi's death, would read themselves into God's apocalyptic timetable just as Olivi had done. The church, an « institution in process » (Burr), was about to make – was already making – big changes. That fact of history is what made of our beloved Olivi – heretical or not – some kind of a true prophet.

Did Olivi have the clairvoyance of « second sight » ? Did he have his ear down on the railroad tracks of history ? Was he merely but sufficiently in tune with his times to see which ways the straws in the wind were blowing ? Even a positivistic historian can say that Olivi – who died during the pontificate of Boniface VIII – predicted more or less accurately the Babylonian Captivity of the Church at Avignon, the break-up of the Holy Roman Empire, the Protestant Reformation,

1. Apoc 3 : 1, 5 : 6.
2. At Apoc 20 : 3, *L.S.A.*, p. 918-919.

and the emergence of the so-called Third Force in Christendom. Olivi's ecclesiology was a self-fulfilling prophecy of the pentecostal charismatic free-church movement that has eventuated in a millennial change of Christendom : the acute democratization of Christianity. Only when Joachite thinking turns political – as it did at Münster and with *il Duce* and *der Führer*, does it become scary; so long as it remains merely religious, it abides benign and can even be generative of social progress [1].

Sometime in late 1297, Olivi lay down his quill, having penned the final amen to his Apocalypse commentary. Now, he was watching to see the Ten Kings appear on the horizon and waiting to hear the voice of the next angel. Our Friar was already spiritually separated from Rome; sitting comfortably in Narbonne, he was listening for the rumor of war and the call to come out and be separate in every way from the Babylonian Whore. Although the scheduled moment on God's timetable for that drastic exodus had not yet quite arrived, it would inevitably come, for it had been foreseen on Patmos. Whoever the Ten Kings might be and whenever they might fall upon Rome, that would be the moment of *kairos* when Christ, the heavenly bridegroom, would put away his centuries-old wife of adultery and marry his new Bride of Poverty, thereby paralleling what his Father in Heaven had done when he had put away the Synagogue of the Jews in favor of the Church of Christ.

According to Olivi's sectarian logic, because the Church of Rome had now become unfaithful, a meretricious fornicator in her opposition to the Gospel of Evangelical Perfection as restored in Francis, she thereby qualified for marital annulment according to the canonical rule of Matthew 19 : 9. Olivi, a Franciscan sectarian of absolute poverty, was heretical because he did not understand that, in the words of the eight masters of Avignon, « the body of Christ corresponds to the entire mystical body of the Church, and not to some singular or separate portion of it » [2]. Olivi thought like a Protestant.

The apocalyptic logic runs like this : Even if the reigning pope were not yet fully heretical, he might soon become the very antichrist himself, for the Church of Rome was already showing her true Babylonian colors as the bloodthirsty continuation of the Roman Empire, and enemy of true faith and true poverty, sitting on her seven hills, a Petrine bureaucracy that had usurped the cruciform life of Christ and Francis. Papal Rome was not yet quite so perverted as Olivi read the Apocalypse to say that she would in time become, but the eschatological train had, nevertheless, already left the station. It was only a matter of time until the Ten Kings would take God's vengeance on the doomed city in the opening of the seven seals and the pouring out of the seven vials of divine wrath. The pattern of misbehavior in the Church was already apocalyptically clear, and, Olivi said, things were « now getting worse ».

1. See Warren Lewis, « Coming-again : How Society Functions through Its New Religions », in *New Religious Movements : A Perspective for Understanding Society*, Eileen Barker ed., New York & Toronto, Edwin Mellen Press, 1982, p. 191-215.

2. Article XXVI.

What *would* Olivi have said had he lived to see the burning at the stake of the four Franciscan Spirituals in Marseilles in 1318? What event could more clearly summarize the anti-Franciscan evil in the Church that Olivi was targeting in the cross-hairs of his Apocalypse commentary? Olivi might well have prophesied the rising of Francis himself from the ashes of those stubborn Friars who died for their defiance of Pope John XXII and for wearing their *usus pauper* miniskirts! What, moreover, would Olivi have said had he lived to see the day of William of Nogaret (in the service of the Ten Kings?) or of Cola di Rienzo (the *novus dux* of the Third Age?). As diametrically opposed ecclesiastically politically as these two figures were, Olivi might well have found space for each of them as characters on the pages of his Apocalypse commentary. No wonder that the Beguines, some of whom had known Olivi personally, made him posthumously their cult leader. No wonder that the Hutterite Brethren two hundred years later were still reading the *L.S.A.* and canonized Olivi an Anabaptist saint, remembered for his anti-papal teaching about poverty [1]. No wonder that Olivi's Joachite understanding of Babylon in the Apocalypse became grist for the Protestant anti-Roman mill, shot for the Protestant anti-papal cannon, proof-texts for a million Protestant sermons in which « the city that sits on seven hills » was identified as the Roman headquarters of a persecuting enemy. Although it is essentially an unhistorical statement, it is not too much to say that our pious Catholic Franciscan Friar, who remained a member of the Church of Rome in good standing until the day he died, had become a Protestant before there were Protestants, a Radical Reformer before there was a Reformation.

Olivi struggled to understand God's apocalyptic timetable for eschatological trains as published in the fine print of John's seven visions. Our Friar was planning, in company with the *nova sponsa* – but contrary to his advice in 1295 to Conrad of Offida – to hop on board the last train out of meretricious Rome.

At Apoc 18 : 4, Olivi wrote about the angelic voice that was to cry out, calling on the saints to flee from the great Babylon. That text, he said, refers primarily to spiritual separation from the bloody Whore; after the Ten Kings attacked and destroyed her, however, then the angelic voice would command the saints to leave her physically and literally, as well.

Olivi did not want innocent Franciscans and their associates suffering as the innocents had suffered with the guilty when the Catholic forces of the North, shouting their battle cry : « Kill them all – God will know His own ! » had ridden against the Albigensian forces of the South at Toulouse and Béziers (1208-1213). The crusade against the heretics had taken place a scant generation before Olivi's birth and partly in the town where twelve-year-old Olivi had entered the Franciscan Order ca. 1260. Olivi knew at close range what it meant for a city set on a hill to fall beneath the sword of divine vengeance and be burned on account of her apostasy.

1. K. Braitmichel, *Geschicht-Buch der Hutterischen Brüder*, R. Wolkan ed., Standoff Colony near Macleod, Alberta, Canada and Vienna, 1923), introduction.

Olivi knew with apocalyptic foresight that Rome was going to fall and burn, and that the voice of the angel – like an Heavenly station master – would call out the final departure : « Come ye out and be separate ! » Olivi was content to remain within the Church of Rome until the engine of the train of history might begin to move. Waiting in Narbonne for the apocalyptic departure time and the angelic : « All aboard ! » our Olivi heard, instead, the voice of « another angel », the Angel of Death.

POVERTY AS VIRTUE, POVERTY AS WARNING, AND PETER OF JOHN OLIVI

David Flood, O.F.M.

Peter of John Olivi proposed a Franciscan poverty which was both legitimate and dissident. It enjoyed approval and it questioned society. Franciscan poverty warned the Christian world which recognized its admissibility. In the first part of this text, I explain Franciscan poverty's social legitimacy. In the second I explain its critical edge. The critical edge to Olivi's Franciscan ideas even made some of his brothers uneasy.

I

Peter Olivi wrote his extensive treatise on Franciscan poverty in the late 1270s. The text predated *Exiit qui seminat*, the papal bull published in August 1279. Olivi defined poverty as the right way to deal with temporal things. With a wide variety of arguments, he explained to his fellow Franciscans their good reasons for living poorly. Olivi followed up his masterful treatment of Franciscan poverty with a further treatise, this one on *usus pauper*. One did not profess such poverty, he argued, without handling material things accordingly. To his mind, that approached the tautological. Not everyone agreed. Peter Olivi had to answer regularly for his views on poverty and on *usus pauper* in particular [1].

Although Peter Olivi occasionally refers to the extensive treatise on poverty as « the first question on poverty », the treatise and its logical adjunct belong to a set of questions, and in this set the two studies on Franciscan poverty occupy the eighth and the ninth place. They are *Quaestio VIII* and *Quaestio IX* in the *Quaestiones de perfectione evangelica*. Consequently they belong to a larger

1. J. Schlageter has edited the treatise on poverty : *Das Heil der Armen und das Verderben der Reichen*, Dietrich-Coelde-Verlag, 1989. D. Burr, the treatise on material restraint : *Petrus Ioannis Olivi. De usu paupere. The* Quaestio *and the* Tractatus, Olschki, 1992. In the *Quaestio* on *usus pauper*, Olivi offers this notion : « A good man living purposefully seeks only what he needs to pursue his good purposes. Now that is *usus pauper* » (lines 778-781 : « *Rectitudo etiam naturalis voluntatis nostre non querit nisi quantum est necessarium sustentationi nature et prout expedit naturali rectitudini conservande et promovende. Hoc autem non est aliud quam querere pauperem usum* »). My thanks to Margaret Carney (The Franciscan Institute) for pointing out weaknesses in the penultimate draft of this text.

argument about Franciscan life. In that larger argument, two further pieces fit Olivi's theory of Franciscan poverty into the social realities of late thirteenth century life. Olivi's treatise on obedience (*Quaestio XI*) locates his poor Franciscans within the church, whereas his treatise on mendicancy (*Quaestio X*) locates them within Christian society, where they expect material support in return for their spiritual services.

Obedience

Peter Olivi's treatise on obedience lodges his poor Franciscans resolutely within the Church. Does the vow of obedience, he asks, made to another man, really belong to gospel life? Though he is questioning individual behavior, in truth Olivi is handling the relation of a subordinate institution to the authority which legitimates it. For the order as a whole enjoys the Church's approval as a duly constituted religious order; and it will in fact remain that subordinate institution insofar as it enjoys the submission of its members.

Olivi introduces his argument for obedience by declaring that obedience belongs to the very substance of gospel life. It frees individuals to pursue right action. Once Franciscans declare their commitment to God's service, they have answered Jesus' summons to follow him. They have put themselves firmly in the context of fidelity. One answers God's summons best by the Franciscan vow of obedience.

Obedience binds individual Franciscans together into their community. « The bonds of religious life arise first of all out of the vow of obedience »[1]. Obedience results in a fraternity, animated by one spirit and one will[2]. Just as the apostles obeyed Jesus Christ and after his death Peter, so do Franciscans obey their minister general. Thereupon Olivi quotes Chapter Ten of the order's rule, to the effect that Franciscans deal openly with each other as members of one community.

In the opening section of his treatise on poverty (*Quaestio VIII*), where he describes poverty's virtuous consequences, Olivi establishes the link between poverty and obedience[3]. No material circumstances restrain the movements of a Franciscan, so that his obedience knows no limits. It knows no limits save when it runs contrary to its formal purpose of submission to God. When Peter Olivi makes the connection between poverty and obedience in the treatise on poverty, he immediately sums up the limitations on obedience. Thereby he refers to the explanation of these limits in the present treatise, on obedience[4]. Obedience and poverty go together easily as facets of Franciscan life. Consequently Peter Olivi

1. *Quaestio XI*, 376, 3 : « *Tenet [oboedientia] principatum in connectendo regularem statum* ». The treatise has been edited as an appendix to Peter of John Olivi on the Bible, The Franciscan Institute, 1997.

2. *Quaestio XI*, 377, 8.

3. *Quaestio VIII*, 118, 7ff.

4. *Quaestio XI* (obedience) refers to *Quaestio VIII* (poverty) and *vice versa*. Olivi crossreferenced them, as he did other of his writings.

observes that anyone can spell out obedience's many services to Franciscan life, along the pattern of poverty's virtuous consequences[1]. He builds obedience into his Franciscan perspective. His Franciscan perspective belongs to a corporate body and not to a fascinated following : he was, in principle, an obedient brother and not, as some said, the head of a sect.

Once Olivi has established the primacy of obedience in gospel life, he goes into the limits on obedience. He explains its limits at greater length than its legitimacy and importance. It is easier to prove the importance of obedience than it is to draw the line between virtuous obedience and destructive submissiveness. Olivi places three limits on obedience, and with each limit draws closer to a Franciscan's responsibility to keep his eyes open and his conscience quick. A Franciscan will not obey and commit sin. A Franciscan will not obey and approach a clear danger of mortal sin. A Franciscan will not obey by engaging in behavior manifestly contrary to his Christian commitment. By reaching the third limit, Peter Olivi assures the control of conscience and open discussion on obedience to superiors. For people within the order have authority over others to ensure that all follow the rule. Superiors, or ministers to use the Franciscan term, are bound to favor Franciscan action and not to hinder it. They have no authority to demand action which would sully the Franciscan commitment.

Peter Olivi has an easy time explaining and justifying the three limits to obedience and the third one in particular, no matter how disruptive such a control on obedience should become. He refers to Chapter Ten in the order's rule. That chapter goes much further than Olivi's three limits in binding obedience into the Franciscan community's basic purposes. The rule chapter also has the authority of a Church-approved text[2].

Peter Olivi raises and answers a second question on obedience. His considerations and his conclusions to his subordinate query show his strict sense of institutional order. He wants to know if a perfectly obedient Franciscan may appeal from a lesser to a higher superior. In his response[3], Olivi begins by excluding a use of law to escape the rigors of Franciscan life. He quotes the canons and he quotes the order's constitutions to that effect. Even if superiors should handle their subjects roughly, in a fashion which might be appealed canonically, a Franciscan will not initiate the process. The canons do make concessions to human weakness; but a Franciscan professes the highest form of obedience. The Franciscan way « demands a sovereign disregard [...] of all ambition »[4]. Peter Olivi offered the precision after his less than satisfactory stay in Paris. There is no evidence he backed off from his observation in the 1280s. Once, however, he has excluded appeals against disagreeable superiors for

1. *Quaestio XI*, 379, 5-10.

2. In 1241-1242, the Four Masters explained the rule passage referred to by Olivi with the same restrictions on obedience. See L. Oliger, ed., *Expositio Quatuor Magistrorum [...]*, Rome 1950, p. 165, 2-11. The Masters' commentary exercised great influence on later understanding of the rule. Hugh of Digne quoted it extensively in his commentary, as did Peter Olivi.

3. *Quaestio XI*, 399-402.

4. *Quaestio XI*, 399, 26-28.

personal reasons, he lays out the grounds for questioning unsatisfactory governance and for bringing weaknesses and abuses, errors and dangers to Franciscan life to the attention of higher authorities.

Olivi lists the grounds for an appeal: the quality of Franciscan life; the Catholic faith; the good of one's community and one's spiritual progress. When he suffers abuse, the Franciscan brings the abuses and the dangers to the attention of the authorities. Olivi does not consider here, as did the canons, the case of papal failure. (He did not have to face papal intransigence, as did Michael of Cesena and Bonagratia of Bergamo with Pope John XXII). The considerations expect comprehension, support, and redress from the order's ministers, the cardinal protector, and the Roman curia. Olivi's obedience, which he brings into play forcefully and clearly in his response to the censure by Bonagratia of San Giovanni in Persiceto, unfolds within the rules and with due respect for the authority of the church.

Olivi does not only admit of appeal in the interests of the order and of the church. He considers it a duty: a clear expression of one's responsibility for the lofty meaning of one's Franciscan commitment. Olivi offers as example fire in town. Should fire threaten, one sounds alarm. Should a Franciscan see his order in danger, he raises a hue and cry. Obedience has its own *actio oboediens*, its *submissio activa*, to match *usus pauper*. Olivi has an activist and not an institutional understanding of Franciscan life.

So Peter Olivi gives the rules, the usages, the lofty purposes of his Franciscan organization strong theoretical confirmation. His obedience makes the order functional as a church organization. By sanctioning the order's organizational details, he solidifies its institutional place within the Church. Franciscans pursued in their day the life led by Jesus, reported in the gospels. To this purpose the brothers first gathered around Francis, to whom Olivi refers as a warrant for his proposals; and given the organization's success they continued to come together as the continuation of that original community. Olivi's argument on obedience told them they had formed holy bonds; and his justification of appeal served clarity of organization as well as forthrightness of obedience. Given the perfect lineaments of his order, given as well the freedom and duty of each Franciscan to see to it that the system worked, Olivi never needed a different social body for a perfectly poor life in service to God's designs. The church approved warmly the brothers' embodiment of Christ's truth. So did Brother Peter of John.

Mendicancy

Peter Olivi followed up his major treatment of Franciscan poverty (*Quaestio VIII*) with a subordinate one on poverty's material consequences (*Quaestio IX*). He then completed his consideration on poverty by addressing mendicancy (*Quaestio X*). He put the question whether those poor by the gospel should beg or labor for their sustenance. He was not really discussing the question but writing an apology for the Franciscan way; and Franciscans had long abandoned their commitment to labor and turned to mendicancy to cover their needs. Olivi argued the superiority of the order's mendicant economics[1].

Olivi makes his case for mendicancy with a variety of considerations. He follows the professional method of opening with a barrage of arguments against the desired conclusion. The barrage draws out the dangers of mendicancy as well as the soundness of labor. Having put much information on the table, he can explain Franciscan mendicancy in detail while arguing for its worth. He does so vigorously, while handling manual labor kindly. These positive presentations of both mendicancy and work allow him to conclude, in a careful and circumstantial way, to the superiority of the Franciscan practice of mendicancy.

In the course of his argument for Franciscan mendicancy, Peter Olivi considers the possibility of abuse. Already in his question on *usus pauper* he had told how, as a young Franciscan, he recognized the devastation caused by begging for more than the modest means of life.

Olivi lists possible abuses in his seventh (of nineteen) argument against mendicancy. He posits the principle that mendicancy readily occasions a series of moral failures : injustice and flattery, hypocrisy and laziness, and so on. He runs the list to twelve such forms of low behavior and then goes into the details. Questionable mendicancy existed then, as it exists today, and not only in the dirty streets of large cities. Olivi well knew that Franciscans regularly violated the limits of virtuous mendicancy. He does not bring that troubling data into play here. He is covering Franciscan policy, and Franciscans beg.

When he gets to the refutation of the arguments against mendicancy, Peter Olivi treats each form of reprehensible mendicancy listed in the seventh argument. He does not hesitate to hark back to his major statement on Franciscan poverty, *Quaestio VIII*, and there to the first part of his argument. For in the first of the five parts of the question's body, Olivi listed fifteen forceful patterns of behavior which Franciscan poverty favors and supports; and insofar as mendicancy expresses that poverty, as Olivi duly demonstrates, mendicancy belongs to a social dynamic which never slips into the low behavior detailed in a dozen dismal patterns by argument seven. Poverty favors generosity and piety, for example. A poor Franciscan gives joyously without expecting, without even wanting any return. He gives with concern for the recipient (which Olivi understands here as piety), and Olivi goes on to offer four reasons for a Franciscan's surplus of compassion. Mendicancy helps unleash such sensitive liberality. One cannot say Peter Olivi does not make a good case. As he refutes the varieties of mendicant misbehavior, we readily understand his emphasis on *usus pauper*.

Olivi's case for Franciscan mendicancy relies, as is understandable, on the brothers' spiritual services. If Franciscans have to get jobs for wages to put food on the table and keep a roof over their heads, they will not have time for study and prayer, and their words of instruction and of encouragement will lack point and force. He puts it at one point as follows : « Those who give [to gospel beggars] [...]

1. The text has been published in *A.F.H.* 87, 1994, p. 299-347.

are supporting men who pray to God for them [...]; they are encouraging contemplation and preaching »[1]. Certainly good Christians, and Christians less than virtuous, readily take note of good and humble men who live and keep alive Jesus' law of love and care for others. Olivi refers to the Apostle's words, in *II Corinthians 8, 14*, whereby some help others in their material need who, in return, help them in their spiritual need[2].

Olivi's argument on poverty locates Franciscans among Christians as the very exemplars of the gospel truth which they propose in their preaching and in their counsel. The Franciscans' poverty supplies their organization a dynamic which reaches out to others and strengthens them on their Christian way[3]. And mendicancy expresses and preserves their poverty.

Olivi's persuasive argument not only locates poor Franciscans among Christians as effective laborers of spiritual truth. It puts them under the control of those who have the means to give them (or withhold) the alms of their sustenance.

Poor Brother Peter of John had no great admiration for the rich. Rich people, for the most part, he notes in passing, take what they can get, with little heed for justice[4]. Possessions distort the relations which should exist among people. Yet Peter Olivi accords these people control over the Franciscans' economics. In praising the behavior induced by the mendicant state, Olivi says mendicancy leads to humility and submission[5]. He says it in a way, especially when he praises his mendicants' « universal-obedience », which easily pushes Franciscans towards the hypocrisy and flattery so roundly rejected in argument seven. And yet he persists in claiming that mendicancy bolsters poverty, for those who give do not intend to subsidize laziness and laxity among Franciscans[6].

We have here a discrepancy between a theory of helplessness (mendicancy) and the social movement of goods. Although, theoretically, mendicancy might well see to it that the brothers abide by their humility and poverty, the social movement of goods will not hesitate to censure their performance and bend it to the expectations of rich Christians. The Franciscans are coming close to sacrificing poverty's intrinsic message to the social order of wealth.

If we put the best face on Olivi's demonstration, as he undoubtedly would wish, then his proposals amount to a division of labor, with Franciscans contributing spiritual services for material provision. They expect the means of life from a society they serve well by their example and by their word. Olivi says nothing about the danger of economic dependency. He does not consider the fate of an irate prophet.

With *Quaestiones X* and *XI*, on mendicancy and on obedience, Peter Olivi ties Franciscan poverty into the church and into society. Obedience sees to it that

1. *Quaestio X*, 309, 33-310, 1.

2. *Quaestio X*, 310, 33-35.

3. *Quaestio VIII*, 85 : *Paupertas valet « ad status [...] dilatationem [...][et] ad animarum conversionem et spiritualem gubernationem »*.

4. *Quaestio X*, 300, 29-30. Even though Olivi is setting up arguments here for later dismissal, his brief image of the wealthy agrees with his idea of the mechanics of excessive appropriation.

5. *Quaestio X*, 308, 22-23.

6. *Quaestio X*, 309, 33ff.

Franciscans heed instruction from church authorities. Their mendicancy (as explained by *Quaestio X*) binds them into society as those who provide spiritual uplift (and not disturbing correction).

II

Apocalyptics

At the same time as Peter of John's treatises on obedience and mendicancy integrated his poor Franciscans into Christian society, his *Quaestiones* also assigned them a challenging role among Christians. For their poverty was intrinsically critical, given its eschatological dimension. That is, Franciscan poverty handled temporal things in terms of a perfect and final order. It reminded Christians, and forcefully on occasion, that « we have here no abiding home ». It told them « what to seek and whither to tend, what to flee and how to hold to course » [1].

Moreover, *Quaestio VIII* gave particular historical reasons for living poorly. Although gospel poverty had subsided in recent centuries, in the church, Francis of Assisi brought it back to full vigor. He did so as part of the Franciscan effort to save what could be saved in the trials of the final times.

Apocalyptics in the Rule Commentary

The eschatological accent completes the simple explanation of the Franciscan rule which Peter Olivi wrote as practical corollary to the *Quaestiones de perfectione evangelica* [2]. He introduced the commentary by distinguishing it from the *Quaestiones*. Whereas in the *Quaestiones* he explained the great wisdom of the Franciscan rule (that is, he supplied Franciscan life theoretical justification), here, in the commentary, he tells simple brothers how to live the rule. His extensive theoretical exercise serves no purpose unless brothers put the rule into practice. The rule needs honest brothers the way poverty needs usus pauper.

Once Olivi has characterized the commentary and stated its purpose, he adds : « May the shrewd and simple spirit of Christ, of his servant Francis, of Francis' companions, of the whole order and of the church of God, help and guide us in our study of the rule ». Brother Peter of John gathers his simple brothers about him. They shall study the rule and carry on the life. In the succeeding chapters he draws from the rule the poor, the mendicant, the obedient life in service to the Christian community so eloquently argued in the *Quaestiones*.

At the end of his commentary, in his explanations of the rule's twelfth and final chapter, Peter Olivi proposes that Franciscans have an historical mission among those still ignorant of the gospel. He understands the mission in terms of

1. *Quaestio VIII*, 120, 27-28.
2. *Peter Olivi's Rule Commentary*, Steiner Verlag, 1972.

the great events which will mark history's end. In this context, without engaging in any extensive exegesis, he evokes Francis as the angel of the sixth seal. Quite clearly, wholly in the logic of his commentary on the rule, he associates those who live by the rule with Francis' role in history. Then, after Chapter Twelve, he ends his commentary with a brief prayer. The prayer sums up the Franciscan style and the Franciscan purpose : true Christians, obedient to the pope, render the Spirit present among believers and unbelievers.

Peter Olivi viewed life by the rule, with its obedience to the pope and with the poverty enjoined by Christ's gospel, in eschatological terms. Those who profess and live by the rule have the task of completing evangelization of the world before the end. They have the task of helping the Christian community through the travail of those final times.

Olivi took his eschatological perspective from « the order's masters »[1], in particular from Bonaventure of Bagnoregio. Bonaventure represented the order's masters as no other. And he it was who formally identified Francis of Assisi as the angel of the sixth seal, a key figure in the apocalyptic scenario of the *Book of Revelations*. That book Peter Olivi read with his students. He read it in the context of Franciscan apocalypticism. He read the rest of Scripture as well. And all of it, the Apocalypse included, he read in the context of his theory on Scripture.

Neither Olivi's theses on poverty, nor his apocalyptical reflections, nor the combination of the two, lay beyond the Franciscan pale. Brother Peter of John had the Franciscan life and the cognitive abilities which gave him the task of bringing poverty back into the Franciscan conscience and into Franciscan life. The minister general's cover letter to *Exiit qui seminat* suffices to prove the necessity of the task (whereas his moral exhortation did little to carry it out). The minister general insisted that much more on improving the Franciscan performance as Pope Nicholas III let him know that the improvement was his part of the bargain : Nicholas' *Exiit* strengthened the order's position within the church considerably. Olivi drew up solid theses on Franciscan poverty, theses which never suffered condemnation, in good part because they had tradition on their side. His proposals on poverty, with its social role in the order and its place in the order's mission, even if contested by other Franciscans, belong to Franciscan history. Nor does the easy fit between his ideas on poverty and his apocalypticism lie outside Franciscan tradition. Peter Olivi's apocalyptical writings and his commentary on the Apocalypse in particular handled questions of Franciscan tradition. More important, he handled them within his understanding of Scripture and of Scripture's role in Franciscan life. In the interests of his theses on poverty, lodged effectively within church and Christian society, it is useful to offer a social apology for his apocalypticism as well.

Apocalyptics and the Legenda maior

Bonaventure of Bagnoregio defined Francis of Assisi as « the angel of the sixth seal ». By that declaration, he both interpreted his times as the age of the

1. See *Statuta generalia ordinis* VII 22, as in *A.F.H.* 34, 1941, 73.

final crisis and accorded Franciscans a cardinal role in rescuing the Christian community from destruction.

Bonaventure defined Francis of Assisi as the angel of the sixth seal, a key figure in the passage from the fifth to the sixth age, in the opening lines of the *Legenda maior*. He announced that he and his readers were living in the final times : « In these last days the grace of God our Savior has appeared in his servant Francis ». Bonaventure also made sure he defined the audience of the so promising appearance : « [...] appeared [...] to the true friends of holy poverty ». Poor Franciscans, given their poverty, understand the signs of the times. Bonaventure uses other images and references to evoke the Franciscan turning point in history. He concludes by stating explicitly that the Apostle John, in the Apocalypse (7, 1), meant Francis when he announced the arrival of the angel of the sixth seal, marked with the sign of the living God. His introduction done, the tone given, Bonaventure wrote his account of Francis in that key [1].

With the *Legenda maior*'s proposals on history and history's demands on Franciscans, Bonaventure made a public and political declaration. He wrote the *Legenda maior* because the general chapter of 1260, over which he presided, gave him the task. He presented his account of Francis at the following general chapter (1263) and at the subsequent general chapter (1266) the *Legenda maior* was declared the official account of Francis – not only for the order but for the church as well. All other accounts of Francis, in the order and outside the order, were to be run down and destroyed. Bonaventure saw to it, politically, that his life of Francis turned into the most public of Franciscan texts. The order's previous problems with Joachimism made his apocalyptical identification of Francis that much more political [2].

Bonaventure's account was well received and widely distributed. M. Bihl supposes [3] that Bonaventure had a copy for each minister when he presented the *Legenda maior* to the general chapter of 1263. The thirty-four ministers had a sure text to take home with them for further copying. At the following chapter the order's ministers ratified the account, both for the order and for Christendom.

Bonaventure's account was further distributed through the *Legenda minor*. The *Legenda minor* abbreviated the text, turning the story into the sixty-three lessons of the feast and octave of Saint Francis [4]. When M. Bihl presented his edition of the *Legenda maior*, he said it would be easy to add further manuscripts

1. R. Emmerson and R. Herzman devote a chapter to the *Legenda maior* in their book on *The Apocalyptic Imagination in Medieval Literature* (U. of Pennsylvania Press, 1992). In an introductory chapter they claim that apocalypticism, views deriving from the Apocalypse and its interpretation, pervade the medieval mind, more specifically the learned mind of theologian and poet. As their first case, they turn to Bonaventure of Bagnoregio's *Legenda maior*. They propose that apocalypticism « informs the structure » (33) of Bonaventure's account of Francis.

2. The traditional line which plays down Bonaventure's *Legenda maior* as neutered apocalypticism would mistake Handel's *Alleluia* for Brahms's *Lullaby*. Even after such studies as that of Emerson and Herzman, we have : A. Pompei, « La storiografia di San Francesco dal Celano al Bonaventura » in *Frate Tommaso da Celano*, Tagliacozzo, 1995, p. 39.

3. *Analecta Franciscana* X, Quaracchi, 1941, LXXII.

4. In VII 1 of the *Legenda minor* Francis is designated as the angel of the sixth seal. That paragraph also mentions Francis' desire to work again among the lepers.

of the *Legenda maior* to the ninety-three in Latin and forty-three in translation listed by the Quaracchi editors in 1898. The explanation for the text's wide distribution raises no problem.

We do have a problem with the influence of Francis' historical role, as defined by the *Legenda maior*, on the thought and life of the order and its members[1]. Matthew of Aquasparta readily labeled Francis of Assisi the angel of Apocalypse 7, 1 at the beginning of a sermon. A man of great learning, Matthew knew well the traditions of the order, and here he did the eschatological tradition some satisfaction. He had no need of an eschatological scenario himself. He held office in the order and in the Church; he addressed problems of administration and not crises of history. People need an apocalyptical scenario when the times are out of joint. So it was when the biblical authors developed the apocalyptical mode. Oppression reigned, corruption flourished. In the face of such evil, they promised final victory and salvation, and did so with extravagant imagery. Not every Franciscan in the late thirteenth century felt seized by Francis' role as harbinger of history's end, nor moved by a language of crisis.

Francis played a pivotal role in salvation history. Bonaventure said it, the chapter of 1266 ratified the theory, and the order's teachers had to transmit the lesson. By the time Peter of John read the Apocalypse with his students, in 1297, Bonaventure's identification of Francis had received some development. Olivi summarized the discussion and offered his own inclusive, and inconclusive, review of the question. He at least, in contrast to other Franciscan lectors, worked over the conceptual machinery of the order's apocalyptical tradition, as was a lector's duty. Olivi had a much stronger sense of the order's identity than did other Franciscan lectors about whom we are informed. The *Quaestiones de perfectione evangelica* offer us abundant evidence of his very Franciscan cast of mind, especially as corroborated by some of his exegesis. Given the acuity of his sense of Franciscan mission, he could less easily dodge the challenge implicit in God's word in Francis to the friends of holy poverty.

Scripture

However seriously Peter Olivi took Franciscan apocalypticism, he had a theory of Scripture to contain his own reflections on history and its stages. His theory helps us understand his refusal to commit himself on future events. Moreover, the basic drama of his life, the soul of his study and teaching, lay in the conflict between gospel truth and contemporary philosophy, between Jesus' story and Aristotle's teachings, between the folly of the cross and the wisdom of the world. Whereas his theory of Scripture allows us to contextualize his work on the Apocalypse, his distinction between biblical truth and university learning defines his Franciscan teaching and consequently his place in the Franciscan community.

1. For some information and analysis, see : Stanislao da Campagnola, *L'Angelo del sesto sigillo e l'« alter Christus »*, Rome, 1971.

Peter Olivi explained how he understood Scripture in a major professional text. I call it « a major professional text », for it introduced Olivi's theology : « What is the subject of sacred Scripture and of this book », the book being the *Sentences*. His answer to the question explained the nature, the form, the purpose both of Scripture and of his own theological writings. When he addressed the question of Scripture's forms, he raised, by implication, the problem of John's Apocalypse. He could make sense out of the Apocalypse if he understood the manner of its rhetoric. As for Scripture's purpose, it pursued the sort of education which Peter of John had spelled out in the *Quaestiones de perfectione evangelica*. The *Quaestiones* laid out the finest lessons of Jesus' gospel.

E. Stadter has made Peter Olivi's question on Scripture available, both by his edition and by his thorough study of the text[1]. Stadter draws out Olivi's decisive rejection of Aristotelianism as Olivi refuses to turn study of Scripture into a science. To make his point, Olivi had but to play up the importance of the event in contrast to Aristotelian abstraction. Stadter also details Olivi's understanding of Scripture as God's slow education and repair of humankind. Given Stadter's other studies on Peter Olivi, he hears well the resonance of key terms in the Franciscan's reflection[2]. He praises the coherence of Olivi's thought[3], wherein he explores Olivi's understanding of Scripture, revelation, and eschatology. In *Quaestio I*, he declares, « we have a tightly argued and summary lesson on the relation between the substance of faith and the Aristotelian notion of science as discussed in the thirteenth century »[4].

Once Peter Olivi has explained and justified Scripture's great variety in *Quaestio I*, he uses a simple example to concretize his argument[5] :

> Let us suppose that a father wants to give his sons and his friends in writing a distinctive way of going about life. So he compiles for them a brief text which contains some medical and nutritional data, something about mathematics and physics, and a few new stories about ancestors of theirs, and all of this with advice, rules, warnings and corrections, all of it useful, written in a clear and balanced style. He adds as well forecasts of coming events. We cannot say then that his compilation has any one subject, as sciences have a single subject, seeing

1. E. Stadter, « Offenbarung und Heilsgeschichte nach Petrus Johannis Olivi », *Franziskanische Studien* 44, 1962, 1-12 ; p. 129-191. The text is on pages 2-12. Stadter had only one manuscript to work with. However major the text, it has reached us by the thinnest of bridges. In his study of Olivi's « Offenbarung und Heilsgeschichte », along with his edition of *Quaestio I*, Stadter uses Olivi's *Principia in sacram Scripturam*. Olivi refers to the *Principia* when discussing the subordinate question of Scripture's form. We should distinguish between the two. Olivi puts his case more clearly and tightly, more technically, in the *Quaestio* than in his often rambling *Principia*.

2. See for example what Stadter has done with the word *adhaerere* in « Das Glaubensproblem in seiner Bedeutung für die Ethik bei Petrus Johannis Olivi O.F.M. (+1298) », *Franziskanische Studien* 42, 196, p. 225-296. See pages 237 and 258. The term helps us understand Olivi on belief, and Olivi on belief helps us understand his ideas on history.

3. « Offenbarung und Heilsgeschichte », 191 : « [...] ein System von einer erstaunlichen Geschlossenheit [...] »

4. « Offenbarung und Heilsgeschichte », 130.

5. The consensus is that he is presenting his own thoughts, with what referents is not known.

> as it contains much about many particular and general bodies of learning. And it contains much else which has nothing to do with the notion of science [1].

The example sums up Olivi's idea of Scripture well, especially insofar as it brings a father into play. For earlier in the *Quaestio*, Olivi pointed out that the scriptures in their great variety were handed down as things to believe :

> The unity of faith does not require that whatever is believed about anything has to have one scientific rationale or one subject, as the unity of science requires. By the faith in which I believe my father I can believe many assertions and negations of various kinds, in their very difference, and much that is factual.

And earlier still Olivi used the verb *adhaerere* to indicate the mode of belief in Scripture's particulars. *Adhaerere* plays an important role in Olivi's understanding of faith. Olivi's relation of faith to God involves stepping over into God's company as one continues on one's way. In *Quaestio I* he adheres to the God who educates him in Scripture. He goes along with Scripture's action. That action finds foremost expression in the life of Jesus, the embodiment of gospel perfection (and the heart of his *Quaestiones de perfectione evangelica*). At the end of his treatment[2], Olivi does not feel he has to go into the purposes of Scripture. What he has said up to that point, and his example of a household head preparing a manual of instruction for his dependents, explains well to what end Scripture has come about.

In *Quaestio I*, Peter Olivi also raises the question about Scripture's form. In answering his query, toward the end of the *Quaestio*, he refers to what he has written while detailing the variety of Scripture's contents. Scripture uses the different ways in which human beings communicate : Scripture contains history and legislation, prophecy and wise reflection. Peter Olivi devoted much thought to defining Scripture's ways in order to read Scripture well. He wanted to know what was going on. Although he refers to his *Principia in sacram Scripturam* as the locus of his work on Scripture's modi[3], he did so as well in several introductions to particular books of exegesis[4]. Although he did not do so, Peter of John could have easily located his role as lector in his brief answer to Scripture's purposes[5]. The Father educating his Franciscan children through Scripture (and not through philosophy) needed someone well versed in reading Scripture. That is what Brother Peter of John did. He helped his fellow Franciscans live as poor and obedient men of the gospel in apocalyptic times.

Peter Olivi had a difficult time figuring out how to handle some parts of the Bible. Once he began reading Isaiah, who labeled his book a vision, Olivi tried to figure out what went into that particular mode of communication. At its core lay a question of epistemology. Olivi had his problems with the apocalyptical books of

1. *Quaestio I*, 7, 34-38.
2. *Quaestio I*, 11, 34-37.
3. *Quaestio I*, 11, 29.
4. Olivi's notabilia to his *Lectura in Apocalypsim* is especially well known. He proceeded similarly with his *Isaiah* and *Acts Commentaries*.
5. *Quaestio I*, 11, 34-37.

Scripture as well. In his study of Olivi's *Quaestio I*, E. Stadter points out that Olivi knew the literature germane to his study[1]. As a Franciscan scholar, consequently, with the task of sorting out progress towards history's consummation and the Franciscans' role therein, he studied and used Joachim of Fiore. A Franciscan who studied the Apocalypse and did not use Joachim of Fiore was passing on general and accepted learning instead of wrestling with Franciscan apocalyptics. Peter Olivi used Joachim of Fiore's scriptural work. Yet no one has yet explained how Joachim of Fiore fits into Peter of John's exegetical labors. Olivi's labors as Franciscan lector, taken up with his order's role in the day's events, wary of the dangers of an overweening Aristotelianism, removed him from the context of Joachim of Fiore's own history. Joachim was a visionary (in a politically agitated southern Italy) in the late twelfth century, whereas Olivi was a Franciscan lector a century later.

Scriptural Wisdom

Although his commentary on the Apocalypse took on a life of its own, Peter Olivi defined his history by a dialectics of knowledge and not within an apocalyptic scenario. He explained himself in that way to his friends in the early 1280s when a major effort was mounted to quiet him[2]. He was called to serve the Franciscan conscience and not to succeed in the world of learning.

Peter Olivi developed the intrinsic incompatibility between the wisdom of the cross and the wisdom of the world in his commentary on Paul's first letter to the Corinthians. Olivi was reading the letter with his students, and the section where Paul draws the distinction between the folly of the cross and the wisdom of the world, when death put an end to his labors.

Peter Olivi divides the letter into eight parts and begins going through them. The first part (1, 10-4, 21) he subdivides into three. He only gets into the second of the three (1, 17-3, 2), but in this second part Paul challenges the world's learning, and Olivi distinguishes and examines the Apostle's five arguments (as Olivi divides up the text).

First Paul explains that the learned simply do not understand how the passion and death of Christ has redefined the conditions of life in this world. The learned and the savvy might think they are imposing themselves on the world as winners. In truth, seeing as their knowledge is erroneous, they lose out on life. At this point Olivi makes the distinctions about non-Christian learning with which he regularly functioned.

> Note that the wisdom of the world includes things simply false and erroneous. These the wisdom of Christ rejects outright. It includes things true in themselves but uses the knowledge pompously and presumptuously to false purposes. These the wisdom of Christ sets aside, not insofar as they are true but for their

1. « Offenbarung und Geschichtstheologie », 130.

2. Olivi took the sudden end of his Parisian sojourn as a lesson in gospel wisdom. The letter and its passages are well enough known to dispense with their analysis here.

> misconstrued programs. The wisdom of Christ takes what is true in worldly learning, but as handmaid and not as mistress, as a dull lamp, inadequate to light up the way to eternal life [1].

As he reads Paul, Olivi explains how the learned have not found the way to God. The Jews are shocked by the cross; the Greeks see no point to it. At the end of this argument, Olivi explains our need of faith, would we be saved. In our great need, we have to let love of God captivate our mind. Then we see what lies before us [2].

After the third and fourth argument (God favors the lowly; Paul shuns any hint of self-importance), the Apostle extolls, in his fifth argument, the wisdom he shares with those prepared to receive it: « We speak wisdom among the perfect [...] » Olivi immediately excludes any high spiritual claims: « Here Paul calls perfect not those who understand perfectly and need no instruction; he means those perfectly suited to learn wisdom from perfect teachers » [3]. Thereupon Olivi distinguishes five phases in this, the fifth and final argument (of the second of three parts to the first of the whole epistle's eight parts). He continues to subdistinguish his way to further reflection on the incompatibility of the Franciscan mind (as he defines it) with the age's learning. His lesson had to do with Franciscan identity; it had to do with scriptural support for Franciscan poverty. *Usus pauper* was not *usus opulentus*, as Olivi once defined the term, and one stayed poor if one refused to think as did society's preceptors.

With an ideal text for his lesson before him, Olivi extends his lesson on the learning which is of God. At the second phase of his fifth argument, he gets into the seven qualities of the wisdom in question. As the fifth quality Olivi designates the inaccessibility of this wisdom. To make his point, he proposes a twofold proof. After handling three objections to the first proof, he advances to the second. The second proof he offers with a threefold argument. And there the commentary breaks off, with Olivi offering as his final observation:

> No man heavy with this world and especially no one proud of his evanescent knowledge can ascend to ecstatic contemplation of what surpasses the mind: only one taught and led and taken by the Spirit of Christ [4].

From the point of view of his labors as lector, Brother Peter of John died while delving ever further into the wisdom to which poverty threw open the door. Only after finishing the series of seven qualities and the five arguments to the second point would he be able to turn his attention to the completion of the opening chapter of his commentary on the letter to the Corinthians. He had ventured far into divine wisdom. And there he died, surrounded by his brothers, to whom with this text he left abundant material for their prayerful study.

1. *Olivi on the Bible*, 357, 8-14.

2. Olivi refers to faith here in terms which he develops and defines in his systematic reflections on faith. See E. Stadter. « Das Glaubensproblem ». Olivi's exegesis enjoyed the support of well-textured theory.

3. *Olivi on the Bible*, 361, 5-7.

4. *Olivi on the Bible*, 364, 3-7.

At the beginning of the letter to the Corinthians (1, 7-8), Paul referred to the final times. The passage readily admitted of at least a few words on the crisis of the age. Peter Olivi did the lines no apocalyptic reverence. He explained how Paul opened his message with praise for the Corinthians. Then Olivi took up the commentary of the letter's first (of eight) part, which began (1, 10) : « I appeal to you [...] » As he had observed in *Quaestio I* (On Scripture), Scripture spoke in many ways for the instruction of the faithful. The initial lesson, the basic lesson, consisted in studying its « various lessons » [1], for they fashioned the true Franciscan [2], a brother to all, with no stake in this world [3].

Peter Olivi's troubles with the Franciscan administration in the early 1280s are the troubles the Franciscan organization was having with itself and with its past. When he looked at his troubles, Olivi had difficulty understanding how they could happen to him, given his devotion and service to order and church [4]. And that was their point : the troubles happened to him because he devoted himself too inventively and too influentially, and perhaps too disputatiously, to the order's high ideals. When he got his chance to answer the accusations lodged against him [5], he acted as a poor and obedient Franciscan. He did not flee into a private history (even though he was dealing with men « *reverendi et metuendi* »). That is, he did not abandon the Franciscan cause, as represented in his views, and do what had to be done to allay administrative displeasure. By his response he carried his troubles into the order's tasks of self-scrutiny and self-correction. The order and its masters had to take account of what one (unofficial) master was saying and doing in their common interest. We see Olivi's insistence on making his case a Franciscan case, as opposed to a private or individual one, in the presentation of his response [6].

Even though Peter Olivi opened with a reflection of principle, on obedience to God and God's Church, he did get around to telling his critics that they had not handled his case according to the rules (They had acted as his judges. He answered them as his critics). He pointed out that they had flouted proper procedure at the beginning of his response; he repeated his point at the end. He had in mind both Church law as well as the order's rules. He had but to mention it; he needed no reference. His critics knew he was right.

Olivi began his defense by explaining his submission to God and to God's authority on earth, the Church. In such submission lay the justification for any obedience in doctrinal matters within the order. Olivi insisted on locating the discussion with his critics within their common devotion to the laws of the Lord God and the truth of Jesus Christ : « Far be it from us », he concluded a severe paragraph on philosophy, « that we abandon the laws of God for the traditions of

1. *Quaestio I*, 6, 37.
2. See *Quaestio I*, 11, 35.
3. Such his theory of poverty : *Quaestio VIII*, p. 125-128.
4. So ended his letter to his friends.
5. « Responsio fratris Petri Ioannis » *A.F.H.* 28, 1935, p. 130-155 and 374-407.
6. « Responsio », p. 130-135 and 407.

any men [...] »[1]. In the interests of church doctrine, he called for study and discussion on points of doctrinal difference. Given the principled way he did so, he also argued for human dignity, and not only his own, and for open intellectual exchange in the order.

In sum, Peter Olivi corrected his critics and pushed the discussion onto the open stage of Franciscan life. He abided by his resolution of service, as expressed at the end of his letter to his friends. We can take his rehabilitation by Matthew of Aquasparta as implicit acknowledgment of his case : not necessarily of its proposals but of the admissibility of his defense. For that reason, Olivi continued to represent his views on Franciscan poverty among his brothers. His views belonged to the analysis and interpretation which went into a life by the Franciscan rule.

Olivi's views on poverty and on *usus pauper* in particular renewed the traditional challenge of Franciscan life, of its challenge both to the brothers and to Christian society. Brother Peter of John proposed a poverty capable of cleansing and renewing the order in its selfless service to others. Franciscan poverty, as the order's socioeconomic mechanism, made Franciscan life work. For Franciscan life needed a critical distance towards society in order to point to another world. The first Franciscans embraced that distance in Chapter Nine of their first rule and their practice continued to rumble deep within the Franciscan memory. Some heard it, others not. Peter Olivi drew it into open view. A man of conscience, and in this Olivi was one, remains a judgment on his age.

1. « Responsio », p. 406.

OLIVI ET LE POUVOIR DU PAPE

Marco Bartoli

Le lundi de Pâques 1282, éclata à Palerme une révolte qui bientôt serait connue sous le nom de « révolte des vêpres ». De Palerme, la rébellion s'élargit rapidement à Messine et aux autres villes de l'île. Les Angevins ne réussirent pas à l'arrêter, et bientôt, tout le monde se rendit compte que la révolte avait pris un aspect international. Quelques mois plus tard les Siciliens saluaient avec la plus grande faveur l'arrivée de Pierre d'Aragon sur l'île.

Bien avant que Pierre d'Aragon n'arrive en Sicile pour soutenir la rébellion, le pape Martin IV, faisant preuve d'une sensibilité politique aiguë, fit lire publiquement, sur la place majeure de Viterbe, le jour de l'Ascension (le 7 mai) et entouré des cardinaux, sa lettre *Cogit nos temporis qualitas*, dans laquelle il menaçait quiconque oserait envahir le Royaume de Sicile.

Dans cette lettre le pape racontait toute l'histoire de la défense du royaume de Sicile par le Saint Siège contre la famille de Frédéric II et ses successeurs (famille à laquelle était lié Pierre d'Aragon) ; enfin le pape menaçait :

> [...] les laïcs, de toute dignité, condition ou état, et tout spécialement ceux qui sont soumis à la juridiction de l'église romaine afin qu'ils obéissent aux ordres et aux admonitions du pape ; en cas contraire, ils seraient privés de leurs fiefs et de tous leurs biens, leurs sujets seraient relevés de leur vœu de fidélité et leur personne serait en danger de mort ou de mutilation [...][1].

C'est vraisemblablement dans ce contexte que quelqu'un eut l'idée de poser une question à Pierre de Jean Olivi qui disputait ses questions quodlibétiques, probablement à Montpellier[2]. Cette question était la suivante : « Faut-il obéir au pape s'il demande d'aller faire la guerre pour défendre des biens temporels ? ». C'était une question délicate, surtout dans une région où les sentiments politiques contre les Angevins devaient être aussi assez forts. Le seul argument opposé à ce pouvoir était le conseil évangélique : « *ego autem dico vobis non resistere malo*

1. *Cf.* O. Raynaldi, *Annales ecclesiastic [...] [continuatio Baronii]*, III, Lucca, 1748, p. 535-538. Voir aussi Martin IV, *Cogit nos temporis qualitas*, 7 mai 1282, dans Potthast, II, 21895.

2. Sylvain Piron a récemment proposé une datation différente des questions quodlibétiques : « En faisant l'hypothèse que les cinq premiers *Quodlibets* correspondent à cinq années successives d'enseignement, on serait amené à placer les trois premiers à Montpellier (1289-92), et les deux suivants à Narbonne (1292-94). Cette hypothèse a pour elle une certaine convergence avec la date probable de mise en ordre de la *Summa*, que l'on a suggéré de placer dans ces années. Cette rédaction finale aurait alors été contemporaine d'une édition des premiers *quodlibets* ».

sed si quis te percusserit in dextera maxilla tua praebe illi et alteram » (Mt. V, 39) [Je vous dis de ne pas tenir tête au méchant, au contraire, quelqu'un te donne-t-il un soufflet sur la joue droite, tends lui encore l'autre]. Les arguments en faveur d'un tel pouvoir du pape, cités par Olivi, étaient au nombre de deux : l'un théorique, l'autre, historique. Pour le premier, Olivi cite Hugues de Saint Victor en disant que si le roi a le pouvoir de défendre ses sujets lorsqu'ils sont injustement attaqués, à plus forte raison, le pape a le même pouvoir dans la mesure où le pouvoir spirituel est supérieur au pouvoir temporel. Le deuxième argument est historique : les papes ont, plusieurs fois dans l'histoire, appelé leurs sujets à la défense armée, et Olivi cite Grégoire le Grand.

Pierre de Jean ne pouvait que répondre que le pape avait le pouvoir d'ordonner à des laïcs de faire la guerre, si cette guerre était juste et pouvait éviter un mal plus grand; mais il ajoutait que, en tout état de cause, le pape n'avait pas l'autorité d'ordonner une telle chose à des hommes évangéliques ou à des ministres de Dieu. C'était une question assez disputée à l'époque : les prêtres peuvent-ils tuer? Dans la *Summa* d'Alexandre de Halès, on trouve cette même question : « *queritur an habentes spiritualem potestatem prohibeatur occidere* », dans laquelle on cite Léon IV (qui avait participé à une expédition contre les Sarrasins), mais aussi Ambroise de Milan, qui avait écrit « *Adversus milites Gothos lacrymae meae arma sunt; talia enim munimenta sunt sacerdotis, aliter nec debeo, nec possum resistere* » [1].

Olivi, en reprenant cette question sur l'interdiction de tuer pour tout homme évangélique (donc non seulement pour les prêtres, mais aussi pour les frères), donne une forme très marquée aux charges de la hiérarchie ecclésiastique : « *Predicatio etiam divine reconciliationis et pacis ad eorum ordinem spectat* ». Ce qui veut dire que, si le pape ordonne à des laïcs de faire la guerre, il faut la faire; quant au pape, il doit se rappeler qu'il est le successeur de Pierre auquel Jésus avait dit : « *Converte gladium tuum in vaginam* » et que sa charge spécifique est de prêcher la réconciliation et la paix [2].

Olivi n'avait pas besoin d'en dire davantage, car il venait de parler du pouvoir du pape dans la *quaestio* quodlibétique immédiatement précédente, dans laquelle on posait la question : « *utrum papa habeat universalissimam potestatem* ». Dans cette *quaestio*, Pierre de Jean avait répondu à la position de certains qui disaient que le pape était le seigneur temporel de tout bien temporel dans le monde entier. Les idées de Olivi sont à l'opposé de cette position, car dit-il :

1. Ambroise, *Sermo contra Auxentium*, n 2, *P.L.* XVI, c. 1008; voir aussi Gratien, *Decretum*, c. 21, § 2, et c. 3 (Friedberg, vol. I, 960, 954).

2. [*Solutio*] *Dicendum quod eos, quibus ex suo laicali et seculari statu competunt bella reipublice agere, potest papa suis preceptis compellere ad bellandum, prout iustitia exigit et expedi cultui chirstiano et ecclesie Dei. Virum vero evangelicum aut Dei ministros et sacerdotes, aut volens statum evangelicum confestim intrare non potest ad hoc cogere. De sacerdotibus enim Deus per apostolum precipit et diffinit quod non sint percussores. Et pro hac re Christus Petro dixit : Converte gladium tuum in vaginam. Nec mirum quia, IIad Thimoteum II generaliter dicit apostolus : Nemo militans Deo implicat secularibus negotiis. Et hoc ipsum per plura capitula consiliorum et summorum pontificum docetur in causa prefata, q. VIII, utrusque autem horum fuit decens et expediens.* Les diverses citations de Pierre Jean Olivi proviennent de Q.L., 1, 18, f° 8r-9r, 1, 19, f° 9r-9v, 1, 20, f° 9v.

> Tout cela irait à l'encontre des conseils évangéliques du Christ. En effet si le pape, par un droit évangélique absolu et par une délégation absolue du Christ, était le roi temporel et le seigneur du monde, alors le Christ n'aurait pas confié à Pierre, prince des apôtres, l'état et le conseil de très haute pauvreté, mais plutôt celui des plus hautes richesses et biens temporels, ce qui est le contraire de ce qu'il a dit dans l'évangile : 'Ne vous procurez ni or, ni argent, ni menue monnaie pour vos ceintures [...]' (Mt. X, 9), et aussi : 'Vous savez que les chefs des nations dominent sur elles en maîtres [...]. Il n'en doit pas être ainsi parmi vous [...]' (Mt. XX, 25-26)[1].

Mais la force la plus grande des argumentations de Pierre de Jean Olivi est surtout son humour. Il fait voir le ridicule de certaines positions, en disant par exemple : « Selon cette manière de penser, le pape serait aussi le seigneur des vers ou des étoiles, de l'éther ou des sphères inférieures, des reptiles ou des crapauds et de toutes les femmes (quant à tout ce qui revient à leurs époux) [...]. Si donc le Christ lui avait donné tout son pouvoir, alors il pourrait, comme le Christ, détruire tous les sacrements et en faire de nouveaux, ou encore, dispenser de tous les préceptes de Dieu. Toutes ces choses sont absurdes et fausses. Le pape est le vicaire universel du Christ, non pas de cette façon mais à la manière que j'ai déjà expliquée dans la *queastio* où je demande si tout le monde doit croire en toutes choses comme en une règle infaillible de foi »[2].

LA *QUAESTIO* SUR L'INDULGENCE DE LA PORTIUNCULE

Pierre de Jean Olivi s'était déjà occupé maintes fois du problème du pouvoir du pape ; la première fois, ce fut probablement vers 1279, lorsqu'il se rendit à

1. *Veruntamen dicto istorum contradicitur. Primo quia hoc esset contra evangelica Christi consilia et apostolorum suorum apostolica instituta. Si enim papa ex absoluto iure evangelico et ex absoluta Christi commissione esset temporalis rex et dominus mundi, tunc Petrus apostolorum principi non commississe statum et consilum altissime paupertatis, sed potius summarum divitiarum et terrene temporalitatis, cuius oppositum patet ex textu, quia precepit eis dicens : Nolite possidere aurum, etc. Et iterum dixit eis : Scitis quia principes gentium dominant eorum, et qui potestatem exercent super eos benefici vocantur. Vos autem non sic, sed qui maior est in vobis sit sicut minor et sicut minister. Petrus etiam in hoc gloriatur dicens : Ecce nos reliquimus omnia, e iterum : Argentum et aurum non est mihi. Et Bernardus ad Eugenium papam, liber II, dicit : Nec locutus est ocio, scilicet, tibi, ubi sedula urget sollicitudo ecclesiarum numquid aliud dimisit tibi sanctus apostolus. Quod habeo, inquit, hoc tibi do, quid illud hoc unum scio : non aurum neque argentum, cum ipse dicat Argentum et aurum non est mihi : esto ut alia quacumque ratione hoc tibi vendices, sed non apostolico iure, nec enim ille tibi dare potuit, que non habet.*

2. Ad primum *autem in contrarium dicendum quod secundum illam rationem papa esset dominus vermium et stellarum et etheris et inferiorum ac reptilium et buffonum et omnium mulierum ad usus quoscumque licitos viris suis. Si etiam Christus commisit sibi simpliciter totum posse suum, ergo potest sicut Christus omina sacramenta destruere et condere nova et in tot preceptis dispensare in quot potest et Deus ; que omnia falsa sunt et absurda. Est ergo vicarius eius universalis, non sic, sed modo superius pretaxato, quem in questione an Pape in omnibus tanquam regule inerrabili sit credendum plenius explicavi.*

Assise et eut l'idée d'écrire une *quaestio* sur l'indulgence de la Portiuncule[1].

Par un destin bizarre, plusieurs des œuvres de Pierre de Jean Olivi ont fait l'objet de polémiques, étrangères à leur contenu. C'est aussi le cas de cette *quaestio* qui a été utilisée dans la dispute sur l'authenticité du pardon d'Assise. Certains spécialistes ont fait de Pierre de Jean Olivi l'inventeur de cette indulgence, en soutenant que « c'est dans le groupe des Spirituels que l'indulgence de la Portiuncule a pris naissance et Pierre Olivi n'écrivit son traité (cette *Quaestio*) que pour lui fournir une base théologique »[2]; ou bien que Olivi « avait composé son texte dans le but évident de faire de l'église de la Portiuncule le centre de l'Ordre franciscain » contre le Sacro Convento et les frères de la Communauté[3].

On a peut-être ainsi prêté peu d'attention au contenu de la *quaestio* qui présente, au contraire, une théologie de l'indulgence plutôt originale, comme l'a bien montré Pierre Péano :

> Notre languedocien préconise donc un renouvellement du sens de l'indulgence, qui n'est plus une contrepartie religieuse d'une somme d'argent offerte en échange du pardon, ni la rémission de quelques mois et jours de la faute et de la peine «*culpe et pene*» sur terre ou dans le ciel (résurgence des livres pénitentiaux avec leurs tarifs pour les péchés), mais le pardon de toutes les fautes commises en vue d'une conversion pour recevoir en abondance la grâce du Seigneur miséricordieux, par l'intercession de Notre Dame[4].

La doctrine sur les indulgences était forcement liée à celle du pouvoir du Pape. Le souverain pontife avait-il le pouvoir de donner un pardon si général et absolu? Plusieurs théologiens, à la moitié du XIIIe siècle, en doutaient[5]. Ces doutes ont été repris par Pierre de Jean Olivi dans le neuvième argument *in contrario*. Ces sont les mêmes argumentations que l'on retrouve, par exemple, dans le *Supplementum* de la *Summa Theologiae* de Thomas d'Aquin. Ils soutenaient l'un et l'autre que l'autorité du pape étant seulement pour l'édification et non pas pour la destruction (selon un fameux passage de la deuxième lettre de Paul aux Corinthiens[6]), celui-ci ne pouvait pas détruire la satisfaction pénitentielle qui avait été annoncée et promulguée par les saints Pères de l'Église [...] On disait aussi que le Pape

1. Selon le père Péano, Olivi fut «mandé par son ministre de venir à Rome à l'époque de la composition de la Constitution « *Exiit qui seminat* » sur la Règle des Mineurs; il passa alors par Assise soit à l'aller, soit au retour; revenu à son enseignement au Studium général de Montpellier, il écrivit sa leçon [...] » : P. Pèano, « L'indulgence de la Portiuncule, origine et signification », dans *Indulgenza nel Medioevo e perdonanza di papa Celestino*, L'Aquila, 1987, p. 56. Mais la question de la datation des œuvres de Pierre de Jean Olivi est encore ouverte. Sylvain Piron y travaille actuellement.

2. A. Fierens, «La question franciscaine. Le manuscrit II 2326 de la Bibliothèque Royale de Belgique (Bruxelles)», *Revue d'Histoire Ecclésiastique* 9, 1908, p. 40-46.

3. K. Müller, *Der Portiuncula-Ablass. Eine kritisch-historiche Studie*, Tubingen, 1906, p. 92.

4. Péano, *op. cit*, p. 58.

5. Voir A. Janssen, «La doctrine des scolastiques sur l'efficacité des indulgences», *Nouvelle Revue de Théologie* 49, 1922, p. 173-185, 241-257, 303-315; C. Balic, «De indulgentiis in disputationibus scholasticis 'Quolibet' nuncupatis», *Antonianum* 25, 1950, p. 79-98; O. Capitani, «L'indulgenza come espressione teologica della 'communio sanctorum' e nella formazione della dottrina canonistica», dans *Indulgenza nel Medioevo [...], op. cit.*, p. 17-32.

6. «*[...] de potestate nostra quam dedit Dominus in aedificationem et non in destructionem vestram [...]*», II Cor. 10, 8.

détenait son pouvoir soit en raison de l'ordre sacerdotal, soit de sa juridiction; [...] or, les indulgences sont des actes sacramentels qui ne sont soumis, ni à l'ordre, ni à la juridiction[1].

Malheureusement cette *quaestio* est incomplète; nous ne savons donc pas comment Pierre de Jean Olivi aurait voulu répondre à ces arguments. Nous pouvons seulement rappeler ici que Thomas d'Aquin répondait exactement aux mêmes arguments en disant :

> *[...] non est in destructionem indulgentias dare, nisi inordinate dentur*[2] ou encore, *clavis est duplex: scilicet ordinis et iurisdictionis* [...] *et huius clavis* [iurisdictionis] *est remissio quae est per indulgentias: cum non pertineat ad dispensationem sacramentorum talis dimissio, sed ad dispensationem bonorum communium Ecclesiae*[3].

La *quaestio* sur l'indulgence serait donc le témoin d'un moment de convergence entre les théologiens des différents ordres mendiants dans l'effort d'établir avec plus de certitude une nouvelle doctrine sur le pouvoir du pape.

Cette convergence n'empêcha pas Pierre de Jean Olivi d'écrire un certain nombre de passages d'une très grande originalité, notamment quand il en vient à parler du lieu de Sainte Marie des Anges à la Portiuncule. Dans le cinquième argument *in contrario*, on déclarait impossible le choix d'un tel lieu pour accorder une indulgence pareille, à la place des sanctuaires traditionnels de Rome ou de Jérusalem[4]. Dans la *responsio*, Olivi soutient au contraire que, justement, le choix d'un lieu humble souligne pleinement l'autorité de celui qui concède une indulgence si grande :

1. « *Preterea si papa hoc non potuit clarum est quod nec conveniens fuit. Quod autem non potuerit, probo quinque modis. Primo quia potestas eius non est in destructionem sed in hedificium secundum Apostolum secunda Corinthios* (X, 8), *sed per hoc destrueretur vindicta peccatorum a sanctis patribus dictata et observata scilicet pena seu satisfaccio penitencialis. Secundo quia indulgencie causam convenientem exigunt. Causa enim convenencie tante indulgencie non videtur posse dari. Tertio quia secundum hoc posset tollere a sacramento penitencie aliquid quod est de substancia eius, scilicet satisfactionem sacramentalem, et sic pro consequens posset destruere sacramenta. Quarto quia secundum hoc posset dei iusticiam exigentem aliquam penam de peccatis nostris et totum statum pene purgatorie penitus evacuare. Quinto quia papa potest aut racione ordinis aut racione iurisdiccionis aut racione utriusque simul; non racione ordinis quia sic omnis sacerdos vel saltem episcopus hoc posset, cum omnis episcopus sit sibi equalis in ordine, non etiam racione iurisdiccionis quia iurisdictio non se extendit ad sacramenta, alias habens iurisdictionem sine ordine posset ordine posset administrare sacramenta. Sed huiusmodi indulgencie sunt sacramentales quia includunt in se condicionem culpe et reatus et quia relaxant penitencias sacramentales; non racione utriusque simul quia iurisdiccio non potest facere quod ordo se extendat ad id ad quod de se nullam habet potestatem, non enim ampliat ordinem nec consecracionis caracterem nec ordinis essentialem potestatem, videtur ergo quod papa nullo modo hoc possit* ».

2. *Summa Theologiae*, Suppl. q. 25, a. 1.

3. *Summa Theologiae*, Suppl. q. 25, a. 2, *ad primum*.

4. « *Quinto quia hoc non invenitur factum in loco solempniori ecclesie scilicet Rome ubi tamen est sedes beati Petri et Christi, et ubi tot corpora sanctorum iacent nec alibi nisi ex aliqua causa maxima scilicet in terra sancta ubi hoc concessum est propter utilitatem expugnandi inimicos fidei et propter singularem reverentiam nostre redempcionis ibi celebratam et propter difficultatem accessus. Et quia hic contra inimicos crucis Christi exponit se morti aut iuvat exponentes se, quorum nullum est dare in proposito, ergo etc.* »

> Si cela avait été sur le Siège de Pierre, on aurait pu croire que cela était possible en raison du Siège et donc que ce serait impossible ailleurs. Et pour la même raison, il ne convenait pas que cela soit accordé dans le lieu de la Passion du Christ [...] Le choix du lieu de l'humilité de François était bien opportun pour montrer encore plus clairement un tel pouvoir.

Olivi souligne ici pour la première fois le lien spécial qui unit le pape à l'ordre dont il fait partie. Il le fait par deux réflexions : la première est que l'obéissance spéciale que François a observée vis-à-vis du pape, lui vaut un don spécial en faveur du lieu qui est son siège ; en second lieu, la famille évangélique de François étant liée au vicaire du Christ, non pas pour ce qui concerne son autorité mais pour ce qui concerne sa sainteté de vie et sa grâce, il était nécessaire que le don associé à ce lieu fût non pas un privilège d'autorité, mais plutôt de grâce [1].

LA *QUAESTIO* SUR L'INFAILLIBILITÉ DU PAPE

La *Quaestio* sur l'infaillibilité du pape [à laquelle, comme on l'a vu, Olivi fait référence même dans la *quaestio* quodlibétique sur l'« universalissima potestas »] a connu le même destin que la *Quaestio* sur l'indulgence : celui de faire l'objet d'une polémique historique parmi les plus virulentes. Il s'agit d'une des *Quaestiones de perfectione evangelica,* publiée par Michele Maccarrone en 1949, qui lui donna le titre « *Quaestio de infallibilitate Romani Pontifici* ». Dans sa préface, l'éditeur soulignait l'importance de ce texte dans l'histoire de la

1. « *Octavo etiam patet hoc ex parte ipsius dantis scilicet summi pontificis. Considero enim de eo potestatis ecclesiastice plenitudinem. Charitatis suscepte reddendam gratitudinem. Proli singulariter genite et singulariter proprie communicandam paternam similitudinem. Ex primo enim non solum constat quod hoc potuit sed etiam quod valde decuit quod eius potestas super universali remissione culpe et pene in tempore consummante notificacionis sue in alico (sic) sic debuit revelari quod indubitabilis foret. Licet autem apercius fieri potuit in loco humili quam in sede Petri quia si hoc ibi factum fuisset posset credi quod racione sedis hoc fieret ita quod alibi hoc non posset. Et eadem racione non suffecit hoc fieri in loco passionis Christi quia posset credi quod racione ipsius loci hoc fieret et ita quod alibi hoc non posset. Convenienter electus est locus humilitatis Francisci ad huiusmodi posse plenissime ostendendum. Ex secundo vero decuit quod sicut Franciscus se et statum suum super omnes alios quantum fuit possibile se subiecit obediencie romani pontificis et romane sedis sicut ex regula patet, quod sic ille aliquid ad exuberanciam sedis sue locum et quasi sedem istius singulariter pre aliis derivaret, et tale quod conveniret humilitati et sanctitati sue professionis et saluti tocius ecclesie ad cuius hedificacionem a deo totaliter destinabatur, hoc autem inter cetera unde de pluribus potuit esse. Ex tertio etiam decuit quod sicut proles Francisci evangelica et eius status et regula per Christi vicarium ad Christi et apostolorum ymaginem est singulariter propagata et hoc non quantum ad auctoritatem sed pocius ad vite et gracie sanctitatem, quod sic ad privilegium gracie pocius quam auctoritatis a Christo vicario obtineret, miroque modo sequebatur ex hoc exaltacio sedis Petri quia per hoc ostensum est quod sicut testamentum vetus et totus patriarcharum cetus ad propagandum dei filium tamquam proprium finem semper intendit et finaliter est assecutus. Sic sedes Petri et totus apostolicus cetus ad propagandum Franciscum et statum eius semper intendit et finaliter hoc perfecit. Communicacio etiam huius gracie non derogat sed actestatur auctoritati Petri et sedis eius sicut fluvius a fonte derivatus actestatur dignitati fontali fiebatque in hoc quedam mutua equalitas inter patrem et filium quia ille sic singulariter servaverat dignitatem originis huic vero singulariter communicaverat plenitudinem remissionis omnium peccatorum* ».

théologie du Primat romain et surtout dans l'histoire de l'infaillibilité pontificale. Mais cette *quaestio* est, malheureusement, inachevée elle aussi. On pourrait même dire qu'elle s'arrête au moment le plus délicat, là où l'auteur, après avoir parlé de l'obéissance qu'on doit au pape comme à une règle « infaillible », conclut ses réflexions en évoquant le cas, déjà bien connu chez les canonistes, du « pape hérétique ». Il dit :

> Au cas où le pape tomberait dans cette erreur, c'est à dire une erreur commune [et pas seulement une erreur concernant sa propre personne] il serait impossible que ce pape fût le véritable pape et le véritable chef de l'église. Donc, selon le droit, aucun hérétique connu publiquement comme hérétique – ce qui correspond au cas dont on parle – n'a le droit de bénir ou de maudire dans l'église, car tout fidèle est plus grand que lui [1].

Olivi donc, comme le soutenait déjà Raoul Manselli, élabore ici une théorie assez équilibrée, selon laquelle il faut toujours obéir au pape comme à une règle « infaillible » de foi, mais sans oublier que le pape reste toujours un homme et qu'il peut donc tomber dans l'hérésie : dans ce cas, mais seulement dans ce cas, il faut le considérer comme hérétique et ne pas lui obéir.

L'approche du problème était tout à fait traditionnelle à l'époque à laquelle Olivi écrivait. Au point que le cardinal Ehrle, qui, le premier, avait signalé l'existence de cette *quaestio* sur l'obéissance au Pontife en matière de foi et de morale, avait soutenu que son auteur dans cette matière ne s'écartait pas trop de la doctrine commune de ses contemporains. Mais le titre choisi par Maccarrone, dans lequel on parlait d'infaillibilité, a attiré l'attention des spécialistes, au point que Pierre de Jean Olivi est devenu tout récemment l'« inventeur » de la doctrine de l'infaillibilité pontificale. L'histoire de cette transformation a commencé en 1972, lorsque Brian Tierney publia un volume intitulé *The Origins of Papal Infallibility*, dans lequel il soutenait que Olivi avait été le premier théologien à écrire un texte sur l'infaillibilité du pape [2]. On peut résumer de cette façon les conclusions de Tierney :

Cette *quaestio* fait partie des *quaestiones de perfectione evangelica*, c'est à dire d'une œuvre consacrée à la vie franciscaine; il faut donc la lire dans le contexte des disputes qui ont marqué la vie de l'ordre au milieu du XIIIe siècle ;

Olivi a écrit cette *quaestio* probablement autour de 1280, juste après la rédaction de la Bulle *Exiit qui seminat*, la décrétale dans laquelle le pape Nicolas III déclarait que la règle de François était parfaitement évangélique, et où il réaffirmait la valeur de la pauvreté ;

1. « *Papa autem sic errans, errore scilicet communi, cum habeat rationem capitis erronei, et non solum persone singulariter et quoad se errantis, impossibile est quod papa sic errans sit verus papa et verum capud ecclesie. Et ideo, secundum iura, nullus hereticus publicus seu in quantum hereticus, quod idem est in proposito, habet potestatem benedicendi et maledicendi in ecclesia, quia omnis fidelis est maior eo* ».

2. « *In a fumbling and hesitant way perhaps, and yet quite explicity, Olivi was trying for the first time to formulate a viable theory of papal infallibility* », B. Tierney, *Origins of Papal Infallibility 1150-1350. A Study on the Concepts of Infallibility, Sovereignty and Tradition in the Middle Ages*, Leyde, 1992, p. 96.

Olivi voulait souligner l'autorité de ce texte pontifical, face aux adversaires internes ou externes à l'ordre;

la doctrine de l'infaillibilité aurait été élaborée par Olivi en prévoyant la possibilité qu'un pape différent pourrait faire une autre décrétale, en prenant une position différente de celle de Nicolas III;

la doctrine de l'infaillibilité aurait donc été créée par Olivi pour limiter et non pas pour élargir le pouvoir du pape.

Le livre de Tierney sortait peu de temps après les conclusions du Concile Vatican II, lors duquel on avait réaffirmé la doctrine de l'infaillibilité pontificale, promulguée par le Concile Vatican I. La discussion qui s'ensuivit fut considérable. En effet, pour les adversaires de cette doctrine, il était même curieux de voir que le premier théologien à avoir parlé d'infaillibilité aurait été un franciscain spirituel, qui, après sa mort, avait été condamné pour hérésie.

Le seul problème, c'était qu'Olivi n'avait jamais parlé d'infaillibilité. Il avait utilisé le terme « *inerrabilitas* » qui, pour lui, n'était pas équivalent. Les spécialistes qui se sont disputés sur les thèses de Tierney ont sans doute été victimes du manque d'éditions critiques des œuvres du frère languedocien. En lisant leurs différentes contributions, on a l'impression que l'on a parlé d'Olivi sans beaucoup lire ses œuvres. On n'avait pas lu, par exemple, le texte de la lettre à Conrad de Offida (bien que ce texte ait été publié depuis des années); Olivi, pour répondre aux frères italiens qui refusaient l'abdication de Célestin V et disaient que le Christ est présent dans la personne du pape d'une façon inséparable, comme dans l'Hostie consacrée, disait:

> [...] sur ce qu'ils disent, à savoir que, si le pape est l'image du Christ éternel et inéchangeable, alors le pape devrait être éternel et immuable [...] On devrait donc penser que, dès que le pape, en tant qu'évêque, est l'image du Christ, il devrait en être l'image dans tout autre domaine? Ils devraient dire alors qu'il est incréé, immense, sans péché et infaillible et omniscient, comme le Christ, chose que seul un dément pourrait dire ou penser [1].

Si l'on revient donc à la *quaestio* sur l'« infaillibilité », il faut dire que, là où il abandonnait soudainement son travail, Olivi laissait ouvertes de nombreuses questions. S'il ne faut pas obéir au Pontife qui devient hérétique, qui va le juger hérétique? Ou bien, dans quels cas concrets un pape devient-il hérétique? Maccarrone pensait que Olivi avait laissé sa *quaestio* incomplète justement parce qu'il était trop jeune et encore trop peu formé en théologie pour répondre à de telles questions [2].

1. « *Quod vero dicunt, quod papa est ymago Christi eterni et immutabilis, ergo papa debet esse eternus et immutabilis [...]. Unde autem sequitur quod, quia papa vel episcopus est quoad aliquid Christi Ymago, ergo quoad omnia est Christi ymago? Dicant ergo quod est increatus et immensus et impeccabilis et* infallibilis *et omnium prescius, sicut Christus, quod nullus dicet vel sapiet nisi demens!* », QPE 14, p. 368.

2. « *la questione affronta un tema nuovo, che sino ad allora non era stato direttamente e da solo trattato dai teologi; ora bisogna dire che la parte propriamente nuova viene precisamente al punto che si presenta interrotto, e qui l'Olivi non trova più modelli o tracce da seguire [...] Venendo a parlare specificatamente della natura dell'infallibilità papale e poi dei suoi limiti e delle sue*

LA QUAESTIO SUR LE POUVOIR DE RELEVER DES VŒUX

Pierre de Jean Olivi n'a pas évité ces questions; simplement, s'il n'y a pas répondu dans cette *quaestio*, c'est parce qu'il a préféré y répondre dans d'autres *quaestiones*, avec plus d'ampleur. C'est le cas, par exemple, de la *quaestio XIV De perfectione evangelica*, intitulée «*An papa possit in omni voto dispensare et specialiter an in votis evangelicis*»: «Le pape peut-il relever de tout vœu et surtout des vœux évangéliques?»

C'est une question de grande actualité au moment où Olivi écrit. C'est seulement à la fin du XIIe siècle et au début du XIIIe que les vœux religieux commencèrent à faire l'objet d'un travail théologique systématique. La raison en est évidente: la naissance des ordres mendiants. Si pour les moines, les vœux ne faisaient pas l'objet d'une attention spéciale, car leur identité était bien marquée par le choix de vivre en dehors du monde, pour les frères, le problème des vœux devint central, car ils vivaient dans le monde et sentaient le besoin de clarifier leur identité par rapport aux laïcs. C'était un langage que les laïcs pouvaient bien comprendre: le XIIIe est le siècle pour lequel on a parlé de «civilisation du serment»[1]. Les serments étaient le fondement de toute nouvelle structure sociale, le fondement des universités, des communes. Or, le serment est une promesse solennelle entre les hommes, tandis que le vœu est une promesse faite à Dieu. Sur cette base, il était simple pour les frères mendiants de se présenter comme des hommes qui avaient fait leurs promesses directement à Dieu. Le modèle était toujours celui des chevaliers qui faisaient le vœu d'aller à la croisade, mais les vœux des frères étaient encore plus remarquables, car ils y restaient liés pour toute leur vie.

Le problème fut bientôt associé à celui de l'autorité du pontife romain. Il s'agissait de savoir si le Pape avait le pouvoir d'intervenir dans la vie des ordres religieux ou, pour mieux dire, quelles étaient les limites de ce pouvoir d'intervention. Le cas s'était déjà posé au temps de Bernard de Clairvaux pour quelqu'un qui voulait passer d'un monastère de moines blancs (cisterciens) à un monastère de moines noirs. Bernard dit *expressis verbis*, qu'il n'était jamais licite, même avec une permission papale, de passer d'une forme de vie plus parfaite à une plus imparfaite[2]. On revient ainsi sur le thème de l'autorité donné par Dieu «pour l'édification et non pas pour la destruction»[3].

conseguenze, per il giovane teologo francescano il tema si faceva più arduo, sia per l'argomento assai delicato che per la sua novità, e questo può aver determinata la interruzione della questione, non più ripresa e lasciata nel suo getto primitivo».

1. P. Prodi, *Il sacramento del potere*, Bologna, 1992, p. 161-225.

2. «*Bernardus in* Epistula ad Robertum puerum, *dicit quod nullo modo ei licuit, etiam per dispensationem seu licentiam papalem, transire de statu monachorum alborum ad statum nigrorum*».

3. «*Bernardus,* De consideratione ad Eugenium Papam, *libro tertio in fine dicit: 'Non sum tam rudis ut ignorem dispensatores nos positos, sed in edificationem non in destructionem, nisi necessitas urget excusabilis dispensatio est. Ubi utilitas provocat dispensatio laudabilis est. Utilitas dico communis non propria. Nam, cum nichil horum est non plane fidelis dispensatio, sed crudelis dissipatio est'*».

Le problème devenait toujours plus important dans la mesure où les frères étaient liés au pape par une obéissance spéciale. Le pape avait-il le pouvoir de dispenser des vœux, c'est-à-dire de permettre de sortir des nouveaux ordres? Pouvait-il par exemple demander à des frères prêcheurs de devenir des prêtres séculiers ? Ou à des frères franciscains de devenir chanoines ?

On comprend alors pourquoi la doctrine des vœux n'a pas grande place dans les *Sentences* de Pierre Lombard, tandis qu'elle devient toujours plus importante chez les auteurs dominicains, comme Raymond de Peñafort et Vincent de Beauvais, pour finir avec la très grande place qui lui est réservée dans la *Summa* de Thomas d'Aquin [1]. Ce furent les dominicains, d'abord, qui élaborèrent une théorie cohérente qui liait les vœux de croisade aux vœux religieux, et le tout au problème de l'obéissance au pape [2].

Chez les franciscains, l'intérêt pour la question naquit avant tout des commentaires sur la Règle. On touchait ici un point fondamental de l'identité franciscaine : celui de l'obéissance évangélique. Comme on le sait, la Règle de François s'ouvre par ces mots : « *Regula et vita minorum fratrum haec est, scilicet Domini nostri Iesu Christi sanctum Evangelium observare, vivendo in obedientia, sine proprio et in castitate* » [3].

En réalité, dans cette Règle, comme d'ailleurs dans toutes les autres Règles anciennes, on ne fait pas mention d'un vœu de chasteté, de pauvreté ou d'obéissance ; on y établit simplement, que :

> Après une année de noviciat, ils seront reçus à l'obéissance, promettant d'observer toujours cette vie et cette règle. Il ne leur sera plus permis dès lors, en aucune façon, de quitter notre Ordre [4].

Déjà en 1230, le pape Grégorie IX, sollicité par les frères mineurs eux-mêmes, dut intervenir, avec la décrétale « *Quo elongati* », pour éclairer les

1. Thomas d'Aquin, *Summa Theologiae*, II-II, q. 88 et la *Summa Contra Gentiles*, l. III, c. 139, mais aussi *Quodlibet III*, a. 2, et *Contra impugnantes Dei cultum et religionem : « sicut autem in baptismo quo homo per fidei religionem deo ligatur, peccato moritur; ita per votum religionis non solum peccato, sed saeculo moritur, ut soli deo vivat in illo opere in quo se deo ministraturum devovit : quia sicut per peccatum vita fidei tollitur, ita per occupationes saeculi christi ministerium impeditur : II ad Tim.* II, 4 : *nemo militans deo implicat se saecularibus negotiis. et ideo per religionis votum illis abrenuntiatur quibus humanus animus maxime occupari consuevit, et a divinis obsequiis praepediri* » ; voir aussi *Contra pestiferam doctrinam hominum retrahensium a religionis ingressu*, cap. 11.

2. Pour ne donner qu'un exemple, dans le *Speculum doctrinale* de Vincent de Beauvais les chapitres 68-94 du neuvième livre sont consacrés à la doctrine des vœux, il s'agit de vingt-six chapitres ainsi répartis : 1. Qu'est ce qu'un vœu ? 2. Les vœux simples et les vœux solennels ; 3. Les vœux solennels de ceux qui restent dans le siècle ; 4. Le vœu solennel de chasteté ; 5. Le vœu de croisade (3 chapitres) ; 6. La *irritatio votis* (déclaration de nullité) ; 7. Les vœux des moines et des religieux (6 chapitres) ; 8. Les vœux des évêques et des serfs ; 9. Les vœux des mineurs (3 chapitres) ; 10. Les vœux des mariés (8 chapitres) : Vincent de Beauvais, *Speculum Doctrinale*, l. IX, cap. LXVIII-XCIV.

3. Regula Secunda (Bullata) Fratrum Minorum, I, 2, dans *Concordantiae verbales opusculorum S. Francisci et S. Clarae assisiensum [...] cura* et studio Fr. Io. M. Boccali dispositae, S. Mariae Angelorum-Assisii 1976.

4. *Idem*, 2, 12 : « *Finito vero anno probationis, recipiantur ad obedientiam, promittentes vitam istam sempre et regulam observare. Et nullo modo licebit eis de ista religione exire, iuxta mandatum domini papae* ».

sens de cette obéissance évangélique promise dans la Règle. Le pape, qui était un bon juriste, soulignait que les frères :

> [...] ne devaient pas obéir à d'autres conseils évangéliques, en plus de ceux qui sont exprimés par des ordres ou des interdictions expressément cités dans la Règle; [...] aux autres en effet, ils sont tenus de la même façon que les autres chrétiens, et encore davantage, car ils se sont voués eux-mêmes comme holocauste précieux au Seigneur, à travers le mépris des choses du monde [1].

Selon Grégoire IX donc, la règle ne fixait pas une obligation juridique d'obéissance à chaque précepte évangélique, mais elle fixait tout de même une obligation spirituelle, car ceux qui faisaient profession de cette règle, s'offraient eux-mêmes, devenant ainsi « *de-voti* », voués au Seigneur.

Cependant, dans les commentaires à la règle, on souligne toujours que cette obligation spirituelle est quand même une obligation. C'est le cas, par exemple, de Hugues de Digne, qui insiste en disant que :

> *Retro ergo aspicit quisquis alta professus sponte ad inferiora descendit. Regno Dei consequenter indignus, iuxta evangelicam et divinam sententiam* (Lc. 9, 62), *quam nulla, ut volunt, potest dispensatio irritare. Nullus inquiunt supra Dominum est, nullus contra Dominum esse debet* [2].

Si on pense que, comme l'a démontré Jacques Paul, le commentaire de Hugues de Digne sur la règle a été probablement écrit pour répondre à la bulle *Ordinem vestrum* de Innocent IV afin de contester certaines de ses affirmations, on peut comprendre l'importance qu'avait cette phrase selon laquelle personne, pas même le pape, n'est au-dessus du Seigneur et personne ne peut aller contre le Seigneur [3]. Le vœu d'obéissance à la règle devenait ainsi la plus importante défense de la liberté de conscience du simple frère, que personne, pas même le pape, ne pouvait empêcher de vivre selon l'évangile.

La même réflexion se retrouve dans l'œuvre théologique d'Alexandre de Halès. Ce maître, en effet, dans ses *Quaestiones antequam fuit frater* ne disait encore rien sur les vœux. Il en parle en revanche dans ses *Quaestiones postquam fuit frater*, qui sont encore malheureusement inédites. Il y a donc une *quaestio* dans laquelle Alexandre se demande « *utrum religiosus in hoc quod vovet obedientiam abneget propriam volutatem in omnibus aut in aliquibus solum* » [4]. Il pose ici avec clarté le problème des limites du vœu d'obéissance. Et la réponse est celle qui vient directement de la règle des mineurs : « *in omnibus teneatur, dummodo non fuerint contraria regulae aut animae suae* ». Alexandre fixe encore une fois le primat de la conscience personnelle de chaque simple frère, qui

1. Le texte de la Bulle est dans H. Grundmann, « Die Bulle *Quo elongati* Papst Gregors IX », *Archivum Franciscanum Historicum* 54, 1961, p. 1-25.

2. Voir D. Flood, *Hugh of Digne's Rule Commentary*, Grottaferrata, 1979, p. 108.

3. J. Paul, « Le commentaire de Hugues de Digne sur la Règle Franciscaine », *R.H.E.F.* 61, 1975, p. 231-41 (spécialement p. 233); *id.* Hugues de Digne, dans *Franciscains d'Oc. Les Spirituels ca. 1280-1324*, *Cahiers de Fanjeaux* 10, 1975, p. 69-97.

4. Je dois remercier le Collège Saint Bonaventure de m'avoir laissé utiliser une transcription de cette *quaestio*, faite par les frères de Quaracchi en 1941 sur la base du Ms. Bologna 2554, f°s 38b-43c : *De obedientia religiosorum, ad tertium*.

est appelé à juger quand un ordre d'un supérieur est contraire à la Règle ou à son âme.

Le produit de cette réflexion fut une « ecclésiologie du bas » qui se présente non pas comme opposée, mais comme complémentaire à cette ecclésiologie du haut, qui, chez les mêmes auteurs, présente l'église comme une structure hiérarchique qui a son point de légitimation au sommet de la pyramide. La doctrine des vœux représente un aspect complémentaire de cette vision de l'église[1] : obéissance et liberté sont, dans cette ecclésiologie, les deux faces de la même médaille.

Tout au cours du XIIIe siècle, on peut voir donc, chez les théologiens dominicains comme chez leurs confrères franciscains, un intérêt grandissant pour le thème des vœux[2].

S'il est vrai qu'à un certain moment, il y eut des discussions entre Prêcheurs et Mineurs sur le thème du vœu d'obéissance, et que Thomas d'Aquin souligna que la formule utilisée dans la Règle des dominicains était meilleure que celle des franciscains[3], il est vrai cependant que les points de contact entre les deux écoles

1. Le premier à établir ce lien entre la querelle entre les mendiants et les séculiers et l'ecclésiologie a été Y. Congar, « Aspects ecclésiologiques de la querelle entre les mendiants et les séculiers dans la moitié du XIIIe siècle et le début du XIVe », *A.H.D.L.M.A.* 28, 1961, p. 35-151. On peut voir aussi P.M. Gy, « Le statut ecclésiologique de l'apostolat des Prêcheurs et des Mineurs avant la querelle des Mendiants », *R.S.P.T.* 59, 1975, p. 79-88.

2. Le développement le plus important interviendra surtout dans la deuxième moitié du siècle, à la suite des polémiques ecclésiologiques qui deviendront très vives à cette période. La doctrine des vœux se trouvera alors au centre d'un double polémique : d'un côté celle des maîtres séculiers (surtout Guillaume de Saint-Amour et Gérard d'Abbeville) contre les mendiants, de l'autre, la polémique entre les dominicains (en particulier Thomas d'Aquin) et les franciscains. La première de ces polémiques a été amplement éclaircie par les travaux fondamentaux de Y. Congar; voir aussi D.L. Douie, *The Conflict between the Seculars and the Mendicants at the University of Paris in the Thirteenth Century*, London 1954; P. Glorieux, « Pour une édition de Gérard d'Abbeville », *R.T.A.M.* 9, 1937, p. 56-84; M.-M. Dufeil, *Guillaume de Saint-Amour et la polémique universitaire parisienne 1250-1259*, Paris, 1972 (avec bibliographie); la seconde polémique a été bien présentée par le F.M. Delorme éd., « Fr. P. J. Olivi quaestio de voto regulam aliquam profitentis », QPE, *Antonianum* 16, 1941, p. 131-164.

3. En effet, dans son premier *Quodlibet*, Thomas d'Aquin avait soutenu que « *Est ergo considerandum quid sit illud ad quod religiosus voto professionis se astringit. Et si quidem religiosus profitendo voveret se regulam servaturum, videretur se obligare voto ad singula quae continentur in regula et sic, contra quodlibet eorum agendo, pecaret mortaliter, et ex hoc sequeretur quod religionis status esset religiosis in laqueum peccati mortalis, quod vix aut numquam possent declinare. Sancti ergo patres qui Ordines instituerunt, nolentes hominibus iniicere damnationis laqueum, des magis viam salutis, ordinaverunt talem professionis formam in qua periculum esse non posset, sicut in Ordine fratrum Praedicatorum est cautissima et securissima forma profitendi, qua non promittit servare regulam, des obedientiam secundum regulam* » : Thomas d'Aquin, *Quodlibet* 1, a. 20; voir aussi *Summa Theologiae*, II-II, q. 186, a. 9 : « *Videtur quod religiosus semper peccet mortaliter transgrediendo ea quae sunt in regula. facere enim contra votum est peccatum damnabile, ut patet per id quod apostolus dicit, I ad Tim. V, quod viduae quae volunt nubere damnationem habent, quia primam fidem irritam fecerunt. Sed religiosi voto professionis ad regulam adstringuntur. ergo peccant mortaliter transgrediendo ea quae in regula continentur* ». Celui qui répondit à Thomas fut Guillaume de la Mare (*Correctorium Fr. Thomae*, a. 74 et 106) ; suivit la réplique connue sous le titre *Correctorium corruptorii* (a. 74 et 106). La polémique fut un peu aplanie par l'intervention du pape Nicolas III, avec sa bulle *Exiit qui seminat*, à laquelle les dominicains réagirent en disant que « *intentio est summi pontificis et voluntas magistri Ordinis quod de his quae ad regulam et statum Fratrum Minorum pertinent, caute loquamur* » (Lettre de Bernard Geraldi, prieur de la province de Provence

sur ce sujet sont très forts : le premier est constitué par la valeur de la liberté humaine[1] ; le second réside dans les limites du pouvoir du Pape.

Pour tous, le pape n'a pas le droit de dissoudre des vœux religieux. La doctrine élaborée par les mendiants, qu'on retrouve soit dans les *Quodlibeta* de Thomas d'Aquin, soit dans la *Summa Alexandri*, est qu'il y a une différence entre les vœux simples (ou privés, c'est-à-dire formulés dans la solitude) et les vœux solennels (c'est-à-dire prononcés face à une personne publique de l'église). Si on peut être relevé des vœux simples, car il s'agit seulement de promesses, on ne peut plus être relevé des vœux solennels, car il s'agit d'un don fait à Dieu et, même si on peut donner à d'autres ce qu'on a promis à quelqu'un, on ne peut pas donner à d'autres ce qu'on a déjà donné à quelqu'un[2].

Quand il commence à écrire une *quaestio* sur le pouvoir qu'a le pape de relever des vœux, Pierre de Jean Olivi a déjà consacré à la doctrine des vœux plusieurs *quaestiones* dans son traité *De perfectione evangelica*[3]. Il connaît donc très bien le débat sur cette doctrine. L'originalité de la *quaestio* sur le pouvoir du pape consiste dans une distinction, non pas entre vœux simples ou solennels, mais entre vœux évangéliques et vœux non évangéliques. C'est une différence non formelle mais substantielle : pour Olivi le problème n'est pas de savoir si le vœu a été prononcé face à quelque personne publique de l'église, mais si son contenu est évangélique. Il réalise de cette façon une synthèse nouvelle entre la doctrine de la

du 5 janvier 1280. Voir B. M. Reichert, *Litt. encycl.*, n. 30, p. 114-116 ; Mortier, *Histoire des Maîtres généraux*, II, p. 162-seq.

1. *Cf.* Thomas d'Aquin, *De perfectione vitae spiritualis*, cap. 10 : « *Nihil autem est homini amabilius libertate propriae voluntatis. Per hanc enim homo est et aliorum dominus, per hanc aliis uti vel frui potest, per hanc etiam suis actibus dominatur. unde, sicut homo dimittens divitias, vel personas coniunctas, eas abnegat ; ita deserens propriae voluntatis arbitrium, per quod ipse sui dominus est, se ipsum abnegare invenitur. Nihilque est quod homo naturali affectu magis refugiat quam servitutem : unde et nihil posset homo pro alio amplius impendere post hoc quod se ipsum in mortem pro eo traderet, quam quod se servituti eius subiugaret : unde, ut dicitur Tob. ix, 2, Tobias iunior dixit ad angelum : si me ipsum tradam tibi servum, non ero condignus providentiae tuae. Huius autem voluntatis libertatem aliqui sibi propter deum particulariter adimunt, dum quodcumque particulare votum emittunt de quocunque faciendo vel non faciendo. Per votum enim necessitas quaedam voventi imponitur, ut id de cetero non liceat quod prius licebat ; sed quadam necessitate constringitur ad reddendum quod vovit : unde in psal. lxv, 15, dicitur : reddam tibi vota mea, quae distinxerunt labia mea ; et eccl. V 3 dicitur : si quid vovisti Deo, ne moreris reddere : displicet enim ei infidelis et stulta promissio* ».

2. Thomas d'Aquin, *Quodlibet X*, ar. 5 : « *Nam per votum solemne transfert se vovens quasi in corporale obsequium ipsius dei per susceptionem ordinis vel introitum religionis. Quod autem aliquis semel uni dedit, non potest postmodum alteri dare ; et ideo post votum solemne non potest aliquis se tradere in potestatem uxoris matrimonium contrahendo. Sed in voto simplici est sola promissio. Qui autem aliquid alicui promittit, potest idem alteri dare, licet fidem promissionis non servet ; et ideo ille qui simplex votum emittit, potest postmodum matrimonium contrahere* ».

3. 1) *An sit melius aliquid facere ex voto quam sine voto ;* 2) *an votum vitandi suspectum consortium vel colloquium implicetur in consilio evangelico ;* 3) *An usus pauper includatur in consilio seu in voto paupertatis evangelice ;* 4) *An vovere alteri homini obedientiam in omnibus, que non sunt contraria anime et evangelice regule seu perfectionis sit perfectionis evangelicae ;* 5) *An vovens evangelium vel aliquam regulam simpliciter et absque determinatione, teneatur observare omnia que in eis sunt contenta :* Sur l'importance des *Quaestiones de perfectione evangelica* dans l'ensemble de l'œuvre de Pierre Jean Olieu, voir D. Burr, *Olivi and Franciscan Poverty. The Origins of the* Usus Pauper *Controversy*, Philadelphia, 1989.

valeur de la liberté humaine et celle des limites du pouvoir du pape. Pour Olivi le vœu évangélique n'est pas seulement le lieu du renoncement à sa propre liberté, mais aussi le point de départ d'une nouvelle liberté. Seul celui qui a renoncé à sa propre volonté devient libre d'obéir seulement à l'évangile.

Le vœu évangélique fixe, selon Pierre de Jean Olivi, la limite devant laquelle même le pouvoir du pape doit s'arrêter :

> *Dicendum est quod papa a nullo voto licito potest simpliciter absolvere, in votis autem evangelicis nec absolvere nec dispensare potest nec multo minus contrarium precipere*[1].

Le pape ne peut pas ordonner d'aller à l'encontre des vœux évangéliques. On revient ici à la limite déjà rencontrée dans la *quaestio* sur l'indulgence : le pouvoir du pape n'est destiné qu'à l'édification et non à la destruction. Or, s'il ordonne à quelqu'un de renoncer aux vœux évangéliques, il le pousse à descendre dans l'échelle de la perfection, ce qui n'est pas dans son pouvoir. Aucun pape ne peut aller contre une promesse, même privée, faite à Dieu selon l'évangile.

Ici Olivi utilise des mots forts, en faisant l'hypothèse d'un pape qui désirerait détruire tout ordre religieux. Il dit :

> L'état de religion en commun est plus utile à l'église que l'état séculier. Et normalement, un état plus haut et plus parfait est meilleur et plus utile qu'un état plus bas. C'est la raison pour laquelle, faire disparaître [*tollere de medio*] l'état le plus haut, en le transformant en un état inférieur, reviendrait à bouleverser l'ordre et la perfection des états. Et si le pape le faisait, il devrait être jugé comme hérétique[2].

On répond donc ici à une des questions qu'Olivi avait laissées ouvertes dans la *quaestio* sur l'inerrabilité. On dit clairement que ceci est un cas dans lequel le pape doit être jugé hérétique. Olivi ajoute :

> En effet, si tout destructeur de l'église et de son bien commun doit être tenu non seulement comme schismatique, mais encore comme plus que schismatique, à plus forte raison, devrait-on tenir également pour tel celui qui, ayant la charge de chef [*rationem capitis*] et de pasteur, créerait une confusion entre les états de l'Église et exercerait publiquement une tyrannie à l'égard de son bien commun. Et ce d'autant plus si ses actes erronés sont faits d'une façon solennelle et s'il établit, promulgue, défend et met en œuvre le schisme[3].

1. Voir Ms. Borgh. 357, f° 124r.

2. « *Constat enim quod status Religionis in communi utilior est Ecclesie Dei et divino cultui, quam status secularis, et universaliter status altior et perfectior est melior et utilior statu inferiori; ergo tollere de medio totum statum altiorem, commutando ipsum in statum inferiorem, esset commune bonum Ecclesie dissipare et ordinem statuum et perfectionem subvertere. Quod factum in Papa pro heresi iudicari* ».

3. « *Si enim omnis subversor Ecclesie et boni communis eius debet censeri non solum schismaticus, sed plus quam schismaticus, multo magis hoc esset in eo qui, cum deberet habere rationem capitis et pastoris, potestative status Ecclesie confunderet et contra bonum eius commune publice tyrannidem exerceret. Et maxime cum hoc facere, esset sollempniter facti sui erronei sententiam statuere, promulgare, defensare et executioni mandare* ».

Le frère languedocien n'a pas peur de dire encore : « Pour cette raison je ne doute pas que, s'il continuait avec obstination [*pertinaciter*], il ne devrait pas être obéi et que, au contraire, il devrait être évité des fidèles en tant que pontife hérétique et que loup »[1].

Comme on peut le voir, l'objet réel de cette *quaestio* n'est pas le vœu, mais le pouvoir du pape. Ainsi, Olivi consacre plusieurs pages aux limites de l'autorité ecclésiastique et il présente ici quatre limites, qui étaient traditionnelles chez les théologiens de son époque, mais il ajoute des observations originales :

– Avant tout, l'objet de l'autorité ecclésiastique (qui, comme on l'a vu, peut seulement s'appliquer pour édifier et non pour détruire) est le bien et non le mal ; [et Olivi ajoute : « si le pouvoir du pape s'étendait jusqu'à la capacité de détruire l'état évangélique, alors il pourrait même détruire l'église et aller contre les conseils évangéliques, ce qu'il pourrait faire seulement si Dieu n'avait soumis même cela à son pouvoir »][2] ;

1. « *Unde non dubito quod ex quo pertinaciter in hoc persisteret quod ei non esset obediendum tamquam Pape, immo esset tanquam schismaticus et tanquam hereticus precisus et tamquam lupus a fidelibus totaliter evitandus* ». Selon l'interprétation traditionnelle, les « loups » dont parlent les Ecritures sont les hérétiques. C'est le cas, par exemple, dans les Actes des apôtre 20, 29 : « *scio quoniam intrabunt post discessionem meam lupi rapaces in vos* » qui interprétait la Glose : « *haeretici callidi in fraude, fortes in disputatione, crudeles in occisione* » ; voir aussi Matthieu 7, 15 : « *intrinsecus autem sunt lupi rapaces* » commenté ainsi par la Glose : « *specialiter hoc intelligitur de haereticis, qui venenato animo et intentione nocendi lupi sunt rapaces vel exterius, si copia datur, persequendo vel interius corrumpendo* ». Cependant, il est intéressant de noter que, à l'époque où Olivi écrivait, on accusait les membres des ordres mendiants d'être des loups, comme en témoigne cette phrase de Thomas d'Aquin extraite des *Contra impugnantes*, Ps 5, Cp. 4 : « *lupos autem rapaces eos dicunt, per hoc quodque, accedunt ad ministrandum fidelibus christi alimenta spiritualia, intrinsecus autem intendunt refici de bonis carnalibus eorum; sicut lupi accedunt ad oves, ut de carnibus earum reficiantur* ». Olivi renverse donc l'accusation et traite en « loup » le pape qui se serait opposé aux Mendiants. Par la suite, cette définition du pape hérétique comme un loup sera fréquemment reprise par les disciples des Spirituels dans la France méridionale ; c'est, par exemple ainsi que les nomme Bernard Gui lorsqu'il y fait référence : « *Item, graviter et ignominiose oblocuntur contra dominum papam vicarium Jhesu Christi, quem dicunt insani mente et schismatici vocant et dicunt esse misticum Anti-Christum maioris Anti-Christi, precursorem et preparatorem eius. Item, vocant eum lupum rapacem a fidelibus evitandum et prophetam luscum seu cecum et Caypham pontificem qui Christum condemnavit et Herodem qui Christum illudendo derisit, quia, ut dicunt, ipse dondemnat vitam Christi et deridet Christum in pauperibus suis* » : Bernard Gui, *Manuel de l'inquisiteur*, éd. G. Mollat, vol. I, Paris, 1964, p. 152.

2. « '*Attendendum est ergo iam aliquid ex parte potestatis ecclesiastice. Ad quod quattuor regule sunt attendende. Quarum prima est quod non potest in destructionem sed in edificationem, nec* contra veritatem, *sed* pro veritate, *sicut expresse vult Apostolus, loquens de potestate sua et aliorum Apostolorum*', II Cor., *ultimo. Unde Bernardus, De consideratione ad Eugenium Papam, libro tertio in fine dicit : 'Non sum tam rudis ut ignorem dispensatores vos positos, sed in edificationem non in destructionem. Ubi necessitas urget excusabilis dispensatio est. Ubi utilitas provocat dispensatio laudabilis est. Utilitas dico communis non propria. Nam, cum nichil horum est non plane fidelis dispensatio, sed crudelis dissipatio est [...] ? Prima autem regula sic est intelligenda, quod eius obiectum per se et primum est bonum et non malum, et eius actus specificus est secundum naturam suam bonus et non malus. Impossibile enim est quod potestas a Deo data, ac per consequens a Deo ordinata, secundum Apostolum, Rom. XIII, possit primo et per se in malum obiectum et in malum actum, et ita oportet quod nullo modo nisi forte per accidens se extendat ad malum faciendum. Ut, verbi gratia, potestas conficiendi corpus Christi per se nunquam habet nisi optimum obiectum et optimum actum, per accidens tamen ad malum actum potest ordinari, sed si potestas Pape posset statum evangelicum destruere et homines a statu perfectionis revocare, hoc directe esset posse in*

– le pouvoir ecclésiastique dépend du Christ et il est soumis à ses lois, comme le pouvoir des préfets ou des baillis[1] dépend du pouvoir et des lois du Roi [Olivi ajoute : « les lois du Christ ne sont pas seulement celles que l'on trouve dans les Ecritures Saintes, mais aussi celles qui sont instituées par l'Esprit Saint dans le cœurs des fidèles »][2] ;

– le pouvoir ecclésiastique ne peut pas se diminuer lui-même [encore une affirmation traditionnelle, suivie par une observation originale : « je suis en train de parler – dit Olivi – des choses spirituelles et non pas des temporelles », dont il souhaitait la réduction dans l'Église][3] ;

– enfin le pouvoir ecclésiastique ne concerne pas les choses que Dieu a laissé à la liberté de chacun [ici Olivi donne libre cours à son sens de l'humour en disant : « Si le pape avait le pouvoir d'obliger toute chose et si, sur toute chose qui ne soit pas contraire à son âme, chacun était tenu de lui obéir, alors il pourrait obliger tous les hommes à la pauvreté, ou à la chasteté ; le pape pourrait, par exemple, les obliger à ne jamais rire, ou à donner tout ce qu'ils ont ; il pourrait encore interdire à tous de se marier, ou de passer un contrat sans son autorisation préalable, toutes choses qui sont ouvertement fausses car Dieu a promis à chacun la liberté d'utiliser ce qui lui appartient et chacun peut, en pleine liberté, donner ce qui est en sa propriété, sans devoir demander la permission et le consentement à quiconque »][4].

destructionem Ecclesie et posse contra veritatem consiliorum evangelicorum. Non enim hoc posset nisi Deus etiam hoc sue potestati subiecisset' ».

1. Il est intéressant de noter que, à Narbonne, à l'époque où Olivi écrit, le bailli est le fonctionnaire royal.

2. « *Secunda autem regula de se patet. Universaliter enim potestas prefecti seu baylivi dependet a potestate regia et est subiecta eius legibus et statutis. Leges autem Christi non solum sunt ille quas in Scripturis sacris expressit, sed etiam ille quas in corde fidelium per Spiritum Sanctum instinguit. Sub nomine etiam legum et statutorum intelliguntur quecumque sanctiones et consultationes sollempnes et universales. Unde et inferiores potestates non solum debent procedere in suis iudiciis secundum precepta regum, sed etiam secundum sollempnes et universales consultationes eorum, quas pro utilitate totius rei publice ediderunt. Ergo Papa in suis absolutionibus et dispensationibus et in quibuscumque suis decretis nullo modo potest contraire preceptis et consiliis Christi, immo necessario tenetur ea sequi et secundum ea in suis iudiciis regulari et quicquid contrarium faceret non esset ex potestate sibi a Christo data, sed ex usurpatione nequiter presumpta. Sed in statu evangelico cum nullo potest dispensare quin evidenter Christi consiliis contrariaretur. Et etiam Christi sanctionibus et statutis, quibus statum evangelicum instituit et ordinavit, hoc modo quod ante eius assumptionem esset omnibus in consilio, post assumptionem vero esset in immobili* precepto ».

3. « *Tertia est quod non potest se ipsam diminuere, et loquor de potestate Ecclesie spirituali et non temporali* ».

4. *Quarta regula etiam patet. Si enim Papa posset cogere ad illa que Deus permisit in plena libertate uniuscuiusque, tunc posset omnes homines cogere ad paupertatem et castitatem, et in omnibus que non sunt contra animam teneretur sibi quilibet obedire, et sic posset precipere unicuique quod numquam rideret et consimilia et posset omnibus auferre quecumque habent propria aut communia. Et tunc etiam sequeretur quod nullus potuit uxorem ducere aut aliquem contractum facere sine eius consensu. Que omnia manifeste sunt falsa, quia huiusmodi sic Deus permisit in libertate uniuscuiusque, quod nec per se nec per alium voluit homines ad ista astringi et cogi. Constat autem quod unusquisque potest libere dare illa que sunt in sua plena libertate, irrequisito consensu cuiuscumque alterius, et maxime talis cui quoad hoc in nullo est subiectus. Ergo unusquisque poterit dare Deo per professionis votum se ipsum et omnia sua, pro quanto erant prius in sua libertate posita, absque omni consensu Pape.*

LA QUAESTIO SUR L'ABDICATION DU PAPE CELESTIN

La deuxième question à laquelle Petrus Johannis n'avait pas répondu dans la *quaestio* sur l'infaillibilité du pape, était la suivante : qui a le pouvoir de juger le pape ? La position presque unanime des théologiens et des canonistes était que le pape, qui juge le monde entier, ne peut être jugé que par Dieu [1].

Olivi touche ce problème dans la *quaestio sur l'abdication du pape Célestin.* Le cas d'un pape qui veut renoncer est tout à fait semblable à celui d'un pape hérétique : pour l'un comme pour l'autre, se pose le problème de savoir qui va accepter cette abdication ou bien juger le pape comme hérétique. Comme Olivi le répète dans le troisième argument *in contrario*,

> [...] aucune abdication n'a de valeur si elle n'est reçue par le supérieur de celui qui renonce, mais personne n'est supérieur au pape si ce n'est Dieu lui-même et Dieu ne manifeste pas sa volonté d'accepter une telle abdication, à moins qu'il n'en donne des signes indubitables [2].

Et, ailleurs,

> [...] personne ne peut jouer le rôle de supérieur et de prélat pour sa propre personne, de même que personne ne peut se baptiser lui-même ou pardonner ses propres pêchés, ou se donner les ordres sacrés [...] pour cette même raison un pape ne peut pas se juger lui-même ni se condamner [...] [3].

Olivi répond à ces questions en disant qu'il existe déjà un collège d'hommes qui jouent dans l'église un rôle spécial : le sacré collège des cardinaux. Puisque le pape est un homme et que, donc :

> [...] il peut mourir, tomber malade, ou être empêché d'exercer le gouvernement de l'église pour diverses raisons, il est bien qu'il existe ce collège d'hommes très sages et solennels, qui a le pouvoir de créer le pape ou bien d'exercer les fonctions du pape, au cas où il viendrait à mourir ou serait empêché [4].

1. On peut voir, par exemple, Alexandre de Halès, *Summa Theologica*, Pars II, Inq. III, tract. II, sect. II, qu. I, tit. I, vol. IV, Quaracchi, 1948, p. 612a : « *Utrum possit esse aliqua humana potestas, quae habeat diudicare Summum Pontificem, dicendum quod* [sicut ostendebatur] *Summus Pontifex non potest ab alio quam a Deo iudicari, sicut dicit* Canon, Causa IX, quaest. 3 [voir can. 15, *Decretum*, I, 610] « *facta subditorum a nobis iudicantur, nostra vero a Domino iudicantur. Ex quo accipitur quod Summus Pontifex iudex est ordinarius singulorum, et nullus est qui eum iudicat nisi Deus* » ; dans la même *Summa* les références sont à 1 Cor. 2, 15 : '*Spiritalis autem iudicat omnia et ipse a nemine iudicatur*' ; et à Hugues de Saint-Victor, *De sacramentis Christianae fidei*, II, p. 2, c. 4, *P.L.* 176, p. 418.

2. « *Item nullius renuntiatio valet, nisi acceptetur a superiori suo; sed nullus est papa superior nisi Deus, de quo non constat an eam acceptet, nisi signo indubitabili hoc sue ecclesie declaret* ».

3. « *Item nullus habet rationem prelati et superioris respectu proprie persone et nullus potest se ipsum baptizare, aut a peccatis absolvere, aut sacros ordines sibi conferre et sic de aliis, nec re vel iudex potest se ipsum ordine iudiciario pro quocumque crimine occidere, sicut potest alios reos ; ergo papa non gerit vicem prelati et superioris respectu proprie persone ; ergo per modum condempnantis vel renuntiantis non potest se ipsum a papatu deponere* ».

4. « *Quantum autem ad secundum principale, quam scil. potestatem habet super hoc ecclesia Dei et specialiter illud collegiunn, quod eligit papam, sciendum, quod ea ratione, qua oportuit papam mori et multipliciter infirmari et a regimine ecclesie necessario ex causis variis impediri, oportuit*

Olivi explique que :

> [...] pour la même raison pour laquelle le collège des cardinaux tient le rôle du supérieur dans la substitution d'un pape, il tient le même rôle en acceptant l'abdication du pape, au moins quand elle est évidemment utile et nécessaire, comme lorsque le pape meurt; et pour cela, n'est-il pas vrai que, dans le cas où le pape tomberait dans l'hérésie et où glisserait dans l'impiété, ce serait leur charge spécifique de discerner et juger tout cela? Certainement; et dans ce jugement là, ils auraient le rôle de supérieurs [1].

Olivi tient à tel point à cette doctrine sur le rôle des cardinaux, qu'il n'hésite pas – une des très rares fois – à citer l'autorité d'Aristote pour soutenir sa thèse [2].

Mais l'aspect le plus intéressant de cette doctrine est celui qui concerne le rapport entre le pape et le Siège apostolique. Pour Olivi il y a en même temps une distinction et une très forte relation. A ceux qui disaient que l'autorité du pape était plus grande que l'autorité du Siège apostolique, car elle vient directement de l'autorité donnée à Pierre par Jésus, Olivi répond en disant que cela est vrai dans un sens absolu, mais pas en relation à la personne du pape car, dans ce sens là, la durée de la permanence de chaque pape sur le siège apostolique ne peut pas être aussi grande que le siège lui-même, et la personne du pape peut facilement se corrompre ou devenir inutile pour le gouvernement de l'Église [3].

CONCLUSIONS

On revient ainsi sur le portrait du pape qui émerge de la lecture des œuvres de Pierre de Jean Olivi. Il faut dire avant tout qu'il s'agit d'un homme fragile. Cet homme peut évidement tomber malade, mais aussi commettre des fautes, et de graves. Olivi évite toute identification simpliste entre le pape et le Christ. La papauté n'est pas une garantie contre le péché. Olivi n'est pas naïf : il sait que les

aliquod collegium discretorum et sollempnium virorum habere potestatem creandi papam et interim gerendi vicem pape defuncti saltem in casibus necessariis, alias totum regimen ecclesie posset sepe et sepius multipliciter discrimen et dampnum incurrere ».

1. *Qua ratione collegium cardinalium quo ad quid participat vim superioris in substituendo papam, eadem ratione debet eam consimiliter participare in acceptando renuntiationem pape, saltem quando evidenter est eque utilis et necessaria, sicut est creatio succedentis post mortem pape. Preterea nonne si papa in heresim publice et contumaciter laberetur, ad ipsos spectaret precipue, hoc discernere et iudicare? certo; ymmo ergo ipsi in hoc iudicio haberent quo ad quid rationem superioris.*

2. « *Preterea etiam philosophis paganis, puta Aristoteli in libro Politicorum, recta ratio dictavit, quod illud civile regimen est optimum, quod erat commixtum ex monarchico et ex eo, in quo partim maiores et meliores plebis, partim tota plebs conparticipat. Nam sicut unitas capitis valet contra scismata et scissuras et etiam quia facilius est invenire unum perfecte sapientem et bonum quam plures, propter quod monarchicum regimen est utilius; sic minores fraudes possunt a monarcha committi, quando in quibusdam precipuis oportet eum uti consilio plurium et meliorum* ».

3. *Ad* V[um] *dicendum, quod potestas pape potest considerari vel secundum se, et sic est maior sede papali tanquam imperans et presidens ei, vel potest considerari per respectum ad personam, in qua est, et sic quo ad diuturnitatem perdurandi, non est maior sua sede, quia persona pape potest facilius corrumpi aut ad regimen ecclesiarum inutilis reddi quam deses romana.*

papes prennent quelquefois de mauvaises décisions et il dit que, s'ils les prennent consciemment et s'ils sont obstinés dans leurs mauvaises décisions (comme ce serait le cas si le pape voulait dissoudre l'ordre des frères mineurs), il faudrait les considérer comme des schismatiques et des hérétiques.

Il est vrai cependant que cet homme fragile a, selon Olivi, un pouvoir immense, car il est la règle de la foi. Olivi le répète plusieurs fois : « *apud papam residet summa potestas diffiniendi questiones et dubia fidei* ». C'est un pouvoir, évidemment, spirituel, mais les conséquences de ce pouvoir spirituel peuvent se voir dans tous les aspects de la vie humaine. En tant que successeur de Pierre, le pape a reçu directement du Christ le pouvoir de pardonner, sur la terre comme aux cieux. C'est pour cela qu'Olivi défend avec force le pouvoir du pape de concéder l'indulgence de la Portiuncule. Dans l'humilité de cette petite église, on peut recevoir, grâce à ce pouvoir du Christ, transmis aux hommes à travers du pape, le pardon pour toute leur vie, présente et future.

Le pape, l'homme faible, devient alors un homme angélique. C'est ce qu'Olivi dit dans sa *Lecture sur l'Apocalypse*, là où il parle de la vision, au milieu des sept candélabres de quelqu'un semblable à un Fils d'homme. Olivi dit ici qu'il s'agit du Christ, mais aussi de tout pasteur qui a une charge dans l'église et, tout spécialement, de tout pape. Le commentaire d'Olivi dit : « ici on ne parle pas d'un fils d'homme, mais de quelqu'un semblable à un fils d'homme, c'est pour cela que Richard [de saint Victor] dit qu'il s'agit d'un ange » [1].

L'attente d'un pape angélique fut une des caractéristiques de la génération postérieure à celle d'Olivi. Peut-être ce passage a-t-il contribué à créer cette attente.

Ce qui touche toujours notre sensibilité en lisant les textes d'Olivi sur le pape est donc cette apparente contradiction entre un homme fragile et un homme doué d'un pouvoir immense. Mais c'était probablement une contradiction seulement apparente, car pour Pierre de Jean, le pouvoir du pape, comme celui de tout chrétien, n'est pas un pouvoir personnel, mais n'est que le pouvoir de Dieu lui-même. Pour Olivi, le pape n'est que l'instrument du pouvoir de Dieu : s'il suit la volonté de Dieu, son pouvoir reste immense, s'il s'en écarte, il redevient le plus faible et le plus misérable des hommes. En tout cas le pouvoir de Dieu n'est pas comme les pouvoirs des hommes : il ne s'impose pas par la force. Dieu a choisi de séduire les hommes à travers l'amour; le pape, s'il veut en être le Vicaire, doit toujours choisir le chemin de la réconciliation et de la paix.

1. *Ex hoc autem, quod non dicit « filium hominis » sed « similem filio hominis » arguit Ricardus quod angelum vidit.*

LA DIFESA DELL'ORDINE FRANCESCANO DI FRONTE ALLE CRITICHE DEI SECOLARI IN OLIVI [1]

Roberto Lambertini

INTRODUZIONE

In una questione conservata nel codice 2094 della Bibl. Univ. di Padova, Pietro di Giovanni Olivi prende posizione a proposito del conflitto tra clero secolare ed ordini mendicanti a riguardo dell'interpretazione della bolla di Martino IV, *Ad fructus uberes*[2]. Il suo giudizio è severo : la *controversia magna*, sorta già da tempo e tuttora in corso, è da ascriversi forse più all'emulazione che non allo zelo per le anime[3]. Questa valutazione morale non impedisce però ad Olivi di comporre un testo del tutto sbilanciato a favore dei mendicanti. Egli si inserisce appieno nella linea apologetica del suo Ordine, di cui possediamo altre testimonianze, senza lasciare alcuno spazio alle rivendicazioni del clero secolare. Olivi condivide una concezione ecclesiologica prevalente tra i teologi francescani di quegli anni, secondo la quale il pontefice romano possiede su ciascun fedele un'autorità maggiore e più immediata di quanto non abbia ciascun prelato inferiore, che va inteso come suo incaricato. Ne deriva che l'autorità di confessare dei sacerdoti parrocchiali non ha alcuna precedenza rispetto a quella che può essere conferita da un privilegio papale. Non è difficile immaginare che qualsiasi difesa da parte del clero secolare, anche fondata sull'appello al canone *Omnis*

1. Per ragioni di spazio il presente saggio riproduce quanto letto a Narbona con l'aggiunta delle sole note essenziali, che non aspirano ad alcuna completezza. Sono grato a Sylvain Piron per le osservazioni critiche ed i preziosi suggerimenti. E' per me un piacere ringraziare il mio maestro, Carlo Dolcini, gli organizzatori ed i partecipanti al colloquio di Narbona, senza i quali non sarebbe stato possibile questo mio lavoro, che dedico a Gedeon Gál, *in memoriam*.

2. Per un'introduzione al problema, si veda L. Hödl, « Theologiegeschichtliche Einführung », a Henrici de Gandavo *Tractatus super facto prelatorum et fratrum* (Qdl XII, q. 31), L. Hödl – M. Haverhals edd., *Opera Omnia* 16, Leuven, 1989, p. VII-CXVII.

3. *Comm. Sent.*, IV, d. 17, q. 12, ms. Padova, Bibl. Univ., 2094, f° 188v : « *Dicendum quod circa questionem istam forsitan ex emulatione potius quam ex zelo animarum iamdiu fuit et est in presenti controuersia magna inter quosdam clericos seculares et quosdam religiosos habentes privilegium supradictum secularibus asserentibus quod populi tenentur eadem peccata numero que religiosis confessi sunt confiteri nihilominus ex integro proprio sacerdoti ; religiosis autem e contrario quod in nullo sunt obligati a deo uel a iure positiuo ad illa peccata suis propriis sacerdotibus iterum confitenda. Quia uero ueritatis uia semper est zelanda et pro posse sequenda dicendum est quod opinio clericorum illorum falsa est et erronea nec habet pro se aliquam rationem cogentem, habens contra se euidentissimas rationes et instantias euidentes* ».

utriusque sexus, sia facilmente superabile in Olivi, come in Peckham, Ruggero Marston o in Riccardo di Mediavilla[1]. Neanche la sua apertura alla positività di una ripetizione della confessione dei medesimi peccati, che pure risulta dal IV *Quodlibet*[2], gli fornisce, in questo contesto, ragioni di comprensione nei confronti della rivendicazione del clero secolare, secondo la quale era comunque necessario riconfessare al proprio sacerdote tutti i peccati commessi in un anno. Anzi, rispetto alle prudenti distinzioni di un Riccardo di Mediavilla[3], Olivi si mostra molto più deciso, e non privo di durezze nei confronti dei Secolari. Attribuisce ben poca importanza alle implicazioni pastorali, giurisdizionali ed anche, in ultima istanza, economiche della questione. A suo modo di vedere, il fedele che si è già confessato in modo completo ad un religioso privilegiato non è neppure strettamente tenuto – se non richiesto – a farlo sapere al proprio parroco. Non senza un malcelato disprezzo, Olivi aggiunge che il fedele ottempera meglio alla prescrizione della costituzione *Omnis utriusque sexus* confessandosi frequentemente ad un religioso all'altezza del compito piuttosto che facendolo una volta sola con un parroco ignorante e dai costumi corrotti[4].

Questa immagine di un Olivi pienamente partecipe della linea di difesa del suo Ordine nei confronti degli attacchi dei Secolari si è andata affermando – nonostante la giustificata attenzione alle questioni intrafrancescane – nella consapevolezza storiografica anche a proposito di alcune tra le sue più importanti questioni sulla perfezione evangelica. Così, Johannes Schlageter evidenzia che, composta all'esaurirsi del cosiddetto *Mendikantenstreit*, la questione ottava si inserisce appieno nella tradizione francescana[5]. Da parte sua, David Burr ha potuto presentare la questione ottava come tarda incursione nella controversia Secolari-Mendicanti ed indicarne la stretta dipendenza dalla tradizione francescana precedente, con una netta preferenza per materiali provenienti dal *Tractatus*

1. *Ibidem*: «*Sed non minus auctoritatis habet papa immediate super quemlibet fidelem quam proprius sacerdos, ymmo longe plus et magis immediate, quia ab ipso dependet auctoritas inferiorum ministrorum et sacerdotum. Ergo multo minus tenentur confiteri proprio sacerdoti confessi his qui a papa habent licentiam et ita plene satisfecerunt illi constitutioni sicut si de* [f° 189r] *licentia sacerdotis confessi fuissent*». *Cfr.* Ioannis Pecham *Quodlibeta Quatuor*, IV, 47, F. Delorme – G.I. Etzkorn edd., Grottaferrata, 1989, p. 274-280; Rogeri Marston *Quodlibeta Quatuor*, G.I. Etzkorn – I.C. Brady edd., Grottaferrata, 1994, III, 25, p. 359-366; Richardi de Mediavilla *Quaestio disputata de privilegio Martini papae IV*, F. Delorme ed., Ad Claras Aquas, 1925, p. 1-78.

2. *Quodl.* IV, q. 25, *An peccata de quibus aliquis est sufficienter absolutus possit idem teneri iterum confiteri; et an de eisdem non reiteratis possit iterum absolvi*, f° 31va-b.

3. *Cfr.* Richardi de Mediavilla, *Questio disputata*, *ed. cit.*, p. 48-49.

4. *Comm. Sent.*, IV, d. 17, q. 12, ms. Padova, Bibl. Univ., 2094, f° 189r: «*Dicendum ergo quod ex quo aliquis legitime confessus est habentibus priuilegium a papa non tenetur unquam illa peccata sacerdoti proprio confiteri; sed alia si habet confiteatur ei semel in anno propter mandatum ecclesiasticum implendum; si uero non habet, quia perfecte de omnibus confessus est, sufficit quod inquisitus a sacerdote presentet se sacerdoti suo, dicendo se legitime confessum habenti potestatem, et ille credere debet sicut ei crederet in propria confessione; si uero non requiratur nec se ei presentet non est magna uis, dummodo hoc non faciat ex contemptu, quia preceptum decretalis etiam aliter implet perfectius confitendo frequenter pure et integre discreto religioso habenti auctoritatem ex priuilegio quam si solum semel sacerdoti inscio et miserabilis uite confessus fuisset*».

5. J. Schlageter, *Das Heil der Armen und das Verderben der Reichen. Petrus Johannis Olivi O.F.M. Die Frage nach der höchsten Armut*, Werl/Westfalen, 1989, in part. p. 19-22 e nota 9.

pauperis di Giovanni Peckham[1]. Anche per la questione decima, dedicata alla difesa della mendicità, David Flood ha saputo mostrare il debito di Olivi nei confronti della tradizione apologetica dell'Ordine, ed in particolare di Bonaventura e di Peckham[2]. Nello stesso tempo, a questi studiosi non è sfuggita la peculiarità di Olivi rispetto alla tradizione in cui egli nondimeno si inserisce. Schlageter ha concentrato la sua attenzione sulla connessione tra teoria della povertà e critica della situazione della Chiesa e dell'Ordine francescano stesso[3]. Flood ha rimarcato, da parte sua, una maggiore valorizzazione del lavoro manuale in Olivi rispetto a quanto accade in Bonaventura o Peckham[4].

Ponendosi sulla scia di queste indagini, partendo dal dato assodato del pieno inserimento di Olivi in una tradizione apologetica dell'Ordine, questo contributo si propone di evidenziare alcuni punti in cui il francescano della Linguadoca si è discostato dalla linea tradizionale di difesa del suo Ordine proprio nei confronti della critica dei Secolari. Lo farò focalizzando l'attenzione in primo luogo sull'Ottava questione *de perfectione evangelica*, vera e propria *summa* delle discussioni precedenti. Poiché la disputa tra Secolari e Mendicanti è stata anche uno scambio di argomenti e controargomenti, concentrerò la mia attenzione non sulle grandi questioni che gli esperti hanno da tempo analizzato, ma su alcuni elementi apparentemente marginali, legati ad altrettanti *topoi* della tradizione apologetica dell'Ordine. Adotterò il metodo di rilevare mutamenti anche minori all'interno del ripetersi quasi infinito di medesimi *pro* e *contra*. Ne emergeranno alcune originalità di Olivi apologeta dell'Ordine ed anche una possibile connessione, nelle opere del teologo francescano, tra difesa dell'ideale francescano e genesi della teoria dell'*usus pauper*.

CONDESCENSIO INFIRMORUM

Un primo esempio di questa indipendenza di Olivi rispetto alla tradizione apologetica dell'Ordine è fornito da un aspetto della difesa della teoria francescana della povertà : quello della *condescensio infirmorum*. L'importanza della tesi richiamata da questa espressione risulta chiara se si pone mente al fatto che, non appena trascinati nel campo della polemica contro i Secolari, gli autori francescani si videro costretti a confrontarsi con brani evangelici dai quali l'espropriazione di Cristo e degli apostoli risultava tutt'altro che scontata. Si potrebbe dire che lo specchio apostolico, nel quale i Francescani vedevano riflessa la perfezione della propria scelta, rischiava di finire in frantumi già nel corso dei primi confronti critici. E' noto che una delle pietre d'inciampo era

1. D. Burr, « Introduction » a Petrus Ioannis Olivi, De usu paupere. *The* Quaestio *and the* Tractatus, D. Burr ed., Firenze-Perth, 1992, in part. p. XXVI-XXXII.

2. D. Flood, « Peter Olivi. *Quaestio de mendicitate*. Critical Edition », *A.F.H.* 87, 1994, p. 287-293.

3. Schlageter, *Das Heil*, *op. cit.*, p. 24-26.

4. Flood, *Peter Olivi*, *op. cit.*, p. 293.

costituita da un brano che avrebbe accompagnato tutta la disputa sulla povertà, ben oltre il XIII secolo, vale a dire quel versetto del Vangelo di Giovanni (12, 6) dai quali emerge che Cristo e gli apostoli avrebbero avuto una borsa per il denaro, i *loculi*. Fin dallo scontro tra Guglielmo di Sant'Amore e Bonaventura, i teorici francescani hanno lottato con questa evidenza scritturistica, al fine di dimostrare che quel dato di fatto non aveva una valenza propriamente esemplare. In questo sforzo hanno trovato sostegno in una tradizione patristica già assorbita e tramandata dalle Glosse, secondo la quale Cristo avrebbe assunto comportamenti per accondiscendere alla debolezza di coloro che sono definiti *infirmi*. Questi elementi sono già presenti nella seconda questione *De perfectione evangelica* di Bonaventura, in cui il dottore serafico vuole mostrare che per tre motivi si può sostenere che Cristo ebbe i *loculi* senza per questo venir meno all'altissima povertà. Tra queste ragioni, accanto all'aiuto agli altri poveri ed al caso di necessità, campeggia infatti, con due citazioni dalla *Glossa*, la condiscendenza verso i deboli. Nei medesimi anni, la stessa linea di difesa incontra il favore di altri apologeti degli Ordini mendicanti : per esempio, lo stesso Tommaso d'Aquino la utilizza nel suo *Contra impugnantes*[1]. Ma, soprattutto, assume notevole importanza nel trattato attribuito a Tommaso di York, in cui costituisce il nerbo di quella che lo stesso autore ritiene essere la *facilior responsio* alla questione dei *loculi* di Cristo. In questa opera, infatti, le ragioni del possesso dei *loculi* sono quasi raddoppiate rispetto a Bonaventura, ma la prima resta quella dell'aver compassione per i deboli, o come suggerisce il testo più avanti, per gli imperfetti[2]. Se questa moltiplicazione delle spiegazioni sia espressione della forza di una interpretazione esegetica (o non piuttosto della sua debolezza) è questione non facile da dirimere. Certo è che essa si basava sulla possibilità di distinguere, all'interno dei comportamenti di Cristo, quelli aventi una valenza di perfezione e quelli che invece potevano fungere da modello, per così dire, per chi non fosse in grado di raggiungere quella perfezione.

Con la sua *Apologia pauperum* Bonaventura dovette fare i conti con le critiche di Gerardo d'Abbeville[3], rivolte anche contro la tesi della *condescensio*, specificando anche in modo significativo la propria posizione. Ma la *condescensio* restò. L'*Apologia pauperum* osserva infatti che la Provvidenza ha avuto molti fini nel fare sì che la comunità apostolica fosse fornita di *loculi*, pur affidandoli a colui che infine tradì. Tra questi campeggia la condiscendenza verso coloro che non sono in grado di rinunciare, anche se Bonaventura si affretta a precisare che, segno di imperfezione per gli uni, i *loculi* sono invece componente della

1. S. Bonaventurae *Quaestiones de Perfectione evangelica*, II, art. 1, *Opera Omnia*, V, Ad Claras Aquas, 1891, p. 131 : « *Habuit etiam loculos condescendendo infirmis, sicut dicitur in Glossa super illud Psalmi : Producens foenum iumenti : 'Dominus loculos habebat vel habuit[...] in his infirmorum personam suscipiens'* ». *Cfr.* Thomas de Aquino, *Contra impugnantes Dei cultum et religionem*, *Opera Omnia*, Editio leonina, XLI/A, Romae, 1970, p. 101.

2. Thomas Eboracensis, *Manus quae contra Omnipotentem*, M. Bierbaum ed., in *Id.*, *Bettelorden und Weltgeistlichkeit an der Universität Paris*, Münster/Westfalen, 1920, p. 59-60, 63.

3. A questo proposito mi permetto di rimandare a R. Lambertini, *Apologia e crescita dell'identità francescana (1255-1279)*, Roma, 1990, p. 65-106.

perfezione dei prelati[1]. Emerge qui forse la preoccupazione più viva degli apologeti francescani dopo le obiezioni di Gerardo, quella di evitare di scivolare in un'accusa indiretta di imperfezione nei confronti dei prelati della Chiesa. Si può osservare, però, che la tensione non pare del tutto superata : se portare denaro è segno di compassione nei confronti dei deboli, di coloro che non riescono a sopportare il rigore della perfezione, allora risulta difficile allontanare il sospetto di un'implicita svalutazione della dignità dei vescovi. In effetti, Bonaventura sostiene che la medesima azione può essere elemento di imperfezione per gli uni (i deboli) e non per gli altri (i prelati, che hanno doveri nei confronti della comunità). Una posizione analoga è presente nelle numerose opere di Peckham, nel *Tractatus pauperis*, nella questione sulla perfezione evangelica, nel *Quodlibet romanum*, perfino nel *Canticum pauperis*, dove significativamente, la parola *infirmus* è usata come sinonimo di *imperfectus*. Anche l'*Expositio regulae* che a ragione è stata avvicinata a Peckham non esita a parlare di *imperfecti*[2]. Ma quali valenze – ben più polemiche – potesse ancora chiaramente assumere questa dottrina è mostrato appieno da un ulteriore scritto di Peckham, a rigore non pertinente in senso stretto alla polemica contro i Secolari, ma con essa strettamente connesso, il trattato *Contra Kilwardby*. Qui, prendendo spunto dal medesimo brano di Ugo di San Vittore utilizzato anche nel *Tractatus pauperis* (e presente anche nella *Expositio regulae*) Peckham non esita a tacciare i frati Domenicani di imperfezione. La forma di vita alla quale i Predicatori si conformano altro non è che l'imperfezione alla quale accondiscese Cristo per amore dei deboli e quindi non è una perfezione di cui ci si possa gloriare, come invece vorrebbe fare Kilwardby[3]. La tesi della *condescensio* è quindi sempre potenzialmente aperta a ribaltarsi da difesa in accusa.

Ripreso così *per summa capita* lo sviluppo di un vero e proprio *locus* apologetico francescano, risulta in modo ancora più chiaro la lucidità teorica di Pietro di Giovanni Olivi, che affronta il tema risolvendo l'11° argomento in contrario (seconda serie) di *QPE VIII*. Qui Olivi apre la sua trattazione presentando l'argomento tradizionale e attribuendolo ai soliti *quidam*, nei quali possiamo includere un'ampia tradizione francescana, anche se è molto probabile che egli avesse presente in particolare la formulazione di Giovanni Peckham, come ha opportunamente segnalato Johannes Schlageter. Non ci stupiamo nel trovarlo ben consapevole delle discussioni precedenti, ma ci colpisce il fatto che proponga

1. S. Bonaventurae *Apologia pauperum*, VII, *Opera Omnia*, VII, Ad Claras Aquas, 1898, p. 284-285.

2. Johannes Peckham, *Tractatus pauperis*, IV, A. van den Wyngaert ed., Paris, 1925, p. 45 ; *id.*, *Utrum perfectio ewangelica consistat in renuntiando vel carendo divitiis propriis et communibus*, L. Oliger ed., *Franz. Stud.* 4, 1917, p. 161 ; *id.*, *Canticum pauperis*, in *Stimulus Amoris fr. Jacobi Mediolanensis – Canticum pauperis fr. Johannis Pecham*, Ad Claras Aquas, 1949, p. 141 ; *Id.*, *Quodlibeta quatuor*, IV, q. 48, p. 284-285. *Cfr. id.* [?], *Expositio super regulam*, IV, in S. Bonaventurae *Opera Omnia*, VII, *cit.*, p. 414.

3. Johannes Peckham, *Contra Kilwardby*, in *Fratris Johannis Pecham quondam archiepiscopi Cantuariensis tractatus tres de paupertate*, C.L. Kingsford – A.G. Little – F. Tocco edd., Aberdeen, 1910, p. 133. In anni non lontani si appella alla *condescensio* anche Guglielmo de la Mare, *Correctorium fratris Thomae*, 75, in P. Glorieux, *Les premières polémiques thomistes, I, Le Correctorium Corruptorii Quare*, Kain, 1927, p. 315-317.

un'altra via, pur non parlando in prima persona. « Quibusdam tamen non inconvenienter visum est », con questa formula Olivi introduce una tesi diversa, secondo la quale non si può affermare che Cristo abbia compiuto qualche cosa che possa essere considerato imperfetto secondo il nostro *status* di *viatores*. In breve, Cristo non ha fatto nulla che possa essere giudicato imperfetto per lui durante la sua vita o per i perfetti dei nostri giorni. Il possesso dei *loculi* va ricondotto unicamente alla situazione di necessità, che non deroga alla perfezione. In questo senso, si può affermare che mai Cristo ha accondisceso a possedere beni in comune in un modo contrastante con l'altissima povertà[1]. In *QPE IX* Olivi sarà ancora più esplicito : il possesso dei *loculi* è connesso con un caso di inevitabile necessità. Parlando questa volta in prima persona, dirà che alcuni si riferiscono a questo proposito alla *condescensio infirmorum*, ma questa tesi gli pare priva di ogni sostegno testuale : « *ex textu non video unde probari possit* »[2]. Anche in *QPE X* Olivi conferma la sua distanza dalla tesi della *condescensio*[3], mentre nella *Lectura super Iohannem* rimanda esplicitamente a quanto scritto nelle Questioni sulla perfezione evangelica, ribadendo che Cristo ha costituito un modello perfetto, al quale invero possono ispirarsi anche comportamenti in parte manchevoli[4]. Il dissenso di Olivi nei confronti di quel *topos* apologetico può quindi essere considerato una costante del suo atteggiamento[5].

1. *QPE VIII*, J. Schlageter ed., p. 181-182 : « *Christus in nullo condescenderit, quod communitati hominum secundum statum huius vitae esset imperfectum, sed in illis dictus est condescensisse quae existentibus in statu perfectionis propter infirmitatem humanae naturae contingere possunt [...] Secundum autem hanc viam Christus numquam condescendit in habendo communia secundum illum modum, secundum quem repugnat altissimae paupertati. Secundum primos autem, etsi condescendit, non tamen in hoc exemplum dedit perfectis, sed solum imperfectis* ».

2. *QPE IX*, Burr ed., p. 52.

3. In questo contesto – seppure da un angolatura un poco diversa – emerge di nuovo la questione dei *loculi* ed Olivi evita completamente di appellarsi alla tesi della condiscendenza nei confronti dei deboli : qui, l'unica ragione per la quale Cristo e gli apostoli ebbero la borsa dei denari è per sovvenire altri poveri : *Cfr. QPE X*, D. Flood ed., p. 328 ; il medesimo atteggiamento emerge nella *Lectura super Actus Apostolorum*, ms. Firenze, Biblioteca Marucelliana, C 276, f° 26r : « *et Christus aliquando habuit pro ceteris pauperibus loculos* ». Devo anche la conoscenza di questo manoscritto alla gentilezza di Sylvain Piron ed alle sue indicazioni, che arrichiscono il contributo di Antonio Ciceri, contenute in S. Piron, « Compléments à l'inventaire des manuscrits d'Olivi », *A.F.H.* 90, 1997, p. 591-596.

4. *Lectura super Iohannem*, 12, 6, ms. Firenze, Bibl. Med. Laur., S. Croce, Plut. X dext., cod. 8, f° 66vb-66^{bis}ra : « *De questione autem quare Christus loculos habuit aut qualiter et quando in questionibus et tractatibus de euangelica paupertate satis habunde est dictum. [...] Tertia (scil. causa habendi loculos) est secundum Augustinum ad dandum formam ecclesiastice pecunie que clericis et monachis in suis ecclesiis et collegiis temporalia habentibus est concessa. Scito tamen quod huiusmodi formam dedit eo modo quo in perfecto et exemplari sygillo est forma, scilicet omnium impressionum seu sygillarium figurarum perfectarum et imperfectarum; nam absque omni imperfectione sciuit in se dare <exemplum> infirmis et imperfectis tam in loculis quam in fuga [...]* ».

5. Nella *QPE XV*, il testo in cui forse l'opposizione alla tesi della *condescensio* è meno marcata, sembra emergere la preoccupazione che da quella interpretazione non si possa comunque far derivare alcun elemento contrario alle più rigorose scelte di perfezione ; *Cfr.* ms. Firenze, Bibl. Med. Laur., C. S. 448, f° 100va : « *Ex hiis autem condescensionibus nichil potest concludi contra uias rigidiores et perfectiores de sui natura* ». *Cfr.* D. Flood, *Peter Olivi*, *op. cit.*, p. 347.

Il cambiamento di rotta rispetto alla tradizione precedente poneva Olivi in contrasto con le grandi *auctoritates* dell'Ordine, ma consentiva di superare le ambiguità precedenti e di presentare, con maggiore eleganza argomentativa, l'esempio di Cristo come unitario, e come univocamente orientato all'esercizio di quella somma povertà che costituiva la perfezione. Nello stesso tempo, questa soluzione non implicava, in verità, l'accusa implicita di imperfezione a chi avesse posseduto i *loculi*, fatto salvo, naturalmente, che ciò fosse avvenuto nelle medesime modalità della comunità apostolica. Inoltre, escludeva con nettezza che si potesse parlare di imperfezione dei prelati in ragione del fatto che amministrano beni. Olivi avrebbe infatti ribadito che è inscritto nel diritto naturale, e quindi non va a detrimento della perfezione, il fatto che chi esercita autorità sugli altri – in particolare i prelati – debba anche amministrare i beni necessari al suo ufficio [1].

MULTITUDO CREDENTIUM

Un caso analogo mi pare essere costituito dall'interpretazione dei brani iniziali degli Atti degli Apostoli che descrivono la comunione dei beni tra i primi credenti. Guglielmo di Sant'Amore vi faceva riferimento già nella *Quaestio de quantitate eleemosinae* [2]. Spinto con tutta verosimiglianza dalla polemica di Gerardo d'Abbeville, che tanto aveva insistito sul carattere comune del possesso per tutti gli ecclesiastici, Bonaventura affronta questo versetto nell'*Apologia pauperum*. A suo modo di vedere, esso va interpretato secondo una fondamentale distinzione interna già alla prima comunità cristiana. Da una parte la *turba credentium*, dall'altra il collegio apostolico. Solo quest'ultimo viveva secondo una povertà assoluta; i restanti fedeli possedevano beni in comune. Questa distinzione assolveva ad una molteplicità di funzioni, non ultima quella di fondare nella medesima comunità dei primi tempi sia il modello della proprietà comune dei beni – cui secondo Bonaventura si sono rifatte le comunità monastiche – sia quello della espropriazione totale [3]. Anche questa interpretazione gode di una notevole eco. Peckham la fa sua nel *Tractatus Pauperis*, nella Questione sulla perfezione evangelica e nel *Quodlibet romanum* dove la contrapposizione della *Glossa* tra *doctores* ed *auditores* viene ricondotta anche alla diversità di regime economico. Pure l'*Expositio regulae* vicina a Peckham adotta il medesimo punto di vista : la comunità dei santi di Gerusalemme condivideva il dominio, mentre gli apostoli non avevano in comune che l'uso [4].

1. *Cfr. QPE VIII*, J. Schlageter ed., p. 178.
2. Guillelmus de Sancto Amore, *Quaestio de quantitate eleemosynae*, in A.G. Traver, « William of Saint Amour's Two disputed questions *De quantitate eleemosynae* and *De valido mendicante* », *A.H.D.L.M.A.* 62, 1995, p. 295-342, in part. p. 328.
3. Bonaventura, *Apologia pauperum*, VII, *ed. cit.*, p. 273.
4. Johannes Peckham, *Tractatus pauperis*, IV, *ed. cit.*, p. 56 ; *id.*, *Utrum perfectio*, *ed. cit.*, p. 171 ; *id.*, *Quodlibeta quatuor*, IV, q. 48, *ed. cit.*, p. 285. *Cfr. id.* [?], *Expositio super Regulam*, VI, *ed. cit.*, p. 422.

L'atteggiamento di Olivi mostra notevoli analogie con la trattazione del caso precedente. Nelle *rationes in contrarium* compare la citazione dei brani degli Atti da cui emerge il possesso comune della prima comunità. La risposta si apre anche qui con la presentazione della soluzione inaugurata da Bonaventura, anche se – come annota con precisione Schlageter – la forma utilizzata da Olivi è piuttosto quella di Peckham[1]. Ma all'opinione di questi *quidam*, secondo la quale la *multitudo credentium* viveva in modo conforme ad un regime proprietario, Olivi oppone un'altra interpretazione: « *Quibusdam autem non indocte visum est* ». Anche in questo caso, viene rifiutata una linea apologetica di origine bonaventuriana. Per Olivi la soluzione va cercata altrove, nella ripresa integrale del tema secondo il quale nella comunità dei primi tempi è stato radicalmente rinnovato lo stato d'innocenza. Articolando ulteriormente questa intuizione, Olivi sostiene espressamente che nello stato d'innocenza e durante il suo rinnovamento apostolico, diversamente da quanto accade oggi, la comunità non possedeva sui beni che usava diritti tali da escludere gli altri uomini da quei medesimi beni. La comunità dei primi tempi – e qui Olivi passa significativamente a parlare in prima persona – non aveva nessuno *ius, nec in re, nec in usu*, nei confronti dei beni che usava[2]. Come il teologo francescano si potesse immaginare il rapporto della comunità apostolica con i beni materiali è suggerito da quanto, poco più avanti, dice delle vesti e degli altri beni dell'apostolo Pietro: esse non erano sottoposte alla giurisdizione di alcuno, come i pesci del mare e gli uccelli del cielo[3]. Che sia proprio Olivi a nascondersi dietro i *quidam* che non accettano l'interpretazione bonaventuriana è confermato anche dal corpo della questione. Lì, appellandosi alla dottrina di Platone mediatagli dal *Decretum* e da Aristotele, Olivi sostiene la concezione di uno stato di innocenza originario in cui non solo gli individui, ma anche i gruppi hanno in comune con gli altri l'uso dei beni di questo mondo[4]. Anche in *QPE IX* Olivi si oppone ad un tentativo di risposta che postuli una differenziazione di modi di vivere la povertà all'interno della chiesa primitiva[5]. La *Lectura super Actus Apostolorum* (commentando Atti 2, 44-45) ribadisce questa sua posizione con dovizia di argomentazioni che contengono anche un esplicito rinvio a quanto sostenuto nelle « *quaestiones de paupertate* »[6]. In questo

1. *QPE VIII*, J. Schlageter ed., p. 79, 178.

2. *Ibidem*, p. 178-179 : « *Quibusdam autem non indocte visum est quod alia fuit communitas illius temporis et alia illa que usque hodie durat. Illa enim fuit communitas extendens se ad omnes homines – qualis fuit in statu innocentiae – ita quod unum speciale collegium non plus habebat iuris quibus utebantur, quam quicumque alius homo [...] Unde illi, ut credo, solum usum habebant in illis communibus, non autem aliquod ius nec in re nec in usu* ».

3. *Ibidem*, p. 180 : « *Ad septimum dicendum quod ea quae Petrus portabat, in nullius iurisdictione erant. Hoc enim est possibile etiam secundum iura civilia. Nam aves caeli et pisces mari secundum se in nullius iure sunt* ».

4. *Ibidem*, p. 98-99.

5. *QPE IX*, D. Burr ed., p. 40.

6. *Lectura super Actus Apostolorum* 2, 44-45, ms. cit, f° 18v-19r; si veda in particolare l'opinione di Olivi al f° 18v : « *[...] aliqui istius opinionis distinguunt inter apostolos et ceteros credentes. Dicunt enim quod apostoli nihil habebant penitus in proprio uel in communi. Cetera uero multitudo credentium carebat tunc quidem proprio sed habebat alica in communi. [...] Alii uero dicunt quod hec communitas omnem proprietatem, seu ius proprietatum excludebat non solum a singulis sed etiam a*

commento Olivi si mostra molto attaccato all'idea dell'unità fondamentale della comunità apostolica, impegnandosi perfino in una serie di discussioni per dimostrare come si possa sostenere che gli apostoli rispettarono pienamente il loro voto di povertà, senza ricorrere all'ipotesi di Bonaventura e Peckham che la proprietà comune e l'uso del denaro siano stati prerogativa dei membri della comunità che non facevano parte del collegio apostolico [1].

Si potrebbe così riassumere l'immagine alternativa proposta da Olivi : la prima comunità è stata modello integrale di perfezione : non ha compiuto atti al fine di *condescendere infirmis*, né ha distinto al suo interno modi diversi di usare dei beni. I brani evangelici che possono sembrar militare in senso contrario, e che hanno affaticato gli esegeti francescani, vanno intesi come se si esprimessero in modo improprio : in verità, nella chiesa primitiva non v'erano né proprietà né compravendita [2].

Usu consumptibilia : un silenzio da interpretare

Nei due casi sopra indicati Olivi si discosta apertamente da una linea apologetica rilevante nell'Ordine, per proporre modalità alternative di concepire la comunità apostolica cui vuole rifarsi il suo Ordine. In entrambe le sue risposte emerge una netta tendenza all'unificazione del modello apostolico, che fa riferimento privilegiato al rapporto tra povertà e necessità naturale : è la necessità a spiegare i *loculi*, alla necessità primigenia è ritornata la prima comunità.

In questa prospettiva si può affrontare un terzo caso di distanza di Olivi da una linea apologetica dell'Ordine ; un caso particolare, perché si esprime non con un dissenso aperto, seppure relegato nelle *responsiones ad rationes in contrarium*, ma in una strana assenza. E' fin troppo noto che uno degli argomenti principali utilizzati da Gerardo d'Abbeville per asserire la contraddittorietà della scelta francescana è quello dell'inseparabilità di uso e dominio nelle cose che si consumano con l'uso. L'*Apologia* di Bonaventura ne coglie il mordente, e vi contrappone, come eccezione in cui si verifica la separabilità, la circostanza in cui chi usa non ha autorità sul bene usato. L'esempio è quello del *filiusfamilias* [3].

tota communitate eorum ita quod, si aliqui de externis gentilibus uel iudeis aliqua eis aufferret, nequaquam repetissent illa ab eis tamquam propria uel communitatis... illa communitas non appropriabat illi collegio aliquid in communi ymmo erat talis qualis in statu innocentie apud totam communitatem hominum fuisset et qualis inter omnes homines esse deberet si non esset corruptio et infirmitas originalis uel actualis peccati, et qualis est illa qua aer et sol omnibus sunt communes ».

1. *Cfr. Lectura super Actus Apostolorum* 4, 32-35, ms. cit., f° 25v-27v. Qui Olivi si pone la questione « *Cuius aut quorum erant illa precia rerum uenditarum que afferebantur* » e risponde (f° 26r) : « *Dicendum quod sicut non est necesse quod aues celi et pisces maris sint alicuius domini specialis aut quod sint appropriati alicui collegio speciali, sic non fuit hoc necesse de illis pecuniis* ». *Cfr. supra*, n. 30. Olivi si chiede anche se gli apostoli abbiano amministrato anche denaro o solamente i beni necessari acquistati con quel danaro, e propende per la prima soluzione, attribuendola ancora una volta alla *grandis et manifesta necessitas* che caratterizzava la comunità.

2. *QPE VIII*, J. Schlageter ed., p. 179.

3. Bonaventura, *Apologia Pauperum* XI, *ed. cit.*, p. 312.

Peckham, nel *Tractatus pauperis* (o meglio nella versione più estesa del *Tractatus pauperis*)[1], si richiama invece al caso del servo che usa il denaro del padrone. La questione gli pare di tale importanza da inserirla perfino nella polemica contro Kilwardby, il quale in verità non ne aveva fatto esplicita menzione[2]. In *QPE VIII*, però, non si trova traccia di questo argomento e della sua confutazione. Lo stesso accade nello scritto *Quod regula fratrum minorum excludit omnem proprietatem*[3]. Questa assenza non può mancare di suscitare un certo stupore, se si pone mente al fatto che la trattazione di Olivi intende certamente essere una sorta di *summa* della discussione sulla povertà condotta fino a quel momento. Se Burr ipotizza, ed a ragione, che il francescano provenzale abbia attinto ad un qualche di centone di argomenti *pro* e *contra* i Francescani, risulta difficile pensare che non vi fosse contenuto un riferimento ad un argomento così incisivo. E certo, per lo meno in fase di stesura definitiva, Olivi aveva a disposizione l'*Apologia pauperum*, dove l'argomento pure compariva. Lo stesso – credo – si può osservare a proposito del *Tractatus pauperis* di Peckham, cui Olivi attribuisce una grande autorevolezza[4]. Escluso quindi – almeno con grande verosimiglianza – che Olivi ne fosse all'oscuro, il suo silenzio diventa ancora più difficile da spiegare, ma nello stesso tempo ancora più interessante, richiamando alla mente le osservazioni di Malcolm Lambert a proposito della medesima assenza, ben più foriera di conseguenze, che si può riscontrare nella stessa decretale *Exiit qui seminat*. Dovremmo pensare, come suggerisce Lambert per Niccolò III, che anche Olivi abbia considerato l'argomento troppo forte per poter essere confutato adeguatamente e l'abbia proprio per questa ragione passato sotto silenzio[5]?

Dai testi emergono alcuni indizi che possono aprire una prospettiva diversa. Quando, in *QPE VIII*, Olivi si avvicina maggiormente al problema, mostra non solo di condividere la distinzione, sviluppata dalla tradizione precedente, tra *usus* e *ius*, ma la approfondisce ulteriormente, contrapponendo, come avrebbe poi fatto la *Exiit*, l'*usus* allo *ius utendi*. Ebbene, anche in questo contesto che lo suggerirebbe da vicino, – pur citando l'esempio ormai « canonico » del servo, utilizzato da altri per contrastare l'obiezione di Gerardo – egli non fa riferimento esplicito allo statuto delle cose che si « consumano con l'uso »[6]. In verità,

1. Forse sarebbe più esatto parlare della versione più estesa del *Tractatus*, testimoniata solo da alcuni codici. Manchiamo, purtroppo, di un'edizione condotta su tutta la tradizione menoscritta. *Cfr.* Johannes Peckham, *Tractatus pauperis*, X, in *Johannis Pecham tractatus tres*, *cit.*, p. 51-52.

2. J. Peckham, *Contra Kilwardby*, p. 140.

3. Oltre alla consultazione di un edizione a stampa (*Firmamenta trium ordinum*, Parisius 1512, f° 109r-111r) ha dato esito negativo anche il controllo, compiuto con squisita gentilezza per me da Eva Wittneben, sulle seguenti copie manoscritte del trattatello : Città del Vaticano, Bibl. Ap. Vat., Borgh. lat. 357, f° 74r-76r ; Borgh. lat. 358, f° 201r-202r ; Vat. lat. 4986, f° 47v-48v.

4. D. Burr, « Introduction » a Petrus Iohannis Olivi, *De usu paupere*, *cit.*, p. 26.

5. M.D. Lambert, *Povertà francescana. La dottrina dell'assoluta povertà di Cristo e degli Apostoli nell'Ordine francescano (1210-1323)*, trad. it. aggiornata dall'autore al 1995, Milano, 1995, p. 140, 226.

6. *QPE VIII*, J. Schlageter ed., p. 195 : « *Ad vigesimum nonum dicendum quod usus et ius non sunt idem. Possumus enim uti re absque hoc quod habeamus ius in ea vel in usu eius, sicut servus utitur re domini sui, qui tamen nec est dominus nec ususfructuarius [...] In minori tamen huius rationis non fit*

l'argomento a cui Olivi risponde parlava di *res necessarie*, sostenendo che nel caso di quei beni uso e diritto d'uso si identificano. Ma il teologo francescano risponde limitandosi a rimarcare che quell'identificazione è valida solo nel campo del diritto naturale, non in quello del diritto positivo, evidenziando che in quest'ultima sfera l'uso ed il diritto all'uso rimangono ben distinti[1]. Il silenzio (in verità non facile da comprendere) a proposito dei *bona usu consumptibilia* e la mancanza del ricorso ad argomentazioni volte a sostenere la separabilità di uso e dominio anche per questo tipo di beni potrebbero però essere posti in relazione con quanto Olivi dice nel suo *tractatus* sui contratti usurari. Qui, infatti, tra le argomentazioni contro la liceità dell'usura, si ritrova la *ratio* secondo la quale l'uso del danaro, così come quello del grano o dell'olio, coincide con la loro alienazione e consunzione. Ne deriva che l'uso è inseparabile dalla sostanza di questo genere di cose e vendere l'uno è necessariamente vendere l'altro[2]. Pur considerando la diversità dei contesti, il brano può far pensare che Olivi avesse qualche difficoltà ad ammettere nel campo della teoria dell'usura l'idea dell'inseparabilità tra uso e dominio per le cose consumabili ed a rifiutarla poi nelle polemiche in favore dell'Ordine.

Di fronte a questi elementi, parziali ad anche sfuggenti, in quanto tratti da contesti diversi (sappiamo quanto gli autori medievali fossero sensibili alla diversità dei contesti argomentativi), può comunque porsi spontanea la domanda se appunto Olivi non considerasse la questione in una prospettiva diversa. Anche se l'esito del mio sondaggio non può dirsi conclusivo, mi sento di avanzare un'ipotesi : che a giudizio di Olivi la garanzia del fatto che l'uso dei frati non si traducesse in una forma qualsivoglia di diritto sulla cosa non fosse autenticamente fondata sulla separabilità di uso e dominio in ogni caso[3]. Piuttosto, a fare la differenza potrebbe essere il fatto che la scelta della povertà altissima pone il

bona assumptio, quia pro uti sumitur usum habere, cum tamen multum differant, quia usum habere est idem quod habere ius utendi vel simpliciter vel ad tempus ».

1. *Ibidem* : « *Sciendum tamen quod est potestas iuris naturalis, et de tali iure non loquimur hic ; et est potestas iuris positivi, et de tali non est verum quod uti re sit idem quod posse eam licite consumere* ».

2. *TC*, p. 71 : « *[...] usus ibi non differt a rei utibilis consumptione vel alienatione : est sic inseparabilis enim a substantia rei quod perinde est dare vel vendere eius substantiam quod dare vel vendere eius usum et econtrario. Sed usus pecunie vel nummorum in quantum talium et usus bladi et olei, et consimilium est idem quod eorum alienatio vel consumptio, ergo idem est huiusmodi res dare vel vendere <quod dare vel vendere> earum usum et econtrario* ». Sull'opportunità di non disgiungere la produzione di Olivi sulla povertà francescana da quanto scritto dal medesimo sui problemi di etica-economica ha insistito più volte G. Todeschini ; ricordo solo *Il prezzo della salvezza*, Roma, 1994, p. 215-216.

3. Non è forse irrelevante il fatto che in *QPE XV* siano gli avversari a proporre, per sostenere l'accidentalità della modalità dell'uso rispetto alla professione di povertà, il caso del « *Pauper uero pauper manens saepe utitur copiose, ut patet in bayulo alicuius magni domini* », caso non dissimile da quello del servo che usa dei beni del suo padrone, molto diffuso nell'apologetica francescana ; Olivi risponde distinguendo in modo netto tra ciò che vale per la *paupertas* religiosa e quella mondana ; si veda ms. Firenze, Bibl. Med. Laur., C.S. 448, f° 98rb : « *Quod autem subdit quod usus tenuis est accidentalis paupertati sicut usus habundans est accidentalis diuitibus, si loquatur de paupertate uulgari que nullam professionem regularem aut euangelicam includit, uerum dicit; et talis est paupertas bayliui de quo dabat exemplum. Si vero loquatur de paupertate euangelica non solum dicit falsum sed petit quod debet probare* ». *Cfr.* D. Flood, *Peter Olivi*, *op. cit.*, p. 341.

francescano *ipso facto* all'interno di una sfera non giuridica, di quel diritto naturale che vigeva nello stato d'innocenza ed era stato rinnovato dalla primitiva comunità apostolica e dai suoi imitatori. In quella condizione puramente naturale, lo abbiamo già visto, l'uso di una cosa non si configurava in alcun modo come appropriazione, perché l'accesso ai beni del mondo non escludeva un pari accesso di tutti gli altri. D'altra parte, questa dimensione naturale era caratterizzata anche dall'ancoraggio alla necessità. La *naturalis necessitas*, scrive Olivi, non implica né lo *ius in rebus* né la sovrabbondanza [1]. La *rectitudo naturalis* della nostra volontà non chiede se non quello che è necessario al sostentamento della natura, come ribadisce *QPE IX* [2]. In altre parole, la vera linea di demarcazione passerebbe tra i due tipi di rapporto con le cose del mondo, quello che è estrinsecazione della libertà naturale e quello che invece, attraverso l'appropriazione dei beni, coarta quell'originale *naturalis libertas* [3]. Di conseguenza, il principio che, per le cose consumabili, l'uso dei frati non si identifichi con il dominio non andrebbe difeso andando alla ricerca, come facevano Bonaventura e Peckham, di un caso in cui anche il diritto positivo ne contempli la separabilità, ma piuttosto evidenziando che nella dimensione della necessità naturale uso e dominio hanno valenze radicalmente diverse rispetto a quanto accade nel campo del diritto positivo e la questione della separabilità non si pone.

Mi rendo conto che la mia ricostruzione – come del resto in generale accade per molti tentativi di interpretazione di silenzi – è altamente congetturale. Ciononostante, vorrei evidenziare che, accettandola seppure come ipotesi di lavoro, si istituisce un legame molto stretto tra alcuni aspetti della teoria oliviana dell'espropriazione francescana e quella dell'*usus pauper* [4]. In effetti, se è l'ancoramento alla dimensione della necessità a rendere possibile l'espropriazione da ogni diritto sulle cose ed il loro uso, allora essa rischia di essere messa in discussione da ogni comportamento che infranga l'uso povero delle cose, definito proprio dalla sua limitazione rigorosa, seppur non rigida, ai beni necessari. In altri termini, il francescano si muove in quella sfera in cui il diritto naturale alle cose non si traduce in uno *ius* positivo nella misura in cui non oltrepassa la soglia della necessità.

Se questa mia interpretazione del silenzio di Olivi potesse essere confermata, si potrebbe indicare un'ulteriore fonte della teoria oliviana dell'*usus pauper*, vale

1. *QPE VIII*, J. Schlageter ed., p. 127 : « *Qui vero quaerit ea propter naturalem necessitatem, ex hoc non habet quaerere ius in rebus nec rerum abundantiam, cum ista non sint necessaria ad hominis vitam* ».

2. *QPE IX*, D. Burr ed., p. 25-26 : « *Rectitudo etiam naturalis voluntatis nostre non querit nisi quantum est necessarium sustentationi nature et prout expedit naturali rectitudini conservande et promovende* ». *Cfr. QPE VIII*, J. Schlageter ed., p. 125-128.

3. *QPE VIII*, J. Schlageter ed., p. 125.

4. Devo le prime suggestioni in questo senso a O. Capitani, « Ipotesi sociali del francescanesimo medievale : orientamenti e considerazioni », in *San Francesco. Giornata Lincea indetta in occasione dell'VIII centenario della nascita* (Roma, 12 novembre 1982), Roma, 1985, p. 39-47. Fondamentali ed insuperate rimangono le riflessioni di A. Tabarroni, *Paupertas Christi et Apostolorum. L'ideale francescano in discussione (1322-1324)*, Roma, 1990, in part. p. 113-119.

a dire il lavorio teorico di difesa dell'ideale francescano di *abdicatio* assoluta[1]. Oltre alla profonda esperienza religiosa personale – quella narrata da Olivi in *QPE IX* – accanto alle motivazioni indagate da Burr ed alla necessità di precisare lo *status* dei francescani divenuti vescovi[2], si configurerebbe così anche una connessione abbastanza stretta, in Olivi, tra difesa della povertà francescana dalle critiche dei Secolari e sviluppo di una teoria dell'*usus pauper*. Come se, riflettendo sulla tradizione apologetica dell'Ordine e fornendo il proprio contributo, Olivi si fosse persuaso della imprescindibilità di un uso povero dei beni anche per la coerenza teorica del concetto francescano di *abrenuntiatio* assoluta. L'*usus pauper* apparirebbe così non solo come istanza ulteriore rispetto alla rinuncia alla proprietà, ma anche come una sua condizione di possibilità. Devo ammettere che non è Olivi ad esplicitare i passaggi di questa connessione; ma resta vero che in questa prospettiva diventa ancora più chiara la sua insistenza sull'impossibilità di disgiungere *abrenuntiatio* ed *usus pauper*, tra i quali sussisterebbe un rapporto come di materia e forma[3].

Per concludere, suggerisco che nell'opera di Olivi esista un filo rosso che collega le peculiarità della sua difesa dell'Ordine e lo sviluppo della sua così controversa teoria dell'uso povero. Di una certa continuità, seppure in negativo, mi pare fosse ben cosciente lo stesso Olivi quando, nell'apertura del suo *Tractatus de usu paupere*, affermava che è stata la medesima *serpentina astucia* dell'antico Nemico a suscitare prima gli attacchi dei clerici contro lo *status mendicantium*, e poi ad inviare alcuni pseudo-apostoli, questa volta francescani, a contestare l'uso povero[4]. Olivi vi vedeva quindi un'unica, continua battaglia, nella mischia della quale intendeva buttarsi con la spada sguainata del verbo di Dio. Forse mi è riuscito di evidenziare una delle ragioni di questa continuità.

1. Questa prospettiva potrebbe suggerire di riesaminare anche la concezione secondo la quale le discussioni sull'*usus pauper* non avrebbero grande rilevanza per la questione dell'*abdicatio* francescana ad ogni forma di proprietà. Idea che si ritrova, p. es. ancora in A.S. Brett, *Liberty, right and nature. Individual rights in later scholastic thought*, Cambridge, 1997, in part. p. 52.

2. D. Burr, *Olivi and Franciscan Poverty: the origins of the usus pauper controversy*, Philadelphia, 1989.

3. *QPE IX*, D. Burr ed., p. 35 : « *Sicut autem forma ad sui existentiam preexigit materiam tanquam sue existentie fundamentum, sic professio pauperis usus preexigit abdicationem omnis iuris tanquam sue grandissime existentie et ambitus capacissimam materiam et altissimum fundamentum [...]* ». Credo che alcune interessanti pagine di L. Parisoli, « *Come affiorò il concetto di diritto soggettivo inalienabile nella riflessione francescana sulla povertà, sino ai fraticelli de opinione e Giovanni XXII* », *Materiali per una storia della cultura giuridica* 38, 1998, p. 93-137, in part. p. 118-119, vadano rilette alla luce di brani come questi. Concordo comunque sull'idea della peculiarità della fondazione oliviana della povertà francescana.

4. *Us Paup.*, p. 89-90.

PETER OLIVI ON THE CONVERSION OF THE JEWS *

Robert Lerner

Although medieval Christian theologians were obliged to believe with St. Paul that « all Israel shall be saved », they customarily taught that the conversion of the Jews would occur at the edge of time as part of the Last Judgment. Peter Olivi, on the contrary, expected the conversion to accompany the establishment of an imminent final salvational-historical era – humanity's greatest fulfillment on earth. For him one of the several biblical proofs could be found at the conclusion of the story of the prodigal son (Luke 15 : 11-32). When the father prepared a banquet for his younger son, the older son was angry « and would not go in ». As he complained to his father, « Lo, these many years do I serve thee, neither transgressed I at any time thy commandment; and yet thou never gave me a kid, that I might make merry with my friends ». But the father reassured his firstborn by saying « thou art ever with me, and all that I have is thine ». For Olivi this was a promise that the Jews would join the gentiles in their father's banquet with « singular joy » [1].

David Burr has observed that « the ultimate conversion of the Jews [is] a Biblical motif which assumes tremendous importance in Olivi's eschatological scenario » [2]. Pursuing this remark I wish to examine Olivi's conception of the joyful millennial calling in of the Jews in terms of its place within a larger tradition. My purpose is first to compare Olivi's thought on the subject with that of his mentor, Joachim of Fiore, and then to look briefly at how Olivi's influence was exerted on others.

* The following essay treats material that I will be discussing further in a book-length study. I wish to thank the Woodrow Wilson International Center for Scholars, the Max-Planck-Gesellschaft, and Northwestern University for research support.

1. Olivi, *QPE 8*, ed. J. Schlageter, *Das Heil der Armen und das Verderben der Reichen*, Werl/Westphalia, 1989, p. 159 : « *Si in introitu gentium ad fidem factum est grande gaudium et convivium et fieri decuit, secundum quod tangit Christus Luce* XV° *in tribus parabolis, et maxime in illa de adolescente, consimilis ratio et condecentia clamat quoddam singulare gaudium futurum et convivium in introitu omnis Israelis [...]* ». The application of the last verses of Luke 15 to the final conversion of the Jews is found in standard medieval exegesis, but Olivi diverges in viewing the event as part of the coming earthly sabbath. A similar millenarian interpretation is implicit at the end of Joachim of Fiore's *Adversus Judeos* but there is no evidence that Olivi knew this source.

2. D. Burr, *The Persecution of Peter Olivi*, Philadelphia, 1976, p. 22b.

To gain a basis for comparing the views of the abbot and the friar on the conversion of the Jews we may look at passages in two works by Joachim to which Olivi often referred, the *Concordia* and the *Expositio in Apocalypsim*[1]. In the *Concordia* Joachim treated the peripaties of the patriarch Jacob (Gen. 27-35) as an image for the movement of God's chosen « spiritual men » through time. In fleeing his homeland to avoid the wrath of his brother Esau, Jacob stood for the progress of the spirituals who moved from the synagogue of the Jews to the Christian Church of the gentiles. But after dwelling and prospering in the land of his uncle Laban, Jacob began to incur the enmity of Laban's sons. For Joachim this referred to a tension existing in his own day between God's chosen spiritual men, monastic contemplatives, and the corrupt clergy: the clergy resented the contemplatives because of their « prosperity in the gifts of God ». Hence it was necessary for Jacob to flee again, and now back to his home. In the words of Genesis : « the Lord said unto Jacob : return to the land of thy fathers, and to thy kindred, and I will be with thee » (Gen. 31 : 3). Jacob's consequent return to the land of Canaan was a movement Joachim understood as a final return of the spirituals to the Jews, « as if to our parents »[2].

For Joachim the return to the homeland by no means meant that « spiritual » Christians would revert to Judaism; on the contrary he believed that the Christians would convert the Jews to Christianity. But he portrayed the conversion of the Jews in the most uplifting terms by making it a crucial constituent of the divine plan. Since the Jews were initially God's chosen people it was fitting that divine favor would return to them at the culmination of the history of salvation. In the first status the Jews could see providential truth more clearly than others, but then, around the time of Christ, most became blinded. In the second status a few Jews who were not blinded to Christ's messiahship converted the gentiles, whereupon the gentile populace replaced the Jews as the Lord's favored. But now, in Joachim's own day, the Church of the gentiles was becoming blinded to the spiritual truth seen by monastic contemplatives. Thus the imminent conversion of the Jews by the contemplatives would mark the opening of the third status and would parallel the previous conversion of the gentiles[3]. With the balance redressed there would be no need for any further conversions : the sequence of three would be completed and the entire world

1. It is well known that Olivi frequently cited these two works in his *Lectura super Apocalypsim*, but less familiar that he referred to them in his early Isaiah commentary, dating from about 1280; see D. Flood and G. Gal, *Peter of John Olivi on the Bible*, St. Bonaventure (N.Y.), 1997, p. 197.

2. Joachim of Fiore, *Liber de concordia novi ac veteris testamenti*, Venice, 1519 (repr. Frankfurt, 1964), V, 50, f° 84va-vb : « *Iacob [...] cepit reverti ad patriam suam, maxime quia hoc ipsum preceperat illi angelus Domini qui apparuerat ei. Sed et viri spirituales qui presunt hiis diebus collegiis monachorum eo magis [Venice ed. mistakenly : Et magis] debent cogitare qualiter cum suis omnibus revertantur ad suos, quo magis vident nonnullos clericorum invidere sibi super prosperitate donorum Dei. [...] Quasi enim ad parentes nostros revertimur ut eis iungamur, cum de illius antiqui populi cogitamus salutem de quo processerunt prophete et apostoli qui nos in fide genuerunt* ».

3. *Ibid.*, f° 84vb : « *Ut autem eo tempore quo ceperunt intrare gentes cecitas ex parte contingit in Israel, et delictum incredulitatis eorum factum est quodammodo salus gentium, ita cecitas quo contigit nunc ex parte in populo gentili illius hactenus ceci populi preostendit salutem* ».

would have sight until the final blindness, or « cooling of charity » to come immediately before the Last Judgment.

At one point in his exegesis of Jacob's journies Joachim compared the movement of divine energy from Jews to gentiles and back to a farmer rotating his fields[1]. As if explaining the Mediterranean two-field system to undergraduates, he observed that when wheat gives way to thorns it is time to alternate the field. But the image of rotation or balance was only one way of envisaging the story, for Jacob's move from Canaan to the land of Laban and back to Canaan was also a march of progress, a movement toward the apotheosis of the « spiritual men ». Elsewhere in the *Concordia* the abbot enunciated the progressive principle in the clearest terms : « the letter of the Old Testament was given to the Jewish people; the letter of the New to the Roman people; and the spiritual intelligence that proceeds from both to the spiritual men »[2]. Seen from this point of view, salvational history was not an alternation of wheat and thorns, but, in Joachim's own language, a progression from « blades to ears to wheat »[3].

The linked principles of balance and progress raise the question of how Joachim understood the relationship between Jews and gentiles in the third status. For an answer we may turn to a section of exegesis in his *Expositio in Apocalipsim*. In reference to the foundations and gates of the new Jerusalem (Rev. 21 : 10-21), Joachim explained that there are three steps in building a city : finding a location and digging the ditches; laying the foundations and building the walls; and erecting the gates and building the houses. Correspondingly, there are three historical « statuses » that culminate in building the houses of Jerusalem. In the first the « people of Israel » found the location. In the second their successors, the apostles, who were « spiritual sons of the patriarchs » laid the foundations and built the walls so that « their sons in faith from the gentile people » could enter. That left the third status, still to come, when the gates would be erected so that « the entire faithful populace » could enter[4]. So far there is a clear historical progression toward the goal of merger – from Jewish people, to gentile people, to all the faithful people.

Yet if the Jews were the people of the first status, the gentiles of the second, and « all the faithful » of the third, Joachim still faced the question of who would lead the faithful into the third status. He addressed this question in recognition of the fact that the apostles who led the gentiles into the second status were themselves Jews. If Jews led gentiles into the second status, then it would be fitting for gentiles to lead Jews into the third. Yet, on the other hand, not only Jews were to enter Jerusalem but remaining gentiles who, with the Jews, would comprise « all the faithful ». Given that merger, it might inhere in the divine plan

1. *Ibid.* : « *Nunquid non et agricola alternat agros cum fessa ex diutino labore terra, pro tritico ferre incipit tribulos et spinas, igitur cum vident viri spirituales recedere donum Dei a filiis Laban [...] intelligunt approprinquare tempus quod predixit apostolus de conversione Israel* ».

2. Joachim, *Liber de concordia*, ed. E.R. Daniel, Philadelphia, 1983, II, 1, 8 : « *Sciendum quod littera veteris testamenti commisa fuit populo Iudeorum, littera novi populo Romano, spiritualibus autem viris spiritualis intelligentia que ex utraque procedit* ».

3. *Concordia*, V, 84, f° 112rb : « *prius herbas, secundus spicas, tertius triticum* ».

4. Joachim of Fiore, *Expositio in Apocalypsim*, Venice, 1527 (repr. Frankfurt, 1964), f° 220ra.

for the evangelists of the third status to arise from both the Jewish and gentile peoples. Joachim considered these options in terms of the « twelve gates » of Jerusalem and the « twelve pearls » at the twelve gates. For him the gates were « similar to the twelve apostles », but Scripture provided no answer as to whether they stood for Jews, gentiles, or an even number of both[1]. The pearls, however, were another matter. The « twelve pearls » at each of the gates (Rev. 21 : 21) stood for 144 « helpers » (*adjutores*), who would preach the gospel of the kingdom throughout the world. These 144 helpers were equivalent to the 72 elders who accompanied Moses in the exodus[2], and the 72 disciples who were chosen by Christ. The number of disciples in the second status was the same as the number of elders in the first because one people simply replaced another, but in the third status there would be a doubling because the two peoples would be conjoined[3]. Thus, to sum up Joachim's position about the relationship of Jews and gentiles in the third status, his emphasis was on equality. Not only did he foresee the millennial conjoining of the peoples, but he was ready to grant the Jews an equal role with the gentiles as bearers of enlightenment – in his language, as « helpers » of the gospel of both Testaments illumined by spiritual intelligence[4].

Turning now to Olivi's formulations about the conversion of the Jews, these appear regularly over the full term of his mature literary activity within a scenario that reveals his debt to the abbot Joachim[5]. Invariably Olivi places the conversion within a coming joyful sabbath on earth. For him, as for Joachim, the event is to be part of the transfiguration of the world that will have its own temporal duration apart from the Last Judgment. Thus he foretells how Christ will return « to the fathers, whence he came, that is, the Jewish people » thence « to linger with them

1. *Ibid.* : « *Utrum autem de populo Iudaico eligendi sint viri qui designantur in portis, an potius de gentili, an communiter ex utroque incertum est* ».

2. Joachim is evidently thinking here of Exodus 24 : 1, 9, which, however, refers to seventy elders rather than seventy-two. Presumably he arrived at the seventy-two by adding the two names that were linked with the seventy in these verses, Nadab and Abihu.

3. *Ibid.*, f° 220rb : « *Si enim in primo statu post duodecim patriarchos filios Israel in quorum vice duodecim principes de singulis tribubus constituti sunt in deserto septuaginta duo seniores electi sunt pariter a Moyse, et nihilominus post electionem duodecim apostolorum septuaginta duo discipuli electi sunt a Christo, oportunius videretur ut in hoc tertio statu parimodo septuaginta duo viri potius quam centum quadraginta quatuor, id est septuaginta duo et septuaginta duo vocarentur pariter a spiritu sancto quatenus in singulis statibus summa equalitas inesse videretur. Sed notandum quod restitutus Job pristine sanitati septem quidem filios pro ammissis obtinuit, id est simplices pro simplicibus, cetera omnia duplicata recepit [Job 42 : 10], sic in primo statu seculi quasi simplicia recepit Dominus de populo Israel, simplicia nihilominus in secundo de populo qui dicebatur gentilis, in tertio vero quasi duplicata, quia de utroque populo colligentur electi* ».

4. Verbs of joining also appear in Joachim's exegesis of Jacob's travels. *Concordia* V, 50, f° 84va-b : « *Quasi enim ad parentes nostros revertimur ut eis iungamur [...]* ». *Ibid.*, f° 85va : « *completo itinere sexti temporis sexte huius etatis in quo et sextum signaculum aperitur, coniungetur gentilis populus cum Hebreo* ».

5. I do not mean to exclude the possibility that Olivi was also endebted to Bonaventure's *Collationes in Hexaemeron*, which foretells a millennial « calling of the Jews » : see Coll. XV, 24-25, in Bonaventure, *Opera omnia*, 5, Quaracchi, 1891, p. 401-402. While Olivi never cited this work explicitly, and while manuscript copies were very rare, the likelihood that he knew it nevertheless appears to me to be strong.

until the end »[1]. Similarly he refers to the period of the final conversion of the Jews as a « tempus », and indicates that this period itself will have its own « solemn times and works »[2].

The same event occurs in Olivi's writings regardless of different schemes of periodization. In the commentary on Lamentations he offers a scheme of « three Churches ». The holy city of Jerusalem was conquered by the Chaldeans and later by the Romans. Both times the majority of the inhabitants were justly punished, but both times there was also a concurrent founding of a « Church » – first, the government of the people of God by priests until the time of Christ; then the founding of the Church of Christ. Completing the triad there would soon be a third onslaught, by Antichrist, to be complemented by the founding of the « final Church ». And just as the first Church consisted of Jews and the second of gentiles, so the third would consist of Jews and gentiles in one flock[3].

Olivi's better known periodization is that of the seven periods of Church history. In the fifth period the Church becomes ever more carnal, but starting around 1200 comes the overlapping of the sixth period with the fifth. The sixth period, one of evangelical renewal, pertains to the third age of the world (Joachim's third status) and sees the conversion of the Jews at the time of the great battle against Antichrist[4]. The seventh period occurs thereafter and is the fulfillment of the sabbath on earth. It is in terms of this periodization that Olivi expresses his version of Joachim's principle of balance. The carnal Church is becoming ever more corrupt and will be blinded like « a second synagogue ». But apostles from the gentiles will convert all the Jews when nearly the whole Church

1. *Expositio in Genesim* in *Sancti Thomae Aquinatis [...] Opera Omnia*, 23, Parma, 1869, p. 112b : « *Postremo autem redibit Christus, scilicet per gratiam, ad patres, id est ad Judeorum populum, unde exivit, moriturus cum eis usque ad finem, ut per mortem extremi judicii ducat eos in celum* ».

2. *Lectura super Apocalypsim*, ed. W. Lewis, *Peter John Olivi : Prophet of the Year 2000*, Diss. Tübingen, 1972, p. 52 : « *circa finem seculi aliquod solemne tempus sue universali conversioni et magnificationi esset reservandum* » ; p. 53 : « *Si in conversione gentilis populi fuit solemnis renovatio totius orbis habens sua solemnia tempora et opera, non minus decet quod in universali conversione Israelis renovetur iterum solemniter totus orbis* ». The « times and works » are specified in the *Lectura*, p. 88 : « *[...] oportet habere tantum temporis spatium quod totus orbis et totus Israel convertatur ad Christum; et quod illud tempus crescat a mane per gradus congruos usque ad meridiem ac deinde per gradus congruos descendat ad tantam vesperam et noctem iniquitatis quod vix inveniatur fides in terra* ».

3. *Postilla super Lamentationes Ieremie prophete*, ed. M. Bartoli, *La caduta di Gerusalemme : Il commento al Libro delle Lamentazioni di Pietro di Giovanni Olivi*, Rome, 1991, p. 31-32 : « *Sicut illa fuit finis prioris status synagoge sub regibus gubernati usque ad Christum, sicut secunda fuit finis legis veteris et initium explicite fidei Christi ecclesie eius, sic etiam tertia erit initium finalis ecclesie ex reliquiis Iudeorum et gentium in unum Christi ovile collecte* ». For Olivi the first « Church » in this context was founded by Jeremiah, Ezechiel, and Daniel, and their successors.

4. *Lectura super Apocalypsim*, ed. Lewis, p. 59 : « *in sexto statu ecclesie debet plenitudo gentium intrasse et omnis Israel converti ad Christum* ». For an expert review of the details of Olivi's system of seven periods of the Church, see D. Burr, *Olivi's Peaceable Kingdom : A Reading of the Apocalypse Commentary*, Philadelphia, 1993.

has become a second synagogue, just as apostles from the Jews converted the gentiles when the Jewish synagogue was blinded[1].

Olivi thus follows Joachim, not only in placing the conversion of the Jews within a coming earthly sabbath but in conceiving of a reciprocity of blindings and gainings of sight. Despite the intense anti-Judaism of his age, he does not back away from the view that God will return his favor to the Jews and that their conversion will be indispensable for the future of Christianity insofar as it will provide a means for superseding the corruption of the carnal Church. Above all he places the highest premium on the coming reunion of Jews and gentiles because he considers this event, as did Joachim, to provide the context for the height of ecstatic contemplation which is the ultimate fulfillment of God's plan for humanity on earth. Olivi tells of the « great feats of glory and opulence » that will take place at the time of the conversion of the Jews as the result of an « ineffable outpouring of heavenly delight »[2]. Elsewhere he glosses St. Paul's « three heavens » to denote respectively the militant, contemplative, and triumphant Churches; of these the first consists of the gentiles, the second of the gathering together of the gentiles and the remaining people of Israel, and the third the life in the beyond[3]. Most clearly of all he offers a Joachite triad whereby the time of the written law « under Moses and the prophets » is that of « regulative justice », the time of the gentiles converted by faith « under Christ and the apostles » that of « regenerative grace », and the time of « both parts, the Jews and the gentiles, gathered in the flock of love and unity under Elijah » that of « contemplative intelligence »[4].

Well might Alexander of Alessandria in a remark dating from around 1300 have identified Olivi's master as Joachim[5]. Yet careful attention reveals one difference between the abbot and the friar concerning the role of the Jews in the

1. *Lectura super Apocalypsim*, ed. Lewis, p. 61 : « *Item ex prophetis probatur quod maior pars Israelis erat excecanda in primo Christi adventu et totus orbis gentium tunc convertendum ad Christum, et quod post quamdam plenitudinem temporis debet iterum totus mundus precellentius converti et cum toto Israele iocundari in Christo. Ex quo etiam habetur quod mundus primo conversus debuit fere totus a Christo averti ante generalem conversione Israelis* ». For the « second synagogue », see Olivi, *Quodl.*, 7, f° 14ra : « *[...] carnalis ecclesia quasi altera synagoga erat excecanda et universitas Iudeorum et ceterorum infidelium convertenda* ». I wish to thank Deeana Klepper for providing me with a copy of the rare printed edition of Olivi's *Quodlibeta* (Biblioteca Apostolica Vaticana, Prop. Fide IV 134).

2. *QPE 8*, ed. Schlageter, p. 158 : « *tanta magnalia glorie et opulentie promittuntur eis pro tempore conversionis sue quod spiritualiter compleri non potest sine quadam ineffabili inundatione celestium suavitatum* ».

3. *Principium*, « *De Doctrina* », ed. D. Flood and G. Gal, *Peter of John Olivi on the Bible*, St. Bonaventure (N.Y.), 1997, 94 : « *in triplici celo, scilicet in celo Ecclesie de gentibus converse, et in celo Ecclesie contemplative de reliquiis Israelis et gentium collecte, et in celo triumphantis Ecclesie* ».

4. *Principium*, « *De Causis* », in *ibid.*, p. 49 : « *Et hierarchia legis scripte sub Moyse et prophetis, correspondens veritati essentie integrantis. Et hierarchia gentis ad fidem converse sub Christo et apostolis, correspondens veritati gratie regenerantis. Et hierarchia utriusque partis, Iudeorum scilicet et gentium, in ovile caritatis et unitatis collecte sub Elie, [...] correspondens veritati intelligentie contemplantis* ». After the time of Elijah comes the « hierarchy of the celestial curia » : « *correspondens veritati glorie beatificantis* ».

5. Cited by V. Doucet, « P.J. Olivi et l'Immaculée Conception », *A.F.H.* 26, 1933, p. 561 : « *magister eius Joachim* ».

sabbath. This rests on Olivi's more emphatic Christocentrism – his insistence on the conversion of the Jews « to Christ ». For him the Jews are to be brought into « Christ's Church » and led to « Christ's chair » ; Elijah will « bring back the tribes of Jacob to Christ » [1]. In his frequent references to Jewish conversion Olivi never tires of invoking Christ's name : the Jews will « delight in Christ » ; they will be led back to « the true cult of Christ » ; they will be « under Christ and in Christ » ; they will even have « transformative and ecstatic union with Christ » [2].

It is this emphasis on converting « to Christ » that makes Olivi, in contrast to Joachim, unwilling to grant the Jews an active role in the economy of the third status. For him, as for Joachim, Jacob's return to the land of his fathers denotes the meeting of « spirituals » with Jews in the sabbath, but the occasion is marked by the preaching of the former to the latter [3]. Similarly, Olivi adheres to the main terms of Joachim's exegesis of the three levels of the new Jerusalem while making subtle changes that reduce the Jewish people into being recipients of salvation rather than active participants in a new way of life. Specifically he neglects to pose Joachim's open question of whether the twelve gates of the third status stand for Jews, gentiles, or an equal number of both, and he omits Joachim's proposition about the 144 pearls being equally Jews and gentiles. Apparently he simply cannot imagine that the « apostles » of the third status or their « helpers » might be Jews because of his preoccupation with the entry of the Jews « into Christ ». Instead, for him the gates are simply « doctors of the third status » who expound « Christian wisdom », and although the pearls might be « helpers », as Joachim said, they might also be « privileges of perfect purity » [4].

1. Cynthia Kilmer et Elsa Marmursztejn, « *Petrus Ioannis Olivi. Epistola ad fratrem R.* », introduction and comment by Sylvain Piron, *A.F.H.* 91/1, 1998, p. 63, l. 380 and 384-385 : « *Ordo Francisci [...] reliquias Iudeorum ac gentium in Christi ecclesiam introducat et ad Christi sedem adducat* » ; *Lectura super Mattheum*, MS Oxford, New College 49, f° 110rb : « *Alter vero [Elias] ad litteram qui restituat et reducat ad Christum tribus Iacob* ». (The latter passage was called to my attention by Kevin Madigan, who generously provided me with his transcription). In contrast, one of Joachim's locutions is that the converted Jews will accept the « word of life » : *Concordia*, ed. Venice, f° 85va.

2. *Lectura super Apocalypsim*, ed. Lewis, p. 61 : « *debet iterum totus mundus precellentius converti et cum toto Israele iocundari in Christo* » ; *ibid.*, p. 927 : « *post conversionem et reductionem Israelis ad verum cultum Christi* » ; *QPE 8*, ed. Schlageter, p. 158 : « *quam debent habere sub Christo et in Christo* » ; *Expositio in Canticum Canticorum*, c. 8 : « *ad Christi transformativam et exstaticam unionem dabitur ei* ». The last passage was kindly communicated to me by Father Schlageter, whose edition of this text will soon appear.

3. *Expositio in Genesim*, p. 106b : « *in fuga a Laban designatur finalis discessus spiritualium a carnalibus [...] unde et in fine ad Judeos convertendos redibit predicatio* ».

4. *Lectura*, p. 968-970 : « *Licet per apostolos et alios sanctos secundi generalis status ecclesie intraverit multitudo populorum ad Christum tanquam per portas civitatis Dei, nihilominus magis appropriate competit hoc principalibus doctoribus tertii generalis status per quos omnis Israel et iterum totus orbis intrabit ad Christum. Sicut enim apostolis magis competit esse cum Christo fundamenta totius ecclesie et fidei Christiane, sic istis plus competit esse portas apertas apertores seu explicatores sapientie Christiane [...]. Possunt etiam per has XII margaritas designari XII privilegia puritatis perfecte* ». See also Olivi's selective borrowing from Joachim, *Lectura*, p. 956, where he mostly follows the abbot verbatim but says nothing about a contribution of the Jews to the founding of the second status, omits Joachim's statement that the apostles and their gentile progeny were « spiritual sons of the patriarchs », and omits the supporting quotation from St. Paul that « if ye be Christ's then are ye Abraham's seed » (Gal. 3 : 29).

Granted that Olivi gives no active role to the Jewish people in the third status, he lays greater emphasis on their ancient capital of Jerusalem than did Joachim because he conceives of the Jerusalem of the sabbath not merely metaphorically but concretely. In Olivi's scenario the future of Jerusalem has no direct bearing on the role of the Jews *per se*, but, as we will see, such a connection was made in the prophecies of one of his heirs. Olivi speaks confidently of the future rebuilding of Jerusalem as promised by the words of Isaiah : « I will lay thy stones with fair colors and lay thy foundations with sapphires » (Isaiah 54 : 11). In reference to the verse in the Apocalypse, « and I looked, and lo, a Lamb stood on the mount Zion » (Rev. 14 : 1), he states that « the most sublime worship of Christ will be literally on Mount Zion »[1].

For Olivi the only question is whether the restored Jerusalem will replace Rome as the principle seat of the faith. At one point in his Apocalypse commentary, apparently not wishing to offer a gratuitous insult to Rome, he says that an answer cannot be determined from Scripture or from any certain dogma. But elsewhere in the commentary he argues for the likelihood of the exaltation of Mount Zion over « all other places of the earth » because « that place will be more suitable to the highest rulers of the world for the conversion of the world and for the governing of all those converted since it is the center of the habitable world ». His own position finally becomes explicit at the end of the commentary, when he removes doubt by stating that Jerusalem will be « the principle city and seat of God and the saints »[2].

Olivi's position about the role of the Jews in the future is of particular interest because his prophecies became a conduit of Joachite thought to a wider public in the later Middle Ages. Although this influence has been adequately recognized, specific applications of Olivi's prophecies regarding the Jews have been overlooked. Thus while it is well known that his teachings were transmitted to the Béguins of Languedoc by means of vernacular translations and public readings, it has never been noticed that these included his millenarian conception of Jewish conversion.

The proof is clear from two independent trial depositions of the 1320s. Maria de Serra, a tertiary from the town of Cintegabelle near Toulouse, stated in her testimony of 1322 that she believed many teachings she had heard from a male tertiary from Narbonne. Among these was the prediction that upon the imminent destruction of Antichrist and transformation of the world the Jews would be baptized to become « as great and high » as at any prior time in history[3]. Maria's

1. *QPE 8*, ed. Schlageter, p. 160; *Lectura*, ed. Lewis, p. 751 : « *post mortem Antichristi, forte etiam ante mortem, erit sublimissimus cultus Christi ad litteram in monte Sion* ». Olivi's source for the restoration and exaltation of Jerusalem could very well have been Bonaventure's *Collationes in Hexaemeron*, XVI. 30. See Bonaventure, *Opera omnia*, 5, Quaracchi, 1891, p. 408.

2. *Lectura*, p. 858, 751, 945 : « *vocatur vero Ierusalem quia ibi erit visio summe pacis et principalis metropolis et sedis Dei et sanctorum* ». The first two passages are treated by Burr, Olivi's Peaceable Kingdom, p. 193-194, but Burr overlooks the third.

3. P. van Limborch, *Liber sententiarum inquisitionis Tholosanae*, Amsterdam, 1692, p. 319 : « *quod de Judeis aliqui baptisarentur qui ita magni et alti essent sicut aliis temporibus precedentibus unquam fuerunt* ». My student Louisa Burnham kindly called my attention to this passage.

view was particularly poignant because she must have known about the terrible pogroms perpetrated by the Pastoureaux in and around Toulouse in 1320[1]. The second deposition is that of Na Prous Boneta of Montpellier, who told of her beliefs to an inquisitorial court in 1325. Although Prous's deposition has recently become the subject of much interest, no attention has been paid to a remark about the Jews that shows a clear debt to Olivi's *Lectura*. Specifically, Na Prous foretold the coming of a new order of preachers, « who are called in Holy Scripture twelve gates », by means of whom God would « restore the Jewish people »[2]. Here an echo of Olivi's position that doctors denoted by the twelve gates would accomplish the entrance of the Jews into the New Jerusalem seems indisputable[3].

After the suppression of the Béguins, Olivi's prophecies regarding the Jews lived on by means of their adaptation in the writings of John of Rupescissa. In his *Liber secretorum eventuum* of 1349 the imprisoned Franciscan prophet enthusiastically reaffirmed Olivi's expectation of the imminent conversion of the Jews[4]. According to him, immediately upon the destruction of Antichrist all the Jews would be miraculously converted, for « that which the Church was not able to do in thirteen hundred years, she will accomplish in one day » (§ 98-99). Rupescissa also stated without qualification that during the millennial sabbath Jerusalem would be rebuilt « most grandly » in order to house all the people who would flock there (§ 119). For him the city would be the seat of the faith and the capital of the world, and it would remain so for a thousand years (§ 123). The restoration of Jerusalem would be most fitting because whereas the Jews had once lost the « general seat of the general Church » as a result of their incredulity, the corrupt Italians would now lose it because of their league with Antichrist and it would revert to the realm of the now converted Jews (§ 115-116)[5].

1. In June of 1320 the Pastoureaux murdered 152 Jews in towns to the north of Toulouse, and, in a single day, 115 more in Toulouse itself. One Jew, Baruch, accepted forced baptism but then managed to flee to the south, where he was stopped by a band of Pastoureaux near Maria de Serra's home town of Cintegabelle, and then taken to Pamiers, where Maria herself was tried two years later. See M. Barber, « The Pastoureaux of 1320 », *Journal of Ecclesiastical History* 32, 1981, p. 143-166, esp. 149-152.

2. W. May, « The Confession of Prous Boneta », in *Essays in Medieval Life and Thought*, J.H. Mundy *et al.* ed., New York, 1965, p. 23-24 : « *Item quod sicut filius Abrahe genitus a libera habuit duodecim filios, qui fuerunt patriarche, ita iste ordo Predicatorum novus, si servetur ut prius, habebit duodecim filios ab isto spiritu, qui sunt vocati duodecim porte in sacra scriptura, et ita reparabit Deus populum Judeorum per ordinem istum* ».

3. *Cf.* D. Burr, « Na Prous Boneta and Olivi », *Collectanea Franciscana* 67, 1997, p. 477-500, without reference to this borrowing. Burr reminds us that Prous managed to learn Olivi's doctrines very well even though she was unable to read his Latin.

4. See the edition and commentary by R.E. Lerner and C. Morerod-Fattebert, *Johannes de Rupescissa, Liber secretorum eventuum*, Fribourg, 1994. I refer in parentheses to paragraphs numbers from this edition.

5. Another heir of Olivi's prophecies, the anonymous author of the Pseudo-Joachite *Breviloquium*, who wrote in Catalonia in the 1350s, also foretold the rebuilding of the temple and the walls of the city of the universal Church so that there would be one sheepfold and one shepherd. See H. Lee *et al.*, *Western Mediterranean Prophecy*, Toronto, 1989, p. 297.

As can be seen from the foregoing, Rupescissa directly linked the restoration of Jerusalem with the fortunes of the Jewish people. For him the blessings of the millennium would include special blessings for the Jews, for then the prophecy of Zachariah would be fulfilled that the Lord would « pour upon the house of David and upon the inhabitants of Jerusalem the spirit of grace and supplication » (§ 99, citing Zach. 12 : 10). The Jews would not replace the gentiles as bearers of the faith but they would replace the Romans as bearers of empire. After the death of Antichrist tyrants associated with the Roman Empire would remain for forty-five years, but the converted Jews led by an « Augustus from the seed of Abraham » would destroy these enemies and gain just power over the world (§ 106-107, 122). No nation thereafter would succeed the Jews as world rulers, in fulfillment of Daniel's words that « the kingdom shall not be left to other people » (§ 112, citing Dan. 2 : 44). Indeed, when the End came the Jews would still be the champions of the faith, this time against the gentiles from the tribes of Gog and Magog (§ 131-36).

Whether or not there is a step progression in content from Joachim to Olivi to Rupescissa depends on what aspect of the three men's thought one wishes to emphasize. On the one hand, Joachim awarded a greater dignity to the Jews than did Olivi in making them equal to the gentiles in accomplishing the synthesis of the third status, but on the other Olivi was more concrete than Joachim in foreseeing the central place of Jerusalem in the earthly sabbath. Rupescissa in turn foretold the exaltation of both the Jewish people and the city of Jerusalem, but his conception of the millennial role of the converted Jews was military and political rather than theological. Rupescissa's prophecies about the Jews had their own late-medieval resonances, but these take us too far away from Olivi to be considered here. Suffice it to say that if there was a triad of « father, son, and holy spirit » in the history of late-medieval millennial philo-Semitism, Olivi was the son, an analogy with which the devoutly Christological friar from Sérignan might have been pleased.

OLIVI E IL *MERCATOR* CRISTIANO

Giacomo Todeschini

« *[...] Confiteor quod notabiles excessus locorum et edificiorum quantum ad pretiositatem materie et curiositatem forme et politure, et quantum ad quantitatem vel sumptuositatem et quantum ad multiplicationes questus, quos in sui fabricatione exigunt, est periculosa impuritas [...] pro eo quod sunt longe et sempiterne durationis quasi, et quia semper in totam multitudinem se diffundunt, et quia mundo prebent malum exemplum et exemplar vite Christi offuscant; et consimiliter litigare aut causidicare pro [...] quacumque re temporali est notabilis impuritas et precipue ubi est horum frequentia et multiplicatio et longa continuatio et multitudinis Fratrum ad hoc inviatio et fervida et animosa incitatio, quia hoc est etiam in secularibus maior imperfectio quam proprium possidere aut quam lucrum mercationum facere et sectari, preterquam in aliquis casibus, et hoc sub certis circumstantiis imperfectum eius pro magna parte tollentibus* ». (*De obitu dicti fratris Petri et quid receptis sacramentis dixit [...]*, B. Laurenz, S. Crucis, pl. 31 sin., cod. 3, f° 206 [175a-b], ed. Heysse, *AFH* XI, 1918, p. 268)

La possibilità odierna di attribuire un senso storicamente verosimile alle concezioni economiche e sociali dell'Olivi dipende, prima di tutto, dalla capacità storiografica di reinserire la testualità etico-economica o economico-politica oliviana, dunque l'immagine delle dialettiche di mercato rintracciabile nel *corpus* dottrinale oliviano, nel sistema complessivo costituito dal discorso pauperista dell'Autore, inteso come sistema fitto di importanti implicazioni teologiche e canonistiche [1].

Già muovendosi da questa premessa si potrà scoprire che di sintassi sociale ed economica l'Olivi scrive non soltanto nel tripartito trattato *de contractibus* (*de emptionibus et venditionibus, de usuris, de restitutionibus*), ma anche, come ha

1. La più recente ricostruzione della riflessione economica oliviana è quella contenuta in O. Langholm, *Economics in Medieval Schools: Wealth, Exchange, Value, Money and Usury according to the Paris Theological Tradition, 1200-1350*, Leiden, 1992; ma *Cfr.* ora la notevole impostazione di J. Kaye, *Economy and Nature in the Fourteenth Century. Money, Market Exchange, and the Emergence of Scientific Thought*, Cambridge, 1998. Importante messa a punto dei criteri metodologici utili a comprendere la complessità oliviana in R. Lambertini, *Apologia e crescita dell'identità francescana (1255-1279)*, Roma 1990; *Idem*, « *Usus* and *Usura*: Poverty and Usury in the Franciscans' Responses to John XXII's *Quia vir reprobus* », *Franciscan Studies* 54, 1994-97 (Essays in honor of f. G. Gál), p. 185-210. *Cfr.* D. Burr, *Olivi and Franciscan Poverty. The Origins of « Usus Pauper » Controversy*, Philadelphia, 1984.

ben rilevato Odd Langholm[1], nel denso percorso concettuale e semantico costituito dalle *quaestiones de perfectione evangelica*, nell'ottava, nella nona e nella decima specialmente, come pure nell'ambito della questione *quid ponat ius* ben nota per il suo decisivo carattere metodologico[2]. Il «tipo» del *mercator christianus* e lo schema di un mercato cristiano eticamente corretto come vengono tratteggiati dall'Olivi potranno dunque risultare comprensibili solo a considerare, nel complesso testuale citato, la logica degli elementi linguistici e concettuali che li compongono e la natura della loro derivazione dal patrimonio teologico e giuridico che l'Olivi intese come suo proprio : un'eredità concettuale e terminologica pervenutagli, fra l'altro, grazie a due precedenti sintesi testuali francescane, la *Summa* attribuita ad Alessandro di Hales e la *Summa confessorum* di Monaldo di Capodistria[3].

1

Occorrerà, prima di tutto, ricordare che caratteristica essenziale della scelta di povertà è, in Olivi, il manifestarsi terreno di un così alto grado di libertà del volere, da consentire il distacco da tutti gli oggetti che, nella quotidianità temporale, potrebbero costituire l'obiettivo concreto della volontà stessa. I *temporalia* non sono che *puncti*, « *immo sicut nihil* », di fronte alla sterminata *capacitas* della libera volontà umana : ne consegue che l'apice del *dominium* esercitabile sulle cose del mondo consiste nell'annullamento del desiderio nei confronti di tali inconsistenti obiettivi, consiste, quindi, nel manifestarsi, come potenza assoluta, in una tensione smisurata verso le perfezioni celesti, le *coelestes divitias*, ossia in una affermazione della capacità di volere tanto profonda da trascendere la forma

1. *Op. cit.*, p. 345-373 ; decisive conclusioni sul senso e la datazione (1294-95) del de contractibus oliviano in S. Piron, « Marchands et confesseurs. Le *Traité des contrats* d'Olivi dans son contexte (Narbonne, fin XIIIe siècle) », in : *L'argent au Moyen Age*, Paris, 1998, p. 289-308 ; *Idem*, « Vœu et contrat chez Pierre Olivi », *Cahiers du Centre de Recherches Historiques* 16, 1996, p. 43-56.

2. *Cfr.* Petrus Johannis Olivi, *Quid ponat ius vel dominium* in F. Delorme, « Question de P.J. Olivi '*Quid [...]*' ou encore, '*De signis voluntariis*' », *Antonianum* 20, 1945, p. 309-330 (=4Sn) ; *Idem, De emptionibus et venditionibus, de usuris, de restitutionibus* in G. Todeschini, *Un trattato di economia politica francescana*, Roma 1980 (=TC) ; la prima parte del trattato anche in A. Spicciani, *La mercatura e la formazione del prezzo nella riflessione teologica medievale*, Roma (Accademia dei Lincei, Memorie, Classe di sc. morali, storiche e filologiche, s. VIII, 20 3), 1977 ; *Idem, Q. VIII de perfectione evangelica*, in J. Schlageter, *Das Heil der Armen und das Verderben der Reichen*, Werl/W, 1989 (=QPE VIII) ; *Idem, Q. IX de perfectione evangelica*, in D. Burr ed., *De usu paupere. The Quaestio and the Tractatus*, Firenze-Perth (West Australia Univ.- Italian Medieval and Renaissance St., 4), 1992 (=QPE IX) ; *Idem, Q. X de perfectione evangelica*, in D. Flood ed., « Peter Olivi *Quaestio de mendicitate*. Critical edition », *A.F.H.* 87, 1994, p. 287-347 (=QPE X) ; *Idem, Q. XVI de perfectione evangelica*, in D. Burr – D. Flood, « Peter John Olivi : On Poverty and Revenue », *F.S.* 8, 1980, p. 18-58 (=QPE XVI).

3. Alexander Halensis, *Summa theologica I-IV*, Firenze, Quaracchi 1924 ss. ; Monaldus Iustinopolitanus, *Summa de casibus conscientiae*, Lione, 1516 ; sulla Summa di Monaldo, *Cfr.* A.M. Hamelin, *Pour l'histoire de la théologie morale : l'école franciscaine de ses débuts jusqu'à l'occamisme*, Louvain 1961 ; M. Turrini, *La coscienza e le leggi : morale e diritto nei testi per la confessione della prima età moderna*, Bologna, 1991 ; Langholm, *op. cit.*, p. 447.

stessa del *dominium* nelle sue concrete manifestazioni. Il *verus dominus temporalium*, dunque, a imitazione di Cristo e della sua *universalis potestas*, sarà *contemptor et conculcator* dei beni terreni :

> *Naturalis enim rectitudo voluntatis nostrae clamat eam [paupertatem] altam et sibi consonam; tum quia naturalem habet libertatem qua omnibus mundanis superfertur et superferri appetit per modum cuiusdam dominii naturalis. Unde per naturam non determinatur voluntas nostra nec persona nostra plus ad hoc quam ad illud nec ipsa re de vi naturae plus ad hunc quam ad illum. Tum quia tantam habet secundum naturam capacitatem quod omne temporale est sibi sicut punctus, immo sicut nihil; tum quia tantam habet secundum naturam ad mundana difformitatem quod secundum naturam suam magis est eis inassociabilis.*
> *Unde paupertas haec magis fuit ostensiva universalis potestatis Christi quam esset affluentiam quarumcumque humanarum divitiarum, cum etiam verus dominus temporalium sit eorum contemptor et conculcator*[1].

La più intima sostanza teologico-giuridica del dominio è, per l'Olivi teorico dell'*usus pauper*, una disciplina del desiderio così affinata da consentire alla volontà del singolo di negare ogni forma di controllo della realtà, di negare ogni rivendicazione di *ius* che non siano realizzate in se stesse come assolute e totali, dunque eccedenti le forme particolari della realtà e dello *ius*. Il potere sui beni del mondo, sui *temporalia*, sulle ricchezze, risulta essere, insomma, la manifestazione degradata, relativa e convenzionale, «politica» si potrà dire, di una *potestas* dominativa la cui unica possibile compiutezza risiede nel non avere oggetto finito[2].

Sarebbe, tuttavia, un errore ritenere tale concezione oliviana della *potestas* un'astrazione filosofica di generica derivazione agostiniana o aristotelica : sono invece chiare, nella testualità dell'Olivi, le radici teologiche e canonistiche di alcuni aspetti fondamentali della sua dottrina dominativa e, di conseguenza, della sua dottrina sociale ed economica. Non si dovrà sottovalutare, in primo luogo, il peso che sulla riflessione sociale oliviana hanno esercitato le discussioni ecclesiologiche riguardanti l'acquisizione simoniaca del carisma sacerdotale e delle sostanze ecclesiastiche, discussioni svoltesi, come è noto, con grande intensità, in ambito canonistico soprattutto italiano e francese fra XI e XIII secolo, e sedimentate testualmente nel *Decretum Gratiani* prima, nelle *Decretales Gregorii IX* poi, e infine in commentari di gran successo come quelli del cardinale Ostiense e di Innocenzo IV[3]. Questa tipologia del discorso ecclesiologico contenne e produsse

1. *QPE VIII*, p. 125, 135; *QPE IX*, p. 29 : «*Rationes etiam que ibi afferuntur ad ostendendum paupertatem altissimam Christo summe convenire non verificantur complete sine paupere usu, nam sine ipso non apparuisset Christus perfectus contemptor et conculcator temporalium ac per consequens nec tamquam dominus plene ei superpositus*». *Cfr.* F. Simoncioli, *Il problema della libertà umana in Pietro di Giovanni Olivi e Pietro di Trabibus*, Milano, 1956; e il classico P. Grossi, *Usus facti in Idem, Il dominio e le cose. Percezioni medievali e moderne dei diritti reali*, Milano, 1992, p. 123-189.

2. *Cfr. 4Sn.*

3. La nozione di *libertas ecclesiae* come concetto complessamente politico-dominativo è ben spiegata in B. Szabò-Bechstein, *Libertas ecclesiae. Ein Schlüsselbegriff des Investiturstreits und*

da un lato un sempre più specifico vocabolario della analisi dei comportamenti economici, a cominciare da quello creditizio[1], mentre, d'altro canto, giunse progressivamente a distinguere con accuratezza fra pratiche economiche lecite e illecite ad ecclesiastici e laici[2]. La storiografia della questione ha, sino ad oggi, messo in evidenza troppo poco il nesso assai stretto che lega queste discussioni con l'interdizione della prassi usuraria tipica della testualità canonistica, penitenziale ed etico-economica, soprattutto a partire dalla seconda metà del XII secolo. Il divieto di usura, in effetti, sia pur radicandosi in antiche prescrizioni patristiche e carolingie sull'argomento[3], rinasce contestualmente fra XII e XIII secolo, non soltanto, come spesso si disse, in conseguenza della trasformazione economica di questo periodo, ma anche per effetto di una riflessione ecclesiologica gregoriana e post-gregoriana che imponendo l'assoluta inalienabilità delle *res ecclesiarum* e la natura assolutamente non privata della conduzione di tali entità economiche, giungeva a individuare nella prassi usuraria di *clerici* e *layci* una dialettica economica lesiva per i patrimoni ecclesiastici e in grado di allentare i vincoli di fedeltà che univano i laici alle gerarchie sacerdotali, come, sin dal X secolo, era stato messo in evidenza da Atto di Vercelli nella sua descrizione del malcostume sacerdotale, fatto di interessi privati anteposti all'utilità ecclesiale e tali da implicare e giustificare la prassi usuraria determinando così il discredito e l'impoverimento delle Chiese :

> *Sic sacrae aedes publicantur, et a vulgo deridentur [...]. Quoties namque huiuscemodi mulieres vel earum spurii cum aliquibus litigant, ipsi [sacerdotes] abiecta omni sacerdotali reverentia sese opponunt; iniurias et contumelias quae possunt, inferre, et deteriora minantur. Insuper, ut talis ditetur familia, ipsi cupidi, rapaces, usurarii, avari et invidi, ac fraudulenti efficiuntur. Unde non modicum Ecclesia patitur detrimentum. Nam populus hoc considerans, decimas et primitias ipsis exigentibus reddere Deo contemnunt, nullumque obsequium sanctae Dei Ecclesiae persolvere volunt, unde ipsi sacerdotes aliquod consequi possint emolumentum. Et inde populus sacrilegus efficitur*[4].

Più specificamente, una caratteristica centrale di questa elaborazione ecclesiologica, lampante in Pier Damiani nell' XI secolo e in Graziano e nei suoi commentatori nel XII, e mirante a una codificazione della economia ecclesiastica in termini di consacrazione e di utilità pubblica, si concretizzò nella decisa

seine Vorgeschichte, 4.-11. Jh., Roma, 1985 (= « *Studi Gregoriani* » XII) ; la controversia su *symonia*, i suoi significati e le sue implicazioni economiche e politiche è stata spesso analizzata dagli storici : *Cfr.* J.H. Lynch, *Simoniacal Entry into Religious Life from 1000 to 1260. A social, economic and legal Study*, Columbus/Ohio, 1976; O. Capitani, *Tradizione ed interpretazione : dialettiche ecclesiologiche del sec. XI*, Roma, 1990.

1. *Decretum Gratiani X* 2, 2 = Friedberg, I, p. 618-619; per cui *Cfr.* G. Todeschini, « Linguaggi economici ed ecclesiologia fra XI e XII secolo : dai Libelli de lite al *Decretum Gratiani* », in *Studi in onore di Mario Del Treppo*, Napoli (in corso di stampa).

2. Langholm, *op. cit.*, pur notando di frequente la connessione esistente fra discussioni del problema usurario e di quello simoniaco nella testualità degli Scolastici, non sembra dare importanza alla cosa.

3. H. Siems, *Handel und Wucher im Spiegel frühmittelalterlicher Rechtsquellen*, *M.G.H. Schriften* 35, Stuttgart, 1992.

4. « Atto Vercellensis, Epistola IX ad omnes sacerdotes dioecesis Vercellensis », *P.L.* 134, p. 117.

affermazione della natura istituzionale degli enti ecclesiastici, dei loro beni e delle transazioni definibili come utili alla conservazione e alla crescita economica di tali soggetti collettivi o *personae fictae*[1]. Da Graziano al IV concilio lateranense, in altre parole, la polemica antiusuraria si radicò in una ecclesiologia che nel prestito su pegno gestito dai laici e nella dialettica creditizia non controllata dalle chiese vedeva un pericolo per l'integrità dei patrimoni consacrati analogo alla minaccia simoniaca. Da questo punto di vista, la natura ereticale, sacrilega ed *infidelis* dell'usuraio nella testualità, oltre che canonistica, penitenziale, dei secoli XII-XIII, deriverà direttamente dal fatto che l'etica economica di derivazione antisimoniaca percepisce, proprio nell'usuraio, un soggetto economico esterno e, per ciò stesso, ostile al circuito consacrato della ricchezza ecclesiale[2]. Due sembrano essere le chiavi di volta di questo edificio concettuale e linguistico: l'*utilitas ecclesiarum* e la capacità amministrativa, *dispensativa*, dei consacrati poggiante d'altronde sulla risoluta negazione e condanna del loro desiderio personale di ricchezza. E' dunque la povertà, intesa prima di tutto come atteggiamento mentale di rinuncia al possesso privato, a fondare nella testualità canonistica di radice antisimoniaca la possibilità di una ordinata gestione dei beni ecclesiastici, ossia di una loro gestione istituzionalmente utile e razionale[3].

Con la nitidezza che abitualmente caratterizza la sua scrittura, Olivi mostra di collegarsi direttamente e rigorosamente alle suddette discussioni canonistiche. La povertà come abitudine economica perfetta coincide, infatti, nelle questioni VIII, IX e X *de perfectione evangelica* con la perfezione potestativa di cui sopra si disse, ma è anche l'unica condizione che possa realmente consentire l'utilità dei comportamenti amministrativi di cui gli ecclesiastici, i vescovi in particolare, sono protagonisti, la garanzia della loro estraneità alle transazioni simoniache, alle *quasdam vias spiritualium mercationum*, la premessa di un'abitudine gover-

1. Petrus Damiani, *Epistolae* 73, 74, 98, in K. Reindel ed., *Die Briefe des Petrus Damiani*, II, München, 1988 (*M.G.H. Epistolae* 2, *Die Briefe des deutschen Kaiserzeit*, 4); *Cfr.* P. Grossi, *L'ordine giuridico medievale*, Bari, 1995; O. Capitani, « 'Ecclesia romana' e riforma: 'utilitas' in Gregorio VII », 1986, ora in Capitani, *op. cit.*, p. 185-232; I. Scaravelli « 'Utilitas' nella libellistica dell'XI secolo; un primo sondaggio », *Studi Medievali* XXXII/1, 1991, p. 191-229. Sul problema, *Cfr.* A. Boureau, « Droit et théologie au XIIIe siècle », *Annales* 47/6, 1992, p. 1113-1125; *Idem*, « Pierre de Jean Olivi et l'émergence d'une théorie contractuelle de la royauté au XIIIe siècle », in *Représentation, pouvoir et royauté à la fin du Moyen Âge*, Paris, 1995, p. 165-175.

2. Fonti e riferimenti in G. Todeschini, « '*Judas mercator pessimus*'. Ebrei e simoniaci dall'XI al XIII secolo », in *Zakhor. Rivista di storia degli ebrei d'Italia*, Firenze, Giuntina, I, 1997, p. 11-23; *Idem*, « 'Usura' ebraica e identità economica cristiana: la discussione medievale », in *Ebrei in Italia*, C. Vivanti ed., I, Torino, 1997, p. 291-318. *Cfr.* A. Sapir Abulafia, « Theology and the Commercial Revolution: Guibert of Nogent, St. Anselm and the Jews of northern France », in *Church and City 1000-1500. Essays in Honour of Christopher Brooke*, A.S. Abulafia, M. Franklin, M. Rubin ed., Cambridge, 1992, p. 23-40.

3. Continuano ad essere utili le osservazioni di L.K. Little, « L'utilité sociale de la pauvreté volontaire », in AA. VV., *Etudes sur l'histoire de la pauvreté*, *cit.*, I, Paris, 1974, p. 447-459; *Idem*, Religious Poverty and the Profit Economy in Medieval Europe, London, 1979; B.H. Rosenwein – L.K. Little, « Social Meaning in the Monastic and Mendicant Spiritualities », *Past and Present* 63, 1974, p. 4-32; G. Todeschini, « I vocabolari dell'analisi economica fra alto e basso medioevo: dai lessici della disciplina monastica ai lessici antiusurari », *Rivista Storica Italiana* 110/3, 1998.

nativa non *subditis iniuriosa* ma *utilis et fructuosa*, in grado dunque di generare, fra l'altro, una *maior utilitas temporalium Dei ecclesie* :

> *Quia subditi minus gravabuntur in exactione sumptuum et redditus ecclesie poterunt tam pauperibus quam cultui ecclesie habundantius ministrari et divites ad erogationem elemosinarum per huiusmodi exempla fortius trahi*[1].

Tutto il nesso *paupertas-simonia* è, del resto, fondamentale in Olivi e gli consente di sviluppare una riflessione sulla relazione (contrattuale) fra *spiritualia* e *temporalia; intentio* e *utilitas* giocano con ogni evidenza, per l'Olivi, un ruolo importante nel momento della valutazione etica di *paupertas* come comportamento in grado di determinare benefici economici o favori. E' nel caso di una *ordinatio ad futurum* della *exhibitio spiritualium* che si determina « *de facto aut de iure* » una *obligatio seu pactum expressum vel tacitum et interpretativum* e che, quindi, si crea, molto probabilmente, una relazione simoniaca; anche in questo caso, però, la *voluntas* di colui che, in sede più propriamente economica, si chiamerà « *contraente* », dovrà essere attentamente indagata per stabilire :

> *[...] an voluntas tunc feratur in causam sine qua non sicut in principale motivum an solum sicut in annexum principali motivo. Et etiam quando fertur in eam sicut in annexum principali difficile est videre an sit annexum sicut comprincipale aut sit annexum nihil habens de principalitate aut de comprincipalitate.*

Visibilmente, qui, l'analisi delle dialettiche simoniache di radice canonistica, mediata dal volontarismo contrattualista oliviano, diventa la base di una analisi casistica funzionale alla valutazione dell'eticità dei *lucra* in generale, e introduce, pertanto, in particolare, criteri di analisi dell' *intentio* in grado, eventualmente, di legittimare i profitti mercantili :

> *Sciendum tamen quod multis modis potest quis ordinare praedicta ad temporalia. Uno modo in respectu ad praeteritum, non ad futurum, utpote quando aliquis ex beneficiis iam receptis incitatur ad gratiam rependendam benefactori, non intendens per hoc eum inclinare ad benefaciendum in futurum quamvis forte intendat eum elevare ad maiorem pietatem prout est quaedam perfectio ipsius benefactoris aut prout est utilis aliis pauperibus potius quam*

1. *QPE IX*, p. 66 : la *paupertas* degli episcopi non è in contrasto con la *reverentia* loro dovuta, anzi ne è la base più certa. Essa infatti consente sia una *utilitas spiritualis* derivante dallo *status episcopalis* che una *maior utilitas temporalium Dei ecclesie.* Il prestigio generalmente sociale degli episcopi, secondo l'Olivi, sarà in ogni caso, e in contrasto con un apprezzamento meramente 'quantitativo' del loro valore, direttamente proporzionale al grado della loro povertà : « *Concedo autem quod familiaritas quando est nimia parit contemptum. Sed isti ex ipsa humilitate paupertatis erunt condescensivi et benigni et ex altitudine ipsius status et sollicitudine contemplationis sic erunt ab aliis segregati quod sicut angeli dei et ac si ipse Christus a fidelibus conspicientur* », *loc. cit.*, p. 65-66. Non sfuggiranno né, da un lato, le analogie con alcuni, importanti, passaggi testuali di Pier Damiani dedicati alla povertà personale del clero (Petrus Damiani, *op. cit.*) e in particolare dei vescovi (*Idem, Epistola* 97, *ed. cit.*, III, p. 64 ss.) o di Bernardo di Clairvaux sulla povertà monastica come base di un'ordinata aministrazione (*Apologia ad Guillelmum abbatem* in *Opere I*, Milano, 1984, p. 210 ss.), né, d'altro canto, il valore di modello esemplare che la povertà ecclesiastica assume in Olivi, come in Damiani, nei confronti della gestione patrimoniale dei laici orientata verso forme di sistematica largitio ovvero fluidificazione della ricchezza (Petrus Damiani, *Epistola* 110, *ed. cit.*, III, p. 223 ss.).

> *prout est temporaliter utilis sibi et suis. Et hic modus nihil sapit simoniae, immo summe condecet viros perfectos*[1].

Da questo punto di vista, in Olivi, *paupertas* è fondamento di ogni costruzione economico-istituzionale corretta dal punto di vista ecclesiologico e si oppone direttamente alla gamma di comportamenti denotati dalle parole *avaritia* e *simonia*. *Paupertas*, allora, non significherà nell'ipotesi di *perfectio evangelica* dell'Olivi semplicemente e genericamente privazione, una *vacua seu vana et infructuosa abdicatio omnis iuris*, ma piuttosto realizzazione effettiva, attuazione dell'*usus pauper*, ossia di uno stato di controllo dominativo, la cui indispensabile premessa dovrà in ogni caso essere l'analisi ravvicinata dei bisogni, delle necessità e del superfluo che compongono il quotidiano reale o ipotetico del cristiano che aspiri alla perfezione, ossia alla imitazione di Cristo :

> *[...] sciendum quod sicut forma se habet ad materia, sic usus pauper se habet ad abdicationem omnis iuris. Unde sicut materia sine forma est informis et confusa, instabilis, fluxibilis et vacua seu vana et infructuosa, sic abdicatio omnis iuris sine paupere usu se habet. [...] et ideo quia per formam devenimus in cognitionem materie, et posita forma necessario intelligitur materiam positam esse, tam Christus in evangeliis quam sancti in dictis suis principalius intentionem verbi ferunt ad expressionem pauperis usus*[2].

In altri termini, nella testualità oliviana, ancor prima che essa si manifesti come esplicitamente economico-sociale, *paupertas* in quanto formalmente concretizzata da *usus pauper* impone l'esigenza di discorsi in grado di catalogare e valutare i comportamenti economici, impone dunque come fondamento etico e teologico della rievangelizzazione sociale francescana una razionalizzazione economica del sistema sociale cristiano occasionata in particolare, e con specifico vigore linguistico, dalla volontà di definire la *necessitas* in termini di previsione verosimile dei bisogni :

> *[...] dicendum quod necessarium de presenti et necessarium pro presenti non sunt omnino idem, nam de presenti potest esse aliquid necessarium pro tempore futuro, ut est necessarium tempore sementis seminare pro tempore messium, et sic contingit in provisione domus et vestium. Si enim non provideret homo sibi de presenti vestes pro toto tempore durabilitatis ipsarum vestium sed potius quolibet die vestes mutaret, ridiculosum quemdam statum effigiaret, et ad perfectionem nichil prodesset, sed potius obesset. Quantum etiam ad usum pauperem in nullo prodesset quia ita asperam et vilem vestem potest quis habere ad usum continue deportationis sicut et cum commutationibus crebris. Nec est in hoc alia differentia nisi quod isti una vestis continue commodatur, illi vero semper alia et alia. Et consimile est in domo et in omnibus que absque sui multiplicatione ad usum diuturnum valent. Aliud tamen est in hiis que necessario habent alia et alia esse in tota successione usus eorum, sicut oportet alium et*

1. *QPE X*, p. 320-321.

2. *QPE IX*, p. 35. L'*usus pauper* è dunque, oltre che una concretizzazione-attuazione di *paupertas*, anche il modo di conoscerla effettivamente. Il rinvio oliviano è a Bonaventura, *Apologia pauperum* (VII, XII, in *Opera VIII*, Firenze Quaracchi 1882 ss., p. 272 ss., p 322 ss.) in quanto attestante *paupertas* come « forma » attuabile giuridicamente.

alium esse cibum in tota successione comestionum. [...] Quecumque igitur de presenti sunt manifeste necessaria, quamvis non sint necessaria pro presenti, provideri licite possunt et etiam haberi, salva tamen semper condescentia pauperis usus, quod idcirco adiungo quia non est estimandum esse necessarium de presenti quod convenienter estimatur posse provideri et procurari in tempore sequenti seu in temporibus suis[1].

Nelle *quaestiones* VIII, IX e X in effetti, è presente una serie di complessi ragionamenti che, esaminando la gamma dei possibili *usus* che da quello *pauper* raggiungono quello *tenuis*, quello *communis* e infine quello *dives*, mostra con chiarezza che la testualità pauperistica oliviana implica in sé tutta una serie di possibili analisi della ricchezza alle quali si perviene attraverso la via di una sistematica verifica dei bisogni e delle utilità relative : la determinazione dell'*excessus quantum ad usum* dipende esplicitamente da un'attenta valutazione della *diversitas* e delle *conditiones rerum utibilium* nonché da una precisa valutazione del senso dei bisogni individuali e collettivi :

Sciendum etiam quod de excessu quantum ad usum secundum diversitatem rerum utibilium est diversimode iudicandum. Nam quedam sunt quibus frequenter et in magna quantitate indigemus et que communiter conservari possunt et communiter conservantur, ut panis et vinum. Quedam vero sunt quibus frequenter et in competenti quantitate indigemus et tamen communiter conservari et haberi non possunt nisi per continuam generationem ipsorum, ut sunt herbe ortolane. Quedam vero quibus raro et tunc in modica quantitate, indigemus, ut oleum et legumina. Quedam etiam quorum conservatio plus sapit divitias et plus opponitur defectui inopie etiam secundum communem usum et estimationem mundi quam multorum aliorum, ut conservatio bladi in horreis et vini in cellariis, quam conservatio olei vel lignorum, nisi forte oleum in quantitate et pretio eis equaretur. Iterum quedam sunt que secundum communem usum de facili assidue dari possunt et dantur, ut elemosina panis et vini et consimilium. Hec enim communiter ab omnibus habuntur et apud omnes semper in usum veniunt. Quedam sunt que a paucis habuntur et in modica quantitate respectu communis usus earum, ac per hoc a paucissimis dari possent communiter et frequenter et maxime pluribus, ut sunt holera et herbe ortolane. Secundum autem has tres divisiones seu diversitates rerum utibilium necessitas de presenti respectu eorum et diversimode est pensanda. Conservatio enim leguminum aut olei pro una parte anni non sapit divitias, nec communiter veniunt in usum saltem in magna et pretiosa quantitate, ne communiter de facili inveniri possent per modum doni aut etiam per aliam viam, maxime ad opus unius magne societatis, et ideo talis conservatio non repugnat pauperi usui, et maxime quia ipsis assistentibus adhuc deest principalis victus, panis scilicet et vinum. Erbe vero hortolane nisi ad usum orti habeantur communiter a multitudine aliqua haberi non poterunt commode iuxta communem et frequentem earum exigentiam, et ideo ortos ad ususm habere non repugnat usui pauperi, ad minus ubi rationem possessionis non sapiunt sed potius habitationis [...] In omnibus autem istis semper attendenda est quantitas multitudinis seu societatis. Quod enim saperet divitias uni vel duobus sapit usum pauperem et inopem

1. *QPE IX*, p. 39-40.

triginta vel centum hominibus. Preter has autem divisiones sunt adhuc alique alie conditiones rerum utibilium, quia quedam sunt que in utilitatem hominis non cedunt nisi per continuam sui consumptionem, ut cibus et potus. Quedam autem eadem numero diu durant ad hominum servitium et utilitatem, ut vestes et domus, et talia ad ususm continuum secundum suam totam durabilitatem possunt haberi, ita tamen quod in hoc presentem necessitatem non excedant [...][1].

Ma l'esposizione oliviana della *raritas* o della frequenza dell'uso dei beni necessari al sostentamento, se da un lato determina un'acuta percezione del variare della necessità, dunque del valore relativo dei beni, d'altro canto introduce il lettore nell'universo concettuale della valutazione economica delle cose del tutto palese nel *de contractibus :*

> *[...] commune verbum est* quod omne rarum est carum et preciosiorum preciosum. *Et quod* nimia familiaritas et abundantia parit contemptum. *Quanto enim rarius et difficilius adire possumus et habere tanto super nostram facultatem altius et admirabilius extimamus. Ardua enim nobis et insolita admiramur. Et ideo ubi aurum vel triticum communiter multum habundat non tanti pretii extimatur; sicut quando communiter grandis inopia est ipsorum. Et idem est ubi est communis inopia vel inopia medicorum vel advocatorum aut pugilum vel fossorum*[2].

In particolare, il binomio *familiaritas-raritas*, che nel trattato sulle compravendite, le usure e le restituzioni è fra gli elementi che, decisamente, fondano la dinamica del prezzo di mercato, appare, e non è un caso, nella citata *quaestio* IX nell'ambito di una riflessione sul valore e sul prestigio sociale degli ecclesiastici[3]. In effetti un semplice confronto testuale mostra che tanto nel *de emptionibus*, quanto nella *quaestio* IX la nozione di valore, indipendentemente dall'oggetto a cui si applichi, appare, cifrata appunto dai lemmi *familiaritas* e *raritas*, nella medesima logica: quella di una valutazione dipendente dalla desiderabilità e dalla frequenza dell'apprezzamento collettivi, radicata però, a differenza di quanto sostenne Langholm[4], non nell'antico truismo dell'equivalenza fra *rarus* e *pretiosus*, ma piuttosto in un preciso assunto ecclesiologico di Girolamo, ripreso nella *distinctio 93* del *Decretum Gratiani*, in un testo cioè che connetteva il valore di mercato alla qualità del carisma :

1. *Ivi*, p. 47-48; *cfr*. *QPE X*, p. 341 : « *Usus ergo est quaedam actio competens tam divitibus quam pauperibus ut est actualis inhabitatio domus aut actualis induitio vestimenti aut actualis commestio cibi et consimilia. Quod autem subdit quod usus tenuis est accidentalis paupertati sicut usus abundans est accidentalis divitibus : si loquitur de paupertate vulgari quae nullam professionem regularem aut evangelicam includit verum dicit. [...] Si vero loquatur de paupertate evangelica non solum dicit falsum, sed petit quod debet probare* ». *Cfr*. anche *QPE VIII*, p. 195 : « *[...] usus et ius non sunt idem. Possumus enim uti re absque hoc quod habeamus ius in ea vel in usu eius, sicut servus utitur re domini sui, qui tamen nec est dominus nec usufructuarius [...]* ». L'argomento bonaventuriano è precisato, *ivi*, come fondato su principi di diritto positivo « *et de tali non est verum quod uti re sit idem quod posse eam licite consumere* ».

2. TC, *De emptionibus et venditionibus*, p. 56.

3. *Cfr*. sopra nota 1, p. 222.

4. *Op. cit.*, p. 359.

> *Sed dicis, quomodo Romae ad testimonium diaconi presbiter ordinatur? Quid mihi profers unius urbis consuetudinem? Quid paucitatem, de qua ortum est supercilium, in leges ecclesiae vendicas? Omne quod rarum est plus appetitur. Pulegium apud Indos pipere preciosius est. Diacones paucitas honorabiles, presbiteros turba contemptibiles facit*[1].

2

Il denaro in quanto oggetto inquietante, ma per ciò stesso epistemologicamente avvincente, è scoperto nel *de usuris*, nel *de restitutionibus* e nella *quaestio* XVI del *quodlibet* I, come oggetto dotato di sorprendenti capacità di riprodursi, se sia inscritto nello spazio mercantile di una potenziale *probabilitas lucri*, inscritto com'è, in questo caso, in una *ratio seminalis lucri* :

> *[...] patet quod quando quis ex gratia speciali prestat vel vendit bladum in tempore, quo communiter minus valet, quod tamen firmiter proponebat servare et vendere in tempore communiter et probabiliter magis caro, potest idem pretium exigere quod in hora prestationis vel venditionis probabiliter creditur affuturum in illo tempore magis carum. Sic tamen quod aliquem dictum diem illius temporis determinate prefigat, quia ipse non erat illud venditurus nisi in aliquo uno die [...]. Causa autem quare sub tali pretio potest illud vendere vel commutare est, quia is cui prestatur tenetur sibi ad probabiliter equivalens, seu ad preservandum ipsum a damno probabilis lucri, tum quia illud quod in firmo proposito domini sui est ordinatum ad aliquod probabile lucrum non solum habet rationem simplicis pecunie seu rei, sed ultra hoc quamdam seminalem rationem lucrosi quam communiter capitale vocamus, et ideo non solum habet reddi simpliciter valor ipsius sed etiam valor superadiunctus. Item ex hoc patet quod quando aliquis pecuniam de qua firmiter mercari proponitur, prestat alicui ex sola pietate et necessitate illius, sub tali pacto quod quantum consimilis summa apud talem equivalentem mercatorem lucrabitur vel perdet, tantum ipse lucretur vel perdat, non committit usuram, sed potius facit aliquam gratiam salva tamen sua indemnitate. Sicut in quadam questione de quolibet fuit ostensum*[2].

Ed è ancora il denaro, in tutta la sua ambigua fascinazione, ad essere rappresentato nella IX questione *de perfectione evangelica* come pure nel commento a Matteo, e dunque nel decennio 1270-1280 che vede anche la stesura della bolla *Exiit qui seminat*. Negli scritti pauperistici ed esegetici dell'Olivi, la *pecunia* è raffigurata, certo, in una luce quanto mai ambigua : la sua natura *multiplicabilis, tractabilis, aggregabilis in infinitum*, la caratteristica che le è propria di essere *ad*

1. *Decretum Gratiani* 93, 25 = Friedberg I, p. 329. *Cfr.* Todeschini, *Linguaggi economici ed ecclesiologia, cit.*

2. TC, *De usuris*, p. 84-85 *Cfr. Idem, Quodl.* I, 17, f° 7v-8r ; A. Spicciani, « Gli scritti sul capitale e sull'interesse di fra Pietro di Giovanni Olivi », *S.F.* 73, 1976, p. 317-321, ora in *Idem*, *Capitale e interesse tra mercatura e povertà nei teologi e canonisti dei secoli XIII-XV*, Roma, 1990.

omnem contractum valde ductilem sottolineata nel commento a Matteo[1], la *facilitas utendi* che la qualifica, la maneggevolezza del suo *usus*, la caratteristica che le è propria di concretizzare e rappresentare numeralmente il valore delle cose, ne fanno un oggetto pericoloso, negato dalla *abdicatio* e dal *contemptus* dei *pauperes voluntarii :*

> *Sicut enim in divitiis omnia desiderabilia mundi implicite continentur, ac si fructus in radice, et propter hoc radix omnium malorum est cupiditas, sic quicquid fere est appetibile in divitiis et omnis earum facultas in pecunia aggregantur, sicut enim habetur Ecclesiastis decimo, communis est hominum conceptio quod* pecunie obediunt omnia. *Unde quicquid homo vult, sive divitiarum, sive delitiarum, sive vindicarum, sive dignitatum, sive obsequiorum et comitivarum, sive honorum et laudis, totum per pecunias admirabiliter obtineri potest et facilius quam per aliquod aliud genus divitiarum et ideo super omnia alia amabiles se ingerunt et illecebrosissime amorem hominum ad se trahunt. Super omne etiam aliud genus divitiarum earum amor est infinitum et in infinitum excrescens non solum ratione predicta, sed etiam quia amplius sunt multiplicabiles et aggregabiles et thesaurizabiles etiam in infinitum. [...] Quantum etiam ad usum eius hoc ipsum patet. Usus enim pecunie in quantum talis per se et immediate non est hominibus utilis, propter quod ab Aristotele in politicis, facultas earum divitie inutiles vocantur. Ad solos enim contractus eorum utilitas directe se extendit. Contractibus autem faciendis intendere mercationem sapere videtur et iurisdictionem et vix possunt esse sine peccatis. [...] Usus etiam earum super omnia facillime ad manum habetur. Sunt enim facillime ad portandum et ad abscondendum et ad conservandum et ad commutandum et ideo multe fraudulentie et mala per eas facillime perpetrari possunt. Secundum autem omnia ista omnino sunt dedecentes virum et statum apostolicum. Pro eo enim quod per se sunt inutiles, non potest eius usus directe et per se necessarius ostendi, qui solus decet professores pauperis usus : Pro eo autem quod sunt principale instrumentum contractuum, adhuc multo minus eos decent. Ex facilitate autem utendi eis non solum multa furta et alia mala possent perpetrari a viris religiosis [...] sed etiam posset altissima paupertas simulatione ypocrisis falsificari [...] et e contrario in earum contemptu et abdicatione summus refulget divitiarum contemptus [...]*[2].

Ma è, d'altronde, evidente, che questi stessi *pauperes* proprio perché maestri dell'*usus*, sono i meglio indicati, nella dottrina dell'Olivi, a cogliere i più interni misteri della *pecunia*, a cominciare da quanto, nel denaro risulta più particolare dal punto di vista di un'etica del possesso : la inafferrabile mobilità, il dinamismo astratto, la possibilità, quindi, tipica della moneta, di esistere e di aver senso socialmente al di fuori della sfera del *dominium*, una possibilità affermata dall'Olivi, ma già presupposta in Bonaventura :

1. P.J. Olivi, *Lectura super Matthaeum X*, Padova, Bibl. Antoniana, ms. 336, f° 100v. La definizione del denaro come antitetico all'*usus pauper* è qui situata nell'ambito della nota polemica oliviana nei confronti di Tommaso d'Aquino, per cui *Cfr.* M.T. D'Alverny, « Un adversaire de Saint Thomas : Petrus Iohannis Olivi », in *St. Thomas Aquinas, 1274-1974*, Toronto, 1974, p. 207-218. Sull'opera, *cfr.* D. Douie, « Olivi's Postilla super Matthaeum », *Franc. Stud.* 35, 1975, p. 66-92 ; D. Burr, « The Date of Petrus Johannis Olivi's Commentary on Matthew », *C.F.* 46, 1976, p. 131-138.

2. *QPE IX*, p. 50-51.

> *Non oportet pecuniam habere dominum. Multa enim sunt a nullius dominio possessa in mari et in aere et in terra. Dispensator tamen habet auctoritatem dispensandi eam, non simpliciter sed secundum voluntatem testatoris. Licet autem dominus eius pauperibus eam dare intenderit, non propter hoc sequitur quod sit ipsorum pauperum, tum quia ad hoc quod donatio valeat exigitur a parte recipientis potestas recipiendi et actualis consensus, que non possunt habere huiusmodi pauperes, tum quia nullus sane mentis credet eum dare aliquid vel legare sanctis pauperibus nisi eo modo quo ab eis decenter recipi potest seu in eorum usus utiliter cedere. [...] Dispensatores autem predicti in receptione pecunie pauperibus legate non sunt bailivi ipsorum pauperum sed potius dominorum dantium aut legantium, et maxime cum ipsi pauperes ex vi talis doni vel legati nullam penitus iurisdictionem in pecuniam acquirant*[1].

La straordinaria funzionalità e potenzialità sociale del denaro, come, d'altra parte, la relatività dei valori e delle necessità, sono dunque, nella testualità oliviana, pertinenti alle procedure epistemologiche di coloro che scelgono la perfezione attuabile nell'*usus pauper:* tali elementi di economia, cioè, devono essere conosciuti e compresi dai *pauperes voluntarii* poiché costituiscono gli strumenti mentali stessi che consentono la realizzazione quotidiana, politica della *abrenuntiatio.* E' notevole – da questo punto di vista – la precisione con la quale l'Olivi, sia nella *quaestio* X *de perfectione evangelica*, commentando il testo della bolla *Exiit qui seminat*, sia nella sezione *de emptionibus et venditionibus* del suo trattato sull'economia dei laici, applica il medesimo vocabolario della *latitudo* del valore e della necessità, della variabilità delle *circumstantiae*, dunque della approssimazione razionale (*variabile iudicium*, *variabilis opinio*) della valutazione di prezzi e bisogni, tanto al problema della definizione quantitativa dell'*usus* pauper (*quantitas usus pauperis*), quanto al problema della definizione dei prezzi di mercato (*precium rerum venalium*) :

> *Ecce quod etiam de pecunia cuius usus ad nos non spectat non vult quod possimus facere alicui tradi nisi solum pro usu necessario necessariarum rerum,* necessitate tamen pensata iuxta probabile iudicium *quia in hac materia non potest semper haberi certitudo infallibilis.*
> *Licet enim usus mediocris vel tenuis vel excedens non possit sciri omnino a nobis in puncto, sumpto tamen medio non secundum rem sed potius secundum quod recta ratio determinat et hoc in quadam rationali latitudine sicut fit in mediis ceterarum virtutum, satis potest sciri a nobis. Non igitur oportet quod quantitas usus pauperis determinetur in puncto nec secundum uniformitatem realem sed potius secundum quod recta ratio dictat pensatis debitis circumstantiis secundum diversitatem personarum negotiorum temporum et locorum.*

1. *Ivi*, p. 54 ss., in risposta al decimum argomento contrario alla pratica dell'*usus pauper* (« *Item pecuniam pauperibus huiusmodi legatam oportet habere dominum. Sed non est dare alios qaum ipsos pauperes, quoniam ille qui legavit mortuus est et qui eam dono obtulit vere ipsam dare intendit. Nec potest dici quod ille qui tenet eam ad dispensandum huiusmodi pauperibus sit eius dominus, quia tunc licite posset eam retinere, maxime si ea indigeret, aut aliis personis iuxta beneplacitum proprium dare* ». *Ivi*, p. 9. A questa è connessa la argomentazione di Duns Scoto che esemplificherà la distinguibilità di uso e proprietà del denaro appunto con la possibilità accertata dei Minores di rifiutare lo ius sui denari loro donati, *Cfr.* A.B. Wolter, *Duns Scotus Political and Economic Philosophy*, Santa Barbara, Cal., 1989; Lambertini, *Usus* and *Usura, cit.*

> *Item tertio sciendum quod huiusmodi pensatio valoris rerum usualium vix aut numquam potest fieri a nobis nisi per coniecturalem seu probabilem opinionem, et hoc non punctualiter, seu sub ratione seu mensura indivisibili in plus et minus, sed sub aliqua latitudine competenti circa quam etiam diversa capita hominum et iuditia differunt in extimando. Et ideo varios gradus et paucam certitudinem, multumque ambiguitatis iuxta modum opinabilium in se includit quamvis quedam plus et quedam minus. His igitur prenotatis, dicendum quod res non possunt licite vendi plus quam valeant nec minus emi, pensato earum valore etiam in respectu ad usum necessarium et ad probabilem iudicium humane extimacionis mensurantis valorem rei infra limites latitudinis competentis*[1].

3

Ma è appunto questa conoscenza pauperista delle dinamiche economiche a consentire, d'altronde, all'Olivi di stabilire nel mondo sociale dei laici un campo di prova nel quale possa manifestarsi la capacità evangelizzatrice dei *pauperes Christi*.

Si stabilisce dunque, in primo luogo, che, fra coloro che non sono così forti da *abdicare* al *dominium* dei beni temporali, meno imperfetti sono coloro che esercitano il *dominium proprietatis* come anche coloro che si guadagnano le ricchezze terrene *mercando et per alias vias et negociaciones mundanas :*

> *Preterea cum quattuor gradus circa temporalia videamus in imperfectione et periculo per ordinem se habentes et exercentes quorum primus est possidere temporalia cum dominio proprietatis, secundus procurare et acquirere ipsa mercando et per alias vias et negociationes mundanas, tertius causidicare repetendo ipsa et defendendo, quartus bellare pro ipsis inferendo aut repellendo, si altissime paupertatis est prima due minus imperfecta minusque periculosa, nec ita directe caritati proximi et mutue paci contraria in summa fortitudine a se abdicare et elongare, et in tantum quod etiam iurisdictionem rerum in communi et superfluum usum a se totaliter abdicat, mirabile esset si tertium, videlicet causidicare, summe prout fieri potest a se non debeat totaliter et perpetuo abdicare etiam amplius quam prima, et maxime cum quartum, scilicet bellare, quo ad aliqua in malo seu in imperfectione excedat, utpote in astuciis, dolositatibus et fraudulentiis, et in maioribus occasionibus spiritualium peccatorum*[2].

È questa gradazione casistica dell'esistere economico laicale, in effetti, a rendere comprensibile il percorso che conduce la testualità oliviana a determinare le basi etiche di una società cristiana, fondandone l'eticità su una sempre più celere dialettica degli scambi, e a stabilire nel *mercator christianus* l'interlocutore ed oggetto ideale del discorso economico-politico pauperista. Nel momento in cui il testo oliviano si dedicherà ad esperire e correggere lo stato di

1. *QPE X*, p. 338 : (con riferimento a *Exiit qui seminat IX*); *ivi*, p. 343; TC, *De emptionibus et venditionibus*, 53, sottolineature nostre. *Cfr.* Kaye, *Economy and Nature*, *cit.*, p. 116 ss.
2. *QPE IX*, p. 77-78.

relativa imperfezione dei laici cristiani, stato nel quale, come chiarisce la *quaestio* IX, la *pecunia* ha una sua intrinseca *utilitas*, il *pauper voluntarius* sarà in grado di proporre al *mercator* una sintesi delle proprie conoscenze che, impostate dal rifiuto del *dominium*, consentono però, quando si giunga allo spazio semantico della contrattualità e dello scambio, la compiuta articolazione di un lessico del profitto catalogabile come cristiano e dunque come moralmente accettabile :

> *Ad octavum dicendum quod aliqua sunt utilia imperfectis et in statu imperfectorum que tamen sunt mortifera in statu perfectorum, ut in incontinentibus melius est nubere quam uri, et sic in proposito. Statui enim habentium propria et habere volentium utilis esse potest usus pecuniarum, licet hoc ipsum sit de imperfectione ipsius status quod indigeat usu earum tot periculis annexo. In professoribus autem pauperis usus predicta locum non habent, tum quia paucis indigent tum quia proprie ius faciendi contractus non habent, et tamen ubi casus ardue necessitatis eis emergeret, sicut iam satis dictum est, eis uti possent*[1].

Come è noto, negli scritti oliviani dedicati alla analisi dell'economia dei laici, il *quodlibet I*, il trattato sulle compravendite, le usure e le restituzioni e, per quanto attiene alla ragione formale del rapporto contrattuale, la questione *quid ponat ius*, il *mercator christianus* è indubbiamente il principale protagonista del discorso. Questo avviene non semplicemente perché, come a volte intesero, equivocando, alcuni storici, Olivi sia (o non sia) genericamente un paladino della modernità economica, ma piuttosto perché è nella figura del *mercator* che culmina l'ipotesi di virtù civica laicale messa a punto dalla catena testuale teologico-canonistica già riassunta dalla *Summa* attribuita ad Alessandro di Hales e ora, nel fuoco della polemica pauperista, ripresa e rifusa dall'Olivi nella sua produzione testuale[2]. Da questo punto di vista, la *sollicitudo*, la capacità monetaria, la puntuale conoscenza dell'equilibrio dei valori e dei prezzi di mercato, l'insieme delle attitudini professionali che del mercante fanno, in Olivi, un professionista del mercato utile al consorzio civile, dovranno essere riconnesse al progressivo decantarsi teologico e canonistico, fra XII e XIII secolo, di una normativa cristiana per i soggetti giuridici economicamente attivi che, pur riprovandone alcuni comportamenti, ne potenziasse e valorizzasse tuttavia altri, a cominciare dall'abilità a costruire il benessere economico della città[3]. Già in Graziano, d'altronde, la spesso fraintesa *palea* « Eijciens » non

1. *Ivi*, p. 53. Questi *casus*, che eccezionalmente consentono ai *pauperes evangelici* di portare denaro con sé, erano stati accennati poco prima; *ivi*, p. 52, discutendo della questione dei *loculi* detenuti da Cristo e dagli apostoli e rinviavano essenzialmente a due situazioni : « *quando quis vadit per terras ubi res nisi per viam emptionis haberi non possunt* », e « *quando oportet hominem habitare inter inimicos ubi res haberi commode non possunt, et sine periculo nisi per occultos emptionis contractus* ».

2. *Cfr*. R. De Roover, *La Pensée économique des Scolastiques*, Montréal-Paris, 1971 ; Langholm, *op. cit.*, p. 117-141 ; Spicciani, *Capitale e interesse*, *cit.* ; Todeschini, « Œconomica franciscana » I-II, *Rivista di Storia e Letteratura Religiosa* XII/1, 1976, p. 15-77; XIII/3, 1977, p. 461-494; *Idem*, Il *prezzo cit.* Testi salienti in TC, p. 63 ss.

3. *Ivi :* le caratteristiche positive dei *mercatores* utili alla *respublica* ossia idonei al loro compito professionale sono riassunte dalle espressioni *industrii in rerum valoribus et pretiis et*

condannava come spesso si è preteso l'attività mercantile nel suo complesso, ma soltanto le prassi mercantili che non facessero delle merci un oggetto socialmente utile e produttivo, una *materia operandi*, il principio dunque di un'utilità pubblica[1]. Nei circa ottant'anni che intercorrono fra il IV concilio lateranense e gli scritti economici dell'Olivi, d'altra parte, il diritto canonico aveva sempre più chiarito che il nemico da battere per la *ratio* economica cristiana era l'*usurarius alienigena* o *judeus*, ma comunque nettamente distinguibile per le sue abitudini tesaurizzatrici e improduttive dal *campsor*, il cambiavalute, e dal *mercator*, intesi al contrario sempre più come presenze utili alla felicità pubblica, al *bonum commune*. E bisognerà, qui solo brevemente, ricordare che questa stessa nozione di pubblico benessere scaturisce, nel periodo suddetto, dal più generale processo di autoidentificazione cristiana gradualmente manifestatosi in età postgregoriana come risultato dell'avvenuta equazione fra la nozione teologica di *corpus mysticum* e quella invece tutta politica di *societas christiana*[2].

commoditatibus subtiliter extimandis; honorabiles et fide digni; pecuniosi; il pregio (*raritas*) dei mercanti è sottolineato dalla frase : « *Pauci enim habent ad hoc industriam et peritiam competentem* ». Il profitto mercantile, in Olivi, dipende ed è giustificato dalla capacità del mercator di valutare la già ricordata *latitudo* del valore-prezzo delle merci : « *Ex latitudine vero, quia sicut ars et industria artificis sibi licite fit lucrosa, sic industria mercatoris in rerum valore et pretio prudentius examinando et ad subtiliores minutias iustum pretium producendo, potest licite sibi valere ad lucrum et maxime cum in hoc, salva latitudine iusti pretii, aliis communiter prosit, etiam in hoc solo quod per hoc adiscent subtilius pensare rerum pretia et valores* ». (*ivi*, p. 64) Il profitto è, insomma, non solo la retribuzione del « lavoro » svolto dal mercante ma anche la quantificazione ipotetica della sua abilità mentale nel valutare il sistema dei valori, capacità dalla quale principalmente dipende la possibilità sociale di una determinazione della latitudo dei prezzi ovvero di una dialettica degli scambi comunemente accettata. Critica della *Eijciens*, *ivi*, 65.

1. *Decretum Gratiani*, *ed. cit.*, distinctio LXXXVIII 11, *ed. cit.*, p. 308-309 : « *Quicumque rem conparat, non ut ipsam rem integram et inmutatam vendat, sed ut materia sibi sit inde aliquid operandi, ille non est negotiator; qui autem conparat rem, ut illam ipsam integram et inmutatam dando lucretur, ille est mercator, qui de templo Dei eicitur. Unde super omnes mercatores plus maledictus est usurarius; ipse namque rem datam a Deo vendit, non conparatam, ut mercator, et post fenus rem suam repetit, tollens aliena cum suis, mercator autem non repetit rem venditam* ». *Cfr. Ps. Crisostomo, Opus imperfectum in Matthaeum*, prefazione all'ed. critica a cura di J. Van Banning, Turnhout, CC, 87B, 1988 ; Todeschini, *Linguaggi economici ed ecclesiologia, cit.*

2. *Cfr.* R. De Roover, *Business, Banking and Economic Thought in Late Medieval and Early Modern Europe*, Chicago-London, 1974; U. Santarelli, *La categoria dei contratti irregolari. Lezioni di storia del diritto*, Torino, 1984; E.D. English, *Enterprise and Liability in Sienese Banking, 1230-1350*, Cambridge, Mass., 1988; Todeschini, *Il prezzo, cit.* Per il nesso fra società cristiana e *corpus mysticum* ecclesiale, *Cfr.* H. De Lubac, *Corpus mysticum. L'Eucharistie et l'Église au Moyen Age*, Paris, 1949; M. Rubin, *Corpus Christi. The Eucharist in Late Medieval Culture*, Cambridge, 1991 ; S. Beckwith, *Christ's Body : Identity, Culture and Society in Late Medieval Writings*, London – New York, 1993. Il contributo francescano, e oliviano, alla questione eucaristica è studiato da D. Burr, *Eucharistic Presence and Conversion in Late Thirteenth-Century Franciscan Thought*, Philadelphia, 1984.

4

E' comunque evidente, in Olivi, il ripensamento di queste complesse riorganizzazioni del concetto e del linguaggio sociale alla luce di una teoria-prassi della *paupertas* che, nella testualità oliviana, fa del *mercator* non solo una figura pubblicamente utile, ma, di più, un esperto laico del sistema dei valori economici, un conoscitore della bilancia delle necessità e dei bisogni relativi, e, per ciò stesso, il detentore di una ricchezza attiva perché circolante; fruttifera perché, ed è fondamentale, *probabilmente* e *abitualmente* immessa nel circuito degli investimenti. Il denaro del mercante, da questo punto di vista, contiene in sé una *probabilitas lucri*, la già citata *ratio seminalis lucri*, è dunque un denaro qualitativamente differente da quello dell'*usurarius*, come sarà chiaro a tutta la tradizione francescana successiva fino all'epilogo osservante quattrocentesco, proprio perché il *mercator* da inquieto conoscitore del mercato, benché il suo fine ultimo sia il lucro, deve in ogni caso, appunto per conseguire il suo premio terreno, il guadagno, attivare il proprio denaro prima di tutto mentalmente, scoprendo e catalogando cioè, *sollicitus* e *industrius* com'è, bisogni reali e bisogni superflui, utilità soggettive, oggettive o presunte: questa costante attitudine analitica fa del suo denaro un oggetto potenzialmente infinito, e del suo profitto non un semplice *stipendium laboris*, come in Tommaso d'Aquino[1], ma piuttosto la misura del valore che lui e il suo denaro pubblicamente possiedono.

A ben guardare, tuttavia, è appunto questo impegno mentale, questa inquietudine mercantile, questa, insomma, oggettiva competenza economica del mercante che lo rende protagonista della ricchezza ipotetica, continuamente ricalcolata, a fare del *mercator christianus*, in Olivi, un chiaro interlocutore del *pauper voluntarius*.

Tre sembrano gli aspetti fondamentali che caratterizzano il nesso percepito dal testo oliviano fra *paupertas voluntaria* e ricchezza mercantile.

In primo luogo, si potrà stabilire che la gamma di attributi mercantili che ne qualificano metodologicamente la capacità professionale, ed espressi dai lemmi *sollicitudo*, *industria*, e correlati, ha il suo più vicino riferimento nel vocabolario monastico del perfezionamento attivo, denso com'è – soprattutto fra XI e XIII secolo – di immagini e terminologie dell'attenzione e dell'impegno quotidiano: e si vorrà qui soltanto ricordare un notevole passaggio del *de speculo caritatis* del benedettino Aelredo di Rievaulx, autore del XII secolo assai letto negli ambienti pauperisti del XIII, che proprio servendosi dei lessici e delle

1. Della copiosa bibliografia sulle concezioni economiche dell'Aquinate, si ricorderanno soltanto A. Sapori, « Il giusto prezzo nella dottrina di san Tommaso e nella pratica del suo tempo », *Archivio Storico Italiano*, s. VII, 18, 1932, p. 3-56; O. Capitani, « La 'venditio ad terminum' nella valutazione morale di S. Tommaso e di Remigio de' Girolami », *B.I.S.I.M.E.* 70, 1958, p. 299-363; O. Langholm, *Price and Value in the Aristotelian Tradition. A Study in Scholastic Economic Sources*, Oslo, 1979; *Idem*, *Wealth and Money in the Aristotelian Tradition. A Study in Scholastic Economic Sources*, Oslo, 1983; *Idem*, *Economics*, *cit.*

metafore dipendenti da *industria* e *sollicitudo* descrive la perfezione monastica come forma di inesauribile attivismo :

> *[...] sed sicut piger quis, ac desidiosus, ac agriculturae imperitus, agrum suum, parva licet ex parte tribulis, ac spinis obsitum, tardius evacuat et emundat; impiger autem ac sollicitus, ac huius disciplinae industrius, etiamsi omnem agri superficiem occupaverit, veprium densitatem citius eradicat, ac de sterili et infecundo pinguem reddit et uberem : sic nimirum abrenuntians quis mundo, si tardus, si tepidus, si suae purgationis minus fuerit curiosus, quamquam in saeculo minus exstitit inquinatus, tardius in conscientiae serenitatem, ac caritatis proficiet libertatem; at si fervens spiritu, si diligens ac sollicitus, si discretionis virtute fundatus, assumptis spiritalium exercitiorum instrumentis, vitiorum germina ab agro cordis sui potenter evellat, in auras conscientiae purioris citius respirabit, ac iugo cupiditatis excusso, ac onere deposito passionum, inveniet quia iugum domini suaue est, et onus eius leve est*[1].

In secondo luogo si noterà che uno dei nodi centrali della dottrina economica oliviana, la nozione di valutabilità del tempo (*tempus proprium rei proprie*) a sua volta connessa al concetto di denaro fruttifero perché abitualmente e professionalmente investito in affari produttivi per la comunità civica, la nozione dunque di una temporalità che, come il denaro, ha una sua dimensione qualitativa e dunque un valore specifico, non può essere scissa dalla complessa riflessione svolta dall'Olivi sul tempo come entità che la scelta dell'*usus pauper*, che la scelta pauperista specializza sia in termini mistico-religiosi che in termini più propriamente politico-economici :

> *[...] tempus proprium venditoris possit licite vendi, si temporalem utilitatem temporali pretio appretiabilem in se includat. Et ideo si quis debeat tibi centum libras solvere post tres annos, ita quod antea non tenetur, potest tibi vendere tempus illud paciscendo tecum quod det tibi mox LXXX, et propter tempus trium annorum intercurrens retineat seu acquirat sibi viginti. Quod vero contra a quibusdam arguitur quod tempus est res omnibus communis; tale autem non debet vendi quasi sit proprium venditoris. Dicendum quod hic non arguitur de tempore prout est omnibus commune, sed potius de proprio tempore rei proprie, et prout respectu alicui rei est de iure vel iurisdictione huius vel illius. Iuxta quod annus equi mihi accomodati ad annum est eo ipso de meo iure, et consimiliter tres anni pecunie quam non teneor solvere usque post tres annos, sunt quoad hoc mei iuris, propter quod et possum vendere valorem ipsius. Si enim nichil valeret, non pluris esset teneri ad mox solvendum usque post tres annos et non ante. Si vero adhuc obicias quod qua ratione pecunia mutuata nichil ultra se habet valoris vendibilis, eadem ratione nec pecunia ad tres annos solvenda et ideo vendere tempus eius XX libras videtur esse usura; dicendum quod hic non venditur pecunia, sed tempus solutionis, quod utique est venditoris*[2].

1. *Cfr.* Aelredus Rievallensis, *Compendium speculi caritatis* 56, in *Idem*, *Opera ascetica*, Hoste, Talbot, Vander Plaetse, Wilmart ed., I, Turnhout 1971, *C.C.C.M.* 1. *Cfr.* Todeschini, *Il vocabolario dell'analisi economica*, *cit.*

2. TC, *De usuris*, p. 80-81. Sulla concezione oliviana di tempo soggettivo e oggettivo, *Cfr.* in questo stesso volume il saggio di R. Imbach e F.X. Putallaz.

E', infatti, il tempo del *pauper voluntarius*, un tempo di prova, un tempo, per dirlo con Sylvain Piron, di voto[1], giocato nella scommessa della realizzabilità dell'astensione giuridica dal *dominium;* ma questo tempo povero, d'altra parte, è anche la dimensione specifica, determinata, in cui si gioca, anche nel rapporto con i poteri secolari ed ecclesiastici, l'esperimento di rievangelizzazione sociale minorita orientato, nel complesso, da un'attesa apocalittica[2]. Il tempo del mercante, in effetti, in questo caso è molto vicino, almeno metodologicamente, al tempo del rigorista della povertà : entrambi sperimentano una quotidianità fatta di attimi altamente apprezzabili ; se il tempo della povertà ben speso ha come valore la Salvezza propria ed altrui, il tempo della ricchezza vale quanto la possibilità di moltiplicazione della ricchezza stessa, ha dunque il valore di un'utilità individuale e collettiva.

Si vorrà poi, in terzo luogo, di nuovo sottolineare che la capacità mercantile di esperire e conoscere i valori delle cose, ossia delle merci e del denaro, che costituiscono gli strumenti del lavoro mercantile, è descritta nella testualità oliviana in termini di complementarità alla complessa capacità di cui il *pauper voluntarius* deve dar prova nel conoscere il sistema dei bisogni e delle necessità primarie, attitudine esperta che, sola, può consentirgli di determinare, insieme con il valore relativo dei beni, la distanza che intercorre fra necessario e superfluo, i termini concreti, allora, dell'uso povero. *Mercator* e *pauper voluntarius*, nel testo oliviano, a differenti altezze dell'edificio sociale, compongono una mappa dei valori relativi delle cose, ed è la sottigliezza della loro analisi a consentire tanto un immanente bene comune quanto la prospettiva di una Salvezza. Il denaro, che il *pauper voluntarius* non usa e che il *mercator* utilizza invece come principale utensile della propria arte non appare in questo quadro un elemento di contraddizione fra il mondo dei perfetti e il mondo degli imperfetti : al contrario, la sua natura sfuggente, la sua natura di oggetto risolto nella mobilità, in grado di esistere socialmente, secondo Olivi, anche in assenza di un *dominus*, ne fanno un ente fruibile indirettamente tanto dal *pauper voluntarius* quanto dal *mercator*. Non a caso l'immagine del denaro-*instrumentum*, trasmessa, alla fine del XV secolo, da Summenhart al mondo moderno, per fondare la dinamica del profitto determinato da un *lucrum cessans*, rivela un'origine, lessicale e concettuale, nitidamente oliviana :

> *Modo inducens mercatorem in casu huius conclusionis ad mutuandum, impedit huius industriam, ne pariat fructum, quem nata est producere, quia cum illa industria non possit fructificare nisi mediante pecunia, quam ille mutuo recipit, sequitur quod impossibilitat eius industriam non minus si quis peritum artificem mechanicum non quidem ligaret in carcerem, attamen ei attolleret instrumenta artis suae ad tempus, sine quibus eius industria vel ars in actum exire non posset. Similiter si quis peteret ab artifice, ut sibi suae artis instrumenta accomodaret et artifex non teneretur alias ex praecepto Dei ei ea accomodare, sed esset supererogationis, tunc poterit illa accomodando petere ut relevet sibi interesse*

1. Piron, *Vœu et contrat*, *cit.*

2. *Cfr.* E. Randolph Daniels, *The Franciscan Concept of Mission in the High Middle Ages*, Lexington, 1975, p. 27 ss.

lucri cessantis, quod patitur ex carentia suorum instrumentorum suae artis. Ergo eadem ratione cum mercator in aliquo casu dabili non teneatur sub praecepto pecuniam suam mutuare proximo, et tamen proximus petit eam mutuo, ex quo mutuo mercator carere incipit quasi instrumentis suae artis, et etiam incipit eius ars scilicet industria quasi in carcere detineri, vel suspendi a sua executione actuali, et etiam circa suas res scilicet industriam et pecuniam (quae simul aptae sunt natae fructificare) incipit pati talia a mutuatario, ex quibus impeditur ab assecutione fructuum, qui alias provenirent ex rebus illis, igitur si ei talia concedit de rebus suis, poterit inter concedendum exigere ut sibi satisfaciat pro illo fructu cessante[1].

In Olivi in effetti, e questo pare un nucleo centrale della sua riflessione etico-economica, il denaro e il valore ossia la ricchezza non coincidono : i bisogni del *pauper* sono soddisfatti in assenza di denaro, e questa soddisfazione è l'esito di una rete di relazioni che cede percentuali minime di ricchezza all'universo dei perfetti, così da consentirgli la sussistenza, l'*usus arctus*, ma, d'altro canto, non è il denaro del mercante a costituirne la ricchezza, ma piuttosto il susseguirsi degli investimenti, il continuo riaccendersi della speranza di lucro, la probabilità del guadagno, in una parola il credito. Nell'attimo stesso in cui il denaro venisse a concretizzare, accumulato, la ricchezza mercantile, il *mercator* decadrebbe, in Olivi, ad *avarus* presumibilmente *usurarius*. La consuetudine, la *fama* che in ambito di diritto canonico, dal III concilio lateranense (1178) al secondo concilio di Lione (1274)[2], avevano fatto della tesaurizzazione e dell'usura un comportamento dimostrato dalla notorietà della trasgressione, stabiliscono nel XIII secolo, in Olivi come nel diritto comune, un analogo pubblico riconoscimento come prova dell'attitudine imprenditoriale, dunque non tesaurizzatrice, del *mercator christianus*. In questo senso, il *consensus contrahentium*, l'accordo contrattuale, fonda, per Olivi, non solo il mercato, ma anche la credibilità del mercante come figura produttiva e socialmente utile. Dal punto di vista oliviano, e in questa prospettiva, la pubblica volontà di ricchezza del mercante, del cambiavalute, scopre nel denaro un oggetto utile ma non in grado di soddisfarla compiutamente : il denaro, lungi dall'essere qui una semplice invenzione atta a facilitare gli scambi al modo aristotelico[3], si rivela dunque, proprio per l'ambiguità dei modi del suo uso e del suo possesso, dunque in conseguenza della sua totale scambiabilità, del suo essere sempre uguale e sempre diverso, l'oggetto che misura i valori, che cifra la ricchezza e la sua possibile moltiplicazione, senza tuttavia poterne quantificare l'infinita eventualità. Come tale esso è ignorato dal *pauper voluntarius* che può tuttavia usufruirne indirettamente, e può essere utilizzato dal *mercator* che ne metta a punto il significato sociale di simbolo e

1. C. Summenhart, *De contractibus licitis et illicitis*, II 30, Venezia, 1580, p. 132-133. *Cfr.* H. Ott, « Zur Wirtschaftsethik des Konrad Summenhart (*ca. 1455, † 1502) », *Vierteljahresschrift für Sozial- und Wirtschaftsgeschichte* 53, 1966.

2. Concilio di Lione II, canone 26 *Usurarum voraginem*, leggibile, oltre che in *Conciliorum Oecumenicorum Decreta*, Alberigo ed., Bologna, 3ra ed. 1973, in *Decretales, liber sextus* V 1 = Friedberg II, 1081.

3. *Cfr.* Langholm, *Wealth and Money*, *cit.*

misura sociale della ricchezza senza, però, mai identificarlo con la ricchezza intesa come potenzialità pura.

5

Il significato etico-sociale del *mercator* è dunque, in Olivi, strettamente dipendente da un lessico, di radice teologico-canonistica, in grado di esprimere l'utilità quotidiana, concreta, di scelte, di ipotesi di perfezione spirituale e metafisica. L'organizzazione del mercato cristiano, riconducibile, in Olivi, tanto al protagonismo mercantile, quanto al consenso contrattuale dei contraenti, condizionato eticamente dalla legislazione canonica e penitenziale, si offre oggi alla interpretazione storiografica come universo nel quale fu pensata in chiave pauperista una possibile realizzazione delle dialettiche sociali cristiane. La dinamica economica cittadina, rinnovata fra XI e XIII secolo dalla accelerazione dei movimenti delle monete ma anche da nuove forme dell'iniziativa finanziaria e commerciale delle istituzioni ecclesiastiche [1], dei poteri territoriali laici e delle « super-companies » commerciali cristiane ben visibili fra Montpellier e Narbonne [2], fu in grado di apparire, all'ipotesi di riorganizzazione evangelica oliviana, come un contesto in cui verificare le possibilità tanto di un'economia della povertà tutta giocata sul credito di un'avanguardia intensamente carismatica come quella francescana, quanto di un'economia della ricchezza tutta dipendente dalla sempre crescente variabilità e incertezza dei valori di scambio. Per un intelletto come quello oliviano, che a Narbonne o a Montpellier aveva potuto conoscere lo scatenarsi della tensione intorno ai prestiti gestiti dagli ebrei così tipica del Duecento francese, e ben attestata fra l'altro dal *Mil'hemet Mizwah* di Me'ir ben Simeon di Narbonne [3], che a Montpellier e a Firenze non aveva certo potuto ignorare il decollo commerciale e finanziario di compagnie capaci ormai di vivere la ricchezza in termini di giro internazionale dei valori, per un intelletto teologicamente e giuridicamente affilato come questo la dialettica fra *habun-*

1. P. Spufford, *Money and its use in medieval Europe*, Cambridge, 1988 ; C. Violante, « I vescovi dell'Italia centro-settentrionale e lo sviluppo dell'economia monetaria », in *Vescovi e diocesi in Italia nel Medioevo (sec. IX-XIII)*, Padova, 1964, p. 193-217 ; *Idem*, « Monasteri e canoniche nello sviluppo dell'economia monetaria (secoli XI-XIII) », in *Istituzioni monastiche e istituzioni canonicali in Occidente, 1123-1215*, Milano, 1980, p. 369-416.

2. E.S. Hunt, *The medieval super-companies. A study of the Peruzzi company of Florence*, Cambridge, 1994 ; Piron, *Marchands et confesseurs*, *cit.*

3. *Cfr.* S. Stein, *Jewish-Christian Disputations in Thirteenth Century Narbonne (1964)*, London, 1969; R. Chazan, « A Jewish Plaint to Saint-Louis », *Hebrew Union College Annual* 45, 1974, p. 287-305 ; *Idem*, « Anti-usury Efforts in Thirteenth Century Natbonne and the Jewish Response », *Proceedings of the American Academy for Jewish Research* 41-2, 1973-74, p. 47-67; *Idem*, « Confrontation in the Synagogue of Narbonne : A Christian Sermon and a Jewish Reply », *Harvard Theological Review* 67, 1974, p. 437-457 ; *Idem*, « A Medieval Hebrew Polemical Mélange », *Hebrew Union College Annual* 51, 1980, p. 89-110 ; K. Reyerson, *Business, Banking and Finance in Medieval Montpellier*, Toronto, 1985 ; W. Chester Jordan, *The French Monarchy and the Jews : from Philip Augustus to the Last Capetians*, Philadelphia, 1989; J. Shatzmiller, *Shylock Reconsidered. Jews, Moneylending, and Medieval Society*, Berkeley, 1990.

dantia, *raritas*, *valor*, *beneplacitum voluntatis*, *probabilitas* e *fructus* giungeva a significare che la prassi della ricchezza mercantile poteva o avrebbe potuto radicarsi nel vocabolario di un'ecclesiologia volontarista, poteva o avrebbe potuto essere l'analogo imperfetto, non sacro, laico, di un'economia della Salvezza fondata sulla critica a ogni forma del *possidere immobiliter*[1].

1. *Cfr. QPE VIII* e *XVI*.

LE JEU COMME CONTRAT ET LE *RISICUM* CHEZ OLIVI

Giovanni Ceccarelli

Pourquoi associer Olivi au jeu? Parce que le théologien franciscain, même dans un domaine marginal comme le jeu de hasard, apporte une contribution de haut niveau à la réflexion médiévale. Tout d'abord il soutient que le jeu de hasard est une forme contractuelle; cette définition, qui à nos yeux peut désormais apparaître intuitive, est d'un côté le fruit d'une longue sédimentation conceptuelle, de l'autre, à travers des itinéraires tortueux, en arrivant directement aux théologiens du XVIe siècle, elle jette les bases de la réflexion juridique et économique moderne sur les phénomènes aléatoires; non seulement sur le jeu donc, mais également sur les assurances, la spéculation financière, etc.[1]

Olivi ne se borne pas à considérer l'incidence des phénomènes accidentels dans le domaine du jeu; le *risicum*, le *periculum*, c'est-à-dire l'élément d'incertitude qui caractérise la plupart des relations économiques, et qu'aujourd'hui on pourrait définir comme le risque d'entreprise, occupe un rôle important dans la réflexion du théologien languedocien. Cela caractérise et éloigne la réflexion franciscaine des autres lexiques de morale économique du bas Moyen Age, en particulier du lexique thomiste[2]. Le lien entre le risque commercial et le risque du jeu est fréquent parmi les penseurs de l'ordre; ce fait a déjà été souligné par Alonzo Hamelin à propos d'un autre «économiste» franciscain: Alexandre d'Alexandrie[3]. Cependant il est évident que sans une large analyse des rapports qui existent parmi les phénomènes aléatoires, le commerce et la finance, Olivi n'aurait pu aboutir à la définition de *contractus ludi*. Dans cette brève étude on

1. *Cf.* P.J. Olivi, *TC*, p. 91-92; *Id.*, *Quodl.* I, 17, f° 7rb-8rb. Sur la pénétration des idées oliviennes dans la pensée théologique aux XVIe-XVIIe siècles, *cf.* A. Spicciani, «Gli scritti sul capitale e sull'interesse di fra Pietro di Giovanni Olivi. Fonti per la storia del pensiero economico medievale», *S.F.* 73, 1976, p. 292; Dominicus Sotus, *De iustitia et iure*, Lyon, 1569, f° 112r; Leonardus Lessius, *De iustitia aliisque virtutibus morum*, Lyon, 1630, p. 313-315. Pour une définition juridique et théologique moderne du contrat aléatoire, *cf.* F. Deshayes, «Aléatoires (Contrats)», dans A. Vacant, E. Mangenot, éds., *Dictionnaire de Théologie Catholique*, Paris, 1909, t. 1, col. 695-703.

2. On utilise le terme «morale économique» pour traduire le concept d'*etica economica*; *cf.* O. Capitani, «Sulla questione dell'Usura nel Medioevo», *Bullettino dell'Istituto storico italiano per il Medioevo* 70, 1958, p. 539-566; G. Todeschini, «Oeconomica franciscana. Proposte di una nuova lettura delle fonti dell'etica economica medievale», *Rivista di storia e letteratura religiosa* 12, 1976, p. 15-77; O. Capitani, ed., *L'etica economica medievale*, Bologne, 1974.

3. *Cf.* A.M. Hamelin, *Un Traité de morale économique au* XIVe *siècle. Le Tractatus de usuris de maître Alexandre d'Alexandrie*, Louvain-Montréal-Lille, 1962, p. 99-101.

essayera de dépasser cette simple constatation et d'établir si le théologien languedocien pense le *periculum* comme une catégorie économique abstraite, dont on peut faire descendre une typologie contractuelle spécifique des phénomènes aléatoires, soumise à des règles univoques d'évaluation de morale économique. Pour répondre à cette question, on analysera la réflexion sur le *risicum* dans les opérations commerciales et financières et simultanément dans le jeu de hasard. Cette analyse ne se bornera pas à la pensée d'Olivi. Le frère mineur se situe d'une part au point de formalisation de thèmes précédemment formulés non seulement par des franciscains, mais encore par des canonistes et des théologiens; d'autre part, précisément pour sa grande capacité de synthèse, il constitue un réservoir immense de concepts à la lumière desquels l'on peut mieux considérer les thèmes économiques.

Le *periculum* ou *risicum* est déjà présent dans les analyses économiques des canonistes et scolastiques qui précèdent l'ouvrage d'Olivi; il est considéré dans ses aspects qui le lient au crédit en tant qu'élément de légitimation ou de non-légitimation des différentes formes d'investissement financier[1]. Dans les milieux franciscains parisiens vers la moitié du XIIIe siècle a lieu un changement qualitatif de la réflexion sur le risque économique. Ce changement est encore plus significatif, parce qu'il se produit dans un contexte culturel où des tendances déterministes, fruit de l'aristotélisme et de l'averroïsme radicaux, portaient à nier l'existence des phénomènes accidentels[2].

Chez les théologiens du groupe qui rédigent la *Summa* attribuée à Alexandre de Halès (*Summa Alexandri*), le problème du risque est posé non seulement pour les opérations de crédit, mais surtout à partir de l'analyse des opérations commerciales[3]. Ayant à faire face au problème de la légitimité ou de la non-légitimité du commerce, dans les termes posés par le pseudo-Chrysostome dans son interprétation de l'expulsion des marchands du temple (la prétendue *palea Eiciens*), les auteurs de la *Summa Alexandri* donnent une double interprétation au rôle du marchand dans une société dite chrétienne[4]. On a un thème d'origine aristotélicienne, probablement filtré à travers Averroès, grâce auquel le marchand est considéré dans sa fonction de médiateur des besoins de consom-

1. Sur le droit canon et les canonistes, *cf.* T.P. McLaughlin, « The Teaching of the Canonists on Usury. (XIIth, XIIIth, and XIVth Centuries) », *Medieval Studies* 1, 1939, p. 103-105, 144-147; sur la théologie, *cf.* O. Langholm, *Economics in the Medieval Schools. Wealth, Exchange, Value, Money and Usury, according to the Paris Theological Tradition. 1200-1350*, Leyde-New York-Cologne, 1992, p. 50-51, 56, 61, 85-86, 96-97.

2. Dans les thèses condamnées en 1277 par l'évêque de Paris Etienne Tempier, la n° 21 disait : « *quod nichil fit a casu, sed omnia de necessitate eveniunt* », *cf. Chartularium Universitatis Parisiensis*, H. Denifle, A. Chatelain, éds., Paris, 1891, t. 1, p. 545; pour l'origine de cette thèse, *cf.* R. Hissette, *Enquête sur les 219 articles condamnés à Paris le 7 mars 1277*, Louvain-Paris, 1977, p. 172-173.

3. Sur la *Summa Alexandri* comme ouvrage collectif, *cf.* O. Langholm, *Economics, cit.*, p. 119-120; G. Todeschini, *Il prezzo della salvezza. Lessici medievali del pensiero economico*, Rome, 1994, p. 195-196.

4. *Cf.* Alexandre de Halès, *Summa theologica*, Florence-Quaracchi, 1928, t. 4, p. 721-724; *cf.* Pseudo-Chrysostomus, *In Mattheum, homilia* 38; *PG* 56, col. 839, passé dans le *Decretum Gratiani* (D. 88, c. 11); *cf.* Friedberg, p. 1, col. 308-309.

mation de la collectivité; mais on a aussi un thème d'origine augustinienne, qui considère le marchand non seulement dans son rôle social, mais aussi dans sa dimension individuelle[1]. Le *mercator* a le droit de commercer et de tirer profit de son travail parce que, s'appuyant uniquement sur ses capacités spécifiques et individuelles, il doit faire face à toute une série de risques: «*ex consideratione incertitudinis eventus futuri et susceptione periculi*»[2]. Dans la tradition dominicaine, au contraire, le rôle du *risicum* en tant qu'élément de légitimation du commerce est beaucoup moins important. Chez Thomas d'Aquin cette double interprétation est seulement effleurée, presque insignifiante; le marchand peut obtenir une rémunération, un «*stipendium laboris*», non seulement parce qu'il court des risques personnellement («*propter periculum, cui se exponit*»), mais encore parce que le commerce est nécessaire à la vie de la collectivité: «*propter publicam utilitatem, ne scilicet res necessariae ad vitam patriae desint*»[3].

Reprenant les thèmes présents dans la *Summa Alexandri*, Olivi, dans le *Tractatus de emptionibus et venditionibus, de usuris, de restitutionibus*, les applique à la plupart des analyses économiques. Même avant d'aborder le thème de la légitimité du commerce, le risque devient un élément important dans la description typique du *mercator christianus*, faite par Olivi dans la première partie de son œuvre. Le marchand utile à la collectivité, affirme le théologien, doit posséder ces qualités, cette «*sollicitudo mentalis*», qui lui permet de se débrouiller correctement dans le monde des affaires, et ces capacités se développent à travers une expérience faite de risques et d'incertitudes: «*multo et diuturno studio ac peritia et labore, multisque periculis et expensis [...] acquiritur peritia et industria talis*»[4]. On a l'impression que, pour le franciscain, le marchand a droit à une récompense non seulement pour les risques d'entreprise qu'il court, mais encore parce qu'il montre sa capacité à évaluer et à «maîtriser» les dangers que comporte la pratique commerciale. Le *mercator christianus* d'Olivi se heurte au risque et cherche à le limiter de quelque manière, en se fondant sur sa capacité professionnelle, afin de l'orienter vers l'utilité collective; le marchand joue pour la communauté le rôle de médiateur rémunéré entre *bonum commune* et *periculum*.

Pour ce qui est du problème de la légitimité du commerce, d'après le théologien languedocien, la condamnation consacrée par l'*Eiciens* ne concerne pas les phénomènes économiques dans leur ensemble, mais seulement ceux qui relèvent de la spéculation, ce qui, dans l'analyse olivienne, tend à se polariser sur

1. *Cf.* Alexandre de Halès, *Summa theologica cit.*, p. 723: «*Cum ergo connegotiatio inter homines sit ad supplendam indigentiam mutuae necessitatis, negotiatio non erit illicita nec mala*». *Cf.* Aristote, *Ethique à Nicomaque*, V, 5 et Averroès, *Aristotelis Opera cum Averrois commentariis*, Venise, 1562, v. 3, fol. 72a-72b. Pour la médiation d'Averroès, *cf.* O. Langholm, *Economics cit.*, p. 132-135. Pour l'influence augustinienne, *cf.* Alexander de Halès, *Summa theologica cit.*, p. 722; *cf.* Augustin, *Enarratio in Psalmum*, 70, 16-17, *PL* 36, col. 886-887 passé dans le *Decretum Gratiani* (D. 88, c. 12); *cf.* Friedberg, p. 1, col. 309-310.

2. *Cf.* Alexandre de Halès, *Summa theologica, cit.*, p. 724.

3. *Cf.* Thomas d'Aquin, *Opera omnia*, Rome, 1897, t. 9, col. 153a-154b.

4. P.J. Olivi, *TC*, p. 57.

le terme d'*usura*[1]. Le marchand, d'après Olivi, peut vendre une marchandise à un prix plus élevé que celui auquel il l'a achetée aussi bien parce qu'il a une fonction socialement utile (« *ex manifestis commodis et necessitatibus provenientibus communitati* »), que pour son caractère entreprenant, ses capacités professionnelles en plus des risques auquels il doit faire face : « *ex honerosis laboribus ac periculis et expensis et industriis* ». Sans une juste rémunération économique, dit le franciscain, l'incitation individuelle cesse et, par conséquent, la fonction sociale même du marchand est mise en crise : « *umquam inveniretur qui absque lucro vellet huic operi inservire* »[2].

Les thèmes de la *Summa Alexandri* sont formalisés et renforcés par le théologien languedocien, qui développe un véritable binôme lexical et conceptuel, fondé sur les termes *periculum* (risque commercial) et *industria* (capacité professionnelle), binôme qui occupe une bonne partie du traité et qui devient le point de départ de chaque interprétation des phénomènes économiques.

Par exemple, dans l'analyse olivienne de la formation du prix, ce binôme joue un rôle fondamental; les deux éléments *periculum* et *industria*, dûment estimés par la collectivité, par la « *communis taxatio* », permettent de donner au prix une valeur qui change selon les circonstances, sans tenir compte des critères simplement objectifs. Le *mercator*, dit le franciscain, ne viole pas la loi ni le *bonum commune*, en revendant les marchandises à un prix majeur, parce que cette majoration est justifiée par les « *pericula et onera* » envisagés[3]. Le bien commun est au contraire attaqué quand l'élément de risque dans un achat-vente n'est pas pris en considération, par exemple, dit Olivi, en cachant les dangers que l'acheteur peut courir en utilisant une marchandise défectueuse; dans ce cas, la relation commerciale retombe immédiatement dans une dimension partielle et spéculative[4]. Le théologien propose donc un modèle de *risicum* qui, grâce à la médiation d'un marchand à même d'estimer et d'évaluer le risque, peut devenir utile, en tendant vers le bien commun.

Ce modèle reste fondamental même quand le théologien passe de l'exégèse de l'achat-vente à l'analyse du crédit. Pour Olivi, les activités de crédit mêmes doivent être orientées vers le *bonum commune*, elles doivent être faites en fonction des opérations commerciales utiles à la collectivité. La ligne de partage entre investissement productif et spéculation est liée en dernière analyse à la possibilité d'investir l'argent dans le commerce[5]. Globalement le théologien

1. Sur le concept d'usure chez Olivi, *cf.* G. Todeschini, *Un trattato di economia politica francescana : il « De emptionibus et venditionibus, de usuris, de restitutionibus » di Pietro di Giovanni Olivi*, Roma, 1980, p. 18, 22-24, 33-36.

2. *Cf.* P.J. Olivi, *TC*, p. 63.

3. *Cf.* P. J. Olivi, *TC*, p. 64-65 : « *dicitur quod licet in commutatione mercatoria secundum absolutam sui considerationem sit deffectus perfecte adequationis pretii ad rem emptam vel venditam, non tamen in comparatione ad communem utilitatem rei publice vel ad mercatorum pericula et onera superius tacta, predictus etiam adequationis deffectus : non sic recedit ab equalitate quin aliquo modo contineatur sub ipsa* ».

4. *Ibid.*, p. 59 : « *deffectus illos ex quibus emptor ultra iustum pretium enormiter falleretur tenetur venditor pandere sibi si tamen eos novit vel probabiliter opinatur, et precipue ubi ex hoc aliquod grande periculum contingere posset emptori* ».

5. *Cf.* G. Todeschini, *Un trattato*, *cit.*, p. 16-20, 26-29 ; A. Spicciani, « Gli scritti », *cit.*, p. 298.

affirme que l'usure se produit quand on obtient un bénéfice sans avoir couru aucun «*periculum*», mais cela ne veut pas dire forcément que le risque en soi puisse légitimer le profit[1]. Olivi nie la légitimité de n'importe quelle forme de prêt commercial sans distinction : il ne suffit pas, affirme le théologien, que celui qui fournit les capitaux assume toute une série de risques d'entreprise, il doit aussi participer en personne à la gestion du capital. Pour être utile, et s'intégrer dans un mécanisme productif dont la collectivité puisse bénéficier, l'entreprise commerciale doit être menée par celui qui possède le capital, puisque le *risicum* est pour l'acteur économique le banc d'essai de son *industria* individuelle[2].

La situation se complique quand on se trouve face à l'analyse de cas contractuels typique de la deuxième partie du traité d'Olivi. Il existe en effet quelques modèles de contrat où l'incidence du risque est totalement insignifiante (dépôt, louage) et d'autres où l'élément aléatoire non seulement est fondamental, mais encore doit être de quelque façon quantifié (achat-vente à terme, achat-vente des rentes, emprunt d'Etat, société et jeu)[3]. La typologie du *contractus societatis* est celle où apparaît le mieux la nécessité d'évaluer le *periculum*; on s'y trouve face à deux sujets autonomes, chacun avec sa capacité professionnelle, avec son capital initial, qui s'associent sur la base d'un partage raisonnable des profits et des pertes; par conséquent ils devront supporter la même dose de risque d'entreprise, puisque, dit Olivi «*contractus [...] societatis exigit equalitatem proportionis*». Si au contraire on s'éloigne de ce modèle paradigmatique et, si, par exemple, seulement l'une des deux parties supporte tout le risque d'entreprise, sans une juste rémunération («*equalitas proportionis*»), alors, d'après le frère languedocien, on retombe dans la spéculation. Si l'on n'attribue pas sa juste valeur (en termes de rétribution) au binôme *risicum-industria*, c'est le mécanisme même de productivité économique, orientée vers le *bonum commune*, qui s'en ressent et on n'aura plus de risque utile, mais un non-risque, c'est-à-dire l'*usura*[4].

1. *Cf.* P.J. Olivi, *TC*, p. 71-72 : «*Item de lucro incerto et contingente, ac cum periculo perditionis futuro exigere certum lucro sine omni periculo cuiuscumque perditionis vel damni est aperte iniustum, saltem quando certum lucrum per se non provenit ex re tradita pro illo lucro, sed hoc fit in contractu usurario*».

2. *Cf.* P.J. Olivi, *TC*, *cit.*, p. 82 : «*Predictorum autem radicalis ratio est quia periculum tollens usuram, debet apud lucrantem ex eo includere dominium et usum rei periclitans. Dominium quidem, quia ex re sua debet lucrari, non autem ex re ut est iam alterius. Usum vero, quia usus rei ex quo lucrum provenit, debet mediate vel immediate esse lucrantis. Quandocumque autem in ipso actu mercandi periculum mercium vel pecunie non spectat ad primum traditorem pecunie vel mercium, sed solum ad illum cui sunt tradite, tunc eo ipso earum usus vel dominium, quoad actum illum mercandi, spectat ad solum illum cuius periculo currunt*».

3. On a observé que l'analyse olivienne de l'économie est fondée sur l'idée d'une «*pluralità di forme contrattuali*», chacune avec un propre paradigme de contrat; le risque, donc, pourra être plus au moins important selon les différents types contractuels; *cf.* G. Todeschini, *Un trattato*, *cit.*, p. 21-22. Sur les contrats de dépôt, *cf.* P.J. Olivi, *TC*, *cit.*, p. 80; sur le louage, *Ibid.*, p. 86; sur l'achat-vente à, terme *Ibid.*, p. 80-81 ; sur l'achat-vente des rentes, *Ibid.*, p. 83-84; sur l'emprunt d'Etat, *Ibid.*, p. 84-85; sur les contrats de société, *Ibid.*, p. 86-87; sur le contrat de jeu, *Ibid.*, p. 87.

4. *Ibid.*, p. 86 : «*Si vero arguatur in suprascripto casu non esse usuram, quia conductor potest simul in se suscipere periculum et casus fortuitos rei conducte quantum est de natura contractus : respondetur quod in prefato casu non tam est contractus locationis et conductionis, sed etiam*

Après Olivi, le binôme *risicum-industria* devient le point de départ d'une bonne partie de la réflexion franciscaine en matière économique; il s'agit d'une véritable ligne textuelle qui d'Olivi arrive jusqu'en plein XVe siècle (Bernardin de Sienne, Matthieu d'Agrigente), surtout à travers la médiation d'« économistes » franciscains comme Duns Scot, Alexandre d'Alexandrie, Guiral Ot[1].

Même en ce qui concerne le thème du jeu il n'est pas juste de parler d'Olivi en tant qu'auteur isolé, mais il est nécessaire de l'insérer dans un contexte plus vaste; il faut donc faire un bref préambule pour expliquer ce qu'est concrètement le jeu de hasard au bas Moyen Age, quelle est la norme et quelle est la réflexion sur le *ludus* avant l'intervention du frère languedocien[2].

De récentes recherches ont mis en valeur combien les phénomènes ludiques étaient importants dans les sociétés médiévales[3]. Si importants que, à partir du XIIIe siècle, en Europe occidentale, les autorités politiques définissent des lieux députés juridiquement au hasard, des maisons de jeux, des tavernes, où les gains sont pris en tutelle[4]. Cependant, bien que les activités ludiques fussent soumises à une grande œuvre de réglementation écrite, avant la réflexion d'Olivi, aucun document public ou privé ne définit formellement le *ludus* en tant que contrat[5].

Initialement, entre situation concrète et élaboration théorique, il y a un profond hiatus. Dès la fin du XIIe siècle, le problème des gains au jeu est analysé par les experts en droit romain; malgré quelques opinions opposées, à partir du

contractus societatis in periculo ac melioratione et deterioratione bovis. Contractus enim societatis exigit equalitatem proportionis, ut, scilicet, quantum ego in societate do, vel facio, tantum proportionaliter inde recipiam. Si autem, propter mutuum michi factum, pars mee societatis deterioretur est ibi pro tanto usura ».

1. *Cf.* J. Duns Scotus, *Opera Omnia*, Paris, 1894, v. 18, p. 317; Duns Scot (*Opus Oxoniense*, IV, 15, 2), en énonçant les règles à suivre dans la «*commutatio negotiativa*», affirme: «*quod talis commutatio sit utilis Reipublicae [...] quod talis iuxta diligentiam suam et prudentiam et sollicitudinem et pericula accipiat in commutatione pretium correspondens*». *Cf.* Mattheus Agrigentinus, *Sermones varii*, A. Amore, ed., Roma, 1960, p. 146-152; dans son sermon *De mercancia*, ce frère sicilien du XVe siècle propose une distinction entre usuriers et marchands, en utilisant le concept de risque. *Cf. Ibid*, p. 148 : «*usurari [...] recipiunt sanguinem alienum sine labore et risico [...] mercatores [...] cum laboribus multis et risico lucrantur*». *Cf.* Giraldus Odonis, *De contractibus, de excommunicationibus et de casibus reservatis*, ms., Sienne, Biblioteca comunale, cod. U. V. 8, fol. 82v, 85v-86r; Bernardinus Senensis, *Opera Omnia*, Florence-Quaracchi, 1950, t. 3, p. 140-162, 265-277. *Cf.* aussi G. Todeschini, « Testualità francescana e linguaggi economici nelle città italiane del Quattrocento », *Quaderni medievali* 40, 1995, p. 21-49.

2. Nous analyserons seulement le problème des gains du jeu de hasard; sur le sujet plus vaste du loisir dans la société et la pensée médiévale, *cf.* G. Ortalli, « Tempo libero e medio evo : tra pulsioni ludiche e schemi culturali », dans *Il tempo libero. Economia e società (Loisirs, Leisure, Tiempo Libre, Freizeit) secc. XIII-XVIII*, Firenze, 1995, p. 31-54.

3. *Cf.* J.M. Mehl, *Les Jeux au royaume de France du* XIIIe *au début du* XVIe *siècle*, Paris, 1990; *Gioco e giustizia nell'Italia di Comune*, G. Ortalli, ed., Treviso-Rome, 1993; A. Rizzi, *Ludus/ludere. Giocare in Italia alla fine del medio evo*, Treviso-Roma, 1995. *Cf.* aussi les recherches menées à la fin de XIXe siècle par Lodovico Zdekauer; voir L. Zdekauer, *Il gioco d'azzardo nel medioevo italiano*, G. Ortalli, ed., Firenze, 1993. En matière de jeu de hasard, il faut préciser que jusqu'au XVe siècle, lorsque commence la diffusion des cartes, l'instrument principal est le dé; *cf.* J.M. Mehl, *Les Jeux, cit.*, p. 76-98, L. Zdekauer, *Il gioco, cit.*, p. 19-25.

4. *Cf.* J.M. Mehl, *Les Jeux, cit.*, p. 376-387, L. Zdekauer, *Il gioco, cit.*, p. 95-133.

5. *Ibid.*, p. 31-44, 116-120. Les intuitions de Zdekauer à la fin du XIXe siècle, bien qu'elles restent toujours à vérifier, sont encore très efficaces.

grand juriste bolonais Azo, se formalise la tradition juridique romaine qui prévoyait pour le perdant le droit de réclamer (*repetitio*) la somme perdue au jeu [1]. Même la jurisprudence ecclésiastique s'occupe de cette matière; le droit canonique qualifie le jeu de hasard de péché, personne chez les canonistes et les théologiens ne mit jamais en cause ce point. Mais la condamnation est ambiguë; d'un côté elle n'explique pas ce qui dans le *ludus* constitue le péché, de l'autre, canons et décrétales n'envisagent pas le problème du gain. Pour combler cette dernière lacune, la plupart des canonistes, grâce au principe de l'*utrumque ius*, c'est-à-dire de la complémentarité entre les lois ecclésiastiques et les lois romaines, adaptent ce qui a été élaboré par les experts en droit civil, l'appliquant aussi au for interne; on établit ainsi le principe de la restitution des gains au jeu [2].

Vers le milieu du XIIIe siècle, un changement s'opère, les points fermes auxquels ont abouti les jurisprudences civile et canonique sont mis en doute. Par exemple, Thomas d'Aquin résoud le problème des profits au jeu en affirmant que c'est la compétence du droit positif; pour le dominicain, l'obligation de restitution est valable seulement dans les zones où la loi romaine est encore en vigueur [3].

Pour ce qui est de la réflexion d'origine franciscaine, dans ce cas aussi, on retrouve les éléments les plus intéressants dans la *Summa* attribuée à Alexandre de Halès. Comme pour la plupart des relations économiques, le rapport qui lie deux joueurs est interprété à la lumière de la conception volontariste du droit, typiquement franciscaine; conception qui plonge ses racines dans le débat sur la pauvreté absolue [4]. Dans la *Summa Alexandri*, on affirme que deux sujets, agissant sans contraintes, peuvent déroger aux lois de la jurisprudence latine à travers un *pactum*, d'après lequel celui qui perd au jeu doit payer au vainqueur la somme établie à l'avance: «*pactum [...] intervenit inter partes [...] secundum pactum illud [...] nec ille qui amisit de iure potest repetere, nec ille qui lucratus est, tenetur restituere*» [5].

Une telle approche, de même que celle de Thomas d'Aquin, ne prend pas le dessus, mais est maintenue parallèlement à celle qui s'était précédemment affirmée. On a ainsi le développement et l'approfondissement de véritables lexiques sur le jeu qui coexistent et qui divergent selon celui qui envisage la

1. *Cf. Corpus Iuris Civilis*, P. Kreuger, T. Mommsen, eds., Berlin, 1954, v. 1, p. 185 (D. 11, 5, 2); Azzo, *Aurea summa*, Torino, 1578, f° 103b-104a. Pour une position discordante, mais minoritaire, *cf.* Petrus Placentinus, *Summa in Codicem*, Mayence, 1536, p. 129.

2. *Cf.* Friedberg, p. 1, col. 131 (D. 35, c. 8); *Decretum Gratiani [...] cum glossis*, Venise, 1591, p. 165; Raimundus de Pennaforte, *Summa de poenitentia*, X. Ochoa, A. Diez, eds., Rome, 1976, col. 566-567, 571-574; Henricus de Seguso, *Summa aurea*, Venise, 1574, col. 1857.

3. *Cf.* Thomas Aquinas, *Opera omnia*, Rome, 1895, t. 8, col. 256a-257b.

4. *Cf.* P. Grossi, «*Usus facti*. La nozione di proprietà nella inaugurazione dell'età nuova», *Quaderni fiorentini* 1, 1972, p. 287-355; A.M. Hamelin, *L'école franciscaine de ses débuts jusqu'à l'occamisme*, Louvain-Montréal-Lille, 1961.

5. *Cf.* Alexander de Halès, *Summa theologiae in partes quatuor*, Venise, 1575, t. 4, f° 365v-366r, 460r.

problématique : romanistes, canonistes, franciscains, dominicains, experts en droit coutumier[1].

D'un point de vue formel, l'idée olivienne de *contractus ludi* peut être ainsi résumée : deux sujets, agissant sans contraintes et avec une pleine disponibilité de leurs biens, conviennent d'un transfert de propriété d'après un risque équitablement partagé. Sur cette conception pèsent sans doute aussi bien la *Summa Alexandri* que la notion de *risicum* commercial; mais importent aussi des éléments de la réflexion canoniste et de l'analyse franciscaine sur la pauvreté absolue.

Olivi reprend une longue tradition textuelle du droit canon (d'Innocent III à Raymond de Peñafort, à Henri de Suse, cardinal d'Ostie), que l'on retrouve par la suite dans la réflexion théologique sur l'analyse des *lucra turpia*, c'est-à-dire des modalités illicites d'acquisition de biens (opérations simoniaques, usuraires, prostitution, jeu, etc.)[2]. Le résultat de cet itinéraire analytique conduit à la distinction entre le gain illicite en soi, par exemple le prêt à usure, et le gain tiré de pratiques illicites, par exemple les revenus de la prostitution, distinction mise en évidence par Bonaventure et surtout par Thomas d'Aquin[3]. Le théologien languedocien reprend ce thème, en l'utilisant comme point de départ pour une exégèse bien plus vaste. En posant que le *ludus* est une activité qui engendre un *turpe lucrum*, il procède à une différenciation typologique minutieuse qui fait une distinction entre prêt à usure, simonie et vol (activités coupables de par soi, dont les gains sont à restituer) et prostitution, jeu de hasard et opérations commerciales licites, commencées avec un capital usuraire (activités moralement blâmables, mais engendrant un gain légitime)[4]. A la base de cette différence il y a une ferme distinction entre sphère éthique et sphère juridico-économique, que le théologien languedocien approfondit en termes philosophiques. Pour Olivi, en dernière analyse, entre matière et forme du *contractus* il y a une profonde différence, ce qui implique la révision du problème de la morale économique à la lumière d'une analyse spécifique des formes contractuelles : « *aliud est contractum esse in forma vitiosum et nullum, et aliud in sua materia vel causa motiva seu effectiva, non tamen in sua intrinseca forma* »[5]. Même si, dit Olivi, la *cupiditas* était cause efficiente d'une relation contractuelle, dans un achat-vente comme dans le jeu de hasard, au cas où il n'y aurait pas de violations du paradigme du contrat lui-même, l'obligation aurait pleine validité juridico-économique : « *quamvis cupiditas ad*

1. On peut donc parler, même pour le jeu, d'une *pluralità di lessici* économiques, ne communiquant pas nécessairement les uns avec les autres; *cf.* G. Todeschini, *Il prezzo*, *cit.*, p. 192, 199, 205 n.

2. *Cf.* Innocentius III, *De eleemosyna*, *PL* 217, col. 758 ; Raimundus de Pennaforte, *Summa*, *cit.*, col. 566-567, 571-574.

3. *Cf.* Bonaventura, *Opera Omnia*, Florence-Quaracchi, 1885, t. 4, p. 370a-371b; Thomas Acquinas, *Opera*, *cit.*, t. 8, col. 256a-257b.

4. *Cf.* P.J. Olivi, *TC*, p. 91 : « *secundum quosdam est quod omne turpiter et indecenter ac vitiose acquisitum est restituendum [...] utpote si simoniace aut meretricio vel histrionatu aut ludo aut quocumque modo turpi lucrandi seu mercandi fuerit acquisitum [...] Sed istis a magnis contradicitur, et credo quod vere, nisi solum ubi per iura canonica vel civilia est huiusmodi reiectio in penam criminum imposita et statuta sicut est in simoniace acquisitis* ».

5. *Ibid.*

ludum movens ad emendum agros vel merces sit vitiosa, non propter hoc sequitur quod emptio sit vitiosa de se»[1]. Cela permet au frère mineur de rapprocher les gains du jeu de ceux qui sont engendrés par la prostitution, sur la légitimité desquels les traditions juridique et théologique n'ont jamais objecté[2].

Olivi fait écho, en second lieu, à la conception volontariste du droit et de l'économie, déjà vue dans la *Summa Alexandri*, qui caractérise la réflexion de l'ordre. Le théologien languedocien, dans son exégèse sur le jeu de hasard, utilise le langage typique de l'analyse de la morale économique des frères mineurs[3]. Aussi bizarre que cela puisse paraître, même dans le cas du *ludus*, s'appliquent les règles qui sont à la base du choix de la pauvreté absolue franciscaine. Le théologien met l'accent sur la liberté dont jouit un sujet dans la gestion de ses biens qu'il juge la plus opportune, pourvu que cette gestion ne soit pas en désaccord avec les lois divine et naturelle[4]. En effet, dit Olivi, étant donné qu'aucune loi, humaine ou divine, ne prive un homme de son droit, pris comme *iurisdictio* et *potestas*, de donner ses biens à un autre homme, si les parties agissant sans contraintes le décident, un transfert de propriété juridiquement légitime pourra se produire même à la suite d'un coup de dés : « *si [...] iure divino vel humano, non aufertur alicui iurisdictio vel potestas dandi aliquid [...] colludendi pro [...] victoria ludi, non oportet [...] quamdam equalitatem et licentiam annullari* »[5]. La législation romaine, voire la coutume, restent aux marges de l'analyse olivienne : « *quamvis [...] alique leges civiles quondam edite fuerunt contra...ludum, hodie [...] per contrariam consuetudinem abolite reputantur* » ; le déclin de la première et l'affirmation de la seconde ne sont qu'une confirmation indirecte d'une théorie juridico-économique plus vaste, qui, étendant le contractualisme à la sphère ludique, légitime les gains au jeu : « *quia repetenti perdita per ludum in foro civili*

1. *Ibid.*, p. 91-92 : « *quamvis autem in contractu mercedis pro meretricio sit materia meretrici vitiosa et voluntas ad meretricium et ad contractum sue mercedis movens, forma tamen contractus habet in se aliquid veri iuris [...] et multo magis potest hoc sub fortuita sorte ludi quamvis cupiditas ad ludum movens ad emendum agros vel merces sit vitiosa, non propter hoc sequitur quod emptio sit vitiosa de se. Propterea non omnis vitiositas contractus obligat ad restitutionem* ». Sur la base d'un manuscrit inconnu de Todeschini, encore inédit et conservé à Oxford (Bodleian, Bod 52, f° 61r-100v) Sylvain Piron m'a suggéré une version plus étendue du texte : « *Si etiam ludens posset mere gratis rem suam dare, et molto magis potest hoc sub fortuita sorte ludi, quamvis cupiditas ad ludum movens sit aliquando et ut sepius viciosa. Sic licet cupiditas movens ad emendum agros vel merces sit viciosa, non propter hoc sequitur quod emptio sit de se viciosa* ».

2. *Cf.* *Corpus Iuris Civilis*, *cit.*, v. 1, col. 200-201 (D. 12, 5) ; Raimundus de Pennaforte, *Summa*, *cit.*, col. 566-567, 571-574 ; Alexander de Halès, *Summa theologiae*, *cit.*, t. 4, f° 365v-366r, 460r.

3. *Cf.* P. Grossi, « *Usus facti* », *cit.* ; O. Capitani, « San Bernardino e l'etica economica », dans *Id.*, éd., *Una economia politica nel Medioevo*, Bologna 1987, p. 121-141. Pour la notion franciscaine de pauvreté comme « *abrenuntiatio iuris* », *cf.*, par ex., P.J. Olivi, *QPE* IX, D. Burr, ed., p. 14, 24, 29, 32, 34-35.

4. *Id.*, *TC*, p. 91-92 : « *Si autem licitum est michi dare meum gratis, multo magis est licitum michi aliquid dare pro alio michi concesso quamvis illud mihi impie concedatur ; et maxime ex quo aliqua temporalis utilitas sive vere sive secundum iuditium eius et beneplacitum inde provenit danti. Si autem ludens posset michi gratis rem suam dare, et multo magis potest hoc sub fortuita sorte ludi* ».

5. *Ibid.*, p. 92. *Cf.* encore le ms. d'Oxford, Bodleian, Bod. 52 : « *Si igitur iure divino vel humano non aufertur alicui iurisdictio vel potestas dandi aliquid meretrici pro locatione corporis sui, aut ystrioni pro suo ystrionatu, aut colludenti pro fortuita et infraudulenta victoria ludi non oportet [...] quamdam equalitatem et licentiam annullari* ».

et iuditiali non daretur actio nec sententia restitutionibus sibi fiende»[1]. La rémunération des joueurs non seulement est légitime (*licentia*), mais de plus coïncide avec les lois de la justice économique (*aequalitas*)[2].

Pour comprendre ce que Olivi entend par *aequalitas* dans le *contractus ludi* il faut se référer à un bref passage, contenu dans la deuxième partie du traité, qui fait partie de l'analyse, plus ample et déjà citée, des contrats sociétaires. Finalement, le lien entre *ludus* et *risicum* devient évident : Olivi envisage le *casus* où le joueur est obligé de faire face à des conditions de jeu plus risquées («*periculosior sors ludi*») à cause d'un prêt que lui a fait l'autre joueur. Les règles du jeu sont faussées car le risque retombe sur un seul joueur («*preponderat maioritas illius periculi*»)[3]. La différence fondamentale entre *contractus societatis* et *contractus ludi* semble donc due à l'absence, dans ce dernier cas, de capacité professionnelle (*industria*), c'est-à-dire de l'un de deux éléments qui constituent le binôme fondateur de la légitimation des opérations commerciales et, indirectement, de beaucoup des opérations de crédit : le jeu est un contrat de simple *periculum*. Et cependant, même l'élément de risque isolé doit se conformer à un paradigme, à une *aequalitas* qui peut être évaluée par la *communis taxatio*[4]. Pourtant, on a déjà noté que dans d'autres genres de contrats, dans le prêt commercial par exemple, le *periculum* en lui-même ne légitime pas le gain ; pourquoi cela est-il possible dans le cas du jeu de hasard ? On trouve la réponse du théologien dans une *quaestio quodlibetalis*, chronologiquement antérieure au traité[5]. Olivi envisage le *casus* d'une transaction pécuniaire fondée sur le *risicum : « aliquis tradit alteri centum libras [...] sub hoc pacto, quod sicut consimiles centum librae apud [...] mercatorem [...] lucrabuntur vel perdunt, sic istae tradenti lucrentur vel perdent*»[6]. En termes uniquement abstraits, ce contrat pourrait être considéré comme un véritable pari sur gains ou pertes éventuels pour un marchand, pari assimilable au jeu : « *contractus ludentium est huic similis* »[7]. Au contraire Olivi envisage ce contrat comme une forme de prêt et le qualifie d'opération spéculative («*fraus usuraria*»), puisqu'il manque une des qualités essentielles pour le rendre utile à la collectivité : l'intervention en personne de l'acteur

1. *Ibid.*

2. Ce passage logique, très implicite et en effet obscur, peut être mieux expliqué grâce à une nouvelle perspective interpretative du concept de *aequalitas* chez Olivi ; *cf.* J. Kaye, *Economy and Nature in the Fourteenth Century*, Cambridge-New York-Melbourne, 1998, p. 116-152.

3. *Cf.* P.J. Olivi, *TC*, p. 87 : « *Tertius superius dictus contractus potest fieri ut simul concurrat ibi contractus mutui et contractus societatis [...] Item consimilis usura est si quis mutuat alteri C solidos, cum quibus ludat, cum eo sic tamen quod, rationis talis mutui, periculosior sors ludi detur ei cui mutuum illud est factum. Tunc enim ibi est tantum de usura quantum preponderat maioritas illius periculi* ».

4. *Ibid.*, p. 85-88.

5. *Cf.* P.J. Olivi, *Quodl.* I, 17, fol. 7rb-8rb (on utilisera l'édition critique de cette *quaestio quodlibetalis* dans A. Spicciani, « Gli scritti », *cit.*, p. 317-321).

6. *Ibid.*, p. 317. Il ne s'agit pas d'un *casus* abstrait, mais d'un contrat courant à Narbonne dans les années quatre-vingt du XIIIe siècle. *Cf.* S. Piron, « Marchands et confesseurs. Le *Traité des contrats* d'Olivi dans son contexte (Narbonne, fin XIIIe-début XIVe siècle) », dans *L'Argent au Moyen Age, XXVIIIe Congrès de la S.H.M.E.S (Clermont-Ferrand, 30 mai-1er juin 1997)*, Paris, 1998, p. 303-304.

7. *Cf.* P.J. Olivi, *Quodl.* I, 17, fol. 7rb-8rb ; A. Spicciani, « Gli scritti », *cit.*, p. 318.

économique[1]. La raison, et le franciscain l'explique avec une extrême clarté, provient du fait qu'entre le commerce, le crédit et le jeu, il y a des différences substantielles qui transforment les modèles contractuels respectifs. Le contrat du jeu n'est pas assimilable à une opération commerciale quelconque, mais seulement à des formes ludiques codifiées : « *materia [...] contractus ludi est pricipaliter ipse ludus et victoria ludi* ». Dans le *ludus* seul, l'utilité sociale et la capacité individuelle sont des éléments insignifiants, tandis qu'ils deviennent fondamentaux, avec le *risicum*, dans le commerce. L'attitude du franciscain envers le jeu n'est pas le fruit d'une acceptation vague du risque en tant qu'élément économique; c'est pourquoi on n'a pas de formulation parfaite du contrat aléatoire[2].

L'idée olivienne du jeu comme contrat est aussi efficace à nos yeux qu'elle était complexe pour les penseurs médiévaux. Nous bornant ici à fournir des exemples tirés du domaine franciscain, car, comme on l'a déjà dit, romanistes, canonistes et dominicains suivent des itinéraires textuels différents, nous notons que les réactions sont opposées[3]. D'une part la ligne *Summa Alexandri*-Olivi est acceptée en bloc, sans approfondissements : Alexandre d'Alexandrie copie la *Summa* attribuée à Alexandre de Halès, Monalde de Capo d'Istria y fait une brève allusion et Guiral Ot calque littéralement Olivi[4]. Seul Pierre de Trabibus, élève d'Olivi à Florence, développe la thématique plus en profondeur[5]. D'autre part, le lien *ludus-contractus* est refusé en bloc; dans certains cas, cela se passe sans comparaison avec les thèses oliviennes, comme chez Richard de Médiavilla; chez quelques autres, il y a des omissions volontaires, comme chez Bernardin de Sienne qui copie Olivi, mais omet précisément les exemples relatifs au *ludus;* d'autres franciscains, enfin, comme par exemple Astesanus ou François de Meyronnes, opposent aux thèses du contrat rigide, des argumentations juridiques

1. *Ivi*, p. 318 : « *quia in fraudem usurarum tale pactum venisse videtur [...] quia si ex ratione aliqua <pecunia> est lucrosa, hoc non est nisi quia currit ad suum periculum, sicut faceret capitale traditum mercatori* ».

2. *Ibid.*, p. 321 : « *dicendum quod contractus iste quomodocumque fiat non est similis contractui ludi, quia non est alia materia contractus nisi pecunia tradita vel tradenda. Materia vero contractus ludi est principaliter ipse ludus et victoria ludi. Et ideo in contractu ludi nulla est usura quia nulla est ibi ratio mutui ; et si ludus sit licitus et sub debito moderamine factus, potest fieri licite ; et dato quod sit illicitus solum, ex utraque parte plene voluntarius et nulla lege vel consuetudine civili civiliter observata sit prohibitus, non oportet lucrum eius restitui* ».

3. Pour une liste des différentes positions, sauf la contractualiste, voir le premier traité sur le jeu de hasard (XVe siècle); *cf.* Paris de Puteo, *De ludo*, dans *Tractatus in utraque iuris*, Venise, 1584, t. 7, fol. 151v-155r.

4. *Cf.* Alexander de Alexandria, *Tractatus de usuris*, dans A.M. Hamelin, ed., *Un traité, cit.*, p. 204-205 ; Monaldus Iustinopolitanus, *Summa*, Lyon, 1516, fol. 131d-132a; Giraldus Odonis, *De contractibus, cit.*, f° 103r.

5. *Cf.* Petrus de Trabibus, *Quodlibet I, quaestio XL*, ms., Firenze, Biblioteca Nazionale, Conventi Soppressi D. 6. 359, fol. 112c : « *non videtur esse necessarium quod restituatur [...] et maxime si servetur lex ludi. Lex autem ludi videtur esse quod, quando ludentes de pari ludant, quis intendit facere venire quod suum est in possessionem suius consocii, non absolute, sed sub conditione : puta si tale punctum veniet* ».

rigides[1]. L'idée de *contractus ludi* ne prend donc pas le dessus chez les Franciscains, également parce qu'à partir de Richard de Médiavilla, le thème de l'utilité sociale du jeu, lié à une réflexion approfondie sur les jeux agonistiques (généralement ceux qui sont d'origine militaire), oriente le débat dans d'autres directions[2].

Cependant, l'approche d'Olivi remonta à la surface avec force dès que l'on approfondit la réflexion sur le contrat aléatoire par excellence, l'assurance, opération contractuelle qui, il faut le rappeler, se diffuse seulement à partir de la première moitié du XIVe siècle[3]. Le modèle olivien de *contractus ludi* suggère aux théologiens du XIVe siècle le chemin à suivre. Dominique de Soto, dominicain particulièrement sensible à l'approche économique franciscaine, ne se fait pas de scrupules pour réunir sous une même typologie des contrats le jeu de hasard, les paris et les assurances, ni pour les analyser sur la base des principes juridico-économiques formalisés par Olivi : « *quod posset uterque ludentium gratis donare, illa non est simplex donatio, sed quaedam pactio do ut des* »[4].

Il est désormais possible de tirer quelques lignes schématiques de conclusion. Le risque n'est pas un élément abstrait de l'analyse olivienne, mais son incidence est évaluée cas par cas, selon l'incidence économique et sociale de l'élément aléatoire dans chaque forme contractuelle.

Le frère languedocien n'arrive pas à la formulation d'une catégorie univoque des contrats aléatoires parce que le système économique où il vit n'a pas encore identifié de forme d'intervention indirecte dans le commerce clairement distincte de la simple spéculation.

Avec la formule du *contractus ludi*, Olivi fournit un schéma innovateur de relation contractuelle, qui ouvre la voie à une réflexion de grande envergure sur le rôle du *risicum* dans les procédés économiques.

Dès que l'on admit que même l'action indirecte d'un opérateur commercial comme l'assureur peut être utile à la collectivité, puisqu'il est capable de limiter le risque d'entreprise, la notion olivienne de *contractus ludi* put être étendue à d'autres genres de relations contractuelles où l'élément aléatoire était prépondérant.

1. *Cf.* Richardus de Mediavilla, *Super quatuor libros sententiarum Petri Lombardi quaestiones subtilissimae. Quodlibeta*, Brescia, 1591, p. 75-76; Bernardinus Senensis, *Opera*, *cit.*, t. 1, p. 468, 472; Asteanus, *Summa de casibus*, Venise, 1478, f° 301r-301v. Franciscus de Mayronis, *In quatuor libros sententiarum ac quolibeta*, Venise, 1520, f° 203c.

2. *Cf.* Richardus de Mediavilla, *Super quatuor libros*, *cit.*, p. 76 : « *assuefactio ludi taxillorum adducit ocium, quod est fomentum carnalis lasciviae, et in illo ludo non assuescunt homines ad aliquid quod sit utile reipublice, nec ibi exercetur humanum ingenium* ».

3. *Cf.* par ex., F. Melis, *Origini e sviluppi delle assicurazioni in Italia (secoli XIV-XVI), I : Le fonti*, Rome, 1975, p. XIX; sur la France, *cf.* L.A. Boiteux, *La Fortune de mer : le besoin de securité et les débuts de l'assurance maritime*, Paris, 1968.

4. *Cf.* Dominicus Sotus, *De iustitia*, *cit.*, f° 112r : « *multa sunt alia humana negotia licita, quae dubiae illi varietati committitur. Primum divisoriae sortes, videlicet, cum qui de re qualibet dividenda convenire non possunt, rem sorti committunt [...] Atque aliud sortium genus, dum pecunia multorum congesta iocalia coemuntur, quae inter eos sors prolata distribuit. Et contractus assecurationis maritimarum mercium* ».

LA CONTRIBUTION DE L'ÉCOLE FRANCISCAINE A LA NAISSANCE DE LA NOTION DE LIBERTÉ POLITIQUE : LES DONNÉES PRÉALABLES CHEZ PIERRE DE JEAN OLIVI

Luca Parisoli *

DE LA MÉTAPHYSIQUE A LA THÉORIE POLITIQUE

Je veux essayer de montrer le rôle assumé par Olivi dans un grand parcours de l'évolution des idées, l'histoire de la notion de droit subjectif qui est le milieu de naissance de l'idée de liberté politique : Michel Villey a avancé un puissant paradigme historiographique à propos du développement de la notion de droit subjectif [1] qui a parfois été critiqué [2]. Je l'utilise comme un point de départ : l'idée de droit subjectif a été développée par l'école franciscaine à la suite d'une philosophie volontariste et des querelles concernant la pauvreté évangélique [3]. La position d'Olivi vis-à-vis de la pauvreté évangélique n'est pas la même que celle de Scot ou d'Ockham : ces deux derniers partagent l'idée de la possibilité d'un usage des choses dépourvu de tout droit, alors que Olivi est le partisan de la théorie de l'*usus pauper* [4]. La position d'Olivi, du point de vue de la théorie juridique, est une violation du principe de légalité, car il entraîne la peine du

* Je tiens à remercier le frère Régis Carton, O.F.M. Cap., bibliothécaire de la Province de Paris, pour son aide dans mes recherches (politiques et juridiques) franciscaines, et Maria Michela Marzano, qui a discuté avec moi le contenu de ce travail et a contribué à son intérêt.

1. M. Villey, « La genèse du droit subjectif chez Guillaume d'Occam », *Archives de Philosophie du Droit* 9, 1964, p. 97-127 ; dans la même ligne, M. Bastit, *La Naissance de la loi*, Paris, 1990 (pour l'opposition entre l'école thomiste et l'école franciscaine, *Idem*, *Les Principes des choses en ontologie médiévale (Thomas d'Aquin, Scot, Occam)*, Bordeaux, 1997).

2. Pour des indications générales, nous renvoyons notamment aux travaux de Brian Tierney, S.G. Swanson, « The Medieval Foundation of John Locke's Theory of Natural Rights : Rights of Subsistence and the Principle of Extreme Necessity », *History of Political Thought* 18, 1997, p. 399-459.

3. *Cf.* P.A. Folgado, « La controversia sobre la pobreza franciscana bajo el pontificado de Juan XXII y el concepto del derecho subjetivo », *La Ciudad de Dios* 172, 1959, p. 73-133 ; G. Tarello, *Profili giuridici della questione della povertà nel francescanesimo prima di Ockham*, Milano, 1964 ; P. Grossi, « *Usus facti* », 1972, dans P. Grossi, *Il dominio e le cose*, Milano, 1992 ; L. Parisoli, « Come affiorò il concetto di diritto soggettivo inalienabile nella riflessione francescana sulla povertà, sino ai fraticelli *de opinione* e Giovanni XXII », *Materiali per una storia della cultura giuridica* 28, 1998, p. 93-137.

4. D. Burr, *Olivi and Franciscan poverty : the origins of the usus pauper controversy*, Philadelphia, 1989.

péché mortel pour un comportement indéterminé : certes, il était davantage attiré par la perfection du Ciel que par celle du monde. Mais les trois personnages sont séparés par un décalage temporel assez important, et surtout riche d'événements capitaux : ici je ne veux pas m'interroger sur l'interprétation de la Règle franciscaine, je me limite à souligner que les trois frères mineurs, ainsi que beaucoup d'autres, sont unis par l'idée que le droit est issu d'un acte de la volonté individuelle (et non pas formelle). Une notion clef de la théorie juridique et politique moderne est ainsi issue non pas de la tradition des praticiens du droit, mais de l'évolution de la pensée franciscaine, que je qualifie de volontariste sans lui associer aucune connotation péjorative. La seule différence avec la méthode de Villey est dans le fait que je trouve beaucoup plus intéressant de se plonger dans l'école franciscaine que dans la pensée thomiste, étant donné que l'idée de droit subjectif a finalement connu, au XVIe siècle l'approbation de toute la Seconde Scolastique[1] : je ne veux pas exclure de façon draconienne que des auteurs non-franciscains avant la deuxième moitié du XIVe siècle (Jean Gerson puis Conrad Summenhart, furent les hérauts du droit subjectif, mais non des libertés politiques)[2] aient pu contribuer à l'évolution de la notion de liberté politique. Cette notion est l'application du droit subjectif dans le domaine public, utilisé par le citoyen contre le gouvernement : pour aboutir à cette idée, il faut disposer d'une théorie politique qui fait le lien entre la liberté de tous et la source du pouvoir. Ce n'est pas le cas de Marsile de Padoue[3], ni de Henri de Gand[4] : de toute façon, s'il y avait des auteurs non-franciscains impliqués dans ce parcours des idées[5], ce serait une bonne démonstration de la capacité de l'école franciscaine de s'assurer des partisans, comme elle l'a fait au XVe siècle.

Mon but est de dégager une théorie juridique et politique franciscaine et d'identifier, chez Olivi, les éléments qui seront finalement développés de façon systématique par Scot et Ockham : je dois tout d'abord préciser que je ne suis pas concerné par une exploration, dans les écrits des théologiens, des cas pratiques de la vie sociale qui peuvent être utilisés comme *exempla* d'une solution conceptuelle. Je recherche la formation d'une théorie générale du droit et des droits, et non une énumération de situations pratiques : on a parfois essayé de montrer l'influence d'une institution juridique sur la pensée – c'est le cas de l'institution, en *common law,* du *trust* sur l'idée de l'absence absolue de droits de la part des frères mineurs[6] – mais on a toujours dû constater le caractère hautement

1. *Cf.* A.S. Brett, *Liberty, Right and Nature*, Cambridge, 1997.

2. A.S. Brett, *Liberty, Right and Nature*, cit., p. 86-87.

3. *Ibidem*, p. 63-64, note 43.

4. L'effort de R. Macken, « Henry of Ghent as Defender of the Personal Rights of Man », *Franz. Stud.* 73, 1991, p. 170-181, est la meilleure démonstration de la faiblesse d'une théorie des droits individuels chez Henri de Gand. Mais il ne faut pas nier qu'il y a dans ses écrits des intérêts pour les situations de la vie sociale et politique qui demandent une étude ciblée (*Cf.* la notice de F. Lajard, « Henri de Gand » dans *Histoire littéraire de la France*, Paris, 1895, vol. XX, p. 197-199).

5. Sur la prééminence de l'école franciscaine à propos de l'idée de liberté en général, *cf.* O. Lottin, « Le concept de liberté chez les Maîtres franciscains du XIIIe siècle », *Lumières d'Assise* 3, 1948, p. 52-65.

6. C.B Gray, « Ockham on Trusts », *Franc. Stud* 24, 1986, p. 141-159.

hypothétique du lien inductif. En réalité, la théorie politique et juridique est tout d'abord une philosophie normative : ainsi, la richesse des cas analysés par Olivi dans ses écrits économiques, comme l'ont bien montré ici Todeschini et Ceccarelli, ne correspond pas à une telle situation dans le domaine du droit. D'un côté, nous retrouvons la naissance d'une science (empirique) économique, qui devient une véritable théorie d'économie politique quand elle est associée à la métaphysique générale d'Olivi, c'est-à-dire à l'outil de l'*usus pauper*, lié à l'état de perfection évangélique; de l'autre, nous retrouvons la naissance d'une philosophie normative de la société, qui devient juridique ou économique selon son domaine d'application particulier.

Je préfère montrer que la théorie théologique et métaphysique franciscaine est la meilleure justification, étant donné son caractère volontariste, des solutions politiques envisagées par des frères comme Olivi, Scot ou Ockham. Évidemment, cette attitude méthodologique demande une prudence particulière : comme cela a été bien illustré dans l'histoire des idées d'universel et de singulier [1], le lien entre la métaphysique et la politique peut être parfois trompeur, et même ne pas exister du tout. Je ne veux montrer aucune nécessité entre la métaphysique volontariste et la théorie du droit subjectif et des droits politiques individuels, voire les libertés politiques : il me suffit de montrer que la meilleure justification des idées politiques et juridiques de l'école franciscaine n'est pas dans les événements de l'histoire, mais dans les données préalables de la théologie franciscaine [2]. C'est dans cet esprit que je veux aborder les suggestions de la pensée olivienne pour une nouvelle théorie des libertés politiques : et dans le cas particulier d'une liberté qui est le fondement de la personne et de sa dignité, une liberté qui s'exprime par une volonté qui est cause d'elle-même [3], je crois qu'il y a là un lien sûr entre la théorie métaphysique et la théorie politique.

PRÉCISIONS TERMINOLOGIQUES

Il me semble qu'il faut tout de suite introduire certaines précisions dans les significations des mots, afin d'éviter de discuter à propos d'un objet mal identifié. Quand je dis que « l'école franciscaine a introduit l'idée de droit subjectif » je veux dire que c'est seulement dans l'école franciscaine que nous trouvons :

1. C. Zuckerman, « The Relationship of Theories of Universals to Theories of Church Goverment in the Middle Ages : A Critique of Previous Views », *Journal of the History of Ideas* 36, 1975, p. 579-592.

2. Dans le même sens, A.S. McGrade, *Ockham and the Birth of Individual Rights*, dans *Authority and Power. Studies on Medieval Law and Government*, réunies par B. Tierney - P. Linehan, Cambridge, 1980; J. Coleman, « The Relation between Ockham's Intuitive Cognition and his Political Science », dans *Théologie et droit dans la science politique de l'État moderne*, (Coll. de l'École française de Rome - 147), Rome, 1991.

3. *Cf.* F.X. Putallaz, *Figures franciscaines à la fin du XIIIe siècle*, Paris, 1997; R.R. Effler, *John Duns Scotus and the Principle « Omne quod movetur ab alio movetur »*, New York, 1962.

L'idée d'un droit qui ne soit pas légitimé par un ordre naturel des choses, qui ne soit pas invoqué par le juge au-delà de n'importe quelle demande des parties, c'est-à-dire un droit qui soit non-objectif (le paradigme du droit objectif est central pour Saint Thomas)[1].

L'idée d'un droit qui soit constitué (et non pas simplement déclaré) par une volonté, qui peut être celle de Dieu, du législateur, des participants au contrat – notamment, si le droit en question n'est légitimé que par la volonté compétente; il s'ensuit que le sujet compétent peut renoncer à faire valoir son droit, c'est le cas de Dieu qui renonce à l'application d'une loi qu'il avait établie (la miséricorde), du législateur qui déroge à une loi, de la partie lésée qui renonce à ester en justice contre la partie qui lui a procuré un préjudice.

La primauté de la volonté est une donnée répandue chez tous les auteurs de l'école franciscaine : cette idée qui devient un postulat métaphysique chez Scot[2], associé à la défiance vis-à-vis des nouvelles idées aristotéliciennes[3], peut fonder une philosophie juridique volontariste, qui se résumerait ainsi: la norme (c'est-à-dire, la signification d'un énoncé normatif) est un acte de volonté, et pas autre chose.

Chez Olivi nous pouvons discerner ces deux éléments: Simoncioli a bien illustré le rôle de la volonté dans la construction de la liberté[4], et David Burr a souligné les caractères de la condamnation d'Aristote comme philosophe païen[5]. En particulier, Simoncioli dit une chose très intéressante, en l'attribuant à Olivi comme maître de Gonsalve, lui-même maître de Scot: dans la tradition franciscaine, «*la volontà è libera*» est «*una proposizione analitica*»[6]. Mais si l'affirmation de la liberté de la volonté est une proposition analytique, alors la liberté n'est pas une qualité contingente de la volonté : dire que la volonté est libre signifie définir la volonté, donc la volonté est le *definiendum*, et la liberté est le *definiens*. Une chose qu'on appelle « volonté » et qui n'est pas libre, n'est pas la volonté : de cette idée, va tout naturellement découler la notion du pouvoir du

1. On a parfois essayé de démontrer que saint Thomas utilisait la notion de droit subjectif (*Cf.* J.M. Aubert, *Le Droit romain dans l'œuvre de Saint Thomas*, Paris, 1955, p. 91, avec le renvoi à H. Hering, « De iure subjective sumpto apud S. Thomas », *Angelicum* 12, 1935, p. 295-297), mais le fait qu'il y ait des expressions chez Saint Thomas qui font l'équivalence entre *ius* et pouvoir (et la chose n'est pas du tout évident, *cf.* A. Folgado, « La controversia sobre la pobreza franciscana », *cit.*) ne signifie point qu'il y ait une théorie tommasienne du droit subjectif, comme Aubert lui-même en fait le naïf aveu : « lorsque S. Thomas parle de *'ius'*, sans aucune spécification, ou de façon officielle, il l'entend alors au sens objectif » (*loc.cit.*, note 2, *in fine*).

2. *Cf.* John Duns Scotus, *Contingency and Freedom. Lectura I 39*, Dordrecht, 1994 (texte latin, traduction anglaise, commentaire interlineaire par le *Research Group John Duns Scotus*).

3. F. D'Agostino, *La tradizione dell'epieikeia nel medioevo latino*, Milano, 1976.

4. F. Simoncioli O.F.M., *Il problema della libertà umana in Pietro di Giovanni Olivi e Pietro di Trabibus*, Milano, 1956.

5. D. Burr, « Petrus Ioannis Olivi and the Philosophers », *Franc. Stud.* 9, 1971, p. 41-71.

6. F. Simoncioli O.F.M., *Il problema della libertà umana*, *cit.*, p. 53. La question renvoie au statut ontologique du principe de contradiction, que je ne peux aborder ici, mais qui finalement ne se réduit pas du tout à l'idée simpliste de l'historiographie que « Dieu ne peut pas agir contradictoirement », car il faut préciser de quel niveau ontologique l'on parle (pour un travail récent concernant le milieu franciscain, *cf.* L.M.D. Rijk, « Gerardus Odonis O.F.M. on the Principle of Non-Contradiction and the proper nature of Demonstration », *Franc. Stud.* 54 [1994-1997], p. 51-67).

législateur. Le législateur (c'est-à-dire, le pape) doit établir des normes, donc il doit avoir la compétence et la légitimité pour cela (la *iurisdictio*) : Olivi a toujours proclamé sa fidélité au pape, et je crois qu'il n'envisage pas seulement le respect le plus absolu du vœu d'obéissance, tant souligné dans les écrits de saint François. Le pape étant le titulaire du pouvoir législatif, il a l'autorité de constituer des normes : dans sa méfiance à l'égard de la doctrine d'Aristote, Olivi ne pouvait pas croire que la loi fût un acte de l'intellect, car la liberté est ailleurs, dans la volonté. Donc, le pape constitue des normes par sa volonté (nécessairement libre), et personne ne peut contester sa décision, s'il s'agit d'une décision prise dans le cadre de la compétence nécessaire (la *iurisdictio*), car soit un pouvoir législatif est libre (par la volonté), soit il n'existe pas du tout. Évidemment, s'il ne peut pas établir une norme, parce que la compétence lui manque, le discours change radicalement; pourtant le problème n'est pas dans les conséquences de la norme, mais dans le fait que le pape n'est pas autorisé à assumer une telle décision.

Nous sommes déjà en face du dilemme de la philosophie volontariste : d'un côté, le souverain doit régir la société par un pouvoir absolu, car si sa volonté est bornée, son pouvoir n'est pas vraiment souverain; de l'autre, la liberté du législateur humain, qui garantie la production des normes, existe face à la liberté des subordonnés et la liberté de Dieu, qui est au niveau supérieur dans la hiérarchie des normes. Les deux solutions principales dans l'école franciscaine sont celle de Scot, qui se contente de limiter le législateur absolu par la plus grande fidélité aux devoirs envers Dieu [1]; et celle d'Ockham, qui développe une sphère juridique qui borne l'action du pape dans un cadre à l'intérieur duquel elle reste absolue, mais en dehors duquel elle devient nulle – on est en face de la lutte contre un pape jugé hérétique [2], de même que certains auteurs ont noté un caractère constitutionnel dans la pensée politique d'Ockham [3]. La place d'Olivi dans l'héritage de la pensée juridique et politique franciscaine, bien qu'il ait pu largement inspirer la théologie volontariste de Scot comme on l'a suggéré dans ce Colloque (au moins dans la mesure où cela est possible pour une pensée nominaliste par rapport à une pensée réaliste), est celle d'un précurseur d'Ockham, et peut être que l'édition de l'*Opera edita et inedita* d'Olivi va renforcer au niveau textuel une évidence tout à fait impressionnante au niveau conceptuel [4].

1. A. Soto O.F.M., « The Structure of Society according to Duns Scotus », *Franc. Stud.* 11, 1951, p. 194-212, et 12, 1952, p. 71-90.

2. A.S. McGrade, *The political thought of William of Ockham*, Cambridge, 1974.

3. E.F. Jacob, *Essays in the Conciliar Epoch*, Manchester, 2e éd. 1963 (1re éd. 1943), p. 85-105, ch. 5 « Ockham as a Political Thinker » ; et P. Boenher O.F.M., « Ockham's Political Ideas », *Review of Politics* 3, 1943, p. 462-487, aussi dans le recueil par E.M. Buytaert – P. Boenher, *Collected articles on Ockham*, New York, 1958. Sur la notion de constitutionnalisme au Moyen Age, *cf.* B. Tierney, *Medieval Canon Law and Western Constitutionalism*, 1965, dans le recueil *Church Law and Constitutional Thought in the Middle Ages*, London, 1979, essai XV.

4. Je songe en particulier au texte de M. Bartoli, qui donne l'impression d'un certain nombre d'emprunts importants à la question *De dispensatione votis* dans le *Breviloquium de principatu tyrannico*, l'un des ouvrages les plus explicites et les plus polémiques d'Ockham (*Cf.* A. Hamman O.F.M., *La Doctrine de l'Église et de l'État chez Occam*, Paris, 1942). Il serait intéressant de savoir qu'Ockham a utilisé un matériel olivien, car cela renforcerait la thèse d'une continuité forte dans l'école franciscaine, véritable réservoir d'idées : mais il faut évidemment attendre la parution

Afin d'aborder ce parcours d'Olivi jusqu'à Ockham, pour arriver enfin aux libertés politiques que déjà Lagarde situait dans les écrits du *Venerabilis Inceptor*[1] (et notamment dans le *Breviloquium*), je crois qu'il faut avancer un schéma de l'interprétation de la notion de liberté dans l'école franciscaine, qui va devenir une notion à trois significations principales. Je ne peux détailler ici les raisons d'historiographie philosophique qui soutiennent ce schéma[2] et je me borne à l'utiliser comme instrument pour mieux comprendre le passage de la liberté du cadre philosophique au cadre politique. Donc, je propose de distinguer entre : la liberté métaphysique ; le libre arbitre ; la liberté morale.

Je suis conscient que cette division tripartite n'est pas du tout habituelle, mais j'espère pouvoir la proposer sans équivoques, en rappelant aussi le travail de Wolter qui désigne par *native liberty*[3] ce que, *grosso modo*, j'appelle « liberté métaphysique » : il faut se souvenir de l'observation avancée par Gilson à propos de la liberté chez saint Augustin[4]. Ainsi, bien que nous soyons toujours en face d'un seul mot, *libertas*, saint Augustin fait clairement la différence entre le libre arbitre et la liberté qui consiste dans le fait de faire toujours le bien, c'est-à-dire, la liberté morale : la scolastique franciscaine a ainsi appris que le libre arbitre est un bien moyen, constitué par une nature bonne dont l'effet peut être bon ou mauvais, mais qui, sous l'influence de la Grâce divine, est toujours orienté vers le Bien. Donc, la liberté morale est la conformité au bien, le refus permanent de l'esclavage du péché[5] : le libre arbitre est la faculté de choisir entre le bien et le mal, de sorte que, comme le dira Scot, le libre arbitre *confirmato* (c'est-à-dire, *in patria*) produit toujours la liberté morale, et le libre arbitre *non confirmatus* (c'est-à-dire, *in via*) offre la possibilité de la louange et du reproche[6]. Cette idée même d'un « double » libre arbitre nous conduit à une notion très générale de liberté, la plus générale, étant donné sa constitution métaphysique et ontologique : cette liberté est la constitution de la personne, elle est un cadeau que « *nihil sub Deo est nobis*

définitive, car dans le *Breviloquium* il y a des thèses assez élaborées sur le pouvoir du pape (quand Baudry avait édité le texte d'Ockham, il l'avait intitulé *De potestate papae*) et peu sur la question du vœu.

1. *Cf.* G. de Lagarde, *Naissance de l'esprit laïque au déclin du Moyen Age*, Paris, 1946, vol. VI (*Ockham : la morale et le droit*), p. 71-73 et *passim ;* ensuite, la nouvelle édition *Naissance de l'esprit laïque au déclin du Moyen Age*, Louvain – Paris, vol. IV, 1962 (*Guillaume d'Ockham : défense de l'Empire*) et vol. V, 1963 (*Guillaume d'Ockham. Critique des structures ecclésiales*).

2. J'ai essayé de détailler cette hypothèse historiographique dans deux articles : L. Parisoli, « Guglielmo di Ockham e la fonte dei diritti naturali : una teoria politica tra libertà evangelica e diritti fondamentali ed universali » *C.F.* 68, 1998, p. 5-62 ; « Percorsi della libertà nella Scolastica francescana : dal primato della volontà alla 'naturalizzazione' attraverso la teoria politica dei diritti », *Materiali per una storia della cultura giuridica*, 1999, à paraître.

3. A.B. Wolter O.F.M., *Native Freedom of the Will as a Key to the Ethics of Scotus*, dans *Deus et Homo ad mentem I. Duns Scoti*, Roma, 1972, ensuite dans *Idem*, *The Philosophical Theology of John Duns Scotus*, Ithaca, 1990.

4. E. Gilson, *Introduction à l'étude de saint Augustin*, Paris, Vrin, 1969, partie II, ch. 3.

5. Guillaume d'Ockham, *Ordinatio*, I, d. 1, q. 6 (*Opera theologica*, vol. I) : « *opponitur servituti creaturae rationalis et hoc vel servituti culpae, vel servituti poenae. Et hoc modo beati sunt liberiores quam viatores, quia magis liberi a servitute culpae et poenae* ».

6. Jean Duns Scot, *Reportata parisiensia*, II, d. 7, q. 1-3, n. 25 (éd. Vivès, vol. XXII) ; *Lectura*, II, d. 7, q. unica (ed. Vaticana, vol. XIX).

ita dilectum et carum sicut libertas et dominium voluntatis nostrae»[1]. Sans la liberté nous perdons notre personnalité et nous ne sommes que des bêtes avec un intellect[2].

Cette troisième espèce de liberté est d'importance capitale pour le fondement métaphysique d'une liberté politique : nous pouvons ne pas avoir de liberté morale (parce que nous sommes affaiblis par la chair ou bien parce que nous refusons la vérité morale de la doctrine catholique) ; nous pouvons avoir perdu le libre arbitre (parce que l'exercice de cette faculté est empêché par des causes physiques, ou parce que nous sommes trop jeunes, ou encore par suite de troubles mentaux) ; mais la liberté métaphysique, étant donné qu'elle est la personnalité elle-même (Scot nous dit que la personne est l'« *ultima solitudo* »)[3], nous caractérise jusqu'à notre existence, *in via*, comme l'explique magistralement Olivi dans sa q. 57 in *Secundum Sententiarum*, ainsi que *in patria*[4], car la personne (et sa liberté) n'est pas une entité empirique, mais au contraire métaphysique – et la liberté *in patria* peut arriver jusqu'au point de ne pas vouloir voir Dieu, étant donné que la vision de Dieu est un acte d'amour[5]. Nous pouvons perdre notre liberté morale sous la contrainte extérieure et devenir esclave des autres, nous pouvons perdre notre libre arbitre par des contraintes intérieures et ne plus être capables de choisir l'acte bon, mais nous ne pouvons jamais perdre notre liberté métaphysique : finalement, chaque être humain, croyant ou pas, pécheur ou pas, esclave ou pas, jouit de cette liberté, car cette liberté est lui-même. La conséquence fondamentale est dans le fait que cette liberté n'est pas liée aux valeurs du système moral choisi par une personne : l'infidèle n'a pas de liberté morale, évidemment, de même qu'il utilise mal son libre arbitre, mais sa liberté métaphysique est intacte. Si nous fondons les droits d'une société sur le modèle de la liberté morale, notre conception de la politique est très étroitement liée à la vérité d'un système moral (par exemple, la doctrine catholique); la validité des droits de cette société est conditionnée par la conformité à la bonne morale; au contraire, si nous fondons les droits d'une société sur le modèle de la liberté métaphysique (c'est-à-dire de la dignité de la personne), la validité des droits d'une société d'incroyants et d'infidèles ne peut pas être mise en question. Les libertés politiques trouvent ainsi leur fondement non pas dans un système moral particulier (dont la vérité est toutefois décisive pour le Salut), mais dans une valeur morale universelle, la liberté de l'homme, c'est-à-dire la dignité de la personne. Guillaume d'Ockham, sous la pression des événements historiques, élabora la première version explicite d'un pareil projet.

1. A. Emmen O.F.M., « La dottrina dell'Olivi sul valore religioso dei voti », *SF* 62, 1966, p. 88-108, édition de la *quaestio An sit melius aliquid facere ex voto quam sine voto* (*Cf.* p. 98).

2. F. Simoncioli O.F.M., *Il problema della libertà umana*, *cit.*, p. 106-107 : « *Olivi ripone la dignità dell'uomo nella libertà, costitutivo essenziale della personalità* » (p. 107 n. 4).

3. Jean Duns Scot, *Opus oxoniense*, III, d. 1, q. 1, n. 17 (éd. Vivès, vol. VIII).

4. R. Prentice O.F.M., *Scotus' Voluntarism as Seen in his Concept of the Essence of Beatitude*, in *Studia mediaevalia et mariologica*, Roma, 1971.

5. Jean Duns Scot, *Opus oxoniense*, IV, d. 49 (consacrée à la béatitude), q. 6 (éd. Vivès, vol. XXI) ; Guillaume d'Ockham, *In IV Sententiarum*, q. 16 (*Opera theologica*, vol. VII) : « *voluntas pro statu isto potest nolle finem ultimum sive ostendatur in generali sive in speciali* ».

LES DONNÉES MÉTAPHYSIQUES DES LIBERTÉS POLITIQUES CHEZ OLIVI

La liberté humaine est selon Olivi «*manifestissima veritatis lumina et experimenta*» et sa négation «*exterminat omnia naturae rationalis bona*»[1]. Parmi les évidences en faveur de la liberté de la volonté, la cinquième est l'«*affectus subiectionis et reverentiae et affectus dominationis et libertatis*»[2], qui établit un véritable principe politique. La seule *ratio* du pouvoir, la seule légitimité du pouvoir, est la liberté[3] : s'il n'y a pas de liberté, l'homme ne peut pas devenir souverain et régir les autres, il ne peut pas non plus donner des ordres aux autres ni exercer son *dominium* sur les autres. Il peut le faire *de facto*, par la force, mais il n'y a pas de justification *de iure:* la seule légitimation de l'autorité politique, du fait que les *cives* estiment être soumis aux lois (et l'attitude des citoyens comme celle des esclaves exprime la conscience d'un pouvoir «*dominativum et imperativum*» qui leur est supérieur), est la «*ratio voluntarie subiciendi*». Il faut souligner que, ici comme ailleurs, l'attitude empiriste d'Olivi peut être trompeuse : bien sûr, il fait très souvent appel à notre expérience pour renforcer sa thèse de la liberté comme essence de la dignité humaine, mais il ne faut pas croire qu'il est en train de justifier notre expérience. Au contraire, il essaie de montrer comment sa construction métaphysique n'a aucune difficulté à justifier notre expérience : la *potestas imperativa* et la *potestas dominativa*, qui sont finalement la même chose, ne sont pas seulement établies par expérience humaine, car elles sont aussi établies par l'«*intentione et efficacia obligandi*»[4] qui est la force obligatoire de la norme, étant donné qu'elle est l'expression de la volonté d'une personne dotée de la légitime compétence à régir un nombre donné de personnes. Mais nous sommes en face d'une proposition de philosophie juridique, et non d'une analyse de la psychologie humaine : la loi est définie comme «*mandatum vel statutum cum intentione obligandi datum et publice promulgatum ab eo qui auctoritatem habuit super istis*»[5]. Ailleurs, Olivi nous dit que la *ratio legis* est l'intention du législateur, et que la force contraignante des lois n'est pas la même pour chaque espèce de lois, comme la Tradition nous l'enseigne relativement au Décalogue[6].

De plus, l'homme désire «*naturalissime libertatem*» et «*vehementissime horret totalem suae libertatis ablationem*»[7] : la liberté est donc l'essence même de la nature humaine, jusqu'à son désir de béatitude qui peut être réalisé grâce à son *dominium*. Cette horreur de l'aliénation de toute liberté est la donnée préalable des libertés politiques, comme droits subjectifs publics des individus, opposables au pouvoir qui s'est rendu coupable de négation des droits fonda-

1. Pierre de Jean Olivi, *In II Sent.*, q. 57, t. 2, p. 316.
2. *Ibidem*, p. 321.
3. Bien sûr, la source ultime et directe de tout pouvoir est Dieu, qui peut priver de sa légitimité, à chaque instant, n'importe quel souverain (*Cf.* Pierre de Jean Olivi, *QPE 13*, éd. L. Oliger, p. 359).
4. Pierre de Jean Olivi, *In II Sent.*, q. 57, t. 2, p. 336.
5. *Loc. cit.*
6. Pierre de Jean Olivi, *QPE* 17, éd. F. Delorme, p. 153.
7. Pierre de Jean Olivi, *In II Sent.*, q. 57, t. 2, p. 322.

mentaux. Ce sont ces libertés qui devaient être exaltées par Ockham dans son *Breviloquium* et ses *Octo quaestiones*. L'homme ne peut renoncer complètement à sa liberté, car sa dignité disparaîtrait avec sa liberté. Finalement, nous constatons l'existence d'un sentiment de la force contraignante de la loi : l'idée de « *habere aliquid iuris* » serait vide s'il n'y avait la liberté (qui est « *quid nobilissimum* »), car les *iura*, ces « *voluntaria signa voluntatis interne* » [1], demandent la *facultas dominandi*, et sans liberté, il n'y a pas de *facultas dominandi*. En outre, suivant la thèse de la question *Quid ponat ius*, les droits ne sont pas une qualité de la nature, ils sont une manifestation de la volonté qui « *nichil reale addant* ».

Donc, nous pouvons dire que la liberté et le *dominium* sont le fondement de la notion de droit et de l'autorité politique : nous sommes libres, car nous avons le *dominium* sur les choses et sur nous-mêmes, nous pouvons traduire le *dominium* dans des relations de réel pouvoir, car nous sommes libres. Un individu exerce un pouvoir sur les autres car il dispose d'une *facultas dominandi*, mais il ne peut l'exercer légitimement que parce que les autres ont accepté qu'il l'exerce. Finalement, l'autorité politique et les droits sont justifiés ontologiquement par la liberté ; par ailleurs, l'autorité politique peut être exercée seule à la suite d'un consentement initial, si bien que le pouvoir absolu est justifié par ce consentement initial, car la créature *in naturalibis* ne peut pas faire n'importe quoi [2]. Il faut noter qu'il vaut mieux éviter de parler d'un contractualisme olivien : il y a d'anciennes querelles à propos du contractualisme de Scot, et il est inutile de les reproduire. Il suffit de remarquer que le contrat politique d'Olivi, s'il y a contrat, est un contrat vide, sans contenu, car il ne parle jamais, au moins à ma connaissance, des délibérations concernant les règles que les parties ont établies pour la société. Si bien que le contrat bilatéral qui en découle – le pouvoir politique – est délié de tout lien : je renonce à une partie de ma liberté, et je te la donne afin que tu exerces le pouvoir (c'est-à-dire, la libre *facultas imperativa*), étant donné que tu acceptes ce rôle [3]. Selon Olivi, la renonciation n'est pas un acte qui demande une relation hiérarchique, mais seulement la liberté, car chacun peut renoncer à son droit, également en vue du bien commun : justement, le seul cas qui supprime cette liberté est celui du supérieur qui ordonne l'exercice du droit en vue du bien commun [4].

Seul le consentement est nécessaire, et c'est déjà beaucoup, pour la légitimation de l'autorité politique : ce consentement est défini comme un acte (unilatéral) de la volonté qui est nécessairement « *a nobis, ita quod voluntas tanquam ex se operetur* » et cette modalité de l'opération de la volonté se passe quand « *nullius alterius agentis impulsu, sed solum ex proprio motu agens in*

1. Pierre de Jean Olivi, *QPI*, p. 318.

2. *Ibidem*, p. 319.

3. *Ibidem*, p. 319.

4. Pierre de Jean Olivi, *QPE* 13, éd. L. Oliger, p. 358. Pour moi, cette notion de « bien comun » n'est pas la même chez saint Thomas, mais l'importance de la dignité de la personne est la même (*Cf.* J.M. Trigeaud, « L'ordination du bien commun au respect de la personne dans la philosophie politique thomiste », dans *Actes du IXe Congrès Thomiste International*, Rome, 1991, t. 4, ensuite in J.M. Trigeaud, *Éléments d'une philosophie politique*, Bordeaux, 1993).

actum se accomodat» [1]. Nous sommes face à une thèse de volontarisme politique, mais pas à un contractualisme politique au sens moderne : son issue, par un processus de droit positif (*ex pactione*), est le pouvoir absolu du monarque qui «*potest precipere vel dissolvere leges et precepta diversissima et innumera et precepta spectantia ad bella et alia spectantia ad intrinsecum et pacificum statum civium*» et «*omnia etiam hec facit solo imperio, non per modum naturalis agentis*» [2].

Une fois conféré ce pouvoir absolu, les individus n'ont pas de contrôle direct sur ce pouvoir : ils y ont renoncé, ils ne peuvent plus l'exercer. N'y a-t-il donc aucune limite au pouvoir du souverain ? Nous l'avons déjà suggéré, son exercice est vraiment absolu, mais il peut être borné par les libertés politiques qui sont fondées dans la même liberté qui justifie le pouvoir absolu. Mais la liberté politique n'est pas une modalité de l'exercice du pouvoir, elle est simplement une limite. Afin de mieux comprendre cette idée, il faut se rappeler que dans la *Summa fratris Alexandri* [3], on a avancé l'idée que le péché originel a provoqué une rupture dans le système juridique. L'ordre juridique avant la Chute est constitué par des droits qui sont radicalement différents de ceux qui existent après la Chute : avant la Chute, il n'y avait pas de propriété, il y avait seulement le *dominium* naturel sur les choses. Mais après la Chute, pour remédier à l'inclination mauvaise des hommes, la propriété individuelle a été constituée par le droit positif humain, en établissant aussi un système juridique humain entier. Ainsi, le droit naturel n'est pas la forme du droit de ce monde : la thèse tommasienne est repoussée à l'avance, il n'y a pas une échelle des normes de la loi éternelle à la loi humaine, mais une rupture radicale. Le droit humain ne peut pas s'inspirer du droit naturel, car le droit humain est conçu par une nature pécheresse ; au contraire, le droit naturel est le *status* de la nature humaine sans tache. Comme l'a très bien illustré Tarello à propos de Bonagrazia de Bergamo [4], dans la polémique contre le pape Jean XXII, les franciscains ont poussé l'interprétation du canon *Dilectissimis* [5] jusqu'à proposer la plus explicite différence entre le droit naturel et le droit positif : les franciscains renoncent au droit positif (et à ses protections) et veulent se prévaloir du droit naturel, donc ils peuvent utiliser les choses sans aucun droit (c'est-à-dire, positif). Le pape, qui ne pouvait pas accepter de faire une différence si rigoureuse entre le droit naturel et le droit humain, devait condamner le fondement évangélique de la thèse franciscaine dans la bulle *Cum inter nonnullos*.

Olivi s'était déjà posé la question du pouvoir pontifical et il avait déjà essayé de limiter la plénitude de son pouvoir. Si la liberté politique est la réponse du citoyen au gouvernement oppresseur, il est vrai que, chez Olivi, il n'y a pas de théorie politique de la société civile : il établit la possibilité métaphysique d'une

1. Pierre de Jean Olivi, *In II Sent.*, q. 57, t. 2, p. 329.

2. Pierre de Jean Olivi, *QPI*, p. 322.

3. Alexandre de Halès, *Summa theologica*, l. III, pars 2, inq. 2, q. 4, mem. 3, cc. 2-3 (Ad Claras Aquas, 1948, vol. IV, p. 362-364).

4. G. Tarello, *Profili giuridici della questione della povertà, cit.*

5. Friedberg, c. XII, q. 1, c. 2.

telle réponse, mais il est convaincu que la société la plus importante est la société spirituelle. Il est très attaché, bien sûr, comme tout frère mineur, à l'analyse de la vie concrète des hommes, et ses travaux économiques en sont la meilleure illustration[1]; mais il faudra attendre au moins Scot, sinon Ockham, pour voir se dégager une théorie politique de la société. Chez Olivi il n'y a pas non plus de véritable théorie générale du droit: il anticipe le volontarisme juridique du *De perfectione statuum*[2], de Scot, mais il n'est pas vraiment intéressé par une théorie générale d'un système qui n'a pas une telle importance à ses yeux. Pourtant si on considère le pouvoir spirituel, le problème de la limitation du pouvoir absolu du Pape afin d'éviter le danger de l'Antéchrist devient assez sensible. La réponse politique d'Olivi est *prima facie* surprenante : afin de limiter le pouvoir absolu du Pape, qui représente :

> *[...] summa potestas diffiniendi questiones et dubia fidei et omnes maiores ecclesie causas*[3] et peut *novam legem condere de quocunque [..] et in omni tali et etiam in omni sententiali et autentica expositione dubiorum cristiane legis et fidei est sibi credendum et obediendum, nisi aperte esset contraria fidei Christi et legi*[4],

il arrive à proclamer l'infaillibilité du Pape en ne développant que l'espace de cette clause « *nisi aperte* ».

En premier lieu, il utilise, de façon beaucoup plus implicite que Scot ou Ockham[5], la notion de pouvoir ordonné : « *eo ipso quo Deus vult et pro tempore quo hoc vult, habet in se ordinem predicte voluntatis Dei* »[6], en suggérant que l'action du législateur humain est également ordonnée par ses propres lois. Il avance aussi la différence entre l'action *de iure* et celle *de facto*, à la même manière que Scot, pour justifier la forme du pouvoir humain sur le modèle du pouvoir divin[7]. Ensuite, il récupère la différence entre le droit avant la Chute et le droit après la Chute : l'ordre immuable des lois, « *quod Deus non potest nec debet oppositum eius velle* », est appelé « *ordo naturalis* », et il est opposé à l'ordre du « *dominativo imperio* », l'autre sphère normative qui peut voir ses règles changer « *seu absolute seu conditionaliter pro libitu* »[8].

1. *Cf.* l'introduction de G. Todeschini, *Un trattato di economia politica francescana*, Roma, 1980; *Idem, Il prezzo della salvezza*, Firenze, 1994.
2. Parmi les autres passages de cet ouvrage édité dans l'édition Vivès (Paris, 1895) de l'*Opera omnia* de Scot, on peut voir le paragraphe 49, *ad XIVum*, vol. XXVI, p. 533. L'attribution à Scot est contestée, mais contre l'avis d'Ephrem Longpré (*La philosophie du B. Duns Scot*, Paris, 1924, p. 19-22), on peut croire que le *terminus ad quem* est de 1317 (*Cf.* G.J. Kirby, « The Authenticity of the *De perfectione statuum* of Duns Scot », *The New Scholasticism* 7, 1933, p. 134-152; B. Tierney, *Origins of Papal Infallibility. 1150-1350*, Leiden, 1972, p. 169, in note; il faut aussi souligner que dans la *Summa astesana* (1317 – l. VI, tit. XLVII, a. 1) on trouve la thèse principale du *De perfectione statum*, c'est-à-dire l'idée que l'état de perfection des religieux est supérieur à celui des prélats; l'ouvrage prend position contre Henri de Gand; *cf.* F. Lajard, *Henri de Gand, cit.*, p. 195-196).
3. Pierre de Jean Olivi, *QPE* 13, éd. L. Oliger, p. 347.
4. *Ibidem*, p. 351. *Cf.* aussi *Qind.*, p. 72-73
5. *Cf.* O. Boulnois, éd., *La puissance et son ombre. De Pierre Lombard à Luther*, Paris, 1994.
6. Pierre de Jean Olivi, *QPI*, p. 323.
7. Pierre de Jean Olivi, *QPE* 13, p 363.
8. Pierre de Jean Olivi, *QPI*, p. 324.

J'ai déjà essayé d'illustrer la position d'Olivi concernant l'infaillibilité pontificale[1], dans le but de travailler sur le guide indiqué par Capitani[2]. J'avais défendu la thèse selon laquelle Olivi est le défenseur de l'infaillibilité pontificale, car le Pape est la règle *inerrabili* de l'Église[3]; or, je crois qu'il faut une définition préalable du mot « infaillibilité » pour éliminer de nombreuses équivoques.

Dans un premier sens, qui peut être identifié au dogme actuel de l'infaillibilité pontificale, nous sommes dans la situation d'un sujet qui est sûrement le pape (nous le savons par des critères plus ou moins complexes, qui renvoient à la procédure de son élection ainsi qu'à d'autres normes de procédure) : ses décisions prises en sa qualité d'acteur infaillible sont nécessairement infaillibles. A l'intérieur d'un pareil schéma, l'infaillibilité assure le pouvoir de déterminer la Vérité à un sujet qui a reçu, par des procédures indépendantes, la qualification de pape. Le pape est le dernier juge en matière de foi.

Dans un second sens, nous sommes dans la situation d'un sujet qui est *prima facie* le pape (nous connaissons les procédures de l'élection, mais ces règles ne peuvent pas assurer la qualité de pape, sinon *prima facie*) : ses décisions doivent être infaillibles, il faut ainsi les confronter à la Révélation et à la Tradition de l'Église. Si ces décisions sont conformes à la Révélation et à la Tradition, alors le sujet *prima facie* pape est un vrai pape; si ces décisions ne sont pas du tout conformes à la foi et aux mœurs, alors le sujet *prima facie* pape n'est pas en réalité le pape, car le pape est infaillible. Dans ce schéma, l'infaillibilité agit comme une limite du sujet qui a reçu par élection la qualification de pape. Le pape est jugé par le théologien, et s'il est en conflit avec la foi de l'Église, sans aucun procès[4], il n'est plus pape *ipso facto*.

Donc, dans le second sens, Olivi a cru en l'infaillibilité pontificale; c'était un moyen de limiter le pouvoir absolu du pape. Olivi raisonne de façon classique, mais radicale : traditionnellement on croyait que le pape ne pouvait changer la foi et les mœurs de l'Église, ni les décisions des quatre premiers Conciles Œcuméniques. Cela signifie que le pape n'a pas de *iurisdictio* sur la foi et les mœurs de l'Église : dans toute autre matière, il dispose d'un pouvoir absolu, il peut établir des normes, mais dans le cadre de la Révélation et la Tradition, il ne peut établir aucune norme, il ne peut que déclarer la foi et les mœurs, car elles sont des vérités immuables, présentes dans la Bible, dont l'exégèse n'est pas de la compétence du

1. J'ai illustré ma position dans L. Parisoli, « La formazione del concetto di infallibilità pontificia, da Pietro di Giovanni Olivi a Guglielmo di Ockham », *C.F.* 67, 1997, p. 431-458. Après un échange épistolaire avec Fr. Johannes Schlageter, je suis persuadé de la nécessité d'une analyse qui débarrasse la discussion au moins des plus lourdes ambiguïtés terminologiques : comme le disait Descartes dans son ouvrage *Regulae ad directionem ingenii*, « *si de verborum significatione inter Philosophos semper convenerit fere, omnes illorum controversiae tollerentur* » (*Œuvres de Descartes*, Paris, 1986, t. 10).

2. O. Capitani, « Il francescanesimo ed il papato da Bonaventura a Pietro di Giovanni Olivi : una riconsiderazione », *Ricerche storiche* 13, 1983, p. 595-611.

3. En s'appuyant sur l'usage linguistique d'Olivi (*Cf. QPE* 12, éd. M. Maccarrone, p. 325), on a proposé d'utiliser le mot « inerrable » à la place d'« infaillible ». J'espère justifier ma préférence pour le mot « infaillible » (au moins, c'est un mot de la langue française).

4. Le renvoi à *QPE* 13, éd. L. Oliger, p. 353, montre qu'il n'y a qu'un pouvoir de procédure exceptionnel chez les cardinaux, et non un rôle de juges.

pouvoir pontifical, mais de celle des théologiens. Un autre raisonnement d'Olivi pour assurer sa démonstration est de faire la différence entre le pape comme individu et le pape comme fonction [1], une discussion tout à fait étrangère au droit canonique de l'époque : le premier est le pape qui peut se tromper (selon la Tradition canonique), le second est le pape infaillible, car il est défini comme tel (si le premier se trompe, il n'est plus revêtu de la fonction pontificale).

On trouve la même solution chez Ockham [2], et c'est l'attitude contraire à celle de Scot, qui ne conteste jamais la *iurisdictio* la plus étendue du pape [3]. L'infaillibilité du pape est la première sorte de liberté politique (c'est-à-dire, spirituelle) qu'Olivi confiait aux membres de l'Église en sauvegarde de la Vérité éternelle. Les droits fondamentaux de l'homme ne sont pas que le déplacement au niveau simplement humain de tels schémas, si l'on passe de la défense de l'aspiration à l'état de perfection (avant le péché) des frères mineurs contre les contraintes du droit humain aux *relecciones* de Vitoria, beaucoup plus riches en suggestions franciscaines (dans le domaine juridique et politique) qu'on ne croit.

1. *Ibidem*, p. 361.

2. Le sujet est controversé, à mon avis, par manque de précision analytique dans le langage (*Cf.* J.J. Ryan, « Evasion and Ambiguity : Ockham and Tierney's Ockham », *Franc. Stud.* 24, 1986, p. 285-294 ; B. Tierney, « Ockham's Infallibility and Ryan's Infallibility », p. 295-300. Pour un avis contraire au mien, J. Kilcullen, « Ockham and Infallibility », *Journal of Religious History* 16, 1991, p. 387-409 ; pour une tentative de « banalisation » de la thèse d'Ockham, A.S. McGrade, « William of Ockham and Augustinus de Ancona on the Righteousness of Dissent », *Franc. Stud*, 1994-1997, p. 143-165).

3. E. Longpré, « Le B. Jean Duns Scot pour le Saint-Siège et contre le gallicanisme », *La France franciscaine* 11, 1928, p. 137-162.

AUTOUR DE PIERRE DE JEAN OLIVI. NARBONNE ET LE NARBONNAIS, FIN XIIIe – DÉBUT XIVe SIÈCLE

Gilbert Larguier

« Le contexte historique des difficultés qu'a connues Olivi nous sera compréhensible le jour seulement où nous pourrons acquérir une connaissance de l'environnement immédiat où il a vécu » écrivait naguère un des plus fins exégèses de la pensée de Pierre de Jean Olivi au terme d'un ouvrage qui tentait d'en présenter une synthèse[1]. Cette remarque qui s'inscrit dans l'effort de compréhension de l'œuvre du franciscain, si fascinante par sa profondeur et sa diversité, attire l'attention sur les conditions de son élaboration. La précocité avec laquelle Pierre de Jean Olivi affirme son indépendance, l'originalité de sa pensée – où il faudrait voir la raison pour laquelle il n'obtiendrait pas la maîtrise à l'issue de ses études à Paris ; il a vingt ans à peine alors –, les condamnations dont il fut la cible de la part de son ordre et l'obstination à le réduire au silence, plus encore après sa mort que de son vivant, aiguisent l'intérêt en effet pour les conditions dans lesquelles elle fut produite et connue autour de lui.

On peut s'interroger cependant : cette démarche dont l'ambition est légitime n'est-elle pas prématurée encore et donc aventurée ? Olivi est entièrement absorbé par sa méditation en effet, à la fois humble – ce n'est pas un rebelle, il le montre à Avignon en 1283 –, exigeante, éprise de cohérence et qui ne dévie jamais de la voie qu'elle s'est tracée. Les difficultés qu'il rencontra n'eurent probablement pas pour cette raison d'effet inhibiteur sur son activité intellectuelle. Au contraire, d'où sa richesse et la tension qui la traverse.

On aperçoit mal dans cette œuvre la part des contingences du siècle depuis les premières années de sa jeunesse à Sérignan, opaques, jusqu'à son dernier séjour à Narbonne. Faut-il s'en préoccuper d'ailleurs puisque, on le sait, il y a un « fossé entre la haute culture universitaire et les tensions de la société » que n'ont jamais tenté de réduite les penseurs de ce temps[2] ? Ne court-on pas le risque suivant : solliciter avec trop d'insistance les événements, le contexte local pour rendre compte des inflexions et du développement de la pensée olivienne, ce qui aurait un effet contre-productif car réducteur et contraire à l'indication que donne la

1. D. Burr, *L'histoire de Pierre Olivi, franciscain persécuté*, Fribourg-Paris, 1997, p. 271.

2. F.X. Putallaz, *Insolente liberté. Controverses et condamnations au XIIIe siècle*, Fribourg-Paris, 1995, p. X.

mention de son décès qui veut qu'une « illumination » reçue à Paris ait tracé sa voie à Pierre de Jean. Que fut celle-ci [1] ? on n'en sait rien pour l'instant, mais son emprise orienterait dans le sens d'une cohérence interne forte de la démarche olivienne qui réduirait à peu de choses la résonance des événements étrangers à ses champs de préoccupation, amplifiant au contraire ceux qui les concernaient.

L'ampleur prise par le mouvement béguin à Narbonne, Béziers et Montpellier après la mort du frère Olivi, la liaison étroite entre le courant spirituel et le mouvement béguin, la démarche effectuée en 1316 par les deux consulats de Narbonne et celui de Béziers en faveur des Spirituels obligent à s'interroger sur la réception des idées d'Olivi. On insiste essentiellement sur l'exemplarité de la vie d'Olivi et ses idées sur la pauvreté qui étaient les plus immédiatement accessibles à un public peu au fait des disputes savantes. D'autres aspects de sa pensée sont peut-être concernés. On ne peut qu'être frappé en effet par ce rapprochement : Narbonne fut le théâtre de débats et de luttes de grande ampleur entre 1290 et la fin de la décennie 1320-1330, au moment où Olivi résida à Narbonne et où le mouvement béguin eut son plus grand développement, avant que la répression ne l'épuise. Rien ne permet pour l'instant d'établir formellement une relation de cause à effet. La meilleure approche est de tenter, sans chercher à solliciter de trop près l'œuvre d'Olivi dont le cheminement n'est pas encore complètement élucidé, de décrire le terrain olivien par excellence qui est celui où le béguinisme eut l'intensité la plus forte.

De Sérignan a Narbonne : un espace olivien

Né à proximité de la Méditerranée, à Sérignan, entré à douze ans au couvent franciscain de la ville voisine, Béziers, Pierre de Jean Olivi meurt à Narbonne en 1298. Itinéraire d'une vie longue d'un demi-siècle marquée par ses trois naissances – au monde, à l'ordre et à une mission, à la vie éternelle – au cœur du Languedoc. Ces trois localités de taille différente tracent un territoire aux dimensions réduites, auquel Olivi ne s'est pas borné puisqu'il est à Paris dès 1266 – il a dix-huit ans à peine – mais auquel il est resté fidèle.

Sérignan, Béziers et Narbonne sont tout à fait représentatifs du Languedoc en cette fin du XIIIe siècle. Sérignan est proche du littoral, d'un fleuve – l'Orb –, d'un étang côtier – celui de Vendres. Une position très avancée sur le bord du golfe du Lion qui n'a fixé en bordure de la mer aucune communauté d'habitants. Sérignan, probablement, était plus proche de la côte qu'elle n'est aujourd'hui, à proximité d'une passe – *gradus de Serinhano* – par où s'effectuait la communication avec la

1. S'agit-il d'une intuition centrale, comparable à celle qu'eut Descartes le 10 novembre 1619 alors qu'il était dans son poêle – une pièce chauffée près d'Ulm –, au cours d'une véritable nuit d'exaltation mystique, on le sait, qui lui assigna une véritable mission : trouver le principe de la science en lui-même, appliquer le raisonnement mathématique aux phénomènes de la nature, reconstituer le véritable système de l'univers ?

Méditerranée[1]. Ce grau, l'un des cinq ou six passages permanents que comptait cette côte sableuse du Languedoc, explique Sérignan et lui donne son importance.

Par de modestes embarcations et des allèges, il était possible de pratiquer la pêche côtière, d'atteindre des bateaux marchands qui stationnaient en mer sur lesquels on transbordait les marchandises, de participer à une navigation de cabotage. Sérignan profite de l'absence d'un port important à proximité pour fixer une vie maritime qui était loin d'être négligeable à l'échelle du Languedoc. La bourgade, reliée à Béziers par l'Orb modeste et la voie terrestre, servait de débouché à la ville voisine, se trouvait directement associée par là au développement des échanges. On sait que des marchands biterrois pratiquaient au début du XIVe siècle le commerce avec l'Italie méridionale et le Levant en association avec des Narbonnais et des gens de Montpellier[2]. Le mer offre une ouverture à Sérignan, une facilité de communication avec les îles Baléares et la Méditerranée occidentale[3].

Les sources manquent pour se faire une idée de l'importance exacte de Sérignan, de Béziers, et des communautés voisines au milieu du XIIIe siècle. Béziers comptait 3 619 feux sur les 100 000 de la sénéchaussée de Carcassonne en 1304, soit plus de 15 000 habitants. Sérignan, lors du dénombrement effectué en 1344 à l'occasion du projet de démembrement de la viguerie de Béziers, faisait partie des communautés les plus peuplées du Biterrois, à bonne distance d'Agde, de Montagnac, mais à peu près à égalité avec Pézenas qui avaient tiré parti de l'essor des échanges. Elle devait compter de 1 200 à 1 500 habitants[4]; une population suffisante déjà pour qu'avec sa double vocation maritime et agricole une différenciation sociale y soit nettement perceptible[5]. L'établissement d'une collégiale à Sérignan est un signe indiscutable de l'importance qu'on lui reconnaissait. Dans le diocèse voisin – pour se limiter à un seul exemple –, Capestang qui possédait également une collégiale était à la même date le lieu le plus peuplé après Narbonne. Si l'on n'a pas d'indication précise sur le milieu familial dont Olivi était issu, au moins sait-on qu'il naquit dans une communauté relativement importante, étroitement liée à la ville voisine, ouverte sur l'extérieur.

Celle-ci l'était davantage, ou différemment, qu'aujourd'hui. La mer ou les étangs bordiers pénétraient beaucoup plus à l'intérieur des terres entre l'Orb et le cap Leucate que de nos jours : jusqu'aux abords de Capestang, qui pour cette raison disposait de salines. Narbonne était pratiquement accessible par les étangs depuis Sérignan et Vendres alors que par terre il fallait aller jusqu'à Capestang

1. Le « château de Sérignan qui est à un mille de la mer dans le diocèse de Béziers », dans R. Manselli, *Spirituels et Béguins du Midi*, trad. de J. Duvernoy, éd. Privat, Toulouse, 1989, p. 45 n. 1.

2. J. Combes, « Le port de Sérignan au XIVe siècle et au XVe siècle », *Annales du Midi* 62, 1950, p. 15-20; *Id.*, « Béziers dans les premières décennies du XVe siècle », XLIIIe Congrès de la fédération historique du Languedoc méditerranéen et du Roussillon, *Béziers et le Biterrois*, Montpellier, 1971, p. 222-223.

3. R. Manselli, *op. cit.*, p. 187.

4. M. Bourin-Derruau, *Villages médiévaux en Languedoc: genèse d'une sociabilité (X[e]-XIVe siècle)*, Paris, 1987, 2 vol., t. 2, p. 213-221, carte p. 214-215.

5. Différenciation sociale ancienne, comme on l'aperçoit avec les structures foncières, *cf.* M. Bourin-Derruau, *op. cit.*, t. 1, p. 112.

pour contourner la lagune : une configuration où les fleuves, les étangs et la mer mettaient en communication Sérignan, Béziers et Narbonne [1].

Sérignan ne peut se comparer, certes, aux deux autres villes. Sa dimension la place au seuil à partir d'où s'esquissent des fonctions à caractère urbain, alors que Narbonne qui possédait une communauté juive importante dépassait peut-être 30 000 habitants. Le siège de l'archevêché égale Bordeaux, Toulouse, Montpellier, Marseille. Béziers est au nombre des villes de second rang en Languedoc, avec Carcassonne et Nîmes [2]. Narbonne est ainsi au centre d'un réseau urbain méridional compris entre l'Atlantique et la côte méditerranéenne qui joignait Bordeaux et Valence en Espagne à Marseille, dont l'originalité était d'être hiérarchisé en strates d'organismes d'importance à peu près identique : un premier étage de centres de 5 à 8 000 habitants, un second de 12 à 18 000 habitants dont Béziers faisait partie, des grandes villes peuplées de 30 à 35 000 habitants. Narbonne et Béziers occupaient une place de choix dans ce réseau urbain méridional qui comptait en Europe au début du XIVe siècle. Narbonne tenait en effet un rang honorable parmi les villes du royaume puisque cinq ou six villes seulement possédaient davantage d'habitants qu'elle [3].

Pierre de Jean Olivi est donc un citadin depuis sa jeunesse, qui passe de longues années en Languedoc, au cours de sa formation universitaire à Paris, plus tard à Florence où il enseigne, dans les villes les plus peuplées et les plus actives de l'Occident. Il n'est pas infondé de parler d'un espace olivien, étroit ou plus large, dont les caractères ont contribué sinon à orienter des aspects de la pensée du frère, du moins à conditionner une géographie des sympathies qu'il s'était attirées. Celles-ci sont le fait d'hommes et de femmes originaires ou habitants de villes et de bourgades identiques à celles dont Olivi fut natif et où il vécut [4].

Accumulation de richesse et pauvreté

Insister sur la ville – la grande, voire la très grande ville – comme cadre de vie d'Olivi consiste à revenir encore davantage qu'on ne l'a fait, s'il est possible, sur la pauvreté évangélique dont il s'était fait un des apôtres les plus fervents. Pauvreté, est-il besoin de le rappeler, qui n'est pas le dénuement ou l'incertitude du lendemain, mais le détachement des biens de ce monde – une forme d'abstinence – qui laisse libre et n'interdit pas de s'intéresser avec profondeur et comme de l'intérieur à l'échange des biens ainsi qu'à la valeur du facteur temps dans les échanges. Le paradoxe entre la pauvreté choisie, comme règle de vie, et la réflexion sur la circulation des biens, n'est pas aussi grand qu'il paraît au premier

1. L'Aude traversait Narbonne et avait son embouchure plus au sud. Elle n'emprunte son cours actuel que dans la première moitié du XIVe siècle.

2. Auxquelles il faut ajouter Perpignan qui est alors en pleine croissance.

3. G. Larguier, *Le drap et le grain en Languedoc. Narbonne et Narbonnais, 1300-1789*, Presses universitaires de Perpignan, 2e éd. 1999, p. 61-74.

4. R. Manselli, *op. cit.*, p. 213-218.

abord. La question est davantage de savoir où Olivi acquit sa formation, comment il développa son intérêt et nourrit sa réflexion, car cela suppose des relations suivies avec des gens d'affaires. Il faudrait disposer de noms pour cela, reconstituer des réseaux d'échanges, les pratiques concernant les sujets auquel il s'intéressait, à moins que l'on suggère l'hypothèse – mais on ne dispose d'aucun élément pour la soutenir – qu'Olivi avait été éveillé, à partir de l'observatoire sérignanais, aux techniques du commerce et du crédit que dispensait la ville [1].

Seule certitude: les villes où passe successivement Olivi – Béziers, Montpellier, Paris, Florence, Avignon, Narbonne, etc. – étaient en pleine vigueur ainsi que les campagnes qui les entouraient. Béziers, Narbonne plus encore, sont tout à fait représentatives à cet égard. Narbonne était un centre drapier de premier ordre, le premier assurément du Languedoc dès le milieu du XIIIe siècle, ce qui explique l'importance de sa population. La vieille cité romaine connaissait alors une de ses phases d'expansion les plus remarquables de son histoire. On y faisait toutes les opérations de la fabrication des draps. 41 % des artisans de la Cité, le côté de ville au sommet duquel les franciscains construisirent leur maison, travaillaient le textile en 1278, dont 45 tisserands, 95 pareurs, 114 foulons et 17 teinturiers. La draperie ainsi que le négoce étaient encore plus développés en Bourg, l'autre partie de la ville [2]. La réussite des Narbonnais venait de ce qu'ils étaient parvenus à fabriquer les draps, à les apprêter, à les négocier et même à les écouler dans les lieux jusqu'où ils les transportaient car le principal marché des *blanchs* ou *blanquets* de la fabrique de Narbonne se situait au sud, en Catalogne, dans le royaume de Valence, et de là dans toute l'Espagne. Ces exportations avaient pris de l'ampleur dès le premier tiers du XIIIe siècle. Les plus anciens tarifs des leudes de Catalogne les mentionnent. Du côté de l'est, les *blanquets* de Narbonne furent les premiers produits de l'industrie languedocienne à faire leur apparition sur le marché montpelliérain. Montpellier, via le cycle de foires de Montagnac et de Pézenas qui s'organisait au cours de la seconde moitié du XIIIe siècle, en liaison directe avec l'essor de la draperie en Haut-Languedoc, n'était qu'une étape aux mains du négoce local ou de marchands italiens. Les Narbonnais, par contre, se plaçaient en position hégémonique à Valence à la fin du XIIIe siècle puisqu'ils vendaient 90 % des draps qui s'y négociaient [3]. Olivi fut donc le témoin direct ou indirect des conquêtes de la draperie languedocienne, de la mise en place des circuits économiques dont on aperçoit à peu près les routes, les points de rencontre, mais beaucoup plus mal le volume ainsi que les modalités des transactions financières auxquelles elles donnaient lieu.

1. M. Bourin-Derruau, *op. cit.*, vol. 2, p. 84-85. Pour Narbonne nous ne connaissons à peu près rien sur le commerce et quelques noms à peine avant le XIVe siècle, aucun registre de notaire n'a été conservé avant l'extrême fin du XVe siècle.

2. Narbonne était composée de deux parties distinctes, Cité et Bourg, de part et d'autre de l'Aude. Chacune a son consulat. L'union des deux consulats n'interviendra qu'en 1338.

3. G. Romestan, « Les marchands languedociens dans le royaume de Valence pendant la première moitié du XIVe siècle », dans *Bulletin philologique et historique*, 1969, vol. 1, p. 115-192.

L'élaboration des statuts de métiers dont les premiers qui sont rédigés à Narbonne datent de 1254[1], témoigne de la maturation de la draperie. Les attributions de chacune des spécialités sont soigneusement distinguées à la fin du XIIIe siècle. La rédaction des statuts contribue à sanctionner et à accuser la division du travail ainsi que les écarts sociaux. L'organisation de la production et le développement du négoce vont de pair en effet. Des pareurs forment de véritables entreprises à caractère familial. On ne peut saisir complètement à cause de l'insuffisance des sources, les corrélations exactes entre la croissance de la population, l'immigration, le développement des différentes spécialités dans les villes, voire à Narbonne le déplacement des activités d'un quartier à l'autre, qui n'ont pas été sans effet sur le mouvement des idées, ne serait-ce qu'en leur offrant un public réceptif. On sait les liens qui se nouent précocement entre les Spirituels et certains milieux du textile. Le développement connexe d'une accumulation du capital et de thèses radicales n'est pas fortuit.

Une tension identique, dont l'expression est différente, est perceptible dans les campagnes proches de la ville. Le Narbonnais compte peu de communautés où la population dépasse un millier d'habitants, contrairement aux vallées de l'Orb et de l'Hérault où les sols de bonne qualité sont plus étendus qu'aux abords de l'Aude. Les conflits pour la terre et son utilisation éclatent d'abord et prennent une tournure conflictuelle dans des zones où la densité de la population n'est pas la plus forte, ce qui peut apparaître contradictoire au premier abord. Cela tient à la conjonction d'une série de facteurs qui n'ont guère de relations entre eux au départ. Un marché de la terre où les citadins purent intervenir ne s'est pas constitué jusque très tard dans le XIVe siècle. Les plus anciens compoix ruraux ainsi que les reconnaissances seigneuriales montrent une très faible emprise citadine sur la terre, même à proximité immédiate de la ville. Les marchands les plus en vue possédaient en propre, au plus, quelques parcelles dans le terroir citadin. Les croissances urbaine et rurale restent nettement distinctes à cet égard, ce qui ne sera pas sans effet sur l'image réciproque de la ville sur la campagne et de la campagne sur la ville.

Le vicomte que l'on peut considérer comme un citadin et les seigneurs fivatiers ruraux ne font pas preuve d'un grand dynamisme. Leur position s'était affaiblie au cours du XIIIe siècle. La croisade albigeoise et ses lendemains y avaient contribué. Il y avait eu peu de victimes à Narbonne et en Narbonnais, contrairement à Béziers. Les confiscations des biens des *faidits*, par contre, avaient fragilisé un peu plus des positions qui l'étaient déjà[2]. Ce ne sont pas cependant ces déboires qui eurent le plus de conséquences à terme bien qu'ils soient plus visibles et mieux connus. Ils accentuèrent un processus déjà engagé. L'événement majeur en Narbonnais – que l'on a peut-être tendance à exagérer car il fut producteur d'archives – est l'établissement des cisterciens à Fontfroide.

1. G. Mouynès, *Inventaire des archives communales de Narbonne antérieures à 1790*, Narbonne, 1871, Annexes de la série AA, document XLVI, p. 74-81. L'arbitrage entre les métiers est rendu par les consuls de Cité et de Bourg.

2. R.W. Emery, *Heresy and Inquisition in Narbonne*, New York, 1941, carte p. 171, appendice V, p. 171.

Installés à l'extrémité nord des Corbières, entre de petites communautés rurales aujourd'hui disparues – Saint-Pierre-des-Clars et Saint-Martin-de-Toques – ceux-ci n'avaient pas trouvé une table rase. Proches d'une ville où l'Église jouissait de fortes positions, ils venaient après d'autres fondations monastiques qui avaient eu le temps de se développer, comme celle des bénédictins de Lagrasse dans les Corbières. Certes, ils avaient bénéficié d'un important courant de sympathie qui s'était traduit par de nombreuses donations. Leur rapport à la terre, neuf à bien des égards, qui visait à constituer et mettre en valeur par leurs propres moyens de vastes exploitations d'un seul tenant, les avait engagés à se lancer dans une politique onéreuse d'acquisitions foncières, très active dans la seconde moitié du XIIe siècle et jusqu'au premier tiers du XIIIe siècle, servie par d'importants moyens financiers. Les religieux multiplient les achats dans la diagonale qui va de l'étang de Capestang à l'abbaye et se prolonge vers le sud, mettant à profit la fragmentation des patrimoines des laïcs. Artisans essentiels de la croissance rurale en Narbonnais, qui font produire des territoires restés inexploités jusque là comme les fonds lacustres situés entre l'Aude et l'étang de Capestang, les cisterciens se heurteront à une série de résistances de la part de l'Église citadine peu disposée à favoriser l'expansion de ce concurrent et des communautés rurales en mal d'espace.

Les modalités des croissances urbaine et rurale, très différentes car c'est une communauté religieuse visant à se placer à l'écart pour être maîtresse chez elle qui est la plus dynamique ici, le négoce, les individus et l'initiative privée qui s'imposent là, font se rejoindre la campagne et la ville sur les points suivants : l'accélération de la circulation des biens, l'accumulation de la richesse. Ces processus, nettement engagés dès la première moitié du XIIIe siècle arrivent à maturité, c'est-à-dire au stade où ils aigrissent les relations, suscitent des incidents, produisent des statuts et des règlements, dans la seconde moitié du siècle. L'espace olivien étroit, tel que nous l'avons délimité, constituait donc un observatoire privilégié, tant la rapidité et la netteté des évolutions qui s'y produisaient étaient prononcées. Il convient certainement d'en tenir le plus grand compte pour comprendre – par contraste – les succès franciscains, le prestige du frère Olivi, le choix radical de la pauvreté : une disposition intellectuelle et spirituelle pour mieux prendre ses distances à l'égard du monde tout en y étant immergé ; une proximité avec des milieux que faisaient grossir les écarts sociaux en train de s'accuser.

UNE MULTITUDE DE CONFLITS, EN MARGE DU FRÈRE ET DE SES ADMIRATEURS ?

Des tensions de tous ordres se manifestent donc avec une vigueur croissante au cours du XIIIe siècle. Autant la première moitié du siècle avait été dominée par l'hérésie, la croisade, l'intrusion du pouvoir royal, à la suite des barons français – par des luttes où les agents les plus actifs venaient de l'extérieur –, autant la seconde moitié du siècle voit se multiplier les différends et les difficultés au cœur même de la société urbaine ou rurale[1]. Les conflits qui sont le symptôme autant que l'expression de ces difficultés peuvent apparaître, si on les considère isolément, comme une série de poussées de fièvre indépendantes les unes des autres. Mis en relation, ils ne s'avèrent pas seulement producteurs de violence. Des tractations les accompagnent ou les suivent auxquelles participent des arbitres choisis par les parties, à l'occasion desquelles se développe et s'approfondit une réflexion sur la condition des individus, les relations entre les métiers et les groupes sociaux, les institutions communales. Nous sommes à un moment d'intense activité intellectuelle où la pensée trouve dans la société un champ d'action, d'expérimentation et de projection inédit.

La typologie et la chronologie des heurts qui se produisent en Narbonnais se recoupent largement. Jusqu'à la fin du XIIe siècle, les oppositions dressaient les unes contre les autres les « puissances », l'Église et les seigneurs laïcs, à la ville comme à la campagne. A partir du début du XIIIe siècle, elles sont éclipsées par les conflits entre les populations et ces mêmes « puissances », l'Église plus particulièrement. Les luttes âpres opposant les archevêques aux seigneurs laïcs, anciennes, se déroulaient à partir de la ville où les prélats et les vicomtes étaient face à face[2]. La compétition se transporte à l'intérieur de l'Église, entre les séculiers – l'archevêque et le chapitre cathédral – et les cisterciens. La dernière strate des fondations régulières, urbaine, sera seulement la spectatrice de ces luttes.

On aperçoit ces rapports de force avec la plus grande netteté dès que l'archevêque, le vicomte et les cisterciens se trouvent en contact. Les vicomtes n'opposent pas dans l'ensemble une grande résistance, voire se retirent. Les cisterciens, au contraire, s'engagent dans une vigoureuse offensive de conquête, investissent massivement. Ils parviennent à leurs fins à peu près partout, sauf lorsqu'ils se heurtent aux intérêts de l'archevêque. La lutte entre le prélat et Fontfroide s'engage dès que l'abbaye passe dans l'orbite cistercienne[3]. Les archevêques de Narbonne, à n'en pas douter, prennent rapidement ombrage des succès des cisterciens. S'ils les laissent progresser dans les zones où ils n'avaient que de médiocres intérêts, ils organisent une défense sans concession des territoires qu'ils contrôlaient. Ils font tout ce qui était en leur pouvoir pour décourager les tentatives d'expansion des cisterciens en direction du nord et de la côte, consolident leurs positions avec une persévérance égale à celle dont les moines de Fontfroide font preuve un siècle durant. Ces derniers tentent-ils de progresser en direction de l'étang de Capestang ? Ils achètent massivement pour empêcher de nouvelles acquisitions, si bien que les religieux préfèrent leur

1. Ce contraste, ainsi que le médiocre succès du catharisme à Narbonne alors que la ville sera le principal foyer des Spirituels et des Beguins, n'avait pas échappé à R.W. Emery.

2. E. Magnou-Nortier, *La société laïque et l'Église dans la province ecclésiastique de Narbonne de la fin du VIIIe siècle à la fin du XIe siècle*, Toulouse, 1974 ; J. Caille, « Origine et développement de la seigneurie temporelle de l'archevêque dans la ville et le terroir de Narbonne, IXe – XIIe siècle », dans *Narbonne, archéologie et histoire*, t. 2, Montpellier, 1973, p. 9-36.

3. Fontfroide est rattachée à l'abbaye de Grandselve en 1146.

rétrocéder les biens sur lesquels ils avaient pu mettre la main[1]. Les archevêques font de même dans toutes les communautés littorales où ils s'intéressent aux maisons, aux fiefs, aux tasques, aux censives, aux dîmes, aux salines. La défense du quasi monopole qu'ils exerçaient sur le sel fut une de leurs motivations principales. Cette confrontation séculaire eut une série de conséquences : elle contribua à augmenter considérablement le patrimoine de l'Église en Narbonnais, elle renforça les positions des séculiers et des réguliers dans leurs aires de domination respectives. La spécialisation foncière des cisterciens, à la différence de l'archevêque davantage intéressé par les seigneuries, les dîmes et les salines, explique pourquoi ils seront en première ligne dans les campagnes au cours de la seconde moitié du XIIIe siècle alors que les difficultés de l'archevêque auront la ville pour cadre.

Les archevêques mènent une action préventive à l'égard des cisterciens. Les villageois qui ne jouissaient d'aucun droit collectif ne disposaient pas de moyens pour s'opposer aux réunions de terres destinées à constituer des domaines d'un seul tenant. La rencontre conflictuelle entre les villageois et les religieux interviendra ultérieurement, un siècle après qu'eut débuté la confrontation entre l'archevêque et les cisterciens, lorsque l'espace viendra à manquer. Les besoins de terre augmentent avec la population. L'extension des parcelles mises en culture réduit les terrains de parcours du bétail à laine. Tout aussi graves que l'occupation du sol arable qui pendant longtemps n'avait pas entraîné de graves inconvénients étaient les interdictions de passage et d'accès aux points d'eau. Autant de motifs pour que les villageois se heurtent aux moines, surtout lorsque les pasteurs des différentes communautés se retrouvèrent face à face sur les limites de leurs territoires respectifs. Dire que le Narbonnais se transforma en un champ de bataille serait tout à fait exagéré. Mais partout où les cisterciens s'étaient installés à proximité de villages dont la population dépassait une centaine de feux, des incidents éclatèrent, graves, puisqu'on alla au-delà des rixes, banales : il y eut de véritables expéditions pour arracher des bodules de bornage, des fourches patibulaires[2].

Le consulat du Bourg de Narbonne soutint les habitants qui défendaient contre Fontfroide leurs droits de pacage. La ville a une avance considérable à cet égard. Un des aspects les plus intéressants des luttes rurales de la seconde moitié du XIIIe siècle est la maturation qu'elles paraissent accélérer dans les communautés où elles interviennent. Certes, une communauté comme Ouveillan dans le nord du Narbonnais, la plus populeuse du Narbonnais après Capestang, était au contact des principaux protagonistes des conflits : le vicomte, seigneur de la localité, l'archevêque présent à Montels où les cisterciens avaient dû lâcher prise, les moines de Fontfroide propriétaires du vaste territoire de Fontcalvy où ils édifiaient une grange fortifiée de façon à se défendre contre leurs remuants voisins, ... etc. Les affrontement favorisent l'éclosion des institutions commu-

1. G. Larguier, « Fontfroide et l'espace cistercien en Narbonnais. La grange de Fontcalvy », *L'espace cistercien*, Comité des travaux historiques, Paris, 1994, p. 70-84.

2. G. Larguier, « Un siècle de conflits en Narbonnais, Ouveillan, 1250-1350 », *Bulletin de la Commission archéologique de Narbonne* 38, 1976, p. 79-122.

nautaires – syndicat d'abord, puis consulat –, la rédaction de transactions avec l'abbaye, ainsi que des revendications pour la suppression des mansattes.

La question du droit du sol, des personnes et des collectivités se pose donc avec acuité. On aperçoit mal, malheureusement, même si on les pressent, les interrogations qui eurent lieu à ce sujet. Y eut-il interaction entre ces différents aspects ainsi qu'entre la campagne et la ville? Celle-ci, aussi, est traversée par d'importants débats sur lesquels on est mieux documenté. Comme il est impossible de les passer tous en revue, il vaut mieux en extraire un, celui qui eut les plus fortes résonances car l'ensemble de la population fut concerné. Il s'agit du développement des institutions municipales et de la fiscalité urbaine. On ignore le moment et les conditions exactes de la mise en place des institutions consulaires narbonnaises. Elles paraissent relativement tardives, puisque rares sont les textes explicites à leur égard antérieurs au milieu du XIIIe siècle. A l'inverse, le dernier tiers du siècle voit se multiplier les statuts obtenus sur la pression des habitants. Le premier qui nous intéresse, rédigé à la suite de laborieuses négociations, fut le résultat d'une sentence arbitrale rendue entre les consuls et les habitants du Bourg portant sur le mode, la forme, les époques de l'élection consulaire, ainsi que sur les droits et les obligations des consuls [1]. L'analyse de ce texte, même succincte, n'a pas sa place ici. Remarquons seulement la qualité des arbitres choisis: un juriste, le sacristain majeur de Saint-Paul, l'abbé de Fontfroide. Elle s'explique par leur appartenance au Bourg, où Fontfroide possédait un enclos. Le Bourg se comporte en cité autonome et indépendante où les règles qui le régissent et concernent les citadins sont fixées par contrat. De telles procédures étaient communes : le Languedoc appartient à cette culture de l'arbitrage. Ceux qui les mettent en œuvre avaient-ils une conception claire de la capacité des personnes à agir en association, le sentiment de participer à l'élaboration du droit? Ceci nous rapproche de thèmes éminemment oliviens. Certes, il s'agit de pratique, sollicitée, qui concernait des institutions déjà créées. Les arbitres ne pouvaient intervenir sans références.

La fiscalité était un terrain plus neuf que les institutions, où les pratiques restaient à préciser. Comme pour les institutions, on cerne mal la proto-fiscalité où se déterminent les bases sur lesquelles reposera la fiscalité urbaine. A-t-on affaire à une fiscalité de type méridional, ou chaque ville établit-elle de manière distincte son propre système? Il est trop tôt pour répondre. Des aspects spécifiques existent en effet, même si une convergence de similitudes n'est guère contestable, en particulier le recours, au moins partiel, à une fiscalité directe et par voie de conséquence la pratique des estimes pour évaluer les patrimoines.

Ceci est connu. Plus intéressants sont le moment où le système fiscal finit de se mettre en place ainsi que les péripéties qui l'accompagnent. Rares jusque là et peu précises, les sources concernant la fiscalité municipale augmentent sensiblement de volume à partir de 1290. Pendant plus d'un tiers de siècle, la fiscalité

1. *Archives municipales de Narbonne* (*A.M.N.*), AA 1023, f° 48-50, 11 octobre 1277; 27 mars-24 juillet 1278; G. Mouynès, Annexes de la série AA, *op. cit.*, document LXXXVII, p. 146-150. Quatre capitules font l'objet d'une nouvelle rédaction. Début d'une longue série de textes de même nature : G. Mouynès, documents CXI, CXII, CXIII.

devient l'objet principal des tensions urbaines qui impliquent le consulat, les habitants, les seigneurs de la ville, le pouvoir royal et même la papauté à qui l'on fit appel. Ces derniers, le pouvoir royal notamment auquel on prête généralement un rôle déterminant dans les origines de la fiscalité urbaine, n'intervinrent qu'en second lieu, sur la demande des protagonistes. Faut-il établir un lien entre l'arrivée de Gilles Aycelin sur le siège de Narbonne et le raidissement de l'Église à l'égard des prétentions des consuls à faire contribuer les clercs? L'official de l'archevêque défendit l'immunité des «personnes ecclésiastiques», ainsi que celle de tous les clercs mariés et non mariés, les sergents, des domestiques ou des personnes qui appartenaient à la cour de l'archevêque avec la plus grande énergie[1]. Tous les moyens furent employés : monitoires, censures ecclésiastiques contre les consuls qui avaient exercé leur droit de pignore contre les récalcitrants[2], violences physiques[3], excommunications même. L'épreuve de force entre l'Église et les deux consulats, de Cité et de Bourg, ne connut aucun répit pendant un tiers de siècle. En 1324 encore, les consuls en appelaient au roi des sentences d'excommunication qu'avaient prononcées contre eux l'official de l'archevêque[4].

Parallèlement – complémentairement? – à ces affrontements, s'en déroulent d'autres qui portent sur les taux d'imposition et la manière d'estimer. Deux sentences arbitrales, la première de 1294, la seconde de 1322[5], livrent ce qui posait problème et les réponses qui furent apportées. L'une et l'autre portaient principalement sur la manière d'estimer les biens puisqu'on ne modifiait pas le barème de *la tala de la viela antiqua*. On s'accorda en 1294 pour que tous les types de biens soient pris en compte et mis sur un pied d'égalité. Impôt de quotité proportionnelle, la taille devait être en principe conforme à l'échelle des fortunes. Cette stricte parité fut rapidement contestée. La balance ne parut pas juste dans une ville aussi industrieuse. Les propriétaires de biens immeubles n'acceptèrent pas longtemps sans murmure de se voir traités comme ceux qui tiraient le plus clair de leurs revenus de leurs boutiques et ateliers. Les propositions de Béranger d'Olargues, un chanoine de l'église cathédrale à qui on avait confié le soin de dégager un compromis, firent droit à ces objections: l'usage des biens, les revenus qu'ils procuraient, les plus-values et les moins-values seraient pris en

1. *A.M.N.*, CC 844, 17 octobre 1290. Sur tout ceci, *cf.* G. Larguier, «Genèse, structure et évolution de la fiscalité à Narbonne, XIIIe- XVe siècle», dans *La fiscalité des villes au Moyen Age (France méridionale, Catalogne et Castille)*, II, à paraître.

2. *Ibid.*, CC 1503, 31 mars 1291.

3. *Ibid.*, CC 1506, 5 novembre 1294, bail à ferme de la *quista* imposée sur les habitants de Bourg; les consuls exemptent les hommes et les femmes qui avaient été frappés par la verge vengeresse du seigneur (archevêque).

4. *Ibid.*, CC 1509, 1308 : exécution de lettres du sénéchal de Carcassonne à la suite des plaintes des habitants de Bourg défendant que les consuls soient empêchés d'imposer les tailles sur les habitants taillables; CC 1513, 1313 : exécution des lettres du sénéchal pour enjoindre l'official de l'archevêque de Narbonne de ne pas troubler les consuls dans la libre levée des tailles; CC 4114, 1315, CC 4415, CC 202, etc., 1323-1325 : appels au pape et au roi par les consuls de Bourg contre les censures ecclésiastiques dont ils viennent d'être l'objet, etc.

5. *A.M.N.*, AA 101, f° 47; AA 106, f° 48v, G. Mouynès, Annexes de la série AA, *op. cit.*, document CVII, p. 175-178 (1294); CC 1514, (1322).

considération, les locaux à usage lucratif seraient taxés le double des autres; ce qui impliquait une réflexion d'ordre économique.

Nous sommes au moment où des Béguins viennent d'être livré au bras séculier[1], où la querelle de la Pauvreté bat son plein à Narbonne[2]. Peut-on s'autoriser à établir une corrélation entre tous ces aspects? On en revient à la question initiale, des rapports entre le développement d'une pensée et les sollicitations du monde dans lequel on vit, même si l'on entend s'en dégager par une conception exigeante de la pauvreté. Reconnaissons ceci néanmoins : un regard porté sur un cadre territorial délibérément circonscrit montre qu'il n'était pas besoin de chercher loin, voire d'attendre l'établissement de la papauté à Avignon, pour être sensible à la critique d'une église riche, dominatrice, qui entendait soutenir l'exonération de quelque contribution que ce soit aux charges de la collectivité à tous ceux qui pouvaient se dire clercs, et à la pauvreté franciscaine.

De même, s'il y avait un écart considérable entre les hautes spéculations d'Olivi et les idées véhiculées par les opuscules rédigés après sa mort, entre la poignée d'hommes capables de saisir l'ampleur et la profondeur de sa pensée et le public d'artisans ou de gens humbles qui lui vouaient un culte, un espace existait, où se mouvait la majorité des citadins, voire des ruraux, en train de déterminer avec la participation sollicitée de membres éminents de l'Église locale, leurs modes de gouvernement et la participation solidaire aux charges communes. C'est dans cet intervalle large, au sein de strates intermédiaires auxquelles on s'est peu intéressé encore, que l'on rencontrera ceux qui ont fréquenté les Spirituels, les Béguins, mais également les consuls qui intervinrent en leur faveur, les familiers de l'archevêque ou le prélat lui-même[3]. La multitude, la diversité et les implications des tensions sont telles qu'il est peu imaginable qu'elles soient restées à l'état de débats parallèles, étanches les uns par rapport aux autres. Il convient probablement de les scruter avec un regard neuf, ce qui reviendra à mieux comprendre l'originalité d'Olivi par rapport à son environnement immédiat et à insérer plus correctement les Spirituels et les Béguins dans le contexte où ils vécurent.

1. En 1319 et 1321 ; R. Manselli, *op. cit.*, p. 151-180.

2. J. Paul, « Narbonne et la querelle de la Pauvreté », dans *Narbonne, archéologie et histoire*, t. II, p. 157-162.

3. Il n'est pas besoin d'insister, tant elle est connue, sur la condamnation que Gilles Aycelin et ses suffragants font de Pierre de Jean Olivi et des Béguins au concile de Béziers tenu au mois d'octobre 1299, R. Manselli, *op. cit.*, p. 36-37.

CULTE ET RAYONNEMENT DE PIERRE DÉJEAN-OLIEU EN LANGUEDOC AU DÉBUT DU XIVe SIÈCLE

Jean-Louis Biget

Pierre Déjean-Olieu (*Petrus Johannis Olivi*) fait l'objet d'un véritable culte dans le Languedoc du XIVe siècle. On le considère comme un saint non canonisé [1]. Cette vénération apparaît très clairement dans les registres de l'Inquisition où sont consignées les sentences qui ont frappé les Béguins et les Spirituels [2], car elle fait partie des charges retenues contre eux.

Tous les historiens qui ont analysé le mouvement des franciscains dissidents ont noté le rôle cardinal de référence tenu par Pierre Déjean-Olieu dans la spiritualité de ce groupe, Franz Ehrle, Raoul Manselli et David Burr notamment [3]. La reprise du dossier ne révèle aucun fait nouveau, mais elle permet de modifier et de préciser un peu les perspectives. L'examen des formes du culte de Pierre Déjean-Olieu dans leurs aspects traditionnels et leurs modalités spécifiques permet de déterminer les conditions dans lesquelles il a pris naissance. Il semble également possible de comprendre son développement et son évolution au fil du temps en situant ces derniers dans le cadre urbain du Languedoc, qui détermine sans doute en partie les luttes des Spirituels avec la communauté franciscaine.

1. L'expression revient souvent dans les dépositions faites par les Béguins devant l'Inquisition, par exemple dans celle d'Etienne Gramat de Villeneuve-les-Béziers en novembre 1325 : *dictum fratrem Petrum Johannis credit esse sanctum non canonizatum*, *Doat* 27, 10v (pour cette référence, voir note ci-dessous).

2. Il s'agit, en premier lieu, d'un ensemble de « sermons généraux » de l'Inquisition de Toulouse, alors conduite par Bernard Gui. Ils ont été publiés par Ph. De Limborch en 1692 : *Philippi a Limborch Historia Inquisitionis cui subjungitur Liber Sententiarum Inquisitionis Tholosanae ab anno Christi MCCCVII ad annum MCCCXXIII*, Amsterdam (ouvrage désormais cité Limborch). Le registre original, longtemps considéré comme perdu, a été retrouvé au British Museum (ms Add. 4697), *cf.* J. Duvernoy, « Albigeois et Vaudois en Rouergue », *Cathares, Vaudois et Béguins, dissidents du pays d'Oc*, Toulouse, 1994, p. 102 n. 32. Les textes concernant Spirituels et Béguins se trouvent aux f° 150v-168r et 196r-203r du manuscrit et aux p. 298-233 et 381-393 du livre de Limborch. Un autre ensemble de « sermons généraux » » tenus par Jean de Beaune, puis par Henri Chamayou et Pierre Brun, figure dans les volumes 27 et 28 de la Collection Doat à la Bibliothèque Nationale de France, cités plus bas *Doat* 27, *Doat* 28.

3. F. Ehrle a publié un ensemble d'articles fondamentaux dans *Archiv für Literatur und Kirchengeschichte des Mittelalters* (plus bas *A.L.K.G.*), 1 à 4 (1885-1888). R. Manselli, *Spirituali e Beghini in Provenza*, Rome, 1953. Nous renvoyons (R. Manselli, *Spirituels*) à la traduction française par J. Duvernoy, Toulouse, 1989. D. Burr, *The Persecution of Peter Olivi*, Philadelphie, 1976. Nous citons l'édition française par F.X. Putallaz, Fribourg-Paris, 1997.

Il convient également de s'interroger sur l'impact spatial, social et spirituel effectif de la dévotion à Pierre Déjean-Olieu, pour en mieux connaître les agents et savoir s'il possède ou non un caractère populaire. On peut de la sorte éclairer son sens dans le contexte global des années 1300-1325 et mesurer mieux ses conséquences pour l'ensemble de l'œuvre « olivienne ».

UN SAINT « CANONISÉ PAR DIEU »

Marie Desserre, une Béguine de Cintegabelle[1] au diocèse de Mirepoix, déclare Pierre Déjean-Olieu « père des Béguins et saint non canonisé, car il ne convient pas qu'il soit canonisé par un homme, parce que Dieu l'a canonisé dans sa vie comme dans sa mort »[2]. Le lecteur des Frères mineurs de Narbonne bénéficie, en effet, dans le milieu des Spirituels et des Béguins du Languedoc au cours des premières décennies du XIVe siècle, d'un prestige exceptionnel et du culte ordinairement dévolu à ceux qui jouissent d'une réputation de sainteté. On discerne dans les dépositions faites devant l'Inquisition après 1322 tous les éléments d'un processus ordinaire de sanctification[3]. On peut, bien entendu, poser la question de la validité des témoignages ainsi recueillis et transmis. Les inquisiteurs, par la grille des questions qu'ils imposent aux Béguins, dictent très largement leurs réponses. Ils ont pour but de disqualifier le mouvement et son chef spirituel. Ils peuvent donc chercher à grossir toutes les manifestations d'hétérodoxie par un interrogatoire orienté[4]. En outre, les sources considérées ne rapportent pas le texte des dépositions (*confessiones*), mais les procès-verbaux de « sermons généraux », où figure, avant l'énoncé des sentences, l'acte d'accusation de chacun des prévenus, sa *culpa*. Celle-ci s'appuie sur les aveux du prévenu, mais elle en donne une synthèse entièrement recomposée[5]. Elle met en évidence les charges pesant sur le coupable (qui s'exprime généralement en langue d'oc dans le Midi de la France), avec les habitudes lexicales et stylistiques des notaires du tribunal. Il pourrait en résulter des distorsions importantes entre les faits réels et la formulation qui leur est finalement donnée. En l'occurrence, ce ne semble pas le cas. Le questionnaire de Bernard Gui, s'il évoque la sainteté de Pierre Déjean-Olieu, laisse de côté l'expression traditionnelle de son culte, dont il suggère cependant l'existence, révélant que son corps a été exhumé et caché l'an 1318[6].

1. Aujourd'hui chef-lieu de canton du département de la Haute-Garonne.

2. *Dixit [...] quod dictus frater P. Johannis erat pater eorum et sanctus non canonizatus et non oportebat quod per hominem canonizaretur, quia Deus canonizaverat eum in vita et in morte*, Limborch, *cit.*, p. 319.

3. *Cf.* A. Vauchez, *La Sainteté en Occident aux derniers siècles du Moyen Age, d'après les procès de canonisation et les documents hagiographiques*, Rome, 1988, p. 223-256 et 272-287.

4. Voir « Interrogatoire spécial aux Béguins des temps actuels » in B. Gui, *Manuel de l'inquisiteur*, G. Mollat éd., I, Paris, 1964, p. 157-175.

5. B. Gui, *Ibid.*, II, p. 137.

6. B. Gui, *Ibid.*, I, p. 193.

Un processus classique de sanctification

La première modalité de la sanctification de Pierre Déjean-Olieu, fort usuelle, consiste dans la célébration de sa fête, son *dies natalis*, au jour de sa véritable naissance, celui de son trépas, le 14 mars à Narbonne[1]. Cette fête existe dès 1306, date à laquelle Dame Prous Bonet de Montpellier s'y rend[2]; on l'a sans doute établie l'année suivant le décès de Déjean-Olieu. Elle prend très vite une grande importance. Angelo Clareno en témoigne, qui passe peut-être par Narbonne après avoir séjourné à Majorque auprès de l'infant Philippe[3]. Il écrit en 1313 à ses frères :

> Maintenant, comme nous l'espérons, Célestin va être canonisé et les constitutions faites à Vienne seront publiées : elles contiennent beaucoup de choses favorables aux serviteurs de Dieu et qui réfréneront les hommes pervers. Sachez aussi que notre seigneur le pape a déposé tous les supérieurs des frères qui s'opposaient à la voie de l'Esprit et à la doctrine de frère Pierre Déjean et ils seront punis plus sévèrement encore. Et contre la volonté des frères relâchés (*relaxatorum*), la fête de ce même Pierre Déjean fut célébrée à Narbonne par le clergé et par le peuple tout entier avec tant de solennité que jamais dans cette contrée une fête semblable n'a été célébrée de nos jours aussi solennellement, car le peuple est accouru de toute la province à son tombeau, et pas moins nombreux, dit-on, que celui qui avait l'habitude de se réunir à la fête de Sainte-Marie de la Portioncule. Il apparaît assez, de la sorte, que notre secours est, maintenant et à jamais, au nom du Seigneur qui fit le Ciel et la terre[4].

Plus tard, Nicolau Eymerich signale aussi cette affluence :

> *Petro Johannis in theologia lector famosus et sepultus in ecclesia fratrum Minorum civitatis Narbonensis. Quo mortuo, quidam eum sanctum, quidam eum hereticum, fratres eiusdem ordinis palam et publice praedicabant, propter quod simplices decepti, quamplures de Catalonia, Carcassona, Tolosa et Provincia ad eius tumulum confluebant*[5].

Les témoignages des Béguines et des Béguins consignés dans les registres de l'Inquisition attestent, en effet, qu'ils se sont autrefois déplacés à Narbonne pour la fête du saint. Ils venaient de Lodève, de Limoux[6] ou de Montpellier, comme Na Prous, et de toute la région. Les cérémonies d'usage se déroulaient autour du tombeau. On y prêchait également[7].

1. Date fournie également *Ibid.*, p. 191. Pierre Déjean-Olieu *migravit a seculo* en 1298.

2. Na Prous – dont la confession prend place en août 1325 – déclare avoir fait vœu de virginité vingt ans plus tôt et être allée neuf mois après à Narbonne pour la fête du frère mineur, *Doat* 27, 56r.

3. *Cf.* L. von Auw, « Angelo Clareno et les Spirituels », *Franciscains d'Oc. Les Spirituels ca 1280-1324, Cahiers de Fanjeaux* (plus bas *C.F.*) 10, Toulouse, 1975, p. 248-249.

4. Bib. Naz. Florence, Magliabecchi XXXIX, 75, lettre XXXIV, f° 103r-v. F. Ehrle, *A.L.K.G.* I, 1885, p. 544.

5. *Directorium Inquisitorum*, Rome, 1578, t. 2, p. 76.

6. *Doat* 27, 14 v ; *Doat* 28, 237v.

7. Pierre Tort, de Montréal, *dixit quod tempore quo fiebat festum fratris P. Johannis in Narbona audivit predicari per aliquos fratres*, Limborch, p. 326.

Hors la fête, la sépulture de Pierre Déjean-Olieu fait l'objet d'un pèlerinage. Comme Pierre Massot, de Béziers, Amade Orlac de Lodève, ou bien Etienne Gramat de Villeneuve-les-Béziers, on y vient *causa devotionis*[1]. Mieux, on se fixe auprès d'elle, comme Amade de Limoux vers 1315, pour mener une vie d'ascèse en mendiant[2]. Il s'y produit des guérisons miraculeuses, celle de la fille de Sibille Gazelle, de Gignac, par exemple; malade des écrouelles, elle est amenée par sa mère sur le tombeau de Pierre Déjean-Olieu et elle guérit. Sibille « croit qu'elle a guéri par la prière » de ce dernier[3]. De même, Jean Orlac, de Montpellier, voue son fils à Pierre Déjean-Olieu et vient avec lui à Narbonne; l'enfant recouvre la santé par les mérites du défunt[4].

On forge aussi pour le nouveau saint l'image d'une mort elle-même sainte, après qu'il a reçu l'extrême-onction au milieu de ses frères. Un texte court, le *Transitus sancti Patris*, circule parmi les Béguins[5]. Le début forme une biographie très simple en forme de *légende*, avec des expressions fortes : *pater sanctissimus* et *praeclarissimus doctor*. « La mort du saint Père » exalte ensuite les progrès admirables de Pierre Déjean dans la conversion et la perfection et sa fin glorieuse. Et surtout, elle affirme qu'il a lui-même révélé avant son trépas avoir bénéficié d'une illumination divine, disant « qu'il avait reçu toute sa science de Dieu par révélation » (*per infusionem*) et qu'à Paris, dans une église, à l'heure de tierce, Jésus-Christ l'avait subitement illuminé (*subito se fuisse illuminatum a Domino Jhesu Christo*).

Le *Transitus sancti Patris* marque fortement les consciences des Béguins et l'on en trouve des réminiscences dans leurs déclarations[6]. Il signale que le très saint corps (*sacratissimum corpus*) repose à la place d'honneur, offert à la vénération, au milieu du chœur de l'église des Mineurs de Narbonne. Il y reste jusqu'en 1318. Cette année-là, on célèbre encore la fête devenue habituelle. Bernard Délicieux, qui a été lui-même lecteur dans le couvent narbonnais (en décembre 1301)[7] se trouve alors emprisonné dans les geôles d'Avignon. Un des actes d'accusation auxquels il doit répondre lui fait grief d'avoir, depuis sa prison, pris contact avec les Béguins à l'occasion de la fête, signalant qu'il souffrait pour Pierre Déjean et priant qu'on lui envoyât du secours[8].

1. *Doat* 27, 13 r. *Doat* 28, 194v. *Doat* 27, 9r.

2. *Tempore quo fiebat festum de fratre Petro Johannis sicut de sancto, ivit Narbonam et inibi habitavit [...] querendo panem amore Dei, credens tunc melius facere querendo sic victum suum mendicando quam si laborando lucraretur victum suum et vestitum*, *Doat* 28, 237v.

3. *Quandam filiam suam, quae patiebatur infirmitatem in gutture, scilicet scroellas, ad sepulcrum suum duxit et curata fuit et credidit tunc et adhuc credit quod per orationem dicti fratris Petri curata fuerat*, *Doat* 27, 18r.

4. *Quondam filium suum infirmum dicto fratri Petro*, sicut sancto, *devovit et ad eius sepulcrum portavit, credens ipsum filium fuisse sanatum per dicti fratris Petri merita*, quem reputabat esse sanctum et credebat, *Doat* 27, 25r.

5. Le texte en est donné par B. Gui, *op. cit.*, I, p. 191-193.

6. *Cf*, par exemple, Limborch, p. 306, 329.

7. *Les journaux du trésor de Philippe le Bel*, P. Viard éd., Paris, 1940, n° 5744.

8. [37] *Item quod ipse patiebatur pro fratre Petro Joannis et quod multi venirent ad instantem diem dicti fratris Petri Joannis et quod tunc facerent sibi succurri et adjutorium mitti.* [38] *Item quod praedictas litteras dictus frater Bernardus scripsit manu propria captus in carcere domini papae*

Après la destruction du tombeau de Pierre Déjean-Olieu, en 1318, la fête continue d'être célébrée dans le milieu des Béguins de Montpellier sous forme d'un banquet, un *convivium*. Ces agapes fraternelles soudent la communauté dans la mémoire du saint[1]. Elles ont encore lieu en 1325[2].

Dès 1305, le culte de Pierre Déjean semble s'être élargi à son lieu de naissance, évoqué dans le *Transitus sancti Patris*. En effet, Astrugue Cussac, une Béguine narbonnaise, vient alors faire vœu de virginité dans l'église Sainte-Marie de Sérignan[3].

Ainsi révère-t-on Pierre Déjean-Olieu selon les modalités usuelles du culte des saints, dont on lui attribue les mérites et les vertus, y compris le pouvoir thaumaturgique. Un texte anonyme, issu vers 1316 du milieu des Spirituels, illustre bien le fait. Il veut montrer que les pratiques suivies à Narbonne demeurent conformes à l'orthodoxie, mais son existence même exprime leur ambiguïté. Au demeurant, en même temps qu'il en précise le détail, il révèle qu'elles marquent effectivement une étape sur la voie de la canonisation. Son auteur affirme d'abord que les Béguins ne parlent jamais de saint Pierre ou saint Pierre-Déjean. Ils nomment ce dernier « saint père » ou « saint homme », ce qui n'est pas défendu par les canons : *bene tamen nominant eum et nominare possent* sanctum patrem *vel* sanctum virum; *hoc enim nunquam fuit a sacris canonibus prohibitum.*

En outre on ne porte pas au franciscain de Narbonne la même révérence qu'aux saints canonisés : on ne dit pas de prières solennelles et l'on ne célèbre pas d'offices en son honneur et son nom ne figure ni dans le calendrier, ni dans les litanies. Si au jour de sa mort, ou à d'autres, le peuple vient à son tombeau, c'est pour louer et glorifier Dieu. La messe solennelle est célébrée en l'honneur de la Vierge, Sa mère, et les miracles survenus durant l'année sont attribués à l'invocation et aux mérites de celle-ci. Si de telles manifestations avaient été interdites à l'endroit des saints dernièrement canonisés, François, Dominique, Antoine (de Padoue) et Louis (d'Anjou), l'Église aurait eu moins de motifs de célébrer sur terre ceux que Dieu glorifie au Ciel. Peut-on, d'ailleurs, juger répréhensible une dévotion aussi pieuse, que des cardinaux, des évêques et d'autres prélats ont eux-mêmes exprimée envers le tombeau de Pierre Déjean[4]?

Avinioni, A. Friedlander, *Processus Bernardi Delitiosi. The Trial of Fr. Bernard Délicieux*, Philadelphia, 1996, p. 63.

1. Pierre Orlac assiste à ce banquet et en assume les frais : *In quodam convivio facto ad honorem fratris Petri facto per eos tali die quali dictus frater obierat interfuit et expensas ibi factos de suo proprio ministravit : Doat* 27, 25r. Jean Lapeyre participe à une fête du même type, *Doat* 27, 22r.

2. Pierre de Tournemire, prêtre, arrêté d'abord le 24 juin 1325, puis à nouveau en septembre, déclare avoir pris part à cette fête avec Na Prous Bonet et frère R. Déjean, *Doat* 35, 11-18.

3. *Doat* 28, 224v.

4. *Nec [...] aliquis dicto patri exibet illam reverenciam, que sanctis ab ecclesia canonizatis consuevit. Nom enim facte sunt nec fiunt nec recitantur sollemnes orationes et officia in honorem eius, nec in kalendario nec [in] letonia ponitur nomen eius [...] [Quod si] autem [...] in die sui obitus vel alias ad eius tumulum conveniat populus, laudetur et glorificatur Deus, dicatur missa solempniter ad honorem Virginis matris eius, portentur insignia miraculorum evidentissimorum factorum infra annum ad invocacionem suam [...] Si in sanctis ultimo canonizatis Francisco, Dominico, Antonio, Ludovico, predicta fuissent prohibita, non habuisset sancta mater ecclesia tam evidentia motiva,*

Au total, le culte dévolu à celui-ci resterait assez classique s'il ne comportait aussi la vénération de ses écrits et de leur contenu.

Formes particulières de dévotion :
vénération de la doctrina *et de la* scriptura *de Pierre Déjean-Olieu*

Les Béguins qui comparaissent devant l'Inquisition après 1318 connaissent un grand nombre des ouvrages de Pierre Déjean. Ces *libelli*, traduits *in romancio seu vulgari*, c'est-à-dire en langue d'oc, leur sont en effet accessibles [1]. Ou bien ils les entendent lire et commenter par des Spirituels, ou bien par leurs compagnons plus instruits, cas le plus fréquent; plus rarement, ils savent lire et les déchiffrent eux-mêmes. Toutefois, on lit rarement seul : on se rassemble en petits cénacles où ceux qui en sont capables lisent et commentent tour à tour [2], où quelquefois un Spirituel entré dans la clandestinité ou bien l'un des chefs des Béguins vient porter la bonne parole. Il est notable qu'il n'est jamais question de lecture de la Bible dans la documentation dont nous disposons, mais les traductions occitanes depuis longtemps interdites, en étaient inexistantes.

Les œuvres de Pierre Déjean-Olieu forment donc la base – à peu près exclusive – de la nourriture spirituelle des Béguins. On ignore avec quelle fréquence ils y ont accès : « souvent », disent certains; « quelquefois », affirment beaucoup d'autres. Il est sûr, en tout cas, qu'elles sont lues sous Clément V, après le concile de Vienne, puis au début du pontificat de Jean XXII.

Dans le contexte de cette époque, les opuscules qui composent un directoire de vie spirituelle au quotidien ne font pratiquement l'objet d'aucune mention. Prévalent les traités exaltant la pauvreté et la règle de saint François, ainsi que la

quibus cum precedenti sancta vita inducitur ad reddendum celebres in terris, quos dominus glorificat de excelsis [...] Quis audet reprehendere devocionem piam reverendorum patrum aliquorum dominorum cardinalium et episcoporum et aliorum ecclesie prelatorum, qui meritis dicti patris divina senserunt et ad eius tumulum sollempnia enchenia transmiserunt, Ehrle, *A.L.K.G.* III, 1887, p. 443.

1. Par exemple, Raimond de Bouis, de Belpech au diocèse de Mirepoix, *pluries audivit legi et in diversis locis de libris fratris P. Johannis Olivi* in romancio seu vulgari *per diversas personnas* (Limborch, p. 300). Il parle aussi de la *postilla predicta que fuit sibi lecta* in vulgari (*Ibid.*, p. 298). Les traductions en langue vernaculaire sont encore évoquées aux pages 313, 316, 318 et 325 de Limborch. Et Pierre Dospital, de Montpellier, déclare : *de qua postilla audivit ipse pluries legi, etiam plus quam XXX. vicibus*, in vulgari (*Ibid.*, p. 388). *Cf.* également les extraits cités dans la note suivante.

2. Voici quelques exemples des deux possibilités. Bernarde, épouse de Raimond d'Antusan, de Cintegabelle, *aliquando audivit legi sibi et aliis beguinis de libris P. Johannis in vulgari et specialiter de postilla ejus super apocalipsim* (Limborch, p. 313; autres cas, p. 316, 318). Certains lisent eux-mêmes. Ainsi Pierre Tort de Montréal : *Item dixit [...] se legisse in libro de fine fratris P. Johannis* (Limborch, p. 329); il s'agit sans doute de l'une ou l'autre forme du *Transitus Sancti Petri* (là-dessus, voir D. Burr, p. 205-206). Raimond d'Antusan, de Cintegabelle, accède directement aux livres de P. Déjean : *Credidit et tenuit doctrinam et scripturam fratris P. Johannis Olivi de ordine fratrum minorum est veram et fidelem et catholicam et specialiter postillam ipsius super apocalipsim quam habuit et tenuit transpositam in vulgari et frequenter legit in ea, etiam aliis personis audientibus, et audivit legi aliquociens totam aut majorem partem* (Limborch, p. 311). Fils de notaire, Pierre Gastaud, de Belpech, sait également lire : *de quo libro in postilla ejusdem fratris P. Johannis plura legerat scripta et posita in vulgari* (*Ibid.*, p. 325).

Lectura super apocalipsim, nommée en l'occurrence *Postilla*, bien accordée aux vicissitudes du moment.

A côté de cette dernière, Bernard Gui ne cite dans sa *Practica Inquisitionis* que trois autres œuvres de Pierre Déjean familières aux Béguins : un traité sur la pauvreté, un second sur la mendicité, un troisième sur les dispenses[1]. Ils se trouvent effectivement mentionnés dans les *culpae* enregistrées par l'Inquisition. Raimond de Bouis, de Cintegabelle, a entendu lire *in libro de mendicitate fratris Petri Johannis*[2]. Pour Pierre Guiraud, de Gignac, ce dernier a montré, dans le même livre, que vivre en mendiant permet d'approcher une perfection supérieure à celle atteinte en vivant du travail de ses mains[3]. Pierre Calvet, de Cintegabelle, a entendu commenter la « Postille » et le traité sur la pauvreté[4]. Jean Roger, prêtre – qui parcourt également les œuvres de Barthélemy Sicard – parle d'une *compilationem factam per fratrem Petrum Johannis super paupertate*[5]. Pierre Gastaud sait, lui, que tout frère mineur est tenu par sa règle à ne rien posséder en propre ou en commun, et ne peut être relevé de ses vœux, *sicut frater P Johannis Olivi hoc scripsit et ipse legit in libro de dispensacionibus*[6]. Bernard Maurin, prêtre, évoque d'ailleurs un commentaire de la règle de saint François, sans doute l'*Expositio super regulam*[7]. Un autre prêtre, Jean Roger, mentionne des gloses sur le Psautier[8]. Beaucoup de ces données paraissent renvoyer, en dernière analyse, aux *Quaestiones de perfectione evangelica*[9]. En revanche, un écrit sur les vices et les vertus, parfois évoqué par les Béguins[10] ne semble pas dû à Pierre Déjean[11].

L'ensemble de ces traités forme une œuvre, *doctrina et scriptura* fidèle et catholique, pour quelques Béguins[12]. Beaucoup ajoutent à ces deux qualificatifs

1. *Op. cit.*, I, p. 111. Nous laissons aux spécialistes des écrits de Pierre Déjean-Olieu le soin d'établir une correspondance précise entre les ouvrages cités par Bernard Gui et les Béguins et les œuvres actuellement connues et répertoriées du lecteur de Narbonne.

2. Limborch, p. 300.

3. *Sicut asserit quod probat hoc frater P. Johannis Olivi per aliquas raciones in tractatu de mendicitate*, Limborch, p. 390.

4. *Audivit Petrum Dominici [...] legentem de libris fratris Petri Johannis Olivi, videlicet de postilla super apocalipsim et de libro de paupertate in vulgari*, Limborch, p. 318.

5. *Doat* 27, 74v.

6. Limborch, p. 324. Il s'agit du problème des vœux, de leur caractère contraignant et de savoir s'il peut y avoir des dispenses à cet égard. Ce même livre est cité par P. Estève, du diocèse d'Alet, Limborch, p. 322.

7. *Doat* 35, 32v.

8. *Quaedam glosae super Psalterio [...] quae factae fuerant per fratrem Petrum Johannis*, *Doat* 27, 172v.

9. *Cf.* D. Burr, p. 273-274.

10. Ainsi Pierre Daissan, tailleur de Béziers, qui l'a entendu lire, *Doat* 28, 213v.

11. Il ne paraît pas correspondre aux questions « *de vitiis* » in *Quaestiones in secundum Sententiarum*, mais plutôt à un ouvrage anonyme, signalé par Bernard Gui, la *Somme des vices et des vertus* (*op. cit.*, I, p. 115) et mentionné par Ehrle, *A.L.K.G.* III, 1887, p. 476.

12. Ainsi pour Mathieu Terré de Saverdun (diocèse de Pamiers) : *doctrina et scriptura fratris Petri Johannis [...] erat tota fidelis et catholica*, Limborch, p. 320.

les épithètes de vraie (*vera*) et de bonne (*bona*)[1]. Ainsi Pierre Déjean-Olieu est-il considéré comme *sollempnis doctor ecclesiae*[2]. On le compare aux quatre docteurs de l'église latine, Augustin, Jérôme, Grégoire et Ambroise[3]. Pierre Mourès, de Belpech, va jusqu'à déclarer que, pour ce qui concerne la sainteté de vie et l'autorité de la doctrine, il est au-dessus de tous les docteurs de l'Église, hormis les apôtres et les évangélistes. En dehors de saint Paul et lui, tous ont d'ailleurs été quelque peu censurés par l'Église, alors que sa doctrine doit être entièrement suivie par celle-ci, comme celle de saint Paul, *nec est una littera dimittenda*. Certains Béguins glissent facilement à l'hyperbole; ainsi Guillaume Azémar, tisserand de Narbonne, déclare-t-il que Pierre Déjean-Olieu a composé sur l'apocalypse un ouvrage admirable, « tel que si les têtes de tous les hommes étaient réunies en une seule tête, elles ne pourraient concevoir une telle œuvre, n'était-ce par l'effet du Saint-Esprit »[4].

En tout cas, cette doctrine a été approuvée par le pape Clément (V) et, à part quelques articles, par le concile de Vienne, de sorte qu'il est hérétique de la contester[5]. Les Béguins, instruits par le *Transitus sancti Patris*, affirment d'ailleurs qu'elle résulte d'une révélation de l'Esprit saint. Ainsi Pierre Mourès de Belpech soutient *quod dictus frater P. Johannis doctrinam et scripturam suam habuit ex revelacione Spiritus sancti*[6]. Pierre Tort, de Montréal, dit aussi *quod dum esset Parisius [...] tota veritas Evangelii et vite Christi ei fuerat revelata et quod tota scriptura ejus [...] fuerat revelata, et nichil de suo in dicta scriptura posuerat, set solum quod ei a Deo fuerat revelatum*[7]. On en vient ainsi à la conception d'une *sancta scriptura*[8]. Ce terme de *scriptura*, singulier comme l'a signalé David Burr[9], semble également expressif d'une réalité supraterrestre. Comme l'Ecriture, la *scriptura* olivienne exprime l'incarnation historique de la parole de Dieu; elle est sainte et manifeste la sainteté de son auteur. Bien des Béguins le croient, comme Jeanne Bérenguier, habitante de Narbonne, pour laquelle *fratrem Petrum Johannis et eius scripturam esse sanctum et sanctam* et qui pense *ipsum fratrem Petrum Johannis esse in Paradiso*[10]. Guillaume Doumergue, de Narbonne, verrier, fabricant de chandelles et de lanternes, l'un des animateurs des communautés de Béguins, exprime la même opinion, dans les mêmes termes[11]. Guillaume Serralier, effectivement serrurier, de Lodève, autre

1. *Vera*, pour, entre autres, Bernarde, femme de Raimond d'Antusan, de Cintegabelle, Limborch, p. 313. *Bona*, par exemple, pour P. Calvet, compatriote de la précédente, et pour P. de Mazères, de Belpech, Limborch, p. 318, 302.

2. *Ibid.*, p. 321.

3. *Ibid.*, p. 329.

4. *Doat* 28, 230r.

5. Limborch, p. 302, 308, 316, 318, 329, par exemple.

6. Limborch, p. 306.

7. *Ibid.*, p. 329.

8. Pierre Mourès affirme *quod revelacio sancte scripture facta fuit eidem sicut alicui de sancti doctoribus*, *Ibid.*, p. 306.

9. *Op. cit.*, p. 259.

10. *Doat* 28, 190v; 191r.

11. *Item fratrem Petrum Johannis quondam ordinis minorum credidit esse sanctum in Paradiso, non canonizatum, et eius scripturam seu doctrinam credidit esse bonam et sanctam*, *Doat* 28, 241r.

personnalité marquante, qui dépose en mars 1327, persiste dans cette croyance, malgré les condamnations officielles de Jean XXII[1]. Et Guillaume Rous, de Cintegabelle, assure que la doctrine et la *scriptura* de Déjean-Olieu valent celles de saint Jean l'Evangéliste et qu'il se trouve comme ce dernier au Paradis[2]. Beaucoup de Béguins le croient avec lui.

On peut se demander, une fois encore, si la tonalité de ces déclarations ne procède pas des sollicitations des inquisiteurs, soucieux d'établir l'hétérodoxie et la culpabilité de ceux qu'ils interrogent et d'affirmer avec force leurs fautes dans leurs actes d'accusation. Il semble qu'il n'en soit rien, si l'on en juge par la confession de Na Prous Bonet qui s'est épanchée longuement devant le tribunal sans qu'on lui pose de questions et dont les vaticinations ont été soigneusement consignées par le notaire des inquisiteurs[3].

Envoyé de l'Esprit saint, introducteur à des temps nouveaux

Dame Prous, fille de Durand Bonet de Saint-Michel de La Cadière, dans le diocèse de Nîmes, habite Montpellier[4], avec ses sœurs Alisette[5] et Stéphanie[6] et leur compagne – et, probablement servante, Alaraxis Bedous[7]. Na Prous tient une place cardinale dans le groupe des Béguins montpelliérains et le terme d'hérésiarque apparaît au moins une fois sous la plume du notaire des inquisiteurs pour la qualifier[8]. Il y a des chances, en revanche, qu'il ait, en la transcrivant, affadi la parole de feu de ce personnage extraordinaire. Na Prous présente Pierre Déjean-Olieu comme l'acteur fondamental du devenir spirituel de l'humanité, après le Christ et saint François. Elle le cite douze fois dans sa confession[9]. C'est auprès de son tombeau que le Seigneur l'a enfantée en esprit, le 14 mars 1306. Elle y a fait l'objet d'un « ravissement » mystique, accompagné de larmes, de parfums suaves et d'une chaleur douce[10]. Elle attribue à Pierre Déjean un rôle essentiel dans l'économie du salut.

1. *Item dixit se credere doctrinam et scripturam fratris P. Johannis Olivi esse sanctam [...] non obstante quod sibi fuit dictum expresse quod dominus Johannes Papa vicesimus secundus condemnavit dictam scripturam et specialiter postillam quam ipse frater Johannes fecit super apocalipsim*, *Doat* 28, 248r ; 249r.

2. Limborch, p. 385.

3. *Gratis et sponte et sine interrogatione deposuit*, *Doat* 27, 51v.

4. Sur Na Prous, *cf.* l'article de Louisa Burnham dans le présent recueil. Voir également W.H. May, « The Confession of Prous Boneta, Heretic and Heresiarch » in *Essays in medieval life and thought presented in honour of Austin Patterson Evans*, J.H. Mundy, R.W. Emery et B.N. Nelson éd., 1955, p. 3-30 et R. Manselli, *Spirituels*, p. 196-202. Le texte de la confession de Na Prous est traduit dans l'édition française, p. 274-289.

5. Sa *culpa* figure dans *Doat* 27, 26r – 29v.

6. Celle-ci apparaît tardivement, à l'occasion du sermon général tenu en septembre 1329 à Carcassonne, *Doat* 27, 186r. Elle abjure (225r), mais est cependant condamnée au mur perpétuel (228r, 229r).

7. Confession, *Doat* 27, 30r-32r.

8. *Doat* 27, 25v.

9. A vrai dire très longue, *Doat* 27, 51v-79r.

10. *Doat* 27, 56r-v.

En effet, après la mort salvatrice de Son Fils, Dieu a instauré – sous la forme de l'Église – le Paradis terrestre, qui prépare à la vie éternelle. En ce Paradis, Il a placé saint François et Pierre Déjean-Olieu comme Elie et Enoch [1]. Saint François a rendu témoignage de la vie de pauvreté dont le Christ a donné l'exemple et Pierre Déjean a porté le témoignage de la divinité dans l'Ecriture sainte. Grâce à la vertu de l'Esprit Saint, que Dieu avait déposé en lui et auquel toute la Sainte Trinité avait conféré son pouvoir [2], il a pu y rechercher toutes les paroles inspirées aux saints par le Christ [3].

La « *scriptura* » de Frère Pierre a donc été composée par la main de Dieu : *scriptura dicti fratris Petri Johannis erat scripta per manum divinitatis* [4].

Na Prous assimile le franciscain de Narbonne à l'un des trois anges que Jean a vus, selon l'Apocalypse. Le premier, porteur du signe du Dieu vivant, était saint François; le second à la face comme un soleil était le saint docteur (et le troisième, tenant les clés de l'abîme, personnifiait le Saint-Esprit descendu sur Na Prous [5]).

Celle-ci, finalement, fait du héros des Béguins un nouveau Christ, dans un parallèle vigoureux. De même que saint Jean Baptiste, affirme-t-elle, a préparé la voie au Fils de Dieu, saint François l'a préparée au Saint-Esprit. Et le Seigneur a pourvu Pierre Déjean d'autant de grâces et de gloire qu'il en a données à Son Fils en tant qu'il fut homme. Il l'a fait pour sauver l'humanité [6]. Mais, ainsi que le Christ a combattu seul à seul avec le diable, Pierre Déjean a dû lutter seul à seul avec l'Antéchrist [7]. Saint Thomas déjà, autre Caïn, l'a mis à mort spirituellement [8]. On a tué dans le Christ sa nature humaine en le crucifiant et sa nature divine en condamnant la *scriptura* de Pierre Déjean. Jean XXII, Caïphe du temps présent, a renouvelé la crucifixion [9]. Son péché excède de beaucoup celui d'Adam quand il mangea la pomme. Pour cette raison, il a perdu son pouvoir pontifical et le sacrement de l'autel n'a plus aucune vertu [10]. Ceux qui croiront la *scriptura* de Pierre Déjean-Olieu seront baptisés dans l'Esprit saint et le Seigneur pardonnera

1. *Doat* 27, 64v.
2. *Doat* 27, 67r.
3. *Doat* 27, 65r.
4. *Doat* 27, 61r.
5. *Item dixit sibi dominus, ut asserit, quod sanctus Joannes vidit tres angelos quorum primus portabat signum Dei vivi et hic erat Sanctus Franciscus, secundus vero habebat faciem solis et erat frater Petrus Ioannis; tertius vero portabat claves abyssi et hic est sanctus Spiritus quod Deus dedit sibi loquenti; Doat* 27, 79r. D'autres Béguins opèrent cette assimilation de Pierre Déjean au second ange de la vision de Jean, ainsi Pierre Rous, de Cintegabelle (Limborch, p. 316), Pierre Tort de Montréal (*Ibid.*, p. 329) ou Pierre Gastaud, de Belpech. Ce dernier affirme : *quod non fuisset major doctor eo ab apostolis citra et audivit dici et legi inter beguinos ipsum fuisse et esse spiritualiter illum angelum de quo scribitur in apocalipsi quod facies ejus erat sicut sol et habebat librum apertum in manu sua, quia singulariter inter omnes alios doctores fuit aperta ei veritas Christi et intelligencia libri apocalipsis;* Limborch, p. 325.
6. *Doat* 27, 69v.
7. *Doat* 27, 66v.
8. *Doat* 27, 72r.
9. *Doat* 27, 58r.
10. *Doat* 27, 61r.

leurs péchés[1]. Et quiconque veut être sauvé doit croire les paroles de cette Ecriture[2]. Avec Pierre Déjean commence un temps nouveau, celui de l'Église de l'Esprit: *Tempus novum dicti Spiritus sancti et novus status ecclesie habuit initium in dicto fratre Petro Johannis et consequitur in ipsa*[3].

On le voit, Na Prous s'arroge un rôle identique à celui de Pierre Déjean pour l'avenir céleste de l'humanité. En le glorifiant, elle sert sa propre gloire. Il faut aussi tenir compte de l'exaltation du personnage qui pousse ses formules à l'hyperbole, voire à l'excès. Quand elle dépose devant les inquisiteurs, en août 1325, elle n'en traduit pas moins avec force la réputation de sainteté et la vénération exceptionnelle dont jouit Pierre Déjean-Olieu parmi les Spirituels et les Béguins. La plupart des témoignages qui subsistent de ce culte extraordinaire sont postérieurs à 1320. On peut, cependant, formuler quelques hypothèses sur ses origines, son évolution chronologique et les conditions dans lesquelles il se développe.

Une figure emblématique

Le culte de Pierre Déjean-Olieu s'inscrit, bien évidemment, au centre des conflits qui opposent les Spirituels aux frères de la communauté de l'ordre de saint François; très tôt, ceux-ci ont désigné Pierre Déjean comme le chef de leurs adversaires, constitués en « secte ». Une telle personnalisation ressortit aux usages de l'époque; elle traduit aussi une influence effective; mais la vénération dont Pierre fait l'objet paraît également en rapport direct avec les condamnations qui frappent à la fois son œuvre, les Spirituels et les Béguins. Au cœur des luttes qui se déroulent dans l'ordre des Mineurs, dans l'Église et dans les villes du Languedoc, Narbonne tout particulièrement, il devient la figure emblématique d'un mouvement de protestation qui confère à ses ouvrages et à sa personne un caractère militant, dépassant à coup sûr ses intentions propres.

« Maître » des Spirituels

Le contraste s'avère total entre saint Louis d'Anjou, autre saint franciscain objet d'une dévotion populaire considérable[4], et Pierre Déjean-Olieu. Louis se soumet à des macérations, sert les malades et les lépreux, il est révéré pour sa vie d'ascèse et de charité. Or les Béguins qui voient Pierre dans le Paradis, n'évoquent jamais son existence. Un seul, Pierre Mourès, de Belpech, déjà cité, met en parallèle la sainteté de sa vie et l'autorité de sa doctrine :

1. *Doat* 27, 76r.
2. *Doat* 27, 70r.
3. *Doat* 27, 76r-v.
4. *Cf.* J. Paul, *C.F.* 7, *Les Evêques, les clercs et le roi (1250-1300)*, 1972; *C.F.* 11, *La Religion populaire*, 1976, et *C.F.* 15, *Le Pèlerinage*, 1980.

[...] credidit quod dictus frater P. Johannis quantum ad sanctitatem vitae et auctoritatem doctrine cuicumque sancto doctori ecclesie sit equalis, nullo excepto praeter apostolos et evangelistas[1].

La sainteté d'Olieu ne procède donc pas d'une dévotion suscitée par une existence exemplaire. Ses œuvres seules en sont constitutives (à cet égard, son cas n'est pas totalement différent de celui de saint Thomas). Il est donc promu d'abord comme intellectuel et son culte ne peut être de source populaire. Il est en premier lieu reconnu pour maître par les Spirituels qui trouvent dans ses écrits des arguments pour défendre leurs positions. Ainsi se noue le paradoxe qui fait de Pierre Déjean-Olieu, penseur orthodoxe, le chef apparent d'une dissidence violemment contestataire[2].

La « rencontre » des Spirituels et de Pierre Déjean survient très tôt. En effet, si l'on en croit Raimond de Fronsac, procureur ultérieur de l'ordre des Mineurs, Arnaud de Roquefeuil et trente-cinq autres frères dénoncent ce dernier comme chef d'une secte d'hérétiques dès les alentours de 1285[3]. Il existe donc à ce moment un groupe constitué qui se réclame de lui et de sa doctrine sur la pauvreté franciscaine, exposée dans ses *Quaestiones de perfectione evangelica* et son traité *De usu paupere*[4]. En 1279, il a participé à la préparation de la bulle *Exiit qui seminat*. Il apparaît à la fois comme un maître à penser et comme une victime des frères de la communauté, en raison de la mise en cause de certaines de ses conceptions. Pour les Spirituels, qui considèrent intangibles et saintes la règle franciscaine et la pauvreté qu'elle implique, celui qui soutient une position identique à la leur et compte parmi les frères de leur ordre, devient en toute logique un personnage sacré et quasiment un saint. Cela d'autant plus qu'il polémique avec les penseurs de la communauté, ainsi Vital du Four, lecteur à Montpellier en 1292. Il jouit d'un grand prestige, puisque les fils de Charles II d'Anjou envisagent au printemps 1295 de le faire venir auprès d'eux en Catalogne, où ils se trouvent retenus comme otages[5]. Bien que la lettre qu'il adresse à Conrad d'Offida, en 1295 également, atteste qu'il n'est pas un rigoriste extrémiste et qu'il se borne à défendre les termes d'*Exiit qui seminat*[6], les protagonistes de la communauté le définissent comme le chef des Spirituels et ceux-ci le reconnaissent pour tel, car ils puisent dans sa doctrine de quoi alimenter leurs convictions et leur argumentation. Lui-même ne s'est jamais proclamé,

1. Limborch, p. 306.

2. Paradoxe souligné par J. Paul, « Les Spirituels, l'Église et la Papauté », *Chi erano gli Spirituali ?* Atti del III convegno internazionale, Assisi, 1975, p. 224. Le même auteur affirme dans le même article : « Ni sur le pouvoir pontifical, ni sur l'histoire de l'Église, ni sur la perfection évangélique, Pierre Déjean-Olieu n'a enseigné les erreurs que l'on reproche aux Spirituels », p. 253.

3. Raimond de Fronsac compose dans la première moitié de l'année 1318 le plan d'un ouvrage destiné à relater « le combat du dragon et antique serpent, assisté de ses anges apostats, contre le peuple de Dieu ». La seconde partie, vouée à raconter l'histoire des sectes *ex quibus orta est secta fratris P. Jo. Olivi* (Ehrle, *A.L.K.G.* 3, 1887, p. 8), devra comporter le texte d'un grand nombre de documents, témoignages sur cette lutte. Raimond de Fronsac prévoit d'y mettre en bonne place la lettre d'Arnaud de Roquefeuil, Ehrle, *Ibid.*, p. 14.

4. D. Burr, *op. cit.*, p. 21-40.

5. *Cf.* la formule terminale de l'épître qu'il leur adresse en mai de cette année-là, *C.F.* 10, p. 137.

6. D. Burr, *op. cit.*, p. 201.

voulu, ni même senti peut-être, chef d'école ou de parti. Il reste qu'il prend cette qualité aux yeux des Spirituels comme à ceux de leurs adversaires et sa gloire se trouve inévitablement renforcée après sa mort, quand s'affirment les divisions et les conflits dans l'ordre des frères Mineurs.

Dans ces luttes, le renoncement de Célestin V, pape durant quelques mois de juillet à décembre 1294, marque une inflexion décisive, car il entraîne une offensive appuyée contre les Spirituels, leur guide et leurs principes. « Le grand refus » s'accompagne en mai 1296, à l'initiative de Boniface VIII, de la relève de Raimond Jauffret par Jean de Morrovalle comme ministre général. Suit bientôt une répression accentuée à l'égard des contestataires et de leur tuteur intellectuel et spirituel. Le chapitre général tenu à Lyon en 1299 condamne et interdit les œuvres de Déjean-Olieu. Jean de Morrovalle envoie dans toutes les provinces une lettre par laquelle il mande de disperser les sectateurs du frère de Narbonne : *sectam fratris Petri Johannis extingui et sectatores dispergi, etiam extra provinciam emittando eos*[1]. Par une série d'autres lettres, il ordonne de rassembler ses ouvrages et de les faire brûler[2]. Bien des frères récalcitrants sont jetés dans des cachots où certains périssent, tel Ponce Carbonnel, antérieurement précepteur des fils de Charles d'Anjou.

On comprend bien que dans un tel contexte, les Spirituels tendent à sanctifier leur maître à penser. Cela vient dans le droit fil des événements et des « alliances » du quart de siècle antérieur, de l'importance prise par les écrits de Pierre Jean-Olieu dans l'élaboration de leur doctrine et de la nécessité de donner à leur combat une auréole de sainteté.

Il existe entre les couvents des Mineurs et les membres du Tiers-Ordre de saint François, une étroite symbiose. Il en résulte que le maître des Spirituels devient le patron des Béguins.

Patron des Béguins

Dans la seconde moitié du XIIIe siècle, les Frères mineurs jouissent à Narbonne d'une audience certaine. On conserve malheureusement peu de testaments de l'époque, mais la connaissance fragmentaire des dons consentis par les testateurs – pour moitié membres de l'aristocratie traditionnelle et pour moitié marchands ou artisans – témoigne de leur attraction. Le montant des legs qui leur sont destinés s'élève à 57,5 % du total des donations faites à l'ensemble des ordres mendiants[3].

Il est sûr en outre qu'il existe une véritable conjonction entre les Spirituels et toute une population de laïcs gravitant autour du couvent narbonnais[4]. Cette osmose tient, en particulier, au fait que les frères jouent le rôle de directeurs spirituels de multiples petits groupes. Lors de leur comparution devant les

1. Lettre mentionnée par Raimond de Fronsac dans le sommaire évoqué note 80 ci-dessus. Elle devait composer le chapitre XL de la seconde partie de son ouvrage, Ehrle, *A.L.K.G.* 3, 1887, p. 15.

2. *Ibid.*, p. 16.

3. R.W. Emery, *Heresy and Inquisition in Narbonne*, New-York, 1941, Appendix II, p. 163.

4. Signalée par R. Manselli, *Spirituels*, p. 79.

inquisiteurs, plusieurs béguines signalent avoir eu pour confesseur un des Mineurs cités à Avignon en avril 1317. Or, dans ces relations proches et familières, les Frères peuvent s'appuyer sur plusieurs opuscules de Pierre Déjean, rédigés afin de constituer des guides de spiritualité. On n'a pu jusqu'à présent dater ces traités. Raoul Manselli en a publié quatre dans son ouvrage sur les Spirituels du Languedoc[1]. *La façon dont chacun peut rendre grâces à Dieu des bienfaits qu'il a reçus de Lui*[2], énumérant tous ces derniers, cherche à provoquer la conversion du pécheur. *L'Instruction de Pierre Déjean* (*Informatio Petri Johannis*), par une série d'arguments, exhorte à une vie plus haute. *Les remèdes contre les tentations spirituelles* évoquent les conduites à tenir et celles à éviter. Enfin, le *Miles armatus*, aussi dénommé *Lo cavalier armat*, stipule que le chrétien doit être un soldat du Christ, qui s'arme et se bat spirituellement pour se protéger du péché[3]. Des versions en langue d'oc de tous ces traités, élaborées au Moyen Age, existent encore au XXe siècle[4]. Elles montrent qu'ils ont été rédigés pour un public assez large, comme le confirme la simplicité de leur style et l'emploi d'images accessibles à chacun. Elles contrastent sur ces plans avec la lettre aux fils de Charles II, plus complexe quant au langage et aux termes théologiques. Ces œuvres d'édification montrent que Déjean-Olieu a eu le souci de construire le christianisme dans et par les fidèles regroupés autour de ses frères, en favorisant l'élévation spirituelle de chacun. Elles ont sans doute contribué à modeler la conscience religieuse des Béguins. Il est possible également qu'elles aient servi le rayonnement de Pierre Déjean hors du cercle des Spirituels. Malheureusement, sur ce point, les sources actuellement disponibles restent muettes ; il est vrai que ces traités – absolument orthodoxes – n'intéressent pas l'Inquisition.

Il faut ajouter que Pierre Déjean, pour former ses frères dans leur rôle de confesseurs, rédige des ouvrages de morale pratique bien accordés au milieu narbonnais. Il met ainsi à leur disposition, vers 1294-1295, un traité sur les contrats où il avalise les usages des marchands en justifiant la plupart des prêts à intérêt[5] ; cela montre des relations suivies avec le milieu des fidèles narbonnais.

De toute manière, en contact étroit avec les Spirituels qui leur enseignent les préceptes de la vie évangélique et leur donnent à connaître leur vérité, Béguins et Béguines ne peuvent ignorer Déjean-Olieu. Au demeurant, les porte-parole de la communauté les intègrent aux membres de sa secte. Et il est vrai que ceux-ci

1. R. Manselli, *Spirituali*, 1959, Appendice I, « Quattro operette ascetiche di Pietro di Giovanni Olivi del cod. Guarnacciano di Volterra 5230 », p. 267-290. Dans ce codex les textes sont en latin. Ils sont édités ainsi par R. Manselli. Traduction française par J. Duvernoy, *op. cit.*, p. 239-256. *Lo cavalier armat* fait l'objet d'une publication en langue d'oc par R. Manselli, avec traduction du P. M.H. Vicaire, *C.F.* 11, 1976, p. 203-216.

2. *Modus quomodo quilibet referre gratias Deo de beneficiis ab eo receptis.*

3. Analyse précise, dans R. Manselli, *Spirituels*, p. 39-44. *Cf.* aussi *Id.*, « Les opuscules spirituels de P.J. Olivi et la piété des béguins de langue d'oc », *C.F.* 11, *La Religion populaire en Languedoc*, 1979, p. 189.

4. Pour ces versions occitanes, R. Manselli, *Spirituels*, renvoie à D. Zorzi, « Testi inediti francescani in lingua provenzale », *Miscellanea del centro di studi medievali*, 6e année, p. 249-268.

5. S. Piron, « Marchands et confesseurs. Le *Traité des contrats* d'Olivi dans son contexte (Narbonne, fin XIIIe – début XIVe siècle) », dans *L'argent au Moyen Age*, Paris, 1998, p. 289-308.

démontrent, à travers le culte développé sans doute dès 1300 et dans leurs confessions devant les inquisiteurs, une vénération sans bornes pour celui qu'ils considèrent comme leur saint patron.

Il existe des signes de la présence d'une communauté de Béguins à Narbonne en 1288. On arrête alors – sur le soupçon qu'elle pourrait être vaudoise – une veuve, animatrice spirituelle d'un groupe de femmes, lié à une « Dame », Na Jordana Maynard, et qui compte deux béguines, Sicarde et Alissende, avec l'épouse de Guillaume Hulart[1]. L'importance des Béguins se marque nettement quand la répression s'abat sur eux, au moment même où elle frappe les Spirituels. En octobre 1299, l'archevêque de Narbonne, Gilles Aycelin, préside à Béziers un concile provincial qui interdit les communautés de Béguins et leurs réunions[2]. Ces tribulations entraînent rapidement l'actualisation de la *Lectura super apocalipsim*.

Auteur d'une vision prophétique : la Postilla super apocalipsim

Le quatrième canon du concile de Béziers expose que les Béguins, satellites des Frères mineurs, prêchent que la fin du monde est proche et que le temps de l'Antéchrist est ouvert, ou presque. On discerne dans ce texte l'écho d'une eschatologie probablement inspirée des œuvres de Pierre Déjean et popularisée par les Spirituels, sans doute.

L'idée de l'avènement d'un monde meilleur, enfanté dans la douleur, s'accorde bien à l'état d'esprit et à la situation des Spirituels et des Béguins au sein de l'Église. Il semble toutefois qu'une eschatologie fortement contestataire, associée à une spiritualité exigeante, ne peut se développer, comme le mouvement de la rigueur franciscaine lui-même, sans l'existence dans la société méridionale d'un contexte favorable. Le culte de Pierre Déjean-Olieu participe non seulement de cadres religieux, mais aussi d'un ensemble de conditions propres aux villes du Bas-Languedoc autour de 1300.

Nous avons nous-même esquissé déjà cette analyse[3]. Nous la reprenons sommairement. Elle mériterait une recherche approfondie.

Les Béguins – on y reviendra plus bas – appartiennent pour l'essentiel aux milieux aisés de l'artisanat, auxquels se joignent quelques marchands. Les problèmes de ces groupes sociaux sont simples : développer leur fortune, assurer la pérennité de leur famille par une stratégie appropriée (*i.e.*, par une forme de contrôle des naissances), maîtriser le pouvoir urbain, afin de sauvegarder leurs intérêts et d'accroître leur capital de prestige. Quant à l'argent et au sexe, la pratique ordinaire des marchands et des artisans enrichis entre en contradiction avec la doctrine et les exigences de l'Église.

1. *Cf.* I. Dollinger, *Beiträge zur Sektengeschichte des Mittelalters*, II, Munich, 1890, p. 706, 711. On retrouve un Bérenger Hulart parmi les Béguins après 1320 ; R. Manselli, *Spirituels*, p. 312.

2. Mansi, t. XXIV, c. 1215-1218 ; R. Manselli, *op.cit.*, p. 36-37.

3. J.-L. Biget, « Autour de Bernard Délicieux. Franciscanisme et société en Languedoc entre 1295 et 1330 », *Mouvements franciscains et société française, XIIIe-XXe siècle*. Etudes présentées à la Table ronde du C.N.R.S., réunies par A. Vauchez, Paris, 1984, p. 74-93.

Le problème de l'usure reste entier au début du XIVe siècle. L'Église donne au terme une acception très large qui recouvre non seulement le crédit usuraire, mais aussi tous les prêts à intérêt, les bénéfices et les subtilités propres à fournir du gain introduites dans les contrats. En juillet 1314, l'official de Narbonne ordonne aux paroissiens de la ville – sous peine d'excommunication – de venir lui dénoncer tous les faits d'usure dont ils auraient connaissance. Le problème est sans doute rendu plus aigu par l'expulsion des Juifs, prêteurs traditionnels, survenue en 1306[1]. Il semble se poser à Béziers[2] comme à Narbonne.

Les dépositions des Béguins attestent que la non-procréation se trouve également au cœur de leurs préoccupations. Elles expriment souvent une dévaluation de l'union conjugale[3], qualifiée de *lupanar privatum*[4], et occasionnellement la volonté d'atténuer la gravité de l'onanisme : il ne serait pas un péché, mais une simple *purgatio corporis*[5]. Certains, pour exalter la continence, vont jusqu'à imiter l'essai probatoire des troubadours, l'*assag* ou *jazer*[6]. De nombreuses Béguines font aussi vœu de chasteté ou de virginité et le respectent[7]. Ces affirmations et ces conduites traduisent des problèmes auxquels l'Église répond seulement par des sanctions. Les citadins en voie d'ascension sociale dans le Languedoc des années 1280-1320, vivent donc un malaise spirituel, en raison de l'opposition entre les exigences du clergé et le maintien de leur statut économique et social. La situation politique et les antagonismes sociaux des villes ajoutent à ces tensions.

A Narbonne, à Béziers, à Lodève, à Agde, les seigneurs temporels principaux sont d'Église. Les consulats cherchent évidemment à élargir leurs droits au détriment des prérogatives seigneuriales. L'intervention du roi de France à la fin du XIIIe siècle, complique la situation et les alliances (hors Montpellier qui appartient au royaume de Majorque).

A l'intérieur des consulats, le pouvoir se répartit de manière très inégale entre l'oligarchie et les gens de métier. Narbonne est une ville double; la Cité compte cinq consuls, dont deux pour les artisans et les marins; le Bourg en a six, dont deux seulement représentent l'artisanat. A Béziers, comme à Montpellier, fonctionne un système d'échelles qui permet la surreprésentation au consulat des grands marchands, des changeurs et des hommes de loi, et place les artisans,

1. S. Piron, *art.cit.*

2. Si l'on en juge par les dires du Prêcheur R. Barrau, *cf.* P. Botineau, « Les tribulations de R. Barrau O.P. (1295-1338) », *Mélanges d'archéologie et d'histoire publiés par l'Ecole Française de Rome* 77, 1965.

3. R. Barrau (*Cf.* note précédente) dit qu'un Frère mineur a prêché à Villeneuve-les-Béziers *quod matrimonium erat proscribile.*

4. Guilhem Marti le pense et *credebat etiam quod homo cognoscendo carnaliter propriam uxorem peccaverat mortaliter; Doat* 28, 162 v.

5. L'opinion est attribuée à un prêtre; il s'agit d'un faux témoignage, qui n'en est pas moins significatif, *Doat* 28, 202 r-v.

6. Limborch, p. 382-383.

7. Ermessende Gros, une veuve de Gignac, vers 1308, *induta per quosdam fratres, Doat* 27, 14 r. Astrugue Cussac de Narbonne, *Doat* 28, 224v, et, naturellement, Na Prous Bonet, *Doat* 27, 56r.

même les maîtres, en position subordonnée [1]. Or Narbonne, entre autres villes, est une grande cité drapante. En 1278, 40 % de la population de la Cité – 38 % de celle du bourg vers 1330 – vit des activités lainières. Celles-ci sont prospères, grâce à une forte exportation vers la péninsule ibérique [2]. Cette prospérité, assortie quelquefois de crises passagères ou de données nouvelles comme diverses impositions mises sur les draps par le roi de France [3], rend pugnaces les classes moyennes, non intégrées ou minoritairement représentées dans le système communal – ce qui ne leur permet pas de maîtriser les conditions de leur travail, équivaut à un déficit de prestige et les rend tributaires hors de tout contrôle [4]. Un front social et politique oppose (comme en Flandre ou en Toscane), les marchands drapiers aux maîtres du textile [5], car les artisans sont organisés en métiers [6], mais ne disposent pratiquement d'aucun pouvoir dans le gouvernement de la ville ni d'aucune possibilité de défendre leurs intérêts vitaux.

L'ouverture des Franciscains en général, et des Spirituels en particulier, aide sans aucun doute les milieux urbains taraudés par le malaise né de leur attitude à l'égard de l'argent ou du sexe. Ils offrent aux besoins nouveaux des fidèles une pastorale adaptée, un autre visage de l'Église, et c'est probablement un des facteurs de leur audience. Leur ascétisme n'est pas contradictoire d'une forme d'acceptation du monde, comme l'indique le *Traité des contrats* de Pierre Déjean, évoqué plus haut. Au contraire, limité à une élite, il se convertit en bienfaits spirituels pour ses parents et ses amis et s'étend de proche en proche à la ville tout entière. Il offre une alternative positive à l'intercession conditionnelle des clercs séculiers ou des membres des ordres anciens [7]. Il reste que la situation économique et politique des milieux où se recrutent les Béguins demeure bridée. Dynamiques et conquérants, ils sont en même temps contraints et non reconnus. Cet état et l'étroitesse de leurs liens avec les Spirituels, les disposent à recevoir une version actualisée de l'eschatologie de Pierre Déjean-Olieu, où s'exprime l'idée que la souffrance, signe de la condition humaine, permet de progresser dans la lutte vers le salut et dont le pessimisme à l'égard du présent s'accompagne d'un optimisme absolu quant à l'avenir.

1. *Cf.* P. Dognon, *Les Institutions politiques et administratives des pays de Languedoc du XIIIe siècle aux guerres de religion*, Toulouse, 1895.

2. G. Larguier, *Le Drap et le grain. Narbonne et Narbonnais 1300-1789*, Perpignan, 1996, t. I, ch. I et Annexe 1, t. III, p. 1245.

3. *Cf.* G. Larguier, *op. cit.*, et G. Romestan, « La gabelle des draps en Languedoc (1318-1333) », dans *Hommage à André Dupont. Etudes Médiévales languedociennes*, Montpellier, 1974, p. 197-237.

4. A Narbonne, pour le Bourg, en 1312, un accord prévoit l'accroissement de la représentation des métiers « mécaniques » dans le consulat, à la suite d'un appel au roi formulé par ces derniers, mais l'opposition des marchands drapiers fait échec à son application ; R.W. Emery, *op. cit.*, p. 36. A Montpellier, en 1324, le « populaire » proteste contre la répartition de la taille et forme un « syndicat » exigeant l'examen des comptes consulaires depuis vingt ans ; il demande aussi la réduction des taxes sur le blé ; P. Dognon, *op. cit.*, p. 166.

5. En 1254, à Narbonne, un conflit oppose les tisserands aux drapiers ; R.W. Emery, p. 38.

6. On en compte dix-neuf dans le Bourg et quinze dans la Cité pour Narbonne, entre 1290 et 1317, *Ibid.*, p. 39.

7. Nous partageons cette analyse de S. Piron, donnée en conclusion de son article, cité plus haut.

Ajoutons que règne d'une manière générale dans le Midi à la fin du XIIIe siècle une spiritualité de l'attente, bien illustrée par le succès du jubilé de 1300[1] et par la circulation des *Vaticinia de summis pontificibus*[2].

Tous ces éléments font que la *Lectura super apocalipsim* constitue très tôt pour les Béguins un livre de consolation et d'espérance et qu'il en résulte pour Pierre Déjean-Olieu toute la considération due à celui qui a su prophétiser les événements à venir.

Le quatrième canon du concile de Béziers, évoqué plus haut signale, de manière indirecte, l'audience de la *Postilla* dès 1299. Il ne fait aucun doute que celle-ci s'élargit dans la décennie suivante[3], puisqu'en 1311 Raimond de Fronsac et Bonagrazia de Bergame mettent explicitement l'ouvrage en cause. A la fin d'un libelle dirigé contre les Spirituels, ils accusent Olieu d'avoir multiplié dans ses écrits, principalement son *Commentaire sur l'Apocalypse*, « des prophéties sur l'Église, fausses et produites par son imagination », « la qualifiant de grande putain ». Ils développent ensuite un intéressant excursus sur les opinions des sectateurs de Pierre Déjean. On y trouve toutes les thèses exprimées par les Béguins après 1317-1318 et notamment l'identification de leur « patron » à l'ange au visage de soleil de l'Apocalypse[4]. Il est parfaitement clair que tout le système de croyances des Béguins est dès lors constitué et que la *Postilla super apocalipsim* y a trouvé sa place, concourant à renforcer la vénération pour son auteur, prophète de l'Esprit saint. Quand la crise de l'ordre franciscain s'accentue, après 1314, puis lorsqu'une répression brutale frappe Spirituels et Béguins, à partir de 1317-1318, il n'est donc pas étonnant que Pierre-Déjean Olieu fasse l'objet de condamnations répétées et devienne la référence emblématique des victimes de la persécution.

Emblème et caution d'une dissidence radicalisée

Sous le pontificat de Clément V, Spirituels et Béguins bénéficient de quelque répit. Le culte de Pierre Déjean prend alors son essor, dans son expression la plus traditionnelle. Le concile de Vienne donne au problème franciscain une solution mitigée, puis les couvents de Béziers, Narbonne et Carcassonne sont assignés aux Spirituels qui les occupent, non sans résistance de leurs ennemis. La mort du pape et celle d'Alexandre d'Alexandrie redonnent vigueur aux prétentions des frères de la communauté. Des supérieurs de leur mouvance sont rétablis dans les couvents concédés aux Spirituels; ils s'en trouvent bientôt expulsés, *manu militari*, par ceux-ci et leurs amis. En mai 1316, Michel de Césène est élu général; en août, Jacques Duèse devient pape. La situation change radicalement.

1. Sur ce jubilé, voir A. Frugoni, « Il giubileo di Bonifazio VIII », *Bolletino del Istituto storico per il Medio Evo*, 62, 1950, p. 1-121. Sur son écho dans le Languedoc, voir, « A propos de l'Albigeois », d'après Arch. Vaticanes, Collectorie 404, la thèse de l'Ecole des Chartes de Julien Théry, 1999.

2. *Cf.* H. Millet et D. Rigaux, dans *C.F.* 27, *Fin du monde et signes des temps. Visionnaires et prophètes en France méridionale (fin XIIIe – début XVe siècles)*, 1992.

3. Nous nous rangeons pleinement sur ce point à l'avis de D. Burr, *op. cit.*, p. 210.

4. Ehrle, *A.K.L.G.* 3, 1887, p. 370-371.

1317 est pour les Spirituels et les Béguins une année terrible. Le 17 février, Jean XXII ordonne aux inquisiteurs de traiter ces derniers comme des hérétiques. Le 27 avril, il fait citer devant lui les Spirituels de Narbonne et de Béziers qui refusent d'obéir aux supérieurs de l'ordre des Mineurs. Conduits par Bernard Délicieux, ils comparaissent le 13 mai. Vingt-cinq irréductibles sont jetés en prison. Le 7 octobre, la bulle *Quorumdam exigit* condamne le port des habits courts et autorise les frères mineurs à constituer des réserves de grains et de vin. Le 8 novembre, le pape remet les Spirituels qui refusent de se soumettre au jugement de Michel le Moine, inquisiteur de Provence, membre de la communauté. Le 30 décembre, il supprime toute congrégation de frères et sœurs du Tiers-Ordre, Béguins et Béguines. Le 23 janvier 1318, la bulle *Gloriosam Ecclesiam* inaugure une nouvelle année terrible, préface de beaucoup d'autres. Elle fait des Spirituels des hérétiques schismatiques et, bien qu'elle concerne avant tout un groupe italien, elle énumère des « erreurs » ayant cours en Languedoc, dont la formulation première est attribuée à Pierre Déjean-Olieu [1].

Survient une rupture définitive : le 7 mai 1318 flambe à Marseille un premier bûcher où meurent quatre frères restés fidèles à leur idéal. La sentence de Michel le Moine comporte non seulement la condamnation des Spirituels impénitents, mais aussi celle des ouvrages de Pierre Déjean-Olieu, principalement la *Postilla super apocalipsim*, dans lesquels l'inquisiteur discerne le principe de l'hérésie de ceux qu'il a jugés :

> *Constat nobis quod prefati hereses manifeste processerunt sive originem habuerunt a venerato fonte doctrine, immo verius seductrine, quam frater Petro Johannis Olivi, Biterensis diocesis, super Apocalypsi et in quibusdam ejus opusculis contra honorem sancte Romane ecclesie et auctoritatem ejusdem temere scriptitavit*[2].

Une telle diatribe prouve à l'envi que les années 1317-1318 ne constituent pas le moment déterminant pour l'actualisation de la *Lectura super apocalipsim* et que l'application de celle-ci au temps présent a depuis longtemps commencé, ainsi que l'attestait déjà *Gloriosam Ecclesiam*. Seul fait nouveau : Jean XXII s'identifie à l'Antéchrist mystique. Michel le Moine précise dans la suite de sa sentence que le pape a commis certains cardinaux et des maîtres en théologie à l'examen des ouvrages de Pierre Déjean-Olieu. A ce propos, il se livre à une attaque en règle contre lui :

> *[...] qui de erroribus adversantibus fidei catholice, honori et auctoritati summi pontificis vicarii J.-C. et sanctissime Sedis ejus, diu est graviter et a personis maturis et peritis notatus, maxime a prelatis, magistris, ministro et communitate fratrum dicti ordinis, qui prefati Petri Johannis et doctrine ejus lubricos, calles et tortuosas semitas exploratius cognoverunt.*

1. Eubel, *Bullarium franciscanum* V, n. 302.

2. Cette sentence est dans Baluze, *Miscellanea novo ordine digesta*, Mansi éd., Lucques, 1761, t. 2, p. 248-251.

L'inquisiteur juge donc tout à fait déplacé le culte dont jouit ce chef d'une secte abominable : *absonum nimis esse videtur quod ipsi Petro Johannis [...] sicut sancto seu viro approbato et catholico reverentia exhibeatur.* Il semonce chacun, puisqu'une enquête est en cours et l'affaire pendante, de ne pas manifester à Pierre Déjean la révérence due à un saint ou même à un bon catholique[1]. Tout contrevenant se trouverait, *ipso facto*, pris dans les entraves de l'excommunication.

Cette condamnation péremptoire met à la fois en évidence le culte rendu à Pierre Déjean et l'importance de ses œuvres pour les Béguins et les Spirituels. La destruction du tombeau érigé dans le chœur des franciscains de Narbonne[2] l'accompagne ou lui fait suite. Bernard Gui signale que le corps de Pierre fut « exhumé, transporté ailleurs et caché, l'an du Seigneur 1318 »[3]. Il ajoute que l'on ne sait où il se trouve et que les opinions varient à cet égard. Nicolau Eymerich déclare plus tard que Jean XXII fit brûler à Narbonne ses os avec les images de cire et les draps que ses fidèles avaient apportés sur son tombeau[4]. Quoi qu'il en fût, il est clair que le traitement réservé à Déjean-Olieu fut celui des hérétiques privés de sépulture. Ses restes furent en outre anéantis afin de rendre impossible toute forme de dévotion à leur sujet.

A partir du printemps 1318 s'engagent les poursuites contre les Béguins[5]. Ce sont les cours épiscopales qui en prennent apparemment l'initiative. Le fait n'est pas surprenant, car les enjeux[6] ecclésiastiques de la dissidence débordent largement le cadre de l'ordre franciscain, comme on l'a signalé déjà. En outre, l'archevêque de Narbonne et les évêques de Béziers, d'Agde ou de Lodève, détiennent la juridiction seigneuriale sur tout ou partie de leurs villes, et il y va de la paix sociale et de leurs intérêts temporels.

1. *Nullus presumat prenominato Petro Johannis tanquam sancto aut viro catholico et approbato reverentiam exhibere* (*Ibid.*). Notons au passage l'insistance mise sur l'approbation nécessaire des œuvres et de la sainteté par le Souverain Pontife.

2. Ehrle, *A.K.L.G.* 2, 1886, p. 293 et 3, 1887, p. 443.

3. *Fuit autem corpus ejus inde extractum et alibi portatum et absconditum sub anno Domini M° CCC° XVIII°*, *op. cit.*, p. 192-193.

4. Il précise : *Idem dominus Papa Ioannes fecit exhumari ossa dicti fratris Petri Ioannis et omnia, tam cereos imagines quam pannos, per manus simplicium ad eius tumulum deducta, Narbonae fecit publice concremari. Aliqui tamen volunt dicere quod, licet ossa fuerint exhumata, non tamen cum predictis concremata, sed Avinionem deducta et de nocte in Rhodanum proiecta, pro eo quia repertum extitit quod libros suos praedictos supposuerant correctioni sacrosanctae Romanae Ecclesiae*, dans *Directorium Inquisitorum*, Rome, 1578, t. 2, p. 77. Notre attention a été attirée sur ce texte par S. Piron, que nous remercions. Le passage a été publié par Francisco de la Peña au sein de son commentaire du *Directorium*, à partir de manuscrits donnant une version différente de celle de la première partie de ce dernier. Josep Perarnau l'a signalé dans une communication parue dans *A.F.H.* 91, 1998.

5. Certains sont condamnés au port de croix, en novembre 1318, *Doat* 27, 4r-v.

6. Nombreux témoignages de cette offensive dans les confessions. En 1320, Bernard Maurin comparaît devant les vicaires généraux de l'archevêque de Narbonne, *Doat* 35, 24r. C'est aussi le cas de Jacques Castillon, *Doat* 28, 120r. Des Béguins sont emprisonnés *in curia domini archiepiscopi; Doat* 28, 225r. Les Béguins de Lodève sont tous interrogés une première fois en 1320 dans la cour de l'évêque, *Doat* 28, 1-27. Certains sont alors absous sans pénitence, que l'Inquisition retrouve plus tard, *Doat* 28, 247r-v. Amade, femme de Durand Orlac, jure alors n'avoir rencontré aucun Béguin, *quia timebat perdere corpus suum si recognosceret veritatem*, dit-elle plus tard, *Doat* 28, 194r. Certains sont aussi jetés dans les prisons de Maguelonne, *Doat* 27, 20r.

On dresse à Narbonne un premier bûcher pour trois Béguins, le 14 octobre 1319[1]; d'autres suivent, à Capestang, à Béziers en 1320[2], à Carcassonne en 1321[3]. Cette année-là on brûle à Lunel, un dimanche comme toujours, le 18 octobre, fête de saint Luc, dix-sept Béguins, parmi lesquels deux femmes et un prêtre, au moins[4]. A Béziers, le 10 janvier 1322, la foule arrache deux condamnés au supplice, mais ils n'échappent pas à leur châtiment, après un transfert à Agde[5]. Un grand exemple est encore donné à Narbonne, dans les fossés de Saint-Paul, le 28 février 1322, premier dimanche de Carême: seize hommes et cinq femmes y sont brûlés[6]. Un bûcher de moindre importance flambe encore à Pézenas[7] et puis, à l'été de 1322, la répression change de style. Les Inquisiteurs – dont Bernard Gui – en prennent la direction et pour une dizaine de sermons généraux, échelonnés jusqu'en 1329, on ne compte plus qu'une quinzaine de remises au bras séculier. En outre, bien des condamnés au mur perpétuel sont élargis après deux ou trois ans.

Parallèlement, se poursuivent les condamnations des écrits de Pierre Déjean-Olieu. Dès 1318, comme le soulignait Michel le Moine, Jean XXII confie au cardinal Niccolà Albertini da Prato, un Prêcheur, une enquête sur la *Postilla super apocalipsim*. Ce dernier en soumet soixante extraits à une commission de huit maîtres, qui émettent, en 1319, un jugement défavorable[8]. La même année, le chapitre général des Mineurs, tenu à Marseille, condamne une fois de plus les écrits oliviens et déclare excommuniés les frères qui en détiendraient[9]. En septembre 1322, après la vague des bûchers, le pape soumet à des « experts » quatre articles tirés de la *Postilla;* ils expriment une opinion négative. En parallèle, Jean XXII porte des coups très durs à la tradition franciscaine. Il lève l'interdiction de gloser la Règle (*Quia nonnunquam*, mars 1322); il transfère à l'ordre les biens dont le Saint-Siège était (fictivement) propriétaire (*Ordinem vestrum*, décembre 1322). Enfin, il proclame hérétique la théorie de la pauvreté absolue du Christ et des apôtres (*Cum inter nonnullos*, 12 novembre 1323). Il condamne le *Commentaire sur l'Apocalypse* en consistoire, le 8 février 1326 seulement[10]. Il se débarrasse d'une telle vision de l'histoire, au moment où le mouvement des Béguins est près de son anéantissement et où Louis de Bavière tend à reprendre leur conception actualisée de la *Postilla*.

Tous ces événements, principalement ceux des années 1316-1322, jouent un rôle pour l'évolution du culte voué à Pierre Déjean-Olieu. A partir de 1318, en

1. Baluze, *Miscellanea*, I, Paris, 1678, p. 211; *Doat* 28, 225 r, 250.

2. Le bûcher de Capestang est évoqué très souvent: *Doat* 28, 17r, 192v, 196, 205r, 231, Limborch, p. 313. Pour celui de Béziers, où figure une *juvencula*, *cf. Doat* 28, 196r.

3. *Doat* 28, 21r.

4. *Doat* 28, 14r, 18r, 21v.

5. *Doat* 28, 824r; Limborch, p. 313.

6. Chronique de Saint-Paul de Narbonne, *Histoire générale de Languedoc*, t. V, c. 45-46; Limborch, p. 309, 313; *Doat* 28, 22r, 117r-v, 225v, 250v.

7. Limborch, p. 368.

8. B. Gui, *op. cit.*, p. 112-113.

9. D. Burr, *op. cit.*, p. 250.

10. Eubel, *Bullarium franciscanum*, t. V, n. 601.

effet, il n'existe plus de monument concret auquel le rattacher. En outre la cause des Spirituels compte désormais ses martyrs et les formes traditionnelles de la dévotion des Béguins tendent à se fixer sur ces derniers. On admire leur mort sainte [1], car l'on tient à cœur d'assister à leur supplice, à Capestang, à Lunel ou à Béziers [2]. On achète leurs vêtements au bourreau [3] et l'on prélève des reliques dans les bûchers éteints [4]. Certaines donnent lieu à des ostensions [5]; d'autres, plus petites, sont conservées dans une bourse [6]. Des prêtres célèbrent des offices en l'honneur des saints martyrs, présents dans le Paradis. Et même, un des Béguins principaux de Narbonne, Pierre Doumergue, introduit leurs noms dans les litanies, sollicitant leurs prières et leurs suffrages. On en compose ailleurs un martyrologe [7].

Dans de telles conditions, la vénération pour Olieu glisse logiquement, après 1318, de son tombeau vers ses écrits, et se concentre presque exclusivement sur eux. Toutefois, le poids des circonstances s'avère tel qu'ils reçoivent un sens très largement différent de leur lettre et de leur esprit originels. Ce processus d'interprétation a commencé très tôt, dès 1300 probablement, comme nous l'avons dit, peut-être avant dans certains cas. Il aboutit sous le pontificat de Jean XXII à la radicalisation extrême des positions de Pierre Déjean.

Malgré sa volonté d'éliminer les Béguins, Bernard Gui demeure un intellectuel suffisamment cohérent pour constater lui-même qu'ils ajoutent beaucoup aux écrits de leur « saint ». Pierre Déjean, dit-il, énonce de manière générale dans ses opuscules des jugements que les Béguins interprètent et s'appliquent à eux-mêmes, en altérant le sens. Aussi vont-ils d'erreur en erreur et tombent-ils dans le pire [8].

Le message de salut de Pierre Déjean n'est a priori ni contestataire ni révolutionnaire. Pour lui, la transformation de l'Église charnelle, engagée dans le monde, en l'Église spirituelle s'opère au quotidien, selon le mode de la

1. *Nunquam vidi homines ita dulciter mori*, déclare un boucher de Lodève, qui a vu brûler trois Béguins à Capestang; *Doat* 28, 17r.

2. *Doat* 28, 15v, pour Béziers. Nombreux exemples pour Lunel.

3. *Doat* 28, 24v.

4. *Doat* 28, 11r, 12v, 20v, 21r; Limborch, p. 312.

5. Martin Allègre, de Clermont, a pris à Lunel le cœur d'Esclarmonde Durban; des Béguins viennent périodiquement l'embrasser, en signe de vénération, *Doat* 28, 16r.

6. Ainsi le fait Guilhem Serralier, de Lodève, qui déclare avoir conservé des restes des Béguins brûlés à Lunel : *in sua bursa portavit tanquam reliquias martirum Christi et sanctorum de Paradiso*, *Doat* 28, 247r. On peut légitimement se demander pourquoi l'Inquisition laisse libre l'accès aux bûchers. C'est probablement dans l'intention de repérer ceux qui viennent y prélever des vestiges, d'identifier de la sorte d'autres Béguins et de les compromettre gravement, manœuvre qui réussit parfaitement.

7. Limborch, p. 385-386. Le martyrologe existe à Béziers, *Doat* 28, 26v.

8. *Nonnulla quoque ipsi Bequini, per adinventiones proprias seducti, addiderunt [...] et quamplura que generaliter dicta aut scripta inveniuntur in dictis opusculis aut in quibusdam aliis scriptitatis per complices et sequaces prefati fratris Petri Johannis, ipsi Bequini, secundum suum intellectum depravatum, sibi ipsis applicant [...], et ita ex uno errore in plures alios prolabuntur proficientes in pejus, Op. cit.*, p. 112-113.

concurrentia[1]. Cette évolution dialectique peut s'effectuer à l'intérieur des cadres ecclésiastiques traditionnels. Il reste que cette théologie du mouvement s'oppose au dogme qui pose l'Église établie dans sa perfection depuis les temps apostoliques.

Surtout, Spirituels et Béguins ne peuvent lire les ouvrages d'Olieu qu'à la lumière des combats qu'ils mènent et des persécutions qu'ils subissent. Cela, avant 1314, mais plus encore après. Les prophéties de Pierre Déjean leur semblent réalisées. Ils y découvrent leur lutte, leur justification et la promesse de leur élection. C'est, sans aucun doute, cette possibilité de transposition dans le présent et cette actualité de son œuvre, principalement la *Postilla super apocalipsim* qui, pour les Béguins donnent à Pierre Déjean-Olieu la stature d'un précurseur, revêtu de l'Esprit saint, seul capable de percevoir la fin des temps et de guider les fidèles. En opposition à l'Église romaine, la grande prostituée de Babylone, il a su donner vie à l'Église spirituelle, celle des véritables fils de Dieu. Ce rôle providentiel et prophétique l'élève au rang des saints et lui vaut une vénération que traduisent avec force les mots de Na Prous Bonet, mais que tous les Béguins, ou presque, lui portent.

On touche ici à une question fondamentale. Les Béguins vénèrent profondément Pierre Déjean-Olieu, les frères de la communauté franciscaine, puis l'Église d'Avignon tout entière le combattent avec une vigueur extrême. Cette intensité et cette âpreté traduisent-elles une large diffusion de son culte? Il convient de mesurer l'importance des milieux qui se réclament de lui, afin d'établir son audience. Cela revient à définir le cercle où se meuvent les Spirituels et les Béguins.

UNE AUDIENCE RESTREINTE

Une pétition de principe assimile, chez beaucoup d'historiens, le mouvement des Béguins à un phénomène de masse, populaire et de large diffusion. Le culte de Pierre Déjean serait en conséquence affecté des mêmes caractères. Les documents produits par l'Inquisition de Toulouse et de Carcassonne constituent les sources fondamentales sur ce point, en l'absence de toute étude précise sur chacune des villes concernées[2]. Elles ne fournissent, de toute évidence, que des données incomplètes. En effet, on peut logiquement supposer que tous les Béguins n'ont pas été poursuivis. On sait aussi que les condamnations prononcées dans les cours épiscopales entre 1318 et l'été de 1322 ont peu laissé de traces dans les archives.

1. Sur cette notion, qui vaut d'abord pour les âges, *cf.* Giulia Barone, *C.F.* 27, *Fin du monde et signe des temps. Visionnaires et prophètes en France méridionale (fin XIII*e *– début XV*e *siècle)*, 1992.

2. Seule Narbonne fait exception, grâce au livre de R.W. Emery, *op. cit.* Mais il est ancien et bref, de sorte que la monographie mériterait d'être reprise, car Narbonne constitue le pôle essentiel du monde des Béguins.

Il ne semble pas, malgré tout, qu'il faille renoncer à tenter une évaluation quantitative du mouvement des Béguins à partir des registres inquisitoriaux. Institution efficace, l'Inquisition s'est toujours efforcée d'en savoir le plus possible sur les cercles hétérodoxes et d'en recenser tous les membres [1]. En outre, bien des accusés mentionnés à partir de juillet 1322 dans les procès-verbaux des inquisiteurs faisaient déjà partie des comparants devant les juges épiscopaux autour de 1320, comme ils le confessent eux-mêmes. En tout état de cause, et pour éviter toute sous-estimation, il semble qu'on puisse approcher le nombre exact des Béguins en multipliant celui que livrent les comptages opérés dans la documentation disponible par un coefficient oscillant entre cinq et dix.

En revanche, il ne fait aucun doute que les sermons généraux de Bernard Gui, de Jean de Beaune et des autres responsables de l'Inquisition qui livrent seulement une image partielle de la population béguine, donnent une image complète de son implantation géographique et de l'extension dans l'espace du culte de Pierre Déjean-Olieu.

Un espace étroit

Premier constat : il n'est de Béguins que dans les villes. Le culte de Pierre Déjean-Olieu ne concerne absolument pas les campagnes. Il touche une vingtaine de localités. Les unes sont de grandes cités, comme Narbonne, Béziers ou Montpellier; d'autres apparaissent alors comme des agglomérations importantes, ainsi Lodève, Carcassonne, Limoux; beaucoup appartiennent au monde des petites villes, ainsi Clermont (l'Hérault), Montréal (d'Aude), Capestang, Pézenas, Montagnac, Olargues, Belpech, Cintegabelle ou Saverdun, et peut-être Alet. Villeneuve-les-Béziers, Sauvian, Gignac ou Mazères sont de gros bourgs, que leur statut, leur activité économique et leur structure sociale placent à la frontière du monde urbain. Les seuls Béguins habitant les campagnes sont des prêtres, titulaires de paroisses rurales.

Deuxième constat : les villes citées se répartissent dans une région relativement étroite qui s'étend des pays de la Basse-Ariège à l'ouest (Saverdun, Mazères, Cintegabelle) à Montpellier et de Lodève, au nord, à Narbonne. Elle forme une bande de deux cents kilomètres sur cinquante, dont Narbonne constitue le centre.

Dans cette zone, on peut considérer les sources utilisées comme indicatives du poids relatif de chacune des communautés de Béguins. Elles se répartissent en quelques gros noyaux. Narbonne et ses environs immédiats regroupent 39,5 % de leur effectif. Le Biterrois en rassemble 22 %; le Lodévois (Clermont, Gignac, Lodève), 13,5 seulement. Viennent ensuite la région de Carcassonne (11,5 %),

1. Il est vrai – *Cf. supra* – que nous ne disposons pas des aveux enregistrés (*confessiones*), mais seulement des *culpae*. On y relève fréquemment l'indication qu'un Béguin ou une Béguine a rencontré un sympathisant, *quem nominat*. Cet anonymat fait peser une lourde menace sur les coupables non encore poursuivis et les incite à une conversion rapide. La recension de ce type de mention, qui peut concerner des personnes apparaissant plus tard nominalement dans les registres, n'augmente pas de plus d'une centaine le nombre des Béguins donné plus bas.

les pays de la Basse-Ariège (Mazères, Saverdun, Belpech, Cintegabelle) qui regroupent 7,5 % des Béguins, puis Montpellier qui ne compte que 6 % de leur nombre.

Narbonne apparaît vraiment comme la capitale du mouvement avec 36 % du total des dévots de Pierre Déjean. Béziers en est le second pôle, où vivent 12,75 % de ceux-ci. Lodève (8,50 %), Montréal (7,25 %) viennent ensuite, puis Montpellier (6 %), Clermont (4,20 %), Capestang (3,6 %) et Belpech (3,6 % également), enfin Cintegabelle (3 %). Carcassonne ne compte de Béguins que dans le Bourg et en très faible nombre ; l'hétérodoxie s'y manifeste avant tout par le catharisme. La prépondérance de Narbonne n'est pas surprenante, car il s'agit d'une très grande ville et le couvent des Frères mineurs est le cœur du mouvement des Spirituels et le lieu de la sépulture de Pierre Déjean-Olieu. Que Béziers soit la seconde capitale des Béguins, le fait est confirmé par tout un ensemble de données. En revanche, la faiblesse du mouvement à Montpellier, illustré pourtant par la forte personnalité de Na Prous, étonne. Tient-elle à un effet de la documentation, les poursuites inquisitoriales ayant été bornées par la très large autonomie du consulat montpelliérain et l'appartenance de la ville au Royaume de Majorque ? Il se peut aussi qu'elle dépende d'une différence de climat social et spirituel.

On observe en effet que la carte des centres du béguinisme coïncide pour partie avec celle des cités drapantes du Languedoc[1] et des centres de redistribution des produits textiles régionaux, parmi lesquels Montagnac et Pézenas, appelés à un bel avenir. Le groupe lodévois, mais aussi Montréal, Belpech et Cintegabelle, comptent parmi les plus actives des petites villes marquées par l'essor d'une draperie légère, destinée à l'exportation. Il serait intéressant de reconstituer le réseau de relations du monde du textile dans la région, afin de voir si les courants commerciaux, les rapports de travail et les migrations des artisans du textile, ne jouent pas un rôle important dans la propagation du béguinisme et celle du culte de Pierre Déjean.

Pour ce qui concerne ce dernier, les registres de l'Inquisition donnent l'impression de contrastes régionaux assez marqués. Les Béguins de Cintegabelle et de Belpech ont tous lu ou entendu lire les œuvres du frère narbonnais, moins directement évoquées à Béziers, à Montpellier, à Montréal ou bien à Lodève. Chacune de ces trois villes compte cependant un vulgarisateur des idées oliviennes : Pierre Trencavel, Na Prous Bonet ou Raimond Déjean, l'un des Spirituels. Ceux-ci prêchent souvent et il apparaît dans le plus grand nombre des confessions que la version béguine des œuvres de Pierre Déjean a marqué les esprits. Tout dépend donc, en l'occurrence, du questionnaire des inquisiteurs. Celui de Bernard Gui, rapporté dans son *Manuel*, met Olieu en cause à de multiples reprises. En conséquence, les Béguins du ressort de l'Inquisition de Toulouse sont prolixes à son endroit. Ceux qu'interrogent, selon une grille différente, les inquisiteurs de Carcassonne, le citent moins.

1. *Cf.* Ph. Wolff, « La draperie languedocienne », dans *Regards sur le Midi*, Toulouse, 1979.

On peut conclure sur ce point que l'aire de diffusion du culte de Pierre Déjean-Olieu coïncide avec celle du béguinisme, qui se limite à un espace régional étroitement circonscrit. Le nombre des Béguins paraît lui-même relativement faible.

Un monde étroit

Les sources à notre disposition permettent de décompter entre 166 et 170 Béguins [1]. En vertu des coefficients définis plus haut, la population des Béguins oscille – dans le meilleur des cas – entre 850 et 1700 pour l'ensemble de la région considérée. Pour Narbonne, le nombre des Béguins répertoriés s'élève à 60; si l'on estime entre 300 et 600 celui des Béguins effectifs dans la ville, cela représente entre 1 et 2 % d'une population globale de 30.000 habitants, entre 1,5 et 3 % d'une agglomération de 20.000 citoyens. Le pourcentage est du même ordre pour Béziers (21 Béguins recensés, 10.000 habitants), pour Lodève (14 Béguins, 6.000 résidents); il s'élève un peu à Montréal (12 Béguins, 3.000 habitants?); il s'avère très bas à Montpellier (11 amis des Spirituels, 15.000 habitants?).

Il est donc très clair que le mouvement des Béguins n'est pas un phénomène de masse et que le culte de Pierre Déjean-Olieu reste sans doute un fait minoritaire.

On compte 37 % de femmes dans l'entourage des Franciscains spirituels. Cette forte proportion s'explique sans doute par l'existence d'un tiers-ordre féminin. On connaît «l'état civil» de 44 d'entre elles (sur 62); les femmes mariées dominent (19); les célibataires sont nombreuses (18); les veuves forment un contingent non négligeable (7).

Il est possible de définir l'appartenance sociale des Béguins; le notaire de l'Inquisition a consigné leur état ou leur profession dans 40 % des cas. On ne compte parmi eux aucun noble et l'on y trouve un seul travailleur de la terre, un jardinier, vivant en ville au demeurant, car il habite Narbonne. En revanche, prêtres et clercs sont nombreux (32 % du total), mais les marchands (7 %) et les notaires (5 %) appartiennent à des milieux peu représentés. Les artisans composent 51 % de la population béguine. Parmi eux dominent ceux du textile: tisserands, pareurs, tailleurs, qui forment un peu plus du quart de l'effectif dont la profession se trouve répertoriée. On y remarque aussi des artisans des cuirs et peaux et du fer, mais un seul représentant des métiers de l'alimentation (un boucher, de Lodève) et deux membres des professions du bâtiment (des charpentiers, de Narbonne).

La détermination professionnelle, cependant, ne suffit pas à définir le niveau social des Béguins. On en peut juger par le cas des Narbonnais. Parmi eux, un pareur de draps, un tisserand, un tailleur se placent au premier rang des élites

1. Cette variation résulte de quelques incertitudes de la documentation.

urbaines[1]. Des notations diverses montrent que beaucoup de Béguins vivent dans une aisance certaine; parmi les femmes, « Dame » Prous Bonet et Alaraxis Bias, la nièce de Pierre Déjean; puis beaucoup de chefs de famille, tel Bernard Castillon de Montpellier qui achète des maisons pour les réfugiés de Lodève et d'ailleurs[2]. Raimond d'Antesan, de Cintegabelle, a donné pour la défense des Spirituels 100 gros d'argent, 50 sous de toulzas et d'autres sommes. Il confie aussi en commande à Pierre Trencavel, animateur de la communauté béguine, 350 deniers d'or, tant en agnels qu'en florins[3]. Les comptes du procureur du roi pour les encours d'hérésie révèlent, sinon la richesse du moins la fortune honorable de plusieurs Narbonnais et de Pierre Baron de Montréal[4]. Il ne suffirait à rien de multiplier les exemples, tous vont dans le même sens : les Béguins se recrutent essentiellement dans une classe moyenne active, déjà riche et puissante, et parmi les métiers les plus dynamiques. S'y adjoignent parfois des membres de l'oligarchie citadine; à Narbonne, ce sont les Hulard, les Rouch[5] ou les Raseire[6], entre autres. Il est à cet égard intéressant de relever qu'un Bernard Mathieu de Bouzigues, chanoine de Narbonne, occupe la fonction de vicaire général de l'archevêque autour de 1320; il appartient sans doute à la famille du Béguin Mathieu de Bouzigues, auteur vers 1300, après s'être exilé en Italie, d'une confession de foi tout à fait remarquable[7].

On ne repère donc, parmi les fidèles de Pierre Déjean-Olieu, aucun de ces malheureux, sans travail, obligés pour subsister de vendre leurs outils ou de mendier et qui se comptent 1100 en 1304 dans la seule Cité de Narbonne[8]. L'exigence de la pauvreté évangélique pour la vie franciscaine n'est pas le fait des pauvres, que leur dénuement rend incapables de se préoccuper de la venue de l'Antéchrist. Le cercle social du béguinisme, bien loin de se situer chez les humbles, dans le menu peuple, s'inscrit dans la partie la plus aisée des classes moyennes et il intègre quelques membres des oligarchies citadines.

Le monde des Béguins se compose de noyaux relativement homogènes et formant bloc à l'intérieur des villes. Entre cités voisines, ils sont en contact grâce à des liens familiaux, des relations d'affaires ou des rencontres assez fréquentes. Une recherche approfondie permettrait sans doute de découvrir dans l'univers des Béguins un tissu assez dense de parentés, mais il en est certaines qui se repèrent aisément et en laissent deviner d'autres.

Un groupe particulièrement fourni est celui des Baron. Toutes les rencontres de Béguins se font à Montréal dans la maison de Pierre Baron. Non loin, à Mazères, un Bernard Baron a pris la fuite par crainte de l'Inquisition, à laquelle Agnès Baron du Bourg de Carcassonne n'a pas échappé, non plus qu'un autre

1. Jean Davignon, Bernard Roger, Blaise Boyer. *Cf.* R.W. Emery, *op. cit.*, Appendix IV, p. 166-169.

2. *Doat* 27, 20r.

3. Limborch, p. 310.

4. *Doat* 34, 189-197v.

5. R.W. Emery, *op. cit.*, Appendix IV, p. 166-167.

6. S. Piron, *art. cité.*

7. F. Delorme, « La confession de foi de Mathieu de Bouzigues », *Etudes franciscaines* 279, 1937.

8. R.W. Emery, *op. cit.*, p. 142.

Bernard Baron, consul de Narbonne[1]. On repère également des liens d'affaires unissant les Béguins d'une ville à l'autre. Ainsi le même Pierre Baron a-t-il dix agnels d'or en commande chez Jean Torroselle, hôtelier et consul de Narbonne[2].

Il existe toutefois de véritables agents de liaison, qui sont aussi des propagateurs de la bonne parole. Ils vont *occulte* de maison amie en maison amie. Le plus important d'entre eux est assurément Frère Raimond Déjean, un Spirituel, perpétuellement fugitif. Originaire de Montréal, où vit son neveu et homonyme, pareur de draps, il est le parent d'Alaraxis Bias, de Sauvian, nièce de Pierre Déjean, et probablement aussi de ce dernier[3]. Il s'exile un temps Outre-mer, puis revient dans le Midi où il prêche dans la plupart des centres importants. Pierre Trencavel, de Béziers, apparaît comme le plus actif des Béguins gyrovagues. Il s'est échappé des prisons inquisitoriales de Carcassonne et joue le rôle d'animateur des communautés citadines. Il organise des quêtes pour les Spirituels et les Béguins en fuite. Il prêche. Il assure la conservation des œuvres de Pierre Déjean-Olieu. On le voit partout : à Olargues, à Narbonne, à Béziers et à Montpellier. Deux autres « missionnaires » assurent un apostolat du même type : Guilhem Doumergue, verrier et lanternier de Narbonne, et Guilhem Serralier, de Lodève. De temps à autre, ces hommes intrépides vont se reposer en Provence, où il existe une communauté d'exilés, répartie entre Apt, Manosque, Marseille et Brignoles[4], puis ils reprennent leur tâche en Languedoc. Leur venue est l'occasion de rassemblements locaux, dans des maisons privées où ont lieu prêches et repas, ce qui traduit la faible importance de l'effectif de leurs fidèles. Ainsi les Béguins de Lodève se rendent-ils à Montpellier ou bien à Aniane, et encore à Béziers[5]; les Biterrois vont à Narbonne et à Montpellier. Etienne Gramat, de Villeneuve-les-Béziers, se déplace, quant à lui, à Montpellier et à Marseille. Une Béguine de Carcassonne, pour entendre Raimond Déjean, se rend, elle, à Montréal.

Cette ville offre l'exemple d'une communauté particulièrement soudée. Si Raimond Déjean cache son oncle, tous les Béguins se rassemblent autour de ce dernier dans la même maison, celle de Pierre Baron. Avec lui, le groupe comporte ses deux filles, Fleur et Paule, deux femmes de la famille Estève et deux autres Béguines[6].

Tout cela donne l'impression d'un cercle étroit et relativement fermé. On retrouve toujours les mêmes Béguins autour des mêmes guides. Cela tient, bien sûr, aux obligations de la clandestinité, mais cela paraît aussi correspondre à une

1. Sur ce dernier, *cf.* R.W. Emery, *op. cit.*, p. 166. Un autre noyau familial important est celui des Durban, réparti entre Clermont et Lodève. Il compte Bernard Durban, forgeron établi à Lodève, Jean Durban brûlé à Lunel en 1321, Esclarmonde Durban aussi brûlée et Raimond Durban, mari de cette dernière. Notons aussi qu'il existe à Lodève une Amade, veuve de Bernard Orlac, et un Jean Orlac à Montpellier.

2. *Doat* 34, 197v.

3. *Cf. Doat* 27, 36r, et R. Manselli, *Spirituels*, p. 187.

4. *Cf.* déposition de Bernard Maurin, prêtre de Narbonne, *Doat* 35, 26v. Elle est publiée par R. Manselli, *op. cit.*

5. *Doat* 28, 193 v, 194 v. *Doat* 28, 20, 24r.

6. *Doat* 28, 191r, 192r, 196r, 198v, 199r.

réalité sociale. Le milieu où se développe le culte de Pierre Déjean-Olieu est numériquement limité ; il ne possède aucun caractère populaire et il s'organise en petits cénacles animés par quelques individualités marquantes. On comprend ainsi que la dévotion à Pierre Déjean ne s'épanouisse pas en culte civique.

Absence d'un culte civique

Pierre Déjean-Olieu, saint des classes moyennes supérieures et d'une faible partie de l'oligarchie narbonnaise, apparaît davantage comme le saint d'un « parti » que celui d'une ville entière. On pourrait penser que les formes traditionnelles et « populaires » qu'il affecte entre 1300 et 1318 en font le patron de tous les Narbonnais, mais cela ne semble pas le cas.

En août 1309 émane de Narbonne un appel à Clément V. Il affirme que les livres de frère Pierre Déjean ont été injustement condamnés. Il dénonce les manquements à la Règle qui se constatent dans l'ordre de saint François et signale que ceux qui voudraient l'observer sont jetés en prison. Il demande en outre que soit accordée à la dépouille de frère Pierre Déjean une révérence toute spéciale [1]. Cette pétition n'est pas le fait du consulat, apparemment, mais de citoyens de Narbonne (*civium Narbonnensium* dit l'original). Elle est donc l'expression d'une catégorie d'habitants, non des représentants de la ville, et elle ne semble pas traduire une symbiose avancée entre le consulat et les dévots de Pierre Déjean.

Sept ans plus tard, un supérieur de la communauté a été replacé à la tête du couvent des Mineurs de Narbonne. Son expulsion par les Spirituels a entraîné l'excommunication de ces derniers. Alors le 27 février 1316, le consulat du Bourg proteste contre une telle mesure qui empêche les Narbonnais d'aller se confesser aux Frères – point important, comme on l'a souligné plus haut, en raison de leur accueil compréhensif – d'entendre des messes dans leur église et d'en faire dire pour le repos des morts, nombreux, ensevelis dans leur couvent. Le 3 mars, les deux consulats de la ville et les Frères font appel au pape de l'excommunication. Les consuls de Béziers se joignent à eux.

Il n'est pas question de Pierre Déjean-Olieu dans la procédure, mais les consuls de la Cité et ceux du Bourg se solidarisent, cette fois, avec les Spirituels. Ce rassemblement, qui n'implique pas l'adhésion de toute la ville – les frères de la communauté semblent y posséder de solides appuis – mais qui exprime l'accord des détenteurs du pouvoir urbain à ce moment pourrait aboutir au développement d'une religion civique à Narbonne, autour du tombeau d'Olieu, dont le culte atteint probablement son moment le plus fort.

La situation générale évolue dans un sens contraire. On sait la cascade de condamnations qui suit l'accession de Jean XXII au Souverain Pontificat. Les consuls de Narbonne ne défendent ni les Spirituels ni le culte de Pierre Déjean, dont le tombeau disparaît sans qu'il en résulte des troubles. Cela marque bien

1. *Petierunt etiam quod corpori fratris Petri Johannis [...] exhiberetur reverentia specialis*, Ehrle, *A.L.K.G.* 3, 1887, p. 18. C'est à tort que R. Manselli évoque un appel parallèle au roi (*op. cit.*, p. 79-80) en s'appuyant sur la table d'actes de R. de Fronsac (*Cf.* n. 80 ci-dessus) ; celle-ci évoque le seul appel au pape.

qu'il n'existait pas d'union de tous les habitants de Narbonne autour de la sépulture du patron des Béguins.

BILAN ET PERSPECTIVES

Le culte de Pierre Déjean-Olieu semble devoir sa promotion à l'initiative des Spirituels, qui reconnaissent en lui leur maître. Le phénomène prend sans doute naissance de manière spontanée. Les adeptes de l'observance stricte de la règle de saint François et de la pauvreté évangélique en sanctifient le défenseur intellectuel, celui dont les œuvres leur fournissent des arguments contre leurs adversaires.

Au cours de la première décennie du XIVe siècle, la dévotion à Pierre Déjean affecte des formes traditionnelles; elle s'étend alors à l'ensemble des Béguins. Pour autant, elle n'en devient pas un culte de masse très populaire et ne suscite pas une religion civique à Narbonne. Son extension se borne à une vingtaine de villes du Languedoc et à de petites communautés, limitées en nombre, qui rassemblent des artisans aisés auxquels s'associent parfois des membres de l'oligarchie citadine. Après 1317-1318 et la destruction du tombeau d'Olieu, elle se concentre exclusivement sur les œuvres de ce dernier.

La constitution de Pierre Déjean en figure emblématique d'un parti minoritaire, protestataire et contestataire, entraîne la condamnation de son culte, éprouvé dangereux par tous les pouvoirs de l'époque. Ce sentiment ressort bien dans le *Manuel de l'Inquisiteur* de Bernard Gui, qui consacre aux Béguins et à leur chef charismatique presque la moitié du texte concernant l'ensemble des dissidences hérétiques[1].

En effet, au moment où la Papauté commence d'avoir des rapports difficiles avec les monarchies « nationales », où son assise territoriale en Italie est évanescente, où s'élabore une « fiscalité pontificale » nouvelle, les Béguins, à l'abri d'une radicalisation et d'un abâtardissement des idées d'Olieu et notamment de son eschatologie, prétendent astreindre le pouvoir pontifical au respect d'impératifs extérieurs à lui et le déclarent nul s'il se refuse à cela; dans un raccourci saisissant, ils entendent même le soumettre aux écrits de Pierre Déjean dans leur version nouvelle[2]. Les enjeux sont tels que ces prétentions ne peuvent qu'aboutir à la condamnation sans appel du lecteur des Franciscains de Narbonne. Il est à celle-ci d'autres causes, moins directement perceptibles à travers les sources inquisitoriales, mais bien réelles.

On se trouve entre 1280 et 1320 en pleine gestation de la monarchie moderne en France; cette mutation s'accompagne et se traduit par des crises aux formes

1. Dans l'édition Mollat, *op. cit.*, 43 pages. En comparaison, 12 pages traitent des « Nouveaux Manichéens », 25 des Vaudois et 17 des Pseudo-Apôtres.

2. Un seul exemple de cette exigence, parmi beaucoup d'autres. Alissette Bonet, sœur de Na Prous, dépose avoir entendu les Béguins dire que *dominus Papa perdiderat suam potestatem papalem ex quo condempnaverat scripturam fratris Petri Joannis. Doat* 27, 28r.

multiples : famines, dévaluations monétaires, guerres, fiscalité croissante; la mort de Philippe le Bel est suivie de turbulences aristocratiques, puis des prédicateurs soulèvent des foules incontrôlées et violentes comme les Pastoureaux. On cherche des boucs émissaires : les lépreux sont brûlés. Na Prous met en parallèle ces derniers et les Béguins [1]. Le risque n'est pas négligeable d'une inflexion politique de l'eschatologie de Pierre Déjean. Surtout la monarchie ne peut tolérer aucune forme d'irrédentisme spirituel. Les mouvements religieux hors normes doivent être éradiqués. Gilles Aycelin, futur chancelier de France, l'archevêque qui fait édifier la belle tour d'angle du palais de Narbonne, est le premier à prendre l'initiative d'une condamnation des Béguins à Béziers en 1299.

Pour la monarchie capétienne, le Languedoc, zone récemment et partiellement incorporée à son domaine, constitue en effet une zone sensible. Il a été troublé par l'affaire Bernard Saisset et puis par toute une série de révoltes contre l'Inquisition, suivies par la trahison des consuls de Limoux et de Carcassonne qui ont fait acte d'allégeance au fils du roi de Majorque. Narbonne et Béziers se trouvent au cœur d'une région névralgique – et stratégique – entre le Roussillon et Montpellier, intégrés dans le royaume majorquin et situés dans la mouvance catalano-aragonaise. Le temps est proche de la croisade contre l'Aragon (1285) et la Sicile, enlevée aux Capétiens de Naples, a pour souverain un prince aragonais. Or le mouvement des Béguins ignore les frontières : il s'étend à la Catalogne [2], opérant une unité spirituelle qui pourrait favoriser le passage du Narbonnais et du Biterrois sous la domination aragonaise.

La prise en compte de ce contexte d'ensemble montre que le mouvement des Béguins inscrit de manière malencontreuse Pierre Déjean-Olieu dans la géopolitique du temps. Ils l'intègrent dans la coalition de l'Aragon, de la Sicile, des Gibelins et de l'Empereur, contre le pape, les Angevins de Naples et le roi de France [3]. Il sert le schisme et les Aragonais. Le franciscain reconnu pour saint,

1. *Doat* 27, 58r.

2. Sur les Béguins catalans, *cf.* J. Pou y Marti, *Visionarios, beguinos y fraticellos catalanos (siglos XIII-XV)*, Vich, 1960 et les travaux de Josep Perarnau. La symbiose entre les Béguins catalans et ceux du Languedoc apparaît nettement et de plusieurs façons dans les dépositions devant l'Inquisition. R. de Bouis, de Belpech, évoque les tertiaires Béguins brûlés à Gérone (Limborch, p. 299). Par ailleurs, Astrugue et Marie de Runderia, originaires du diocèse de Gérone, habitent Narbonne (*Doat* 28, 203v-205r, 224v-226v), où se réfugie un Béguin de Perpignan. La collusion avec la Sicile et avec l'aire catalano-aragonaise est mise en évidence dans la confession de la nièce de P. Déjean-Olieu. Elle reçoit deux émissaires venus de Sicile (*Doat* 28, 217v), qui embarquent deux jours plus tard six Spirituels fugitifs et les conduisent à Majorque (*Ibid.*, 218).

3. Les Béguins ont pleinement conscience de ce fait. Voici ce que rapporte, en 1322, un habitant de Belpech : *Opinabantur etiam quod dictus falsus papa constituerat imperatorem dictum dominum Fredericum, qui imperator factus cum rege Aragonie et aliis octo regibus venirent contra regnum Francie et regnum domini Roberti et destruerunt ipsa et dominus rex Francie devinceretur per eos [...] determinant etiam personam que erit major Antichristus, scilicet dominum Philippum de Majoricis... et predicta opinantur instructi et informati per doctrinam fratris Petri Johannis, ut dicunt*, Limborch, p. 309. Plus tard, après l'élection de l'antipape franciscain, Germain Frettier, de Carcassonne, est condamné par l'Inquisition, parce que *multa verba, blasfema dixerat et protulerat contra dominum Johannem Papam vicesimum secundum et in favorem Bavari qui se gerit pro imperatore ac illius fratris minoris qui dicebatur esse factus novus Papa*, *Doat* 27, 18v-19r.

Louis d'Anjou, appartient, lui, au camp adverse et l'illustre[1]. L'évolution du problème des Spirituels et des Béguins transforme Pierre Déjean-Olieu en adversaire du pape, de l'Église et du roi de France. Il se trouve dans une position homologue à celle de Bernard Délicieux, condamné pour son opposition aux mêmes pouvoirs en décembre 1319, mais circonstance aggravante, il alimente les Béguins en « opinions pestilentielles », *opiniones pestiferas*[2]. La sainteté que lui reconnaissent ses amis se révèle empoisonnée. Elle vaut à ce penseur de la modernité à la fin du XIIIe siècle et à ses œuvres, non point l'Enfer où leurs ennemis les plongeraient volontiers, mais un long temps de Purgatoire.

1. Les Béguins le savent, qui sont réservés à l'égard de Louis d'Anjou. Ainsi Pierre Guiraud, de Montpellier, qui s'exprime en 1322 : *Predictum fratrem Petrum Johannis credit et asserit firmiter se credere esse sanctum, quamvis non canonizatum. Et interrogatus de sancto Ludovico confessore canonizato per ecclesiam, si reputat eum sanctum, noluit hoc simpliciter confiteri set dixit quod hoc credebat sicut ecclesia Dei*, Limborch, p. 390.

2. L'expression est de Bernard Gui, *op. cit.*, I, p. 11.

DID THE BEGUINS UNDERSTAND OLIVI?

David Burr

Olivi was of central importance to the béguin movement. Bernard Gui and extant verbal processes provide us with a sense of how influential he was. Gui says, « they took their pestiferous errors and opinions partly from the books and other writings of Brother Peter John Olivi, [...] [and] from oral tradition, teachings which they say he imparted to his close associates and to the Béguins during his lifetime ». As for which of Olivi's works the béguins found useful, Gui gives us much the same list we could derive from the verbal processes. He says,

> They took these errors from his commentary on the Apocalypse, which they have both in Latin and in a vernacular translation : from some treatises on poverty, begging and dispensations that the Béguins say and believe he wrote : and from certain other writings they attribute to him, all of which they have in vernacular translations [1].

We find the same works mentioned in the processes in the Collection Doat and in those published by Limborch[2]. In other words, the béguins developed a number of their more inflammatory ideas from his Apocalypse commentary and certain of his *Questions on Evangelical Perfection.* To this list we should also add the series of essentially devotional and ascetic works edited by Manselli in an appendix of his book, *Spirituali e beghini in Provenza.* We know they were used by the béguins because they were translated into the vernacular[3].

How well did the béguins understand Olivi, though? In an article published in 1981, Raoul Manselli offered an answer. Speaking of Bernard Gui, he says,

> *Bernard a bien pénétré l'élaboration que les béguins ont fait subir aux idées d'Olivi, lorsqu'ils ont réellement appliqué à leurs propres personnes les idées impersonnelles et théoriques de leur maître, par un procédé d'adaptation et de*

1. *Practica inquisitionis heretice pravitatis*, Paris, 1886, p. 265 : *Quod errores suos et opiniones hujusmodi pestiferas ipsi habuerunt et collegerunt partim quidem ex libris seu opusculis fratris Petri Johannis Olivi qui fuit oriundus de Serinhano prope Bitterim, videlicet ex postilla ejusdem super Apocalipsim quam habent tam in latino quam etiam transpositam in vulgari; item ex aliquibus tractatibus quos ipsum fecisse Beguini dicunt et credunt, unum videlicet de paupertate et alium de mendicitate, et quemdam alium de dispensationibus, et ex quibusdam etiam aliis scriptitatis que sibi attribuunt, et que omnia habent in vulgari transposita.*

2. P. a Limborch, *Historia inquisitionis* and *Liber sententiarum inquisitionis tholosanae*, Amsterdam, 1692, *Liber sententiarum*, p. 290, 314, 318, 322, 324, 326.

3. R. Manselli, *Spirituali e beghini in Provenza*, Rome, 1959, Appendix 1.

> *concrétisation de ce qui était abstrait. Ceci est tout à fait caractéristique et manifeste les rapports entre religion savante et religion populaire*[1].

Manselli explains that this alteration was aided by the medium through which they received Olivi's thought.

> *Il faut préciser sur ce point que celui qui a directement influencé les fidèles, les béguins, n'était pas Olivi lui-même, ce vrai théologien, grand exégète et frère mineur de haut format, mais, le groupe des frères qui le suivaient entre Narbonne et Béziers. Ce sont eux qui ont condensé les œuvres du maître, les ont résumées, traduites en termes accessibles à une mentalité simple et, quelquefois, en soi et par soi des plus modestes*[2].

In the following article I will argue, in essence, that Manselli was partly right and partly wrong. He was right in suggesting that the béguins came to know Olivi primarily through the spiritual Franciscans. He was also right in suggesting that the resultant image of Olivi's thought was not entirely accurate. Nevertheless, my own reading of various béguin processes leaves me less willing than Manselli to describe the change as one of translating complex ideas into terms accessible to the simple.

In order to appreciate how they came to know Olivi we might concentrate on a single figure, Pierre Tort, whom we encounter in one of the processes published by Limborch. Pierre's confession is dated May with no year given, but it was probably 1322[3]. The son of a cutler from Montréal, Pierre was a third-order Franciscan. His confession offers us little in the way of narrative concerning his own life as a heretic. We merely learn that he harbored fugitive spiritual Franciscans and béguins in his home. Other processes shed light on his capture, which occurred in Cintegabelle. After being arrested and imprisoned he refused to cooperate for a few days but finally confessed all and was sentenced to perpetual imprisonment[4].

However little Pierre's confession may tell us about his heretical career, it speaks volumes about what the béguins believed and how they came to believe it. Pierre was voluble on Olivi and his orthodoxy :

> He said he had heard someone named in his confession preach a public sermon at Narbonne in which he said the whole doctrine of Petrus Iohannis Olivi and all his writings were good, faithful and catholic, and at the council of Vienne they as

1. R. Manselli, « Bernard Gui face aux spirituels et aux apostoliques », in *Bernard Gui et son monde*, Cahiers de Fanjeaux, Toulouse, 1981, p. 271.

2. *Ibid.*, p. 270.

3. Limborch, *Liber sententiarum*, p. 325-329. Pierre's confession is one of a group of thirteen, some undated and some dated 1321. Another of the undated ones is that of Marie de Serra, which will be considered later. Pierre, Marie and some of the confessions dated 1321 all refer to the May 1318 execution of the four spiritual Franciscans at Marseilles as having taken place *four years earlier*. The confessions dated 1321 are all from before Easter, so it was probably 1321 by their reckoning and 1322 by ours. In fact, two confessions including Marie's (*Ibid.*, p. 313, 314, 318) refer to executions which, according to Richard Emery, *Heresy and Inquisition in Narbonne*, New York, 1967, p. 132f., occurred on February 28, 1322.

4. Limborch, *Liber sententiarum*, p. 331f.

well as Olivi himself had been excused from all error and praised, except for five doubtful articles which the pope reserved to himself, although even these five he did not declare erroneous [1].

This allusion to Vienne, far from being unique, was repeated in a series of béguin testimonies, although with variations. Some simply stated that Olivi's writings had been approved as holy and orthodox at Vienne : others deduced from this that those who condemned Olivi were themselves guilty of heresy : and still others acknowledged that, while most of Olivi's thought had been approved, some of it had not. Of the latter group, some spoke of three articles, some of five, and some merely rounded it off at « a few » [2].

Pierre also heard in Franciscan sermons a ringing endorsement, not only of Olivi's apocalyptic scenario, but of Olivi himself as an apocalyptic figure :

> He also said he had heard in sermons by Friars Minor at Narbonne during the feast of Friar Petrus Iohannis that his doctrine and writings were more necessary to the Church of this final time than those of any other holy doctor except the apostles and evangelists, because, as he said, more had been revealed to Friar Petrus Iohannis than to any other holy doctor about what would happen toward the end of the world. The whole world would be in darkness and ignorance of the truth were it not for Friar Petrus Iohannis and his writings, especially regarding this modern age. They considered him to be on a par with Augustine, Jerome, Gregory and Ambrose [3].

What Pierre heard from spiritual Franciscans in sermons and conversation was supplemented by what he himself read. He was one of the few béguins who seems to have been literate, or at least one of the few who spoke of having read things as well as having heard them read. His reading included the narrative of Olivi's death cited by Bernard Gui. Gui says the béguins « frequently and willingly read or have read to them » from « a certain small work entitled *The Passing of the Holy Father* ». According to this document, on his deathbed Olivi,

> [...] after he had received holy unction and with the entire convent of Brothers Minor of Narbonne standing about, said all of his knowledge had been infused in

1. *Ibid.*, p. 329 : *Item dixit quod audivit predicari in publico sermone Narbone a quodam quem in sua confessione nominat, quod tota doctrina fratris Petri Johannis Olivi et ejus scriptura erat bona fidelis et catholica, et fuit in concilio Viennensi excusata ab omni errore et laudata, et etiam persona ipsius, exceptis v. articulis acceptis de dicta doctrina dubiis, quos sibi retinuerat dominus papa, non tamen declaraverat dictos articulos esse erroneos.*

2. For varieties of interpretation see Manselli, *Spirituali*, p. 321, 326; Limborch, *Liber sententiarum*, p. 301, 302, 306, 308, 316, 318, 329.

3. Limborch, *Liber sententiarum*, p. 329 : *Dixit etiam audivisse in sermonibus factis per fratres minores de Narbona tempore quo fiebat festum de dicto fratre P. Joh. quod doctrina et scriptura sua erat magis necessaria ecclesie pro isto tempore finali quam doctrina cujuscumque sancti doctoris, exceptis apostolis et evangelistis, quia ut dicebant magis fuerant sibi revelata illa que circa finem mundi fieri debebant quam alicui sancto doctori, et quod totus mundus fuisset in tenebris et ignorancia veritatis, nisi dictus frater P. Joh. fuisset et scriptura ejus, maxime in hiis que pertinent ad ipsa moderna equiparantes vel proponentes eum Augustino Jeronimo Gregorio et Ambrosio.*

> him by God, and that in the church at Paris at the third hour he had suddenly been illumined by the Lord Jesus Christ[1].

Pierre's version adds context. He announces that

> [...] just before he died Olivi called the friars minor together and told them that while he was in Paris, at the moment when he was washing his hands to administer the eucharist to a certain priest, the entire truth concerning the gospel and Christ's life was revealed to him, and that all his writings were true and had been revealed to him, and that he had put nothing in his writings on his own, but had written only what had been revealed to him by God[2].

Pierre's reading also included Olivi's own writings translated into the vernacular, particularly the Apocalypse commentary, which he admitted to having read frequently. Here we encounter a problem, though. On one occasion he mentions having read that Olivi « was that angel of whom it is said in the Apocalypse that his face was like the sun, and he had an open book in his hand, because he clearly had knowledge of the truth ». This identification, though of course not found in Olivi's Apocalypse commentary, was current among Olivi's followers even before Vienne, and it was found in the Catalan apocalyptic work condemned by Guido Terreni and Pierre de Palu in 1318 or 1319[3]. The latter work consisted mostly of Olivi's Apocalypse commentary, but with additions like this one. What sort of work was Pierre reading then ? He does not say.

Another citation sharpens the problem. Pierre admits that « informed by the writings of Petrus Iohannis, he had believed that Lord Pope John XXII, the present pope, was the mystical Antichrist ». Olivi, of course, never said John was anything of the kind. One assumes that Pierre simply means to credit Olivi with a picture of the mystical Antichrist which he and other béguins found it easy to apply to John, but it is not clear Pierre means only that.

Other passages add another dimension to the problem. Pierre notes that, « informed by others and by the writings of Friar Petrus Iohannis, he had believed the Preaching Friars were pharisees ». Elsewhere he observes that he

> [...] believed for two years something he had heard from certain apostates and fugitives of the Order of Friars Minor and from certain béguin associates whom he names, and which he himself had read in the books of the aforesaid Petrus Iohannis translated into the vernacular, namely that the Roman Church as far as the reprobates within it was Babylon the great whore, of which it is said in the Apocalypse that she had a gold chalice in her hand filled with abominations and

1. *Practica inquisitionis*, 287 : *Post sacram inunctionem receptam, astante sibi conventu fratrum Minorum Narbone, dixit totam scientiam suam per infusionem recepisse a Deo, et Parisius in ecclesia hora tertia subito se fuisse illuminatum a Domino Jhesu Christo.*

2. Limborch, *Liber sententiarum*, p. 329 : *Item dixit dictus P. Tort se legisse in libro de fine fratris P. Johannis, quod dum apropinquaret morti dictus frater P. Johannis convocatis fratribus minoribus dixit eis quod dum esset parisius et ablueret manus ut cuidam sacerdoti ministraret in missa tota veritas evangelii et vite Christi ei fuerat revelata et quod tota scriptura ejus erat vera et sibi fuerat revelata, et nichil de suo in dicta scriptura posuerat, set solum illud quod ei a Deo fuerat revelatum.* Reference to washing his hands is also found at Limborch, p. 308 in another process.

3. See my *Olivi's Peaceable Kingdom*, Philadelphia, 1993, ch. 9, especially p. 200, 210.

> was drunk with the blood of the martyrs of Jesus Christ, taking the Roman Church to mean the church which is in Rome and also diffused throughout the world as far as the Roman Empire extended. It was the great whore, according to them, because it involved itself in carnal delights, pride, luxury, cupidity and simony. It was called « Babylon » because of its great power, and because it sinned confusedly and all things were confused in it. It was said to be drunk with the blood of the martyrs of Jesus Christ because it persecuted those who maintained the poverty and life of Jesus Christ, and killed them. This Roman Church would be destroyed and rejected in this time, they said, through the ten kings, some of which he names [1].

In these last two citations Pierre combines what he has read and what he has heard in such a way as to make it unclear where he is getting his material. Some of it is traceable to Olivi and some is not. The passage just quoted goes on to identify John XXII with the mystical Antichrist and predict that the great Antichrist will arrive while John is still reigning. There will be two popes for a while. That great Antichrist, he says,

> [...] will be an apostate from the Order of Friars Minor, because it is the highest state in the church, as they say. They say it will be Friar Angelo, who is an apostate from the order. Others say the Lord Philip of Majorca is Antichrist. Many of them say Frederick the king of Sicily will be emperor and persecute the Roman Church, causing the Antichrist to be adored by all. Some of them say the Antichrist will finish his career within three years, others say within thirteen [2].

This scenario reflects Olivi in one way (the Antichrist as an apostate Franciscan) : expands him in another (application of that general prediction to a specific Franciscan, Angelo) : and straightforwardly contradicts him in still others (the two Antichrists as concurrent, and the king who aids Antichrist as arising from within the Christian realm, instead of being from Islam as Olivi

1. Limborch, *Liber sententiarum*, p. 329-330 : *Item dixit se credidisse a duobus annis citra tam per ea que audivit a quibusdam apostatis et fugitivis ordinis fratrum minorum et a quibusdam sociis suis beguinis quos nominat quam per ea que ipsemet legit in libris dicti fratris P. Johannis positis in vulgari quod ecclesia Romana quantum ad reprobos erat Babilon meretrix magna de qua dicitur in apocalipsi quod habebat calicem aureum in manu sua, plenum abhominacionibus et erat ebria de sanguine martirum Jesu Christi, exponendo ecclesiam Romanam pro ecclesia que est in Roma et est diffusa per mundum quantum se extendebat latitudo Romani imperii que est magna meretrix secundum eos, quia miscebat se delectacionibus carnalibus et involvebat in superbia luxuria cupidatate et symonia quam vocabant Babiloniam propter magna potestatem quam habebat, et etiam quia confuse peccabat et omnia confundebantur in ea, quam dicebant esse ebriam de sanguine martirum Jesu, quia persequitur illos qui manutenebant paupertatem Jesu Christi et vitam ejus, et eos interficit, que ecclesia Romana debet destrui et deici isto tempore ut dicunt per x. reges, quorum aliquos nominat.*

2. *Ibid.*, p. 330 : *Nullus alius papa debet esse ante antichristum, set ipso vivente apparebit antichristus major, et erunt duo pape simul, scilicet iste et dictus antichristus, qui antichristus quando venerit aufferet totum quicquid Christi est in mundo quantum poterit, quem antichristum dicunt esse aliquem apostatam ordinis minorum, quia est alcior status ecclesie ut dicunt dicentes quod erit frater Angelus qui est apostata ordinis fratrum minorum. Alii dicunt dominum Philippum de Majoricis esse antichristum. Dicunt etiam plures ex eis quod Fredericus rex Sicilie erit imperator et persequetur ecclesiam Romanam, et facit quod dictus antichristus ab omnibus adoretur. Dicunt etiam quod dictus antichristus finierit cursum suum secundum aliquos infra tres annos, secundum alios infra xiii.*

implies). The whole scenario has more to do with what « they say » than with what Olivi wrote: yet Pierre rounds off this prediction by noting that he believed all this « informed by the aforementioned apostates and béguins and by Petrus Iohannis' commentary on the Apocalypse ». The point here is not merely that what Pierre read in Olivi was distorted by what he heard from spirituals and béguins, but also that his confession mixes what he read with what he heard in such a way as to make it impossible for us to say whether he was actually reading Olivi or an amalgam like the Catalan text.

In the final analysis even the literate Pierre seems to have been far more reliant on what he heard than on what he read. He provides us with an extended series of radical statements he heard in Franciscan sermons, and he explicitly says some of them were delivered on Olivi's feast day. On that day he heard a friar say the poverty prescribed by the rule had been hidden from those in the community even though Olivi had made it clearly evident: that the pope could not relax the demands made by the rule: and that if he attempted to do so he should not be obeyed. Pierre provides the reasoning behind this claim, and it is straight out of Olivi's *Questions on Evangelical Perfection*.

Olivi's apocalyptic scenario was equally represented in these sermons. On Olivi's feast day Pierre heard friars say Olivi's writings were more important to the church in the final time than were those of any other holy doctor except the apostles and evangelists, because more had been revealed to him about what was to occur at that time. He heard Olivi compared to Augustine, Jerome, Gregory and Ambrose. This much is explicitly attributed to sermons on Olivi's feast day: but in Pierre's testimony it is enveloped in a much longer series of assertions which, though not explicitly identified with that day, are nonetheless said to have been derived from Franciscan sermons in Narbonne. Pierre does not date these sermons, but there is reason to assume that he heard them no later than March 1317, the last Olivi feast day before the Narbonne and Béziers spirituals were summoned to Avignon[1].

Others heard similar sermons. Marie de Serra says she heard a sermon at Narbonne on Olivi's feast day in which she was told Olivi was an uncanonized saint. It was not important whether he was canonized by humans, because God had canonized him[2]. Again, a priest named Mathieu tells of hearing, this time at Montréal rather than Narbonne, a sermon by the spiritual Raymond Déjean. In it Raymond described persecutions of the faith continuing up to the present. After the sermon Mathieu asked Raymond what he had meant when he said in the

1. He says he has believed many of these things for five years, which seems to mean since 1317. Moreover, the whole scene – spiritual Franciscans preaching public sermons at Narbonne on Olivi's feast day in which they warn the laity that in the approaching hour of trial they must observe their vows even in the face of papal commands to the contrary – seems to fit the period between the time the house was forcibly taken over by the spirituals and that last feast day on March 14, 1317. Conversely, it seems very hard to imagine any such defiant messages being preached in public during succeeding years, after Olivi's tomb at Narbonne had been destroyed and John had transformed the spirituals from dissidents into heretics. Nevertheless, even after that date Olivi's feast was still celebrated in private by beguins (*e.g.* at Montpellier as attested in *Collection Doat*, vol. 27, f. 21 v).

2. Limborch, *Liber sententiarum*, p. 319.

sermon that he, Raymond, would suffer for the faith. He was, after all, not going overseas among enemies of the faith. Raymond replied to him and others that:

> [...] enemies of the faith are among us, for the Church by which we are ruled is what is signified by the great whore of which the blessed John speaks in the Apocalypse, and it persecutes Christ's ministers and the poor. Can you not see that we do not dare to appear openly before our own brothers? Later Brother Raymond Déjean said that there had been no true pope in the Roman Church since Celestine[1].

Here we find a remarkably strong indictment of the Church in the Olivian tradition and, more surprising, a view of Celestine's successors much like the one vigorously attacked by Olivi in his 1295 letter to Conrad of Offida. If Mathieu is remembering correctly, Raymond was focusing Olivi's apocalyptic on the present situation and announcing that what Olivi predicted was now occurring: but he was going well beyond Olivi, combining him with completely different influences. When did Raymond say all this? The evidence given us by Mathieu is ambiguous to say the least, but it seems very possible that here too we are dealing with a recollection of words uttered just before the spirituals were called to Avignon[2].

In short, Pierre and others confront us with the picture of an embattled spiritual group around 1317 applying Olivi to their current situation in a way that radicalized his message, not only by applying his general predictions to specific

1. *Collection Doat*, vol. 27, f° 85v-86r: *Inimici fidei sunt inter nos, nam ecclesia qua regimur figuratur nobis per illam magnam meretricem de qua loquitur Bertrandus [sic] Ioannes in apocalipsi, et ista persequitur ministros Christi et pauperes nunquid vos videtis quod nos non audemus ire palam inter nostros fratres. Postea dixit dictus fratres [sic] R. Ioannis quod in Ecclesia Romana non fuit verus Papa citra Celestinum quem ipsi pauperes habebant in Cilicia vel eius successorem, et cardinales, et praelatos, et illa est vera ecclesia.*

2. Mathieu and Raymond were part of a group sentenced on November 11, 1326, but when Mathieu says Raymond said these things « seven years earlier » he presumably means seven years before the confession. Mathieu's confession is dated *millesimo trecentesimo vicesimo*, but one suspects a final number was eliminated. The other confessions are dated between 1324 and 1328, but all the beguins sentenced that day other than Mathieu were interrogated in late 1325 or early 1326, so Mathieu probably was too. If so, then one would assume that in recounting an event that occurred « seven years ago » he was looking back to ca. 1318 or 1319. Raymond Déjean's process, edited by Manselli, *Spirituali e beghini di Provenza*, p. 302-306, says he was one of those spiritual Franciscans cited to Avignon in April 1317. The friars who went to Avignon were apparently held until October, then asked if they would obey the pope. Raymond agreed to do so and was sent to the Franciscan house at Anduze. He remained there « for a while » but eventually left without permission, accompanied by another friar. From Anduze he went to Béziers and remained hidden in a home there « for more than three years ». Thus it is hard to imagine how he could have preached a public sermon at Montréal between April 1317 and late 1320. Raymond's comment that he could not appear openly before his brothers seems to suggest that he was a fugitive, and we know from other processes that he was in Montréal after he apostasized, probably not long after; but if he was a wanted man it seems odd that Mathieu heard him preach a public sermon. Moreover, he is described as « then of the Friars Minor », suggesting a contrast with what he later became, an apostate. Thus a date before April 1317 seems likely.

people and events, but by mixing in elements that were not Olivian at all[1]. That brings us back to our original question : whether the béguins were reading Olivi correctly or distorting him. In saying that the pope should not be obeyed if he ordered the Franciscans to violate their solemn vow of *usus pauper*, they were reading Olivi correctly. He said this much explicitly and rather insistently, not only in his *Questions on Evangelical Perfection* but in his Apocalypse commentary. The only real question is whether Olivi would have recognized the particular relaxations demanded by the pope in 1317 as so obviously in violation of the vow as to demand disobedience, and that is an unanswerable question.

Much the same thing could probably be said of Olivi's apocalyptic scenario as reflected, not merely in the spiritual Franciscan sermons described by Pierre Tort and others, but throughout the béguin processes. Olivi's expectation of future tribulation was very concrete in one sense and very general in another. It was concrete in the sense that he saw the Church as becoming increasingly corrupt and expected that in the relatively near future that corruption would reach the highest possible levels. He saw a new age dawning with Francis and his order and expected that a future carnal pope would lead a carnal power structure in opposing it. He tended to identify that pope with the mystical Antichrist. The carnal Church would be destroyed by a non-Christian army whose goal was to destroy Christianity, not to save the suffering righteous from persecution, and the latter would still find themselves persecuted, but by a new oppressor, the Great Antichrist.

To put the matter in this way is to state it more positively than Olivi ever did. He tended to say « perhaps » a great deal and offer alternative scenarios : yet in the final analysis it is hard to read him without deciding the above scenario is the one he himself favored. That is the sense in which he was fairly concrete. He was general in the sense that he identified the mystical antichrist with a pope, but not with any specific pope. Even the invading non-Christian army, though it looks very Moslem at times, is never definitively labeled. The identity of the great Antichrist is even less clear, although Olivi obviously approved of the notion that he would be a pope and an apostate Franciscan. Nor did Olivi offer a precise timetable, although he assumed that the mystical Antichrist might begin work anytime after the beginning of the fourteenth century and that the great Antichrist would be dead at least by the middle of the century[2].

Olivi's apocalyptic scenario was, in short, a plot line in which the motivation and much of the action were furnished but the names and dates were left unspecified. In the context of 1317 and beyond, a series of people seemed to be

1. Thus Pierre Tort heard from the Narbonne spirituals something they said had been revealed to Saint Francis, namely that the order would be divided into three parts. Two of them, the community and the Tuscan rebels in Sicily under Enrico da Ceva, did not observe the rule and would be destroyed, while the third, the spiritual Franciscans and beguins, would survive their many persecutions and endure until the end of the world. All of this had been revealed to Saint Francis. Limborch, *Liber sententiarum*, p. 326. Here the matter is confused by Pierre's failure to designate this assertion explicitly as one of the ideas he encountered five years earlier, but whenever he heard it we can be sure it did not come from Olivi.

2. For all this see my *Olivi's Peaceable Kingdom.*

auditioning for the major roles. Once the spirituals chose to identify themselves with the vanguard of the new age, their persecutor John XXII automatically became the carnal pope and thus by extension the mystical Antichrist[1]. Here again Olivi's general word had become solid flesh, and here again it is impossible to say whether he himself would have made the same identification. In fairness to the béguins it should be recognized, though, that whether Olivi would have recognized John's credentials as mystical Antichrist or not, he would have had to acknowledge that John was occupying the position Olivi himself had expected the mystical Antichrist to hold : that in undermining Franciscan poverty as Olivi understood it he was doing pretty much what Olivi had expected the mystical Antichrist to do : and that he had appeared just about when Olivi had thought the mystical Antichrist should be expected[2].

When the béguins chose to support the spirituals, they were eligible to join Olivi's persecuted elect, and John soon made sure that they did. Again we find it impossible to say whether Olivi would have recognized this situation as the one he had been anticipating : yet again we find that he might have had good reason to see it as such. After all, he had noted that the gospel preached by harbingers of the new age would be rejected by the wise and powerful but accepted by the simple[3]. Béguin tailors, candlemakers and housewives had every reason to see themselves as the latter group.

Once we move beyond the mystical Antichrist to the great one we find it somewhat easier to see a basic contradiction between the Olivian prediction and its béguin application. In expositing Apoc. 17, Olivi had thought it likely that in the future a pagan ruler would combine forces with an apostate Franciscan pope and the two would gain ultimate control over the Christian world. One or the other, probably the pope, would be the great Antichrist. The béguins adapted this pattern to their own reality in an unexpected way. At least some of them – including Pierre Tort, as we saw – saw it in terms of the Angevin-Aragonese rivalry that characterized European politics at the moment[4]. When we compare this béguin expectation with Olivi's original thoughts on the great Antichrist, we might be excused for suspecting that the béguin scenario simply cannot bear the weight of Olivi's expectation. Olivi was aware that he was projecting the discussion into a time beyond his own imagining. Nevertheless, what he seems to have had in mind, insofar as he could envisage it at all, was much too monstrous to be translated into anything as prosaic as an alliance between Frederick III and Angelo Clareno, although it is impressive that béguins like Pierre Tort respected Olivi's text enough to be on the lookout for an apostate Franciscan.

1. *E.g.* Limborch, *Liber sententiarum*, p. 308 (with reservations), 312, 316, 318, 330, 388; *Collection Doat*, vol. 28, f. 206v, 214v, 220v, 225v, 236r (the final citation says he prepares way for Antichrist, which is taken elsewhere as equivalent to being the mystical Antichrist); Manselli, *Spirituali*, p. 322f., 325.

2. Burr, *Olivi's Peaceable Kingdom*, ch. 7.

3. See his *Lectura super apocalypsim*, in W. Lewis, « Peter John Olivi, Prophet of the Year 2000 », dissertation, Tübingen University, 1972, p. 974.

4. Limborch, *Liber sententiarum*, p. 309, 319, 326, 330; Manselli, *Spirituali*, p. 160-165.

On the other hand, the béguin expectation of life after Antichrist seems essentially in harmony with Olivi's. That is partly because Olivi preferred to leave that period undefined and they said little about it either: yet there is an attractively Olivian ring to Bernard de Na Jacma's suggestion that at that time a young virgin will be able to go from Rome to Santiago da Compostella without anyone making any evil plans concerning her along the way [1].

Nor was the béguin timetable totally out of step with Olivi's. We have seen that Olivi expected the mystical Antichrist to show his hand any time after the beginning of the fourteenth century, so John XXII was none too early for that appearance. The rest of the timetable also has points of contact. Though he was cautious about it, Olivi tended to assume that the great Antichrist would rule sometime during the first four decades of the century [2]. We find various béguins saying in 1321-22 that the Antichrist is now over twenty years old: that he will be in Jerusalem by 1325: and that he will be dead in either three, thirteen or fourteen years [3]. While these numbers do not precisely mirror Olivi, they fit within the range of his expectation. It is hard to say how much the béguins differed on the length of the third age. Olivi thought it would last around seven hundred years. Bernard Gui claims that the béguins expected it to last around a century, and perhaps many of them did. Those whom we meet in inquisitorial processes simply did not say. They and their questioners were too preoccupied with the present tribulation to worry much about the future peace.

In short, the béguins – like the spiritual Franciscans on whom they depended – altered Olivi's teachings not so much by oversimplifying them as by applying them to their concrete situation and combining them with other, very different sources. In the final analysis, however, the most striking thing is not how the béguins followed or departed from Olivi in certain details but how they reflected central themes in his writing, like his sense that the church was heading into a new age and that the pope would stand against it. They were formed by Olivi's strong sense that Christ's age and his own age represented two major turning points of history, and that they were generally similar in structure, with Francis and his order playing the role of Christ and the contemporary Church hierarchy cast as the chief priests, scribes and pharisees. They were informed by Olivi's notion that in this new period Christ was suffering a new passion in his people prior to being resurrected in a new age. These were powerful images that sustained and united the béguins, even when their presentation of the details varied.

1. Limborch, *Liber sententiarum*, p. 308. The same idea is repeated in the investigation concerning Adhémar de Mosset. J. Vidal, « Procès d'inquisition contre Adhémar de Mosset », *Revue d'histoire de l'Église de France* 1, 1910, p. 579.

2. See my *Olivi's Peaceable Kingdom*, ch. 7.

3. Limborch, *Liber sententiarum*, p. 319-320, 330, 388.

THE VISIONARY AUTHORITY OF NA PROUS BONETA

Louisa A. Burnham

Na Prous Boneta probably never expected to become a leader of an underground religious resistance movement. In the decade after 1317, the heretical community of the Beguins of Languedoc, followers of Peter Olivi, gathered together in secret solidarity as the Church intensified its campaign to convert, imprison or execute them. For the Beguins, their persecution was the sign that the dawning of a new age was at hand, an age when spiritual understanding and visionary experience of the divine would increase, and the humble might thereby be exalted. In the midst of the turmoil, Na Prous Boneta had a series of apocalyptic visions which emboldened her to assert an unexpected authority not only over the women of her acquaintance, but also over a widening circle of men. « God put on flesh in the body of a virgin, and in me, he has put the word », she was to tell the inquisitor, « I am the donor *[donatrix]* of the Holy Spirit »[1]. Though her adamant defense of her own central position in the economy of salvation led her to the stake, she remains one of the few examples in Western history of a woman who attained a position of leadership in a resistance movement of both men and women. In this text, I would like to demonstrate three things. First, that Na Prous' extraordinary testimony does in fact have its basis in the Olivian and Joachite traditions. Second, I will show how the reception of her message among her contemporaries was conditioned both by the development of these ideas in the Beguin communities in the Midi and by the atmosphere of persecution. Finally, I will demonstrate that Na Prous exercised a significant influence over the heretical conduct of both men and women, due to the authority of her visions.

1. « *Ut Deus sibi dixit, ut asserit, de virgine cepit corpus suum, et de ipsamet Naprous cepit verbum* ». W.H. May, « The Confession of Prous Boneta, Heretic and Heresiarch » in *Essays in Medieval Life and Thought Presented in Honor of Austin Patterson Evans*, J.H. Mundy *et al.*, eds., New York, 1955, p. 29, 26. Na Prous' testimony is preserved in vol. 27 of the Collection Doat of the Bibliothèque Nationale in Paris (f° 51r-79v). Though the Collection Doat documents are only seventeenth-century copies of the originals, they have the very considerable virtue of existing, since most of the originals were destroyed at the time of the Revolution. Na Prous Boneta's sentence was published by Henry Charles Lea in his *A History of the Inquisition of the Middle Ages*, New York, 1887, vol. III, p. 653-654.

As the Dominican inquisitor Henry de Chamayo rightly called her, and as I will prove in this article, Na Prous Boneta was not only a heretic, but also a heresiarch. Canon law defines « heresiarch » as follows :

> He who defends the error of others is much more damnable than those who err, because not only does he himself err, but he prepares and confirms the stone of offence of error for others. Whence, the teacher of error is said to be not only a heretic, but also a heresiarch [1].

We can assume that Henry de Chamayo was familiar with this usage, and that therefore he understood Na Prous to be a leader in heresy, and a teacher of heresy to others. It is not sufficient to explain that Na Prous' deposition was astonishing to the inquisitors, for other equally original, astonishing, and impenitent heretics were not deemed to deserve the title heresiarch. The condemnation of Limosus Nigri on September 10, 1329, a scant year after Na Prous' execution, is one example that proves the point. The same inquisitor, Henry de Chamayo, described Limosus Nigri, whose cosmology appears akin to Menocchio's, and whose radical ecumenism seems to come straight out of the sixties [2], as merely « a manifestly obstinate and pertinacious heretic » [3]. Though Limosus Nigri tells us himself that he had tried to lead others to follow his beliefs, it would appear that few, if any believed him [4]. The word heresiarch was, however, used by the same inquisitor to describe Raymond Johannis, an apostate friar who preached, heard confessions and carried with him a copy of Olivi's Apocalypse commentary [5] : for the inquisitor of Carcassonne, « heresiarch » appears to describe someone who *succeeds* in leading others into error. As I will show, Na Prous Boneta was indeed a heresiarch as defined by canon law, and as understood by Henry de Chamayo.

Though other scholars have worked with Na Prous Boneta's deposition, few have recognized her influence on others [6]. The most recent general publication in

1. Friedberg, 1, 999. C. 24 q. 3 c. 32. « *Qui aliorum errorem defendit multo est dampnabilior illis, qui errant, quia non solum ille errat, sed etiam aliis offendicula preparat erroris et confirmat. Unde quia magister erroris est, non tantum hereticus, sed etiam heresiarcha dicendus est* ». That this definition was current among inquisitors at the beginning of the fourteenth century is indicated by its use in documents from a Bohemian trial that dates from between 1335 and 1343. « Zwei Rechtsgutachten zum Inquisitionsprozeß gegen den Brünner Goldschmied Heynuš Lugner », in A. Patschovsky, *Quellen zur Böhmischen Inquisition im 14. Jahrhundert.*, Weimar, 1979, p. 289, 302.

2. *Doat* 27, f° 216r-225r. Limosus Nigri, a sixty-year-old man from St Paul-de-Fenouillet in the diocese of Alet, asserted, among other things, that the sun and the moon were corruptible, and made from corruption, but that their intercourse created the earth and mankind. He denied the Church's conception of the Trinity, and the efficacy of most of the sacraments (except as a means of distinguishing among Jews, Muslims and Christians – all of whom he believed could be saved). He told the inquisitors that God had placed this « *scientiam et philosophiam* » in his heart after he had fasted for ten days and ten nights (f°s 223v-224r). For the comparison to Menocchio, see C. Ginzburg, *I formaggio e i vermi : Il cosmo di un mugnaio del '500*, Torino, 1976.

3. *Doat* 27, f° 235r-v.

4. Limosus Nigri, Doat 27, f° 216r. His own nephew fought with him about receiving the eucharist (f° 224r).

5. See below.

6. David Burr's recent article, « Na Prous Boneta and Olivi », *C.F.* 67, 1997, p. 477-500, does indeed consider this point (p. 483-488), and Burr and I come to many of the same conclusions. Though

English on the history of medieval heresy relegates Na Prous to a footnote, in company with eccentrics, madmen, and « suggestible women »[1]. Even William May, whose edition of her deposition has allowed a wider range of scholars to have access to her, considered Na Prous to be of interest primarily to « all concerned with the psychology of religion and the history of millennial hope and expectation »[2]. He considered Na Prous « troubled », and her mission to have failed[3].

Other scholars have accepted May's assessment, including Raoul Manselli, whose *Spirituali e beghini in Provenza* has been the standard work on the subject of the Spirituals and Beguins since its publication in 1959. For Manselli, « the solitude and the incomprehension that Na Prous encountered and found around her is made clear by the particular singularity of her message »[4]. Manselli expressly dismissed any possibility that her message may have found sympathetic listeners, and did not even allude to her most intimate companions. His concern to preserve the orthodoxy of the Beguins forced him to consider a figure like Na Prous, who took Olivi's message to its most radical degree of heterodoxy, a lone, lonely and « psychopathic » heretic[5].

More recently, however, Na Prous has found a place in the literature as a contemporary feminist heroine. Elizabeth Petroff places Na Prous firmly in a certain affective tradition of feminine religiosity[6], and Daniela Müller argues that Na Prous was condemned because she, like Marguerite Porete and Guglielma of Milan, had dared to consider the « powerful masculine Church » useless[7]. In a

I have greatly benefited from discussions with this master of the material, my argument and conclusions were developed independently.

1. M. Lambert, *Medieval Heresy*, Blackwell, Oxford, 1996, p. 188 n. 42. Other general histories of heresy and prophecy have also given Na Prous short shrift. While Henry Charles Lea included Na Prous' sentence in the appendix to his great work on heresy, in his text, he also states that she reached « the heights of religious delirium ». Lea, *A History of the Inquisition*, vol. III, p. 82. Though Gordon Leff considered Na Prous to have been influential (especially to women) because of the revelatory nature of her views, he provided no details of that influence. *Heresy in the Later Middle Ages : The Relation of Heterodoxy to Dissent*, Manchester, 1967, p. 213. Marjorie Reeves juxtaposed her discussion of Na Prous with a more complete treatment of Guglielma of Milan, and considered Na Prous' doctrine to be « strange » and « ill-assorted ». *The Influence of Prophecy in the Later Middle Ages : A Study in Joachimism*, Oxford, 1969, p. 248.

2. W.H. May, « The Confession of Prous Boneta [...] », p. 6.

3. W.H. May, « The Confession of Prous Boneta [...] », p. 4.

4. R. Manselli, *Spirituali e beghini in Provenza*, Rome, 1959, p. 248. Manselli's book has been translated into French by J. Duvernoy as *Spirituels et béguins du midi*, Toulouse, 1989.

5. R. Manselli, *Spirituali e beghini*, p. 247.

6. E.A. Petroff, *Medieval Women's Visionary Literature*, New York, Oxford, 1986, p. 284-290. Her introduction, which is derived essentially from H.C. Lea and W.H. May, is on p. 276-277. Petroff's incomplete translation of the text omits a number of passages especially important to the argument of this paper. A complete translation into French of Na Prous' deposition is contained in Jean Duvernoy's translation of Manselli's *Spirituali e Beghini. Spirituels et Beguins du Midi*, Toulouse, 1989, p. 274-289.

7. D. Müller, « Les Béguines », *Hérésis* 13-14, 1989, p. 351-389. Also, « Der Prozess gegen Prous Boneta : Begine, Ketzerin, Häresiarchin (1325) », in Norbert Höhl ed., *Ius et historia : Festgabe für Rudolf Weigand*, Würzburg, 1989. Though Müller has turned to the Doat originals to find the testimony of Alisseta, Na Prous' sister, and Alaraxis, their companion, her erroneous contention that Na Prous had been executed by November, 1325 does not allow her to consider Na Prous' continued

more intriguing approach, Barbara Newman associates Na Prous with another heresiarch, Guglielma of Milan, in a study which links the two on the issues of gender complementarity, and the feminity of the Godhead : « they breathed new life into the tenuous yet tenacious memory of a Godhead in which the Holy Spirit was no sacred bird, but the heavenly Mother »[1]. Recent studies by both Claudia Rattazzi Papka and David Burr have moved away from a uniquely feminist interpretion of her visions, and have instead taken Na Prous' apocalyptic views seriously. Papka considers Na Prous' transgressive apocalyptic « I » as an important step in the development of the medieval apocalyptic tradition[2], and Burr has conclusively and magisterially established the links that tie Na Prous to Olivi, and eventually Joachim[3]. The work of Newman, Papka, and Burr is particularly valuable in that it acknowledges Na Prous' place in the larger history of western heresy, and no longer relegates her story to the merely curious history of psychopathology. Yet even these important studies treat Na Prous primarily as « heretic »; it is my goal to return to her the more important and influential role which her inquisitors did not hesitate to grant her, that of « heresiarch ».

Na Prous Boneta, the daughter of Durand Boneti[4], was born in La Cadière, a small village in the diocese of Nîmes about 40 km from Montpellier, no later than 1296[5]. At the age of seven, presumably with her family, she moved to Montpellier. We know very little about Na Prous' family, or the motives which led them to relocate to Montpellier, but we do know the attraction of the bustling,

influence in prison (she does not appear to be aware of the papal bull mentioning « *quandam mulierem [...] Boneta* ». See below).

1. B. Newman, *From Virile Woman to WomanChrist: Studies in Medieval Religion and Literature*, Philadelphia, 1995, p. 198.

2. C. Rattazzi Papka, *Fictions of Judgment : The Apocalyptic « I » in the Fourteenth Century*, doctoral dissertation, Columbia University, New York, 1996, especially p. 126-161.

3. Burr has published two recent articles on this subject. D. Burr, « Na Prous Boneta and Olivi », and « Olivi, Prous and the Separation of Apocalypse from Eschatology », in M. Cusato and F.E. Coughlin eds., *That Others May Know and Love : Essays in Honor of Zachary Hayes, O.F.M. ; Franciscan, Educator, Scholar*, St. Bonaventure, NY, 1997. In an earlier work, « Olivi, Apocalyptic Expectation, and Visionary Experience », *Traditio* XLI, 1985, p. 273-288, Burr concludes that Na Prous' visions were unique in the Beguin community, but his more recent work affirms their Olivian content and inspiration.

4. Her deposition calls her « *filia Durandi Boneti de sancto Michaele de la Cadyera* » (W.H. May, « The Confession of Prous Boneta [...] », p. 7), but her sentence reads « *filia quondam Stephani Boneti de Sancto Petro de la Cadiera* » (H.C. Lea, *A History of the Inquisition*, p. 653). A note here on her name, Na Prous Boneta : the title « Na », short for *domina* or *domna* (*i.e.*, « Mistress » or « Lady ») was probably a simple honorific, perhaps used to indicate a female head of household. In Montpellier, several Beguin women are called by this title (see A. Germain, « Une Consultation inquisitoriale au XIVe siècle », *Publications de la Société Archéologique de Montpellier*, IV, 1857, p. 309-344 ; p. 334, « Na Catharina », and p. 338, « Na Bodina »). Emery also notes the existence of two poor women in Narbonne in 1305 called « *na Dossa, beguina and na Guillelma, beguina* ». R.W. Emery, *Heresy and Inquisition in Narbonne*, New York, 1941, p. 131. The original source is A. Blanc, « Le livre de comptes de Jacme Olivier », *Bulletin de la commission archéologique de Narbonne* III-VII, p. 543. Na Prous Boneta's given name is thus Prous ; since all of the sources call her « Na Prous » (frequently in one word, « Naprous »), however, I have chosen to follow their convention.

5. Na Prous tells us that she has lived in Montpellier since she was seven years old (W.H. May, « The Confession of Prous Boneta [...] », p. 7), and her sister Alisseta says she has lived in Montpellier for 22 years (*Doat* 27, f° 26r).

cosmopolitan city of Montpellier for the inhabitants of its « basin » [1]. Montpellier was known primarily as a market, but also for its scarlet wool-dyeing industry, and for silk-finishing, though not, surprisingly, for textile manufacturing [2]. Perhaps a move to Montpellier represented a kind of « gradual upward social mobility » [3]. It is also possible that the move was made for religious reasons : if the Boneti family were already connected with Beguin circles, then a town with an active Franciscan convent such as Montpellier, where Olivi himself had been located from 1289 to approximately 1295 [4], might well be preferable to a tiny village like La Cadière, which had none [5].

It is clear, however, that Na Prous, at least, was « beguinized » at a very young age [6]. In June, 1305, at the age of nine, she took a vow of chastity, a « *votum virginitatis* ». When she told this to the inquisitor, she emphasized, « and I have maintained it » [7]. Though we do not know under what circumstances Na Prous

1. The largest of the towns of lower Languedoc, Montpellier was a busy commercial center, with a flourishing cloth-dying industry, long-distance trade and banking. Its university also contained the finest medical faculty in Europe, which attracted an international clientele. In 1300, its population probably amounted to between 30,000 and 40,000, including very many immigrants, or the immediate descendants of immigrants, from the surrounding countryside and as far afield as Spain and Italy. Though Montpellier itself was under the rule of the Kings of Majorca, a cadet branch of the Crown of Aragon, until 1349, the French king Philip IV had purchased rights over the episcopal quarter of Montpellieret from the bishops of Maguelone in 1293. Kathryn Reyerson has treated the position of Montpellier as a center of financial activity in *Business, Banking and Finance in Medieval Montpellier*, Toronto, 1985, and as a draw for immigration in « Patterns of Population Attraction and Mobility : the Case of Montpellier, 1293-1348 », *Viator* 10, 1979, p. 257-281. Many of her relevant articles are collected in K. Reyerson, *Society, Law and Trade in Medieval Montpellier*, Variorum, London, 1995. Another collection of material concerning mercantile Montpellier is J. Combes, *Montpellier et le Languedoc au moyen âge*, Montpellier, 1990. Detailed analysis of the medieval city is most conveniently available in G. Fabre and T. Lochard, *Montpellier : la ville médiévale*, Paris, 1992.

2. K. Reyerson, « Patterns of Population Attraction », *cit.*, p. 261. Reyerson analyzes the textile industries of Montpellier in « Medieval Silks in Montpellier : The Silk Market ca. 1250 – ca. 1350 », *Journal of European Economic History* 11, 1982, p. 117-140, and « Le Rôle de Montpellier dans le commerce des draps de laine avant 1350 », *Annales du Midi* XCIV, 1982, p. 17-40. The existence of small sewing shops for women is also attested to in a thirteenth-century romance, *Escoufle*, written by Jean Renart, where the heroine, in search of her lover, establishes a sewing shop in Montpellier whereby the lovers are reunited. J. Baldwin, *The Language of Sex : Five Voices from Northern France Around 1200*, Chicago, 1994, p. 26.

3. K. Reyerson, « Population Attraction and Mobility », p. 271.

4. D. Burr, *Persecution*, p. 68, and F. Ehrle, « Petrus Johannis Olivi, sein Leben und seine Schriften », *Archiv für Literatur und Kirchengeschichte des Mittelalters*, III, Berlin, 1887, p. 431. In 1289, Olivi was transferred from Santa Croce to the studium in Montpellier, and we know that he was in Narbonne by 1295.

5. A Franciscan convent dependent on the convent of Montpellier was founded in Ganges, a few kilometers from La Cadière, sometime prior to 1297 (J. Rouquette ed., *Cartulaire de Maguelone*, Montpellier, 1912-1925, vol. III, n° MXLIV). Emery's later date, 1302, is thus in error (R.W. Emery, *The Friars in Medieval France : A Catalogue of French Mendicant Convents, 1200-1550*, New York, 1962, p. 73). It is possible that the Boneti family encountered the Spirituals first in Ganges, and then relocated to Montpellier to a larger Beguin community.

6. This term was used by Olivi himself in a letter to the sons of King Charles of Naples in May, 1295. D. Burr, *Persecution*, p. 72.

7. « *Et servavit* », W.H. May, « The Confession of Prous Boneta [...] », p. 10-11. Though nine seems young to commit oneself to the celibate life, Na Prous was not the only fourteenth-century

took her vow, we do know that nine months later she took part in the popular, but unofficial, celebration of the feast of Peter Olivi, held at his tomb in the church of the Franciscans of Narbonne in March, 1306[1]. There, she had a revelation that God had « given birth to her in spirit », and He gave her three gifts : tears, the sweetest aroma she had ever smelled, and a feeling of warmth as though someone had placed a cloak on her shoulders[2]. From the age of nine or ten, therefore, Na Prous had been a committed member of the Beguin community, and a supporter of the claims to sanctity of Peter Olivi.

Beyond these two events, we know little of Na Prous' young life. Her father was certainly dead by 1328[3], and it appears that Na Prous had lived in her own home for at least ten years in 1325[4]. She did not live alone, but with her sister Alisseta, and a companion called Alaraxis[5]. Though none of the three make their situation explicit, Bernard Gui refers to the tendency of Beguins to live together in homes they call « houses of poverty », and for many of them to work with their hands, and thereby to make enough money to live « a poor life »[6]. It is probable that Na Prous herself, at least, was illiterate, since she describes her religious practice as repeating the *Pater Noster* instead of the offices of the Church[7]. Though we can only speculate about their precise occupation, we do know that the home of these three immigrants was a center for Beguin activity in Montpellier : both Alisseta and Alaraxis refer to a number of Beguins who ate and drank with them[8]. and Sibillia Cazelle, a friend of the Beguins from Gignac, had been meeting Beguins at Na Prous' home for ten years[9]. If the Boneta sisters and Alaraxis were engaged in handiwork, the sedentary, and probably communal,

figure to do so. In their study of medieval saints, Donald Weinstein and Rudolph Bell found that a very large proportion of female saints vowed chastity around the age of seven. Caroline Walker Bynum has written about this disproportionate number of saintly women committed to celibacy at an early age : unlike men, women tended to have seen religious commitment as a steady progression to sanctity. D. Weinstein, and R.M. Bell, *Saints & Society : The Two Worlds of Western Christendom, 1000-1700*, Chicago, 1982, p. 19-47, 123. C.W. Bynum, *Holy Feast and Holy Fast : The Religious Significance of Food to Medieval Women*, Berkeley, 1987, p. 24-28.

1. This festival, which attracted enormous crowds from all over Languedoc, was not countenanced by the ecclesiastical hierarchy.

2. W.H. May, « The Confession of Prous Boneta [...] », p. 11. These three « gifts » are consonant with the idea, expressed by Bernard Gui (*Manuel de l'Inquisiteur*, ed. and trans. by G. Mollat, 2 vols, Paris, 1926-27, vol. 2, p. 138-139), and confirmed by the testimony of so many Beguins, that Petrus Johannis Olivi was a saint, though as yet uncanonized.

3. He is termed deceased in Na Prous' sentence. H.C. Lea, *A History of the Inquisition*, p. 653.

4. Sibillia Cazelle, *Doat* 27, f° 16v.

5. Alaraxis was also an immigrant to Montpellier, from Brequesenhegnes, also in the diocese of Nîmes. A shadowy figure who may well be a third sister to Na Prous and Alisseta (or perhaps their mother), Stephana Boneta, is mentioned briefly in the sources, though her deposition has not survived. Also from St. Michel de la Cadyera, like Na Prous and Alisseta, and an inhabitant of Montpellier, she was apparently sentenced to life imprisonment in September 1329. Deliberations of the judges, *Doat* 27, f° 186r. Abjuration, f° 225r.

6. B. Gui, 1 : 114-117. Reyerson has suggested that many female immigrants to Montpellier worked in the food trades, in needlework and with precious metals. K. Reyerson, « Patterns of Population Attraction », p. 271-272.

7. W.H. May, « The Confession of Prous Boneta [...] », p. 9.

8. Alisseta Boneta, *Doat* 27, f° 26v. ; Alisseta seu Alaraxis, *Doat* 27, f° 30r-v.

9. Sibillia Cazelle, *Doat* 27, f° 16v.

nature of their activity would have provided an ideal opportunity for heretical conversation.

On March 14, 1325, the Beguin community of Montpellier celebrated the feast of Peter Olivi in the home of a certain male Beguin. Though the celebration did not take place in Na Prous' home, the scene related by four unidentified witnesses nevertheless brings us a little closer to the world familiar to her. It is quite possible, even likely, that she and her sisters were guests at the celebration [1]. Many Beguins gathered for a large meal, paid for by a member of a prominent Montpellier family named John Orlach [2], and together they ate, drank, and spoke of Peter Olivi. The Beguin priest Peter de Tornamira blessed the table, gave thanks, and later read aloud from Olivi's Apocalypse commentary. Afterwards, Tornamira, with many others, went to visit William Veyrerii, a fugitive Beguin who was hiding in the home of another Beguin named Na Catharina. Though this scene took place in 1325, mere months before many of these Beguins were taken by the inquisitors, it gives us a sense of the solidarity of the community of Beguins in Montpellier.

This solidarity had been tested very early. The testimony of Peter Calveti of Cintegabelle (1322) preserves the drama of the moment when the Beguins of Languedoc heard the news of the burning of the four Spiritual friars of Marseilles in March, 1318 :

> It was four years ago in Eastertide when Peter Trencavel came to Cintegabelle and told the Beguins that four friars Minor had been condemned as heretics in Marseilles by an inquisitor who was of the Franciscan Order; and after this, he, Peter Calveti and the other Beguins began to speak among themselves in many times and places about the condemnation of the friars, saying that they were condemned badly and unjustly and by the envy of the other friars and of the inquisitor of Marseilles; that they underwent death for the truth and for the Rule which was the same as the life of the Gospels; and then he and the others said that they were holy martyrs, and so he believed it to be [3].

From this moment on, the dynamics of Beguin life in Languedoc were decidedly changed. Though it would be rash to declare that the actual heresy of the Beguins dates from this moment, it is clear that their opposition to the institutional church increased. Claudia Rattazzi Papka calls this the « Catch-22 of

1. Four witnesses (among whom may well have been Na Prous herself, her sister or Alaraxis) testified that Peter de Tornamira, a member of one of the wealthiest families of Montpellier, attended a «*festum de obitu quondam fratris Petri Johannis*» held «*in domo cujusdam beguini*». Peter de Tornamira did himself acknowledge his acquaintance with Na Prous, and with several of her close associates. A. Germain, « Une Consultation inquisitoriale [...] », p. 333-334, 338.

2. John Orlach, *Doat* 27, f° 24v. The Orlach family appears many times in the records of Montpellier. A certain «Johannes de Orllaco» was bailiff of the castle of Montferrand in 1211 (Cartulaire de Maguelone, t. II, n° CCCXIII), and a «Guiraut Dorlach» appears as a member of the *Commune Clôture* in 1262 (AM Montpellier, Petit Thalamus, f° xiiv). Several others (including a «*Johannes de Orlhaco, mercerius*») appear in the 1293 notarial register of Jean Grimaud, AM Montpellier BB1 (M. de Dainville, M. Gouron, L. Valls, eds., *Archives de la Ville de Montpellier, Inventaire Analytique Série BB*, t. XIII, Montpellier, 1984, p. 31). Members of the family appear frequently in association with the merchant elite of Montpellier.

3. Limborch, p. 317.

apocalyptic discourse»: resistance is «not only imperative, but also sanctifying»[1]. Olivi himself had divided the Church into an *ecclesia spiritualis* and an *ecclesia carnalis*, and the persecution of their friends and loved ones must have sharpened this opposition in the minds of Na Prous and her associates. Though the women continued to attend services at the Franciscan Church in Montpellier[2], the friars with the most vocal Spiritual proclivities had been rounded up and silenced. Beguins and friars who had been visitors in their home before might well be fugitives in hiding there now. Other acquaintances were imprisoned, and then condemned to the stake.

An underground network of Beguins began to take shape as the persecutions began. Beguins visited other Beguins in prison, bringing them fellowship, and comforts from home[3]. Those who were suspected by the inquisitors, but not yet captured were hidden in various locations, frequently in large cities[4]. The most intrepid travelled secretly from location to location, reading aloud from Olivi's Apocalypse commentary, hearing confessions, and preaching to the faithful[5]. They also spread the word about « the burned Beguins », whose martyrdoms they witnessed, and whose relics they frequently carried with them[6]. Bernard Gui even reported that the Beguins had created a martyrology of Beguin saints: they had inscribed the names of the martyrs, and the dates of their passions in a calendar, which they used for their litanies[7]. As more and more of the friars were captured or had fled, the burden of preserving the faith increasingly fell on lay shoulders.

1. C. Rattazzi Papka, *Fictions of Judgment*, p. 133.

2. W.H. May, « The Confession of Prous Boneta [...] », p. 7.

3. Sometime before August, 1321, Na Prous and her sisters visited the Beguins imprisoned in the prisons of the bishop of Maguelone, and especially a certain Guillelma of Mirepoix (Alisseta Boneta, *Doat* 27, f° 27v); Bernard Peyrotas, a priest from Lodève, visited five of his former parishioners in the same prison, and dined with them several times (Manselli, *Spirituali e beghini*, p. 317); and Peter de Tornamira also visited Beguins in Maguelone, and gave « *unum turonensem argenti* » to the prison guard, « for wine » (A. Germain, « Une Consultation inquisitoriale [...] », p. 338).

4. A number of Beguins were fugitives in Montpellier itself: Raymond Johannis and « a certain Ataussatus » (A. Germain, « Une Consultation inquisitoriale [...] », p. 338), William Serallerii, who was ill enough to have to be carried on the shoulders of another Beguin from hiding place to hiding place (Berengaria Estorgua, *Doat* 28, f°s 194-196r; Alisseta seu Alaraxis, *Doat* 27, f° 30-30v; John Orlach, *Doat* 27, f° 25r.), and William Domenici Veyrerii (A. Germain, « Une Consultation inquisitoriale [...] », p. 334).

5. The indefatigable Beguin missionary Peter Trencavel (from Béziers) is the most notable example: when he fled across the Rhône, having escaped from prison, he took a number of books by Olivi with him so that their message might not be lost forever (Bernard Maurini, R. Manselli, *Spirituali e beghini*, p. 335). Raymond Johannis was particularly welcomed in his home town of Montréal, where he twice took refuge shortly after 1318. He heard confessions, read from Olivi's *Postilla*, and spoke about the martyred Beguins (Raymond Johannis, *Doat* 27, f° 37r; Johanna Jouconne, *Doat* 28, f° 199v.).

6. The testimony of the Beguins of Lodève is particularly eloquent in this regard (R. Manselli, *Spirituali e beghini*, p. 309-321).

7. B. Gui, 1: 134-135. The priest Bernard Peyrotas of Lodève clearly alludes to this « libellus » in his deposition before the inquisitors, and also mentions celebrating a special office of martyrs for the burned Beguins (R. Manselli, *Spirituali e beghini*, p. 317-318).

It was in this atmosphere of imprisoned friends, fugitive Beguins, and the absence of acknowledged leaders, that Na Prous conceived of a change in her role as a Beguin. On Good Friday, 1321, she was in the Church of the Franciscans in Montpellier, contemplating the passion, when her visions began. Her first visionary experiences (which continued over a period of several days) have a familiar flavor to them, reminiscent of other female mystical experiences. There is even an erotic dimension to certain passages, when Christ declares that he has made his chamber in her, for instance [1]. She converses so familiarly with God, and so intimately, telling him of her fears of being too great a sinner for the honors he is giving her [2], and her fears of falling into the sin of pride [3], that we are drawn into her intensely personal relationship with God. The notary transcribed certain passages in Na Prous' deposition in the vernacular, which preserves for the reader a hint of this intimacy [4]. In a notable break with a more traditional mystical program, however, God tells Na Prous of her most special place in the economy of salvation : « just as the blessed virgin Mary was the *donatrix* of the son of God, so you will be the *donatrix* of the Holy Spirit » [5]. On another occasion, the three members of the Trinity came together to her : « one of them began to run, and on his way put himself on the neck of her who is telling this, and another placed himself on her right arm ». Arm in arm with the triune God, she heard the gift of the Holy Spirit confirmed, and strengthened : « now this promise has been made complete, when I had promised to you saying that I would give you more, because now you have the whole Trinity » [6]. « Every day and night and every hour she sees God in the spirit and he never leaves her », reported the notary [7]. She was continually affirmed in her prophetic purpose through the intimacy of her relationship with God the Father, Christ and the Holy Spirit.

And yet the substance of her visions is not entirely gendered female, but also uses images and vocabulary taken directly from the Apocalypse. It is she who destroys the serpent of *Revelation* 12 who tries to persecute Mary [8]; the Spirit given to her will govern the Church along with the Spirit given to Peter Olivi [9]; she holds the rainbow above her head [10]; she is the horse of *Revelation* 19 : 10, ridden by Jesus Christ himself, who leads the army of God into battle with the Beast [11] While Francis was the angel who carried the sign of the Living God, and

1. « *Ego tociens vado et revertor, quia in te sumpsi et feci cameram meam* », W.H. May, « The Confession of Prous Boneta [...] », p. 10.

2. « Lord, truly I am nothing, for I feel that I am a sinner and sin is nothing », W.H. May, « The Confession of Prous Boneta [...] », p. 8.

3. W.H. May, « The Confession of Prous Boneta [...] », p. 11.

4. W.H. May, « The Confession of Prous Boneta [...] », p. 7, 10, 29.

5. « *Beata virgo Maria fuit donatrix Filii Dei et tu eris donatrix Spiritus Sancti* », W.H. May, « The Confession of Prous Boneta [...] », p. 11.

6. W.H. May, « The Confession of Prous Boneta [...] », p. 10.

7. W.H. May, « The Confession of Prous Boneta [...] », p. 29.

8. W.H. May, « The Confession of Prous Boneta [...] », p. 20.

9. W.H. May, « The Confession of Prous Boneta [...] », p. 22.

10. Apocalypse 10 : 1. This is the same angel whose face is like the sun ; W.H. May, « The Confession of Prous Boneta [...] », p. 25.

11. W.H. May, « The Confession of Prous Boneta [...] », p. 25.

Peter Olivi was the angel whose face shone like the sun, she herself was the angel who held the keys to the abyss : « the abyss will be shut and closed for those who believe in these words, the words of her speaking, and for those who will not believe, the abyss will be opened »[1]. Na Prous was the angel who « laid hold on the dragon the old serpent, which is the devil and Satan, and bound him for a thousand years »[2]. It is with Na Prous herself that the glorious thousand-year reign of the Spirit will begin[3].

According to Olivi's view of history, the apocalyptic crisis was due to happen soon, indeed immediately[4]. For his followers, the burning of the four friars in 1318 had started the persecution of the mystical Antichrist, identified as Pope John XXII, and the flames had already spread to lower Languedoc. Nearly thirty Beguins and friars had died at the stake by April 1321, and the Beguin community expected the advent of the new age of the Spirit at any moment. Na Prous' visions fit directly into Olivi's conception that the third age would be characterized by a new *intellectus spiritualis,* where the meaning of scripture (especially the book of Revelation) and of apostolic poverty would become clearer, and would be spread to those who lived holy lives and delighted in « chaste and sweet contemplation », instead of to those who approached it through scholarship[5]. The progress of spiritual illumination was inevitable with the approach of the third age, and as Robert E. Lerner has pointed out, most believed that « the gift was showered most copiously on the humble »[6].

Disciples of Olivi took this belief in God's preference for the humble to heart, as witnessed by a number of passages in Arnold of Villanova's *Alia Informatio*, a vernacular work intended for Beguins[7]. Arnold warned Beguins about inquiring intellectually into the nature of God : « when he inquires or seeks the truth in such

1. Apocalypse 20 : 1 ; W.H. May, « The Confession of Prous Boneta [...] », p. 29-30.

2. Apocalypse 20 : 2.

3. Na Prous' assertions are reminiscent of the declarations of Guiard de Cressonessart, who called himself the Angel of Philadelphia, a title he took from Apocalypse 3 : 7-13. R.E. Lerner discusses this case in detail in « An 'Angel of Philadelphia' in the Reign of Philip the Fair : The Case of Guiard of Cressonessart », in *Order and Innovation in the Middle Ages : Essays in Honor of Joseph R. Strayer*, W.C. Jordan *et al.* eds., Princeton, 1976, p. 343-364. It is likely that Olivi also influenced Guiard, who was called *beguinus* by the inquisitors of Paris in 1310. See O. Cartagegia and J. Perarnau, « El Text Sencer de L'*Epistola ad Gerentes Zonam Pelliceam* d'Arnau de Vilanova », *Arxiu de Textos Catalans Antics* 12, 1993, p. 7-42.

4. Olivi does not specify a date, but Burr suggests that he anticipated the cataclysmic events to occur at the beginning of the fourteenth century. *Persecution*, p. 24.

5. D. Burr, « Olivi, Apocalyptic Expectation », p. 280.

6. R. Lerner, « Ecstatic Dissent », *Speculum* 67, 1992, p. 54.

7. J. Perarnau, *L'« Alia Informatio Beguinorum » d'Arnau de Vilanova*, Barcelona, 1978. Arnold's Catalan (the *Alia Informatio* was apparently written for the Beguins of Barcelona) would presumably have been comprehensible in Montpellier, an urban center situated at the linguistic crossroads of Provençal, Occitan, and Catalan. As Perarnau has noted, it is overly subtle to distinguish among these three languages in this period : another of Arnold's Catalan works (the « *Informatio beguinorum seu lectio narbone* », in Arnau, *Obres Catalanes*, vol. I, p. 141-166) was in fact written for the Beguins of Narbonne. It is quite possible, given his years of residence in Montpellier (Arnold was a member of the medical faculty from approximately 1290 to his death in 1311), and his involvement in Beguin circles, that Arnold was acquainted with the young Na Prous or her family.

matters through human reason, a person can bring on the devil »[1]. For Arnold, it was better to be blind, deaf and mute in all such matters so as better to remember the passion of Christ through faith alone. *Curiositat* was perilous, but *humilitat* was pleasing to God[2]. Arnold emphasized God's preference for the humble and the unlettered by citing the example of St Francis, who refused the priesthood and « did not wish to have the preeminence or the dominion of the doctorate, nor the dignity of the prelacy, in order to shun any occasion of conceit or pride »[3]. It is probable that these very words were read aloud in the Beguin circles frequented by Na Prous, further establishing the right of the humble to spiritual insight. Arnold himself suggested public readings of « holy words », and one of the executors of Arnold's will, Raymond Conesa, distributed books copied at Arnold's Barcelonan scriptorium in several cities of southern France, including Montpellier, in the years following Arnold's death in 1312[4]. That this activity was made culpable by the condemnation of a number of Arnold's works (including the *Alia Informatio*) in 1316 merely emphasizes the importance of the tract's ideas[5]. Illiterate Na Prous, who had lived chastely, and in pursuit of humility and poverty for twenty years, whose home was a center of the Beguin community, whose visions occurred as she contemplated the passion of Christ on Good Friday, was as likely a vessel for the Holy Spirit as any. Her Beguin contemporaries, strengthened by the words of authorities like Arnold of Villanova, would have recognized her as such.

Though Na Prous' visions appear to be unique in the fourteenth-century community of Beguins in Languedoc[6], that uniqueness did not divorce her from Olivi. Visions were in fact a vital part of Olivi's writings; he attributed visionary authority several times to others, and at least twice to women[7]. One tradition even asserts that Olivi claimed a visionary role for himself, saying that he had received all his knowledge directly from Christ in a church in Paris at the third hour[8]. Others of Olivi's disciples and admirers, notably Ubertino da Casale and Arnold of Villanova, had also claimed visionary inspiration for their writings, and in 1310, the Conventuals accused the Spirituals of promulgating « dreams and

1. J. Perarnau, *L'Alia Informatio*, p. 70-71.

2. The two chapters of the work most relevant to the present discussion are chapters VII and X : J. Perarnau, *L'Alia Informatio*, p. 47-48, 68-73.

3. « *Ne volgren aver preeminència o senyoria de doctorat o de dignitat o de prelació per esquivar les ocasions de elació o de arguyl* », J. Perarnau, *L'Alia Informatio*, p. 47.

4. R. d'Alós, « De la marmessoria d'Arnau de Vilanova », *Miscellania Prat de la Riba*, Barcelona, 1923, p. 289-306 (at. 301). R. Lerner, « Writing and Resistance among Beguins of Languedoc and Catalonia », *Heresy and Literacy, 1000-1530*, ed. by P. Biller and A. Hudson, Cambridge University Press, 1994, p. 194-195.

5. The text of the condemnation of Arnold's works is published in F. Santi, *Arnau de Vilanova : L'obra espiritual*, Valencia, 1987, p. 283-289.

6. D. Burr, « Olivi, Apocalyptic Expectation », p. 287-288.

7. D. Burr, « Olivi, Apocalyptic Expectation », p. 279.

8. B. Gui, 2 : 190-193. Burr dismisses this widely disseminated anecdote (it formed part of a short devotional text) as apocryphal (*Persecution*, p. 73), but Lerner also notes that Olivi did claim inspiration for his writings elsewhere (« Ecstatic Dissent », p. 53 n. 72).

fictitious visions »[1]. As Lerner has shown, a recourse to visions as a justification for unorthodox theology, the « ecstasy defense », as he terms it, was an intrinsic part of the Joachite and Olivian tradition, and hardly unknown at the beginning of the fourteenth century[2].

The substance of Na Prous' visionary program, too, is firmly in the Beguin tradition, with its veneration for both St Francis and his conception of the apostolic life, and for Olivi. Na Prous was especially devoted to the latter, referring to him once as « holy father brother Peter »[3], and saying that « the Lord gave as many graces and as much glory to brother Peter Johannis as he gave to the son of God in his person »[4]. His writings were not merely worthy, they were « written by the hand of divinity »[5]. Just as Jesus did battle with the Devil, just so did Olivi's writings do battle with Antichrist, Pope John XXII[6]. When that Pope condemned Peter Olivi's writings, the sacrament of the altar lost its power[7]. The Pope's sin was as great as Adam's sin when he ate the apple[8]. Lastly, like many other Beguins, she called brother Peter « the angel whose face shines like the sun »[9].

Recent work by Claudia Rattazzi Papka and David Burr make a reiteration of the Olivian and Joachite content of Na Prous' beliefs unnecessary[10]. Along with the many of her contemporaries influenced by Olivi's Apocalypse commentary, which circulated in an abridged vernacular version in the Midi, Na Prous fervently believed that a new age of the Spirit was about to begin. Though the role in that new age which Na Prous took on for herself was unique, the mental world she lived in was common to all the Beguins, and the role she claimed was one which her contemporaries would have easily recognized. Eventually, Na Prous began to proclaim her unique role to a wider audience. The question that remains to us, however is crucially important : was anyone listening ?

1. R. Lerner, « Ecstatic Dissent », p. 42-46, 53 n. 74.

2. R. Lerner, « Ecstatic Dissent », p. 33-57.

3. « *Sanctus pater frater Petrus Joannis* » W.H. May, « The Confession of Prous Boneta [...] », p. 18.

4. « *Quod tot gratias et tantam gloriam dedit Dominus fratri Petro Joannis, quot et quantas dedit Filio Dei in persona* », W.H. May, « The Confession of Prous Boneta [...] », p. 22.

5. « *Quae erat scripta per manum divinitatis* », W.H. May, « The Confession of Prous Boneta [...] », p. 14-15.

6. W.H. May, « The Confession of Prous Boneta [...] », p. 19.

7. W.H. May, « The Confession of Prous Boneta [...] », p. 12, 13, 14-15. Na Prous' testimony would appear to date this event to Christmas, 1323. Presumably, she is referring to the publication of John XXII's bull *Cum inter nonnullos* in November, 1323. This bull condemned as heretical the idea that Christ and his apostles had owned nothing in private or in common. D. Burr, *Persecution*, p. 83. She refers directly to this proposition in the next passage : « This pope confessed that Christ was a sinner, since he said that Christ owned things in private and in common », W.H. May, « The Confession of Prous Boneta [...] », p. 15.

8. W.H. May, « The Confession of Prous Boneta [...] », p. 13.

9. Apocalypse 10 : 1. Manselli dates the use of this description of Olivi to 1318 (after the burnings in Marseilles), but the cult of Olivi clearly dates from considerably before this time. Burr notes that Olivi was identified with an angel of the apocalypse before the Council of Vienne. Manselli, *Spirituali e beghini*, p. 166 ; Burr, *Persecution*, p. 88 n. 48.

10. C. Rattazzi Papka, *Fictions of Judgment*, and D. Burr, « Na Prous Boneta and Olivi ».

When Na Prous began to reveal her visions to others, she was cautious. First came an incredulous notary[1]. Next was committed Spiritual Franciscan Brother Raymond Johannis, who also did not believe her; later, she declared that he was crucifying Christ in secret, as the notary had persecuted her in public[2]. A friar since 1292[3], Raymond Johannis had accompanied his brethren of the convents of Narbonne and Béziers on the fateful trip to Avignon in May, 1317. Like most of the rest, Raymond Johannis « returned to obedience », and was sent to the convent of Anduze in the Cévennes, where he remained until the burnings in Marseilles in March, 1318. Disguised as a secular priest, he was sheltered by his cousin for three years near Béziers, and then began three or four years of clandestine preaching and ministering throughout the Midi and abroad[4]. The inquisitors considered Raymond Johannis a central figure among the Beguins: they called him « heresiarch »[5], and ultimately condemned him to degradation from all clerical and sacerdotal orders, and to strict immurement, which included chains and irons in perpetuity[6]. Some factors indicate that Raymond Johannis may even have been a relative of Peter Johannis Olivi, though perhaps not a close one[7]. Certainly, he was well known in Montpellier, and his company was highly valued. Many depositions refer to him specifically, and he himself admitted to his acquaintance with many of the Beguins, including Na Prous. He preached, read aloud from Olivi's Apocalypse commentary, and was a consistent witness to the cause, as well as a frequent visitor to the home of the Boneta sisters. It seems likely that Na Prous acquired much of her remarkable familiarity with Olivi from this « apostate friar », as she so frequently terms him in her deposition.

Unlike Raymond Johannis, however, the women of her household admitted to believing in Na Prous' visions and in her special status. Alaraxis, the « companion », first told the inquisitor that:

1. W.H. May, « The Confession of Prous Boneta [...] », p. 9, 21, 25.

2. W.H. May, « The Confession of Prous Boneta [...] », p. 21. The most recent work on Raymond Johannis is an article by David Burr to appear shortly in *Franc. Stud.*, « Raymond Déjean, Franciscan Renegade ». I am grateful to the author for having generously sent me a copy of this article prior to its publication.

3. R. Manselli says 1289 (p. 238), but cites no source beyond Raymond Johannis' culpa contained in *Doat* 27, f°s 35v-42r. There, in October 1325, the friar stated that he had entered the Franciscan order thirty-three years before.

4. His first venture abroad may have been to Majorca (Alaraxis Biasse, *Doat* 28, f°s 216v-219v), and he appears to have visited Sicily in 1324 (A. Germain, « Une Consultation inquisitoriale [...] », p. 334, 338), possibly by way of Barcelona and Sardinia (A. Germain, « Une Consultation inquisitoriale [...] », p. 335).

5. *Doat* 27, f° 40v.

6. *Doat* 27, f° 93v. Life imprisonment in solitary, chained confinement was the punishment the inquisitors reserved for the most heinous of repentent heretics; only impenitent or relapsed heretics were burned at the stake.

7. R. Manselli goes so far as to call him Olivi's nephew (p. 226-227, esp. p. 227 n. 1), but other scholars are less certain (personal communication with David Burr). See the testimony of Alaraxis Biasse, Olivi's niece (*Doat* 28, f°s 216v-29v), and Germain, esp. p. 334, 338.

> She believed the errors she had heard from Na Prous, and she believed that what she had heard from Na Prous was true; she believed that everything would happen just as Na Prous said it would, and that this was the work of God[1].

Though Alaraxis apparently abjured rather quickly, Alisseta Boneta was loyal and bold enough to seek to defend her sister to the inquisitors. Questioned, she asserted « that God could do all things, and that he could have inspired his grace in her sister, and that the things her sister said were good, and true, and given by God »[2] though she also admitted that sometimes she thought that perhaps it was all an illusion, and the work of the devil. But Alisseta refused to abjure, though frequently so admonished by the inquisitor's representatives. « She would not swear in any way [that her sister was a heretic and heresiarch and that those condemned and burned were heretics] because she did not know God's judgments, nor to what end they would come »[3]. By appealing to the judgment of God, Alisseta denied the authority of the inquisitors (and consequently the Church as a whole) to judge both her sister and the other martyrs so revered by the Beguins. Alisseta's stubbornness (she held out for almost three years in prison) in the face of the demonstrated might of the inquisitors is worthy of Na Prous' own, and her refusal to acknowledge her sister as a heretic is a categoric refusal to deny the apocalyptic message of Peter Olivi.

Eventually, Na Prous began to evangelize to the world outside the privacy of her own home. Christ ordered her « to a certain town » where she preached to a number of women, and exhorted them to martyrdom, if need be[4]. When her efforts there were unsuccessful, she moved on to another town, where she preached again, this time in the company of a unidentified male ally[5].

Na Prous swiftly became the topic of every Beguin conversation, as we can see from the testimony of two Beguins from Gignac, old friends of Na Prous and the women of her household. Sibillia Cazelle told the inquisitor that when she visited Montpellier,

> [...] from one person she heard that Na Prous had said that she had received the Holy Spirit, and that she said she was just as holy as the blessed Virgin Mary; from another, she heard that Na Prous had said that God had transported her soul to Heaven [...][6].

We can imagine groups of Beguins, like those assembled for the commemoration of Olivi's feast, all talking about the latest news. Pregnant as it was with Olivian ideas and apocalyptic themes, it must have seemed

1. Alisseta seu Alaraxis, *Doat* 27, f° 31v.
2. Alisseta Boneta, *Doat* 27, f° 28v.
3. « *Nescit iudicia Dei qualia sunt* », Alisseta Boneta, *Doat* 27, f° 29v.
4. W.H. May, « The Confession of Prous Boneta [...] », p. 19.
5. Her mysterious evocation of Brother William Giraudi, another « apostate friar » never found by the inquisitors, as the first pope of the new age, consecrated by the Holy Spirit, tempts us to conjecture that her companion was he, but the point is unprovable. W.H. May, « The Confession of Prous Boneta [...] », p. 19-20. William Giraudi was also Raymond Johannis' teacher in matters apocalyptic, *Doat* 27, f° 37r.
6. Sibillia Cazelle, *Doat* 27, f°s 16v-17r.

astonishingly bold and yet remarkably familiar. The expectation of imminent dramatic changes in the Church was widespread among the Beguins, and yet this may have been more than they were prepared to accept. It seems most likely that there was controversy within the Beguin community about the validity of Na Prous' claim.

Sibillia's friend Ermessendis Grossa claimed that she was incredulous on hearing the news: « Na Prous had a foolish way, and held some foolish positions »[1]. Immediately she sought out Na Prous herself, to castigate her, but Na Prous responded with even more vehement assertions[2]. Ermessendis claims she withdrew immediately, making the sign of the cross, « commending herself to her Lord Jesus Christ and his passion ». She knew that Na Prous' opinions were erroneous and heretical, and that her duty was to reveal them to the authorities – but she did and said nothing until she was called before the inquisitor in November, 1325, three months after Na Prous had already confessed.

Both of these women had been closely involved with the Beguins for years. Sibillia, the widow of William Cazelle of Gignac, had been friendly with the Montpellier Beguins for a decade[3]. Ermessendis, the widow of John Castanherii of Lodève, had taken a vow of chastity, and often travelled in Beguin circles : she had heard about the four friars burned in Marseilles when she was visiting in Mauguio, where we know of a Beguin community[4], and it was in Narbonne at the feast of Peter Olivi that she first met Raymond Johannis (though she spoke with him afterwards in Na Prous' home). Sibillia had brought her daughter to Olivi's tomb in Narbonne to be cured of scrofula, and believed that she was cured through his prayers[5]. Both women denied believing in Na Prous' claims, though Sibillia was reputed to have « confessed badly »[6]. It was certainly to their advantage to deny everything in an attempt to exculpate themselves[7]. It is hard to believe, however, that Sibillia Cazelle, that faithful devotee of Olivi and old friend of Na Prous, did not at the very least wonder if it all might not be true.

In the summer of 1325, the inquisitor of Carcassonne appears to have broken the ring of Beguins in Montpellier, and the Beguin community was now largely

1. « *Unum modum fatuum, et aliquas fatuas oppositiones* », Ermessendis Grossa, *Doat* 27, f° 14v.

2. « *Ego nullum errorem teneo imo teneo veritatem quia verie sum a Deo certificata quod habeo Spiritum Sanctum, et quod sacramenta non sunt salutis* » Ermessendis Grossa, *Doat* 27, f° 15r-15v.

3. Sibillia Cazelle said « she had been familiar with some of the [female] Beguins of Montpellier for ten years, among which were Na Prous Boneta, now held in prison, her sister, and their companion, in whose house she had sometimes visited; one of them had visited her in her own house in Gignac », Sibillia Cazelle, *Doat* 27, f° 16v.

4. A. Germain, « Une Consultation inquisitoriale [...] », p. 333.

5. « *Quandam filiam suam quae patiebatur infirmitatem in gutture, scilicet scroellas ad sepulcrum suum duxit et curata fuit, et credidit tunc, et adhuc credit quod per orationem dicti fratris Petri curata fuerit* », Sibillia Cazelle, *Doat* 27, f° 18r.

6. Sibillia Cazelle, *Doat* 27, f° 18v.

7. It worked: both women received the mildest of sentences (« minor pilgrimages without crosses ») at the *Sermo Generalis* in Carcassonne on November 11, 1328, *Doat* 27, f° 90v.

imprisoned in the inquisitorial prison in Carcassonne known as the Wall[1]. Henceforth, Na Prous exercised her authority from within prison. Two important fugitives, William Serallerii and William Veyrerii, had both testified for the first time in May 1325, and it seems likely that their capture led to the roundup of the thirty-nine Beguins from Montpellier, Narbonne and Béziers who all testified between August, 1325 and January, 1326[2]. Among these were Na Prous Boneta and the members of her household.

While the concept of an inquisitorial prison tends to evoke scenes of filth, chains, torture, and what in French are so fittingly called « *oubliettes* », the Wall at Carcassonne was not entirely filled with prisoners chained to the walls in solitary confinement. A commission of two cardinals who examined conditions in the Wall of Carcassonne in 1306 found some prisoners shackled and held in appalling and degradating conditions[3], but the deposition of Manenta Rosa tells a different story. Probably in 1325, this committed Beguin was able to pass on culpable messages from Amorosa Laureti, a visitor, to Amorosa's imprisoned husband, who was held in a different cell from Manenta[4]. This generally lax attitude towards imprisonment does not appear to have made for very tight prison security: at least three heretics are known to have escaped from the Wall at Carcassonne[5]. While we cannot say for certain in what conditions any particular prisoner was actually held in the Wall at Carcassonne, we can assume that many of the prisoners were held in rather relaxed circumstances.

Some of the testimony related to the inquisitors corroborates this hypothesis, and suggests that Na Prous Boneta continued to act as a leader of the Beguins

1. The term *murus*, borrowed from monastic usage, was commonly used to indicate the inquisitorial prison. See E. Peters, « Prison before the Prison : The Ancient and Medieval Worlds », in *The Oxford History of the Prison*, ed. Norval Morris and David J. Rothman, p. 3-47, New York, 1995.

2. Thirty-eight of these *culpae* are found in *Doat* 27 and 28; the last, that of Peter de Tornamira, which alone survives as an original inquisitorial document in the municipal archives of Montpellier due to his wealthy and influential family's successful 1357 bid to have his conviction overturned, has been published by Germain (see above).

3. J. Given, *Inquisition and Medieval Society : Power, Discipline, and Resistance in Languedoc*, Cornell, 1997, p. 65. Given's entire discussion of inquisitorial prisons (p. 52-65) is highly instructive.

4. Manenta Rosa, *Doat* 27, f[os] 79v-82r. The testimony of Bernard Clergue of Montaillou, makes it clear that similarly lax conditions existed in the prison of the Allemans in Pamiers. Clergue was able to wander about at will, continuing to intimidate the inhabitants of his village, and even managed to procure his own set of keys. Men and women do not appear to have been held separately, and could freely move around and speak openly with each other. J. Duvernoy ed. *Registre d'inquisition de Jacques Fournier (1318-1325)*, Toulouse, 1965, II, p. 277-290. Another example which makes this relative freedom clear is the testimony of Blanche de Rodès before the inquisitor of Carcassonne in 1308, concerning the inquisitorial prison in Foix; A. Pales-Gobilliard ed., *L'Inquisiteur Geoffroy d'Ablis et les cathares du comté de Foix (1308-1309)*, Paris, 1984, p. 232-233, 236-237.

5. The Cathar perfecti Jacques Autier and Guillaume Bélibaste (Duvernoy, *Registre*, vol. 2, p. 57, and vol. 3, p. 145; Pales-Gobilliard, *L'Inquisiteur Geoffroy,* p. 77, 342-343; Given, p. 90) and the Beguin Peter Trencavel (Testimony of William Veyrerii, R. Manselli, *Spirituali e beghini*, p. 321). Both Duvernoy and Pales-Gobilliard assert that another Cathar perfectus, Prades Tavernier, also escaped from the Wall, but none of the documentation that they cite is able to confirm that fact; all we can say for sure is that Tavernier and Autier were captured together in 1305, and that Autier, at least, was able to escape before being captured again and burned in 1309. Many others escaped from the inquisitorial prison in Toulouse, most particularly in a mass breakout in 1310. J. Given, *Inquisition,* p. 101.

even in prison. Guillerma Civille, who with her husband Peter Civille, a weaver of Narbonne (now a fugitive), had been closely associated with Beguin circles for some time, testified before the inquisitor of Carcassonne in September, 1325. It does not appear that she had known Na Prous in Montpellier. But though Guillerma had been interrogated before, she had never confessed: it was only when she was called a second time before the inquisitor – and even then only after a long time in prison – that she acknowledged her own heretical beliefs. « She would have told the truth earlier, had it not been for Na Prous Boneta held in the prison near her who restrained her from confessing »[1]. William Ademarii, another Narbonnais weaver, who also appears not to have known Na Prous, told a similar story in his deposition in 1325. Possibly called because of his acquaintance with Guillerma's husband, the fugitive Peter Civille, William confessed his beliefs; released, then called and held again, he denied them « against his own sworn testimony »[2]. Na Prous Boneta, held in the prison with him, had persuaded him to deny everything[3]. By September, 1325, Na Prous had already confessed to Henry de Chamayo, and her beliefs and her visions were no secret to the Beguins imprisoned in the Wall; still, she exerted enough influence on two individuals she had not known before to persuade them to change their testimony. In the early stages of her imprisonment at least, Na Prous also received visits from Beguins still free: John Orlach of Montpellier came to the prison to visit « Na Prous Boneta, heresiarch » sometime before November, 1325[4].

Two other striking examples of heretics changing their minds about their testimony also occurred during Na Prous' incarceration. A longtime fugitive, William Veyrerii of Narbonne was finally captured in the city of Orange, on the far side of the Rhône[5]. His first confession and abjuration (in May, 1325) was in Avignon, and is unremarkable. In the month of October following, however, now in Carcassonne, he declared that he wished to elaborate on the testimony he had given earlier. Here he confessed to the full array of Beguin beliefs: the burned Franciscans and the burned Beguins were « *gloriosi martires* », Olivi was an uncanonized saint, the Rule of St. Francis was the same as the gospel, and the poverty of Christ was absolute. More importantly, this time, he refused to abjure: « Asked if he wished to persevere in these beliefs just stated, he answered yes ».

What had intervened to turn William Veyrerii from penitence to perseverance in his beliefs? Though he does not testify to it himself, we know of his acquaintance with Na Prous through the testimony of her sister Alisseta, who confessed that along with William Serallerii and Raymond Johannis, William Veyrerii had often dined in their home. Though we know that he had been in

1. Guillerma Civille, *Doat* 28, f°s 226v-228r.

2. « *Contra proprium iuramentum* ».

3. William Ademarii, *Doat* 28, f° 228r-231r. We do not know the fate of either William Ademarii or Guillerma Civille: the sentences for this *Sermo Generalis* are missing.

4. See above. *Doat* 27, f° 24r-26r.

5. The testimony of Pontus of Saint Gilles, formerly of Narbonne, who was captured with him allows us to know that while in Provence, Veyrerii was in touch with Peter Trencavel. Pontus and William had travelled together from « eight days after the feast of St. Michael » (*i.e.* October 7, 1324) until just after Easter, 1325, when they were captured. *Doat* 28, f°s 235v-237r.

hiding at the home of a Beguin named Na Catharina[1], it is possible that the small community of women gathered around Na Prous in Montpellier had helped hide him from the authorities on his way to his enforced exile in Provence, as they had fed his friend William Serallerii.

In September, 1325, Guillerma Civille testified that Na Prous had encouraged her not to confess. In October, 1325, William Veyrerii changed his recantation to an affirmation of his Beguin belief – a decision which would cost him his life[2].

> Asked why he had said that he wished to turn away from these things and to repent, he replied that he had then had something else in his heart than he had now, and that afterwards God had placed this other intention in his heart, in which newer intention he wished to remain and to persevere as long as it would be given to him by God.

I propose that in the crowded prison of the Wall of Carcassonne, William Veyrerii encountered the impenitent Na Prous and her sister, and in their refusal to submit, and in the apocalyptic ideology which Na Prous no doubt continued to expound, found the courage to refuse to abjure. The human agent of the voice of God in this matter must have been the charismatic and compelling Na Prous herself. Even if they were held in completely separate parts of the prison, which seems unlikely, Na Prous had certainly contributed to the atmosphere which made his reversal possible.

William Serallerii, a fugitive since before 1323, made an even more dramatic turnaround in his testimony. He had previously testified before the Bishop of Lodève, and had admitted and abjured certain faults, and in Carcassonne in May, 1325, confessed more, and abjured again[3]. While hiding from the authorities in Montpellier, he had certainly been acquainted with Na Prous and her household, though he appears to have lived with a certain Berengaria Estorgua of Lodève[4]. At the last possible moment, however, « *in pleno sermone* » on March 1, 1327, about to be officially absolved and sentenced, Serallerii returned to his errors. The text is laconic, but it appears that he shouted out his beliefs in front of the luminaries gathered, including the inquisitors of Carcassonne and Toulouse. « Those who persecute the poor condemned Beguins are persecutors of the life of

1. A. Germain, « Une Consultation inquisitoriale [...] », p. 338.

2. Though the sentences from the Sermo Generalis of March 1, 1327 are missing, one of the witnesses against Peter de Tornamira confirms that William Veyrerii did in fact die at the stake: « *Guillermum Veyrerii, hereticum obstinatum beguinum fugitivum, et demum combustum* », A. Germain, « Une Consultation inquisitoriale [...] », p. 334.

3. Relapsed heretics were almost inevitably sent to the stake. Serallerii's admission that he had once had a letter from the inquisitor, but had lost it (on purpose) was damning, especially since he acknowledged that he lost it because a priest, probably Bernard Peyrotas, had told him that it was « to his loss and his confusion » to be found carrying it (« *ad damnum suum et confusionem suam* ».) *Doat* 28, f° 248r. Berengaria Estorgua acknowledged that she had kept the letter for Serallerii for a certain time. She also makes the connection with Bernard Peyrotas, burned in Lodève in 1322. *Doat* 28, f°s 195r-195v.

4. Alisseta seu Alaraxis, *Doat* 27, f° 30r-30v. Berengaria Estorgua of Lodève cared for him while he was sick and hiding in Montpellier. *Doat* 28, f°s 194v-196r. His illness must have been serious and enduring, since John Orlach of Montpellier carried him from one hiding place to another on his shoulders. *Doat* 27, f° 25r.

Jesus Christ! They are the enemies of Christ! » Questioned, he stated that he believed the writings and doctrine of Peter Olivi were holy and catholic, approved at the council of Vienne [1]. « He obstinately persevered in each and every one of the opinions and errors contained in his confession ». Like William Veyrerii, in prison he had found the courage to abjure his abjuration, and to declare the faith which, though swiftly vanishing in the world outside, was clearly still alive among the prisoners held in the Wall of Carcassonne. The Register copied in the seventeenth century by the Doat scribes was even then incomplete (the testimony of Peter Espere-en-diu breaks off in the middle of a sentence). Thus we do not know for certain the fate of William Serallerii. We can assume, however, that as an impenitent heretic, he was handed over to the secular arm on March 1, 1327, and burned along with William Veyrerii.

Na Prous had mentioned the possibility of martyrdom many times : when she spoke to an unresponsive crowd of women, she called on them to be ready to be martyred for their beliefs [2]. She also said that just as the Jews had crucified the son of God in person, the « lawyers of the Christians » would crucify the Holy Spirit in person, in her [3]. Her view of the apocalyptic vision, and of the inevitable correlations between the old dispensation and the new, meant that she expected, and perhaps welcomed martyrdom. The apocalyptic script required it. Her final words to the inquisitor make her position clear : « she persevered [in all her errors and heresies], stating that in them, as in the truth, she wished to live and die » [4]. For three long years, her sister Alisseta held out, too, but before the « General Sermon » of November 1328, she finally abjured. We may well wonder why : perhaps her sister was taken away from her and held elsewhere in the prison, or perhaps Na Prous herself encouraged her to abjure, leaving at least one to spread the message of the new age of the Spirit.

We are left with one other clue, but an important one, regarding the reception of Na Prous' ideas, and the nature of her role of leadership within her community. A bull of John XXII of 1327-1328, recommending that « *quandam mulierem [...] Boneta* » be burned at Carcassonne, and not at Montpellier, suggests that the execution in question was likely to cause trouble in Montpellier [5]. Though the first name of the woman to be sentenced is extremely difficult to read because of water damage on the original register, the likelihood that the name is that of

1. This echoes the testimony of his friend William Veyrerii. R. Manselli, *Spirituali e beghini*, p. 321.

2. W.H. May, « The Confession of Prous Boneta [...] », p. 19.

3. « *Ita isti, scilicet legisperiti Christianorum, crucifixerunt Spiritum Sanctum in persona, scilicet in persona ipsius loquentis* », W.H. May, « The Confession of Prous Boneta [...] », p. 21. The « *isti* » used by the notary appears to describe the scornful or derogatory tone she used towards the lawyers, and, perhaps, a pointed finger.

4. « *Perseveravit in eis, asserens in praedictis, tanquam in veritate se velle vivere atque mori* », W.H. May, « The Confession of Prous Boneta [...] », p. 30.

5. « A certain woman named [...] Boneta », J.M. Vidal, *Bullaire de l'inquisition française*, Paris, 1913, p. 128-129. This bull comes not from the Collection Doat, but from a register in the *Archivio Segreto Vaticano* (*Regestum Vaticanum*, vol. cxiv, n. 1795), and is thus a more reliable source. There is an additional lacuna where the actual date was located, but the regnal year of John XXII is indicated, « *anno duodecimo* ». John XXII was elected pope on August 7, 1316.

Na Prous Boneta is great[1]. We know from the testimony of others that supporters of the Spirituals travelled up and down Languedoc to attend the inquisitors' « Sermons » and the *autos-da-fé* that accompanied them, and we know, especially from the *culpae* of the Beguins of Lodève who collected relics at the burnings in Lunel[2], that such occasions could become important foci for heretical devotion. While the inquisitors may have believed that burning Na Prous in the town where she had lived for twenty-two years, and where she had had many friends and acquaintances, even among the most important families[3], would set an example, the pope's advisors in Avignon seem to have felt that it would instead harden the population in error. That Na Prous' case apparently attracted the attention of the papacy is in itself significant. What is certain is that on November 11, 1328, in Carcassonne, Na Prous was handed over to the secular arm, and her sister Alisseta and companion Alaraxis were sentenced to life imprisonment in the Wall of Carcassonne[4].

Especially since a female leader of a resistance movement is such a rare phenomenon, we would like to be able to determine if her social position contributed to Na Prous' authority as a leader of the Beguin community. She exerted influence on a variety of men: was that because they came from lower social strata than she herself? The answer appears to be no. Some of these men are identifiable through the sources: William Serallerii was a locksmith, William Veyrerii was a candlemaker and William Ademarii was a tailor. Raymond Johannis was one of the last remaining Spiritual Franciscan friars, and possibly a relative of Olivi himself, and Peter de Tornamira and John Orlach both came from the political, social and mercantile elite of Montpellier. Many immigrants to Montpellier came from artisanal families, and is highly likely that that is true for Na Prous' family as well. Though we cannot say for certain, it seems probable that unlike that of Guglielma of Milan, a princess of Bohemia[5], Na Prous' influence was not enhanced by her position in society, but rather rested entirely on the authority given her by her holy life and especially her visions.

1. It is just possible that the bull refers to Alisseta instead; but her case does not seem as likely to have attracted the attention of the papacy as that of Na Prous. A recent re-examination of the original register on my behalf by Pietro Cajazza and Maria Galante confirms Vidal's lacuna for the date, and suggests several possibilities for the damaged name: « ...pres », « ...pns », « ...ores », and « ...ons ». They also affirm that the final letter of the last name is decidedly « a », and not « e ». These observations help to confirm the identification with Na Prous (frequently written Naprous, or even Napros in the sources) instead of Alisetta. I am deeply grateful to Professor Roberto Rusconi for his assistance in acquiring this information, and to Dr. Cajazza and Professor Galante for securing it. Manselli accepts the identification with Na Prous Boneta as a given, p. 249.

2. *Doat* 28, f°s 11v-27v. Also printed in R. Manselli, *Spirituali e beghini*, p. 309-321.

3. Peter de Tornamira's family was influential enough to have his trial overturned in 1357. A. Germain, « Une Consultation inquisitoriale [...] », p. 327.

4. Both Alisseta and Alaraxis were released from prison a year later, condemned along with eight other Beguins to « pilgrimages and crosses » at the General Sermon of December 9, 1329. *Doat* 27, f°s 93v-196v.

5. Newman, *From Virile Woman to WomanChrist*, p. 237. She notes: « Although Guglielma was reticent about her past, her royalty must have contributed to the mystique of her holiness ».

As the Beguins watched one friend or acquaintance after another fall to the inquisitors, as the smoke from their pyres rose over more and more towns of the Midi, and as the likelihood that a choice would have to be made soon between apostasy and martyrdom, Na Prous' message of a new age of the Spirit must have provided a glimmer of hope that their desperate and bloody struggle had not been in vain. The content of this visionary message, inspired as closely as it was by the apocalyptic program of Peter Olivi, was likely to provoke a sympathetic response in the charged atmosphere of Montpellier in the early 1320s. The persecuted Beguin community needed new direction, and new leaders. Unlikely figures rose to the occasion and led the Beguins in their final resistance : a layman from Béziers, a candlemaker from Narbonne, a locksmith from Lodève, and especially, a woman from Montpellier. The face of Peter Olivi may have shone like the sun, but it was Na Prous Boneta who held the keys to the abyss, and the promise of salvation.

PIETRO DI GIOVANNI OLIVI E DANTE, OVVERO IL PANNO E LA GONNA

Alberto Forni

Nel 1929, Ernesto Buonaiuti, trascrivendo nella Biblioteca Angelica di Roma la *Lectura super Apocalipsim*, vi ritrovava i sentimenti e le aspirazioni proprie di Dante. Il rapporto tra Olivi e Dante dominò in seguito, agli inizi degli anni '40, le pagine dedicate all'Olivi nella *Storia del Cristianesimo*, nel capitolo appunto intitolato *L'apocalissi dantesca*. Il maestro francescano era per Buonaiuti quasi un simbolo della conoscenza raggiunta attraverso l'amore, allorché la civiltà moderna, pervasa da preoccupazioni strettamente gnoseologiche, dimostrava in modo tragico che la conoscenza uccide l'amore e non lo alimenta. Così Olivi fu per Dante un « vademecum in tribulatione » e gli offrì lo « schema ideale nel quale egli ha potuto inquadrare il suo amore per Beatrice ». Contro i prepotenti ritorni della visione tomistica dell'universo che aveva appreso a Santa Maria Novella da Remigio de' Girolami, gli ritornava in mente, sulla via dell'esilio, l'immagine di quell'« *Ecclesia spiritualis* » gioachimita ed oliviana, che per lui si identificava con Beatrice[1].

Già in precedenza, studiosi come Ignaz von Döllinger, Franz Xaver Kraus, Felice Tocco, Giulio Salvadori avevano posto la questione del profetismo dantesco[2]. Kraus, nella sua grande monografia su Dante, uscita nel 1897, accostava alla *Divina Commedia* alcuni passi dell'*Arbor Vitae* di Ubertino da Casale, ma tratti soprattutto dal libro V, a sua volta rielaborazione della *Lectura super Apocalipsim*[3]. Il più convinto sostenitore dell'influenza di Olivi su Dante fu Raoul Manselli, i cui studi sulla *Lectura* portavano a concludere che entrambi ebbero lo stesso ideale della Chiesa, povera e perseguitata. Nel suo saggio del 1965 su *Dante e l'« Ecclesia Spiritualis »*, Manselli partiva dalla questione dei rapporti tra Dante e Gioacchino da Fiore, questione su cui studiosi insigni come Herbert Grundmann, Michele Barbi e Bruno Nardi si erano pronunciati in senso negativo, limitando, se non escludendo, l'influenza diretta di Gioacchino su Dante. Eppure, si chiedeva Manselli, come negare il rapporto che unisce la religiosità dantesca, la sua critica alla gerarchia ecclesiastica, con uno dei più tormentati filoni della religiosità duecentesca? La risposta è che se Dante non

1. E. Buonaiuti, *Storia del Cristianesimo*, II, Milano, 1941, p. 543-555.

2. *Cfr.* R. Morghen, *Dante profeta. Tra la storia e l'eterno*, Milano, 1983, p. 139-157.

3. F.X. Kraus, *Dante. Sein Leben und sein Werk. Sein Verhältniss zur Kunst und zur Politik*, Berlin, 1897, p. 720-746, 736-746.

conobbe le opere di Gioacchino, ebbe però presente l'idea della «*Ecclesia Spiritualis*» così come si era sviluppata fra gli Spirituali francescani, e ne condivise alcuni degli elementi fondamentali. Olivi, in questo senso, non può considerarsi una fonte di Dante, ma una voce dell'«*Ecclesia Spiritualis*». Il confronto tra i due era un mettere in parallelo le idee, spesso coincidenti, di rinnovamento della Chiesa[1].

Tuttavia, come scriveva Raffaello Morghen nel 1970, «molti aspetti rimangono ancora da chiarire della sfinge dantesca». Le notizie storiche sono troppo evanescenti. Si può supporre un non provato incontro a Santa Croce di Firenze, ove Olivi insegnò dal 1287 al 1289. Dante stesso afferma nel *Convivio* di aver cominciato a frequentare, dopo la morte di Beatrice, avvenuta nel 1290, le scuole dei religiosi di Firenze, ed è probabile che abbia ascoltato discepoli dell'Olivi[2]. In ogni caso, indubbia è la familiarità di Dante con il mondo degli Spirituali, come dimostrano le menzioni nella *Commedia* di Ubertino da Casale e del senese Pier Pettinaio[3]. Ma tutto ciò non consente di avanzare nella ricerca. Non resta dunque altra via da percorrere che quella, più erta ma più sicura, del confronto dei testi. Accosteremo pertanto i testi della *Lectura super Apocalipsim* e della *Divina Commedia*. Precisiamo che qui non si intendono trarre conclusioni definitive, bensì si vuole proporre un metodo di ricerca.

1. R. Manselli, «Dante e l' 'Ecclesia Spiritualis' », in *Dante e Roma. Atti del Convegno di studio, Roma 8-10 aprile 1965*, Firenze, 1965, p. 115-135, ripubblicato in R. Manselli, *Da Gioacchino da Fiore a Cristoforo Colombo. Studi sul francescanesimo spirituale, sull'ecclesiologia e sull'escatologisno bassomedievali*, a cura di P. Vian, Roma, 1997 (Istituto Storico Italiano per il Medio Evo. *Nuovi Studi Storici* 36), p. 55-78. L'opera curata da Paolo Vian contiene numerosi altri saggi concernenti il rapporto tra Olivi e Dante.

2. *Convivio*, II, xii, 1-8, in Dante Alighieri, *Opere minori*, I/2, a cura di C. Vasoli – D. De Robertis, Milano-Napoli, 1988, p. 201-210: «[...] dico che, come per me fu perduto lo primo diletto de la mia anima, de la quale fatta è menzione di sopra, io rimasi di tanta tristizia punto, che conforto non mi valeva alcuno. Tuttavia, dopo alquanto tempo, la mia mente, che si argomentava di sanare, provide, poi che né 'l mio né l'altrui consolare valea, ritornare al modo che alcuno sconsolato avea tenuto a consolarsi; e misimi a leggere quello non conosciuto da molti libro di Boezio, nel quale, cattivo e discacciato, consolato s'avea. E udendo ancora che Tullio scritto avea un altro libro, nel quale, trattando de l'Amistade, avea toccate parole de la consolazione di Lelio, uomo eccellentissimo, ne la morte di Scipione amico suo, misimi a leggere quello. E avvegna che duro mi fosse ne la prima entrare ne la loro sentenza, finalmente v'entrai tanto entro, quanto l'arte di gramatica ch'io avea e un poco di mio ingegno potea fare; per lo quale ingegno molte cose, quasi come sognando, già vedea, sì come ne la Vita Nuova si può vedere. E sì come essere suole che l'uomo va cercando argento e fuori de la 'ntenzione truova oro, lo quale occulta cagione presenta, non forse sanza divino imperio; io, che cercava di consolarme, trovai non solamente a le mie lagrime rimedio, ma vocabuli d'autori e di scienze e di libri: li quali considerando, giudicava bene che la filosofia, che era donna di questi autori, di queste scienze e di questi libri, fosse somma cosa. E imaginava lei fatta come una donna gentile, e non la poteva immaginare in atto alcuno, se non misericordioso; per che sì volentieri lo senso di vero la mirava, che appena lo potea volgere da quella. E da questo imaginare cominciai ad andare là dov'ella si dimostrava veracemente, cioè ne le scuole de li religiosi e a le disputazioni de li filosofanti; sì che in picciol tempo, forse di trenta mesi, cominciai tanto a sentire de la sua dolcezza, che lo suo amore cacciava e distruggeva ogni altro pensiero». Questo passo non esclude che Dante, prima di apprendere la filosofia nelle scuole dei religiosi, avesse ascoltato la teologia, ovvero la sacra scrittura esposta dall'Olivi o dai suoi discepoli.

3. Rispettivamente in *Paradiso* XII, 124-126 e in *Purgatorio* XIII, 127-129.

Il primo esempio è costituito dal capitolo X della *Lectura*, un capitolo centrale, dove si parla dell'angelo che ha la faccia come il sole. Passo capitale, come dimostra l' *Expositio Apocalipsis* già attribuita ad Arnaldo da Villanova, che identifica quest'angelo con il pastore che attuerà la riforma della Chiesa [1]. E' un capitolo ben conosciuto ai sostenitori dell'influenza spirituale su Dante, e già Kraus, che pure lo citava attraverso Ubertino, lo considerò come ispiratore del Veltro. Nel testo allegato a questo saggio sono riportati alcuni dei possibili punti di contatto.

Ad esempio [2], lì dove si dice che Dio illumina le menti, ma dispone sotto di sé degli spiriti e degli uomini angelici per illuminare, il testo di Olivi sembra condurre al *Paradiso* XI, dove si parla dei due principi – Francesco e Domenico – ordinati dalla Provvidenza a guida della Chiesa. E' da notare che se si collaziona il testo del capitolo X della *Lectura* con quello del capitolo XI dove si parla dei due testimoni, Enoch ed Elia, si ritrovano complessivamente, tradotte dal latino in volgare, alcune parole contenute nei versi danteschi. Però il medesimo passo del capitolo X si accosta pure ad *Inferno* VII, dove si dice che la Fortuna è « general ministra e duce » ordinata agli « splendor mondani ».

Più avanti, il capitolo reca la citazione gioachimita del « *predicator fortis* », avvolto in una nube e con la fronte cinta dell'iride. L'accostamento della nube e dell'iride si trova nel *Paradiso* XII, nel momento in cui una seconda corona di spiriti sapienti in cui è san Bonaventura si aggiunge alla prima, in cui è san Tommaso : l'iride, in questo caso, è doppia, perché due sono i principi ordinati. Il riferimento a Giunone che ordina a Iride, sua ancella, concorda con il tema dell'ordinare da parte di Dio ai suoi messaggeri.

Gioacchino afferma che la faccia dell'angelo è simile al sole perché nel sesto stato la contemplazione di Dio deve condurre alla verità coloro che sono designati in Pietro, Giacomo e Giovanni, che vengono interpretati come i Latini, i Greci e gli Ebrei. Il possibile riferimento è a *Purgatorio* XXXII, quando Dante si risveglia nell'Eden dal sonno, come i tre apostoli si risvegliarono dopo essere stati condotti ad assistere alla trasfigurazione : qui si ritrovano nei versi di Dante alcune parole – « splendescere », « perduci » e i nomi dei tre apostoli – ma appropriate ad una situazione del tutto diversa rispetto al testo di Olivi.

L'immagine del carro igneo [3] è accostabile al carro trionfale su due ruote tirato dal grifone nel finale del *Purgatorio* e alla biga, sempre su due ruote, ossia su Francesco e Domenico, di cui parla san Bonaventura in *Paradiso* XII.

L'angelo dal volto solare viene identificato da Olivi in Francesco. Vediamo dunque se il testo della *Lectura* è accostabile o meno ad alcuni passi della mirabile vita del « poverel di Dio » narrata da Tommaso d'Aquino nel *Paradiso* XI. Come si può vedere [4], alcune parole sono presenti nel testo di Olivi : « acqua », « discende », « sole », « terra », « virtute », « spirital », nonché « scura »,

1. *Cfr.* R. Manselli, *Spirituali e beghini in Provenza*, Roma, 1959 (Istituto Storico Italiano per il Medio Evo. *Studi Storici*, 31-34), p. 60-62.

2. *Cfr.* i testi allegati, Esempio I, f° 114rb-va.

3. Esempio I, f° 114vb.

4. Esempio I, ff. 114vb-115ra.

« costante » e « feroce » in riferimento alla povertà. Se si collaziona il capitolo X con il passo del capitolo VII ove si parla di Francesco, angelo del sesto sigillo, « *ascendens ab ortu solis* », si possono individuare altri temi. Olivi cita Isaia, per cui cinque saranno le città nella terra d'Egitto, ma la città del sole sarà solo una. Le città citate da Dante sono cinque : Perugia, Nocera, Gualdo, Ascesi, Oriente ed una sola, l'ultima, può dirsi realmente « *civitas solis* ». Tuttavia, anche nell'elogio di san Domenico, che Bonaventura pronuncia nel canto seguente, si ritrovano parole come « repleta », « mente » e « vertute » presenti nella *Lectura*. L'immagine dell'orologio di Achaz, che Cristo riascende in Francesco sino al mattino, si ritrova al termine di *Paradiso* X, ove l'orologio che chiama il mattutino è appropriato alla corona delle anime beate.

L'angelo del capitolo X sarà impavido come un leone, sia per attaccare che per difendere[1]. Questa qualità sembra appropriata alla vita di Domenico, il cui luogo di nascita, Calaruega, si trova sotto la protezione dello scudo di Castiglia, in cui è rappresentato un leone che sovrasta ed insieme soggiace ad un castello. Come pure il suo impeto contro le resistenze degli eretici ricorre nell'impeto dell'angelo volto alla conversione di tutto il mondo e nel suo ruggire contro l'ostinata resistenza dei carnali.

L'angelo[2], che pone il mare e la terra sotto i piedi per la sua altissima povertà, non si sottomette vilmente alle cose mondane, ed anche Francesco non si rende vile per la sua umiltà. L'angelo tiene in mano il libro aperto, e Francesco « apre » ad Innocenzo III la sua dura intenzione, ottenendo la prima approvazione della Regola.

L'angelo ruggisce come un leone, con forte indignazione : questo ci conduce alla porta del Purgatorio, che ha gli spigoli forti e rugghia. Olivi afferma che l'angelo ruggisce perché i carnali non hanno più alcuna scusa ora che il libro è aperto : anche Dante, secondo l'ammonizione dell'angelo portiere, sa che non deve voltarsi indietro, e che qualora lo facesse, non ci sarebbe degna scusa alla sua colpa. Il tema dell'« *aspicere retro* », dell'apostatare, è pure contenuto nella *Lectura*, ed appropriato alla chiesa di Laodicea.

Quando l'angelo grida, i sette tuoni fanno sentire la propria voce[3] : dopo il rugghiare della porta del Purgatorio, Dante si rivolge attento al « primo tuono », espressione oscura, ma che può significare la prima, o il primo gruppo, delle voci che Dante ascolterà ascendendo la montagna che è distinta, appunto, in sette gironi. In ogni caso, c'è una conseguenzialità di parole tematiche (il ruggire forte, il non poter più invocare scuse per i carnali, il tuonare) che è comune ai due testi.

Giovanni è pronto a scrivere i sensi spirituali dei sette tuoni, ma una voce glielo impedisce, secondo quanto era stato imposto a Daniele, di chiudere le parole e di sigillare il libro fino al tempo stabilito, ossia fino a quando il tempo di questo secolo finirà nel canto della settima tromba[4]. Si può pensare al chiudersi sonando, dietro le spalle di Dante, della porta del Purgatorio. Ma più evidente è la

1. Esempio I, f° 115rb-va.
2. Esempio I, ff. 115vb-116ra.
3. Esempio I, f° 116ra-b.
4. Esempio I, f° 116rb-vb.

connessione con le parole di Cacciaguida, l'avo del poeta, che in *Paradiso* XVII dice cose incredibili di Cangrande della Scala, cose che Dante deve portare scritte nella mente e non rivelare. E Cangrande è « forte » nelle « opere » e nella « sua virtute », come l'angelo del capitolo X.

Questi giudizi di Dio occulti ed incredibili sono preannunziati sotto veli mistici[1]. Il tema del « velamen » ci conduce ad una terzina famosa, ossia all'appello al lettore che precede l'arrivo del messo celeste che apre la porta della città di Dite, chiusa in faccia a Virgilio dai diavoli che non vogliono saperne di farvi entrare Dante, e che anzi lo vogliono rimandare indietro da solo per la buia strada. Le parole di questa terzina risultano quasi tutte da una collazione di un passo del tema introduttivo della *Lectura*, da Isaia 30, 26, con un altro del capitolo XIII. Sotto il velo dei versi strani, che poco prima hanno descritto le Furie ed il Gorgone, si nasconde la dottrina di Cristo, velata perché non è ancora tempo di aperture. E tuttavia coloro che hanno gli intelletti sani, debbono sapere che i santi, pazienti e confidenti nell'aiuto divino, verranno salvati contro quanti vogliono condurli in prigionia. E questo avviene appunto con il fragoroso arrivo del messo celeste.

L'angelo[2] dice a Giovanni di prendere il libro e di divorarlo : esso dapprima provocherà contorsioni amare nel ventre, ma poi sarà dolce alla bocca, perché la contemplazione delle future passioni è dolce e amara insieme, come il ricordo della passione di Cristo. Ancora la compresenza delle parole conduce all'episodio in cui Dante ascolta da Cacciaguida il suo futuro destino e le vicende dolorose dell'esilio, e gusta insieme l'amaro del suo patire con il dolce della fama che gli è riservata. Quest'esser dolce e amaro non è solo nel gusto di Dante che ascolta le parole dell'avo, ma pure negli effetti del libro, molesto nel primo gusto per quanti hanno la coscienza turbata dalla vergogna, ma poi salutare. Così Cacciaguida invita Dante a manifestare senza timore tutta la sua visione, e lo stesso farà san Pietro nel XXVII canto del *Paradiso*. Il testo del capitolo X può essere in questo caso collazionato con il passo del capitolo XXII, in cui a Giovanni viene ingiunto di non occultare quello che ha visto. Dante pertanto assume su di sé il compito di Giovanni, di predicare ai popoli e alle genti e di misurare il tempio : non è casuale che la *Commedia* si concluda con l'immagine del geometra che cerca, e non ritrova, la misura del cerchio[3].

Da questa molto sommaria e superficiale rassegna di alcuni passaggi del capitolo X della *Lectura*, si può, sia pure con cautela, trarre un dato emergente : l'estesa presenza di parole latine tradotte in volgare e appropriate a situazioni e personaggi differenti della *Commedia*. Il che significa che, se Dante ha utilizzato la *Lectura*, quello che in Olivi è concentrato su san Francesco viene diffuso da Dante su spazi, tempi e persone più vasti. D'altronde, l'Olivi stesso non esclude che le figure dell'angelo del sesto sigillo, dell'angelo della sesta tromba e di Giovanni che riceve il libro possano essere applicate a differenti ordini o persone.

1. Esempio I, ff. 116vb-117ra.
2. Esempio I, ff. 117vb-118ra.
3. *Paradiso* XXXIII, 133-135.

Certamente, non basta la compresenza di parole in due testi per affermare che l'uno sia connesso con l'altro. Però, fatto del tutto singolare, questa compresenza di parole si verifica per l'intero testo della *Lectura*, e non soltanto nel capitolo X. Qui si mostrerà solo qualche esempio tratto da punti diversi.

Uno dei temi principali del primo stato è quello del passaggio di mano del candelabro[1]. Alla chiesa di Efeso viene minacciata la traslazione del suo primato, qualora insuperbisca a causa di esso. Lo stesso motivo compare nella sesta chiesa, quella di Filadelfia. La collazione dei due testi ci conduce nel primo girone del Purgatorio, quello dei superbi, ove Oderisi da Gubbio riconosce la superiorità nell'arte della miniatura di Franco bolognese, come Cimabue è stato superato da Giotto nella pittura, Guido Guinizzelli da Guido Cavalcanti nella gloria della lingua che verrà presto traslata ad altri, ossia a Dante stesso. L'essere onorati ed illuminati propri della chiesa di Efeso sono appropriati ad Oderisi e, in senso equivoco, all'arte della miniatura, il francese « enluminer ». Oderisi, con atto di umiltà, afferma che tutto l'onore è di chi gli è subentrato, ed è suo solo in parte. E' lo stesso atto di cortese riconoscimento che i seniori, nel quarto capitolo della *Lectura*, rendono a Dio, in modo totale, in quanto ogni parte non riceve grazie e si conserva se non nel suo tutto. Così Cimabue ha visto oscurata la propria fama, ed il verso relativo è un filo tratto dalla quarta tromba ed intrecciato con altri del primo stato (il testo dal cap. XI). La gloria preparata per la Sinagoga e poi traslata alla Chiesa di Cristo, o quella che dal quinto stato viene passata al sesto, viene appropriata ai due Guidi, Guinizzelli e Cavalcanti, che verranno superati dalle nuove rime di Dante.

Veniamo ora ad alcuni passaggi del capitolo XXI, relativi alla forma e alla dimensione della Gerusalemme celeste. Il confronto proposto[2] è l'arrivo di Dante e di Beatrice sul primo cielo, quello della Luna. Si può notare la coincidenza degli aggettivi : la Luna è « lucida » come la piazza della città celeste, è « solida » come la luce divina, è « pulita », ossia perspicua. Essa appare a Dante coperta da una nube. Olivi afferma che l'oscurità della Luna designa l'umiltà delle menti celesti. Poiché nel X capitolo si dice che l'angelo dal volto solare è ricoperto da una nube, « amictus nube », in quanto umile e povero, ecco che la nube designa l'umiltà della Luna. Non è casuale il fatto che fra poco Beatrice demolirà la teoria delle macchie lunari che Dante crede, con Averroè, fondata sul raro e sul denso, e vi sostituirà una visione sostanzialmente dionisiana. La Luna riceve Dante in se stessa, ossia lo incorpora, come è incorporata la luce nelle gemme. Il poeta si meraviglia dello stare simultaneo di due corpi nello stesso spazio, e lo fa usando due verbi, « ricevere » e « patire », che sono due chiavi di volta del sesto stato dell'Olivi. Il sesto stato, rispetto ai precedenti, avrà infatti la proprietà di « pati seu recipere », piuttosto che quella di « agere vel dare », ossia riceverà maggiori grazie e più familiari segni d'amore da parte di Cristo. Ci si può ricordare del Limbo, ove i cinque poeti si rivolgono a Dante con salutevol cenno e lo fanno

1. Esempio III.
2. Esempio III.

della loro schiera, « sì ch'io fui sesto tra cotanto senno »[1]. La Luna, infine, si presenta a Dante unita, « com'acqua recepe raggio di sole permanendo unita », e qui è il riferimento all'unità concorde della città di Dio, « civium unitas ». I beati, nel cielo della Luna, appaiono come attraverso vetri trasparenti e tersi; la loro volontà, afferma Piccarda, è concorde con quella divina.

Nel primo capitolo della *Lectura*, vengono esaminate dodici perfezioni di Cristo. La quarta[2] consiste nella maturità del consiglio, che è designata dal candore dei capelli. Un accostamento, quello dei crini e del consiglio, che è ben conosciuto dal diavolo preparato in logica che argomenta con successo, di fronte a Francesco, il suo diritto a prendersi l'anima di Guido da Montefeltro. Guido, arrivato alla vecchiaia, si era pentito delle sue opere volpine, e si era cinto del cordone, ma poi, dando a Bonifacio VIII il consiglio fraudolento su come conquistare Palestrina, si era rimesso nelle prime colpe, e da quel momento i suoi crini non sono stati più segno di maturità e di gloria celeste.

I capelli di Cristo sono bianchi come lana e come neve, e significa che la sapienza di Cristo può essere pietosa e calda nel condiscendere alle nostre facoltà, ma pure astratta e rigida in quanto purga le nostre colpe. Beatrice, al suo apparire a Dante nell'Eden, si presenta dapprima come « proterva », ossia rigida, e acerba nella pietà, pronta a rimproverare il poeta, perché si purghi del suo traviamento. Il cuore di Dante intanto si congela come neve, che solo il canto compassionevole degli angeli riesce a sciogliere.

Da tutti questi esempi – che, lo ripetiamo, sono solo una minima parte dei possibili – si può notare sia la compresenza delle parole, sia l'intreccio fra più punti della *Lectura*, sia la trasformazione del senso spirituale del testo teologico in una lettera poetica completamente diversa, ma non tanto che non consenta di ritrovare le tracce della sua origine. A questi accostamenti di testi a modo di sondaggi, si aggiunge un'altra constatazione. I temi che nella *Lectura* sono appropriati ai sette stati della storia della Chiesa, ritornano nella *Divina Commedia* in modo consequenziale e ciclico. Anche in questo caso, non potendo diffonderci a lungo, limiteremo gli esempi. Prendiamo una sezione dell'*Inferno*, a partire dal cerchio dei violenti. Il primo girone, dei violenti contro il prossimo[3], contiene dei temi che sono propri del secondo stato, quello dei martiri. La riviera del sangue corrisponde al cavallo rosso del secondo sigillo, che designa le persecuzioni dei pagani contro i cristiani. Dieci sono le persecuzioni generali, e dieci sono i tiranni immersi nel sangue bollente. I dannati sono guardati da Centauri armati di saette, che minacciano Virgilio e Dante, e la seconda vittoria consiste nel sostenere le saette delle tentazioni e della morte eterna. Il centauro Nesso porta in groppa Dante al di là della riviera, e nella seconda tromba si parla di Niccolò, uno dei sette diaconi, il cui compito è quello di portare sulle spalle il peso della passione di Cristo. Nella seconda battaglia il diavolo viene vinto e gettato a terra « *in infimam deiectionem* », e al termine della scesa dirupata verso

1. *Inf.* IV, 102.
2. Esempio IV.
3. *Inf.* XII

la riviera del sangue « l'infamia di Creti era distesa », ossia il Minotauro. Non si tratta solo di situazioni generiche, ma di situazioni trasformate lavorando sulle parole. Si osservi [1] come ai Centauri vengano applicati dei termini che compaiono nel capitolo quinto della *Lectura* per spiegare i motivi della chiusura del secondo sigillo nell' Antico Testamento. Si tratta del desiderio di vendicare le offese, e questo ben si concorda con le qualità di Nesso, Chirone e Folo.

Il secondo girone dei violenti, quello dei suicidi[2], contiene temi del terzo stato, dei dottori. Tutta la descrizione dei suicidi – che hanno operato una divisione in se stessi – è un « troncare », « schiantare », « scerpere », « dilacerare », « esser monco », che corrisponde allo « scindere », « resecare », « dividere » dei dottori verso le eresie e delle eresie stesse verso le verità della fede cristiana. Il « color fosco » delle fronde, il « sangue bruno » che esce dai tronchi, le « nere cagne » che dilacerano i cespugli conducono all'immagine del cavallo nero del terzo sigillo. La « falsa statera » degli eretici, che Olivi interpreta come « intorta acceptio scripture », è nei rami « nodosi e 'nvolti ».

Si potrebbe continuare, ma qui non è possibile, per tutti gli stati. La progressione settenaria è ben visibile nel *Paradiso*, a partire dal quarto cielo, quello del Sole, per quanto tutta la terza cantica sia il trionfo del sesto e del settimo stato e dei relativi temi. Il cielo del Sole, ove si lodano Francesco e Domenico, corrisponde al rinnovamento della Chiesa primitiva; segue Marte, con Cacciaguida che, martire nella crociata, annuncia a Dante le tribolazioni future; poi Giove, ove l'aquila spiega come un dottore l'incomprensibile profondità della predestinazione divina; quindi Saturno, ove splendono gli anacoreti Pier Damiani e Benedetto; quindi il cielo delle stelle fisse, ove discendono le schiere del trionfo di Cristo – il quinto stato è quello del condiscendere alle umane facoltà; il sesto e il settimo stato si ritrovano nel Primo mobile e nell'Empireo. Il silenzio di Beatrice, all'inizio del XXIX canto, corrisponde al silenzio del settimo stato.

Allo stato attuale delle ricerche, riteniamo di poter avanzare un'ipotesi. La *Divina Commedia*, che si distingue in cantiche e canti e che ordina l'inferno, il purgatorio e il paradiso per cerchi, bolge, gironi, cieli, sembra avere un altro ordine interiore, non corrispondente esattamente a quello che appare al lettore, e fondato sui temi relativi ai sette stati oliviani che ritornano ciclicamente. Non si tratta certamente di corrispondenze rigide o meccaniche, tanto intenso è l'intreccio fra i temi. All'interno di ogni stato, inoltre, si ritrovano temi di tutti gli altri e ciò consente a Dante una pressoché infinita possibilità di variazione dei segni, ossia delle parole, e del loro significato, secondo le diverse appropriazioni. Ciascuno stato ha in sé qualcosa di cristiforme, ossia qualche tema del sesto stato. Il magnanimo Farinata, sentendo il poeta parlare delle sue responsabilità nella battaglia di Montaperti – « lo strazio e 'l grande scempio che fece l'Arbia colorata in rosso » – rompe la sua rigidità iniziale, sospira e scuote il capo, prova cioè in sé quel terremoto che, all'inizio del sesto sigillo, condurrà molti a convertirsi a

1. Esempio V.
2. *Inf.* XIII

Cristo. Non diversamente la fiamma di Ulisse comincia a crollarsi, mormorando, dopo le parole alte e folgoranti di Virgilio. Così ogni stato ha in sé qualcosa del settimo, una sua pace, una sua « quietatio », e questo consente a Francesca di parlare, « mentre che 'l vento, come fa, ci tace »[1]. Ed al settimo stato appartiene il vedere in modo aperto tutto il contenuto del libro che solo Cristo può aprire : « nuda et beata *visio* et fruitio Dei per quam liber vite erit plene *apertus* »[2]. Che è quanto rivendica Farinata :

> Ma fu' *io solo*, là dove sofferto
> fu per ciascun di tòrre via Fiorenza,
> colui che la difesi *a viso aperto*[3].

Già Raoul Manselli sottolineava come il silenzio di Dante su Olivi potrebbe essere connesso con le polemiche e con il giudizio di ortodossia cui erano soggette le opere del francescano[4]. Nel cielo del Sole, Tommaso d'Aquino presenta i suoi undici compagni, tutti spiriti sapienti : Alberto Magno, Graziano, Pier Lombardo, Dionigi, Orosio, Boezio, Isidoro, Beda, Riccardo di San Vittore, e un avversario dell'Aquinate, Sigieri di Brabante. La quinta luce, la più splendente, non ha nome :

> La quinta luce, ch'è tra noi piú bella,
> spira di tale amor, che tutto 'l mondo
> là giú ne gola di saper novella :
> entro v'è l'alta mente u' sí profondo
> saver fu messo, che, se 'l vero è vero,
> a veder tanto non surse il secondo.

Tre canti dopo, nel XIII del *Paradiso*, Tommaso preciserà che si tratta di un re sapiente, ossia di Salomone. E il desiderio del mondo di sapere se fosse salvato o dannato corrisponde alle dispute dei teologi che si interrogavano sugli effetti della sua lussuria. Ma la presentazione che Tommaso fa di Salomone può essere accostata ad alcuni temi contenuti nel capitolo quinto della *Lectura*[5].

L'intelligenza del libro che contiene dentro sé la profonda sapienza divina richiede un'alta mente, e i termini dell'inizio del quinto capitolo della *Lectura* ritornano identici nei versi danteschi relativi a Salomone : « intus », « alta », « mens », « profundiores sententie sapientialium documentorum » / « entro v'è l'alta mente u' sí profondo saver fu messo ». Lo spirare d'amore è tratto dal versetto ottavo dello stesso capitolo, relativo agli atti di lode. E' da notare – come testimonianza della complessità della trasformazione dantesca – che il libro contiene anche le leggi di Dio, sommo imperatore, e si trova alla sua destra : così il quinto capitolo fornisce pure il tessuto per l'alto lavoro svolto da Giustiniano nel raccogliere le leggi, lavoro ispirato da Dio e fatto mentre la destra del cielo

1. *Inf.* V, 96
2. *Lectura*, cap. V
3. *Inf.* X, 91-93
4. R. Manselli, *Olivi*, in *Enciclopedia Dantesca*, IV, Roma, Istituto della Enciclopedia Italiana, 1984, p. 136.
5. Esempio VI.

aiutava le vittorie di Belisario. Altri fili adoperati per Salomone sono presi da altre parti del capitolo quinto, per quanto riguarda il « mettere » e l'« esser vero ». Dalla quarta tromba, nel capitolo ottavo, l'identificazione che fa Gioacchino da Fiore dell'aquila con Gregorio Magno come colui che ha visto più di altri avvicinarsi tempi perigliosi, serve all'espressione « a veder tanto non surse il secondo », come pure presta materia alla descrizione di san Giovanni nell'Empireo, ove il riferimento alla lancia è tutto oliviano. Il desiderio del mondo di aver nuove, di sapere cioè se Salomone sia o meno salvato, corrisponde al desiderio che il libro venga aperto. I golosi, se letteralmente sono coloro che sono affetti da un vizio, spiritualmente sono quelli che aspirano a qualcosa di nuovo. Bonagiunta da Lucca, che purga la gola nel sesto girone del Purgatorio, chiede con grande desiderio a Dante se sia lui il poeta che ha tratto le « nove rime », e la risposta di Dante è che egli segue il dettato interiore quando « Amor mi spira » : una situazione che si può accostare a quella di Salomone. Tanto sottile risulta la trama di Dante nei versi relativi a Salomone, che anche l'« u' » – che letteralmente sta per « ubi » – potrebbe essere un filo spirituale a sé. Nel capitolo XX della *Lectura*, si dice che « u » designa il XIII secolo, poiché si pronuncia aspirando sull'estremo delle labbra, e alla fine del secolo Babilon spirerà. Non è casuale che Tommaso usi frequentemente questa espressione, anche perché, nel citato capitolo XX, si dice che il centenario seguente è designato con *X*, ossia con una lettera che ha la forma di croce, cui seguiranno le lettere che i Latini presero dai Greci, designanti la « dilatatio » della Chiesa ai Greci e a tutte le genti. Ebbene, al cielo del Sole, ove parla Tommaso d'Aquino, succede quello di Marte, ove Dante vede appunto una croce greca[1], e poi quello di Giove, ove i lumi volano cantando e formando dapprima le lettere *D*, *I*, *L*, ossia « *dil*atatio ». Le lettere, insieme ad altre luci, formano un'aquila nella cui pupilla rifulge, fra le altre, la luce di Rifeo troiano[2].

Se questo è vero, se le parole che Tommaso d'Aquino dice di Salomone sono tessute con i fili tratti dalla « pestifera postilla » su cui si accanivano gli inquisitori domenicani, allora nel cielo del Sole si assiste ad una pacificazione generale delle controversie terrene, ad un vero e proprio giubileo : Tommaso d'Aquino presenta a Dante la luce più fulgida, dentro la quale è contenuta la vera sapienza cristiana, e poi Sigieri, un avversario dei Domenicani; quindi narra la vita di Francesco, « poverel di Dio ». Bonaventura, il maestro di Olivi, narra la vita di san Domenico, mentre gli luce accanto Gioacchino da Fiore. Quindi Tommaso insiste nell' elogio della sapienza di Salomone, che non fu rivolta alla filosofia mondana. Nel canto successivo, la luce di Salomone parla su richiesta di Beatrice, per risolvere un dubbio di Dante sulla luminosità dei beati dopo la resurrezione dei corpi. E' « una voce modesta, forse qual fu da l'angelo a Maria »[3]. Una voce forse memore di quanto Olivi scrive nel Commento a Luca, dell'angelo che, nel lodare la Vergine, riferisce tutta la lode a Dio[4].

1. *Par.* XIV, 101-102.
2. *Par.* XVIII, 70-114.
3. *Par.* XIV, 35-36.
4. *Lectura super Lucam*, ad 1, 28, Roma, Biblioteca Vaticana, ms. Ottob. 3302, f° 11v.

Conseguenza di quel che si è mostrato, sia pur assai parzialmente, è la possibilità di una duplice lettura, esterna ed interna, letterale e spirituale, della *Divina Commedia*, poema sacro scritto dentro e fuori. Grande è la meraviglia nel vedere la teologia trasformarsi in poesia, e d'altronde Dante aveva avvertito il lettore che la sua sorpresa sarebbe stata di gran lunga superiore a quella degli Argonauti, allorché videro Giasone, il loro duce, mutato in contadino :

> Que' gloriosi che passaro al Colco
> non s'ammiraron come voi farete,
> quando Iasón vider fatto bifolco

come si afferma all'inizio del secondo canto del *Paradiso*. Ma il lettore che può realmente meravigliarsi non è quello che possiede una « picciolетta barca » e che si perderebbe nel pelago della sacra scrittura, egli appartiene alla cerchia di quei pochi che hanno drizzato il collo per tempo al « pan de li angeli », alla sapienza cristiana, alla teologia.

A questo punto assumono rilevanza i pochi eventi storicamente databili. Tra il 1287 ed il 1289, Olivi insegnò a Firenze, in Santa Croce; nel 1290 morì Beatrice. Di certo, come ha dimostrato Paolo Vian, le opere dell'Olivi si diffondono in Italia subito dopo la morte del suo autore, e la loro circolazione manoscritta sembra essere per buona parte italiana[1]. Se in quegli anni Dante ha cominciato a leggere le opere del maestro francescano, deve essersi reso conto presto delle straordinarie possibilità offerte alla poesia dalla teologia dell'Olivi, nel momento in cui il cristocentrismo di questa veniva applicato alla lode della propria donna, di Cristo imitatrice. E molte sorprese potrebbe rivelare lo studio dei rapporti tra il primo Dante, quello della *Vita Nova* e delle *Rime*, e le opere dell'Olivi diverse dalla *Lectura super Apocalipsim*. Come pure è da verificare l'utilizzazione di altre opere del maestro francescano nella *Commedia*[2].

1. P. Vian, *Appunti sulla tradizione manoscritta della* Lectura super Apocalipsim *di Pietro di Giovanni Olivi*, in *Editori di Quaracchi 100 anni dopo. Bilancio e prospettive*, Atti del Colloquio Internazionale, Roma 29-30 maggio 1995, a cura di A. Cacciotti e B. Faes de Mottoni, Roma, 1997, p. 378-384.

2. Impressionante è ad esempio la somiglianza tra un passo della quinta *quaestio de perfectione evangelica* (« *An sit melius aliquid facere ex voto quam sine voto* », ed. A. Emmen, « La dottrina dell'Olivi sul valore religioso dei voti », *S.F.* 63, 1966, p. 97-98) con il passo di *Paradiso* V, 19-33, sempre relativo al voto :

Non basta comunque confrontare la *quaestio* con i versi danteschi, perché, a rigore, la posizione di Dante non è esattamente quella di Olivi e, così come presentata, avrebbe potuto essere sottoscritta da un qualunque teologo del tempo. Anche in questo caso, il tessuto di tutto *Paradiso V* è tratto ed elaborato dalla *Lectura super Apocalipsim* ed allora il riferimento alla *quaestio* costituisce solo uno dei temi da concordare con quelli presenti nel testo principale.

Nel XXXII canto del *Paradiso*, san Bernardo spiega a Dante la distribuzione dei beati nella candida rosa. Ad un certo punto interrompe la descrizione con la similitudine del sarto che non ha più panno per fare il vestito : è tempo ormai di rivolgere la preghiera alla Vergine per poi drizzare l'occhio al primo Amore :

> Ma perché 'l tempo fugge che t'assonna,
> qui farem punto, come buon sartore
> che com'elli ha del panno fa la gonna [1]

<table>
<tr>
<td>
Si enim aspiciamus ad id quod per votum Deo datur et redditur, inveniemus quod per votum non solum datur ipsum opus dum est, sed etiam tota libertas nostra et totum dominium voluntatis nostrae respectu talis operis. Absque voto autem datur solum opus dum fit, non autem plene pro tempore pro quo erit antequam fiat, nec datur libertas et dominium voluntatis respectu talis operis. Tantum ergo praeponderat votum super simplex propositum, quantum valet libertas et dominium voluntatis, et hoc respectu totius futuri temporis. Hoc autem nullo modo posset per aliquid huius vitae appretiari nec recompensari. Haec autem libertas non solum datur in hora qua votum emittitur, sed omni tempore quo placet sibi vovisse, et in quo cum hac complacentia votum implet. Si ergo votum in sua emissione addebat quamdam valoris et meriti infinitatem, et hoc per totum tempus sequens replicatur et multiplicatur, ergo votum continuatum superaddit multiplicem infinitatem.

Praeterea, tantum Deus appretiatur omne a nobis sibi datum, quantum nobis est dilectum et carum, et quanto ipsa donatio est magis supra naturam voluntatis nostrae. Sed nihil sub Deo est nobis ita dilectum et carum sicut libertas et dominium voluntatis nostrae. Hoc enim infinite appretiamur; appretiamur enim illud plus quam omnia quae Deus posset facere, quae sunt infinita, et plus quam aliquid quod sit in nobis; et istius per votum donatio est super omnia, supra naturam et quodammodo contra naturam voluntatis nostrae. Per hoc enim funditus seipsam abnegat et obliviscitur et a seipsa quodammodo totaliter separatur; et per hoc seipsam totaliter subiugando et se plenissime Deo dando, super se totaliter et altissime tota fertur in Deum. Ergo istud donum super omne aliud a nobis datum vel donabile praeponderat in infinitum.
</td>
<td>
« Lo maggior don *che Dio per sua larghezza*
fesse creando e a la sua bontate
piú conformato e quel ch'e' piú apprezza,
fu de la volontà la libertate ;
di che le creature intelligenti,
e tutte e sole, fuoro e son dotate.
Or ti parrà, se tu quinci argomenti,
l'alto valor del voto, *s'è sí fatto*
che Dio consenta quando tu consenti ;
ché, nel fermar tra Dio e l'uomo il patto,
vittima fassi di questo tesoro,
tal quale io dico ; e fassi col suo atto.
Dunque che render puossi per ristoro ?
Se credi bene usar quel c'hai offerto,
di maltolletto vuo' far buon lavoro ».

Cfr. Le parole di Virgilio a Catone, che ha scelto il suicidio in nome della libertà morale (Purgatorio I, 70-72) :

Or ti piaccia gradir la sua venuta :
libertà va cercando, ch'è sí cara,
come sa chi per lei vita rifiuta.
</td>
</tr>
</table>

1. *Par.* XXXII, 139-141.

Questa immagine, del panno e della gonna, rende esattamente ciò che appare a chi confronti i testi dei due capolavori di Olivi e di Dante: la *Lectura super Apocalipsim* è il panno da cui il buon sartore ha fatto la *Divina Commedia.* Non appare esserci solo un'influenza di idee, più o meno ampia, del teologo provenzale sul poeta fiorentino. Sembra che, per una libera scelta, Dante abbia deciso di partire da un testo teologico e di trasformarlo, con una metamorfosi emula di Ovidio, in un'opera poetica. Questa è un'ipotesi, che le ricerche successive potranno o meno confermare. Se verrà confermata, allora la *Lectura super Apocalipsim* si proporrà come autentica « chiave di Davide, che apre e nessuno chiude, che chiude e nessuno apre ». Diversamente, il confronto dei testi consentirà comunque di penetrare nel laboratorio di Dante e di verificare un lavoro che è insieme traduzione, sintesi, intreccio, metamorfosi, di ripercorrere la creazione di una nuova lingua che, come affermò Eliot, pur essendo italiana e locale, è la più europea mai usata da un poeta. Di Pietro di Giovanni Olivi, perseguitato in vita e in morte da molte bufere, potrebbe forse cantare Ariel, l'etereo spirito della *Tempesta* di Shakespeare:

> Those are pearls that were his eyes;
> Nothing of him that doth fade,
> But doth suffer a sea-change
> Into something rich and strange.

TESTI

Pietro di Giovanni Olivi, *Lectura super Apocalipsim:* si tiene presente il lavoro svolto da Paolo Vian in vista di un'edizione critica. Il testo che qui si presenta si basa sul ms. lat. 713 della Bibliothèque Nationale di Parigi.

Dante Alighieri, *La Commedia*, edizione critica della « vulgata », a cura di Giorgio Petrocchi, Firenze, 1994.

Esempio I *(ex cap. X)*

[114 rb] Quod autem quidam dicunt hunc angelum esse Christum quia solius ipsius est aperire librum prout dicitur supra capitulo V° (5, 2-3), non negamus quin ipse sit principalis reserator libri et precipue in quantum est Deus illuminans interius mentes, sed nichilominus ordinavit sub se angelicos spiritus et angelicos homines ad ministraliter illuminandum inferiores. Qua ergo ratione per septem angelos tuba canentes intelliguntur angelici homines et doctores et etiam spiritus angelici eis presidentes, quamquam Christus principaliter doceat omnia que per tubicinationes angelorum docentur, eadem ratione debet consimiliter intelligi in proposito.

Ioachim dicit hic : Quicumque erit iste predicator veritatis fortis [114va] esse describitur, quia robustus erit in fide et de celo descendet, idest de vita contemplativa ad activam, et amictus erit nube, quia indutus erit scriptura prophetarum, et yrim in capite, quia Spiritum Sanctum et misticum seu spiritalem intellectum scripturarum habebit in mente. Sicut enim archus celestis apparet iunctus nubibus celi, sic scripturis prophetarum iungendus est misticus intellectus ad adversarios convincendos.

Et subdit : Ego autem angelum istum secundum litteram aut Enoch fore puto aut Heliam. Verum, prout hoc Deus melius novit, unum dico pro certo, quod hic angelus significat personaliter magnum aliquem predicatorem, quamvis spiritaliter ad multos viros spiritales tunc temporis futuros competenter valeat intorqueri. Sane facies angeli similis est soli quia in hoc sexto tempore oportet Dei contemplatio in modum solis splendescere et perduci ad notitiam eorum qui

Paradiso, XI, 35-36 :

due principi ordinò in suo favore,
che quinci e quindi le fosser per guida

Inferno, VII, 77-78 :

Similemente a li splendor mondani
ordinò general ministra e duce

Paradiso, XII, 10-12 :

Come si volgon per tenera nube
due archi paralleli e concolori
quando Iunone a sua ancella iube

Purgatorio, XXXII, 71-77 :

e dico ch'un splendor mi squarciò 'l velo
del sonno, e un chiamar : « Surgi : che fai ? ».
Quali a veder de' fioretti del melo
che del suo pome li angeli fa ghiotti
e perpetue nozze fa nel cielo.
Pietro e Giovanni e Iacopo condotti
e vinti, ritornaro alla parola

(11, 4) [121va] Preterea hic dicuntur stare [duo testes] « in conspectu Domini » sicut duo candelabra lucentia seu duo luminaria stant coram uno Domino seu coram altari Dei [121vb] unum a dextris et aliud a sinistris, vel sicut duo principes vel consiliarii unius magni regis stant et incedunt coram eo unus a dextris et alius a sinistris.

designantur in Petro et Iacobo et Iohanne, idest Latinorum et Grecorum et Hebreorum. Primo quidem Latinorum, deinde Grecorum, tertio Hebreorum, ut fiant novissimi qui erant primi et e contrario. Hec Ioachim.

Sciendum etiam quod sanctissimus pater noster Franciscus est post Christum et sub Christo primus et principalis fundator et initiator et exemplator sexti status et evangelice regule eius, sic ipse post Christum designatur [114vb] primo per angelum istum

Unde et in huiusmodi signum in curru igneo apparuit transfiguratus in solem, ut monstraretur venisse in spiritu et ymagine Helye et simul cum hoc gerere perfectam ymaginem veri solis, scilicet Christi.

Purgatorio, XXIX, 107, 115-117 :

un carro, in su due rote, triunfale [...]
Non che Roma di carro cosí bello
rallegrasse Affricano, o vero Augusto,
ma quel del Sol saría pover con ello

Paradiso, XII, 106-107 :

Se tal fu l'una rota de la biga
in che la Santa Chiesa si difese

Paradiso, X, 139-141 :

Indi, come orologio che ne chiami
ne l'ora che la sposa di Dio surge
a mattinar lo sposo perché l'ami

(ex cap. VII, 2)

[85va] Hic ergo angelus est Franciscus evangelice vite et regule sexto et septimo tempore propagande et magnificande renovator et summus post Christum et eius matrem observator, « ascendens ab ortu solis », idest ab illa vita quam Christus sol mundi in suo ortu, idest in suo primo adventu, attulit nobis. Nam decem umbratiles lineas orologii Acacz, Christus in Francisco reascendit usque ad illud mane in quo Christus est ortus.

Ipse enim fuit singulariter fortis in omni virtute et opere Dei, et per summam humilitatem et recognitionem prime originis omnis nature et gratie semper descendens de celo, et per aeream et subtilem seu spiritalem levitatem ab omni pondere terrenorum excussam fuit amictus nube, idest altissima paupertate aquis celestibus plena, idest suprema possessione et inbibitione celestium divitiarum. [...]

Paradiso, XI, 43-57, 61-62 :

Intra Tupino e l'acqua che discende
del colle eletto dal beato Ubaldo,
fertile costa d'alto monte pende,
onde *Perugia* sente freddo e caldo
da Porta Sole ; e di rietro le piange
per grave giogo *Nocera* con *Gualdo*.
Di questa costa, là dov'ella frange
più sua rattezza, nacque al mondo un sole,
come fa questo talvolta di Gange.
Però chi d'esso loco fa parole,
non dica *Ascesi*, ché direbbe corto,
ma *Oriente*, se proprio dir vuole.
Non era ancor molto lontan da l'orto,
ch'el cominciò a far sentir la terra
della sua gran virtute alcun conforto

e dinanzi a la sua spirital corte
et coram patre le si fece unito

Ascendit etiam ab ortu solis quia sui ascensus in Deum fundamentum et initium cepit a sede romana, que inter patriarchales ecclesias est principaliter sedes et civitas solis, idest Christi et fidei [85vb] eius, de qua tipice dicitur Isaie XIX° (Is 19, 18) : « In die illa erunt *quinque civitates* in terra Egipti » et cetera, « *civitas solis vocabitur una* ».

Paradiso, XII, 58-59 : (Domenico)

e come fu creata, fu repleta
sí la sua mente di viva vertute

[115rb] Quia vero hoc et sequentia in futuris eius operibus et discipulis clarius innotescent, idcirco sciendum quod a tempore sollempnis impugnationis et condempnationis evangelice vite et regule sub mistico Antichristo fiende et sub magno amplius consumande, spiritaliter descendet Christus et eius servus Franciscus et angelicus discipulorum eius cetus contra omnes

Paradiso, XI, 64-66, 70-72 :

Questa, privata del primo marito,
millecent'anni e piú dispetta e scura
fino a costui si stette sanza invito

né valse esser costante né feroce

Paradiso, XII, 52-54 :

siede la fortunata Calaroga

errores et malitias mundi et contra totum exercitum demonum et pravorum hominum constans et fortis et impavidus sicut leo, tam ad invadendum quam ad patiendum. Et per profundissimam sui humiliationem et per sue originis a Deo humilem recognitionem et per sui ad inferiores piam condescensionem descendet de celo eritque scientia scripturarum non terrestrium et falsarum, sed celestium et purissimarum quasi nube amictus et etiam agillima et [115va] altissima et fecunda simul et obscura seu humili paupertate. Sicut enim nubes est supra inter nos et celum suscipiens solis radios et contemperans nobis eos et est purgans aquis pluvialibus et fecundis ipsasque ad fructificationem terre nascentium moderate effundens, sic est hec scriptura sacra spiritualiter in caritate et in sapientia Dei erit ut sol ad irradiandum finaliter totum orbem et ad formandum solarem diem tertii generalis status mundi. [...]	sí che, dove Maria rimase giuso, ella con Cristo pianse in su la croce.	sotto la protezion del grande scudo in che soggiace il leone e soggioga.
[115va] Ponit etiam pedem suum dextrum super mare nationum infidelium et sinistrum super terram fidelium, quia principalis impetus et processus eius erit ad totum orbem convertendum ad Christum, sic tamen quod ex hoc non deseret priorem ecclesiam fidelium. Sicut enim tempore apostolorum fuit principalis [115vb] et quasi dexter processus eorum ad conversionem paganorum, secundarius vero et quasi sinister ad plebem Iudeorum, quia censerunt non se ita prosperaturos seu prospere piscaturos in terra Iudeorum sicut in mari paganorum, sic et iste angelus sentiet non se ita prosperaturum in carnali ecclesia Latinorum sicut in Grecis et Sarracenis et Tartaris et tandem in Iudeis. Ponit etiam pedem suum dextrum super mare quia promtior erit ad adversa	(10, 3) [116ra] *Alia ratio est propter nimiam resistentiam et nimiam multitudinem obduratorum.* [...]	*Paradiso*, XII, 100-102 : e ne li sterpi eretici percosse l'impeto suo, piú vivamente quivi dove le resistenze eran piú grosse.

toleranda et ad Antichristi prelia invadenda quam ad prospera temporalis pacis et glorie assumenda. Pro tempore etiam quod a Francisco usque nunc cucurrit plus piscatus est hic angelus in mari laycorum secularibus curis fluctuantium quam in terra regularium et clericalium. Simplices enim et ydiote facilius trahuntur ad penitentiam quam magni clerici vel monachi.

Et nota quod hic angelus non posuit supra se mare et terram, sed potius sub pedibus suis, quia per altissimam paupertatem et austeritatem et humilitatem omnes mundanas divitias et honores et delicias sub suis pedibus conculcavit nullique adulatorie aut de mundano questu se carnaliter seu viliter subdens.

Paradiso, XI, 88-93 :

Né li gravò viltà di cuor le ciglia
per esser fi' di Pietro Bernardone,
né per parer dispetto a maraviglia ;
ma regalmente sua dura intenzione
ad Innocenzio aperse, e da lui ebbe
primo sigillo a sua religione.

Clamaturus autem erit sicut leo rugiens, primo quia contra errores et vitia obduratorum cum forti [116ra] indignatione et increpatione loquetur et terribile iudicium Dei eis in proximo venturum cum summa auctoritate et terribili comminatione predicet, ita ut bestias, idest bestiales, contrimescere faciat. Ratio autem magnitudinis sue indignationis erit ex hoc quia cum clausus erat liber videbantur habere aliquantulam excusationem, ex quo autem est apertus nullum velamen excusationis relinquitur eis. Alia ratio est propter nimiam resistentiam et nimiam multitudinem obduratorum. Tertia est propter superfervidum zelum excitandi eos a sompno mortis ad vitam fidei.

Purgatorio, IX, 133-138 :

E quando fuor ne' cardini distorti
li spigoli di quella regge sacra,
che di metallo son sonanti e forti,
non rugghiò sí né si mostrò sí acra
Tarpea, come tolto le fu il buono
Metello, per che poi rimase macra.

Purgatorio, X, 5-6 :

e s'io avesse li occhi vòlti ad essa,
qual fora stata al fallo degna scusa ?

(10, 2) [115ra] Habuit etiam in manu, idest in pleno opere et in plena possessione et potestate, libellum evangelii Christi apertum, sicut patet ex regula quam servavit et scripsit et ex statu evangelico quem instituit. [...]

Secundo clamabit ut leo rugiens, quia cum leonina constantia et esurie curret ad animarum escam et predam, secundum illud Amos tertio (Am 3, 4) : « Numquid rugiet leo in saltu nisi habuerit predam ? »

« Et cum clamasset, locuta sunt septem tonitrua voces suas » (10, 3). Secundum Ioachim, hec septem tonitrua sunt septem spiritus Dei qui universaliter in omnem terram spiritales et allegoricas voces velut e tertio celo emictunt concordantes rugitui angeli tam in revelando magnalia et archana glorie Dei et operum eius et precipue illorum que fiunt in mentibus contemplativis, quam in tonando terribilia iuditia Dei. Septiformis enim gratia Spiritus Sancti et septiformis intelligentia septem [116rb] etatum mundi et septem signaculorum Veteris Testamenti et septem statuum ecclesie et iuditiorum factorum in hiis qui iam processerunt instar septem tonitruorum clamant maxima dona gratiarum et premiorum esse danda electis et quod horribilia iuditia fienda impiis in sexto statu ecclesie et in fine septimi restant. Dicuntur autem hec tonitrua ad clamorem angeli loqui, tum quia ad efficaciam preclare doctrine ispius quasi per se se ingerent mentibus perfectorum discipulorum, tum quia secundum verbum Christi, Iohannis XIIII° (Io 14, 26), paraclitus Spiritus Sanctus suggeret illis omnia interius que tamen angelus extra dixit eis. Sicut enim spiritus veritatis in cordibus apostolorum perhibebat de Christo testimonium, sic et tunc in cordibus spiritualium discipulorum contestabitur predicationi huius angeli, iuxta quod Actuum X° (Ac 10, 44) dicitur quod Petro predicante cecidit Spiritus sanctus super omnes qui audiebant verbum.

Purgatorio IX, 139 :

Io mi rivolsi attento al primo tuono

Sequitur (10, 4) : « Et ego scripturus eram, et audivi vocem de celo dicentem : signa », idest quasi sigillo firmo in tuo corde claude « illa que locuta sunt tonitrua septem et noli ea scribere ». Hic demonstratur primo pium desiderium spiritalium discipulorum ad propalandum omnibus spiritales sensus septem tonitruorum in eorum cordibus vehementer et stupende resonantium. Secundo monstratur quomodo a Christo et eius [116va] spiritu et a sanctis doctoribus prohibentur ne pandant ea homini carnali et animali quibus non licet talia loqui, iuxta illud Christi (Mt 7, 6 ; Lc 8, 10) : « Vobis datum est nosse misterium regni Dei, ceteris autem in parabolis. Et nolite sanctum dari canibus neque porcis ». Sunt enim quedam sic omnibus communia que sunt omnibus publice predicanda, quedam vero non sunt omnibus dicenda et precipue ante tempus, iuxta illud Matthei XVII° (Mt 17, 9) : « Nemini dixeritis visionem donec filius hominis a mortuis resurgat ». Unde et sub sexto signaculo Veteris Testamenti dicit angelus Danieli : « Tu autem Daniel claude sermones et signa librum usque ad tempus statutum » (Dn 12, 4), quod quidem erat sexta etas in qua apparuit Christus et precipue sextus status ecclesie sue in quo liber erat plenius aperiendus non tamen malivolis aut indispositis. Ante enim mortem magni Antichristi oportebat multa tunc sanctis aperta claudere emulis et etiam fidelibus vel adhuc animalibus.

Sequitur (10, 5-7) : « Et angelus quem vidi stantem super mare et super terram levavit manum suam in celum et iuravit per viventem in secula seculorum, qui creavit celum et ea que sunt in illo, et terram et ea que in ea sunt, et mare et ea que in eo sunt quia tempus amplius non erit sed in diebus vocis septimi angeli, cum tuba ceperit

Paradiso XVII, 76-78, 82-84 :

Con lui vedrai colui che 'mpresso fue,
nascendo, sí da questa stella forte,
che notabili fier l'opere sue. [...]
ma pria che'l Guasco l'alto Arrigo inganni,

(10, 1) [114vb] Ipse enim fuit singulariter fortis in omni virtute et opere Dei, et per summam humilitatem et recognitionem prime originis omnis nature et gratie semper descendens de celo, et per aeream et subtilem seu spiritalem levitatem ab omni pondere terrenorum excussam fuit amictus nube, idest altissima paupertate

canere, consumabitur misterium Dei, sicut evangelizavit per suos servos et [116vb] prophetas ». Iuramentum hoc designat vehementem certitudinem et assertionem quod tempus huius seculi omnino finietur in tempore septime tube. Non enim intendit quod post hoc iuramentum suum non sit tempus amplius, sed quod in voce septimi angeli consumabitur. Iurat autem hoc ita fortiter tum ad fortius perterrendum malos et terrendo convertendum ad penitentiam, tum ad consolandum electos multiplicibus persecutionibus et miseriis vexaturos et de exilio et carcere huius vite cupientes exire et ad eternam patriam iugiter suspirantes.

parran faville de la sua virtute
in non curar d'argento né d'affanni.

aquis celestibus plena, idest suprema possessione et inbibitione celestium divitiarum. [...]

Sciendum etiam quod prout tubicinium septimi angeli refertur ad extremum iuditium de quo secunda ad Thessalonicenses IV° (1 Ts 4, 16) dicitur quod "ipse Dominus in visu et in voce archangeli et in tuba Dei descendet de celo et mortui qui in Christo sunt resurgent primi", est simpliciter verum quod tempus huius seculi tunc omnino cessabit et plene implebitur quidquid Deus per suos prophetas prenuntiavit fiendum, quod vocat "misterium", idest secretum, quia nihil mundanis occultius quam spiritalis gratia et gloria in electis consumanda, futura etiam Dei iuditia sunt eis occulta et quasi incredibilia.

Paradiso, XVII, 91-93 :

« e portera' ne scritto ne la mente
di lui, e nol dirai » ; e disse cose
incredibili a quei che fier presenti.

Dicitur etiam « misterium » quia sub misticis velaminibus sunt prenuntiata, nec intendo quin principalia corpora huius mundi tunc durent, sed solum quod temporalis et mobilis [117ra] cursus eius et temporalis status humani generis in hac vita cessabit. Sumendo vero tubicinium septimi angeli respectu pacis que erit in ecclesia post mortem Antichristi, tunc est sensus quod tempus afflictionis et laboris sex priorum

Inferno, IX, 61-63 :

O voi ch'avete li 'ntelletti sani,
mirate la dottrina che s'asconde
sotto 'l velame de li versi strani.

(*ex Prologo*, Is 30, 26)

[1rb] Hec enim septem sunt velut septem dies solaris doctrine Christi que sub velamine scripta et absconsa fuerunt in lege et prophetis. Eo ipso autem quod doctrina Christi novi testamenti probat se ipsam contineri in veteri sicut nucleum in testa et pullum in ovo et fructum in semine vel radice et sicut lumen in lucerna lucente

statuum, quasi sex dierum quibus laborare et operari oportet, cessabit in sabbato et requie septimi status, tunc quia « consumabitur misterium » per prophetas pronuntiatum quantum in hac vita consumari debet. Et sic exponit hoc Ioachim, subdens quod post tempus sex apertionum huius sexte etatis manet tempus ut ait angelus Danieli « quale non fuit ex eo tempore quo ceperunt homines esse in terram » (Dn 12, 1), tempus utique septimi angeli cui benedicet Dominus dans in eo pacem et letitiam sustinentibus se.

Secundum vero Ricardum, non dicit tempus amplius non esse respectu dampnandorum, quia illorum tempus erit in secula, nam de frigoribus ad calores et de caloribus ad frigora revertentur, sed dicit hoc respectu sanctorum glorificandorum et elementorum innovandorum. Dicit enim hoc ad consolationem sanctorum hic pro Christo multa patientium quibus promittit instabilem mutabilitatem huius seculi transituram et eterne glorie immobilitatem successuram. [...]

[117va] Sequitur (10, 8-9) : « Et vox », suple facta est vel sonuit secundum Ricardum, « quam audivi de celo iterum loquentem mecum et dicentem : vade, et accipe librum apertum de manu angeli stantis supra mare et super terram, et abii ad angelum dicens ei ut daret mihi librum ». Secundum Ioachim, iste ordo qui significatur

[1va] in loco caliginoso, eo ipso promovetur luna, idest vetus lex et scriptura, in lucem solis.

(ex cap. XIII)

[146rb] « Si quis habet aurem » (13, 9), idest sanam intelligentiam dictorum et dicendorum, « audiat », idest attente et prudenter consideret id quod est premissum et etiam id quod mox subditur, quia hoc quod subditur multum ei conferet ad servandam fidem et patientiam in tanta tribulatione. Subditur enim (13, 10) : « Qui in captivitatem duxerit », scilicet sanctos vel quoscumque iniuste, « in captivitatem », scilicet eternam, « vadet », supple : nisi penituerit ; « qui in gladio occiderit », scilicet iniuste, « oportet eum gladio », scilicet divine sententie, « occidi », idest in mortem dampnationis eterne mitti. « Hic », idest in hoc loco seu in veritate huius verbi, « est patientia et fides sanctorum », idest sancti sunt patientes et confidentes in Deo quia indubitabiliter sciunt omnes suos persecutores nisi penituerint esse [146va] dampnandos spiritualiter, quia sciunt Antichristum cito esse occidendum gladio Christi et in inferno eternaliter captivandum, et e contrario se si patienter in fide et caritate perseveraverint esse salvandos et in libro vite indelebiliter scriptos. Le « hic » est adverbium loci prout patet in greco sicut et in fine huius capituli ubi dicitur : « Hic sapientia est » (13, 18).

in Iohanne auditurus est hanc vocem « de celo », idest de scriptura sacra, quia si nusquam esset alia vox in scriptura sacra que hoc preciperet, sufficeret ista vox que de isto celo magno, idest de hoc libro aperto, descendit et etiam illa que hoc ipsum dicit in Ezechielis, scilicet capitulo III° (Ez 3, 1). Ibit autem iste ordo ad angelum cum agnita veritate, de nuntiis veritatis Dei reverenter assentiet eis, prout etiam dicit quod vox ista est omnis inspiratio Dei eos instigans [117vb] vel accendens ut sapientiam libri adiscant a doctoribus sacris per hunc angelum designatis et potissime a Christo. Docebit enim eos Deus non presumere ex propriis viribus et absque huius angeli magisterio posse partecipare sapientiam libri.

[117vb] Sequitur (10, 9) : « Et dixit mihi », scilicet angelus : « accipe librum devora illum, et faciet amaricare ventrem tuum », idest faciet tortiones amaras in tuo ventre, vel postquam erit in ventre faciet versus os exaltationes amaras, « sed in ore tuo erit dulce tanquam mel. Et accepi librum et cetera ». Nota quod non dicit lege sed devora, nec dicit vide sed accipe, quia per superfervidum et rapidum devotionis affectum et gustum vult libri spiritales sensus et intelligentias masticari et saporari et ad intima trahici. Vult etiam illum per manum accipi, idest in operibus poni et servari, ut scilicet opere inpleat ea que in libro docentur. Huius autem libri contemplatio est dulcis ori, idest spiritali gustui, faciet tamen amaricari ventrem quia ducit ad amaritudinem laboris et passionis. Quamvis enim preclara contemplatio futurarum passionum sit suavis menti, in experientia tamen laboris est gemitus et afflictio spiritus. Nihil etiam inconveniens si secundum diversos respectus sit simul dulcis et amarus, sicut et

Paradiso, XVII, 22-23, 58-59, 61, 112-113 :

dette mi fuor di mia vita futura
parole gravi [. . .]

Tu proverai sí come sa di sale
lo pane altrui [. . .]

E quel che piú ti graverà le spalle [...]

Giú per lo mondo sanza fine amaro,
e per lo monte del cui bel cacume [...]

Paradiso, XVIII, 1-3 :

Già si godeva solo del suo verbo
quello specchio beato, e io gustava
lo mio, temprando col dolce l'acerbo

Christi passio [118ra] in quantum triumphalis et nobis salubris est nobis dulcis, in quantum autem nostra viscera transfigit per compassionem est nobis amara.

Sequitur: (10, 11) « Et dixit mihi: Oportet te iterum prophetare in gentibus et populis et linguis et regibus multis ». In ipsa sapientia libri expresse continetur quod oportet iterum predicari evangelium in toto orbe et Iudeis et gentibus et totum orbem finaliter converti ad Christum. Sed quod per istum hoc esset implendum non poterat sciri nisi per spiritualem revelationem, et hoc dico prout per Iohannem designantur hic singulares persone quia, prout per ipsum designatur in communi ordo evangelicus et contemplativus, scitur ex ipsa intelligentia libri quod per istum ordinem debet hoc impleri. Potest etiam dici quod eo ipso quod Dei instinctu et iussu accepit ab angelo singularem intelligentiam libri et cum singulari dulcore ipsam sibi invisceravit et ex hoc cum dolore presensit passiones graves sibi et ecclesie affuturas, satis percepit se ad predicationem gentium destinari, sed nichilominus per sacros doctores hoc amplius asseritur tum ne propter temptationem Antichristi et propter nimiam multitudinem hostium hoc timeant impediri. [...]

Paradiso, XVII, 116-120, 127-132:

ho io appreso quel che s'io ridico,
a molti fia sapor di forte agrume;
e s'io al vero son timido amico,
temo di perder viver tra coloro
che questo tempo chiameranno antico

Ma nondimen, rimossa ogne menzogna,
tutta tua vision fa manifesta;
e lascia pur grattar dov'è la rogna.
Ché se la voce tua sarà molesta
nel primo gusto, vital nodrimento
lascerà poi, quando sarà digesta.

Paradiso XXVII, 64-66: (Pietro)

e tu, figliuol, che per lo mortal pondo
ancor giú tornerai, apri la bocca,
e non asconder quel ch'io non ascondo.

(ex cap. XXII)

[205rb] Sextum est iussio de propalando doctrinam propheticam huius libri tanquam scilicet utillimam et necessariam electis et tanquam certam et gloriosam et Christum et eius opera clarificantem et magnificantem. Unde subdit (22, 10): « Et dixit mihi », scilicet angelus: « ne signaveris », idest non occultes nec sub sigillo claudas, « verba prophetie huius libri », subditque huius duplicem rationem. Prima est ex propinquitate futurorum temporum et iudiciorum et operum de quibus loquitur, propter quod oportet eam cito sciri, unde subdit: « Tempus enim prope est ». Secunda est quia eius revelatio est utilis ampliori iustificationi sanctorum et etiam quantum est ex se correctioni malorum. *Quamvis pluribus ex sua malitia per accidens noceat, propter tales autem non est occultanda, imo in ipsorum inexcusabilitatem et iustam excecationem fortius predicanda.* Et hoc primo tangit cum subdit (21, 11): « Qui nocet », scilicet proximis vel ecclesie ipsam persequendo, « noceat adhuc », idest iustum est ut permittatur amplius insanire et nocere, « et qui in sordibus est », scilicet carnalis luxurie per quam se ipsum fedat, « sordescat adhuc », idest dignus est permitti in ampliores sordes a se ipso immergi.

Esempio II *(ex cap. II, 5, Ephesus)*

[39rb] Si vero queratur plenior ratio sui casus vel translationis predicte, potest colligi ex tribus.

Purgatorio, XI, 79-84, 94-99:

« Oh! », diss'io lui, « non se' tu Oderisi,
l'onor d'Agobbio e l'onor di quell'arte

(ex cap. III, 11, Philadelphia)

[51rb] Item sicut soli primo comminatus est translationem sue ecclesie de loco suo, sic soli sexto

Primum est inanis gloria et superba presumptio de suo primatu et primitate, quam scilicet habuit non solum ex hoc quod prima in Christum credidit, nec solum ex hoc quod fideles ex gentibus ipsam honorabant et sequebantur ut magistram et primam tanquam per eam illuminati in Christo et tracti ad Christum, sed etiam ex gloria suorum patriarcharum et prophetarum et divine legis ac cultus legalis longo tempore in ipsa sola fundati. [...]

Tertium est tota multitudo rationum propter quas Iudei in primo adventu Christi fuerunt excecandi et relinquendi et in imperio gentium fides et sedes Christi ponenda ac per consequens et summa sedes Christi in [39va] principali sede imperii gentium fuit collocanda.

Consimiles fere rationes invenies de ultimo casu novissimi cursus quinti temporis ecclesiastici et translationis primatus Babilonis in novam Ierusalem, et iterum casus et translationis ultime et reprobe partis septimi status in celestem Ierusalem.

Ad humiliationem autem sue superbie et manifestationem primatus Christi super legalia et super omnia secula valet quod premittitur Christus tenere in sua dextera septem stellas, idest omnes preclaros principes et prelatos omnium ecclesiarum presentialiter percurrere ac visitare omnes ecclesias presentes et futuras. Ex quo patet quod Christus est summus rex et pontifex et quod multe alie solempnes ecclesie preter Ierosolimitanam ecclesiam sunt et esse debebant sub Christo, ita quod non oportebat eam superbire de suo primatu.

ch'alluminar chiamata è in Parisi ? ».
« Frate », diss'elli, « piú ridon le carte
che pennelleggia Franco bolognese ;
l'onore è tutto or suo, e mio in parte [...] »
Credette Cimabue ne la pittura
tener lo campo, e ora ha Giotto il grido,
sí che la fama di colui è scura.
Cosí ha tolto l'uno all'altro Guido
la gloria de la lingua ; e forse è nato
chi l'uno e l'altro caccerà del nido.

(ex cap. IV, 9-10)

[62ra] Tertius vero designat totius meriti sui ac triumphii et premii totalem Deo attributionem et visceralem et obsequiosam oblationem. Quia vero mittere coronas coram Deo includit actum deponendi eas de capite proprio, ideo in hoc ipso designatur quod sic vehementer ascribunt eas Deo tanquam earum summo et primo et totali principio quod quasi totaliter eas abnegant a se ipsis et a propria causalitate et merito. Per hoc autem quod dicit eas mitti ante tronum designatur quod etiam eas ascribunt matri ecclesie, unusquisque quidem angelorum celesti ierarchie, sancti vero homines tam celesti quam subcelesti ecclesie. Nec mirum, quia omnis in quantum pars ordinatur ad totum sicut ad suum finem et quod sibi datur datur a Deo propter bonum totius nec accipit gratiam nisi consistendo in toto et in unitate totius nec conservatur nisi in ipso et in sinu totalitatis et unitatis sui totius perficitur et fovetur. [...] significat quod si non perseveraverit eius corona ad alium transferetur. Cuius mistica ratio est quia sicut primus status habuit primatum respectu totius secundi generalis status mundi qui ab Apostolo vocatur tempus seu ingressus plenitudinis gentium, sic sextus habebit primatum respectu totius tertii generalis status mundi duraturi usque ad finem seculi. [51va] Ne ergo de suo primatu superbiant aut insolescant quasi non possint ipsum perdere aut quasi alius nequeat substitui eis et fieri eque dignus, insinuatur eis predicta translatio. Secunda ratio est quia uterque eorum substitutus est alteri. Nam gloria que fuerat sinagoge parata et pontificibus suis si in Christum credidissent translata fuit ad primitivam ecclesiam et ad pastores eius, sic etiam gloria parata finali ecclesie quinti status transferetur propter eius adulteria ad electos sexti status, unde et in hoc libro vocatur Babilon meretrix circa initium sexti status dampnanda. Notandum tamen quod per hoc verbum docemur numerum electorum ad complendam fabricam civitatis superne sic esse prefixum quod si unus per suam culpam corruat alterum oportet substitui ne illa fabrica remaneat incompleta.

(ex cap. XI)

[126va] Quia vero de divinorum scientia et gustu sepe quis superbe presumit, et precipue cum ab aliis glorificatur tanquam peritus et sanctus, idcirco contra tertiam partem lucis superbientis et sanctitatis per vanam gloriam in ypocrisim cadentis est quartum tubicinium. Vel quia ex copia mundane scientie et voluptatis oritur magna fama et gloria apud mundanos, ita quod videntur ceteris presidere et superlucere sicut sol et luna et stelle, ideo hanc gloriam percutit et obscurat quartum tubicinium.

Esempio III *(ex cap. XXI, 11)*

[196va] Formam autem tangit tam quo ad eius splendorem quam quo ad partium eius dispositionem et dimensionem, unde subdit : « a Deo habentem claritatem » (21, 11). « Dei » dicit quia est similis increate luci Dei tanquam imago et participatio eius. Dicit etiam « a Deo » quia ab ipso datur et efficitur. Sicut enim ferrum in igne et sub igne et ab igne coloratur et ignis [196vb] speciem sumit non autem a se, sic et sancta ecclesia accipit a Deo claritatem, idest preclaram et gloriosam formam et imaginem Dei quam et figuraliter specificat subdens : « et lumen eius simile lapidi pretioso tanquam lapidi iaspidis, sicut cristallum ». Lux gemmarum est eis firmissime et quasi indelebiliter incorporata et est speculariter seu instar speculi polita et variis coloribus venustata et visui plurimum gratiosa. Iaspis vero est coloris viridis, color vero seu claritas cristalli est quasi similis lune seu aque congelate et perspicue. Sic etiam lux glorie et gratie est sensibus cordis intime et solide incorporata et variis virtutum

Paradiso, II, 31-42 :

Parev'a me che nube ne coprisse
lucida, spessa, solida e pulita,
quasi adamante che lo sol ferisse.
Per entro sé l'etterna margarita
ne *ricevette*, com'acqua *recepe*
raggio di luce permanendo unita.
S'io era corpo, e qui non si concepe
com'una dimensione altra *patio,*
ch'esser convien se corpo in corpo repe,
accender ne dovria piú il disio
di veder quella essenza in che si vede
come nostra natura e Dio s'unío.

--*(3, 8)* [49ra] Hinc est etiam quod Christus plus commendat promissiones suorum donorum factas angelo sexto quam merita ipsius sexti. Consurgitque ex hoc quoddam mirabile et valde notabile, videlicet quod status sextus quanto maior erit precedentibus in

(ex cap. XXI, 18, 21)

[201ra] Postquam autem dixit quod materia muri erat ex iaspide, dicit (21, 18) : « ipsa vero civitas », scilicet erat, « aurum mundum simile vitro [201rb] mundo ». Et infra, postquam egit de materia portarum, subdit (21, 21) : « Et platea civitatis », scilicet erat, « aurum mundum tanquam vitrum perlucidum ». Et forte secundum litteram primum dixit de domibus ex quibus constabat civitas, ultimum vero de toto fundo seu planitie intra muros contenta. Per utrumque autem designatur generalis ecclesia et principaliter contemplativorum, sicut per muros militia martirum et pugilum seu defensorum interioris ecclesie que est per unitatem concordie civitas, idest civium unitas, et per fulgorem divine caritatis et sapientie aurea, et per puram confessionem veritatis propria peccata clare et humiliter confitentis et nihil falso simulantis est similis vitro mundo, et per latitudinem caritatis et libertatem ac comunitatem evangelice paupertatis est platea celis patula, non tectis clausa, nec domibus occupata, nec

coloribus adornata et divina munde et polite et speculariter representans et omnium virtutum temperie virens. Est etiam perspicua et transparens non cum fluxibili vanitate sed cum solida et humili veritate. *Obscuritas* enim lune *humilitatem* celestium mentium designat*. [...]

**(10, 1)* [115rb] [...] et per profundissimam sui humiliationem et per sue originis a Deo *humilem* recognitionem et per sui ad inferiores piam condescensionem descendet de celo eritque scientia scripturarum non terrestrium et falsarum, sed celestium et purissimarum quasi nube amictus et etiam agillima et altissima et fecunda simul et *obscura* seu humili paupertate.

susceptione gratiarum et [49rb] familiarium signorum amoris Christi ad eum, tanto habebit unde plus Christo et statibus precedentibus humilietur, quia potius prefertur eis in *pati seu recipere* quam in agere vel dare, et potius in felicitate habere spem premii quam in laborioso opere habente rationem meriti. Hec tamen per anthonomasiam et per quandam appropriationem sunt intelligenda, alias omnia in viris perfectis omnium statuum reperiuntur.

Paradiso, III, 10-12 :

Quali per vetri trasparenti e tersi,
o ver per acque nitide e tranquille,
non sí profonde che i fondi sien persi

domorum distinctionibus divisa, nec isti vel illi instar domorum appropriata sed omnibus communis et indivisa. Et quia in tertio generali statu, statutis XII portis eius fulgebit singulariter evangelica paupertas et contemplatio, ideo non fit mentio de platea nisi post portas, et ubi mox subditur [201va] quod solus Deus est templum et sol huius civitatis. Unde et platea non solum dicitur esse « aurum simile vitro mundo », idest perspicuo et polito et nulla macula vel pulvere obumbrato, sed etiam dicitur esse sicut « vitrum perlucidum », idest valde lucidum, quod tunc maior erit cordis et oris puritas et clarior veritas. In ecclesia vero beatorum erit tanta ut omnia interiora cordium sint omnibus beatis mutuo pervia et aperta.

Nota quod secundum doctrinam Dyonisii in libro de angelica ierarchia sane et subtiliter intellectam, hii qui fuerunt fundamenta vel porte in statu meriti seu gratie multo gloriosius hec erunt in statu premii et glorie. Quamvis enim totus habitus glorie inferiorum sit immediate a Deo, sic tamen erit connexus glorie suorum superiorum ac si in ipsis fundetur et conradicetur sicut secundaria membra corporis quasi fundantur et radicantur in virtute cerebri cordis et [capitis]. Inferiores etiam ministerialiter iuvabuntur per intermediam gloriam superiorum, quasi per specula clara et quasi per vitrum perspicuum et quasi per portas intrent in clariorem et altiorem actum visionis et fruitionis Dei. Qualiter autem hoc sit et esse possit declaravi plenius in Lectura super librum angelice ierarchie prefate.

Esempio IV *(ex cap. I)*

[29va] Quarta [proprietas vel perfectio] est reverenda et preclara sapientie et consilii maturitas per senilem et gloriosam caniciem capitis et crinium designata, unde subdit : « caput autem eius et capilli erant candidi tanquam lana alba et tanquam nix » (1, 14). Per caput vertex mentis et sapientie, per capillos autem multitudo et ornatus subtilissimorum et spiritualissimorum cogitatuum et affectuum seu plenitudo donorum Spiritus Sancti verticem mentis adornantium designatur.

Sicut autem in lana est calor fomentativus et mollicies corpori se applicans et candor contemperantior et suavior quam in nive, sic in nive est frigiditatis et congelationis algor et rigor et candor intensior nostroque visui intollerabilior.

>> Est et [29vb] humor sordium purgativus et terre impinguativus per que designatur quod Christi sapientia est partim nobis condescensiva et sui ad nos contemperativa nostrique fomentativa et sua pietate calefactiva, partim autem est a nobis abstracta et nobis rigida nimisque intensa nostrarumque sordium purgativa nostreque hereditatis impinguativa.

Inferno, XXVII, 115-117 :

Venir se ne dee giú tra' miei meschini
perché diede 'l consiglio frodolente,
dal quale in qua stato li sono a' crini

Purgatorio, XXX, 70-72 :

regalmente ne l'atto ancor proterva
continuò come colui che dice
e 'l più caldo parlar dietro reserva

vv. 79-81 :
Cosí la madre al figlio par superba,
com'ella parve a me ; perché d'amaro
sente il sapor de la pietade acerba.

vv. 85-86 :
Sí come neve tra le vive travi
per lo dosso d'Italia si congela

>> Est et [29vb] humor sordium purgativus et terre impinguativus per que designatur quod Christi sapientia est partim nobis condescensiva et sui ad nos contemperativa nostrique fomentativa et sua pietate calefactiva, partim autem est a nobis abstracta et nobis rigida nimisque intensa nostrarumque sordium purgativa nostreque hereditatis impinguativa.

Esempio V *(ex cap. V)*

[65ra] Tertia ratio septem sigillorum quo ad librum Veteris Testamenti sumitur ex septem apparenter in eius cortice apparentibus. [...]

Inferno, XII, 67-72 :

Poi mi tentò, e disse : Quelli è Nesso,
che morì per la bella Deianira,
e fé di sé la vendetta elli stesso.

[65rb] Secundum est bellicositas iniuriarum ultrix ac ire et inpatientie nutrix. Quasi enim ubique narrat et laudat et monet et etiam mandat corporalia bella Israel contra suos hostes. Hanc autem evacuat patientie vigor usque ad tollerantiam omnis persecutionis et mortis in secunda apertione notatus.

E quel di mezzo, ch'al petto si mira,
è il gran Chiròn, il qual nodrí Achille;
quell'altro è Folo, che fu sí pien d'ira.

Esempio VI *(ex cap. V)*

[62vb] « Et vidi in dextera sedentis super tronum librum scriptum intus et foris signatum sigillis septem » *(5, 1)* Preostensa gloria et magnificentia maiestatis Dei, hic accedit ad ostendendum profunditatem incomprehensibilem libri sui.

Qui quidem liber est primo idem quod Dei essentialiter prescientia et totius reparationis universe fiende per Christum predestinatio. Et per appropriationem est ipsum verbum Patris prout est expressivum sapientie eius et prout Pater ipsum generando scripsit in eo omnem sapientiam suam.

Secundo modo est idem quod scientia mentium angelicarum ipsis a Deo data et in eis scripta prout est de totali gratia et gloria electorum et totius cultus Dei consumandi per Christum et multo magis est scientia universorum scripta a Deo in anima Christi.

Tertio est idem quod totum volumen scripture sacre et spetialiter veteris testamenti in quo novum fuit inclusum et sub figuris variis figuratum et velatum.

Visus autem est in *dextera* Dei tum quia est in eius plena potentia et facultate, tum quia continet promissiones Christi *gratie* et glorie et etiam largitiones et preparationes que dicuntur spectare ad dexteram sicut

Paradiso, X, 109-114:

La quinta luce, ch'è tra noi piú bella,
spira di tale amor, che tutto 'l mondo
là giú ne gola di saper novella:
entro v'è l'alta mente *u'* sí profondo
saver fu messo, che, se 'l vero è vero,
a veder tanto non surse il secondo.

(5, 6) [68rb] Mittuntur [septem spiritus] autem in suis effectibus et influxibus. Nomen autem missionis docet hic sumi spiritum Christi pro persona Spiritus Sancti, quia mittere proprie in divinis magis spectat ad personam producentem. Nullus enim plene proprie dicitur mittere se ipsum, quamvis propter eosdem effectus a tota christianitate factos propter quos Filius vel Spiritus Sanctus dicuntur mitti, possit persona missa dici mittere se ipsam. [...]

[72ra] Sequitur *(5, 14)*: « Et quattuor animalia dicebant: amen », idest fiat hoc quod dictum est. Vel « amen », idest vere ita est.

(ex cap. V)

(5, 8) [69ra] Item in prima describitur triplex actus laudantium. Primus est regratiativa et adorativa humiliatio ipsorum ad Christum, et hoc tangit cum ait: « et ceciderunt coram agno », scilicet more adorantium. Secundus est sanctarum adorationum fragrans devotio, et hoc tangit cun ait: « et fialas aureas plenas odoramentorum », scilicet habentes. Quod enim premittitur: « habentes singuli citharas » spectat ad canticum quod postmodum subdit. Cithara enim est musicum instrumentum cum quo cantatur. Secundum vero Ricardum, per citharas designantur bona opera quia manibus pulsantur ut sonent, et secundum hoc [69rb] per citharas significatur virtus vite active. Fiale vero sunt late et lucide et communiter sunt vitree, unde et dicte sunt a fialim grece, quod est vitrum latine, et sunt sicut magne patelle. In templo vero erant auree prout dicitur tertio Regum VI° (3 Rg 7, 50), et secundum Magistrum historiarum ponebatur in eis thus, unde et hic dicuntur plene odoramentorum, idest aromatum odoriferorum. Fiale grece iste sunt corda sanctorum per sapientiam lucida, per caritatem dilatata, et per contemplationem splendida et flamma aurea et per devotarum orationum redundantiam odoramentis plena. Sicut enim

adversa vel bona temporalia dicuntur spectare ad sinistram.

Erat etiam « in dextera sedentis [63ra] super tronum » tum quia continet *leges* et precepta summi imperatoris et sententias et iudicia summi iudicis, tum quia altam et stabilem et maturam et quietam ac recollectam mentem requirit ad hoc quod intellectualiter haberi et intelligi possit, unde et talis est intelligentia Dei.

Est etiam « scriptus intus et foris » propter varios sensus vel intellectus ipsius, quorum quidam sunt magis intrinseci et nobis magis absconsi, quidam vero sunt magis forinseci et noti. Et hoc dico respectu omnium supradictarum apertionum libri prout in primo generali principio edito de hoc verbo super totam scripturam diffusius pertractavi. Liber etiam scripture sacre habet litteralem sensum foris, intus vero anagogicum et allegoricum et moralem. In sensu etiam litterali habet foris istorica gesta et exempla sanctorum et suorum exteriorum operum, intus vero profundiores sententias divinorum preceptorum et sapientialium documentorum.

Paradiso, VI, 10-12, 22-27 :

Cesare fui e son Iustiniano,
che, per voler del primo amor ch'i' sento,
d'entro le *leggi* trassi il troppo e 'l vano. [...]
<...>
Tosto che con la Chiesa mossi i piedi,
a Dio per *grazia piacque* di spirarmi
l'alto lavoro, e tutto 'n lui mi diedi ;

(ex cap. VIII)

[100rb] « Et vidi et audivi vocem unius aquile volantis per medium celum » *(8, 13)*. Vidit quidem ipsam aquilam et audivit vocem ipsius. Per aquilam designatur hic alti contemplativi quarti temporis qui prophetico spiritu precesserunt et predixerunt mala que post finem quarti temporis debebant subsequi. Inter quos credit Ioachim per hanc aquilam specialius designari beatum papam Gregorium, qui utique fuit in quarto tempore prout supra fuit in principio prenotatum. Ipse enim libere [100va] plurima de mundi fine et de pressura seculi scripsisse dinoscitur quique allegoriarum semitas ac si arduas celi vias altius pre ceteris prevolavit, nec enim invenitur alius similis eius qui ista erumpnosa tempora appropinquasse in suis operibus testaretur. Hec Ioachim.

Paradiso, XXXII, 127-129 :

E quei che vide tutti i tempi gravi,
pria che morisse, de la bella sposa
che s'acquistò con la *lancia* e coi clavi

odoramenta per ignem elicata sursum ascendunt totamque domum replent suo odore, sic devote orationes ad Dei presentiam ascendunt et pertingunt eique suavissime *placent* et etiam toti curie celesti et subcelesti. Sicut enim diffusio odoris spiratur invisibiliter ab odoramentis, sic devote affectiones orationum spirant invisibiliter et latissime diffunduntur ad varias rationes dilecti et ad varias rationes sancti amoris, prout patet ex multiformi varietate sanctorum affectuum qui exprimuntur et exercentur in psalmis. Patet autem secundum modum Ricardi quare citharas premisit ante fialas, quia activa communiter precedit [69va] contemplativam. Sequendo etiam alterum modum, premittit convenienter citharas quia nisi corde virtutum sint in cithara mentis disposite prout congruit laudi Dei, non potest haberi fiala cordis plena devotis desideriis et suspiriis et meditationibus ignitis et odoriferis, sicut nec iubilatio laudis potest perfecte exerceri nisi pereat plenitudo odoramentorum.

e al mio Belisar commendai l'armi,
cui la *destra* del ciel fu sí congiunta,
che segno fu ch'i' dovessi posarmi.

(ex cap. V)

[67ra] Attamen hec revelatio et fletus Iohannis potius respicit illa tempora in quibus propter pressuras heresum et terrores imminentium periculorum et propter nescientiam rationis seu rationabilis permissionis talium pressurarum et periculorum iudiciorum *flent et suspirant sancti pro apertione libri* quantum ad illa precipue que pro illo tempore magis expedit eos scire.

(ex cap. XX)

[189va] Nos autem sumus in XX° centenario urbis Rome et in XIII° Christi designato secundum eum per *u*, quod in ultimo labiorum quasi aspirando profertur, unde et secundum eum designat quod in fine huius centenarii carnalis ecclesia seu Babilon expirabit, ut in sequenti centenario designato per x litteram, que habet formam crucis et fuit per Cesarem Augustum circa Christi adventum inventa, renovetur et exaltetur crux Christi, et post hec sequantur littere a Grecis ad Latinos deducte designantes dilatationem ecclesie ad Grecos et ad omnes gentes.

RAYMOND LULLE (1235-1316) ET PIERRE DE JEAN OLIVI (1247-1298) : LA « SCIENCE DIVINE », LES CONFLITS DES SAVOIRS ET DES INSTITUTIONS

Dominique de Courcelles

Le franciscain languedocien Pierre de Jean Olivi est l'exact contemporain du laïc catalan Raymond Lulle. Il s'est trouvé intensément lié aux bouleversements culturels et religieux de l'ordre franciscain et plus généralement de l'Église et de l'Université de la fin du XIIIe siècle, auxquels Raymond, philosophe, mystique, n'a pu lui-même manquer d'être sensible. Raymond ne fait aucune allusion à Pierre de Jean Olivi dans l'immensité de son œuvre, mais il est vrai que les citations nominales d'auteurs anciens ou contemporains sont, de sa part, extrêmement rares pour ne pas dire inexistantes. Pierre de Jean Olivi n'évoque pas non plus Raymond Lulle. Les relations entre Lulle et Olivi, s'il y en eut jamais, restent inaccessibles.

Si différents soient-ils, l'un et l'autre jouissent d'une grande notoriété à l'intérieur de l'Église et dans la tradition franciscaine. Raymond Lulle, laïc, se voue à l'étude et à la conversion des infidèles après sa propre « conversion », et voyage dans toute la chrétienté et en terre musulmane ; il a peut-être appartenu au tiers ordre franciscain à l'extrême fin de sa vie. Pierre de Jean Olivi, franciscain controversé, théologien et spirituel, après des séjours de formation et d'enseignement à Paris et à Florence, demeure en Languedoc la plus grande partie de sa vie et se trouve pris dans les conflits qui déchirent l'ordre franciscain. De façon inattendue le récit de l'illumination de Raymond Lulle, bien connu, semble-t-il, par ses contemporains, fait écho à celui de l'illumination de Pierre de Jean Olivi qui n'est connu qu'après la mort de ce dernier. Selon ces récits tous deux auraient reçu leur science par infusion divine. Les énergies intellectuelles ne sauraient-elles se passer de la foi ? La comparaison, à partir de la précieuse *Vita coetanea* de Raymond Lulle écrite en 1311, de quelques grands événements de la vie de Raymond Lulle et de Pierre de Jean Olivi permet de déceler des convergences et des différences significatives entre les deux personnages et de réfléchir à l'élaboration, à la fin du XIIIe siècle et au début du XIVe siècle, de l'autorité intellectuelle et de la diffusion des savoirs.

La science et la pauvreté franciscaine

Raymond Lulle est né vers 1235 à Majorque récemment conquise sur les musulmans, tandis que Pierre de Jean Olivi, pour qui les indices biographiques sont fort limités, serait né vers 1247 ou 1248 à Sérignan et entré dès 1259 ou 1260 dans l'ordre franciscain, sans doute à Béziers [1]. A cette époque, Raymond vit à la cour de l'infant Jacques, troisième fils de Jacques le Conquérant, lieutenant du futur royaume de Majorque composé des îles Baléares, du Roussillon et de la seigneurie de Montpellier, et y mène une existence mondaine.

Dans les années 1260, Olivi arrive à Paris et y étudie; lui-même a rapporté qu'il a entendu les célèbres *Conférences sur les sept dons de l'Esprit Saint* de Bonaventure en 1268. Bonaventure, alors ministre général d'un ordre présent dans toutes les universités européennes et pourvu d'un corps de doctrine, ancien maître régent du *studium* de Paris, a conscience que sa mission de chef d'ordre et de théologien lui impose de s'élever contre les prétentions rationalistes et les erreurs des philosophes de la Faculté des Arts, en particulier les erreurs averroistes. Il provoque la première condamnation des thèses rationalistes par l'évêque de Paris, Etienne Tempier, en 1270. Dans sa théologie des dons du Saint Esprit, Bonaventure expose que la grâce, « don parfait du Père des lumières », descend jusqu'à l'homme par le « Verbe incarné », « crucifié », « inspiré ». Il définit les dons comme des *habitus*, c'est-à-dire des qualités qui disposent l'homme à suivre les impulsions du Saint Esprit. A propos du don de science, il distingue la philosophie qui est la connaissance certaine de la vérité en tant qu'objet de recherche, la théologie qui est la connaissance pieuse de la vérité en tant qu'objet de foi, la contemplation qui est la connaissance sainte de la vérité en tant qu'objet d'amour, la science reçue dans la gloire du ciel qui est la connaissance éternelle de la vérité en tant qu'objet de désir. Chaque science est une étape vers la science supérieure. Bonaventure critique dans ses *Conférences* de 1268 les treize thèses qui seront censurées en 1270 par l'évêque de Paris [2].

David Burr, à la suite de Valens Heynck, estime qu'« il est évident qu'Olivi n'est jamais parvenu à la maîtrise; il le reconnaît lui-même » [3]. De fait, Olivi n'a jamais enseigné à Paris, ce qu'il aurait fait s'il était devenu bachelier. La carrière d'enseignant d'Olivi a commencé dans les années 1270, à Montpellier où il est *lector* dans le *studium* de l'ordre franciscain. Sa période de formation aurait dû l'amener à lire les *Sentences* à Paris, puis à accéder au *magisterium*, si son orthodoxie n'avait pas été mise en cause. Quoi qu'il en soit, vers la fin des années 1270, Olivi jouit d'une notoriété croissante parmi les universitaires, écrit une œuvre théologique et philosophique importante, s'intéresse au rôle de l'activité intellectuelle dans l'histoire du christianisme. Il n'hésite pas à se situer en dehors du courant dominant la pensée franciscaine de son temps, mais ses idées ne sont

1. Je me réfère ici à l'ouvrage fondamental de David Burr, *L'histoire de Pierre Olivi, franciscain persécuté*, Ed. Universitaires Fribourg Suisse-Ed. du Cerf, Paris France, 1997.

2. *Cf.* Jacques Guy Bougerol, *Introduction à saint Bonaventure*, Paris, Vrin, 1988, p. 230-235.

3. David Burr, *op. cit.*, p. 3-4.

pas isolées et aucune d'elles ne remet véritablement en question le dogme. Extrêmement méfiant à l'égard d'Aristote, il fait preuve d'une originalité étonnante sur des thèmes connus tels le mariage, la grâce baptismale, le caractère sacramentel, l'essence divine, les catégories, l'âme forme du corps. C'est surtout sa pensée de la pauvreté franciscaine, de l'*usus pauper*, pourtant défendue par de nombreux franciscains, qui lui vaut des attaques répétées. En 1274-1277, certains de ses livres sont brûlés sur l'ordre du ministre général des franciscains, Jérôme d'Ascoli, futur pape Nicolas IV. Toutes les informations concernant les tribulations d'Olivi sont fournies par les récits de ses contemporains, en particulier les franciscains de la tendance spirituelle tels Angelo Clareno[1], par ailleurs lié à la famille du roi de Majorque[2], ou Ubertin de Casale.

La *Vita coetanea beati Raymundi Lulli*, rédigée à Paris en 1311 alors que Raymond Lulle a encore quelques années à vivre et de nombreux livres à écrire, est presque une autobiographie. Raymond, dit le texte, « raconta et permit de mettre par écrit » les principaux événements de sa vie. Cette *Vita*, tout en étant très proche des biographies religieuses médiévales, évoque les positions de Raymond dans les grands débats de son temps[3]. En 1265, tandis qu'Olivi se trouve à Paris, Raymond Lulle se convertit à la vue du Christ qui lui apparaît sur la croix en des termes qui, en 1311, ne manquent pas de faire référence aux grands traités bonaventuriens[4] :

> Il vit le Seigneur Jésus comme suspendu à la croix [...] A la quatrième, ou même comme on le croit plutôt à la cinquième apparition, terrifié, il entra dans son lit et passa toute la nuit à se demander ce que pouvaient signifier ces visions tant de fois réitérées [...] Enfin, éclairé par le Père des lumières, il considéra la douceur, la patience et la miséricorde que le Christ avaient eues et continue d'avoir pour tous les pécheurs. Il acquit ainsi la certitude que Dieu voulait que lui, Raymond, quittât le monde et se consacrât de son cœur tout entier au service du Christ[5].

1. « Angelo Clareno : Historia septem tribulationum ordinis minorum », *Archiv für Literatur- und Kirchengeschichte des Mittelalters* 2, 1886, p. 108-336.

2. Lydia von Auw dans *Angelo Clareno et les spirituels italiens*, Rome, 1979, donne des informations sur les relations entre Angelo Clareno et l'infant Philippe de Majorque (p. 171-181 en particulier).

3. La *Vita coetanea beati Raymundi Lulli* se trouve conservée dans deux manuscrits (ms lat. 15450, BNF, Paris et ms S. Petr. 92 de la Bibl. de Karlsruhe) qui ont appartenu au chanoine médecin d'Arras, ami de Raymond, Thomas Le Myésier. Il existe également une version catalane majorquine, précieuse particulièrement pour ses informations topographiques majorquines, conservée dans un unique manuscrit du XVe siècle (ms 16432 du *British Museum*, Londres). J'utilise ici la traduction de Ramón Sugranyes de Franch, effectuée à partir de l'édition de Hermogenes Harada, R.L. Opera latina, VIII, Turnhout, Brepols, coll. « Corpus christianorum » 34, 1980, p. 272-309, et publiée dans *Raymond Lulle : actes du colloque sur Raymond Lulle*, Université de Fribourg, Suisse, 1984, Ed. Universitaires de Fribourg Suisse, 1986, p. 95-116.

4. Pour plus de détails, je me permets de renvoyer ici à mon étude dans *La Parole risquée de Raymond Lulle*, Paris, Vrin, 1993, p. 83 suiv.

5. *Vita*, 2, 4 : « *[...] Et sic intellexit tandem certissime Deum velle quod Raimundus mundum relinqueret Christoque corde ex tunc integre deserviret* ».

Raymond conçoit alors le désir de convertir les « sarrasins » « qui, par leur nombre, menaçaient de toutes parts les chrétiens », mais il se rend compte qu'il n'a pas la « science » nécessaire à cette entreprise. La *Vita* explique alors :

> Tandis qu'il broyait ces idées lugubres, voici que sans qu'il sût comment, Dieu seul le sait, une sorte d'inspiration véhémente remplit son cœur et son intelligence : il devrait dans les temps à venir composer un livre qui serait le plus efficace du monde contre les erreurs des infidèles [1].

Ainsi, selon la biographie lullienne de 1311, au point de départ de la formation intellectuelle de Raymond Lulle, il y a la vision réitérée du Christ sur une croix, l'éclairement par le Père des lumières, enfin une inspiration très forte de composer un livre. De façon significative la *Vita* juxtapose le *dictamen mentis* de Raymond et la pauvreté franciscaine. A la voie positive de l'inspiration mystique est jointe la voie négative de la pauvreté franciscaine.

> Là-dessus il retourna à ses affaires. Mais voici qu'au jour de la fête de saint François, il entendit chez les frères mineurs prêcher un évêque qui montra comment saint François avait tout abandonné et tout rejeté pour adhérer plus fermement au Christ seul. Raymond fut frappé par l'exemple de saint François. Il vendit aussitôt tout ce qu'il possédait, ne réservant qu'une petite partie pour les besoins de son épouse et de ses enfants. Puis s'en remettant totalement au Christ, il se mit en route avec l'intention de ne plus jamais revenir [2].

Le texte latin dit : « *ut soli Christo firmius inhereret* », et le texte catalan utilise la formule « *totalment donat al servei de la creu* », ce qui est très commun aux franciscains spirituels de Catalogne dans la ligne de l'*Arbor vitae crucifixae Jesu* d'Ubertin de Casale. La série de miniatures du *Breviculum* de Karlsruhe, commentaire de la *Vita coetanea*, comporte une représentation de Raymond se dépouillant de ses vêtements entre les mains de l'évêque prédicateur le jour de la fête de saint François (miniature 2). Mais le radical – trop radical ? – désir de pauvreté de Raymond ne peut être parfaitement honoré, puisqu'il doit garder une partie de ses biens pour l'entretien de sa femme et de ses deux enfants. Les documents d'archives font état des plaintes amères de son épouse Blanca Picany qui obtient en 1275 que Raymond soit déchu de l'administration de ses biens et qu'un administrateur soit nommé pour le remplacer.

Rappelons seulement ici que, si l'argumentation d'Olivi en faveur d'une pauvreté absolue contre les défenseurs de la propriété privée ou de la propriété commune, telle qu'elle est exposée dans son traité *De usu paupere* ou dans les *Quaestiones de perfectione evangelica* de la fin des années 1270 et du début des années 1280, vaut pour les franciscains qui ont eu à se défendre contre les attaques du clergé séculier, à la même époque le débat sur la pauvreté se modifie puisque c'est désormais à l'intérieur même de l'ordre qu'il y a lutte sur ce thème. David Burr montre bien qu'Olivi, éloigné de tout extrémisme, accepte alors de

1. *Vita*, 6 : « *Verum dum ipse mente lugubri hoc devolveret, ecce – nesciebat ipse quomodo, sed scit Deus –, intravit cor ejus vehemens ac implens quoddam dictamen mentis, quod ipse facturus esset postea unum librum meliorem de mundo contra errores infidelium* ».

2. *Vita*, 9.

distinguer plusieurs niveaux d'*usus pauper*, sans jamais l'identifier à un total oubli de soi lorsqu'il évoque des situations concrètes [1].

L'ILLUMINATION, DON DE « SCIENCE DIVINE »

De 1265 à 1274, Raymond, après avoir séjourné à Barcelone auprès du célèbre et puissant dominicain Raymond de Penyafort à qui il demeure très attaché, puis à Montpellier, et s'être rendu en pèlerinage à Rocamadour et Saint-Jacques de Compostelle, ne gagne pas Paris comme il le souhaite, car Raymond de Penyafort l'en dissuade, et rentre étudier à Majorque, sans doute à l'abbaye cistercienne de la Real, « ce qui expliquerait, selon Armand Llinarès, sa désaffection envers Aristote, son augustinisme et son exaltation mystique » [2]; il existe également à Palma un *studium* dominicain réputé pour son enseignement de la logique. Raymond distingue à plusieurs reprises dans son œuvre, en particulier dans le *Livre de l'ami et de l'aimé*, la science acquise et la science infuse :

> Disait l'ami que la science infuse vient de la volonté, de la dévotion et de l'oraison, et la science acquise de l'étude et de l'entendement (aphorisme 240).
> Angoissé et en larmes allait l'ami à la recherche de son aimé par les chemins des sens et les voies de l'intellect. Et l'on demande lequel des deux chemins il prit d'abord et dans lequel l'aimé se manifesta à l'ami avec la plus grande clarté (aphorisme 351).

Dans la première des *Questions sur la pauvreté évangélique*, Olivi déclare qu'il n'y a qu'un chemin, qu'un processus. La science acquise et la science infuse, loin de s'opposer, sont, chacune à leur mesure, partie intégrante du même processus :

> L'union de notre esprit avec Dieu, que les saints nomment contemplation, n'est rien d'autre que l'application de notre intellect à Dieu, que la perception et l'appréhension intellectuelles de Dieu, que la pénétration intime qu'on en fait par la ferveur de notre amour, [...] que le goût qu'on en a, [...] qu'un processus commencé dans l'intellect purifié par la foi et consommé dans l'acte d'amour [3].

Dans un ouvrage daté des années 1323-1324, l'inquisiteur dominicain Bernard Gui rapporte en se fondant sur un texte conservé et lu « *libenter et frequenter* » par les béguins et béguines qu'Olivi, avant de mourir le vendredi 14 mars 1298 au couvent de Narbonne à l'âge de 50 ans, dit aux frères présents que « toute sa science » il l'avait reçue « par infusion », ce qui tend à contredire l'affirmation d'Olivi citée plus haut. Le récit transmis par Bernard Gui concorde avec le témoignage du franciscain spirituel, ami d'Olivi, Ubertin de Casale :

1. Je renvoie ici à David Burr, *op. cit.*, p. 21-40.
2. Armand Llinarès, *Ramon Llull*, Barcelone, Ed. 62, 1968.
3. Cité par David Burr, *op. cit.*, p. 93.

> Juste avant de mourir, après qu'il eut reçu l'onction sainte, le vénérable frère dit, en présence des frères mineurs de Narbonne, que toute sa science il l'avait reçue par infusion divine et que, à Paris, dans l'église, à la troisième heure, il avait été soudainement illuminé par le Seigneur Jésus Christ[1].

On se souvient évidemment du témoignage de Joachim de Flore évoquant sa propre illumination alors qu'il composait un commentaire de l'Apocalypse. Olivi en 1297 venait lui-même d'achever son propre commentaire de l'Apocalypse. Raymond Lulle connaît-il en 1311, au moment où il dicte les événements de sa vie, l'étonnant récit de l'illumination d'Olivi ? Le parallèle inattendu qui s'établit ainsi entre les deux hommes, le franciscain et le laïc, est tout à fait remarquable. A Paris, ville de la raison universitaire où ses supérieurs l'ont envoyé étudier, mais dans une église, à une heure matinale, le franciscain Pierre de Jean Olivi reçoit « toute » sa science par infusion divine et se trouve illuminé. A Majorque où il vient d'étudier pendant neuf ans la « grammaire » et « l'arabe », mais sur la montagne de Randa qui n'est pas sans évoquer celle de l'Alverne, également à une heure matinale, le laïc Raymond Lulle connaît en 1275 la grande et décisive illumination :

> Un beau matin, alors qu'il se concentrait en regardant les cieux, le Seigneur illumina subitement son esprit et lui donna la forme et le mode de faire le livre dont il a été question plus haut, contre les erreurs des infidèles. Immensément reconnaissant au Très Haut, Raymond descendit de la montagne et retourna aussitôt à l'abbaye susdite où il entreprit de composer et faire ce livre, qu'il intitula d'abord *Art majeur* mais par la suite *Art général* [...] Quand il eut terminé son livre dans cette abbaye, il retourna sur la montagne [...] priant le Seigneur jour et nuit de daigner dans sa bonté diriger ses pas et assurer le succès de l'*Art* qu'il lui avait donné pour l'honneur de Dieu et le bien de l'Église [...][2].

Grâce à l'illumination divine, Raymond, comme Pierre de Jean Olivi qui en aurait reçu « toute sa science », une science totale, peut concevoir un Art « majeur » et même « général ». Bonaventure, dans le célèbre prologue de son ouvrage au titre explicite *De reductione artium ad theologiam*, a posé l'équivalence entre *illuminatio* et *formatio :* illuminer un être, lui communiquer la lumière, c'est par le fait même lui donner sa forme et l'amener à l'existence[3]. Exister pour Raymond Lulle, c'est écrire, donner « *formam et modum* » à l'Art qui

1. Bernard Gui, *Manuel de l'Inquisiteur*, éd. et traduit par G. Mollat (*Practica officii Inquisitionis heretice pravitatis*, vers 1323-1324), Paris, « Les classiques de l'histoire de France au Moyen Age », Champion, 1926, t. 1, p. 190-193 : « *Unum autem pretermittendum non puto quod dictus pater venerabilis, circa finem sui transitus, post sacram inunctionem receptam, astante sibi conventu fratrum Minorum Narbone, dixit totam scientiam suam per infusionem recepisse a Deo, et Parisius, in ecclesia, hora tertia, subito se fuisse illuminatum a Domino Jhesu Christo* ».

2. *Vita*, 14 : « *[...] Subito Dominus illustravit mentem suam dans eidem formam et modum faciendi librum, de quo supra dicitur, contra errores infidelium. De quo Raymundus immensas gracias reddens Altissimo, descendit de monte illo reversusque mox ad abbatiam supradictam, cepit ibidem ordinare et facere librum illum [...]* ».

3. Saint Bonaventure, Les six lumières de la connaissance humaine – *De reductione artium ad theologiam*, texte latin de Quaracchi et traduction française, introduction et notes de Pierre Michaud-Quentin, Paris, éd. franciscaines, 1971.

lui a été révélé. L'œuvre d'Olivi prouve en revanche que son auteur attache de l'importance à la quête longue et minutieuse du savoir et Olivi lui-même n'a jamais fait allusion dans aucun de ses ouvrages à sa propre illumination. La formule suivante revient fréquemment sous sa plume : « Si l'on étudie attentivement tout ce que les philosophes écrivent sur [...] »[1].

Ces deux récits d'illumination, si différents soient-ils, écrits au tournant des XIIIe – XIVe siècles, après la mort d'Olivi, marquent chacun à sa mesure une nette prise de position dans le débat sur les enjeux de la philosophie aristotélicienne. Depuis la seconde moitié du XIIIe siècle la philosophie aristotélicienne est en effet très vivement discutée : est-elle compatible avec la foi chrétienne ? Selon le dominicain Thomas d'Aquin, la pensée d'Aristote, si elle est correctement interprétée, s'accorde en gros avec la foi. Le franciscain Bonaventure a une conception résolument augustinienne et tend à considérer Aristote avec méfiance. Avec Siger de Brabant, Aristote interprété par Averroès est le représentant de la raison naturelle. Ainsi le débat autour d'Aristote débouche sur les questions fondamentales du rapport entre la foi et la raison, la nature et la grâce, la théologie et la philosophie. En 1277, l'évêque de Paris, Etienne Tempier, condamne certaines des idées de Thomas d'Aquin. Olivi lui-même n'hésite pas à contester en partie telle ou telle position thomiste qui lui semble trop encline aux erreurs aristotéliciennes. En déclarant que leur science provient d'une illumination divine, qu'elle est infuse, Pierre de Jean Olivi et Raymond Lulle, qui n'ont pas de magistère universitaire, se situent – ou sont situés par ceux qui rapportent leurs propos – dans une ligne qui affirme la prééminence de la foi sur l'entendement humain, sur tout magistère humain de la raison. Dans la *Vita*, Raymond affirme sa certitude : « Cela je puis vous le démontrer clairement, avec l'aide de Dieu, en me servant d'un certain Art qui fut révélé d'une manière que l'on croit divine à un certain ermite chrétien »[2].

La vanité de la philosophie et l'exigence missionnaire

Dès 1275, Jacques II roi de Majorque invite Raymond à le rejoindre à Montpellier. Les œuvres lulliennes sont examinées et approuvées par le franciscain Bertran Berenguer, maître en théologie. Raymond rencontre-t-il alors Pierre de Jean Olivi à l'occasion de son séjour d'environ deux ans à Montpellier ? Le célèbre franciscain qui se trouve à Montpellier ou à Narbonne est en butte aux attaques ; certains de ses livres sont confisqués et brûlés sur l'ordre du ministre général Jérôme d'Ascoli entre 1274 et 1277. Raymond, pour sa part, fort de l'appui de Jacques II et de l'approbation franciscaine, donne des lectures publiques de son nouvel ouvrage composé à Montpellier, l'*Art démonstratif*. Il obtient du roi et de Jérôme d'Ascoli la création du collège de Miramar dans lequel

1. *Quaestiones in Secundum librum Sententiarum*, q. 33, éd. B. Jansen, Quaracchi, I, 604.

2. *Vita*, 27 : « *Quod et ego per Artem quandam, cuidam eremitae christiano nuper divinitus, ut creditur, revelatam, vobis demonstrare potero claris rationibus, Domino largiente* ».

treize frères mineurs auront la charge d'apprendre l'arabe afin de pouvoir convertir les musulmans. Mais il y aurait eu dès 1250 un *studium arabicum* à Majorque et l'inspirateur du collège lullien serait principalement le dominicain Raymond de Penyafort qui conseilla Raymond Lulle après sa conversion et à qui Raymond resta fort attaché[1]. A la même époque, Raymond commence à rédiger son œuvre immense à Perpignan, à Montpellier, à Miramar. Peut-être se rend-il en Orient. C'est à Montpellier, entre 1283 et 1285, qu'il compose *Blanquerna*.

En 1283, le nouveau ministre général des franciscains, Bonagratia de S. Jean en Persiceto, commande à une commission de quatre maîtres et trois bacheliers en théologie de Paris d'examiner les écrits d'Olivi : sa position sur la pauvreté franciscaine, ses thèses théologiques et philosophiques sont sévèrement censurées. Olivi est dépossédé de ses œuvres et empêché de se défendre lui-même. En 1285, estimant qu'il a été traité injustement, il décide d'écrire une *Apologie* pour se défendre : il est amené sur certains points à nuancer ses affirmations antérieures, à souscrire prudemment à l'avis de ses censeurs. La même année, le ministre franciscain de la Provence, Arnaud de Roquefeuille, et trente-cinq franciscains présentent Olivi comme le chef d'une secte superstitieuse et un semeur de troubles. Olivi s'explique en ces termes sur ses positions philosophiques et théologiques :

> J'ai seulement mentionné diverses opinions, sans en soutenir l'une plutôt que l'autre [...] il s'agissait de positions qui ne paraissaient pas moins adaptées que d'autres à expliquer ou défendre notre foi [...] A l'inverse, de lourds soupçons me faisaient craindre certaines opinions philosophiques truffées de pièges cachés, de dangers obscurs qui menacent la foi catholique [...] ce qui me décide [...], c'est le zèle pour la foi catholique et l'Église romaine. Il est certain toutefois que je n'adhère pas avec ferveur aux conceptions philosophiques ni aux opinions humaines, que je n'y insiste pas avec entêtement et que je ne les tiens pas en elles-mêmes pour des choses de grande valeur. Je suis au contraire consterné de voir qu'Aristote le païen, Averroès l'arabe, ainsi que d'autres philosophes infidèles, sont tenus par certains en une telle estime, une telle vénération et une telle autorité, surtout dans des discours ou des textes traitant de théologie sacrée[2].

La critique d'Olivi la plus développée contre la philosophie païenne est contenue dans son traité intitulé *Comment lire les livres des philosophes*, mais son attitude demeure celle d'Augustin dans le *De doctrina christiana* : la philosophie a sa valeur, si elle est servante de la théologie. La position de Raymond Lulle diffère : selon lui la philosophie ne peut que s'accorder avec la théologie si elle est véritablement raisonnable. Reprenant les termes mêmes d'Olivi, c'est pour « l'honneur de Dieu et le bien de l'Église » que Raymond Lulle veut assurer la diffusion de son Art et décide de parcourir l'Europe.

Après s'être rendu à Rome pour obtenir sans succès du pape la création de nombreux monastères semblables à Miramar, il gagne enfin Paris en 1288-1289.

1. *Cf.* Laureano Robles, « El studium arabicum del capítulo dominicano de Toledo de 1250. Antecedentes del 'Miramar' de Ramon Lull », *Estudios Lulianos* 24, 1980, p. 23-47.

2. Apologie de 1285, *Responsio II*, p. 405.

> Berthauld était chancelier quand Raymond vint à Paris et c'est dans sa chaire et sur sa demande expresse qu'il commenta son *Art général*. Après la fin de son enseignement et ayant vu à Paris la façon dont les étudiants se comportaient, il revint à Montpellier. Là de nouveau il composa un livre qu'il nomma *Art de trouver la vérité* et il le lut en public [1].

Aucune trace écrite de l'enseignement public en Sorbonne de Raymond Lulle n'est conservée, mais c'est à partir de ce moment que Raymond, qui n'est pas clerc et n'a pas de grade universitaire, commence à se dénommer et à être dénommé *magister*, *mestre*. Il a déjà pour disciple le chanoine médecin d'Arras Thomas le Myésier, et il profite de son séjour parisien pour offrir au roi Philippe le Bel, neveu de Jacques II de Majorque par sa mère, son *Livre de les Bèsties*. Ce n'est qu'à propos du dernier séjour de Raymond à Paris en 1309-1311 que la *Vita* mentionne sa position à l'égard de la philosophie et des écrits d'Averroès, position qui n'est pas sans rappeler celle qui est exprimée en 1285 par Pierre de Jean Olivi :

> Une nombreuse assistance de maîtres et d'écoliers vint l'écouter. Raymond ne leur donnait pas seulement une doctrine établie sur de solides raisons philosophiques, mais il professait aussi une sagesse en plein accord avec les grands principes de la foi chrétienne. [...]. Il remarqua que les écrits d'Averroès, commentateur d'Aristote, avaient fait dévier plusieurs esprits de la rectitude de la véritable foi catholique. D'après eux, la foi chrétienne était impossible quant au mode de l'intellect, mais vraie quant au mode de la croyance, car ils étaient tout de même des gens enracinés dans la communauté chrétienne. Aussi Raymond entreprit-il de réfuter leur opinion par voie démonstrative et scientifique et de diverses manières il les laissait incapables de répondre. Car si la loi catholique ne peut être démontrée quant au mode de l'intellect, il est impossible qu'elle soit vraie. Et il composa des livres sur ce sujet [2].

Ce qui compte pour Raymond Lulle, c'est l'efficacité de son Art pour convertir les infidèles et en particulier les musulmans grâce à la démonstration raisonnable des dogmes du christianisme. Originaire de Majorque, il est particulièrement sensible à la question de la différence religieuse. Pour Olivi, ce qui compte, surtout à partir des années 1270 où l'ordre franciscain a perdu la forte autorité qui a été la sienne auparavant et est en proie à des déchirements dramatiques, c'est de défendre une certaine conception de l'ordre franciscain et de sa mission dans l'Église d'abord et également hors de l'Église.

L'exigence missionnaire est particulièrement importante pour l'ordre franciscain. Olivi souligne dans plusieurs traités, par exemple dans la première des *Questions sur la pauvreté évangélique* ou dans le *Commentaire de l'évangile de Jean*, que la fondation de l'ordre a été un signe majeur du renouveau évangélique de l'Église ; le modèle missionnaire est institué par saint François lui-même avec sa mission auprès des musulmans. Olivi prévoit une entreprise audacieuse chez les Grecs, les musulmans et les juifs – ces protagonistes des plus célèbres

1. *Vita*, 19.
2. *Vita*, 42, 43.

dialogues de Raymond Lulle – dans un proche avenir, et explique que les franciscains sont particulièrement aptes à transmettre leur savoir à autrui. Dans le *Commentaire sur l'Apocalypse* de 1297, il affirme que les franciscains seront les premiers à défendre l'Evangile aussi bien dans la chrétienté que dans des terres lointaines. Arnau de Vilanova, *magister medicinae*, formé à Valence, Naples et Montpellier, laïc marié comme Raymond Lulle, enseigne la médecine à l'Université de Montpellier de 1289 à 1299, tout en étant particulièrement soucieux de contribuer à la réforme de l'Église par la pauvreté et la vie intérieure. Proche des franciscains spirituels, il utilise certaines expressions franciscaines d'Olivi pour évoquer la nécessaire réforme de l'Église et de la chrétienté et qualifier Raymond Lulle de « *portaestendard de la reforma espiritual de la cristiandat* »[1].

La science au risque des concurrences et conflits des institutions

Au chapitre général de Montpellier en 1287, Olivi est réhabilité et le nouveau ministre général de l'ordre, Mathieu d'Aquasparta, le nomme *lector* au *studium* de Santa Croce de Florence. Il s'y lie d'amitié avec Pierre de Trabibus qui deviendra l'un de ses plus fidèles disciples et Ubertin de Casale qui le soutiendra au concile de Vienne en 1311-1312. Olivi regagne Montpellier en 1289, en même temps que Raymond Lulle (rentré de Paris) et qu'Arnau de Vilanova (rentré de Valence), parce que Raymond Gaufredi, nouveau ministre général, le rappelle au *studium* franciscain, et il y enseigne jusqu'à sa mort en 1298. Sa réhabilitation semble avoir été totale de 1287 à 1298. 1289 est l'année de l'érection de l'*Estudi universitari* de Montpellier en *Universitat* par Jacques II de Majorque. Miquel Batllori estime qu'il est probable qu'en 1289, comme en 1275, Raymond Lulle n'enseigne pas son Art à l'Université de Montpellier mais dans le couvent des franciscains, puisque la *Vita* ne fait pas mention de l'Université[2]. Il paraît donc évident que Raymond Lulle et Pierre de Jean Olivi ont eu la possibilité matérielle de se rencontrer, ou plutôt n'ont pas pu éviter de se rencontrer à Montpellier en 1289 dans l'espace du couvent franciscain. 1290 est l'année où Raymond Lulle devient veuf et où le ministre général des franciscains Raymond Gaufredi, favorable à la tendance spirituelle de Pierre de Jean Olivi, Ubertin de Casale, Angelo Clareno, et également lié à Arnau de Vilanova, lui accorde le 26 octobre des lettres de recommandation pour les couvents franciscains d'Italie[3]. Raymond

1. *Cf.* Miquel Batllori, « Dos nous escrits espirituals d'Arnau de Vilanova », *Analecta Sacra Tarraconensia* 28, 1955, p. 45-70.

2. *Cf.* Miquel Batllori, *Obres essencials*, t. I, Barcelona, Ed. Selecta, 1957, introduction, édition et notes de la *Vida coetània*, p. 41, note 73.

3. « *Volo quod vos ministri, si aliqui fratres provintiarum vestrarum audire dictam Artem fuerint consolati, detis ipsis fratribus licentiam et dicto domino Raymundo de conventu idoneo opportunitatem in quo possit fratribus ostendere Artem illam, concedatis* » (Antoni Rubió i Lluch, *Documents per l'història de la cultura catalana mig-eval*, I, Barcelone, 1908, p. 9-10; L. Wadding, *Annales minorum*, éd. Quaracchi, V, 1931, p. 268, n (XVIII).

Gaufredi cite l'Art lullien et recommande aux couvents franciscains d'en favoriser et d'en accueillir la lecture.

La *Vita* de Raymond Lulle relate alors l'étonnante et dramatique tentation que Raymond éprouve à Gênes en 1293, en notant au préalable que : « Les Gênois avaient tous entendu dire que Raymond après sa conversion à la vie pénitente avait reçu de façon divine sur une montagne une science sainte capable de convertir les infidèles »[1].

Alors que ses livres se trouvent déjà sur le bateau qui doit l'emmener en terre musulmane, Raymond est pris d'une peur immense du martyre. Il reste donc à Gênes avec ses livres, persuadé d'avoir scandalisé les Gênois, et tombe malade. Le jour de la Pentecôte, après avoir entendu l'hymne « *Veni Creator* », qui est une invocation du Saint Esprit, dans l'église des dominicains, il demande successivement aux dominicains puis aux franciscains d'entrer dans leur ordre, mais les uns et les autres refusent de l'accepter immédiatement. Raymond est persuadé qu'il s'expose à la damnation personnelle s'il n'entre pas chez les dominicains et que son Art et ses livres, c'est-à-dire sa capacité de prouver les dogmes du christianisme, seront perdus s'il n'entre pas chez les franciscains.

> Raymond se rappela que les frères mineurs avaient accepté l'Art qu'il avait reçu de Dieu sur la montagne et qu'ils l'avaient apprécié davantage que les frères prêcheurs. C'est pourquoi, espérant que les frères mineurs divulgueraient plus efficacement son Art pour l'honneur du Seigneur Jésus Christ et l'utilité de son Église, il pensa entrer chez eux en abandonnant les frères prêcheurs [...]. Raymond choisit, chose merveilleuse, sa propre damnation éternelle plutôt que de laisser se perdre l'Art qu'il avait reçu de Dieu pour le salut d'un grand nombre et surtout pour l'honneur de Dieu même[2].

Ainsi Raymond, l'illuminé, choisit, le jour de la Pentecôte, de rester fidèle à sa mission d'enseignement et de conversion par l'Art que Dieu lui a révélé sur la montagne. En cette fin du XIIIe siècle, le choix de l'ordre franciscain contre l'ordre dominicain a valeur de manifeste philosophique et théologique. Raymond choisit de rester fidèle à une certaine orientation spirituelle et franciscaine, bonaventurienne, propre à apprécier et favoriser la divulgation de son Art qui est un don spirituel, divin, « *quam sibi Dominus dederat in monte* », « *que nostro Senyor li havia inspirada* », répète le texte, contre les dominicains, sans doute davantage méfiants à l'égard de la science infuse et redoutables spécialistes de l'orthodoxie des consciences. Mais le texte de la *Vita* prend soin de rappeler que Raymond a d'abord demandé son admission dans l'ordre dominicain. Raymond semble croire que l'illumination divine, l'infusion divine de la science n'est pas liée à la justification. Les grands théologiens franciscains du XIIIe siècle sont d'accord avec Thomas d'Aquin pour dire que la justification est liée à la grâce infuse. Olivi a été accusé de soutenir le contraire à propos du baptême et doit s'en défendre fermement.

1. *Vita*, 20 : « *scientiam quamdam sanctam pro conversione infidelium* ».
2. *Vita*, 22, 23.

Ayant choisi de ne pas renier l'Art qui lui a été révélé autrefois, Raymond peut désormais poursuivre sa route et partir pour Tunis « avec ses livres ». La *Vita* montre bien que « les livres » de Raymond sont toujours conçus comme des explicitations du premier livre, l'Art qui a été révélé sur la montagne, en raison de « la fragilité de l'intellect humain » qu'il a éprouvée au cours de son premier séjour parisien. Raymond aime-t-il écrire ? Ce n'est pas sûr. Mais il veut divulguer, enseigner sans relâche. Ses livres sont le support de sa prédication. La *Vita* cite à deux reprises (26-27 et 37) le début de l'argumentation lullienne *rationabilissime* en faveur de l'existence de la Trinité.

En 1301, à Chypre, « comme il prêchait et enseignait sans arrêt, il finit par tomber malade [...] »[1]. En 1308, jeté sur le rivage de Pise après un naufrage, ayant perdu tous ses livres,

> [...] là, malgré son grand âge et sa faiblesse, l'homme de Dieu, toujours aussi décidé à travailler pour le Christ, termina son *Dernier art général.* Ce livre est digne d'avoir une immense efficacité et d'être connu et goûté de tout le monde, comme d'ailleurs tous les autres ouvrages du Maître, qui, loin d'avoir en vue la gloire de ce monde ou une vaine philosophie, tint l'amour de Dieu et sa sagesse comme fin dernière et bien suprême[2].

Olivi considère que les recherches intellectuelles constituent une part importante de la vie franciscaine, mais il est conscient que les livres peuvent être l'objet de passion exagérée et qu'il est difficile de repérer les excès en ce domaine. Ses nombreux écrits prouvent bien qu'il fait usage des techniques intellectuelles de son temps sans aucune gêne. Il veut développer un type de science en harmonie avec la foi et les vertus chrétiennes. Paris représente pour lui tous les risques de l'erreur et de la « vanité philosophique ». Le christianisme a besoin de « maîtres humbles » qui méprisent les récompenses de ce monde et interdisent à leurs disciples de les honorer, qui sont des prêcheurs et des apologètes aussi bien que des intellectuels et mettent leur savoir au service de l'activité missionnaire chrétienne. Le franciscain Pierre de Jean Olivi trace ainsi au laïc Raymond Lulle un idéal de *magisterium* qui convient bien à ce dernier.

Olivi appartient à une institution où s'affrontent différents enjeux de savoir et de pouvoir. En tant que franciscain, sans être universitaire, il est producteur de savoir. S'il jouit d'une grande autorité philosophique et théologique dans son ordre et parmi les universitaires de son temps, il doit une parfaite obéissance intellectuelle et spirituelle à ses supérieurs. Considéré comme appartenant à la tendance spirituelle, il n'est pas un homme de pouvoir dans son ordre. Son originalité philosophique et théologique, ecclésiologique en particulier, malgré ses sincères protestations de soumission et d'orthodoxie, ne peut que lui valoir les plus graves soupçons de la part d'autorités soucieuses d'unifier et pacifier l'ordre franciscain et de renforcer son prestige. Il ne saurait avoir la liberté de mouvement et de pensée du laïc Raymond Lulle.

1. *Vita*, 34.
2. *Vita*, 41.

Raymond, qui n'a pas suivi le cursus universitaire traditionnel, qui n'est pas clerc, ne prétend jamais faire œuvre théologique. Sans dépendance institutionnelle, se dénommant ou se faisant dénommer dans sa *Vita* « homme de Dieu », « maître », il répète qu'il veut convertir les infidèles aux dogmes majeurs du christianisme – tels la Trinité, l'Incarnation et la Résurrection du Christ. Il n'est pas véritablement pris au sérieux par ceux qui exercent le pouvoir dans l'Église, comme le montrent bien les échecs de ses démarches à Rome auprès des papes successifs. Voyageur infatigable, il ne cesse de rencontrer et de chercher à convaincre de la justesse de ses vues les hommes, politiques ou religieux, les plus puissants et les plus influents de son temps. Malgré ses plaintes réitérées et ses affirmations de découragement, il est bien loin de connaître les difficultés de Pierre de Jean Olivi, ou même d'Arnau de Vilanova qui, médecin et laïc, ne cache pas ses prétentions théologiques. Le roi de Majorque, avec qui il entretient de confiantes relations, appuie constamment ses entreprises, ne cesse de le protéger et de l'admirer, alors qu'il désavoue Arnau de Vilanova en 1309. Raymond a le soutien de franciscains qui s'opposent, tels Jérôme d'Ascoli et Raymond Gaufredi. Raymond a en effet l'art de ne paraître dangereux à aucun pouvoir, de faire jouer la concurrence des pouvoirs et des institutions.

En 1290 une enquête sur les franciscains spirituels a été ordonnée par le pape Nicolas IV (l'ancien ministre général Jérôme d'Ascoli). En 1295 Boniface VIII, récemment élu, démet Raymond Gaufredi de ses fonctions; lui succède Jean de Murrovalle, ami de Boniface et membre de la commission qui a censuré Olivi en 1283. Mais Olivi, définitivement réhabilité, estime que la défense de la règle franciscaine est étroitement liée à la défense du pouvoir pontifical. Il ne saurait donc se prononcer contre l'action du pape ni remettre en question l'autorité pontificale, et il expose clairement sa position. Jusqu'à sa mort en 1298, il ne cesse d'être l'objet d'une grande admiration et vénération de la part de ses contemporains. Ubertin de Casale affirme que, sur son lit de mort, Olivi a soumis ses œuvres au jugement du pape[1]. Mais son *Commentaire de l'Apocalypse* achevé en 1297, d'abord méconnu, relance la polémique autour de sa personne et de son œuvre à la fin du XIIIe siècle et au début du XIVe siècle dans le cadre plus large des conflits qui déchirent toujours l'ordre franciscain. La bataille autour de la pauvreté s'amplifie en effet après 1298 et l'orthodoxie d'Olivi, parce qu'il est considéré comme le tenant inacceptable d'une stricte pauvreté, est à nouveau attaquée tant sur la question de la pauvreté que sur ses conceptions philosophiques et théologiques.

Le 10 février 1310, au cours de son dernier séjour à Paris, Raymond Lulle a la joie de recevoir l'approbation de ses thèses par quarante maîtres et bacheliers de l'Université[2]; il reçoit des lettres de recommandation de Philippe le Bel le 2 août 1310 et le chancelier François Caraccioli, dit François de Naples, examine sur ordre du roi quelques-unes de ses œuvres et leur donne un avis favorable le

1. « Ubertino da Casale : Sanctitati apostolicae », *Archiv für Literatur- und Kirchengeschichte des Mittelalters* 2, 1886, p. 377-416.

2. *Cf.* Denifle-Chatelain, *Chartularium Universitatis Parisiensis*, t. II, 1897, p. 140.

9 septembre 1311. Alors qu'il n'a cessé durant toute sa vie de solliciter sans succès le soutien des différents papes dans ses entreprises, le concile de Vienne, qui a lieu d'octobre 1311 à mai 1312, est l'occasion pour lui de voir triompher ses principales idées sur la mission, la croisade, la réforme de l'Église, même si elles ne sont pas forcément suivies d'effet[1]; seule sa demande d'interdiction de l'averroisme n'est pas prise en considération. Si ses idées semblent recevoir enfin leur application, c'est parce que les différents pouvoirs du début du XIVe siècle y trouvent leur compte pour des raisons qui ne sont pas seulement spirituelles ou missionnaires. Raymond rentre alors à Montpellier, puis à Majorque où il fait son testament. Il décide de faire copier ses œuvres en latin et en « romanç » et de laisser un exemplaire de chacun de ses livres dans la chartreuse de Vauvert à Paris, chez Perceval Spinola qui a été son hôte et son ami à Gênes, dans le couvent des franciscains de Palma de Majorque. Sans doute appartient-il déjà à cette date au tiers ordre franciscain.

A la même époque, à la tête de l'ordre, Jean de Murrovalle, puis Gonzalve de Valboa, puis Michel de Césène, soutenu par le pape Jean XXII à partir de 1316, s'attaquent décisivement aux franciscains de la tendance spirituelle. En 1318, les premiers bûchers consument à Marseille les spirituels rebelles; un an plus tard, leurs protecteurs laïcs seront brûlés. La même année 1318, il est interdit de posséder ou utiliser des œuvres d'Olivi; entre autres théories, celles qui ont trait à la conversion des musulmans, des juifs et des païens sont taxées de rêve apocalyptique dangereux, dénué de tout fondement scripturaire ni rationnel; sa vision dynamique de l'histoire de l'Église qui suppose un changement réel, une transformation des institutions, est complètement rejetée. En 1318 également, le culte qu'on lui voue à Narbonne sur sa tombe est aboli, car son corps est exhumé secrètement et disparaît. Raymond Lulle est alors mort depuis plus de deux ans à Majorque, entre décembre 1315 et mars 1316, et enterré dans l'église du couvent des frères mineurs de Palma où sa tombe ne cesse de susciter une grande vénération. A la fin du XIVe siècle, l'inquisiteur dominicain Nicolau Eymerich sera le plus déterminé adversaire de la pensée lullienne; mais l'archevêque de Tarragone, la ville de Barcelone et le roi d'Aragon s'opposent à la condamnation de l'œuvre lullienne par le pape Grégoire XI en 1376 et le pape Martin V doit la réhabiliter en 1419.

1. La *Vita* résume ainsi les demandes de Raymond : « *Primum quidem, ut locus constitueretur sufficiens, in quo viri devoti et intellectu vigentes ponerentur, studentes in diversis linguarum generibus, quod omni creature scirent doctrinam evangelicam predicare. Secundum vero, ut de cunctis religiosis militibus christianis fieret unus Ordo, qui ultra mare contra Sarracenos usque ad recuperationem Terre Sancte bella continua retinerent. Tertium autem, ut contra oppiniones Averroys, qui in multis perversor extitit veritatis, dominus papa celeriter ordinaret remedium [...]* » (44). Pour les canons du concile, on se reportera à C.J. Hefele, *Histoire des conciles*, Paris, 1915, t. VI, 2, p. 688-689.

CONCLUSION

Ainsi Pierre de Jean Olivi et Raymond Lulle sont tous deux des personnages importants de la vie intellectuelle et spirituelle de la seconde moitié du XIIIe siècle. A l'époque des grandes affirmations dogmatiques, de la mise en place institutionnelle d'un contrôle des savoirs, de l'émergence de différents pouvoirs, de tendances parfois opposées dans l'Église, ces personnages constituent par leur autorité spirituelle et intellectuelle des enjeux et des dangers potentiels. L'ordre franciscain, en proie aux plus graves déchirements entre spirituels et conventuels, s'attache essentiellement à réinterpréter sa fondation et ne peut admettre l'originalité de Pierre de Jean Olivi qui, sans porter atteinte aux dogmes majeurs du christianisme, propose des solutions ecclésiologiques insolites. En revanche, que Raymond Lulle soit à sa marge, dans son tiers ordre, lui convient, dans la mesure où Raymond l'illuminé, qui a pour principale et insoupçonnable intention de prouver les dogmes incontestables du christianisme, est aussi un homme qui a le soutien des princes et des villes, qui peut faire pièce aux prétentions de savoir et de pouvoir d'institutions rivales, qui peut donner des arguments à ses propres objectifs sans favoriser en son sein un parti plutôt qu'un autre, une tendance ecclésiologique plutôt qu'une autre. Echappant aux conflits des institutions, se mouvant entre les influences diverses et profitant de leurs concurrences, tissant un réseau de puissantes amitiés, Raymond sait offrir peu de prise à la coercition et acquiert ainsi une liberté d'esprit et d'expression tout à fait remarquable et unique qui lui permettra en fin de compte de faire école après sa mort. Entré très jeune dans l'ordre franciscain, Pierre de Jean Olivi est affecté par les luttes acharnées de savoir et de pouvoir qui s'y développent et son activité ne peut que lui valoir les soupçons et les interdictions. Même s'il sait après 1285 et jusqu'à sa mort échapper à la condamnation, jouer des tendances concurrentes, affirmer sa fidélité au pouvoir pontifical, ses œuvres seront après sa mort livrées à des interprétations rivales puis vouées à l'oubli.

Les destins, si différents soient-ils de ces deux hommes, concourent à montrer qu'à la fin du XIIIe siècle et au début du XIVe siècle la recherche philosophique n'est plus seulement à l'Université mais en d'autres lieux. Cette dispersion de la recherche, en marge de l'Université, marque peut-être le début de l'épuisement de l'aristotélisme récusé en ses interprétations les plus extrêmes aussi bien par Pierre de Jean Olivi que par Raymond Lulle. Elle marque aussi que de nouvelles institutions – les cours des princes, les villes, tels ou tels groupes de laïcs, comme les béguins et les béguines, également des individus influents – s'apprêtent à accueillir la recherche philosophique et théologique. Tel est sans doute l'enjeu des récits d'illumination de Pierre de Jean Olivi et Raymond Lulle, plus que l'affirmation de la prééminence de la foi sur la raison, de la théologie sur la philosophie, même si cette affirmation vaut également.

Ainsi s'élaborent de nouveaux fonctionnements de l'autorité intellectuelle et spirituelle dans la société de la fin du XIIIe siècle et du début du XIVe siècle.

BIBLIOGRAPHIE 1989-1998

Les références bibliographiques présentées ici viennent compléter deux bibliographies antérieures publiées respectivement dans :

GIEBEN Servus, O.F.M., *Collectanea Franciscana* 38, 1968, p. 167-195 (pour la période 1885-1967), et

VIAN Paolo (a cura di), *Pietro di Giovanni Olivi, Scritti scelti*, Città nuova ed., Rome, 1989 (pour la période 1967-1989).

ÉDITIONS

SCHLAGETER Johannes, *Das Heil der Armen und das Verderben der Reichen. Petrus Johannis Olivi OFM. Die Frage nach der höchsten Armut*, Werl, Coelde, 1989, 215 p = 8QPE (*an status altissime paupertatis sit simpliciter melior omni statu divitiarum*).

BARTOLI Marco, *La Caduta di Gerusalemme. Il commento al Libro delle Lamentazioni di Pietro di Giovanni Olivi*, Rome, *I.S.I.M.E.* 12, 1991 = *Lectura super Lamentationes Ieremiae*.

BURR David, *De usu paupere. The* Quaestio *and the* Tractatus, Florence-Perth, L.S. Olschki-University of Western Australia Press, 1992, p. LXII-154 = 9QPE (*an usus pauper includatur in consilio seu in voto paupertatis evangelice, ita quod sit de eius substantia et integritate*) et *Tractatus de usu paupere*.

PASNAU Robert, « Petri Iohannis Olivi Tractatus de Verbo », *Franciscan Studies* 53, 1993, p. 121-153 (= *Lectura super Iohannem*, cap. 1, extrait).

FLOOD David, « Peter Olivi. *Quæstio de mendicitate*. Critical édition », *A.F.H.* 87, 1994, p. 287-347 = 10QPE et 15QPE (*an pauperibus evangelicis sit perfectius et convenientius victum suum adquirere per mendicitatis questum aut per manuale opus seu laboritium; an vivere de prebendis vel quibuscumque redditibus vel vivere de possessionibus absque vendicatione cuiuscumque dominii vel iuris possit esse licitum pauperibus evangelicis*).

FLOOD David et GÁL Gedeon, *Peter of John Olivi on the Bible. Principia quinque in Sacram Scripturam. Postilla in Isaiam et in I ad Corinthios*, St Bonaventure (N.Y.), Franciscan Institute Publications, 1997 (contient aussi 11QPE : *an vovere alteri homini obedientiam in omnibus que non sunt contraria anime et evangelice regule seu perfectioni sit perfectionis evangelice*).

PIRON Sylvain, KILMER Cynthia et MARMURSZTEJN Elsa, « *Petrus Ioannis Olivi. Epistola ad fratrem R.* », *A.F.H.* 91/1, 1998, p. 33-64.

MADIGAN Kevin, *Peter Olivi's Lectura super Matthaeum in Medieval Exegetical Context*. Thèse (non publiée), University of Chicago, 1992. (Contient l'édition d'un fragment du Commentaire sur Matthieu).

MURTAGH Thomas, *Peter Olivi's Commentary : A Critical Edition of Chapter 5, verses 1-26 with a Commentary*. Thèse (non publiée), Melbourne College of Divinity, 1992.

TRADUCTIONS

Trad. française de *Modus quomodo quilibet potest referre gratias Deo de beneficiis ab eo receptis, Informatio Petri Iohannis, Remedia contra temptationes spirituales, Miles armatus*, dans MANSELLI Raoul, *Spirituels et béguins du Midi*, trad. fr. J. Duvernoy, Toulouse, Privat, 1989.

Trad. italienne de *Expositio super Regulam fratrum minorum* (extraits), *De perlegendis philosophorum libris*, *Lectura super Apocalypsim* (extraits d'après le ms., Paris, BN, lat. 713, ff. 84v-93v, 113v-118), *Modus quomodo quilibet potest referre gratias Deo de beneficiis ab eo receptis, Informatio Petri Iohannis, Remedia contra temptationes spirituales huius temporis, Miles armatus, Expositio orationis dominicae, Epistola ad R., Epistola ad filios regis Siciliae, Epistola ad Conradum de Offida*, dans Pietro di Giovanni Olivi, *Scritti scelti*, VIAN Paolo trad. et éd., Rome, Città Nuova, 1989.

Trad. italienne du *De contractibus* dans Pietro di Giovanni Olivi, *Usure, compere e vendite. La scienza economica del XIII secolo,* a cura di SPICCIANI Amleto, VIAN Paolo e ANDENNA Gian Carlo, Milan, Europía, 1990, 176 p.

ÉTUDES

Pietro di Giovanni Olivi. Verso una nuova età. Chiesa, società, economia. Studi in occasione delle « Giornate dell'Osservanza » di Bologna, 13-14 maggio 1989, in *Zenit Quaderni*. Supplemento al quarto numero del 1989.

Indulgenza nel Medioevo e perdonanza di papa Celestino V. Atti del Congresso storico internazionale. L'Aquila, 5-6 ottobre 1984 cur. A CLEMENTI, praef. G. SCHIPPA, L'Aquila Centro Celestiniano, Sezione storica, 1987. [Interventi di R. MANSELLI, O. CAPITANI, F. CARDINI, P. PÉANO, E. PÀSZTOR, A. CLEMENTI, S. STICCA]

BARONE Giulia, « L'œuvre eschatologique de Pierre Jean-Olieu et son influence. Un bilan historiographique », dans *Fin du monde et signes des temps. Visionnaires et prophètes en France méridionale (fin XIII*e*-début XV*e* siècle)* (*Cahiers de Fanjeaux* 27), Toulouse, Privat, 1992, p. 49-61.

BARTOLI Marco, « Olivi e il *Sacramento del potere* », *B.I.S.I.M.E* 99, 1993, p. 91-115.

– « Celestino V, il caso del papa eretico e i francescani spirituali », *Aspetti della spiritualità ai tempi di Celestini V. Atti dei Convegni : Ferentino, 23 febbraio e 21 maggio 1992*. Ferentino, Associazione culturale « Gli Argonauti », 1993, p. 57-73.

– « Pietro di Giovanni Olivi nella recente storiografia sul tema dell'infallibilità pontificia », *B.I.S.I.M.E.* 99/2, 1994, p. 149-200.

BÉRIOU Nicole, « Pierre de Limoges et la fin des temps », *Mélanges de l'École française de Rome M.A.* 98, 1986, p. 65-107.

BIANCHI Luca, *L'errore di Aristotele. La polemica contro l'eternità del monde nel XIII secolo*, Florence, La Nuova Italia, 1984.

– « Censure, liberté et progrès intellectuel à l'Université de Paris au XIIIe siècle », *A.H.D.L.M.A.* 63, 1996, p. 45-93.

BIANCHI Luca et RANDI Eugenio, *Le verità dissonanti. Aristotele alla fine del Medioevo*, Rome-Bari, Laterza, 1990, trad. fr. C. POTTIER, *Vérités dissonantes. Aristote à la fin du Moyen Age*, Fribourg-Paris, Presses Universitaires-Le Cerf, 1993.

BIGET Jean-Louis, « Autour de Bernard Délicieux. Franciscanisme et société en Languedoc entre 1295 et 1330 », *Mouvements Franciscains et société française, XIIIe-XXe siècles. Etudes présentées à la table ronde du CNRS, réunies par* André VAUCHEZ, Paris, Beauchesne, 1984, p. 75-93.

BOULNOIS Olivier, « Vouloir, vœu et noblesse de la volonté selon Olieu », *Cahiers du Centre de Recherches Historiques* 16, 1996, p. 57-64.

BOUREAU Alain, « Droit et théologie au XIIIe siècle », *Annales E.S.C.* 47, 1992, p. 1113-1125.

– « Pierre de Jean Olivi et le semi-dormeur. Une élaboration médiévale de l'activité inconsciente », *Nouvelle Revue de Psychanalyse* 48, 1993, p. 231-238.

– « Pierre de Jean Olivi et l'émergence d'une théorie contractuelle de la royauté au XIIIe siècle », dans *Représentation, pouvoir et royauté à la fin du Moyen Age. Actes du colloque organisé par l'Université du Maine les 25 et 26 mars 1994*, ed. Joël BLANCHARD, Paris, Picard, 1994, p. 166-175.

– « Le retour de saint Equitius. Pierre de Jean Olivi et l'usage polémique de l'hagiographie », *Florentissima proles ecclesiae. Miscellanea hagiographica, historica e liturgica Reginaldo Grégoire O.S.B. XII lustra complenti oblata*, Biblioteca Civis, IX, Trento, 1996, p. 41-58.

BRETT A.S., *Liberty, Right and Nature*, Cambridge, 1997.

BURR David, « Olivi, the *Lectura super Apocalypsim* and Franciscan Exegetical Tradition », in *Francescanesimo e cultura universitaria. Atti del XVI Convegno internazionale. Assisi, 13-15 ottobre 1988*, Pérouse, Univ. degli studi di Perugia, 1990, p. 113-135.

– *Olivi e la povertà francescana. Le origine della controversia sull' « usu paupere »*, trad. Luca Bergamaschi, Milano, Edizioni Bibliotecana Francescana, 1992, 209 p.

– *Olivi's Peaceable Kingdom. A Reading of the Apocalypse Commentary*, Philadelphia, University of Pennsylvania Press, 1993, 280 p.

– « Ecclesiastical Condemnation and Exegetical Theory : The Case of Olivi's Apocalypse Commentary », in *Neue Richtungen in der hoch-und spaetmittelalterlichen Bibelexegese* (Schriften des Historischen Kollegs, Kolloquien 32), ed. Robert E. LERNER, Munich, Oldenbourg Verlag, 1996, p. 149-162.

– « Olivi on Prophecy », *Cristianesimo nella Storia* 17, 1996, p. 369-391.

– *L'histoire de Pierre Olivi. Franciscain persécuté*, trad. fr. F.-X. PUTALLAZ, Paris-Fribourg, Cerf-Editions Universitaires, 1997.

– « Na Prous Boneta and Olivi », *Collectanea Franciscana* 67, 1997, p. 477-500.

– « Olivi, Prous and the Separation of Apocalypse from Eschatology », in M. CUSTADO and F.E. COUGHLIN eds., *That Others May Know and Love : Essays in Honor of Zachary Hayes, O.F.M. ; Franciscan, Educator, Scholar*, St. Bonaventure, N.Y., 1997.

– « Mendicant Reading of the Apocalypse », in *The Apocalypse in the Middle Ages*, Richard K. EMMERSON and Bernard MCGINN Eds, Ithaca, N.Y -London, Cornell University Press, 1998, p. 89-102.

CAPITANI Ovidio, « 'Romana Ecclesia' e 'Cathedra Petri' in Michele Maccarrone. A proposito di una raccolta di saggi », *Rivista di storia e letteratura religiosa* 28, 1992, p. 591-606.

– « Duns Scoto e la crisi di un'età » in S. CASAMENTI, ed., *Duns Scoto e suggestioni nel moderno*, Edizioni Francescane Bologna, 1994, p. 7-33.

– « Da una ecclesiologia medievale ad una ecclesiologia moderna : il pensiero di Pietro Olivi », *La presenza francescana trà medioevo e modernità*. ed. A. CHESSA e Marco POLI, Firenze, Vallechi Editore, 1996, p. 213-221.

CAZENAVE Annie, « Conception du temps et de l'histoire chez Pierre-Jean Olieu » in *Knowledge and the Sciences in Medieval Philosophy*, Vol. III, ed. R. TYÖRINOJA *et al.*, Helsinki University Press, 1990.

CELANO Anthony J., « Act of the Intellect or Act of the Will : The Critical Reception of Aristotle's Ideal of Human Perfection in the XIIIth and Early XIVth Centuries », *A.H.D.L.M.A.* 57, 1991, p. 93-119.

CENCI Cesare, « Sermoni anonimi già attribuiti a Pietro di Giovanni Olivi », *Antonianum* 73, 1998, p. 43-77.

CICERI Antonio, « Pietro di Giovanni Olivi : Censimento-inventario dei manoscritti », *A.F.H.* 90, 1997, p. 3-83.

COLZANI Gianni, « Fondamenti teologici per la rappresentazione pittoresca del giudizio finale dal 1100 al 1500 », *Vivens Homo* 7, 1996, p. 75-97.

COURTENAY William J., *Capacity and Volition. A History of the Distinction of Absolute and Ordained Power*, Bergame, Lubrina, 1990.

DAHAN Gilbert, *Les intellectuels chrétiens et les juifs au Moyen Age*, Paris, Cerf, 1990.

– « Réflexion sur l'exégèse des Livres prophétiques à la fin du Moyen Age », *Pensée, image et communication en Europe médiévale. A propos des stalles de*

Saint-Claude, Pierre LACROIX et André RENON eds, Besançon, Asprodic, p. 193-198.

– « L'utilisation de l'exégèse juive dans la lecture des livres prophétiques au XIIIe siècle », in *Neue Richtungen in der hoch- und spaetmittelalterlichen Bibelexegese* (Schriften des Historischen Kollegs, Kolloquien 32), ed. Robert E. LERNER, Munich, Oldenbourg Verlag, 1996, p. 121-138.

DAMIATA Marino, « Olivi inquieto : la cristianità dilacerata dei catari, ortodossi e saraceni », *Studi Francescani* 88, 1991, p. 5-29.

DAVIS C.T., « Roma e Babilonia in Dante », in *Studi americani su Dante*, cur. G.C. ALESSIO, R. HOLLANDER, praef. D. Dellaterza, Milano, F. Angeli, 1989.

DE MATTEIS Maria Consiglia, « Girolamo d'Ascoli : dall'esperienza francescana alla politica ecclesiastica », in Studi in onore di Ovidio Capitani, *Rivista di Storia della Chiesa in Italia* 45, 1991.

DUMONT Stephen, « The Origin of Scotus's Theory of Synchronic Contingency », *Modern Schoolman* 72, 1995, p. 149-167.

EASTMAN John R., *Papal Abdication in the Middle Ages*, Lewiton (N.Y.), Mellen, 1990.

– « Giles of Rome and Celestine V : the Franciscan Revolution and the theology of adbication », in *Cath. Hist. Review* 76, 1990, p. 195-211.

EIJNDEN Jan J.G. (van den), *Poverty on the way to God : Thomas Aquinas on evangelical poverty*, Leuven, 1994.

FLOOD David, « Recent Study on Petrus Johannis Olivi », *Franziskanische Studien* 73, 1991, p. 262-269.

– « The Order's Masters Franciscan Institutions from 1226 to 1280 », in *Dalla « Sequela Christi » di Francesco d'Assisi all'apologia della povertà*. Atti del XVIII Convegno internazionale, Assisi, 18-20 ottobre 1990, praef. Roberto RUSCONI, Spoleto, Centro italiano di studi sull'Alto Medioevo, 1992.

– « The Theology of Peter John Olivi. A search for a theology and anthropology of the Synoptic Gospel », in *The History of Franciscan Theology*, ed. Kenan B. OSBORNE. St. Bonaventure, NY, Franciscan Institute Publications, 1994, p. 127-184.

– « Pietro Olivi : Quando il servo inutile è un pensatore », *Vita Minorum* 66, 1995, p. 409-413.

– « Peter Olivi on Prayer », *The Cord* 48, 1998, p. 3-6.

FORNI Alberto, « Pietro di Giovanni Olivi di fronte alla rinuncia di Celestino V », *B.I.S.I.M.E.* 99, 1993, p. 117-157.

GARNER Jeff B., « The Condemnation of Peter John Olivi's *Lectura super Apocalypsim* as contained in *Littera Magistrorum* : A Translation and Review », Lawrence : University of Kansas, 1993.

GROSSI Paolo, « *Usus facti*. La nozione della proprietà nella inaugurazione dell'età nuova », *Quaderni Fiorentini* 1, 1972, p. 287-355, repris dans Ovidio CAPITANI éd., *Una economia politica nel Medioevo*, Bologne, Pàtron, 1986, p. 1-58, et dans P. GROSSI, *Il dominio e le cose*, Milano, Giuffrè, 1992, p. 123-189.

HÖDL Ludwig, « Olivi, Petrus Johannis, min. », in *Lexikon für Theologie und Kirche 3/VII*, Freiburg-Basel-Wien, Herder, 1998, p. 1045-1047.

HORST Ulrich, *Evangelische Armut und Kirche. Thomas von Aquin und die Armutskontroversen des 13. Und beginnenden 14. Jarhunderts*, Berlin, Akademie Verlag, 1992, 229 p.

JECK Udo Reinhold, *Aristoteles contra Augustinum. Zur Frage nach dem Verhältnis von Zeit und Seele bei den antiken Aristoteleskommentatoren, im arabischen Aristotelismus und im 13. Jahrhundert*, Amsterdam-Philadelphie, B.R. Grüner, 1994.

KAYE Joel, *Economy and Nature in the Fourteenth Century: Money, Market Exchange, and the Emergence of Scientific Thought*, Cambridge University Press, 1998.

KIJAS Zdizisaw Józef, « Ten Arguments of P.J. Olivi in favor of Christological Meaning of Isaiah 7, 14 », *Miscellanea Francescana* 97, p. 565-600.

KIRSHNER Julius, « Les travaux de Raymond de Roover sur la pensée économique des scolastiques », *A.E.S.C.* 30, 1975, p. 318-338.

LAMBERTINI Roberto, *Apologia e crescità dell'identità francescana (1224-1279)*, Rome, *I.S.I.M.E.*, 1989, 196 p.

– « Usus and usura : poverty and usury in the Franciscans' responses to John XXII's Quia vir reprobus », *Franciscan Studies* 54, (1994-97 = Essays in honor of f. G. GÁL), p. 185-210.

LAMBERTINI Roberto et TABARRONI Andrea, *Dopo Francesco : l'Eredità difficile*, Turin, Gruppo Abele, 1989.

LANGHOLM Odd, *Economics in the Medieval Schools. Wealth, Exchange, Value, Money and Usury according to the Paris Theological Tradition, 1200-1350*, Leyde, Brill, 1992.

LEE H., REEVES M., SILANO G. ed., *Western Mediterranean Prophecy. The School of Joachim of Fiore and the Fourteenth Century Breviloquium*. Toronto, Pontifical Institute of Mediaeval Studies, 1989.

LERNER Robert E., « Ecstatic Dissent », *Speculum* 67, 1992, p. 33-57.

– « I 'prelati' dell' 'ecclesia spiritualis' », in *Poteri carismatici e informali : chiesa e società medioevali*, ed. Agostino PARAVICINI BAGLIANI e André VAUCHEZ, Palermo, Sellerio editore, 1992, p. 137-152.

– « Recent Work on the Origins of the '*Genus nequam*' prophecies », *Florensia* 7 (S. Giovanni in Fiore, CS), 1993, p. 141-157.

– « Writing and Resistance among Beguins of Languedoc and Catalonia », *Heresy and Literacy, 1000-1530*, ed. P. BILLER and A. HUDSON, Cambridge University Press, 1994, p. 186-204.

LÉRTORA MENDOZA Celina A., « La cuestiòn de la usura en el contexto de la pobreza voluntaria », *Veritas* 40, 1995, p. 583-598.

LEWIS Warren, « Patron Saints of Reader-Response Criticism », Indiana University, Bloomington : *Simploké* 1/1 (winter, 1993), p. 93-100.

LLORENTE MEGÌAS Paloma, « Hombre y libertad en Petrus Johannis Olivi », *El pensament antropològic medieval en el àmbit islàmic, hebreu icristià. Actes del Simposi Internacional mmedieval de Filosofia de l'Edat Mitjana*, Vic-Girona, 11-16 d'abril de 1993. P. LLORENTE et al. ed., Vic, Patronat d'Estudis Osonencs, 1996.

LLORENTE MEGÌAS Paloma, BOADAS-LLAVAT Agustìn, « Pedro Juan Olivi : sobre la voluntad o el principio activo del conocimiento », *Carthaginensia* 11, 1995, p. 81-91.

MACY Gary, « The Dogma of Transubstantiation in the Middle Ages », *Journal of Ecclesiastical History* 45, 1994, p. 11-41.

MADIGAN Kevin, « Aquinas and Olivi on Evangelical Poverty : A Medieval Debate and its Modern Significance », *The Thomist* 61, 1997, p. 567-586.

MANSELLI Raoul, *Scritti sul Medioevo*, Roma, Bulzoni Editore, 1994.

– *Da Gioacchino da Fiore a Cristoforo Colombo. Studi sul francescanesimo spirituale, sull'ecclesiologia e sull'escatologismo bassomedievali* (*Nuovi Studi Storici* 36), Istituto Storico Italiano per il Medio Evo, 1997, 749 p.

MARAZZI Luca, *Das* iustum pretium *im* Tractatus de emptionibus et venditionibus *des Petrus Iohannis Olivi*, Zürich, Schultess Polygraphischer Verlag, 1990, 105 p.

MAURO Vincenzo, « La disputata *de anima* tra Vitale du Four e Pietro di Giovanni Olivi », *Studi Medievali* 38, 1997, p. 89-139.

MCGINN B., « 'Pastor Angelicus'. Apocalyptic Myth and Political Hope in the Fourteenth Century », in *Santi e santità nel secolo XIV*. Atti del XV convegno internazionale, Assisi, 15-17 ottobre 1987, Napoli, Edizioni Scientifiche Italiane, 1989.

PARAVICINI BAGLIANI Agostino, *Il corpo del Papa*. (Biblioteca di cultura storica), Torino, Einaudi, 1994, 394 p.

PARISOLI Luca, « La formazione del concetto di infallibilità pontificia nella riflessione francescana sulla povertà da Pietro di Giovanni Olivi a Guglielmo di Ockham », *C.F.* 67, 1997, p. 431-458.

– « Come affiorò il concetto di diritto soggettivo inalienabile nella riflessione francescana sulla povertà, sino ai fraticelli de opinione e Giovanni XXII », *Materiali per una storia della cultura giuridica* 28, 1998, p. 93-137.

PASNAU Robert, « Petri Iohannis Olivi Tractatus de Verbo », *Franciscain Studies* 53, 1993, p. 121-153.

– *Theories of Cognition in the Later Middle Ages*, New York, Cambridge University Press, 1997.

– « Olivi on the Metaphysics of Soul », *Medieval Philosophy and Theology* 6, 1997, p. 109-132.

– « Olivi, Peter John » in *The Routledge Encyclopedia of Philosophy*, London, Routledge, 1998.

PASQUINI Emilio, « L'Olivi e Dante : fra idealità religiose e attese profetiche », *La presenza francescana trà medioevo e modernità*, ed. A. CHESSA e Marco POLI, Firenze, Vallechi Editore, 1996, p. 233-245.

PÀSZTOR Edith, « L'escatologia gioachimita nel francescanesimo : Pietro di Giovanni Olivi » in *L'attesa della fine dei tempi nel Medioevo,* O. CAPITANI, J. MIETHKE eds, Bologne, Il Mulino, 1990, p. 169-193.

– « L'apport de Raoul Manselli à l'histoire de l'eschatologie médiévale », *Cahiers de Fanjeaux* 27, *Fin du monde et signes des temps. Visionnaires et prophètes en France méridionale (fin XIII*e*-début XV*e *siècle),* Toulouse, Privat, 1992, p. 21-31.

– « Oracculum angelicum [influxus Spiritualium franc.] », in *Lexikon des Mittelalters,* München-Zürich, Artemis und Winkler Verlag, 1993.

– « Girolamo d'Ascoli e Pietro di Giovanni Olivi », in *Niccolò IV : Un pontificato tra oriente ed occidente. Atti del convegno internazionale di studi in occasione del VII centenario del pontificato di Niccolò IV. Ascoli Piceno (14-17 dicembre 1989),* E. MENESTÒ ed., Spolète, Centro Italiano di Studi sull'Alto Medioevo, 1991, p. 53-72.

PAUL Jacques, « Les Spirituels entre la sainteté et l'hérésie (Historiographie et perspectives d'études) », dans *Gli studi francescani dal Dopoguerra ad oggi. Atti del Convegno di studio, (Firenze 1990),* F. SANTI éd., Spolète, Centro Italiano di Studi sull'Alto Medioevo, 1993, p. 173-212.

PÉREZ-ESTEVEZ Antonio, « La materia en Juan Pedro de Olivo (en las 'Quaestiones in secundum librum Sententiarum') », in *Rev. Filos.* 18 (Universidad del Zulia, Maracaibo), 1993, p. 33-61.

– « El individuo en Pedro Juan Olivi », *Miscellanea Medievalia = Veritas* 41, 1996, p. 435-446.

PIRON Sylvain, « Vœu et contrat chez Pierre de Jean Olivi », *Cahiers du Centre de Recherches Historiques* 16, 1996, p. 43-56.

– « Prêts charitables et opérations capitalistes dans l'éthique franciscaine des contrats monétaires », dans *Des personnes aux institutions. Réseaux et culture du crédit du XVI*e *au XX*e *siècle en Europe*, L. FONTAINE, G. POSTEL-VINAY, P.L. ROSENTHAL et P. SERVAIS éd., Louvain-la-Neuve, Bruylant, 1997, p. 11-27.

– « Compléments à l'inventaire des manuscrits d'Olivi », *Archivum Franciscanum Historicum* 90, 1997, p. 591-596.

– « Marchands et confesseurs. Le *Traité des contrats* d'Olivi dans son contexte (Narbonne, fin XIIIe -début XIVe siècle) », dans *L'Argent au Moyen Age. Congrès de la Société des Historiens Médiévistes Français de l'Enseignement Supérieur Public (Clermont-Ferrand, 1997),* Paris, Publications de la Sorbonne, p. 289-308.

POTESTA Gian Luca, « Gli studi su Angelo Clareno », in ACCROCCA Felice, Angelo Clareno, testimone di Francesco. Testi sulla vita del Santo e dei primi Frati nell' « Expositio Regulae fratrum minorum » e sconociuti alle prime fonti francescane, *A.F.H.* 81, 1989, p. 225-253.

– *Angelo Clareno : Dai poveri eremiti ai fraticelli*, Rome, I.S.I.M.E., 1990.

– « I Frati Minori e lo Studio della Bibbia. Da Francisco d'Assisi a Nicolo di Lyra », dans *La Bibbia nel Medio Evo*, éd. G. CREMASCOLI et C. LEONARDI, Bologne, 1996, p. 269-290.

PUTALLAZ François-Xavier, *La connaissance de soi au XIII*e *siècle. De Matthieu d'Aquasparta à Thierry de Freiberg*, Paris, Vrin, 1991, 444 p.

– « La connaissance de soi au moyen âge. Vital du Four », in *Mélanges Bérubé*, cur. Vicenzo CRISCUOLO, Istituto storico dei Cappucini, Roma, 1991.

– *Insolente liberté. Controverses et condamnations au XIII*e *siècle*, Fribourg-Paris, Presses Universitaires-Le Cerf, 1995.

– « Pierre de Jean Olivi ou la liberté persécutée », *Les philosophies morales et politiques au Moyen Age. Actes du neuvième Congrès International de philosophie médiévale, Ottawa, 17-22 août 1992*, ed. par B.C. BAZÀN, E. ANDÙJAR, L. SBROCCHI (Publications du Laboratoire de la pensée ancienne et médiévale, I/1, 2, 3), Vol. II, New York-Ottawa-Toronto, Legas, 1995, p. 903-921.

– *Figures franciscaines à la fin du XIII*e *siècle*, Paris, Cerf, 1997; tr. it. de C. MARABELLI, *Figure francescane alla fine del XIII secolo*, Milano, Jaca Book, 1996.

REEVES Marjorie, « The *'Vaticinia de Summis Pontificibus'*: A Question of Authority », *in Intellectual Life in the Middle Ages. Essays presented to Margaret Gibson*, ed. by Leysley SMITH and Benedicta WARD, London-Rio Grande, Ohio, The Hambledon Press, 1992, p. 145-156.

RHODES Dennis E., « The *Quodlibeta* of Petrus Joannes Olivi », *Papers of the Bibliographical Society of America* 50, 1956, p. 85-87, repris dans *Id.*, *Studies in Early Italian Printing*, Londres, The Pindar Press, 1982, p. 1-3.

– *Annali tipografici di Lazzaro de' Soardi*, Firenze, Olschki, 1978.

ROBB Fiona, « A Late Thirteenth Century Attack on the Fourth Lateran Council : The *Liber contra Lombardum* and Contemporary Debates on the Trinity », *R.T.A.M.* 62, 1995, p. 110-144.

RUSCONI Roberto, « Alla ricerca delle autentiche tracce di Gioacchino da Fiore nella Francia meridionale », *Florensia* 6, 1992, p. 57-71.

SAVELLI Rodolfo, « Between Law and Morals : Interest in the Dispute on Exchanges during the 16th Century », in Vito PIERGIOVANNI éd., *The Courts and the Development of Commercial Law*, Berlin, Decker & Humblot, 1987, p. 39-102.

SCHLAGETER Johannes, « Die Bedeutung des Hoheliedskommentars des Franziskanertheologen Petrus Johannis Olivi. Argumente für eine neue Edition », *Wissenschaft und Weisheit* 58, 1995, p. 137-151.

– « Evangelisation im Verständnis der frühen franziskanischen Bewegung », Vortrag gehalten auf der Fortbildungswoche Fulda, Kloster Frauenberg, 14.-18. Januar 1996, *Thuringia Franciscana* 51, 1996, p. 311-337.

– « Die Auseinandersetzung zwischen griechischem und biblischem Menschenbild im franziskanischen Freiheitsverständnis des Petrus Johannis Olivi O.F.M. », *Wissenschaft und Weisheit* 60, 1997, p. 65-86.

– « Die neue Aktualität mittelalterlicher Spiritualität am Beispiel des Franziskaners Petrus Johannis Olivi (1248-1298) », *Thuringia Franciscana* 53, 1998, p. 396-400.

SENSI Mario, *Dal movimento eremitico alle Regolare Osservanza francescana. L'opera di fra Paoluccio Trinci*, Assisi, Ed. Porziuncola, 1992, 278 p.

SPICCIANI Amleto, *Capitale e interesse tra mercatura e povertà nei teologi e canonisti dei secoli XIII-XV*, Rome, Jouvence, 1990.

SYLWANOWICZ M., *Contingent Causality & the Foundations of Duns Scotus' Metaphysics*, Leiden, E. J. Brill, 1996.

TABACCO Giovanni, « Il papato avignonese nella crisi del francescanesimo, *Rivista Storica Italiana* 101, 1989, p. 314-375.

THIJSSEN J.M.M., *Censure and Heresy at the University of Paris 1200-1400*, Philadelphia, University of Pennsylvania Press, 1998.

TIERNEY Brian, « John Peter Olivi and papal inerrancy; on a recent interpretation of Olivi's Ecclesiology », in: TIERNEY Brian, *Rights, laws and infallibility in Medieval Thought*, Brookfield, Variorum, 1997.

TODESCHINI Giacomo, « Il pensiero economico di Pietro Giovanni Olivi nella recente storiografia », *La presenza francescana tra medioevo e modernità*. Mario CHESSA e Marco POLI eds, Firenze, Vallechi Editore, 1996, 486 p.

– *Il prezzo della salvezza, Lessici medievali del pensiero economico*, Roma, La Nuova Italia Scientifica, 1994, 290 p.

– « Testualità francescana e linguaggi economici nelle città italiane del Quattrocento », *Quaderni medievali* 40, p. 20-49.

– « I vocabolari dell'analisi economica fra alto e basso medioevo : dai lessici della disciplina monastica ai lessici antiusurari », *Rivista Storica Italiana* 110/3, 1998.

TONNA Ivo, « La 'pars intellectiva' dell'anima rationale non è la forma del corpo (Dottrina di Pierre Jean-Olieu sull'unione tra anima e corpo) », *Antonianum* 65, 1990, p. 277-289.

– *Lineamenti di filosofia Francescana. Sintesi dottrinale del pensiero francescano nei secoli XII-XIV*, La Valette, Tau, 1992, 333 p.

TROTTMAN Christian, « Vision béatifique et intuition d'un objet absent : des sources franciscaines du nominalisme aux défenseurs scotistes de l'opinion de Jean XXII sur la vision différée », *Studi Medievali* 3 ser., 34, 1993, p. 653-715.

– *La vision béatifique : des disputes scolastiques à sa définition par Benoît XII*, Rome, Ecole Française de Rome, 1995.

TURBÉ D., *La « Lectura super Zachariam » de Pierre Jean Olivi*, mémoire de D.E.A., Paris, Ecole pratique des hautes études (section des sciences religieuses), 1996.

VEREECKE L., *Da Gugliemo d'Ockham a Sant'Alfonso de Liguori*, Milano, Paoline, 1990.

VIAN Paolo, « I codici fiorentini e romano della *Lectura super Apocalipsim* di Pietro di Giovanni Olivi (con un codice di Tedaldo della Casa ritrovato) », *A.F.H.* 83, 1990, p. 463-489.

– (a cura di) « Pietro di Giovanni Olivi », in : *Mistici francescani. Secolo XIV*, Milano, Edizioni Biblioteca Francescana, 1997, p. 559-587.

– « Appunti sulla tradizione manoscritta della 'Lectura super Apocalipsim' di Pietro di Giovanni Olivi, in *Editori di Quaracchi 100 anni dopo. Bilancio e prospettive*. Atti del Colloquio internazionale. Roma 29-30 maggio 1995. Scuola Superiore di Studi Medievali e Francescani. Pontificio Ateneo Antonianum. A cura di Alvaro CACCIOTTI e Barbara FAES DE MOTTONI (*Medioevo* 3), Roma, *Edizioni Antonianum*, 1997, p. 373-409.

WOLFF Michael, « Mehrwert und Impetus bei Petrus Johannis Olivi. Wissenschaftlicher Paradigmenwechsel im Kontext gesellschaftlicher Veränderungen im späten Mittelalter », in *Sozialer Wandel im Mittelalter Wahrnehmungsformen, Erklärungsmuster, Regelungsmechanismen*, J. MIETHKE, K. SCHREINER eds., Sigmaringen, J. Thorbeke, 1994, p. 413-423.

ADDENDA

Les fascicules 3-4 de l'*Archivum Franciscanum Historicum*, 91, 1998, qui paraissent aux mêmes dates que le présent volume, contiennent les actes des journées de travail organisées à Grottaferrata en décembre 1997, qui avaient rassemblé les éditeurs de textes d'Olivi, et servi ainsi de préparation au colloque de Narbonne. Nous remercions le père Victor Sànchez de nous en avoir communiqué par avance la table des matières.

BURR David, « L'opera di Pietro di Giovanni Olivi », p. 327-335.

CICERI Antonio, « Pietro di Giovanni Olivi : censimento-inventario dei manoscritti », p. 337-358.

PIRON Sylvain, « Les œuvres perdues d'Olivi : essai de reconstitution », p. 359-396.

VIAN Paolo, « L'opera esegetica di Pietro di Giovanni Olivi : uno *status quaestionis* », p. 397-456.

BARTOLI Marco, « Opere teologiche e filosofiche di Pietro di Giovanni Olivi », p. 457-469.

FLOOD David, « The Franciscan and Spiritual Writings of Peter Olivi », p. 471-475.

RECCHIA Stefano, « Opera 'sancti' Petri Joannis ab admiratore transcripta », p. 477-506.

PERARNAU I ESPELT Josep, « Opere di Fr. Petrus Johannis in processi catalani d'inquisizione della prima metà del XIV secolo », p. 507-518.

SCHLAGETER Johannes, « Von göttlicher in menschlicher Liebe. Petrus Johannis Olivi : *Expositio in Canticum Canticorum* », p. 519-534.

BARTOLI Marco, « Il *Tractatus de septem sentimentis Christi Iesu* di Pietro di Giovanni Olivi », p. 535-551.

BORZUMATO Francesca, « Spunti di ricerca dall'*Expositio in Canticum Canticorum* di Pietro di Giovanni Olivi », p. 553-572.

ABRÉVIATIONS DES DIVERSES ÉDITIONS D'OLIVI MENTIONNÉES DANS L'INDEX

Dans l'impossibilité d'harmoniser les différentes façons de citer les textes d'Olivi employées par chacun des auteurs, nous indiquons ici les abréviations utilisées dans l'index.

QPE = *Quaestiones de perfectione evangelica.*

1QPE = *QPE, q. 1 : An contemplatio sit melior ex suo genere quam omnis alia actio,* ed. A. Emmen-F. Simoncioli, *Studi Francescani* 60, 1963, p. 402-445.

2-4QPE = *q. 2 : An contemplatio sit principalius in intellectu quam in voluntate,* ed. A. Emmen-F. Simoncioli, *Studi Francescani* 61, 1964, p. 113-167 ; *q. 3 : An studere sit opus de genere suo perfectum,* id ; *q. 4 : An aliquod opus vitae activae praeter regimen animarum et praedicationem sit melius ex suo genere quam studium,* id.

5QPE = QPE, *q. 5 : An sit melius aliquid facere ex voto quam sine voto,* ed. A. Emmen, *Studi Francescani* 63, 1966, p. 93-108.

6QPE = QPE, *q. 6 : An virginitas sit simpliciter melior matrimonio,* ed. A. Emmen, *Studi Francescani* 64, 1967, p. 21-57.

8QPE = QPE, *q. 8 : An status altissime paupertatis sit simpliciter melior omni statu divitiarum,* ed. J. Schlageter, *Das Heil der Armen und das Verderben der Reichen, Petrus Johannis Olivi OFM. Die Frage nach der höchsten Armut,* Dietrich-Coelde-Verlag, Werl, 1989.

9QPE = QPE, *q. 9 : An usus pauper includatur in consilio seu in voto paupertatis evangelice, ita quod sit de eius substantia et integritate,* ed. D. Burr, in P.I. Olivi, *De usu paupere, The « Quaestio » and the « Tractatus »,* Olschki-Univ. of Western Australia Press, Firenze-Perth, 1992, p. 1-85.

10QPE = QPE, *q. 10 : An pauperibus evangelicis sit perfectius et convenientius victum suum acquirere per mendicitatis quaestum aut per manuale opus seu laboritium,* ed. D. Flood, *Archivum Franciscanum Historicum* 87, 1994, p. 299-347.

11QPE = *An vovere alteri homini obedientiam in omnibus que non sunt contraria anime et evangelice regule seu perfectioni sit perfectionis evangelice.* Voir *Prin.*

12QPE = QPE, *q. 12 : An romano pontifici in fide et moribus sit ab omnibus catholicis tamquam regule inerrabili obediendum,* ed. M. Maccarone, *Rivista di Storia della Chiesa in Italia* 3, 1949, p. 325-343 ; et *Petri Johannis Olivi quaestio de infallibilitate Romani Pontificis,* ed. M. Roncaglia, *Les Frères Mineurs et l'Église grecque orthodoxe au* XIIIe *siècle (1231-1274),* (Biblioteca bio-bibliografica della Terra Santa e dell'Oriente francescano, s. 4[a], Studi, t. II) Il Cairo, 1954, p. 249-264.

13QPE = QPE, *q. 13 : An papa possit renuntiare papatui (De renuntiatione Papae),* ed. L. Oliger, *Archivum Franciscanum Historicum* 11, 1918, p. 340-366.

14QPE = *An Papa possit in omni voto dispensare et specialiter in votis evangelicis*, ed. Marco Bartoli (sous presse).

15QPE, voir 10QPE

16QPE = QPE, *q. 16 : An professio paupertatis evangelice et apostolice possit licite ad talem modum vivendi reduci, quodammodo sufficienter vivat de possessionibus et redditibus a papa vel mundanis principibus certis procuratoribus commissis*, eds. D. Burr-D. Flood, *Franciscan Studies* 40, 1980, p. 18-58.

17QPE = QPE, *q. 17 : An vovens evangelium vel aliquam regulam simpliciter et absque determinatione teneatur observare omnia, que in eis sunt contenta, ita quod semper peccet mortaliter contra quodcumque illorum agendo*, ed. F. Delorme, *Antonianum* 16, 1941, p. 143-164.

1Sn = *Quaestio de trinitate*, ed. M. Schmaus, *Der Liber Propugnatorius des Thomas Anglicus und die Lehrunterschiede zwischen Thomas von Aquin und Duns Scotus*, Teil 2, Band 2, (*Beiträge zur Geschichte der Philosophie und Theologie des Mittelalters* 29/2) Aschendorff, Münster 1930, p. 143*-228*.

1Sn, 6 = *Utrum Deus potuerit nolle que voluit et vult et velle que noluit nec vult*, ed. Sylvain Piron (sous presse).

2Sn = *Quaestiones in Secundum librum Sententiarum*, ed. B. Jansen, (*Bibliotheca Franciscana Scholastica Medii Aevi* 4-6) 3 vol., Quaracchi, 1922, 1924, 1926.

3Sn = *Quaestiones de Incarnatione et Redemptione. Quaestiones de virtutibus*, eds. A. Emmen-E. Stadter, (*Bibliotheca Franciscana Scholastica Medii Aevi* 24) Collegium S. Bonaventurae, Grottaferrata, 1981.

4Sn = *Quaestio quid ponat ius vel dominium (De signis voluntariis) (Summa IV)*, ed. F. Delorme, *Antonianum* 20, 1945, p. 316-330.

1Resp = *Responsio quam fecit Petrus [Ioannis] ad litteram magistorum, praesentatam sibi in Avinione*, ed. D. Laberge, *Archivum Franciscanum Historicum* 28, 1935, p. 126-130.

2Resp = *Responsio fratris Petri Ioannis [Olivi] ad aliqua dicta per quosdam magistros Parisienses de suis Quaestionibus excerpta*, ed. D. Laberge, *Archivum Franciscanum Historicum* 28, 1935, p. 130-155, p. 374-407.

3Resp = *Amplior declaratio quinti articuli qui est de divina essentia*, ed. D. Laberge, *Archivum Franciscanum Historicum* 29, 1936, p. 98-141, p. 365-387.

4Resp = *Responsio Petri Io[hannis] in capitulo generali [Montpellier 1287] quando fuit requisitus quid de usu paupere sentiret*, ed. A. Heysse, *Archivum Franciscanum Historicum* 11, 1918, p. 264-269.

Borgh. 322 = Codex Vatican Borghese 322 : *Utrum tempus sit aliquid reale extra animam.*

EpistC = *Epistola ad Conradum de Offida*, ed. L. Oliger, *Archivum Franciscanum Historicum* 11, 1918, p. 366-373.

EpistR = *Epistola ad R.*, P.I. Olivi, *Quodlibeta*, Venetiis, 1509, ff. 51 (63)va – 53 (65)rb; *Littera quam misit Parisius rescribendo fratri Raymundo Gaufridi et sociis ejus nondum generali ministro*, ed. fr. Gratien, *Etudes franciscaines* 29, 1913, p. 416-422; édition critique, S. Piron, C. Kilmer, E. Marmursztejn, *A.F.H.*, 91, 1998, p. 33-64.

EpistS = *Epistola ad regis Siciliae filios*, ed. F. Ehrle, *Archiv für Literatur-und Kirchengeschichte des Mittelalters* 3, 1887, p. 534-540 ; *Lettre de Fr. Pierre Jean

Olivi, adressée à Saint Louis d'Anjou pendant sa captivité, ed. C. VIELLE, *Saint Louis d'Anjou, Evêque de Toulouse. Sa vie, son temps, son culte,* Vanves, 1930, p. 469-472.

Impugnatio = *Impugnatio XXXVII articulorum adversus opiniones doctorum quorundam quorum ipse supprimere voluit,* in P.I. Olivi, *Quodlibeta,* Venetiis, 1509, ff. 42r-49v.

In Act = *Lectura super Actus Apostolorum.*

In XII = *Lectura super Duodecim prophetas*

In Ap = *Lectura super Apocalypsim,* ed. W. LEWIS, Tübingen (Diss.), 1972.

In Cor = *Lectura super I. Cor,* voir *Prin.*

In Ct = *Lectura in Canticum Canticorum,* ed. J. SCHLAGETER (sous presse).

In Ez = *Lectura super Ezchielem.*

In Jn = *Lectura super Johannem.*

In Lam = *La Caduta di Gerusalemme. Il commento al Libro delle Lamentazioni di Pietro di Giovanni Olivi,* ed. BARTOLI Marco, Rome, *B.I.S.I.M.E.* 12, 1991 = *Lectura super Lamentationes Ieremiae.*

In Lc = *Lectura super Lucam.*

In Mt = *Lectura super Matthaeum.*

Ind = *Quaestio de indulgentia Portiunculae,* ed. P. PÉANO, *Archivum Franciscanum Historicum* 74, 1981, p. 31-76.

Littera = *'Littera septem sigillorum' contra doctrinam Petri Ioannis Olivi edita,* ed. G. FUSSENEGGER, *Archivum Franciscanum Historicum* 47, 1954, p. 51-53.

Obitu = *De obitu dicti fratris Petri et quid receptis sacramentis dixit, quando et ubi recepit scientiam suam et quid senserit de usu paupere et multa [alia],* ed. A. HEYSSE, *Archivum Franciscanum Historicum* 11, 1918, p. 267-269.

Perl = *De perlegendis philosophorum libris,* ed. F. DELORME, *Antonianum* 16, 1941, p. 37-44.

Prin = *Peter of John Olivi on the Bible. Principia quinque in Sacram Scripturam. Postilla in Isaiam et in I ad Corinthios,* Ed. FLOOD David et GÁL Gedeon, St Bonaventure (N.Y.), Franciscan Institute Publications, 1997

QL = *Quodlibeta,* Venetiis, 1509.

QLO = *Quaestiones logicales,* ed. S.F. BROWN, *Traditio* 42, 1986, p. 337-388.

SupReg = *Expositio super regulam,* ed. D. FLOOD, *Olivi's Rule Commentary,* Wiesbaden 1972.

TC = *Tractatus de Contractibus* ou *De emptionibus et venditionibus, de usuris et restitutionibus,* ed. G. TODESCHINI, *Un trattato francescano di economia politica. Il 'De emptionibus [...]' di Pietro di Giovanni Olivi,* (Studi storici, p. 125-126) Istituto Storico Italiano per il Medio Evo, Roma, 1980.

UsPaup = *Tractatus de usu paupere,* ed. D. BURR, in P.I. Olivi, *De usu paupere, The 'Quaestio' and the 'Tractatus',* Olschki-Univ. of Western Australia Press, Firenze-Perth, 1992, p. 87-148.

LISTE DES ABRÉVIATIONS DE REVUES LES PLUS SOUVENT MENTIONNÉES DANS LES NOTES

A.F.H. : Archivum Franciscanum Historicum
A.H.D.L.M.A. : Archives d'Histoire Doctrinale et Littéraire du Moyen Age
B.I.S.I.M.E. : Bulletino dell'Istituto Storico Italiano per il Medio Evo
R.H.E.F. : Revue de l'Histoire de l'Église de France
R.S.P.T. : Revue des Sciences Philosophiques et Théologiques
R.T.A.M. : Recherche en Théologie Ancienne et Médiévale

INDEX

ABÉLARD 46,
Sic et non 108
Theologia christiana 48
AELRED DE RIEVAULX
Compendium speculi caritatis 232, 233
ALBERT LE GRAND, SAINT 349
De IV coaequavis 31
ALCUIN 117
ALEXANDRE D'ALEXANDRIE 212, 239, 244, 294
Tractatus de usuris 249
ALEXANDRE DE HALÈS
Quaestiones antequam fuit frater 60, 183
Summa 173, 174, 185, 189, 218, 230, 240, 241, 242, 245, 247, 249, 260
ALEXANDRE LE MINORITE
Expositio in Apocalypsim 111
AMBROISE, SAINT 311, 314
Sermo contra Auxentium 174
ANDRÉ DE SAINT-VICTOR 97, 101, 112
ANGELO CLARENO 279, 313, 317, 375, 382
ANSELME 115
De casu diaboli 23-24
ANTOINE DE PADOUE, SAINT 106, 113, 281
ARISTOTE 28, 36, 39, 42, 43, 44, 47, 74, 166, 190, 200, 254, 255, 375, 377, 379, 380
De anima 57
De somno et vigilia 61
Ethique à Nicomaque 101, 241
Métaphysique, Δ 48
Physique 29, 30
ARNAUD DE ROQUEFEUIL 87, 288, 380
ARNAUD DE VILLENEUVE 10, 69, 382, 385
Alia Informatio 328, 329
Expositio Apocalipsis 343
ARNAUD GAILLARD 87, 88
ASTESANUS
Summa de casibus 250
AUGUSTIN, SAINT 32, 35-39, 48, 72, 73, 74, 256, 284, 311, 314
Confessions 25, 31
De consensu euangelistarum, II 119
De Doctrina christiana 380
De genesi ad litteram 57, 61
De Trinitate 54
De vera religione 62
AVERROÈS 35, 36, 39, 80, 346, 379, 380
Aristotelis commentarii 31, 241
AZON
Aurea summa 245

BARTHÉLEMY SICARD 283
BASILE, SAINT 117
BÉATRICE 341, 342, 346, 347, 348, 351
BÈDE, SAINT 120, 349
De tropis et schematibus 99
BERNARD DE CLAIRVAUX, SAINT 352
Apologia ad Guillelmum abbatem 222
De consideratione ad Eugenium Papam 181
Epistula ad Robertum puerum 181
BERNARD DE GOURDON
Lilium medicinae 69
BERNARD DÉLICIEUX 280, 308

BERNARD GUI 277, 283, 300, 309, 311, 318, 377
Manuel de l'inquisiteur 187, 278, 282, 296, 297, 298, 301, 306, 308, 324, 326, 329, 378
BERNARDIN DE SIENNE 244, 250
BIBLE 91, 92, 93
Nouveau Testament 151
Ancien Testament 151, 209, 348
Genèse 91, 106, 208
Rois 58
Isaïe 112, 131, 168, 214, 345
Petits prophètes 93, 94, 97, 102, 1055, 107, 112, 216
Cantique 122, 124, 129
Psaumes 122
Daniel 100, 216
Matthieu 118, 122, 154
Marc 115, 117, 118
Jean 115, 117, 118, 132, 174, 175, 187, 196
Luc 115, 116, 216
Actes des Apôtres 187
Hébreux 103
II. Thessaloniens 146
Romains 130, 131, 144, 187
Corinthiens 125, 162, 170, 171, 177, 187, 189
Apocalypse 107, 135-156, 164, 166, 169, 209, 210, 214, 286, 312, 317, 327, 328, 330
BOÈCE 342, 349
BONAGIUNTA DA LUCCA 350
BONAGRATIA DE BERGAME 160, 260, 294
BONAGRATIA DE S. GIOVANNI IN PERSICETO 87, 115, 160, 380
BONAVENTURE, SAINT 8, 27, 55, 65, 66, 81, 89, 113, 124, 137, 141, 151, 195, 200, 204, 227, 246, 343, 344, 379
Apologia pauperum 196, 197, 199, 201, 223
Collationes in Hexaemeron 210
Collationes de septem donis spiritus Sancti 374
De reductione artium ad theologiam 378
De scientia Christi 85-87
In II librum Sententiarum 58-59
Legenda maior 164-166
Legenda minor 164, 165
Quaestiones de Perfectione Evangelica 196
BONIFACE VIII 140, 146, 289, 347, 385
BURGUNDIUS 119

CÉLESTIN V 138, 140, 180, 279, 289, 315
CHARLES II D'ANJOU 288, 289, 290
CICÉRON 342
CIMABUE 346
CLAREMBAUD D'ARRAS 48
CLEMENT V 282, 284, 294, 305
si furiosus 62
COLA DI RIENZO 155
CONRAD D'OFFIDA 141, 151, 155, 180, 288, 315
CYRILLE D'ALEXANDRIE, SAINT 116, 117

DANTE ALIGHIERI 10
Divina Commedia 341-372
Convivio 342
DENYS (PSEUDO) 106, 107, 349
DESCARTES 8, 266
Regulae ad directionem ingenii 262
DOMINIQUE SOTO
De iustitia et iure 239, 250
DOMINIQUE, SAINT 281, 343, 348
DONAT 48

ETIENNE TEMPIER, ÉVÊQUE DE PARIS 30, 374, 379
EUSÈBE DE CÉSARÉE 117

FRANÇOIS CARACCIOLI, DIT FRANÇOIS DE NAPLES 385
FRANÇOIS D'ASSISE, SAINT 111, 112, 113, 131, 139144, 147, 149-152, 154, 160, 164, 165, 166, 178, 179, 182, 255, 281, 282, 283, 285, 286, 306, 316, 327, 329, 330, 335, 343, 344, 345, 347, 348, 376
FRANÇOIS DE MEYRONNES 249
FRÉDÉRIC II, EMPEREUR 173
FRÉDÉRIC III, ROI DE SICILE 313, 317

GAUTHIER D'AGILON
Summa medicinalis 61

GÉRARD D'ABBEVILLE 58, 184, 196, 201
De cogitatione 59, 60, 62
GILBERT DE LA PORRÉE 46
GILLES AYCELIN 275, 276, 291, 307
GILLES DE ROME
In I Sententiarum 31
GIOTTO 152, 346
GONZALVE DE VALBOA 254, 386
GRATIEN 221, 349
Decretum 62, 174, 220, 225, 231, 240, 245
GRÉGOIRE DE NAZIANZE, SAINT 117
GRÉGOIRE LE GRAND, SAINT 101, 174, 284, 311, 314, 350
Homélies sur Ezéchiel 108
GRÉGOIRE IX
Décrétale « Quo elongati » 182, 183
Decretales 219
GRÉGOIRE XI 386
GUGLIELMA DE MILAN 321, 322, 338
GUIDO CAVALCANTI 346
GUIDO DA MONTEFELTRO 347
GUILLAUME D'AUVERGNE
De anima 60
De trinitate 46
De universo 57, 64
De vitiis et peccatis 60
GUILLAUME D'AUXERRE
Summa aurea 60
GUILLAUME D'OCCAM 8, 41, 45, 55, 72, 251, 252, 253, 255, 256, 261, 263
Breviloqium de principatu tyrannico 255, 259
In IV Sententiarum 257
Ordinatio 256
GUILLAUME DE CONCHES
Chirurgia, XIII 69
GUILLAUME DE LA MARE 96, 97
Correctorium fratris Thomae 19, 75, 84, 184
Scriptum in II librum Sententiarum 58, 59, 61, 64, 88
GUILLAUME DE MÉLITON 55
GUILLAUME DE NOGARET 155
GUILLAUME DE SAINT-AMOUR 184, 196
Quaestio de quantitate eleemosynae 199
GUIRAL OT
De contractibus, de excommunicationibus et de casibus reservatis 244, 249

HENRI DE GAND 8, 36, 43, 45, 58, 67, 71, 252, 261
Quodlibet I 19, 73
Quodlibet III 29, 35, 39
Quodlibet VI 61, 63
Summa (Quaestiones ordinaria) 72
Tractatus super facto prelatorum et fratrum 193
HENRI DE SUSE 219, 246
Summa aurea 245
HENRY DE CHAMAYO 320, 335
HENRY DE HARCLAY 45
HILAIRE, SAINT 115, 117
HUGUES DE DIGNE 183
HUGUES DE SAINT-CHER 100, 120
Postille sur Jonas 97
HUGUES DE SAINT-VICTOR 102, 174, 189

INNOCENT III, Pape 46, 146, 189
De eleemosyna 246
INNOCENT IV, Pape 219
Ordinem vestrum 183
ISIDORE DE PÉLUSE 116
ISIDORE DE SÉVILLE 349

JACQUES AUTIER 334
JACQUES DE VORAGINE 118
JACQUES II, ROI DE MAJORQUE 379, 381, 382, 385
JEAN, SAINT 343, 345, 350
JEAN CHRYSOSTOME, SAINT
(pseudo) Hom. In Mt. 119, 231, 240, 250
JEAN DE MURROVALLE 289, 385, 386
JEAN DE ROQUETAILLADE 216
Liber secretorum eventuum 215
JEAN DUNS SCOT 8, 55, 79, 228, 244, 251-253, 259, 261, 263
Lectura 254
Opus oxoniense 131, 257
Reportata parisiensa 256
JEAN GERSON 252
JEAN PECKHAM 55, 204

Canticum pauperis 197
Contra Kilwardby 197, 202
Expositio super regulam 197, 199
In Canticum Canticorum 126
Quodlibeta Quatuor 53, 54, 62, 64, 194, 199
Tractatus pauperis 194, 195, 197, 199, 202
Utrum perfectio ewangelica consistat in renuntiando vel carendo divitiis propriis et communibus 197, 199
JEAN XXII, PAPE 137, 145, 146, 155, 160, 260, 282, 285, 286, 296, 297, 298, 305, 312, 313, 317, 318, 328, 337, 386
Cum inter nonnullos 330
Gloriosam Ecclesiam 295
Quorumdam exigit 295
JÉRÔME D'ASCOLI 138, 375, 379, 385
JÉRÔME, SAINT 9, 97, 100, 101, 102, 284, 311
JOACHIM DE FLORE 46, 121, 131, 132, 169, 207, 210-213, 216, 322, 341, 343, 350
Commentaire de l'Apocalypse 148, 149, 150, 151, 209, 378
Liber de concordia 208, 209, 210

LELIO 342
LÉON IV 174
LÉON, FRÈRE 143, 151
LESSIUS LEONARDUS,
De iustitia et iure 239
LIMBORCH, P. VAN 325
Liber sententiarum inquisitionis Tholosanae 214, 277-307, 309-318
LOUIS D'ANJOU, SAINT 281, 287, 308
LOUIS DE BAVIÈRE, EMPEREUR 297

MARGUERITE PORETE 321
MARSILE DE PADOUE 252
MARTIN IV, Pape
Ad fructus uberes 193
Cogit nos temporis qualitas 173
MARTIN V, Pape 386
MATTHIEU D'AGRIGENTE
Sermones varii 244
MATTHIEU D'AQUASPARTA 58, 60, 166, 172, 382
Quaestiones disputatae de cognitione 59, 63
MENOCCHIO 320
MICHEL DE CÉSÈNE 160, 386
MONALDE DE CAPO D'ISTRIA
Summa de casibus conscientiae 218, 276

NICÉTAS 115
NICOLAS DE LYRE
Postilla litteralis 114
NICOLAS III, PAPE 202
Exit qui seminat 146, 157, 164, 176, 179, 180, 184, 229, 288
NICOLAS IV 375, 385
NICOLAU EYMERICH 386
Directorium Inquisitorum 279, 296

ODERISI DA GUBBIO 346
ORIGÈNE 118
OROSE 349

PASCHASE RADBERT 101
PERCEVAL SPINOLA 386
PHILIPPE LE BEL, ROI DE FRANCE 307, 323, 381, 385
PIERRE D'ARAGON 173
PIERRE DAMIEN, SAINT 348
Epistolae 220, 221, 222
PIERRE DE JEAN OLIVI
QPE : 157, 163, 166, 167, 168, 185, 309, 314, 316, 376
1QPE 72, 75, 77, 166, 168, 169, 171, 381
5QE 351-352
8QPE 75, 124, 157, 158, 160, 161, 162, 163, 171, 195, 197, 199, 201, 202, 204, 207, 212, 213, 214, 218, 219, 221, 224, 225, 283, 288
9QPE 157, 160, 198, 200, 204, 205, 218, 219, 221-230, 247, 376, 377
10QPE 158, 160, 163, 195, 198, 218, 221, 223-225, 228, 229
11QPE 158, 159, 162
12QPE 178, 179, 186, 262
13QPE 189, 258, 259, 261, 262
14QPE 180, 181

15QPE 198, 203
16QPE 218, 226, 237
17QPE 258
1Sn 47, 75, 78-87, 167
2Sn 15-25, 27, 28, 43, 45, 64-67, 73, 74, 76-80, 83, 87, 123, 257, 258, 260, 379
3Sn 49-52, 78
4Sn 41, 218, 219, 259, 260, 261
Borgh. 322 : 27-39, 88
Commentaire des Sentences 193
In XII 92-96, 99-102, 105-108, 110-113
EpistR 87, 128-129, 213
In Act 198, 200, 201
In Ap 10, 91, 110, 135-156, 168, 191, 208, 211-215, 283, 291-294, 295, 297, 299, 309, 312, 314, 316, 320, 326, 331, 241-372, 378, 382, 385
In Cor 121
In Ct 10, 124, 125, 127, 129, 130, 148, 213
In Is 74, 92-95, 100, 101, 105, 121, 129
In Jn 82, 198, 381
In Lam 93, 95-98, 101, 103, 129, 211
In Lc 350
In Mt 119, 213, 226, 227
Ind. 176, 186
Lectura super De angelica hierarchia 89
Perl. 101
Prin. 44, 93, 105-107, 111, 121, 122, 167, 168, 212
QL 27-29, 32, 34-39, 42, 49, 54, 67-69, 71, 83, 128, 129, 173, 174, 177, 182, 212, 226, 230, 239, 248, 249
Responsio II 177, 380
TC 10, 121, 218, 225, 230, 233, 239, 241-243, 246-248, 293
UsPaup 121, 202, 203, 205, 288
PIERRE DE LIMOGES 44
PIERRE DE TARANTAISE
Commentaire des Sentences II 58, 193, 194
Quodlibet I 61, 62, 63
PIERRE DE TRABIBUS 71
Quodlibet I, quaestio XL 249
PIERRE LE MANGEUR
Historia scholastica 99, 100
PIERRE LOMBARD 46, 48, 349
Sentences 8, 10, 15, 123, 182
PLACENTIN
Summa in Codicem 245
PLATON 200
PRISCIEN 48
PROUS BONETA 10, 153, 215, 279, 285, 287, 292, 299, 301, 303, 306, 319-339

RABAN MAUR
Comm. In Matth 119
RAYMOND DE PEÑAFORT 182, 380
Summa de poenitentia 245-247
RAYMOND GAUFREDI 128, 138, 382, 385
RAYMOND LULLE 10, 373-387
Le livre de l'ami et de l'aimé 377
Vita coetana 373-387
RICHARD DE MEDIAVILLA 44, 147, 250
In II librum Sententiarum 58, 60
Quaestio disputata de privilegio Martini papae IV 194
Quodlibet 61, 63, 64, 88
RICHARD DE SAINT-VICTOR 191, 349
ROBERT DE MELUN 48
ROBERT GROSSETESTE 115
Commentarius in VII libros Physicorum 31
ROGER MARSTON 194
Quaestiones disputatae de emanatione aeterna, de statu naturae lapsae et de anima, q. 7 64
ROGERIUS DE FRUGARDO
Chirurgia, XXII 69

SIGER DE BRABANT 349, 379
Super librum De Causis 30
SUMMENHART, CONRAD 252
De contractibus licitis et illicitis 235

THÉODORE DE MOPSUESTE 125
THÉOPHYLACTE 115-118
THIERRY DE CHARTRES 48
THIERRY DE FREIBERG 75

THOMAS D'AQUIN, SAINT 10, 33, 35, 41, 55, 58, 72, 82, 88, 93, 95, 106, 114, 115, 117, 118, 241, 245, 246, 254, 286, 288, 343, 349, 350, 379, 383
Commentaire des Sentences 31, 92
Compendium theologiae 18
Contra impugnantes Dei cultum et religionem 187, 196
De Perfectione vitae spiritualis 185
In librum De memoria et reminiscentia commentarium 61
Quaestiones de Malo 21
Quaestiones de Veritate 18, 20
Quaestiones de quodlibet 27, 184, 185
Summa contra Gentiles 81, 182
Summa Theologiae 19, 20, 21, 28, 30, 49, 60, 62, 63, 64, 73, 74, 77, 81, 83, 84, 119, 120, 182, 184
Summa Theologiae, Supplementum 176, 177
Catena Aurea 115-120
Expositio in Genesim 211, 213
THOMAS D'YORK 196
Manus quae contra Omnipotentem 196
THOMAS LE MYÉSIER 375
TITUS DE BOSTRA 116, 119

UBERTIN DE CASALE 329, 375, 377, 382, 385
Arbor Vitae 341, 376

VICTOR D'ANTIOCHE 115, 116
VINCENT DE BEAUVAIS
Speculum doctrinale 182
Speculum naturale 69
VIRGILE 345, 347, 349
VITAL DU FOUR, 288

TABLE DES MATIÈRES

Remerciements 7
Introduction
par Alain BOUREAU et Sylvain PIRON 9

Olivi on Human Freedom
par Robert PASNAU 15
Olivi et le temps
par Ruedi IMBACH et François-Xavier PUTALLAZ 27
Le concept de relation chez Pierre de Jean Olivi
par Alain BOUREAU 41
La questione della ratio ligata *e Pietro di Giovanni Olivi*
par Vincenzo MAURO 57
La liberté divine et la destruction des idées chez Olivi
par Sylvain PIRON 71
L'exégèse des livres prophétiques chez Pierre de Jean Olieu
par Gilbert DAHAN 91
Olivi utilisateur de la Catena aurea *de Thomas d'Aquin*
par Louis-J. BATAILLON 115
Von göttlicher in menschlicher Liebe. Überlegungen zum Canticum-Kommentar des Fr. Petrus Johannis Olivi O. Min. (+1298)
par Johannes SCHLAGETER O.F.M. 121
Peter John Olivi, Author of the Lectura Super Apocalipsim *: Was he Heretical ?*
par Warren LEWIS 135
Poverty as Virtue, Poverty as Warning, and Peter of John Olivi
par David FLOOD, O.F.M. 157
Olivi et le pouvoir du pape
par Marco BARTOLI 173
La difesa dell'ordine francescano di fronte alle critiche dei secolari in Olivi
par Roberto LAMBERTINI 193
Peter Olivi on the Conversion of the Jews
par Robert LERNER 207

Olivi e il mercator *cristiano*
par Giacomo TODESCHINI 217

Le jeu comme contrat et le risicum *chez Olivi*
par Giovanni CECCARELLI 239

La contribution de l'École fransciscaine à la naissance de la notion de liberté politique : les données préalables chez Pierre de Jean Olivi
par Luca PARISOLI 251

Autour de Pierre de Jean Olivi. Narbonne et le narbonnais, fin XIIIe, début XIVe siècle
par Gilbert LARGUIER 265

Culte et rayonnement de Pierre Déjean Olieu en Languedoc au début du XIVe siècle
par Jean-Louis BIGET 277

Did the Béguins understand Olivi ?
par David BURR 309

The Visionary Authority of Na Prous Boneta
par Louisa A. BURNHAM 319

Pietro di Giovanni Olivi e Dante, ovvero il panno e la gonna
par Alberto FORNI 341

Raymond Lulle (1235-1316) et Pierre de Jean Olivi (1247-1298) : la « science divine », les conflits des savoirs et des institutions
par Dominique de COURCELLES 373

Bibliographie 1989-1998 389
Abréviations 401
Index 405
Table des matières 411

ACHEVÉ D'IMPRIMER
EN JUIN 1999
PAR L'IMPRIMERIE
DE LA MANUTENTION
A MAYENNE
N° 195-99

Dépôt légal : 2e trimestre 1999